CompTIA A+® Guide: Practical Application

Third Edition
(Exam 220-702)

Mike Meyers'

CompTIA A+® Guide: Practical Application

Third Edition
(Exam 220-702)

Mike Meyers

New York Chicago San Francisco
Lisbon London Madrid Mexico City Milan
New Delhi San Juan Seoul Singapore Sydney Toronto

The McGraw·Hill Companies

Cataloging-in-Publication Data is on file with the Library of Congress

McGraw-Hill books are available at special quantity discounts to use as premiums and sales promotions, or for use in corporate training programs. To contact a representative, please e-mail us at bulksales@mcgraw-hill.com.

Mike Meyers' CompTIA A+® Guide: Practical Application, Third Edition (Exam 220-702)

1 2 3 4 5 6 7 8 9 0   WDQ WDQ   1 0 9 8 7 6 5 4 3 2 1 0

ISBN: Book p/n 978-0-07-173866-8 and CD p/n 978-0-07-173868-2
of set 978-0-07-173869-9

MHID: Book p/n 0-07-173866-5 and CD p/n 0-07-173868-1
of set 0-07-173869-X

Sponsoring Editor
TIMOTHY GREEN

Editorial Supervisor
JODY MCKENZIE

Project Manager
ARUSHI CHAWLA

Acquisitions Coordinator
MEGHAN RILEY

Developmental Editor
LAURA STONE

Technical Editor
CHRISTOPHER A. CRAYTON

Copy Editor
MALINDA MCCAIN

Proofreader
PAUL TYLER

Indexer
WORDCO INDEXING SERVICES, INC.

Production Supervisor
JAMES KUSSOW

Composition
GLYPH INTERNATIONAL

Illustration
GLYPH INTERNATIONAL

Art Director, Cover
JEFF WEEKS

About the Author

Mike Meyers, lovingly called the "AlphaGeek" by those who know him, is the industry's leading authority on CompTIA A+ certification. He is the president and co-founder of Total Seminars, LLC, a provider of PC and network repair seminars, books, videos, and courseware for thousands of organizations throughout the world. Mike has been involved in the computer and network repair industry since 1977 as a technician, instructor, author, consultant, and speaker. Author of numerous popular PC books and videos, including the best-selling *CompTIA A+ Certification All-in-One Exam Guide*, Mike is also the series editor for the highly successful *Mike Meyers' Certification Passport* series, the *Mike Meyers' Computer Skills* series, and the *Mike Meyers' Guide to* series, all published by McGraw-Hill. As well as writing, Mike has personally taught (and continues to teach) thousands of students, including U.S. senators, U.S. Supreme Court justices, the United Nations, every branch of the U.S. Armed Forces, most branches of the Department of Justice, hundreds of corporate clients, academic students at every level, prisoners, and pensioners.

> E-mail: michaelm@totalsem.com
> Facebook: Mike Meyers (Houston, TX)
> Twitter/Skype/most instant messaging clients: desweds
> Web forums: www.totalsem.com/forums

About the Editor in Chief

Scott Jernigan wields a mighty red pen as Editor in Chief for Total Seminars. With a Master of Arts degree in Medieval History, Scott feels as much at home in the musty archives of London as he does in the warm computer glow of Total Seminars' Houston headquarters. After fleeing a purely academic life, he dove headfirst into IT, working as an instructor, editor, and writer. Scott has edited and contributed to dozens of books on computer literacy, hardware, operating systems, networking, and certification. His latest book is *Computer Literacy—Your Ticket to IC^3 Certification*. Scott co-authored the best-selling *CompTIA A+ Certification All-in-One Exam Guide* and the *Mike Meyers' A+ Guide to Managing and Troubleshooting PCs* (both with Mike Meyers). He has taught computer classes all over the United States, including stints at the United Nations in New York and the FBI Academy in Quantico.

About the Technical Editor

Christopher A. Crayton (MCSE, MCP+I, CompTIA A+, CompTIA Network+) is an author, technical editor, technical consultant, security consultant, and trainer. Formerly a computer and networking instructor at Keiser College (2001 Teacher of the Year), Chris has also worked as network administrator for Protocol and at Eastman Kodak Headquarters as a computer and network specialist. Chris has authored several print and online books on topics ranging from CompTIA A+ and CompTIA Security+ to Microsoft Windows Vista. Chris has provided technical edits and reviews for many publishers, including McGraw-Hill, Pearson Education, Charles River Media, Cengage Learning, Wiley, O'Reilly, Syngress, and Apress.

Peer Reviewers

Thank you to the reviewers, past and present, who contributed insightful reviews, criticisms, and helpful suggestions that continue to shape this textbook.

Donat Forrest
Broward County Community College
Pembroke Pines, FL

Winston Maddox
Mercer County Community College
West Windsor, NJ

Brian Ives
Finger Lakes Community College
Canadaigua, NY

Rajiv Malkan
Montgomery College
Conroe, Texas

Farbod Karimi
Heald College
San Francisco, CA

Randall Stratton
DeVry University
Irving, TX

Tamie Knaebel
Jefferson Community College
Louisville, KY

Scott Sweitzer
Indiana Business College
Indianapolis, IN

Keith Lyons
Cuyahoga Community College
Parma, OH

Thomas Trevethan
CPI College of Technology
Virginia Beach, VA

■ Acknowledgments

Scott Jernigan, my Editor in Chief at Total Seminars and boon companion on many an evening, worked his usual magic pulling together this latest edition. My thanks, amigo!

My acquisitions editor, Tim Green, kept me on target to get this book done. Seriously. Who else could motivate me to work on the book while on vacation in Key West, Florida? The sun, the surf, the silliness…all dashed away by a phone call. But I'm not bitter, just happy the book is done and Tim will quit yelling at me.

To Chris Crayton. You went so far beyond the call of technical editor that you should have your very own unique title, like *über technical editor king*! Thank you for helping make this book happen.

To Ed Dinovo. Your contributions of words and ideas helped build this book into a much better work than it could have been without you. Thank you very much.

To Alec Fehl. You did an outstanding job on this new book, and it is always a pleasure working with you.

My in-house photographer and fellow geek, Michael Smyer, contributed in many ways. His gorgeous photographs grace most pages. His tirelessness in challenging me technically on almost every topic both irritated and frustrated me, but the book is much better because of it. Excellent work, Michael.

Ford Pierson, my in-house editor and illustrator, brought outrageous wit and skill to his contributions throughout the book. Plus he has a killer instinct in Counter-Strike that makes the gaming sessions all the better. Great job, Ford.

Aaron Verber came in at the last minute with his red pen to help with page proofs, showing a careful eye that Scott will adore. I look forward to many more projects with you, lad.

On the McGraw-Hill side, the crew once again demonstrated why McGraw-Hill is the best in show as a publisher. With excellent work and even better attitude, this book went smoothly together.

Laura Stone reprised her role as developmental editor for this edition, keeping me on my toes for every detail, fact, illustration, screen shot, and photograph—all this while bouncing the newly born and very cute Maleah on one knee. Laura, you're amazing and a joy to work with. Thanks!

To the copy editors, page proofers, and layout folks—Malinda McCain, Paul Tyler, WordCo Indexing Services, Inc., Amarjeet Kumar, and all the folks at Glyph International—superb work in every facet. Thank you for being the best.

■ To Intel, for making great CPUs—and to AMD, for keeping Intel on the ball.

—Mike Meyers

ABOUT THIS BOOK

■ Important Technology Skills

Information technology (IT) offers many career paths, leading to occupations in such fields as PC repair, network administration, telecommunications, Web development, graphic design, and desktop support. To become competent in any IT field, however, you need certain basic computer skills.

Mike Meyers' CompTIA A+® Guide: Practical Application builds a foundation for success in the IT field by introducing you to fundamental technology concepts and giving you essential computer skills.

Try This! *exercises apply core skills in a new setting.*

Key Terms, *identified in red, point out important vocabulary and definitions that you need to know.*

Tech Tip *sidebars provide inside information from experienced IT professionals.*

Cross Check *questions develop reasoning skills: ask, compare, contrast, and explain.*

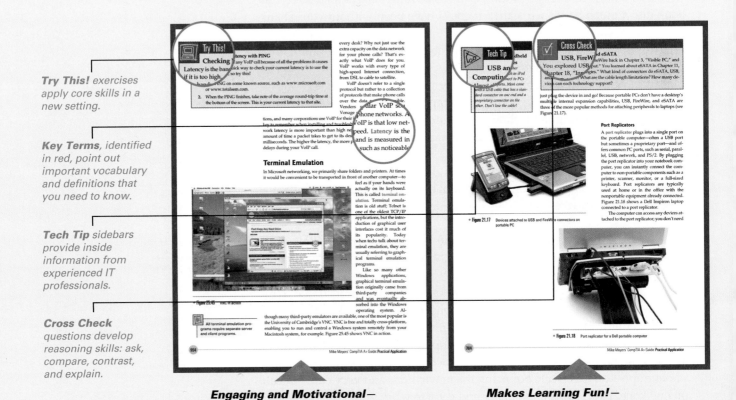

Engaging and Motivational—
Using a conversational style and proven instructional approach, the author explains technical concepts in a clear, interesting way using real-world examples.

Makes Learning Fun!—
Rich, colorful text and enhanced illustrations bring technical subjects to life.

Proven Learning Method Keeps You on Track

Mike Meyers' CompTIA A+® Guide: Practical Application is structured to give you comprehensive knowledge of computer skills and technologies. The textbook's active learning methodology guides you beyond mere recall and, through thought-provoking activities, labs, and sidebars, helps you develop critical-thinking, diagnostic, and communication skills.

Effective Learning Tools

This pedagogically rich book is designed to make learning easy and enjoyable and to help you develop the skills and critical-thinking abilities that will enable you to adapt to different job situations and troubleshoot problems.

Mike Meyers' proven ability to explain concepts in a clear, direct, even humorous way makes these books interesting, motivational, and fun.

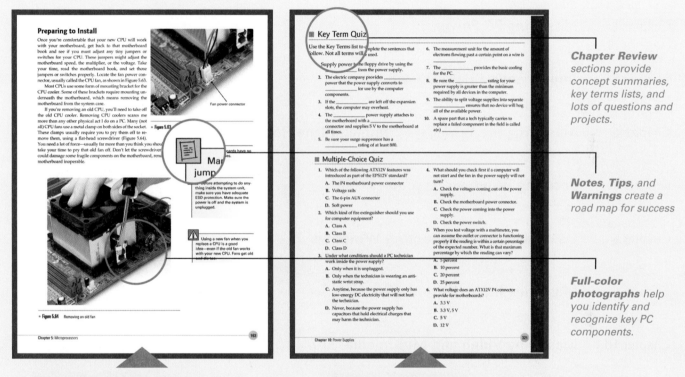

Chapter Review sections provide concept summaries, key terms lists, and lots of questions and projects.

Notes, **Tips**, and **Warnings** create a road map for success

Full-color photographs help you identify and recognize key PC components.

Offers Practical Experience—
Tutorials and lab assignments develop essential hands-on skills and put concepts in real-world contexts.

Robust Learning Tools—
Summaries, key terms lists, quizzes, essay questions, and lab projects help you practice skills and measure progress.

Each chapter includes:

- **Learning objectives** that set measurable goals for chapter-by-chapter progress

- **Try This!**, **Cross Check**, and **Tech Tip** sidebars that encourage you to practice and apply concepts in real-world settings

- Plenty of full-color **photographs** and **illustrations** that provide clear, up-close pictures of the technology, making difficult concepts easy to visualize and understand

- **Notes**, **Tips**, and **Warnings** that guide you through difficult areas

- **Highlighted Key Terms**, **Key Terms lists**, and **Chapter Summaries** that provide you with an easy way to review important concepts and vocabulary

- **Challenging End-of-Chapter Quizzes** that include vocabulary-building exercises, multiple-choice questions, essay questions, and on-the-job lab projects

CONTENTS AT A GLANCE

CONTENTS

Chapter 5
■ Implementing Hard Drives 92

Chapter 6
■ Mastering the Windows Command Line 158

Chapter 7
■ Securing Windows Resources 198

PREFACE

I started writing computer books for the simple reason that no one wrote the kind of books I wanted to read. The books were either too simple (Chapter 1, "Using Your Mouse") or too complex (Chapter 1, "TTL Logic and Transistors"), and none of them provided a motivation for me to learn the information. I believed that there were geeky readers just like me who wanted to know *why* they needed to know the information in a computer book.

Good books motivate readers to learn what they are reading. For example, if a book discusses binary arithmetic but doesn't explain why I need to learn it, that's not a good book. Tell me that understanding binary makes it easier to understand how a CPU works or why a megabyte is different from a million bytes—then I get excited, no matter how geeky the topic. If I don't have a good motivation to do something, then I'm simply not going to do it (which explains why I haven't jumped out of an airplane!).

In this book, I teach you why you need to understand the technology that runs almost every modern business. You'll learn to build and fix computers, exploring every nook and cranny, and master the art of the PC tech. In the process, you'll gain the knowledge you need to pass the CompTIA A+ Practical Application exam.

Enjoy, my fellow geek.

—Mike Meyers

The logo of the CompTIA Authorized Quality Curriculum (CAQC) program and the status of this or other training material as "Authorized" under the CompTIA Authorized Quality Curriculum program signifies that, in CompTIA's opinion, such training material covers the content of CompTIA's related certification exam.

The contents of this training material were created for the CompTIA A+® Practical Application exam (Exam 220-702), covering CompTIA certification objectives that were current as of August 2009.

CompTIA has not reviewed or approved the accuracy of the contents of this training material and specifically disclaims any warranties of merchantability or fitness for a particular purpose.

CompTIA makes no guarantee concerning the success of persons using any such "Authorized" or other training material in order to prepare for any CompTIA certification exam.

■ How to Become CompTIA Certified

This training material can help you prepare for and pass a related CompTIA certification exam or exams. In order to achieve CompTIA certification, you must register for and pass a CompTIA certification exam or exams.

In order to become CompTIA certified, you must:

1. Select a certification exam provider. For more information please visit http://www.comptia.org/certifications/testprep/testingcenters.aspx.

2. Register for and schedule a time to take the CompTIA certification exam(s) at a convenient location.

3. Read and sign the Candidate Agreement, which will be presented at the time of the exam(s). The text of the Candidate Agreement can be found at http://www.comptia.org/certifications/testprep/policies/agreement.aspx.

4. Take and pass the CompTIA certification exam(s).

For more information about CompTIA's certifications, such as its industry acceptance, benefits or program news, please visit www.comptia.org/certification.

CompTIA is a not-for-profit information technology (IT) trade association. CompTIA's certifications are designed by subject matter experts from across the IT industry. Each CompTIA certification is vendor-neutral, covers multiple technologies and requires demonstration of skills and knowledge widely sought after by the IT industry.

To contact CompTIA with any questions or comments, please call (1) (630) 678 8300 or email questions@comptia.org.

chapter 1

For instructor and student resources, check out www.MeyersPracticalApp
.com. Students will find the chapter quizzes from the end of each chapter,
and teachers can access instructor support materials.

■ Additional Resources for Teachers

Resources for teachers are provided via an Online Learning Center that
maps to the organization of this textbook. This site includes the following:

- Answer keys to the end-of-chapter quizzes from this textbook

- Answer keys to the *Mike Meyers' CompTIA A+® Guide: Practical
  Application Lab Manual, Third Edition (Exam 220-702)* lab activities

- Instructor's Manual that contains learning objectives, classroom
  preparation notes, instructor tips, and a lecture outline for each
  chapter

- Engaging PowerPoint slides on the lecture topics (including full-
  color artwork from this book)

- Access to EZ Test online and test files that enable you to generate a
  wide array of tests. EZ Test features automatic grading, hundreds of
  practice questions, and a variety of question types and difficulty
  levels, enabling you to customize each test to maximize student
  progress

- LMS cartridges and other formats may also be available upon
  request; contact your sales representative

The Path of the PC Tech

> "Of everything I've learned during my stint at Maximum PC, one lesson reigns supreme: The PC is what we make of it."
>
> —GEORGE JONES, *MAXIMUM PC*

In this chapter, you will learn how to

- **Explain the importance of gaining skill in managing and troubleshooting PCs**
- **Explain the importance of CompTIA A+ certification**
- **Describe how to become a CompTIA A+ Certified Technician**

Computers have taken over the world, or at least many professions. Everywhere you turn, a quick dig beneath the surface sawdust of construction, the grease of auto mechanics, and the hum of medical technology reveals one or more personal computers (PCs) working away, doing essential jobs. Because the PC evolved from novelty item to essential science tool to everyday object in a short period of time, there's a huge demand for a workforce that can build, maintain, troubleshoot, and repair PCs.

The Importance of Skill in Managing and Troubleshooting PCs

The people who work with computers—the Information Technology (IT) workforce—do such varied jobs as design hardware, write computer programs that enable you to do specific jobs on the PC, and create small and large groupings of computers—networks—so people can share computer resources. IT people built the Internet, one of the most phenomenal inventions of the 20th century. IT people maintain the millions of computers that make up the Internet. Computer technicians (or PC techs, as those of us in the field call each other) make up the core of the IT workforce. Without the techs, none of the other stuff works. Getting workers with skill in building, maintaining, troubleshooting, and fixing PCs is essential for success for every modern business.

In the early days of the personal computer, anyone who used a PC had to have skills as a PC tech. The PC was new, buggy, and prone to problems. You didn't want to rely on others to fix your PC when the inevitable problems arose. Today's PCs are much more robust and have fewer problems, but they're also much more complex machines. Today's IT industry, therefore, needs specialized workers who know how to make the machines run well.

Every profession requires specialized skills. For the most part, if you want to *get* or *keep* a job that requires those specialized skills, you need some type of certification or license. If you want a job fixing automobiles, for example, you get the *Automotive Service Excellence* (*ASE*) certification. If you want to perform companies' financial audits, you get your *Certified Public Accountant* (*CPA*) certification.

Nearly every profession has some criteria that you must meet to show your competence and ability to perform at a certain level. Although the way this works varies widely from one profession to another, all of them will at some point make you take an exam or series of exams. Passing these exams proves that you have the necessary skills to work at a certain level in your profession, whether you're an aspiring plumber, teacher, barber, or lawyer.

If you successfully pass these exams, the organization that administers those exams grants you certification. You receive some piece of paper or pin or membership card that you can show to potential clients or employers. This certification gives those clients or employers a level of confidence that you can do what you say you can do. Without this certification, either you will not find suitable work in that profession or no one will trust you to do the work.

The Importance of CompTIA A+ Certification

Microcomputers were introduced in the late 1970s, and for many years PC technicians did not have a universally recognized way to show clients or employers that they know what to do under the hood of a personal computer. Sure, vendor-specific certifications existed, but the only way to get them was to get a job at an authorized warranty or repair facility first and then get the certification. Not that there's anything wrong with vendor-specific training; it's just that no single manufacturer has taken enough market share to make IBM training, for example, something that works for any job. (Then there is always that little detail of getting the job first before you can be certified....)

The software/networking side of our business has not suffered from the same lack of certifications. Due to the dominance of certain companies at one time or another (for example, Microsoft and Cisco), the vendor-specific certifications have provided a great way to get and keep a job. For example, Microsoft's *Microsoft Certified Systems Engineer (MCSE)* and Cisco's *Cisco Certified Internetwork Expert (CCIE)* have opened the doors for many.

But what about the person who runs around all day repairing printers, repartitioning hard drives, upgrading device drivers, and assembling systems? What about the PC hobbyists who want to be paid for their skills? What about the folks who, because they had the audacity to show that they knew the difference between CMOS and a command prompt, find themselves with a new title such as PC Support Technician or Electronic Services Specialist? On the other hand, how about the worst title of them all: "The Person Who Doesn't Get a Nickel Extra but Who Fixes the Computers"? CompTIA A+ certification fills that need.

What Is CompTIA A+ Certification?

CompTIA A+ certification is an industry-wide, vendor-neutral certification program developed and sponsored by the Computing Technology Industry Association (CompTIA). The CompTIA A+ certification shows that you have a basic competence in supporting microcomputers. You achieve this certification by taking two computer-based, multiple-choice examinations. The tests cover what technicians should know after nine months of full-time PC support experience. CompTIA A+ certification enjoys wide recognition throughout the computer industry. To date, more than 800,000 technicians have become CompTIA A+ certified, making it the most popular of all IT certifications.

Who Is CompTIA?

CompTIA is a nonprofit industry trade association based in Oakbrook Terrace, Illinois. It consists of over 20,000 members in 102 countries. You'll find CompTIA offices in such diverse locales as Amsterdam, Dubai, Johannesburg, Tokyo, and São Paulo.

CompTIA provides a forum for people in these industries to network (as in meeting people), represents the interests of its members to the government, and provides certifications for many aspects of the computer industry. CompTIA sponsors A+, Network+, Security+, and other certifications. CompTIA works hard to watch the IT industry and constantly looks to provide new certifications to meet the ongoing demand from its membership. Check out the CompTIA Web site at www.comptia.org for details on the other certifications you can obtain from CompTIA.

Virtually every company of consequence in the IT industry is a member of CompTIA. Here are a few of the biggies:

Adobe Systems	AMD	Best Buy	Brother International
Canon	Cisco Systems	CompUSA	Fujitsu
Gateway	Hewlett-Packard	IBM	Intel
Kyocera	McAfee	Microsoft	NCR
Novell	Panasonic	Sharp Electronics	Siemens
Symantec	Toshiba	Total Seminars, LLC (that's my company)	Plus many thousands more

CompTIA began offering CompTIA A+ certification back in 1993. When it debuted, the IT industry largely ignored CompTIA A+ certification. Since that initial stutter, however, the CompTIA A+ certification has grown to become the de facto requirement for entrance into the PC industry. Many companies require CompTIA A+ certification for all of their PC support technicians, and the CompTIA A+ certification is widely recognized both in the United States and internationally. Additionally, many other certifications recognize CompTIA A+ certification and use it as credit toward their certifications.

The Path to Other Certifications

Most IT companies—big and small—see CompTIA A+ certification as the entry point to IT. From CompTIA A+, you have a number of certification options, depending on whether you want to focus more on hardware and operating systems or move into network administration (although these aren't mutually exclusive goals). The following three certifications are worth serious consideration:

- CompTIA Network+ certification
- Microsoft Certified Professional certifications
- Cisco certifications

CompTIA Network+ Certification

If you haven't already taken the CompTIA Network+ certification exam, make it your next certification. Just as CompTIA A+ certification shows you have solid competency as a PC technician, CompTIA Network+ certification demonstrates your skills as a network technician, including understanding of network hardware, installation, and troubleshooting. CompTIA's Network+ certification is a natural step for continuing toward your Microsoft or Cisco certifications. Take the CompTIA Network+: it's your obvious next certification.

Microsoft Certified Professional Certifications

Microsoft operating systems control a huge portion of all installed networks, and those networks need qualified support people to make them run. Microsoft Certified Professional certifications are a natural next step after the CompTIA certifications. They offer a whole slew of tracks and exams,

CompTIA A+ is the entry point to IT, though definitely not the only route for learning about computers and having certifications to prove that knowledge. Several certifications cover computer literacy or digital literacy, the phrase that means "what every person needs to know about computers to survive in the 21st century." The most popular computer literacy certification is Certiport's IC^3 certification that tests on general computer knowledge; office productivity applications, such as Word and PowerPoint; and Internet applications such as Web browsing and e-mail.

CompTIA has a pre–CompTIA A+ exam (*not* a certification), called the *CompTIA Strata IT Technology exam*, that's geared a bit more to a user preparing to become a tech. It's designed to check basic knowledge levels for people getting into IT.

ranging from simple specializations in Windows Vista to numerous Microsoft Certified IT Professional (MCITP) certifications and beyond. You can find more details on Microsoft's learning Web site at www.microsoft .com/learning/en/us/certification/cert-overview.aspx.

Cisco Certification

Let's face it, Cisco routers pretty much run the Internet and most intranets in the world. A *router* is a networking device that controls and directs the flow of information over networks, such as e-mail messages, Web browsing, and so on. Cisco provides five levels of certification for folks who want to show their skills at handling Cisco products, such as the Certified Cisco Network Associate (CCNA), plus numerous specialty certifications. See the Cisco certification Web site here for more details: www.cisco.com/web/learning/ le3/learning_career_certifications_and_learning_paths_home.html.

■ How Do I Become CompTIA A+ Certified?

You become CompTIA A+ certified, in the simplest sense, by taking and passing two computer-based, multiple-choice exams. No prerequisites are required for taking the CompTIA A+ certification exams (although there's an assumption of computer literacy, whether or not you have one of the computer literacy certifications). There is no required training course and no training materials to buy. You *do* have to pay a testing fee for each of the two exams. You pay your testing fees, go to a local testing center, and take the tests. You immediately know whether you have passed or failed. By passing both exams, you become CompTIA A+ certified. There are no requirements for professional experience. You do not have to go through an authorized training center. There are no annual dues. You pass; you're in. That's it. Now for the details.

> Previously, CompTIA offered a basic exam and then a choice of three different second exams. CompTIA reverted to the simpler two-exam format in 2009.

The Basic Exam Structure

CompTIA names the two exams introduced in 2009 as CompTIA A+ 220-701 (Essentials) and CompTIA A+ 220-702 (Practical Application). It's common to refer to these two exams as the 2009 exams to differentiate them from older CompTIA exams. Although you may take either of the two exams first, I recommend taking the Essentials followed by the Practical Application. The Essentials exam concentrates on understanding terminology and technology, how to do fundamental tasks such as upgrading RAM, and basic Windows operating system support. The Practical Application exam builds on the Essentials exam, concentrating on advanced configuration and troubleshooting.

Both of the exams are extremely practical, with little or no interest in theory. All questions are multiple choice or "click on the right part of the picture" questions. The following is an example of the questions you will see on the exams:

Your laser printer is printing blank pages. Which item should you check first?

    A. Printer drivers

    B. Toner cartridge

    C. Printer settings

    D. Paper feed

The correct answer is B, the toner cartridge. You can make an argument for any of the others, but common sense (and skill as a PC technician) tells you to check the simplest possibility first.

The 2009 exams use a regular test format in which you answer a set number of questions and are scored based on how many correct answers you give, rather than the adaptive format used in years past. These exams have no more than 100 questions each. (Both exams have 100 questions each at the time of this writing.)

Be aware that CompTIA may add new questions to the exams at any time to keep the content fresh. The subject matter covered by the exams won't change, but new questions may be added periodically at random intervals. This policy puts stronger emphasis on understanding concepts and having solid PC-tech knowledge rather than trying to memorize specific questions and answers that may have been on the tests in the past. Going forward, no book or Web resource will have all the "right answers" because those answers will change constantly. Luckily for you, however, this book does not just teach you what steps to follow in a particular case but also explains how to be a knowledgeable tech who understands *why* you're doing those steps, so that when you encounter a new problem (or test question), you can work out the answer. Not only will this help you pass the exams, you'll also be a better PC tech!

To keep up to date, we monitor the CompTIA A+ exams for new content and update the special Tech Files section of the Total Seminars Web site (www.totalsem.com) with new articles covering subjects we believe may appear on future versions of the exams.

Windows-Centric

The CompTIA A+ exams are exclusively centered on the Microsoft Windows operating systems you would expect at a workstation or home. There are no Linux questions. There are no Macintosh OS X questions. You won't be asked about any version of Windows Server or Windows Mobile (used on smartphones and PDAs). Objectives in both exams clearly focus on the following operating systems:

- Windows 2000 Professional
- Windows XP Professional
- Windows XP Home
- Windows XP Media Center
- Windows Vista Home
- Windows Vista Home Premium
- Windows Vista Business
- Windows Vista Ultimate

Windows 7

CompTIA has the darnedest luck when it comes to the timing of new CompTIA A+ exams compared to releases of new Windows versions. CompTIA released the previous CompTIA A+ exams back in 2006, about four months before Microsoft released Windows Vista. It seems that once again CompTIA is caught missing a new operating system. Just a few months after CompTIA announced the 2009 updates to the CompTIA A+, Microsoft unveiled the next version of Windows: Windows 7.

Assuming CompTIA stays true to form, the chances of Windows 7 making it onto this version of the CompTIA A+ are very small. Adding Windows 7 is a major undertaking that would require CompTIA to change their clearly defined exam objectives. Don't worry about Windows 7. Structurally it is identical to Windows Vista. Even Microsoft has stated that Windows 7 is "a refined version of Windows Vista." If you know Vista, you will know Windows 7—and CompTIA isn't going to ask you about Windows 7 until the next update, probably around 2012.

Essentials (Exam 220–701)

The questions on the CompTIA A+ Essentials exam fit into one of six objectives. The number of questions for each objective is based on the percentages shown in Table 1.1.

The Essentials exam tests your knowledge of computer components, expecting you to be able to identify just about every common device on PCs, including variations within device types. Here's a list:

- Floppy drives
- Hard drives
- Optical drives
- Solid state drives
- Motherboards
- Power supplies
- CPUs
- RAM
- Monitors
- Input devices, such as keyboards, mice, and touchscreens
- Video and multimedia cards
- Network and modem cards
- Cables and connectors
- Heat sinks, fans, and liquid cooling systems
- Laptops and portable devices
- Printers
- Scanners
- Network switches, cabling, and wireless adapters
- Biometric devices

Table 1.1	Essentials (Exam 220-701) Objectives and Percentages	
Domain		**Percentage**
1.0 Hardware		27%
2.0 Troubleshooting, Repair, and Maintenance		20%
3.0 Operating Systems and Software		20%
4.0 Networking		15%
5.0 Security		8%
6.0 Operational Procedure		10%

The Essentials exam tests your ability to install, configure, and maintain all the standard technology involved in a personal computer. You need to be able to install and set up a hard drive, for example, and configure devices in Windows 2000, Windows XP, and Windows Vista. You have to understand drivers. You have to know your way around Windows and understand the tasks involved in updating, upgrading, and installing the operating systems. You need to know the standard diagnostic tools available in Windows—not only so you can fix problems, but also so you can work with higher-level techs to fix things.

You're tested on your knowledge of computer security, including identifying, installing, and configuring security hardware and software. You need to know security tools and diagnostic techniques for troubleshooting. You're not expected to know everything, just enough to be competent.

Finally, the Essentials exam puts a lot of emphasis on operational procedures, such as safety and environmental issues and also communication and professionalism. You need to know how to recycle and dispose of computer gear properly. You have to understand and avoid hazardous situations. The exam tests your ability to communicate effectively with customers and coworkers. You need to understand professional behavior and demonstrate that you have tact, discretion, and respect for others and their property.

Practical Application (Exam 220-702)

The CompTIA A+ 220-702 exam covers four objectives. Table 1.2 lists the objectives and percentages.

The Practical Application exam covers the same hardware and software as Essentials, but with a much more hands-on approach to determining the appropriate technology for a situation—running diagnostics and troubleshooting—rather than identification of hardware or operating system utilities. The exam tests your knowledge of computer components and programs so you can make informed recommendations to customers. You need to understand how all the technology should work, know the proper steps to figure out why something doesn't work, and then fix it.

The first domain, Hardware, provides a stark example of the difference in focus between the exams. Essentials talks about identifying names, purposes, and characteristics of various devices. The Practical Application exam, in contrast, goes into more depth, placing you in real-world scenarios where you must decide what to do. Every sub-objective in the Hardware objective starts with "Given a scenario" and then asks you to do something. Objective 1.1 says, for example, "Given a scenario, install, configure and maintain personal computer components." Objective 1.2 says, "Given a

Table 1.2	Practical Application (Exam 220-702) Objectives and Percentages	
Domain	**Percentage**
1.0 Hardware	38%
2.0 Operating Systems	34%
3.0 Networking	15%
4.0 Security	13%

Even though the Practical Application exam does not specifically cover operational procedures, expect some questions about ethics, proper behavior in the workplace, ways to communicate with customers to get the most information in troubleshooting situations, and more.

scenario, detect problems, troubleshoot and repair/replace personal computer components." The other objectives follow suit.

Another big difference between the two exams is the treatment of the Operating Systems and Software objective in the Essentials exam versus Operating Systems in the Practical Application exam. Essentials tests you on how to use Windows and how to recognize the components, features, and basic utilities of the operating systems. The Practical Application exam goes much deeper. You need to understand intimately how to use the command line to manage the operating systems. You're expected to know all sorts of disk structures and run all the major disk management tools. Finally, the Practical Application exam grills you on operating system recovery tools and techniques so you can help customers get back up and running quickly.

This book covers the 220-702 exam, but many of the concepts and information you'll learn here will help you on the 220-701 exam as well. However, while there is bound to be some overlap of topics between the two exams, there is plenty of information on the 701 exam that is not covered in this book, so be sure to keep studying for that exam once you're finished with this book!

How Do I Take the Exams?

Two companies, Prometric and Pearson VUE, administer the CompTIA A+ testing. There are thousands of Prometric and Pearson VUE testing centers across the United States and Canada, and the rest of the world. You may take the exams at any testing center. Both Prometric and Pearson VUE offer complete listings online of all available testing centers. You can select the closest training center and schedule your exams right from the comfort of your favorite Web browser:

www.prometric.com
www.vue.com

Alternatively, in the United States and Canada, call Prometric at 800-776-4276 or Pearson VUE at 877-551-PLUS (7587) to schedule the exams and to locate the nearest testing center. International customers can find a list of Prometric and Pearson VUE international contact numbers for various regions of the world on CompTIA's Web site at www.comptia.org.

You must pay for the exam when you call to schedule. Be prepared to sit on hold for a while. Have your Social Security number (or international equivalent) and a credit card ready when you call. Both Prometric and Pearson VUE will be glad to invoice you, but you won't be able to take the exam until they receive full payment.

If you have special needs, both Prometric and Pearson VUE will accommodate you, although this may limit your selection of testing locations.

How Much Does the Exam Cost?

The cost of the exam depends on whether you work for a CompTIA member or not. At this writing, the cost for non-CompTIA members is $168 (U.S.) for each exam. International prices vary, but you can check the CompTIA Web site for international pricing. Of course, the prices are subject to change without notice, so always check the CompTIA Web site for current pricing.

Very few people pay full price for the exam. Virtually every organization that provides CompTIA A+ training and testing also offers discount vouchers. You buy a discount voucher and then use the voucher number instead of a credit card when you schedule the exam. Vouchers are sold per exam, so you'll need two vouchers to take the two CompTIA A+ exams. Total Seminars is one place to get discount vouchers. You can call Total Seminars at 800-446-6004 or 281-922-4166, or get vouchers via the Web site: www.totalsem.com. No one should ever pay full price for CompTIA A+ exams.

How to Pass the CompTIA A+ Exams

The single most important thing to remember about the CompTIA A+ certification exams is that CompTIA designed the Essentials exam to test the knowledge of a technician with only 500 hours experience (about three months) and the Practical Application exam to test the knowledge of a technician with only 1000 hours experience (about six months)—so keep it simple! The exams aren't interested in your ability to overclock DDR3 CAS timings in CMOS or whether you can explain the exact difference between the Intel ICH10 and the AMD 790 southbridges. Don't bother with a lot of theory—think in terms of practical knowledge and standards. Read the book, do whatever works for you to memorize the key concepts and procedures, take the practice exams on the CD in the back of the book, review any topics you miss, and you should pass with no problem.

Some of you may be in or just out of school, so studying for exams is nothing novel. But if you haven't had to study for and take an exam in a while, or if you think maybe you could use some tips, you may find the next section valuable. It lays out a proven strategy for preparing to take and pass the CompTIA A+ exams. Try it. It works.

Those of you who just want more knowledge in managing and troubleshooting PCs can follow the same strategy as certification-seekers. Think in practical terms and work with the PC as you go through each chapter.

Obligate Yourself

The very first step you should take is to schedule yourself for the exams. Have you ever heard the old adage, "Heat and pressure make diamonds"? Well, if you don't give yourself a little "heat," you'll end up procrastinating and delay taking the exams, possibly forever. Do yourself a favor. Using the following information, determine how much time you'll need to study for the exams, and then call Prometric or Pearson VUE and schedule them accordingly. Knowing the exams are coming up makes it much easier to turn off the television and crack open the book. You can schedule an exam as little as a few weeks in advance, but if you schedule an exam and can't take it at the scheduled time, you must reschedule at least a day in advance or you'll lose your money.

Set Aside the Right Amount of Study Time

After helping thousands of techs get their CompTIA A+ certification, we at Total Seminars have developed a pretty good feel for the amount of study time needed to pass the CompTIA A+ certification exams. The following table provides an estimate to help you plan how much study time you must commit to the CompTIA A+ certification exams. Keep in mind that these are averages. If you're not a great student or if you're a little on the nervous side,

Table 1.3 | **Analyzing Skill Levels**

Tech Task	None	Once or Twice	Every Now and Then	Quite a Bit
			Amount of Experience	
Installing an adapter card	12	10	8	4
Installing and configuring hard drives	12	10	8	2
Installing modems and NICs	8	6	6	3
Connecting a computer to the Internet	8	6	4	2
Installing printers and scanners	4	3	2	1
Installing RAM	8	6	4	2
Installing CPUs	8	7	5	3
Fixing printers	6	5	4	3
Fixing boot problems	8	7	7	5
Fixing portable computers	8	6	4	2
Building complete systems	12	10	8	6
Using the command line	8	8	6	4
Installing/optimizing Windows	10	8	6	4
Using Windows 2000/XP	6	6	4	2
Using Windows Vista	10	8	4	2
Configuring NTFS permissions	6	4	3	2
Configuring a wireless network	6	5	3	2
Configuring a software firewall	6	4	2	1
Installing a sound card	2	2	1	0
Removing malware	4	3	2	0
Using OS diagnostic tools	8	8	6	4
Using a volt-ohm meter	4	3	2	1

add 10 percent; if you're a fast learner or have a good bit of computer experience, you may want to reduce the figures.

To use Table 1.3, just circle the values that are most accurate for you and add them up to get your estimated total hours of study time.

To that value, add hours based on the number of months of direct, professional experience you have had supporting PCs, as shown in Table 1.4.

A total neophyte usually needs a little over 200 hours of study time. An experienced tech shouldn't need more than 60 hours.

Total hours for you to study: _____.

Table 1.4 | **Adding Up Your Study Time**

Months of Direct, Professional Experience...	To Your Study Time...
0	Add 50
Up to 6	Add 30
6 to 12	Add 10
Over 12	Add 0

A Strategy for Study

Now that you have a feel for how long it's going to take, you're ready to develop a study strategy. I'd like to suggest a strategy that has worked for others who've come before you, whether they were experienced techs or total newbies. This book is designed to accommodate the different study agendas of these two groups of students. The first group is experienced techs who already have strong PC experience but need to be sure they're ready to be tested on the specific subjects covered by the CompTIA A+ Practical Application exam. The second group is those with little or no background in the computer field. These techs can benefit from a more detailed understanding of the history and concepts that underlie modern PC technology, to help them remember the specific subject matter information they must know for the exams. I'll use the shorthand terms Old Techs and New Techs for these two groups. If you're not sure which group you fall into, pick a few chapters and go through some end-of-chapter questions. If you score less than 70%, go the New Tech route.

I have broken most of the chapters into three distinct parts:

- **Historical/Conceptual**   Topics that are not on the CompTIA A+ exams but will help you understand more clearly what is on the CompTIA A+ exams.

- **Practical Application**   Topics that clearly fit under the CompTIA A+ Practical Application exam domains.

- **Beyond A+**   More advanced issues that probably will not be on the CompTIA A+ exams—yet.

 Not all chapters will have all three sections.

The beginning of each of these areas is clearly marked with a large banner that looks like this:

Historical/Conceptual

Those of you who fall into the Old Tech group may want to skip the Historical/Conceptual sections, since they cover information that you may already know. After reading the other sections, jump immediately to the questions at the end of the chapter. The end-of-chapter questions concentrate on information in the non-Historical/Conceptual sections. If you run into problems, review the Historical/Conceptual sections in that chapter. Note that you may need to skip back to previous chapters to get the Historical/Conceptual information you need for later chapters.

After going through every chapter as described, Old Techs can move directly to testing their knowledge by using the free practice exams on the CD-ROM that accompanies the book. Once you start scoring above 90%, you're ready to take the exams. If you're a New Tech—or if you're an Old Tech who wants the full learning experience this book can offer—start by reading the book, *the whole book,* as though you were reading a novel, from page one to the end without skipping around. Because so many computer terms and concepts build on each other, skipping around greatly increases the odds that you will become confused and end up closing the book and firing up your favorite PC game. Not that I have anything against PC games, but unfortunately that skill is *not* useful for the CompTIA A+ exams!

Your goal on this first read is to understand concepts, the *whys* behind the *hows*. Having a PC nearby as you read is helpful so you can stop and inspect the PC to see a piece of hardware or how a particular concept manifests in the real world. As you read about floppy drives, for example, inspect the cables. Do they look like the ones in the book? Is there a variation? Why? It is imperative that you understand why you are doing something, not just how to do it on one particular system under one specific set of conditions. Neither the exams nor real life as a PC tech works that way.

If you're reading this book as part of a managing and troubleshooting PCs class rather than a certification-prep course, I highly recommend going the New Tech route, even if you have a decent amount of experience. The book contains a lot of details that can trip you up if you focus only on the test-specific sections of the chapters. Plus, your program might stress historical and conceptual knowledge as well as practical, hands-on skills.

The CompTIA A+ certification exams assume that you have basic user skills. The exams really try to trick you with questions on processes that you may do every day and not think much about. Here's a classic: "To move a file from the C:\DATA folder to the D:\ drive using Windows Explorer, what key must you hold down while dragging the file?" If you can answer that without going to your keyboard and trying a few likely keys, you're better than most techs! In the real world, you can try a few wrong answers before you hit on the right one, but for the exams, you have to *know* it. Whether Old Tech or New Tech, make sure you are proficient at user-level Windows skills, including the following:

- Recognizing all the components of the standard Windows desktop (Start menu, notification area, etc.)
- Manipulating windows—resizing, moving, and so on
- Creating, deleting, renaming, moving, and copying files and folders within Windows
- Understanding file extensions and their relationship with program associations
- Using common keyboard shortcuts/hotkeys
- Installing, running, and closing a Windows application

Any PC technician who has been around a while will tell you that one of the great secrets in the computer business is that there's almost never anything completely new in the world of computer technology. Faster, cleverer, smaller, wider—absolutely—but the underlying technology, the core of what makes your PC and its various peripheral devices operate, has changed remarkably little since PCs came into widespread use a few decades ago. When you do your initial read-through, you may be tempted to skip the Historical/Conceptual sections—don't! Understanding the history and technological developments behind today's PCs helps you understand why they work—or don't work—the way they do. Basically, I'm passing on to you the kind of knowledge you might get by apprenticing yourself to an older, experienced PC tech.

After you've completed the first read-through, go through the book again, this time in textbook mode. If you're an Old Tech, start your studying here. Try to cover one chapter at a sitting. Don't focus too much on the Historical/Conceptual sections. Get a highlighter and mark the phrases and sentences that bring out major points. Be sure you understand how the pictures and illustrations relate to the concepts being discussed.

Once you feel you have a good grasp of the material in the book, you can check your knowledge by using the practice exams included on the CD-ROM in the back of the book. You can take these in Practice mode or Final mode. In Practice mode, you can use the Assistance window to get a helpful hint for the current questions, use the Reference feature to find the chapter that covers the question, check your answer for the question, and see an explanation of the correct answer. In Final mode, you answer all the questions and receive an exam score at the end, just like the real thing.

Both modes show you an overall grade, expressed as a percentage, as well as a breakdown of how well you did on each exam domain. The Review Questions feature lets you see what questions you missed and what the correct answers are. Use these results to guide further studying. Continue reviewing the topics you miss and taking additional exams until you are consistently scoring in the 90% range. When you get there, you are ready to pass the CompTIA A+ Practical Application exam.

Study Tactics

Perhaps it's been a while since you had to study for a test. Or perhaps it hasn't, but you've done your best since then to block the whole experience from your mind. Either way, savvy test-takers know that certain techniques make studying for tests more efficient and effective.

Here's a trick used by students in law and medical schools who have to memorize reams of information: write it down. The act of writing something down (not typing, *writing*) in and of itself helps you to remember it, even if you never look at what you wrote again. Try taking separate notes on the material and re-creating diagrams by hand to help solidify the information in your mind.

Another oldie but goodie: Make yourself flash cards with questions and answers on topics you find difficult. A third trick: Take your notes to bed and read them just before you go to sleep. Many people find they really do learn while they sleep!

Contact

If you have any problems, any questions, or if you just want to argue about something, feel free to send an e-mail to the author—michaelm@totalsem.com—or to the editor—scottj@totalsem.com.

For any other information you might need, contact CompTIA directly at their Web site: www.comptia.org.

Chapter 1 Review

■ Chapter Summary

After reading this chapter and completing the exercises, you should understand the following about the path of the PC tech.

Explain the importance of gaining skill in managing and troubleshooting PCs

■ The IT workforce designs, builds, and maintains computers, computer programs, and networks. PC techs take care of personal computers, thus representing an essential component in that workforce. As PCs become more complex, the IT workforce needs specialized PC techs.

■ Certifications prove to employers that you have the necessary skills. If you want a job fixing automobiles, for example, you get the *Automotive Service Excellence* (*ASE*) certification. To be certified, you take and successfully pass exams. Then the organization that administers those exams grants you certification. This is particularly important for IT workers.

Explain the importance of CompTIA A+ certification

■ In the early days of the personal computer, you could get vendor-specific certifications, such as IBM Technician, but nothing general for PC techs. Worse, you often had to have a job at that company to get the vendor-specific certification. The software and networking side of IT doesn't have that issue. To prove skill in working with Windows, for example, you could become a Microsoft Certified Technology Specialist (MCTS).

■ CompTIA A+ certification is an industry-wide, vendor-neutral certification program that shows that you have a basic competence in supporting microcomputers. You achieve this certification by taking two computer-based, multiple-choice examinations. The tests cover what technicians should know after nine months of full-time PC support experience. CompTIA A+ certification enjoys wide recognition throughout the computer industry.

■ CompTIA is a nonprofit, industry trade association based in Oakbrook Terrace, Illinois. It consists of over 20,000 members in 102 countries. CompTIA provides a forum for people in these industries to network, represents the interests of its members to the government, and provides certifications for many aspects of the computer industry. CompTIA sponsors A+, Network+, Security+, and other certifications.

■ The CompTIA A+ certification is the de facto entry point to IT. From CompTIA A+, you have a number of certification options, depending on whether you want to focus more on hardware and operating systems or move into network administration. You can get CompTIA Network+ certification, for example, or go on to get Microsoft or Cisco certified. CompTIA Network+ certification is the most obvious certification to get after becoming CompTIA A+ certified.

Describe how to become a CompTIA A+ Certified Technician

■ You become CompTIA A+ certified, in the simplest sense, by taking and passing two computer-based, multiple-choice exams. No prerequisites are required for taking the CompTIA A+ certification exams. There is no required training course and no training materials to buy. You *do* have to pay a testing fee for each of the two exams.

■ The CompTIA exams introduced in 2009 are *220-701* (*Essentials*) and *220-702* (*Practical Application*). It's common to refer to these two exams as the 2009 exams to differentiate them from older CompTIA exams. Although you may take either of the two exams first, I recommend taking the Essentials, followed by the Practical Application.

■ Both of the exams are extremely practical, with little or no interest in theory. All questions are multiple choice or "click on the right part of the picture" questions. CompTIA may add new questions to the exams at any time to keep the content fresh, although the subject matter covered by the exams won't change.

■ Two companies, Prometric and Pearson VUE, administer the actual CompTIA A+ testing. You can schedule exam time and location via the Web site for either company, www.prometric.com or www.vue.com. Check CompTIA's Web site for international links.

- To achieve success with the CompTIA A+ certification exams, think in terms of practical knowledge. Read the book. Work through the problems. Work with computers. Take the practice exams. You should obligate yourself by scheduling your exams. This keeps you focused on study.

- Read the book all the way through once. Experienced techs should then concentrate on the test-specific sections to prepare for the exams. Less experienced techs should read the book all the way through again until everything makes sense.

- If you're reading this book as part of a managing and troubleshooting PCs class rather than a certification-prep course, I highly recommend going the New Tech route, even if you have a decent amount of experience. The book contains a lot of details that can trip you up if you focus only on the test-specific sections of the chapters.

■ Key Terms

certification *(1)* ✓

Certified Cisco Network Associate (CCNA) *(4)*

CompTIA A+ 220-701 (Essentials) *(4)* ✓

CompTIA A+ 220-702 (Practical Application) *(4)*

CompTIA A+ certification *(2)* ✓

CompTIA Network+ certification *(3)*

Computing Technology Industry Association (CompTIA) *(2)*

Information Technology (IT) *(1)* ✓

Microsoft Certified Professional (MCP) *(3)* ✓

network *(1)* ✓

PC tech *(1)* ✓

Pearson VUE *(8)* ✓

Prometric *(8)*

voucher *(9)* ✓

www.comptia.org *(2)* ✓

■ Key Term Quiz

Use the Key Terms list to complete the sentences that follow. Not all terms will be used.

1. You can lump together all the folks who design, build, program, and fix computers into the _Information technology_ workforce.

2. You can become CompTIA A+ certified by passing the _CompTIA A+ 220-701_ and CompTIA A+ 220-702 (Practical Application) exams.

3. A(n) _Certification_ gives clients and employers a level of confidence that you can do what you say you can do.

4. A casual term for a person who builds and maintains computers is _Pc tech_.

5. Prometric and _Pearson Vue_ administer the CompTIA A+ certification exams.

6. You can use a(n) _Voucher_ when you schedule your exam to save some money.

7. Persons desiring to work in Windows-based networking should pursue _Microsoft Certified Professional (mcp)_ certification after completing their CompTIA certifications.

8. You can find the latest information about the CompTIA A+ certification exams here: _www.comptia.org_

9. Typically, techs who attain CompTIA A+ certification then pursue _McP_ to add to their computer credentials.

10. A grouping of computers that enables people to share resources is called a(n) _Network_.

Multiple-Choice Quiz

1. Which of the following is a vendor-specific certification? (Select all that apply.)

    A. Certified Cisco Network Associate

    B. CompTIA A+

    C. CompTIA Network+

    D. Microsoft Certified Systems Engineer

2. Which of the following certifications is the de facto requirement for entrance into the PC industry?

    A. Certified Cisco Network Associate

    B. CompTIA A+

    C. CompTIA Network+

    D. Microsoft Certified Systems Engineer

3. John loves the Internet and wants a career working on the machines that make the Internet work. He has completed both CompTIA A+ and Network+ certifications. Which of the following certifications would make a good next step?

    A. Certified Cisco Network Associate

    B. Certified Cisco Network Professional

    C. CompTIA Security+

    D. Microsoft Certified Systems Engineer

4. Which of the following exams focuses on installing, configuring, and maintaining all the standard technology involved in a personal computer?

    A. Certified Cisco Network Associate

    B. CompTIA A+ 220-701 (Essentials)

    C. CompTIA A+ 220-702 (Practical Application)

    D. Microsoft Certified Systems Engineer

5. At which of the following Web sites can you register to take the CompTIA A+ certification exams?

    A. www.comptia.org

    B. www.microsoft.com

    C. www.totalsem.com

    D. www.vue.com

6. How many exams must you pass to become CompTIA A+ certified?

    A. One

    B. Two

    C. Three

    D. Four

7. How much practical IT experience do you need to become CompTIA A+ certified?

    A. Six months

    B. One year

    C. Two years

    D. None

8. How many questions should you expect on the 220-702 Practical Application exam?

    A. 25

    B. 50

    C. 100

    D. The number of questions varies because the exams are adaptive.

9. The CompTIA A+ certification covers which of the following operating systems? (Select two.)

    A. Linux

    B. OS X

    C. Windows XP Media Center

    D. Windows Vista

10. What percentage of questions should you expect on operating systems in the 220-701 Essentials exam?

    A. 10%

    B. 15%

    C. 20%

    D. 25%

11. What percentage of questions should you expect on operating systems in the 220-702 Practical Application exam?

    A. 10%

    B. 13%

    C. 20%

    D. 34%

12. How much does it cost to take each exam (at the time of this book's publication)?

    A. $100 each

    B. $138 each

    C. $168 each

    D. $150 each

13. What percentage of questions should you expect on Windows 7 in the 220-702 Practical Application exam?

    A. 10%

    B. 13%

    C. 20%

    D. None

14. The 220-701 Essentials exam will *not* test you on which of the following computer components?

    A. Biometric devices

    B. Keyboards

C. Printers

D. Zip drives

15. What is Comp

    A. A vendor

    B. A testin

    C. A for-

    D. A no

■ Essay Quiz

1. Write a short essay on the benefits of certification in the field of computers. Include discussion on how the CompTIA certifications function within the broader category of computer certification.

Why do you suppose people get certifications rather than (or in addition to) two- and four-year college degrees in IT?

Lab Project

• Lab Project 1.1

If you have access to the Internet, do some searching on computer certifications. Make a personal certification tree or pathway that maps out a series of certifications to pursue that might interest you.

What certifications would be useful if you want to be a graphics designer, for example? What if you want to create computer games?

Mastering CPUs and RAM

Computer: a million morons working at the speed of light."
—DAVID FERRIER

In this chapter, you will learn how to

- **Explain the difference between 32- and 64-bit CPUs**
- **Select and install CPUs**
- **Select and install RAM**
- **Perform basic RAM troubleshooting**

No one buys a computer just for the case. Whether you're laying out some spreadsheets in Microsoft Excel or blasting aliens on a planet somewhere in the vicinity of Betelgeuse, it's what's inside your computer that counts. Having the right (not to mention properly functioning) CPU and RAM is the difference between a pleasant evening spent in front of the computer and having to explain to your neighbors why their dog was nearly crushed by a computer flying out of your window.

Because you're interested in becoming a PC tech, you not only need to know what CPUs and RAM do inside a computer, you need to be able to install, maintain, and troubleshoot these devices. Fortunately for you, that is the very information you will learn in this chapter.

CPUs

For all practical purposes, the terms microprocessor and central processing unit (CPU) mean the same thing: it's that big chip inside your computer that many people often describe as the brain of the system. If you've already studied for or taken your CompTIA A+ 220-701 Essentials exam, you know that CPU makers name their microprocessors in a fashion similar to the automobile industry: CPU names get a make and a model, such as Intel Core i7 or AMD Phenom II X4. However, the CompTIA A+ 220-702 Practical Application exam expects you to know not only how a CPU works and the various types of CPUs available, but also how to install and troubleshoot CPUs. Later on in the chapter, you'll also take a look at working with RAM, but for the moment, how about those microprocessors?

Processing and Wattage

To make smarter and faster CPUs, Intel and AMD have had to increase the number of microscopic transistor circuits in the CPU. However, the more circuits you add, the more power the processor needs. CPUs measure their power use in units called watts, just like a common light bulb. Higher wattage also means higher heat, forcing modern CPUs to use powerful cooling methods. Good techs know how many watts a CPU needs, because this tells them how hot the CPU will get inside a PC. Known hot CPUs are often avoided for general-purpose PCs because these CPUs require more aggressive cooling.

 As you read the wattages for the various CPUs, imagine a light bulb with that wattage inside your system unit.

CPU makers really hate heat, but they still want to add more circuits; they constantly try to reduce the size of the circuits, because smaller circuits use less power. CPUs are made from silicon wafers. The electrical circuitry is etched onto the wafers with a process called photo lithography. Photo lithography is an amazingly complex process but basically requires placing a thin layer of chemicals on the wafer. These chemicals are sensitive to ultraviolet light; if a part of this mask is exposed to UV light, it gets hard and resistant. If it isn't exposed, it's easy to remove. To make the circuitry, a mask of the circuits is placed over the wafer, and then the mask and wafer are exposed to UV light. The mask is removed and the wafer is washed in chemicals, leaving the circuits. If you want microscopic circuits, you need a mask with the pattern of the microscopic circuits. This is done though a photographic process. The old 8088 used a 3-micrometer (one millionth of a meter) process to make the mask. Most of today's CPUs are created with a 45-nanometer process, and a 32-nanometer process is appearing in some chips. The same CPU created with a smaller process is usually cooler.

 A nanometer is one billionth of a meter.

Early 64-Bit CPUs

Almost all of the processors manufactured by AMD or Intel these days are 64-bit. A 64-bit CPU has general-purpose, floating point, and address registers that are 64 bits wide, meaning they can handle 64-bit-wide code in one pass—twice as wide as a 32-bit processor. And they can address much, much more memory.

With the 32-bit address bus of the Pentium and later CPUs, the maximum amount of memory the CPU can address is 2^{32} or 4,294,967,296 bytes. With a 64-bit address bus, CPUs can address 2^{64} bytes of memory, or more precisely, 18,446,744,073,709,551,616 bytes of memory—that's a lot of RAM! This number is so big that gigabytes and terabytes are no longer convenient, so we now go to an exabyte (2^{60}). A 64-bit address bus can address 16 exabytes of RAM.

No 64-bit CPU uses an actual 64-bit address bus. Every 64-bit processor gets its address bus clipped down to something reasonable. The Intel Itanium, for example, only has a 44-bit address bus, for a maximum address space of 2^{44} or 17,592,186,044,416 bytes. AMD's Phenom II, on the other hand, can allow for a 48-bit physical address space for 2^{48} or 281,474,976,710,656 bytes of memory.

Multicore CPUs

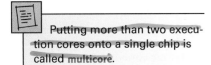
Putting more than two execution cores onto a single chip is called multicore.

CPU clock speeds hit a practical limit of roughly 4 GHz around 2002–2003, motivating the CPU makers to find new ways to get more processing power for CPUs. Although Intel and AMD had different opinions about 64-bit CPUs, both decided at virtually the same time to combine two CPUs into a single chip, creating a dual-core architecture. Dual core isn't just two CPUs on the same chip. A dual-core CPU has two execution units—two sets of pipelines—but the two sets of pipelines share caches (how they share caches differs between Intel and AMD) and RAM.

A multicore CPU can process more than one thread at a time; this is called parallel processing. Through parallel processing, the CPU can more readily juggle the demands of both applications and Windows, making the overall computing experience better. With multithreaded applications (programs written to take advantage of multiple CPUs or CPUs with multiple cores), this parallel processing can dramatically improve the performance of those applications.

■ Installing CPUs

Installing or upgrading a CPU is a remarkably straightforward process. You take off the fan and heat-sink assembly, remove the CPU, put a new CPU in, and snap the fan and heat-sink assembly back on. The trick to installing or replacing a CPU begins with two important questions: Do you need to replace your CPU? What CPU can you put in the computer?

Why Replace a CPU?

The CPU is the brain of your system, so it seems a natural assumption that taking out an old, slow CPU and replacing it with some new, fast CPU will make your computer run faster. No doubt it will, but first you need to consider a few issues, such as cost, cooling, and performance.

Cost

If you have an older CPU, there's a better than average chance that a faster version of your CPU is no longer available for retail purchase. In that case, replacing your CPU with a new one would require you to replace the motherboard and probably the RAM too. This is doable, but does it make sense in terms of cost? How much would this upgrade compare to a whole new system?

Cooling

Faster CPUs run hotter than slower ones. If you get a new CPU, you will almost certainly need a new CPU cooler to dissipate the heat generated by the more powerful processor. In addition, you may discover that your case fans are not sufficient, causing the CPU to overheat and the system to lock up. You can add improved cooling, but it might require a new case.

Performance

A faster CPU will make your computer run faster, but by how much? The results are often disappointing. As you go through this book, you will discover many other areas where upgrading might make a much stronger impact on your system's performance.

Determining the Right CPU

So you go through all of the decision-making and decide to go for a new CPU. Perhaps you're building a brand new system or maybe you're ready to go for that CPU upgrade. The single most important bit of documentation is called the motherboard book (Figure 2.1). Every computer should come with this important book that contains all of the details about what CPUs you can use as well as any special considerations for installing a CPU. Usually in the first few pages, the motherboard book will tell you exactly which CPUs your system can handle (as shown in Figure 2.2).

If you don't have a motherboard book, call the place where you bought the PC and ask for it. If they don't have it, get online and find it—I'll show you where to look in later chapters.

Your first concern is the socket. You can't install an Athlon 64 X2 into a Pentium D's Socket 775—it won't fit! If your motherboard book lists the CPU you want to install, you're ready to start shopping.

● **Figure 2.1**   Sample motherboard books

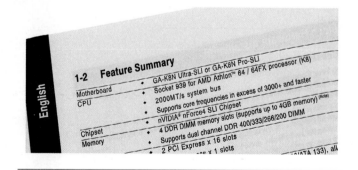

● **Figure 2.2**   Allowed CPUs

Buying a CPU

Buying a CPU is a tricky game because most stores will not accept returns unless the CPU is bad. If you're not careful, you could get stuck with a useless CPU. Here are a few tricks.

CPUs come packaged two ways, as retail-boxed CPUs or OEM CPUs. Retail-boxed CPUs have two advantages. First, they are the genuine article.

There are a surprising number of illegal CPUs on the market. Second, they come with a fan and heat sink that is rated to work with that CPU.

Most stores have an installation deal and will install a new CPU for very cheap. I take advantage of this sometimes, even though it may mean I don't have my PC for a few days. Why does your humble author, the Alpha Geek, have others do work he can do himself? Well, that way I'm not out of luck if there is a problem. Heck, I can change my own oil in my car, but I let others do that too.

If you buy an OEM CPU, you will need the right fan and heat-sink assembly. See "The Art of Cooling" section later in this chapter.

Preparing to Install

Once you're comfortable that your new CPU will work with your motherboard, get back to that motherboard book and see if you must adjust any tiny jumpers or switches for your CPU. These jumpers might adjust the motherboard speed, the multiplier, or the voltage. Take your time, read the motherboard book, and set those jumpers or switches properly. Locate the fan power connector, usually called the CPU fan, as shown in Figure 2.3.

Most CPUs use some form of mounting bracket for the CPU cooler. Some of these brackets require mounting underneath the motherboard, which means removing the motherboard from the system case.

If you're removing an old CPU, you'll need to take off the old CPU cooler. Removing CPU coolers scares me more than any other physical act I do on a PC. Many (not all) CPU fans use a metal clamp on both sides of the socket. These clamps usually require you to pry them off to remove them, using a flat-head screwdriver (Figure 2.4). You need a lot of force—usually far more than you think you

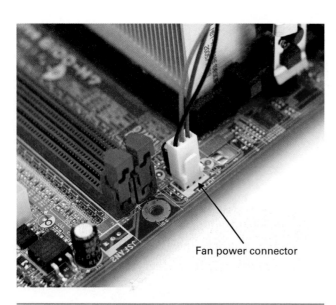

Fan power connector

• **Figure 2.3** Fan connection

 Many motherboards have no jumpers or switches.

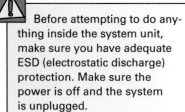 Before attempting to do anything inside the system unit, make sure you have adequate ESD (electrostatic discharge) protection. Make sure the power is off and the system is unplugged.

• **Figure 2.4** Removing an old fan

should use, so take your time to pry that old fan off. Don't let the screwdriver slip; you could damage some fragile components on the motherboard, rendering the motherboard inoperable.

Inserting a PGA-Type CPU

Inserting and removing PGA CPUs is a relatively simple process; just *don't touch the pins* or you might destroy the CPU. Figure 2.5 shows a technician installing a Sempron into a Socket 754. Note that the pins on the CPU only fit in one orientation. These **orientation markers** are designed to help you align the CPU correctly. Although the orientation markers make it difficult to install a CPU improperly, be careful: Incorrectly installing your CPU will almost certainly destroy the CPU or the motherboard, or both!

To install, first lift the arm or open the metal cover. Align the CPU, and it should drop right in (Figure 2.6). If it doesn't, verify your alignment and check for bent pins on the CPU. If you encounter a slightly bent pin, try a mechanical pencil that takes thick (0.9mm) lead. Take the lead out of the mechanical pencil, slide the pencil tip over the bent pin, and straighten it out. Be careful! A broken CPU pin ruins the CPU. Make sure the CPU is all the way in (no visible pins), and snap down the arm or drop over the metal cover.

Now it's time for the CPU cooler. Before inserting the heat sink, you need to add a small amount of

Using a new fan when you replace a CPU is a good idea— even if the old fan works with your new CPU. Fans get old and die too.

• **Figure 2.5**   Orienting the CPU

• **Figure 2.6**   CPU inserted

● **Figure 2.7** Applying thermal compound

● **Figure 2.8** Changing the fan and heatsink

thermal compound (also called *heat dope*). Many coolers come with heat-sink compound already on them; the heat-sink compound on these pre-doped coolers is covered by a small square of tape—take the tape off before you snap down the fan. If you need to put heat dope on from a tube, know that it only takes a tiny amount of this compound (see Figure 2.7). Spread it on as thinly, completely, and evenly as you can. Unlike so many other things in life, you can have too much heat dope!

Securing heat sinks makes even the most jaded PC technician a little nervous (Figure 2.8). In most cases, you must apply a fairly strong amount of force to snap the heat sink into place—far more than you might think. Also, make certain that the CPU cooler you install works with your CPU package.

Testing Your New CPU

The next step is to turn on the PC and see if the system boots up. If life were perfect, every CPU installation would end right here as you watch the system happily boot up. Unfortunately, the reality is that sometimes nothing happens when you press the power button. Here's what to do if this happens.

First, make sure the system has power—we'll be going through lots of power issues throughout the book. Second, make sure the CPU is firmly pressed down into the socket. Get your head down and look at the mounted CPU from the side—do you see any of the CPU's wires showing? Does the CPU look unlevel in its mount? If so, reinstall the CPU. If the system still does not boot, double-check any jumper settings—messing them up is very easy.

As the computer starts, make sure the CPU fan is spinning within a few seconds. If it doesn't spin up instantly, that's okay, but it must start within about 30 seconds at the least.

The Art of Cooling

There was a time, long ago, when CPUs didn't need any type of cooling device. You just snapped in the CPU and it worked. Well, those days are gone. Long gone. If you're installing a modern CPU, you will have to cool it. Fortunately, you have choices.

- **OEM CPU Coolers** OEM heat-sink and fan assemblies are included with a retail-boxed CPU. OEM CPUs, on the other hand, don't normally come bundled with CPU coolers. Crazy, isn't it? OEM CPU coolers have one big advantage: you know absolutely they will work with your CPU.

- **Specialized CPU Coolers** Lots of companies sell third-party heat sinks and fans for a variety of CPUs. These usually exceed the OEM heat sinks in the amount of heat they dissipate. These CPU coolers invariably come with eye-catching designs to look really cool inside your system—some are even lighted (see Figure 2.9).

The last choice is the most impressive of all: liquid cooling! That's right; you can put a little liquid-cooling system right inside your PC case. Liquid cooling works by running some liquid—usually water—through a metal block that sits on top of your CPU, absorbing heat. The liquid gets heated by the block, runs out of the block and into something that cools the liquid, and is then pumped through the block again. Any liquid-cooling system consists of three main parts:

- A hollow metal block that sits on the CPU
- A pump to move the liquid around
- Some device to cool the liquid

And of course, you need plenty of hosing to hook them all together. Figure 2.10 shows a typical liquid-cooled CPU.

A number of companies sell these liquid-cooling systems. Although they look impressive and certainly cool your CPU, unless you're overclocking or want a quiet system, a good fan will more than suffice.

● **Figure 2.9**   Cool retail heat sink

● **Figure 2.10**   Liquid-cooled CPU

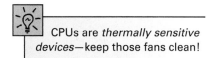
Whether you have a silent or noisy cooling system for your CPU, always remember to keep everything clean. Once a month or so, take a can of compressed air and clean dust off the fan or radiator. CPUs are very susceptible to heat; a poorly working fan can create all sorts of problems, such as system lockups, spontaneous reboots, and more.

■ RAM

So you're pretty familiar with CPUs by this point, and maybe you're thinking about upgrading your PC's processor, but wait! There might be a better, easier upgrade for you.

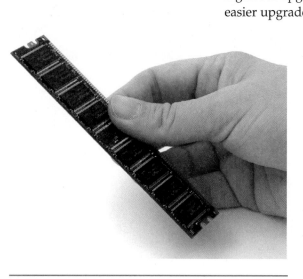

Whenever someone comes up to me and asks what single hardware upgrade they can do to improve their system performance, I always tell them the same thing—add more RAM. Adding more RAM can improve overall system performance, processing speed, and stability—if you get it right. Botching the job can cause dramatic system instability, such as frequent, random crashes and reboots. Every tech needs to know how to install and upgrade system RAM of all types.

To get the desired results from a RAM upgrade, you must first determine if insufficient RAM is the cause of system problems. Second, you need to pick the proper RAM for the system. Finally, you must use good installation practices. Always store RAM sticks in anti-static packaging whenever they're not in use, and use strict ESD handling procedures. Like many other pieces of the PC, RAM is *very* sensitive to ESD and other technician abuse (Figure 2.11)!

● **Figure 2.11**   Don't do this! Grabbing the contacts is a *bad thing*.

Do You Need RAM?

Two symptoms point to the need for more RAM in a PC: general system sluggishness and excessive hard drive accessing. If programs take forever to load and running programs seem to stall and move more slowly than you would like, the problem could stem from insufficient RAM. A friend with a new Windows Vista system complained that her PC seemed snappy when she first got it but started taking a long time to do the things she wanted to do with it, such as photograph retouching in Adobe Photoshop and document layout for a print zine she produces. Her system had only 1 GB of RAM, sufficient to run Windows Vista, but woefully insufficient for her tasks—she kept maxing out the RAM and thus the system slowed to a crawl. I replaced her stick with a pair of 2-GB sticks and suddenly she had the powerhouse workstation she desired.

Excessive hard drive activity when you move between programs points to a need for more RAM. Every Windows PC has the capability to make a portion of your hard drive look like RAM in case you run out of real RAM. This is called the **page file** or **swap file**, as you'll learn in Chapter 8, "Maintaining and Troubleshooting Windows." If you fill your RAM up with programs, your PC automatically starts loading some programs into the page file.

You can't see this process taking place just by looking at the screen—these swaps are done in the background. But you will notice the hard drive access LED going crazy as Windows rushes to move programs between RAM and the page file in a process called disk thrashing. Windows uses the page file all the time, but excessive disk thrashing suggests that you need more RAM.

You can diagnose excessive disk thrashing through simply observing the hard drive access LED flashing or through various third-party tools. I like FreeMeter (www.tiler.com/freemeter/). It's been around for quite a while, runs on all versions of Windows, and is easy to use (Figure 2.12). Notice on the FreeMeter screenshot that some amount of the page file is being used. That's perfectly normal.

System RAM Recommendations

Microsoft sets very low the minimum RAM requirements listed for the various Windows operating systems to get the maximum number of users to upgrade or convert, and that's fine. A Windows XP Professional machine runs well enough on 128 MB of RAM. Just don't ask it to do any serious computing, such as running Doom III! Windows Vista has raised the bar considerably, especially with the 64-bit version of the operating system. Here are my recommendations for system RAM.

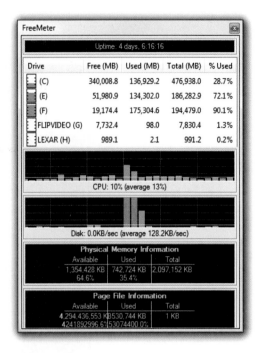

● **Figure 2.12** FreeMeter

Operating System	Reasonable Minimum	Solid Performance	Power User
Windows 2000	128 MB	256 MB	512 MB
Windows XP	256 MB	1 GB	2 GB
Windows Vista	2 GB	4 GB	8 GB

Try This!

Checking the Page File

How much of your hard drive does Windows use for a page file? Does the level change dramatically when you open typical applications, such as Microsoft Word, Solitaire, and Paint Shop Pro? The answers to these questions can give a tech a quick estimation about RAM usage and possibly RAM needs for a particular system, so Try This!

In Windows 2000/XP you can easily glance at your page file usage through the Task Manager. To access the Task Manager, press CTRL-ALT-DEL simultaneously once. Click the Performance tab. The second box on the left, titled PF Usage, displays the amount of hard drive the page file is currently using. In Windows Vista, the process of viewing the page file is exactly the same, but Vista uses a less descriptive way of displaying its usage. In the bottom-right corner of the Performance tab, you'll see the title "Page File," which gives you a numeric representation.

1. How big is the page file when you have no applications open?

2. How much does it change when you open applications?

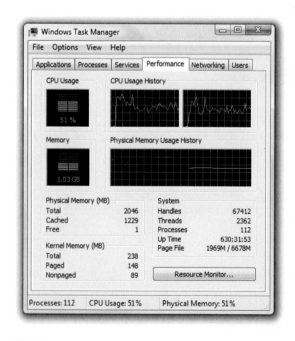

● **Figure 2.13**   Mike has a lot of RAM!

Determining Current RAM Capacity

Before you go get RAM, you obviously need to know how much RAM you currently have in your PC. Every version of Windows works the same way. Just select the Properties for My Computer or Computer to see how much RAM is in your system (Figure 2.13). If you have a newer keyboard, you can access the screen with the WINDOWS-PAUSE/BREAK keystroke combination. Windows 2000, XP, and Vista come with the handy Performance tab under the Task Manager (as shown in Figure 2.14).

Getting the Right RAM

To do the perfect RAM upgrade, determine the optimum capacity of RAM to install and then get the right RAM for the motherboard. Your first two stops toward these goals are the inside of the case and your motherboard manual. Open the case to see how many sticks of RAM you have installed currently and how many free slots you have open. Check the motherboard book to determine the total capacity of RAM the system can handle and what specific technology works with your system. You can't put DDR2 into a system that can only handle DDR SDRAM,

● **Figure 2.14**   Performance tab in Windows XP Task Manager after all, and it won't do you much good to install a pair of 2-GB DIMMs when your system tops out at 1.5 GB. Figure 2.15 shows the RAM limits for my ASUS Crosshair motherboard.

Mix and Match at Your Peril

All motherboards can handle different capacities of RAM. If you have three slots, you may put a 512-MB stick in one and a 1-GB stick in the other with a high chance of success. To ensure maximum stability in a system, however, shoot for as close as you can get to uniformity of RAM. Choose RAM sticks that match in technology, capacity, and speed. Even on motherboards that offer slots for radically different RAM types, I recommend uniformity.

Mixing Speeds

With so many different DRAM speeds available, you may often find yourself tempted to mix speeds of DRAM in the same system. Although you may get away with mixing speeds on a system, the safest, easiest rule to follow is to use the speed of DRAM specified in the motherboard book, and make sure that every piece of DRAM runs at that speed. In a worst-case scenario, mixing DRAM speeds can cause the system to lock up every few seconds or every few minutes. You might also get some data corruption. Mixing speeds sometimes works fine, but don't do your income tax on a machine with mixed DRAM speeds until the system has proven to be stable for a few days. The important thing to note here is that you won't break anything, other than possibly data, by experimenting.

Okay, I have mentioned enough disclaimers. Modern motherboards provide some flexibility regarding RAM speeds and mixing. First, you can use RAM that is faster than the motherboard specifies. For example, if the system needs PC3200 DDR2 SDRAM, you may put in PC4200 DDR2 SDRAM and it should work fine. Faster DRAM is not going to make the system run any faster, however, so don't look for any system improvement.

Second, you can sometimes get away with putting one speed of DRAM in one bank and another speed in another bank, as long as all the speeds are as fast as or faster than the speed specified by the motherboard. Don't bother trying to put different-speed DRAM sticks in the same bank with a motherboard that uses dual-channel DDR. Yes, it works once in a while, but it's too chancy. I avoid it.

Tech Tip

CPU-Z

The freeware CPU-Z program tells you the total number of slots on your motherboard, the number of slots used, and the exact type of RAM in each slot—very handy. CPU-Z not only determines the latency of your RAM, but also lists the latency at a variety of motherboard speeds. The CD accompanying this book has a copy of CPU-Z, so check it out.

Crosshair specifications summary

CPU	Support AMD® Socket AM2 Athlon 64 X2 / Athlon 64 FX / Athlon 64/ Sempron AMD Cool 'n' Quiet™ Technology AMD64 architecture enables simultaneous 32-bit and 64-bit computing AMD Live!™ Ready
Chipset	NVIDIA nForce® 590 SLI™ MCP NVIDIA LinkBoost™ Technology
System bus	2000 / 1600 MT/s
Memory	Dual channel memory architecture 4 x DIMM, max. 8GB, DDR2-800/667/533, ECC and non-ECC, un-buffered memory
Expansion slots	2 x PCI Express x16 slot with NVIDIA® SLI™ technology support, at full x16, x16 speed 1 x PCI Express x4 3 x PCI 2.2
Scalable Link Interface (SLI™)	Support two identical NVIDIA SLI-Ready graphics cards (both at x16 mode) ASUS two-slot thermal design ASUS PEG Link
High Definition Audio	SupremeFX Audio Card featuring ADI 1988B 8-channel High Definition Audio CODEC Support Jack-Sensing, Enumeration, Multi-streaming and Jack-Retasking 8 channel audio ports Coaxial, Optical S/PDIF out on back I/O port * ASUS Array Mic * Noise Filter
Storage	NVIDIA nForce® 590 SLI™ MCP supports: * 1 x Ultra DMA 133 / 100 / 66 / 33 * 6 x Serial ATA 3.0Gb/s with NCQ * NVIDIA MediaShield™ RAID supports RAID 0, 1, 0+1, 5 and JBOD span cross Serial ATA drives Silicon Image® 3132 SATA controller supports: * 2 x External Serial ATA 3.0Gb/s port on back I/O (SATA On-the-Go) * Support RAID 0, 1, JBOD, RAID 0+1(10) and 5 through multiplier

(continued on the next page)

xi

• **Figure 2.15**   The motherboard book shows how much RAM the motherboard will handle.

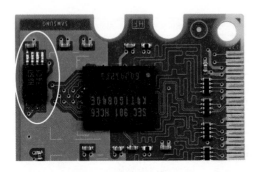

• **Figure 2.16** Inserting a DIMM

Installing DIMMs and RIMMs

Installing DRAM is so easy that it's one of the very few jobs I recommend to non-techie folks. First, attach an anti-static wrist strap or touch some bare metal on the power supply to ground yourself and avoid ESD. Then swing the side tabs on the RAM slots down from the upright position. Pick up a stick of RAM—don't touch those contacts—and line up the notch or notches with the raised portion(s) of the DIMM socket (Figure 2.16). A good hard push down is usually all you need to ensure a solid connection. Make sure that the DIMM snaps into position to show it is completely seated. Also, notice that the two side tabs move in to reflect a tight connection.

Serial Presence Detect (SPD)

Your motherboard should detect and automatically set up any DIMM or RIMM you install, assuming you have the right RAM for the system, using a technology called serial presence detect (SPD). RAM makers add a handy chip to modern sticks called the SPD chip (Figure 2.17). The SPD chip stores all the information about your DRAM, including size, speed, ECC or non-ECC, registered or unregistered, and a number of other more technical bits of information.

When a PC boots, it queries the SPD chip so that the MCC knows how much RAM is on the stick, how fast it runs, and other information. Any program can query the SPD chip. Take a look at Figure 2.18 with the results of the popular CPU-Z program showing RAM information from the SPD chip.

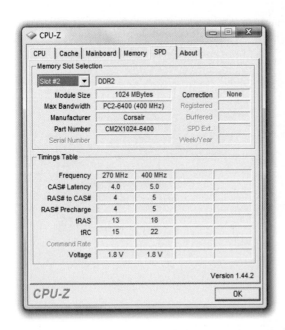

• **Figure 2.17** SPD chip on a stick

All new systems count on SPD to set the RAM timings properly for your system when it boots. If you add a RAM stick with a bad SPD chip, you'll get a POST error message and the system will not boot. You can't fix a broken SPD chip; you just buy a new stick of RAM.

The RAM Count

After installing the new RAM, turn on the PC and watch the boot process closely. If you installed the RAM correctly, the RAM count on the PC reflects the new value (compare Figures 2.19 and 2.20). If the RAM value stays the same, you probably have installed the RAM in a slot the motherboard doesn't want you to use (for example, you may need to use a particular slot first) or have not installed the RAM properly. If the computer does not boot and you've got a blank screen, you probably have not installed all the RAM sticks correctly. Usually, a good second look is all you need to determine the problem. Reseat or reinstall the RAM stick and try again.

• **Figure 2.18** CPU-Z showing RAM information

```
Award Modular BIOS v6.00PG, An Energy Star Ally
Copyright (C) 1984-2005, Award Software, Inc.

GA-K8NP F13

Processor : AMD Athlon(tm) 64 Processor 3200+
<CPUID:0000F4A Patch ID:003A>
Memory Testing : 1048576K OK    <----
CPU clock frequency : 200 Mhz

Detecting IDE drives ...
```

● **Figure 2.19**   Hey, where's the rest of my RAM?!

```
Award Modular BIOS v6.00PG, An Energy Star Ally
Copyright (C) 1984-2005, Award Software, Inc.

GA-K8NP F13

Processor : AMD Athlon(tm) 64 Processor 3200+
<CPUID:0000F4A Patch ID:003A>
Memory Testing : 3145728K OK
CPU clock frequency : 200 Mhz

Detecting IDE drives ...
```

● **Figure 2.20**   RAM count after proper insertion of DIMMs

RAM counts are confusing because RAM uses megabytes and gigabytes as opposed to millions and billions. Here are some examples of how different systems would show 256 MB of RAM:

268435456 (exactly 256 x 1 MB)

256M (some PCs try to make it easy for you)

262,144 (number of KB)

You should know how much RAM you're trying to install and use some common sense. If you have 512 MB and you add another 512-MB stick, you need a number that looks like one gigabyte. After you add the second stick, if you see a RAM count of 524582912—that sure looks like 512 MB, not one gigabyte!

Installing SO-DIMMs in Laptops

It wasn't that long ago that adding RAM to a laptop was either impossible or required you to send the system back to the manufacturer. For years, every laptop maker had custom-made, proprietary RAM packages that were difficult to handle and staggeringly expensive. The wide acceptance of SO-DIMMs over the last few years has virtually erased these problems. All laptops now provide relatively convenient access to their SO-DIMMs, enabling easy replacement or addition of RAM.

Access to RAM usually requires removing a panel or lifting up the keyboard—the procedure varies among laptop manufacturers. Figure 2.21 shows a typical laptop RAM access panel. You can slide the panel off to reveal the SO-DIMMs. SO-DIMMs usually insert exactly like the old SIMMs; slide the pins into position and snap the SO-DIMM down into the retaining clips (Figure 2.22).

Before doing any work on a laptop, turn the system off, disconnect it from the AC wall socket, and remove all batteries. Use an anti-static wrist strap because laptops are far more susceptible to ESD than desktop PCs.

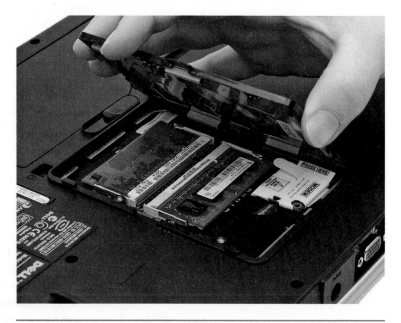

● **Figure 2.21**   A RAM access panel on a laptop

● **Figure 2.22**   Snapping in an SO-DIMM

■ Troubleshooting RAM

"Memory" errors show up in a variety of ways on modern systems, including parity errors, ECC error messages, system lockups, page faults, and other error screens in Windows. These errors can indicate bad RAM but often point to something completely unrelated to RAM. This is especially true with intermittent problems. The challenge for techs is to recognize these errors and then determine which part of the system caused the memory error.

You can get two radically different types of parity errors: real and phantom. Real parity errors are simply errors that the MCC detects from the parity or ECC chips (if you have them). The operating system then reports the problem in an error message, such as "Parity error at *xxxx:xxxxxxxx*," where *xxxx:xxxxxxxx* is a hexadecimal value (a string of numbers and letters, such as A5F2:004EEAB9). If you get an error like this, write down the value (Figure 2.23). A real parity/ECC error shows up at the same place in memory each time and almost always indicates that you have a bad RAM stick.

Phantom parity errors show up on systems that don't have parity or ECC memory. If Windows generates parity errors with different addresses, you most likely do *not* have a problem with RAM. These phantom errors can occur for a variety of reasons, including software problems, heat or dust, solar flares, fluctuations in the Force … you get the idea.

System lockups and page faults (they often go hand in hand) in Windows can indicate a problem with RAM. A system lockup is when the computer stops functioning. A **page fault** is a milder error that can be caused by memory issues but not necessarily system RAM problems. Certainly page faults *look* like RAM issues because Windows generates frightening error messages filled with long strings of hexadecimal digits, such as "KRNL386 caused a page fault at 03F2:25A003BC." Just because the error message contains a memory address, however, does not mean that you have a problem with your RAM. Write down the address. If it repeats in later error messages, you probably have a bad RAM stick. If Windows displays different memory locations, you need to look elsewhere for the culprit.

Every once in a while, something potentially catastrophic happens within the PC, some little electron hits the big red panic button, and the operating system has to shut down certain functions running before it can save data. This panic button inside the PC is called a non-maskable interrupt (NMI), more simply defined as an interruption the CPU cannot ignore. An NMI manifests to the user as what techs lovingly call the **Blue Screen of Death (BSoD)**—a bright blue screen with a scary-sounding error message on it (Figure 2.24).

Bad RAM sometimes triggers an NMI, although often the culprit lies with buggy programming or clashing code. The BSoD varies according to

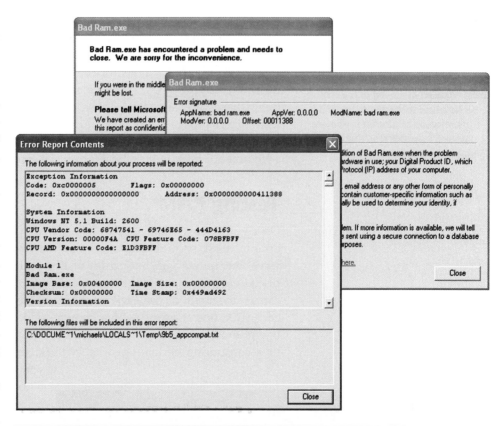

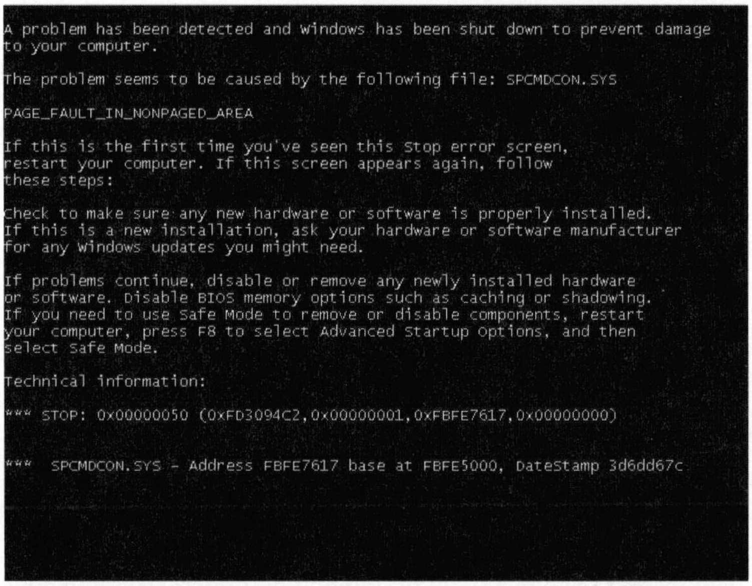

• **Figure 2.23** Windows error message

• **Figure 2.24** Blue Screen of Death

the operating system, and it would require a much lengthier tome than this one to cover all the variations. Suffice it to say that RAM *could* be the problem when that delightful blue screen appears.

A general protection fault (GPF) is an error that can cause an application to crash. Often they're caused by programs stepping on each other's toes.

Finally, intermittent memory errors can come from a variety of sources, including a dying power supply, electrical interference, buggy applications, buggy hardware, and so on. These errors show up as lockups, general protection faults, page faults, and parity errors, but they never have the same address or happen with the same applications. Try the power supply first with non-application-specific intermittent errors of any sort.

Testing RAM

Once you discover that you may have a RAM problem, you have a couple of options. First, several companies manufacture hardware RAM-testing devices, but unless you have a lot of disposable income, they're probably priced way too high for the average tech ($1,500 and higher). Second, you can use the method I use—*replace and pray*. Open the system case and replace each stick, one at a time, with a known-good replacement stick. (You have one of those lying around, don't you?) This method, although potentially time-consuming, certainly works. With PC prices as low as they are now, you could simply replace the whole system for less than the price of a dedicated RAM tester.

Third, you could run a software-based tester on the RAM. Because you have to load a software tester into the memory it's about to scan, there's always a small chance that simply starting the software RAM tester might cause an error. Still, you can find some pretty good free ones out there. My favorite is the venerable Memtest86 written by Mr. Chris Brady (www.memtest86.com). Memtest86 exhaustively checks your RAM and reports bad RAM when it finds it (Figure 2.25).

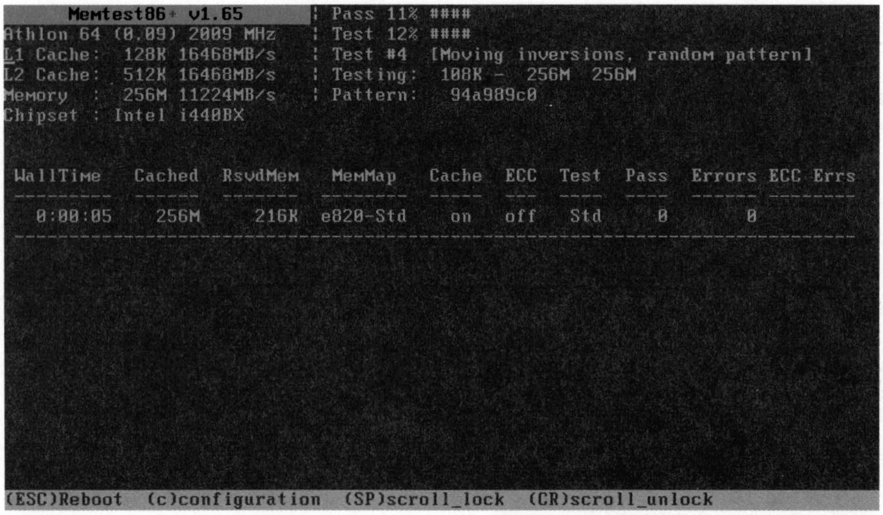

• **Figure 2.25** Memtest86 in action

Beyond A+

Overclocking

For the CPU to work, the motherboard speed, multiplier, and voltage must be set properly. In most modern systems, the motherboard uses the CPUID functions to set these options automatically. Some motherboards enable you to adjust these settings manually by moving a jumper, changing a CMOS setting, or using software; many enthusiasts deliberately change these settings to enhance performance.

Starting way back in the days of the Intel 80486 CPU, people intentionally ran their systems at clock speeds higher than the CPU was rated, a process called overclocking, and it worked. Well, sometimes the systems worked, and *sometimes* they didn't. Intel and AMD have a reason for marking a CPU at a particular clock speed—that's the highest speed they guarantee will work.

Before I say anything else, I must warn you that intentional overclocking of a CPU immediately voids any warranty. Overclocking has been known to destroy CPUs. Overclocking might make your system unstable and prone to lockups and reboots. I neither applaud nor decry the practice of overclocking. My goal here is simply to inform you of the practice. You make your own decisions.

CPU makers dislike overclocking. Why would you pay more for a faster processor when you can take a cheaper, slower CPU and just make it run faster? To that end, CPU makers, especially Intel, have gone to great lengths to discourage the practice. For example, both AMD and Intel now make all of their CPUs with locked multipliers and special overspeed electronics to deter the practice.

I don't think Intel or AMD really care too much what end users do with their CPUs. You own it; you take the risks. A number of criminals, however, learned to make a good business of remarking CPUs with higher than rated speeds and selling them as legitimate CPUs. These counterfeit CPUs have created a nightmare where unsuspecting retailers and end users have been given overclocked CPUs. When they run into trouble, they innocently ask for warranty support, only to discover that their CPU is counterfeit and the warranty is void.

If you want to know exactly what type of CPU you're running, download a copy of the very popular and free CPU-Z utility from www.cpuid.com. CPU-Z gives you every piece of information you'll ever want to know about your CPU (Figure 2.26).

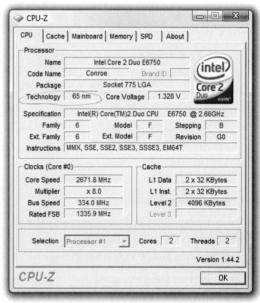

• **Figure 2.26**   CPU-Z in action

Most people make a couple of adjustments to overclock successfully. First, through jumpers, CMOS settings, or software configuration, you would increase the bus speed for the system. Second, you often have to increase the voltage going into the CPU by just a little to provide stability. You do that by changing a jumper or CMOS setting.

Overriding the defaults can completely lock up your system, to the point where even removing and reinstalling the CPU doesn't bring the motherboard back to life. (There's also a slight risk of toasting the processor, although all modern processors have circuitry that shuts them down quickly before they overheat.) Most motherboards have a jumper setting called CMOS-clear (Figure 2.27) that makes the CMOS go back to default settings. Before you try overclocking on a modern system, find the CMOS-clear jumper and make sure you know how to use it! Hint: look in the motherboard manual.

To clear the CMOS, turn off the PC. Then locate one of those tiny little plastic pieces (officially called a *shunt*) and place it over the two jumper wires for a moment. Next, restart the PC and immediately go into CMOS and restore the settings you need.

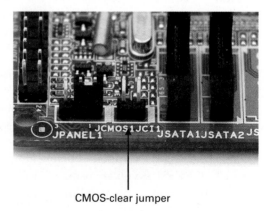

CMOS-clear jumper

• **Figure 2.27**   CMOS-clear jumper

Chapter 2 Review

■ Chapter Summary

After reading this chapter and completing the exercises, you should understand the following about CPUs and RAM.

Explain the difference between 32- and 64-bit CPUs

■ As CPUs have increased in speed and complexity, they have required more and more power. Good techs should know the wattage requirements for any CPU they're planning on installing.

■ 64-bit CPUs have a 64-bit wide address bus capable of recognizing and using over 4 GB of memory, which was not possible with 32-bit CPUs.

■ Almost all modern CPUs are multicore, meaning that they have two or more execution cores on a single die. This vastly improves a CPU's capacity for multitasking.

Select and install CPUs

■ Before upgrading your CPU, consider the implications on your whole system, because an upgraded CPU may require an updated motherboard and RAM.

■ Consult your motherboard documentation to see what CPUs are compatible with your system. Not all CPUs are compatible with all motherboards.

■ Cooling is critical. Make sure you have a fan rated to work with your CPU.

■ Never touch the pins on the underside of a CPU; this can permanently damage the processor.

■ A PGA CPU fits only one way in the ZIF socket. Don't force it. If you find the CPU will not seat properly, take a second look at the orientation markers and verify the CPU is in the correct direction. Check the pins on the underside to make sure none are bent.

■ There should be a small amount of heat-sink compound between the CPU and heat-sink/fan assembly. If your fan came with the compound already applied, be sure to remove the protective tape covering the compound before attaching the fan to the CPU. If you are using your own heat dope from a tube, spread it thinly and evenly.

Select and install RAM

■ You must know what type of RAM (such as regular SDRAM, DDR, DDR2, or DDR3) your motherboard accepts before you purchase a RAM upgrade. You also need to know the maximum amount of RAM your motherboard supports and the maximum supported per slot.

■ Though not required, it is good practice to make sure all sticks of RAM in any system are as close to identical as possible. Matching your RAM modules in technology, capacity, speed, and manufacturer lessens the chance of problems and incompatibility.

■ The serial presence detect (SPD) chip on modern DIMMs automatically supplies all the information about the RAM to the system, such as the size, speed, ECC or non-ECC, registered or unregistered, and other details.

■ To install SO-DIMMs in a laptop, you must remove a panel on the underside of the laptop or remove the keyboard to find the RAM slots. The SO-DIMM slides into the slot and snaps down into position. Unplug the laptop and remove the battery before attempting a RAM upgrade, and protect the RAM from ESD by wearing an anti-static wristband.

Perform basic RAM troubleshooting

■ Symptoms of bad RAM include parity errors, system lockups, page faults, and other error screens in Windows. However, other failing components can cause similar problems. Bad RAM usually results in error screens displaying messages such as "Parity error at *xxxx:xxxxxxxx*," where *xxxx:xxxxxxxx* is a hexadecimal value such as A5F2:004EEAB9. A real parity error shows up in the same place in memory each time—if that hexadecimal code is always the same, you probably have bad RAM.

■ Page faults result in error screens such as "KRNL386 caused a page fault at 03F2:25A003BC." The process that caused the page fault (in this case, KRNL386) may change, but if the hexadecimal address is the same across numerous error screens, you probably have bad RAM.

- If you suspect you have bad RAM and you don't have a hardware RAM-testing device, swap one of the sticks in your system with a known-good stick. If the system works, you've found the bad stick. If the system still has errors, replace the stick you removed and swap a different stick for the known-good stick. Another option is to use a software RAM tester such as Memtest86.

- Disk thrashing is constant hard drive activity symptomatic of insufficient RAM. It occurs when Windows repeatedly uses up all available RAM space and has to move data not immediately needed out of the RAM into a temporary file on the hard drive called a swap file or page file and then swap the data back into RAM when it is needed by the program. You can monitor the size of your swap file in the Task Manager.

- A non-maskable interrupt (NMI) results in a Blue Screen of Death (BSoD). Although BSoDs are often blamed on bad RAM, they are more often caused by buggy application program code.

■ Key Terms

Blue Screen of Death (BSoD) *(33)*
central processing unit (CPU) *(19)*
CMOS clear *(35)*
disk thrashing *(27)*
dual-core *(20)*
general protection fault (GPF) *(34)*
microprocessor *(19)*
multicore *(20)*
non-maskable interrupt (NMI) *(33)*

orientation markers *(23)*
overclocking *(35)*
page fault *(32)*
page file *(26)*
parallel processing *(20)*
serial presence detect (SPD) *(30)*
swap file *(26)*
thermal compound *(24)*

■ Key Term Quiz

Use the Key Terms list to complete the sentences that follow. Not all terms will be used.

1. Systems automatically detect new RAM by polling the module's _SPD_ chip.

2. An Athlon 64 X2 is an example of a(n) _dual-core_ processor.

3. _orientation markers_ help techs properly align a CPU when installing it into a CPU socket.

4. The generic term for a CPU with more than two execution cores is _multicore_.

5. To prevent overheating, _thermal compound_ should always be applied between a CPU and its heat sink.

6. The most dreaded sight in all of Windows, a _BSoD_ could indicate a problem with your RAM.

7. Instead of simply displaying errors or crashing, computers use a _page file_ to maintain proper operation when there is insufficient RAM to do all that the user is trying to do.

8. _parallel processing_ refers to a multicore CPU's ability to run more than one thread simultaneously.

■ Multiple-Choice Quiz

1. What happens if you add two RAM sticks to your PC, and one has a bad SPD?

   A. When your system boots, it will recognize both RAM sticks but will not register any special features (such as ECC) of the stick with the bad SPD.

   B. When your system boots, it will only register the presence of the RAM stick with the good SPD.

   C. When your system boots, it won't register the presence of the RAM stick with the bad SPD until you configure the RAM settings by using the Setup utility.

   D. When you try to boot the system, you will get a POST error message and the system will not boot.

2. If you upgrade your memory but notice that the RAM count does not reflect the additional memory, what should you do?

   A. Remove the RAM and try to reinstall it.

   B. Restart the computer.

   C. Return the memory because it's probably bad.

   D. Go to Setup and configure the memory to reflect the new amount.

3. What does a non-maskable interrupt cause the CPU to produce?

   A. The Blue Screen of Death

   B. A parity error

   C. Excessive heat

   D. An incorrect memory count

4. What steps do you need to take to install an Athlon 64 X2 CPU into an LGA 775 motherboard?

   A. Lift the ZIF socket arm; place the CPU according to the orientation markings; snap on the heat-sink and fan assembly.

   B. Lift the ZIF socket arm; place the CPU according to the orientation markings; add a dash of heat dope; snap on the heat-sink and fan assembly.

   C. Lift the ZIF socket arm; place the CPU according to the orientation markings; snap on the heat-sink and fan assembly; plug in the fan.

   D. Take all of the steps you want to take because it's not going to work.

5. What do 64-bit processors expand beyond what 32-bit processors, such as the Pentium III, have?

   A. System bus

   B. Frontside bus

   C. Address bus

   D. Registers

6. Which of the following statements is true?

   A. If you have an AMD-compatible motherboard, you can install a Celeron processor.

   B. Replacing the CPU is always the upgrade that is most cost effective and that has the strongest impact on your system's performance.

   C. As the size of the address bus increases, the amount of RAM the CPU can use decreases.

   D. You can upgrade your CPU if you make sure that a new CPU will fit into the socket or slot on your motherboard.

7. Which of the following is a consideration when handling sticks of RAM?

   A. Don't touch them with your hands, because their capacitors store a charge that can shock you.

   B. Be very gentle, since RAM sticks are extremely brittle and prone to breaking.

   C. Never touch the gold contacts on the bottom edge of the stick.

   D. Always wash your hands first, because the oil on your fingers can deteriorate the module.

8. If you're thinking about upgrading your PC, what is most likely the cheapest and most efficient upgrade to perform?

   A. Upgrading your RAM to the system's maximum capacity.

   B. Changing your single-core CPU to a dual-core.

   C. Upgrading from a 32-bit CPU to a 64-bit one.

   D. Upgrading your CPU's heat sink.

■ Essay Quiz

1. Your computer is acting funny. Sometimes you get an error message on the screen. Other times data seems to be corrupted. Sometimes the computer just locks up. You suspect that it may be bad memory. How can you find out whether a memory problem or something else is causing your trouble?

2. It is important for the CPU to stay cool. A number of technical advances have been made in the design

of CPUs, along ⋯
keep the CPU fr⋯
two cooling fea⋯

3. Write a brief es⋯
you must have⋯
upgrade your ⋯
list as possible⋯

Lab Projects

● Lab Project 2.1

If your school hardware lab has motherboards and processors for hands-on labs, practice removing and installing PGA processors on the motherboards. Take note of how the mechanical arm on a ZIF socket works. Answer the following about your experience:

- How do you know in which direction to place the CPU?

- How does the mechanical arm lift up? Does it lift straight up or must it clear a lip?

- What effect does lifting the arm have on the socket?

- How does the ZIF socket hold the CPU in place?

● Lab Project 2.2

To learn more about memory, go to the Web site www.kingston.com, select Memory Tools from the buttons at the top of the screen, and examine the "Ultimate Memory Guide." This resource contains information about all aspects of computer memory. After using this guide, answer the following questions:

- Why do memory prices vary so widely?

- What are the differences in tin- and gold-edged memory sticks, and how can you know which to choose when upgrading?

- Describe the notches on a 30-pin SIMM, a 72-pin SIMM, a 168-pin DIMM, and a 184-pin DIMM. What function do the notches serve?

Mastering Motherboards

In this chapter, you will learn how to

- **Troubleshoot the power-on self test (POST)**
- **Maintain BIOS and CMOS properly**
- **Troubleshoot expansion cards**
- **Install expansion cards properly**
- **Upgrade and install motherboards**
- **Troubleshoot motherboard problems**

The **motherboard** provides the foundation for the personal computer. Every piece of hardware, from the CPU to the lowliest expansion card, directly or indirectly plugs into the motherboard. The motherboard contains the wires—called **traces**—that make up the buses of the system. It holds the vast majority of the ports used by the peripherals, and it distributes the power from the power supply (Figure 3.1). Without the motherboard, you literally have no PC.

With that in mind, it makes sense that the CompTIA A+ Practical Application exam would test you pretty heavily on troubleshooting motherboards, CMOS and BIOS, and expansion bus problems. These are skills a tech simply has to know to get by in the world of personal computing, so how about getting your hands dirty?

■ Power-On Self Test (POST)

To start with, here's an overview of the power-on self test (POST) sequence, as this information can prove very helpful when working with a computer that just doesn't want to start up properly. If you've read the Essentials book, this may seem familiar to you, but be assured that this information is helpful for both tests.

When the computer is turned on or reset, it initiates a special program, also stored on the system ROM chip, called the **power-on self test (POST)**. The POST program checks out the system every time the computer boots. To perform this check, the POST sends out a command that says to all of the devices, "Check yourselves out!" All of the standard devices in the computer then run their own internal diagnostic—the POST doesn't specify what they must check. The quality of the diagnostic is up to the people who made that particular device.

Let's consider the POST for a moment. Suppose some device—let's say it's the keyboard controller chip—runs its diagnostic and determines that it is not working properly. What can the POST do about it? Only one thing, really: tell the human in front of the PC! So how does the computer tell the human? PCs convey POST information to you in two ways: beep codes and text messages.

● **Figure 3.1**   Traces visible beneath the CPU socket on a motherboard

Before and During the Video Test: The Beep Codes

The computer tests the most basic parts of the computer first, up to and including the video card. In early PCs, you'd hear a series of beeps—called **beep codes**—if anything went wrong. By using beep codes before and during the video test, the computer could communicate with you. (If a POST error occurs before the video is available, obviously the error must manifest itself as beeps, because nothing can display on the screen.) The meaning of the beep code you'd hear varied among different BIOS manufacturers. You could find the beep codes for a specific motherboard in its motherboard manual.

Most modern PCs have only a single beep code, which is for bad or missing video—one long beep followed by two or three short beeps.

You'll hear three other beep sequences on most PCs (although they're not officially beep codes). At the end of a successful POST, the PC produces one or two short beeps, simply to inform you that all is well. Most systems make a rather strange noise when the RAM is missing or very seriously damaged. Unlike traditional beep codes, this code repeats until you shut off the system. Finally, your speaker might make beeps for reasons that aren't POST or boot related. One of the more common is a series of short beeps after the system's been running for a while. That's a CPU alarm telling you the CPU is approaching its high heat limit.

 You'll find lots of online documentation about beep codes, but it's usually badly outdated.

Tech Tip

Talking BIOS

Some newer motherboards can also talk to you if there is a problem during POST. To use this feature, all that is normally required is to plug a pair of speakers or headphones into the onboard sound card.

PhoenixBIOS 4.0 release 6.0
Copyright 1985-2000 Phoenix Technologies Ltd.
All Rights Reserved

CPU = Pentium III 500MHz
640K System RAM Passed
47M Extended RAM Passed
USB upper limit segment address: EEFE
Mouse initialized

HDD Controller Failure
Press <F1> to resume

• **Figure 3.2**   POST text error messages

Text Errors

After the video has tested okay, any POST errors display on the screen as text errors. If you get a text error, the problem is usually, but not always, self-explanatory (Figure 3.2). Text errors are far more useful than beep codes, because you can simply read the screen to determine the bad device.

POST Cards

Beep codes, numeric codes, and text error codes, although helpful, can sometimes be misleading. Worse than that, an inoperative device can sometimes disrupt the POST, forcing the machine into an endless loop. This causes the PC to act dead—no beeps and nothing on the screen. In this case, you need a device called a **POST card** to monitor the POST and identify which piece of hardware is causing the trouble.

• **Figure 3.3**   POST card in action

POST cards are simple cards that snap into expansion slots on your system. A small, two-character light-emitting diode (LED) readout on the card indicates what device the POST is currently testing (Figure 3.3). The documentation that comes with the POST card tells you what the codes mean. BIOS makers also provide this information on their Web sites. Manufacturers make POST cards for all types of desktop PCs. POST cards work with any BIOS, but you need to know the type of BIOS you have so you can interpret the readout properly.

I usually only pull out a POST card when the usual POST errors fail to appear. When a computer provides a beep or text error code that doesn't make sense, or your machine keeps locking up, some device has stalled the POST. Because the POST card tells you which device is being tested, the frozen system stays at that point in the POST, and the error stays on the POST card's readout.

Many companies sell POST cards today, with prices ranging from the affordable to the outrageous. Spend the absolute least amount of money you can. The more expensive cards add bells and whistles you do not need, such as diagnostic software and voltmeters.

Using a POST card is straightforward. Simply power down the PC, install the POST card in any unused slot, and turn the PC back on. As you watch the POST display, notice the hexadecimal readouts and refer to them as the POST progresses. Notice how quickly they change. If you get an "FF" or "00," that means the POST is over and everything passed—time to check the operating system. If a device stalls the POST, however, the POST card displays an error code. That's the problem device! Good technicians often memorize a dozen or more POST codes because it's much faster than looking them up in a book.

So you got a beep code, a text error code, or a POST error. Now what do you do with that knowledge? Remember that a POST error does not fix the computer; it only tells you where to look. You then have to know how to deal with that bad or improperly configured component. If you use a POST card, for example, and it hangs at the "Initializing Floppy Drive" test, you'd better know how to work on a floppy drive.

Sometimes the POST card returns a bizarre or confusing error code. What device do you point at when you get a "CMOS shutdown register read/write error" beep code from an older system? First of all, read the error carefully. Let's say that on that same system you got an "8042—gate A20 failure" beep code. What will you do? Assuming you know (and you should!) that the "8042" refers to the keyboard, a quick peek at the keyboard and its connection would be a good first step. Beyond that specific example, here is a good general rule: If you don't know what the error means or the bad part isn't replaceable, replace the motherboard. Clearly, you will stumble across exceptions to this rule, but more often than not, the rule stands.

The Boot Process

All PCs need a process to begin their operations. Once you feed power to the PC, the tight interrelation of hardware, firmware, and software enables the PC to start itself, to "pull itself up by the bootstraps" or boot itself.

When you first power on the PC, the power supply circuitry tests for proper voltage and then sends a signal down a special wire called the **power good** wire to awaken the CPU. The moment the power good wire wakes it up, every Intel and clone CPU immediately sends a built-in memory address via its address bus. This special address is the same on every Intel and clone CPU, from the oldest 8086 to the most recent microprocessor. This address is the first line of the POST program on the system ROM! That's how the system starts the POST. After the POST has finished, there must be a way for the computer to find the programs on the hard drive to start the operating system. The POST passes control to the last BIOS function: the bootstrap loader. The **bootstrap loader** is little more than a few dozen lines of BIOS code tacked to the end of the POST program. Its job is to find the operating system. The bootstrap loader reads CMOS information to tell it where to look first for an operating system. Your PC's CMOS setup utility has an option that you configure to tell the bootstrap loader which devices to check for an operating system and in which order (Figure 3.4).

Almost all storage devices—floppy disks, hard disks, CDs, DVDs, and even USB thumb drives—can be configured to boot an operating system by setting aside a specific location called the **boot sector**. (Later chapters show you how to do this.) If the device is bootable, its boot sector contains special programming designed to tell the system where to locate the operating system. Any device with a functional operating system is called a **bootable disk** or a **system disk**. If the bootstrap loader locates a good boot sector, it passes control to the operating system and removes itself from memory. If it doesn't, it goes to the next device in the boot order you set in the CMOS setup utility. Boot order is an important tool for

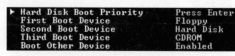

• **Figure 3.4** CMOS boot order

techs because you can set it to load in special bootable devices so you can run utilities to maintain PCs without using the primary operating system.

■ Care and Feeding of BIOS and CMOS

BIOS and CMOS are areas in your PC that you don't go to very often. BIOS itself is invisible. The only real clue you have that it even exists is the POST. The CMOS setup utility, on the other hand, is very visible if you start it. Most CMOS setup utilities today work acceptably well without ever being touched. You're an aspiring tech, however, and all self-respecting techs start up the CMOS setup utility and make changes. That's when most CMOS setup utility problems take place.

If you mess with the CMOS setup utility, remember to make only as many changes at one time as you can remember. Document the original settings and the changes on a piece of paper so you can put things back if necessary. Don't make changes unless you know what they mean! It's easy to screw up a computer fairly seriously by playing with CMOS settings you don't understand.

A Quick Tour through a Typical CMOS Setup Program

Accessing the CMOS setup utility for a system is perfectly fine, but do not make changes unless you fully understand that system!

Every BIOS maker's CMOS setup program looks a little different, but don't let that confuse you. They all contain basically the same settings; you just have to be comfortable poking around. To avoid doing something foolish, *do not save anything* unless you are sure you have it set correctly.

As an example, let's say your machine has Award BIOS. You boot the system and press DEL to enter CMOS setup. The screen in Figure 3.5 appears. You are now in the Main menu of the Award CMOS setup program. The setup program itself is stored on the ROM chip, but it edits only the data on the CMOS chip.

If you select the Standard CMOS Features option, the Standard CMOS Features screen appears (Figure 3.6). On this screen you can change floppy drive and hard drive settings, as well as the system's date and time. You will learn how to set up the CMOS for these devices in later chapters. At this point, your only goal is to understand CMOS and know how to access the CMOS setup on your PC, so don't try to change anything yet. If you have a system that you are allowed to reboot, try accessing the CMOS setup now. Does it look anything like these examples? If not, can you find the screen that enables you to change the floppy and

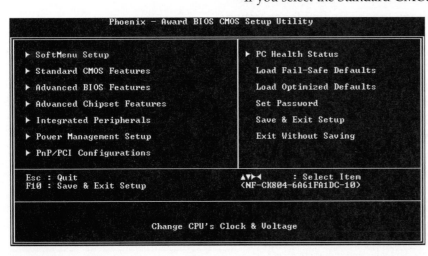

● **Figure 3.5** Typical CMOS Main screen by Award

hard drives? Trust me, every CMOS setup has that screen somewhere! Figure 3.7 shows the same standard CMOS setup screen on a system with Phoenix BIOS. Note that this CMOS setup utility calls this screen "Main."

The first BIOS was nothing more than this standard CMOS setup. Today, all computers have many extra CMOS settings. They control items such as memory management, password and booting options, diagnostic and error handling, and power management. The following section takes a quick tour of an Award CMOS setup program. Remember that your CMOS setup almost certainly looks at least a little different from mine, unless you happen to have the *same* BIOS. The chances of that happening are quite slim.

Phoenix has virtually cornered the desktop PC BIOS market with its Award Modular BIOS. Motherboard makers buy a boilerplate BIOS, designed for a particular chipset, and add or remove options (Phoenix calls them *modules*) based on the needs of each motherboard. This means that seemingly identical CMOS setup utilities can be extremely different. Options that show up on one computer might be missing from another. Compare the older Award screen in Figure 3.8 with the more

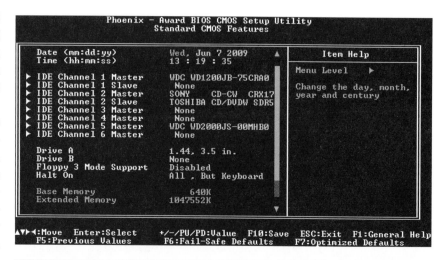

● **Figure 3.6**   Standard CMOS Features screen

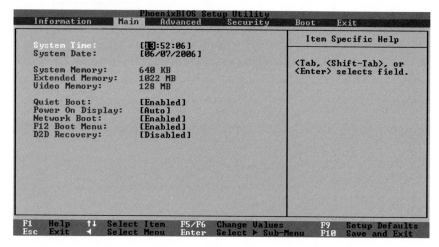

● **Figure 3.7**   Phoenix BIOS CMOS setup utility Main screen

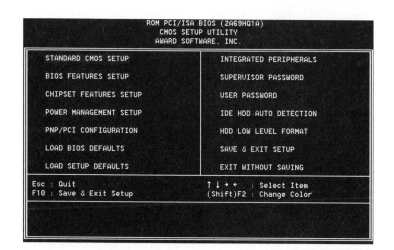

All of these screens tend to overwhelm new techs. When they first encounter the many options, some techs feel they need to understand every option on every screen to configure CMOS properly. Relax: every new motherboard comes with settings that befuddle even the most experienced techs. If I don't talk about a particular CMOS setting somewhere in this book, it's probably not important, either to the CompTIA A+ Practical Application exam or to a real tech.

● **Figure 3.8**   Older Award setup screen

modern Award CMOS screen in Figure 3.5. Figure 3.8 looks different—and it should—as this much older system simply doesn't need the extra options available on the newer system.

The next section starts the walkthrough of a CMOS setup utility with the SoftMenu, followed by some of the Advanced screens. Then you'll go through other common screens, such as Integrated Peripherals, Power, and more.

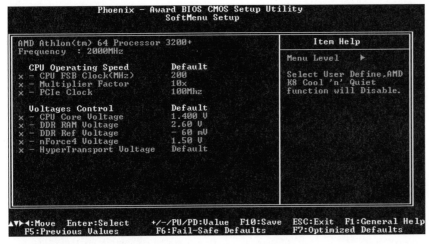

• **Figure 3.9** SoftMenu

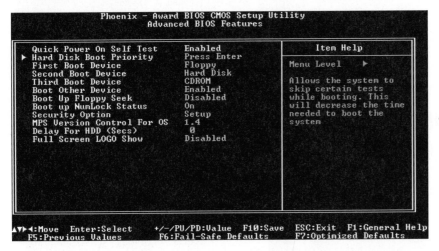

• **Figure 3.10** Advanced BIOS Features

> On some older motherboards, you may notice your CPU running slower than it should. If this happens, check in Advanced Chipset Features to see if your frontside bus is set to the correct speed.

SoftMenu

You can use the SoftMenu to change the voltage and multiplier settings on the motherboard for the CPU from the defaults. Motherboards that cater to overclockers tend to have this option. Usually you just set this to Auto or Default and stay away from this screen (Figure 3.9).

Advanced BIOS Features

Advanced BIOS Features is the dumping ground for all of the settings that aren't covered in the Standard menu and don't fit nicely under any other screen. This screen varies wildly from one system to the next. You most often use this screen to select the boot options (Figure 3.10).

Chassis Intrusion Detection Many motherboards support the **chassis intrusion detection** feature provided by the computer case, or chassis. Compatible cases contain a switch that trips when someone opens the case. With motherboard support and a proper connection between the motherboard and the case, the CMOS logs whether the case has been opened and, if it has, posts an appropriate alert to the screen on the subsequent boot. How cool is that?

Advanced Chipset Features

The Advanced Chipset Features screen strikes fear into most everyone, because it deals with extremely low-level chipset functions. Avoid this screen unless a high-level tech (such as a motherboard maker's support tech) explicitly tells you to do something in here (Figure 3.11).

Integrated Peripherals

You will use the Integrated Peripherals screen quite often. Here you configure, enable, or disable the onboard devices, such as the integrated sound card (Figure 3.12).

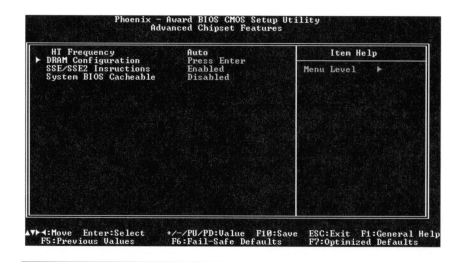

● Figure 3.11   Advanced Chipset Features

Power Management Setup

As the name implies, you can use the Power Management Setup screen to set up the power management settings for the system. These settings work in concert (sometimes in conflict) with Windows' power management settings to control how and when devices turn off and back on to conserve power (Figure 3.13).

PnP/PCI Configurations

All CMOS setup utilities come with menu items that are for the most part no longer needed, but no one wants to remove them. PnP/PCI Configurations is a perfect example. Plug and play (PnP) is how devices automatically work when you snap them into your PC. PCI is a type of slot used for cards. Odds are very good you'll never deal with this screen (Figure 3.14).

And the Rest of the CMOS Settings ...

The other options on the main menu of an Award CMOS do not have their own screens. Rather, these simply have small dialog boxes that pop up, usually with "Are you sure?" messages. The Load Fail-Safe/Optimized default options keep you from having

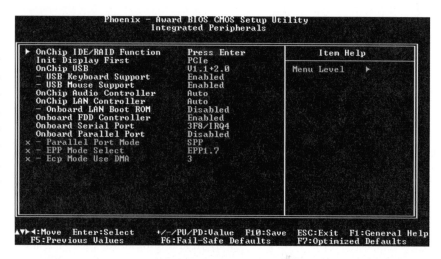

● Figure 3.12   Integrated Peripherals

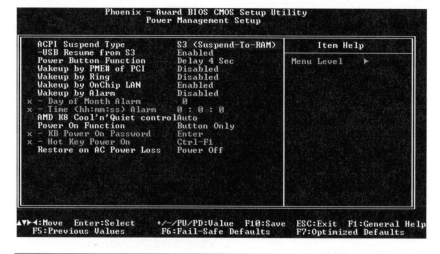

● Figure 3.13   Power Management Setup

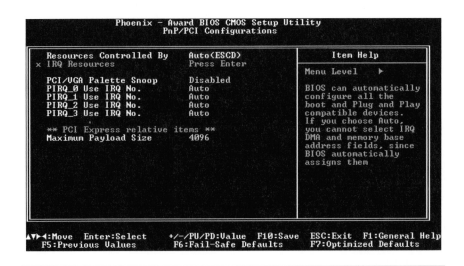

● **Figure 3.14** PnP/PCI Configurations

● **Figure 3.15** CMOS password prompt

to memorize all of those weird settings you'll never touch. Fail-Safe sets everything to very simple settings—you might occasionally use Fail-Safe when very low-level problems such as freeze-ups occur and you've checked more obvious areas first. Optimized sets the CMOS to the best possible speed/stability for the system. You would use Optimized after you've tampered with the CMOS too much and you need to put it back like it was!

Many CMOS setup programs enable you to set a password in CMOS to force the user to enter a password every time the system boots. Don't confuse this with the Windows logon password. This CMOS password shows up at boot, long before Windows even starts to load. Figure 3.15 shows a typical CMOS password prompt.

Some CMOS setup utilities enable you to create two passwords: one for boot and another for accessing the CMOS setup program. This extra password just for entering CMOS setup is a godsend in, for example, schools, where non-techs tend to wreak havoc in areas (such as CMOS) that they should not access!

Drive Lock Passwords On some motherboards, the CMOS setup program enables you to control the ATA Security Mode Feature Set, also commonly referred to as drive lock or **DriveLock**. ATA Security Mode is the first line of defense for protecting hard disks from unwanted access when a system is lost or stolen. It has two passwords, a user password and a master password, and two modes, high security mode and max security mode. In high security mode, the drive can be accessed by both the master and user passwords. In addition, the master can reset the user password in CMOS setup.

In max security mode, the drive is accessible only with the user password. In this mode, the master can reset the user password, but all of the data on the drive is destroyed. Note that in either mode, if the master and user passwords are both lost, the drive is rendered unusable; these passwords are stored in the hard disk's control circuitry and cannot be reset by clearing CMOS.

Trusted Platform Module The Trusted Platform Module (TPM) acts as a secure cryptoprocessor, which is to say that it is a hardware platform for the acceleration of cryptographic functions and the secure storage of associated information. The specification for the TPM is published by the Trusted Computing Group, an organization whose corporate members include Intel, Microsoft, AMD, IBM, Lenovo, Dell, Hewlett-Packard, and many others.

The TPM can be a small circuit board plugged into the motherboard, or it can be built directly into the chipset. The CMOS setup program usually contains settings that can turn the TPM on or off and enable or disable it.

TPMs can be used in a wide array of cryptographic operations, but one of the most common uses of TPMs is hard disk encryption. For example, the BitLocker Drive Encryption feature of Microsoft's Windows Vista can be accelerated by a TPM, which is more secure because the encryption key is stored in the tamper-resistant TPM hardware rather than on an external flash drive. Other possible uses of TPMs include digital rights management (DRM), network access control, application execution control, and password protection.

Exiting and Saving Settings

Of course, all CMOS setups provide some method to Save and Exit or to Exit *Without* Saving. Use these as needed for your situation. Exit Without Saving is particularly nice for those folks who want to poke around the CMOS setup utility but don't want to mess anything up. Use it!

The CMOS setup utility would meet all of the needs of a modern system for BIOS if manufacturers would just stop creating new devices. That's not going to happen, of course, so let's turn now to devices that need to have BIOS loaded from elsewhere.

Losing CMOS Settings

Your CMOS needs a continuous trickle charge to retain its data. Motherboards use some type of battery, usually a coin battery like those in wrist watches, to give the CMOS the charge it needs when the computer is turned off (Figure 3.16). This battery also keeps track of the date and time when the PC is turned off.

If the battery runs out of charge, you lose all of your CMOS information. If some mishap suddenly erases the information on the CMOS chip, the computer might not boot up or you'll get nasty-looking errors at boot. Any PC made after 2002 will boot to factory defaults if the CMOS clears, so the chances of not booting are slim—but you'll still get errors at boot. Here are a few examples of errors that point to lost CMOS information:

• **Figure 3.16**   A CMOS battery

- CMOS configuration mismatch
- CMOS date/time not set
- No boot device available
- CMOS battery state low

Here are some of the more common reasons for losing CMOS data:

- Pulling and inserting cards
- Touching the motherboard

- Dropping something on the motherboard
- Dirt on the motherboard
- Faulty power supplies
- Electrical surges
- Chip creep

Most of these items should be fairly self-explanatory, but chip creep might be a new term for some of you. As PCs run, the components inside get warm. When a PC is turned off, the components cool off. This cycling of hot and cold causes the chips to expand and contract in their mounts. Although the chip designers account for this, in some extreme cases this thermal expansion and contraction causes a chip to work out of its mount and causes a failure called chip creep. Chip creep was a common problem in the earlier days of PCs, but after more than a quarter century of experience, the PC industry has done a pretty good job of designing mounts that hold all of your chips in place dependably.

If you encounter any of these errors, or if the clock in Windows resets itself to January 1 every time you reboot the system, the battery on the motherboard is losing its charge and needs to be replaced. To replace the battery, use a screwdriver to pry the battery's catch gently back. The battery should pop up for easy removal. Before you install the new battery, double-check that it has the same voltage and amperage as the old battery. To retain your CMOS settings while replacing the battery, simply leave your PC plugged into an AC outlet. The 5-volt soft power on all modern motherboards provides enough electricity to keep the CMOS charged and the data secure. Of course, I know you're going to be *extremely* careful about ESD while prying up the battery from a live system!

Cross Check

Clearing CMOS

All techs invariably do things in CMOS they want to undo, but sometimes simply making a change in CMOS prevents you from getting back to the CMOS setup utility to undo the change. A great example is when someone sets a CMOS password and then forgets the password. If you ever run into a system with an unknown CMOS password, you'll need to erase the CMOS and then reset everything.

You'll recall from Chapter 2, "Mastering CPUs and RAM," that all motherboards have a CMOS-clear jumper, so check your memory. How do you find out where the CMOS-clear jumper is located? What steps do you take to clear the CMOS? What scenario would definitely require you to clear the CMOS jumper?

Flashing ROM

Flash ROM chips can be reprogrammed to update their contents. With flash ROM, when you need to update your system BIOS to add support for a new technology, you can simply run a small command-line program, combined with an update file, and voilà, you have a new, updated BIOS! Different BIOS makers use slightly different processes for *flashing the BIOS*, but in general you must boot from a floppy diskette and then run the relevant updating command from the A:\> prompt. This example shows how simple it can be:

```
A:\> aw athxpt2.bin
```

Some motherboard makers provide Windows-based flash ROM update utilities that check the Internet for updates and download them for you to install (Figure 3.17). Most of these utilities also enable you to back up your current BIOS so you can return to it if the updated version causes trouble. Without a good backup, you could end up throwing away your motherboard if a flash BIOS update goes wrong, so you should always make one. Other motherboards have drivers to read flash ROM-based USB drives and have a flashing utility built into ROM. You can download an update, put it on a thumb drive, and boot to the CMOS setup utility to update the firmware. Nice!

Finally, don't update your BIOS unless you have some compelling reason to do so. As the old saying goes, "If it ain't broke, don't fix it!"

● **Figure 3.17**   ROM updating program for an ASUS motherboard

■ Installing Expansion Cards

Installing an expansion card successfully—another one of those bread-and-butter tasks for the PC tech—requires at least four steps. First, you need to know that the card works with your system and your operating system. Second, you have to insert the card in an expansion slot properly and without damaging that card or the motherboard. Third, you need to provide drivers for the operating system—that's *proper* drivers for the *specific* OS. Fourth, you should always verify that the card functions properly before you walk away from the PC.

Step 1: Knowledge

Learn about the device you plan to install—preferably before you purchase it! Does the device work with your system and operating system? Does it have drivers for your operating system? If you use Windows, the answer to these questions is almost always "yes." If you use an old operating system such as Windows 98 or a less common operating system such as Linux, these questions become critical. A lot of older, pre-XP hardware simply won't work with Windows XP or Vista at all. Check the device's documentation and check the device manufacturer's Web site to verify that you have the correct drivers. While you're checking, make sure you have the latest version of the driver; most devices get driver updates more often than the weather changes in Texas.

For Windows systems, your best resource for this knowledge is the Windows Logo'd Product List. This used to be called the Hardware Compatibility List (HCL), and you'll still hear lots of people refer to it as such. You can check out the Web site (http://winqual.microsoft.com/hcl/Default.aspx) to see if your product is listed, but most people just look on the box of the

Tech Tip

Installation Order

Some manufacturers insist on a different order for device installation than the traditional one listed here. The most common variation requires you to install the drivers and support software for an expansion card before you insert the card. Failure to follow the manufacturer's directions with such a card can lead to hours of frustration while you uninstall the card and reinstall the drivers, sometimes manually removing some drivers and software from the system. The bottom line? Read the instructions that come with a particular card! I'll provide more specific examples of problem devices in later chapters.

SERIAL A·T·A LIFE TIME Manufacturer Warranty

PCI › EXPRESS® Works with Windows® 2000 · XP · Server 2003

PCIe RAID
eed, & security to PCIe equipped desktops

• **Figure 3.18** Works with Windows!

The Windows Vista Compatibility Center (www.microsoft .com/windows/compatibility/) is also a great resource to check whether a particular software program works with Windows Vista.

device in question (Figure 3.18)—all Windows-certified devices proudly display that they work with Windows.

Microsoft keeps the Logo'd Product List available for all supported operating systems, so you'll see Windows 7, Windows Vista, and most likely Windows XP (depending on when you're reading this book). Windows 2000 is already gone.

Step 2: Physical Installation

To install an expansion card successfully, you need to take steps to avoid damaging the card, the motherboard, or both. This means knowing how to handle a card and avoiding electrostatic discharge (ESD) or any other electrical issue. You also need to place the card firmly and completely into an available expansion slot.

Optimally, a card should always be in one of two places: in a computer or in an anti-static bag. When inserting or removing a card, be careful to hold the card only by its edges. Do not hold the card by the slot connectors or touch any components on the board (Figure 3.19).

Use an anti-static wrist strap if possible, properly attached to the PC. If you don't have a wrist strap, you can use the tech way of avoiding ESD by touching the power supply after you remove the expansion card from its anti-static bag. This puts you, the card, and the PC at the same electrical potential and thus minimizes the risk of ESD.

Modern systems have a trickle of voltage on the motherboard at all times when the computer is plugged into a power outlet. Chapter 4, "Mastering PC Power," covers power for the PC and how to deal with it in detail, but here's the short version: *Always unplug the PC before inserting an expansion card!* Failure to do so can destroy the card, the motherboard, or both. It's not worth the risk.

• **Figure 3.19** Where to handle a card

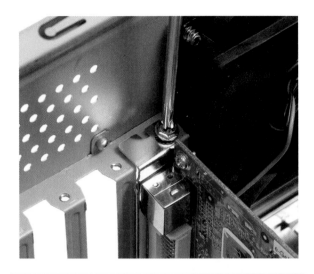

● **Figure 3.20**   Always screw down all cards.

Never insert or remove a card at an extreme angle. This may damage the card. A slight angle is acceptable and even necessary when removing a card. Always screw the card to the case with a connection screw. This keeps the card from slipping out and potentially shorting against other cards. Also, many cards use the screw connection to ground the card to the case (Figure 3.20).

Many technicians have been told to clean the slot connectors if a particular card is not working. This is almost never necessary after a card is installed and, if done improperly, can cause damage. You should clean slot connectors only if you have a card that's been on the shelf for a while and the contacts are obviously dull. *Never use a pencil eraser for this purpose.* Pencil erasers can leave behind bits of residue that wedge between the card and slot, preventing contact and causing the card to fail. Grab a can of contact cleaning solution and use it instead. Contact cleaning solution is designed exactly for this purpose, cleans contacts nicely, and doesn't leave any residue. You can find contact cleaning solution at any electronics store.

A fully inserted expansion card sits flush against the back of the PC case—assuming the motherboard is mounted properly, of course—with no gap between the mounting bracket on the card and the screw hole on the case. If the card is properly seated, no contacts are exposed above the slot. Figure 3.21 shows a properly seated (meaning fitted snugly in the slot) expansion card.

● **Figure 3.21**   Properly seated expansion card; note the tight fit between case and mounting bracket and the evenness of the card in the slot.

Step 3: Device Drivers

All devices, whether built into the motherboard or added along the way, require BIOS. For almost all expansion cards, that BIOS comes in the form of device drivers—software support programs—loaded from a CD-ROM disc provided by the card manufacturer.

Installing device drivers is fairly straightforward. You should use the correct drivers—kind of obvious, but you'd be surprised how many techs mess this up—and, if you're upgrading, you might have to unload current drivers before loading new drivers. Finally, if you have a problem, you may need to uninstall the drivers you just loaded or, with Windows XP or Vista, roll back to earlier, more stable drivers.

Getting the Correct Drivers

To be sure you have the best possible driver you can get for your device, you should always check the manufacturer's Web site. The drivers that come with a device may work well, but odds are good that you'll find a newer and better driver on the Web site. How do you know that the drivers on the Web site are newer? First, take the easy route: look on the CD. Often the version is printed right on the CD itself. If it's not printed there, you're going to have to load the CD in your CD-ROM drive and poke around. Many driver discs have an AutoRun screen that advertises the version. If nothing is on the pop-up screen, look for a Readme file (Figure 3.22).

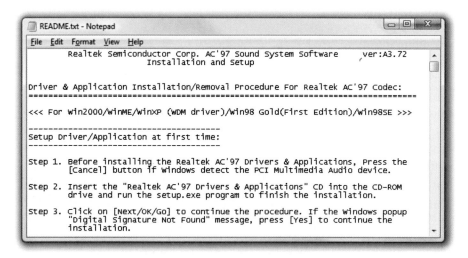

• **Figure 3.22**   Part of a Readme file showing the driver version

Driver or Device?

In almost all cases, you should install the device driver after you install the device. Without the device installed, the driver installation will not see the device and will give an error screen. The exceptions to this rule are USB and FireWire devices—with these you should always install the driver first.

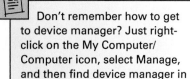
Don't remember how to get to device manager? Just right-click on the My Computer/Computer icon, select Manage, and then find device manager in the list of snap-ins on the right.

Removing the Old Drivers

Some cards—and this is especially true with video cards—require you to remove old drivers of the same type before you install the new device. To do this, you must first locate the driver in the Device Manager. Right-click the device driver you want to uninstall and select Uninstall (Figure 3.23). Many devices, especially ones that come with a lot of applications, will have an uninstall option in the Add/Remove Programs (Windows 2000), Add or Remove Programs (Windows XP), or Programs and Features (Windows Vista) applet in the Control Panel (Figure 3.24).

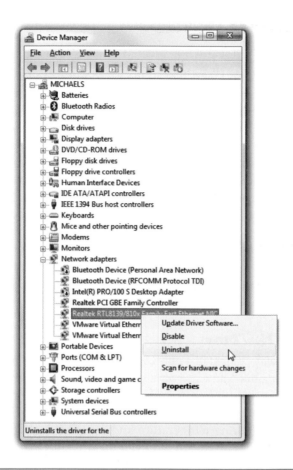

• **Figure 3.23**   Uninstalling a device

Unsigned Drivers

Microsoft wants your computer to work, truly, and the company provides an excellent and rigorous testing program for hardware manufacturers called the **Microsoft Windows Logo Program**. Developers initially use software to test their devices and, when they're ready, submit the device to the **Windows Hardware Quality Labs (WHQL)** for further testing. Hardware and drivers that survive the WHQL and other processes get to wear the *Designed for Windows* logo.

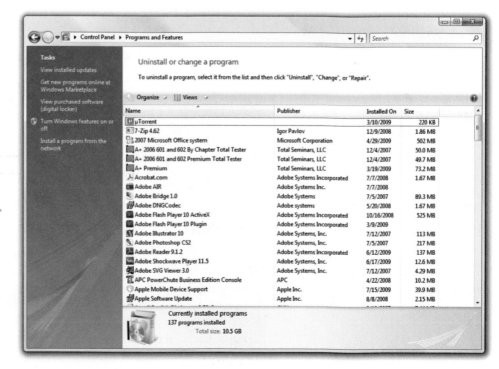

• **Figure 3.24**   The Change/Remove option in Add or Remove Programs

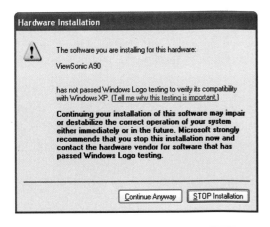

Figure 3.25   Unsigned driver warning

The drivers get a digital signature that says Microsoft tested them and found all was well.

Not all driver makers go through the rather involved process of the WHQL and other steps in the Windows Logo Program, so their software does not get a digital signature from Microsoft. When Windows runs into such a driver, it brings up a scary-looking screen (Figure 3.25) that says you're about to install an **unsigned driver**.

The fact that a company refuses to use the Windows Logo Program doesn't mean its drivers are bad—it simply means they haven't gone through Microsoft's exhaustive quality-assurance certification procedure. If I run into this, I usually check the driver's version to make sure I'm not installing something outdated, and then I just take my chances and install it. (I've yet to encounter a problem with an unsigned driver that I haven't also seen with Designed for Windows drivers.)

With Windows Vista 64-bit, Microsoft tightened the rules to try to provide the most stable platform possible. You simply cannot install unsigned drivers. Microsoft must approve each one.

Installing the New Driver

You have two ways to install a new driver: by using the installation CD directly or by using the Add Hardware Wizard in the Control Panel. Most experienced techs prefer to run from the installation CD. Most devices come with extra programs. My motherboard comes with a number of handy applications for monitoring temperature and overclocking. The Add Hardware Wizard does not install anything but the drivers. Granted, some techs find this a blessing because they don't want all of the extra junk that sometimes comes with a device, but most installation discs give clear options so you can pick and choose what you want to install (Figure 3.26).

Tech Tip

Permissions

To install drivers in a Windows computer, you need to have the proper permission. I'm not talking about asking somebody if you're allowed to install the device. Permissions are granted in Windows to enable people to do certain things, such as add a printer to a computer or install software, or to stop people from being able to do such tasks. Specifically, you need administrative permissions to install drivers. Chapter 7, "Securing Windows Resources," goes into a lot of detail about permissions, so no need to worry about them here.

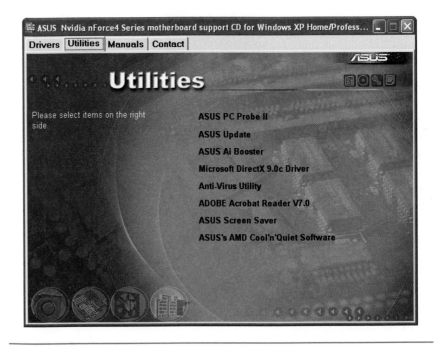

Figure 3.26   Installation menu

The other reason to use installation CDs instead of the Add Hardware Wizard stems from the fact that many expansion cards are actually many devices in one, and each device needs its own drivers. Some sound cards come with joystick ports, for example, and some video cards have built-in TV tuners. The Add Hardware Wizard will install all of the devices, but the installation CD brings them to your attention. Go for the CD program first and save the Add Hardware Wizard for problems, as you'll see in the next section.

Driver Rollback

Windows XP and Windows Vista offer the nifty feature of rolling back to previous drivers after an installation or driver upgrade. If you decide to live on the edge and install beta drivers for your video card, for example, and your system becomes frightfully unstable, you can back up to the drivers that worked before. (Not that I've ever had to use that feature, of course.) To access the rollback feature, simply open the Device Manager and access the properties for the device you want to adjust. On the Driver tab (Figure 3.27), you'll find the Roll Back Driver button.

Step 4: Verify

As a last step in the installation process, inspect the results of the installation and verify that the device works properly. Immediately after installing, you should open the Device Manager and verify that Windows sees the device (Figure 3.28). Assuming that the Device Manager shows the device working properly, your next check is to put the device to work by making it do whatever it is supposed to do. If you installed a printer, print something; if you installed a scanner, scan something. If it works, you're finished!

Tech Tip

Beta Drivers
Many PC enthusiasts try to squeeze every bit of performance out of their PC components, much as auto enthusiasts tinker with engine tunings to get a little extra horsepower out of their engines. Expansion card manufacturers love enthusiasts, who often act as free testers for their unpolished drivers, known as beta drivers. Beta drivers are fine for the most part, but they can sometimes cause amazing system instability—never a good thing! If you use beta drivers, make sure you know how to uninstall or roll back to previous drivers.

● **Figure 3.27**   Driver rollback feature

● **Figure 3.28**   Device Manager shows the device working properly.

■ Troubleshooting Expansion Cards

A properly installed expansion card rarely makes trouble; it's the botched installations that produce headaches. Chances are high that you'll have to troubleshoot an expansion card installation at some point, usually from an installation you botched personally.

The first sign of an improperly installed card usually shows up the moment you first try to get that card to do whatever it's supposed to do and it doesn't do it. When this happens, your primary troubleshooting process is a reinstallation—after checking in with the Device Manager.

Other chapters in this book cover specific hardware troubleshooting: sound cards and video cards in Chapter 10, "Mastering Video and Multimedia," for example. Use this section to help you decide what to look for and how to deal with the problem.

The Device Manager provides the first diagnostic and troubleshooting tool in Windows. After you install a new device, the Device Manager gives you many clues if something has gone wrong.

Occasionally, the Device Manager may not even show the new device. If that happens, verify that you inserted the device properly and, if needed, that the device has power. Run the Add/Remove Hardware Wizard and see if Windows recognizes the device. If the Device Manager doesn't recognize the device at this point, you have one of two problems: either the device is physically damaged and you must replace it, or the device is an onboard device, not a card, and is turned off in CMOS.

The Device Manager rarely completely fails to see a device. More commonly, device problems manifest themselves in the Device Manager via error icons—a black "!" or a red "X" or a blue "i."

● **Figure 3.29** An "!" in the Device Manager, indicating a problem with the selected device

- A black "!" on a yellow circle indicates that a device is missing (Figure 3.29), that Windows does not recognize a device, or that there's a device driver problem. A device may still work even while producing this error.

- A red "X" indicates a disabled device. This usually points to a device that's been manually turned off, or a damaged device. A device producing this error will not work.

- A blue "i" on a white field indicates a device on which someone has configured the system resources manually. This only occurs on non-ACPI systems. This symbol merely provides information and does not indicate an error with the device.

The "!" symbol is the most common error symbol and usually the easiest to fix. First, double-check the device's connections. Second, try reinstalling the driver with the Update Driver button. To get to the Update Driver button, right-click the desired device in the Device Manager and select Properties. In the Properties dialog box, select the Driver tab. On the Driver tab, click the Update Driver button to open the updating wizard (Figure 3.30).

A red "X" error strikes fear into most technicians. If you get one, first check that the device isn't disabled. Right-click on the device and select Enable. If that doesn't work (it often does not), try rolling back the driver (if you updated the driver) or uninstalling (if it's a new install). Shut the system down and make triple-sure you have the card physically installed. Then redo the entire driver installation procedure, making sure you have the most current driver for that device. If none of these procedures work, return the card—it's almost certainly bad.

As you look at the errors in the Device Manager, you'll notice error codes for the device that does not work properly.

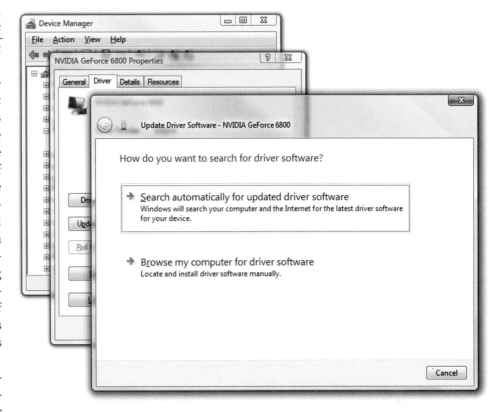

• **Figure 3.30**   Updating the driver

Windows has about 20 error codes, but the fixes still boil down to the same methods just shown. If you really want to frustrate yourself, try the Troubleshooter. It starts most fixes the same way: by reinstalling the device driver.

Upgrading and Installing Motherboards

To most techs, the concept of adding or replacing a motherboard can be extremely intimidating, much more so than merely installing an expansion card. It really shouldn't be; motherboard installation is a common and necessary part of PC repair. It is inexpensive and easy, although it can sometimes be a little tedious and messy because of the large number of parts involved. This section covers the process of installation and replacement and shows you some of the tricks that make this necessary process easy to handle.

Choosing the Motherboard and Case

Choosing a motherboard and case can prove quite a challenge for any tech, whether newly minted or a seasoned veteran. You first have to figure out the type of motherboard you want, such as AMD- or Intel-based. Then you

How to select and install a motherboard appropriate for a client or customer is something every CompTIA A+ technician should know.

Building a Recommendation

Family, friends, and potential clients often solicit the advice of a tech when they're thinking about upgrading their PC. This solicitation puts you on the spot to make not just any old recommendation but one that works with the needs and budget of the potential upgrader. To do this successfully, you need to manage expectations and ask the right questions, so Try This!

1. What does the upgrader want to do that compels him or her to upgrade? Write it down! Some of the common motivations for upgrading are to play that hot new game or to take advantage of new technology. What's the minimum system needed to run tomorrow's action games? What do you need to make multimedia sing? Does the motherboard need to have FireWire and high-speed USB built in to accommodate digital video and better printers?

2. How much of the current system does the upgrader want to save? Upgrading a motherboard can very quickly turn into a complete system rebuild. What form factor is the old case? If it's a microATX case, that constrains the motherboards you can use with it to microATX or the smaller FlexATX. If the desired motherboard is a full-sized ATX board, you'll need to get a new case. Does the new motherboard possess the same type of CPU socket as the old motherboard? If not, that's a sure sign you'll need to upgrade the CPU as well. What about RAM? If the old motherboard was using DDR SDRAM and the new motherboard requires DDR2 SDRAM, you'll need to replace the RAM. If you need to upgrade the memory, it is best to know how many channels the new RAM interface supports, because performance is best when all channels are populated. What if the old motherboard was using an AGP graphics accelerator that the new motherboard does not support, but you don't want to splurge on a PCI Express graphics accelerator right now? In this situation you might want to consider moving to a motherboard with integrated graphics. What's great about integrated graphics is that if the motherboard also possesses a ×16 PCI Express slot, you can upgrade to a more powerful discrete graphics accelerator later.

3. Once you've gathered information on motivation and assessed the current PC of the upgrader, it's time to get down to business: field trip time! This is a great excuse to get to the computer store and check out the latest motherboards and gadgets. Don't forget to jot down notes and prices while you're there. By the end of the field trip, you should have the information to give the upgrader an honest assessment of what an upgrade will entail, at least in monetary terms. Be honest—in other words, don't just tell upgraders what you think they want to hear—and you won't get in trouble.

need to think about the form factor, which of course influences the type of case you'll need. Third, how rich in features is the motherboard and how tough is it to configure? You have to read the motherboard manual to find out. Finally, you need to select the case that matches your space needs, budget, and form factor. Now look at each step in a little more detail.

First, determine what motherboard you need. What CPU are you using? Will the motherboard work with that CPU? Because most of us buy the CPU and the motherboard at the same time, make the seller guarantee that the CPU will work with the motherboard. If you can, choose a motherboard that works with much higher speeds than the CPU you can afford; that way you can upgrade later. How much RAM do you intend to install? Are extra RAM sockets available for future upgrades?

A number of excellent motherboard manufacturers are available today. Some of the more popular brands are abit, ASUS, BIOSTAR, DFI, GIGABYTE, Intel, MSI, and Shuttle. Your supplier may also have some lesser-known but perfectly acceptable brands of motherboards. As long as the supplier has an easy return policy, it's perfectly fine to try one of these.

Second, make sure you're getting a form factor that works with your case. Don't try to put a regular ATX motherboard into a microATX case!

Third, all motherboards come with a technical manual, better known as the motherboard book (Figure 3.31). You must have this book! This book is your primary source for all of the critical information about the motherboard. You heard a bit about this book in the

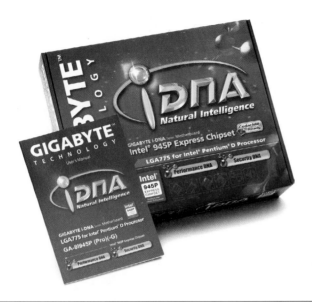

• Figure 3.31   Motherboard box and book

previous chapter, but the motherboard book contains much more information than what kind of RAM and CPU your motherboard can use. For example, if you set up CPU or RAM timings incorrectly in CMOS and you have a dead PC, where would you find the CMOS-clear jumper? Where do you plug in the speaker? Even if you let someone else install the motherboard, insist on the motherboard book; you will need it.

Fourth, pick your case carefully. Cases come in six basic sizes: slimline, desktop, mini-tower, mid-tower, tower, and cube. Slimline and desktop models generally sit on the desk, beneath the monitor. The various tower cases usually occupy a bit of floor space next to the desk. The mini-tower and mid-tower cases are the most popular choices. Make sure you get a case that fits your motherboard—many microATX and all FlexATX cases are too small for a regular ATX motherboard. Cube cases generally require a specific motherboard, so be prepared to buy both pieces at once. A quick test-fit before you buy saves a lot of return trips to the supplier.

Cases come with many options, but three more common options point to a better case. One option is a removable face (Figure 3.32)—many cheaper cases screw the face into the metal frame with wood screws. A removable face makes disassembly much easier.

Another option is a detachable motherboard mount. Clearly, the motherboard has to be attached to the case in some fashion. In better cases, this is handled by a removable tray or plate (Figure 3.33). This enables you to

• Figure 3.32   Removable face

• **Figure 3.33**   Motherboard tray

• **Figure 3.34**   Case with both front-mounted ports and an add-on flash memory card reader

attach the motherboard to the case separately, saving you from sticking your arms into the case to turn screws.

The third option—front-mounted ports for USB, FireWire, and headphones—can make using a PC much easier. Better cases offer these ports, although you can also get add-on components that fit into the increasingly useless floppy drive bay to bring added front connectivity to the PC. Figure 3.34 shows a case with both types of front connectors.

Power supplies often come with the case. Watch out for "really good deal" cases because that invariably points to a cheap or missing power supply. You also need to verify that the power supply has sufficient wattage. This issue is handled in Chapter 4, "Mastering PC Power."

Installing the Motherboard

If you're replacing a motherboard, first remove the old motherboard. Begin by removing all of the cards. Also remove anything else that might impede removal or installation of the motherboard, such as hard or floppy drives. Keep track of your screws—the best idea is to return the screws to their mounting holes temporarily, at least until you can reinstall the parts. Sometimes you even have to remove the power supply temporarily to enable access to the motherboard. Document the position of the little wires for the speaker, power switch, and reset button in case you need to reinstall them.

Unscrew the motherboard. *It will not simply lift out.* The motherboard mounts to the case via small connectors called **standouts** that slide into keyed slots or screw into the bottom of the case (Figure 3.35). Screws then go into the standouts to hold the motherboard in place. Be sure to place the standouts properly before installing the new motherboard.

If you drop any screws into a hard-to-reach place inside the case while installing the motherboard, use an extension magnet to remove them.

Watch out for ESD here! Remember that it's very easy to damage or destroy a CPU and RAM with a little electrostatic discharge. It's also fairly easy to damage the motherboard with ESD. Wear your anti-static wrist strap.

● **Figure 3.35**   Standout in a case, ready for the motherboard

When you insert the new motherboard, do not assume that you will put the screws and standouts in the same place as they were in your old motherboard. When it comes to the placement of screws and standouts, only one rule applies: anywhere it fits. Do not be afraid to be a little tough here! Installing motherboards can be a wiggling, twisting, knuckle-scraping process.

Once you get the motherboard mounted in the case, with the CPU and RAM properly installed, it's time to insert the power connections and test it. A POST card can be helpful with the system test because you won't have to add the speaker, a video card, monitor, and keyboard to verify that the system is booting. If you have a POST card, start the system, and watch to see if the POST takes place—you should see a number of POST codes before the POST stops. If you don't have a POST card, install a keyboard, speaker, video card, and monitor. Boot the system and see if the BIOS information shows up on the screen. If it does, you're probably okay. If it doesn't, it's time to refer to the motherboard book to see where you made a mistake.

Wires, Wires, Wires

The last part of motherboard installation is connecting the LEDs, buttons, and front-mounted ports on the front of the box. These usually include the following:

- Soft power
- Reset button
- Speaker
- Hard drive activity LED
- Power LED
- USB

Tech Tip

Before the Case

A lot of techs install the CPU, CPU fan, and RAM into the motherboard before installing the motherboard into the case. This helps in several ways, especially with a new system. First, you want to make certain that the CPU and RAM work well with the motherboard and with each other—without that, you have no hope of setting up a stable system. Second, installing these components first prevents the phenomenon of flexing the motherboard. Some cases don't provide quite enough support for the motherboard, and pushing in RAM can make the board bend. Third, attaching a CPU fan can be a bear of a task, one that's considerably easier to do on a table top than within the confines of a case. Finally, on motherboards that require you to set jumpers or switches, you can much more easily read the tiny information stenciled on the PCB before you add the shadows from the case. If necessary, set any jumpers and switches for the specific CPU according to information from the motherboard manual.

Pay attention to the location of the standouts if you're swapping a motherboard. If you leave a screw-type standout beneath a spot on the motherboard where you can't add a screw and then apply power to the motherboard, you run the risk of shorting the motherboard.

● **Figure 3.36**   Motherboard wire connections labeled on the motherboard

● **Figure 3.37**   Sample of case wires

- FireWire
- Sound

These wires have specific pin connections to the motherboard. Although you can refer to the motherboard book for their location, usually a quick inspection of the motherboard will suffice for an experienced tech (Figure 3.36).

You need to follow a few rules when installing these wires. First, the lights are LEDs, not light bulbs; they have a positive and negative side. If they don't work one way, turn the connector around and try the other. Second, when in doubt, guess. Incorrect installation only results in the device not working; it won't damage the computer. Refer to the motherboard book for the correct installation. The third and last rule is that, with the exception of the soft power switch on an ATX system, you do not need any of these wires for the computer to run. Many techs often simply ignore these wires, although this would not be something I'd do to any system but my own.

No hard-and-fast rule exists for determining the function of each wire. Often the function of each wire is printed on the connector (Figure 3.37). If not, track each wire to the LED or switch to determine its function.

■ Troubleshooting Motherboards

Motherboards fail. Not often, but motherboards and motherboard components can die from many causes: time, dust, cat hair, or simply slight manufacturing defects made worse by the millions of amps of current sluicing through the motherboard traces. Installing cards, electrostatic discharge, flexing the motherboard one time too many when swapping out RAM or drives—any of these factors can cause a motherboard to fail. The motherboard is a hard-working, often abused component of the PC. Unfortunately for the common tech, troubleshooting a motherboard problem can be difficult and time consuming. Let's wrap this chapter with a look at symptoms of a failing motherboard, techniques for troubleshooting, and the options you have when you discover a motherboard problem.

Symptoms

Motherboard failures commonly fall into three types: catastrophic, component, and ethereal. With a **catastrophic failure**, the PC just won't boot. This sort of problem happens to brand-new systems because of manufacturing defects—often called a **burn-in failure**—and to any system that gets a shock of electrostatic discharge. Burn-in failure is uncommon and usually happens in the first 30 days of use. Swap out the motherboard for a replacement and you should be fine. If you accidentally zap your motherboard when inserting a card or moving wires around, be chagrined. Change your daring ways and wear an anti-static wrist strap!

Component failure happens rarely and appears as flaky connections between a device and motherboard, or as intermittent problems. A hard drive plugged into a faulty controller on the motherboard, for example, might show up in CMOS autodetect but be inaccessible in Windows. Another example is a serial controller that worked fine for months until a big storm took out the external modem hooked to it and now doesn't work anymore, even with a replacement modem.

The most difficult of the three types of symptoms to diagnose are those I call *ethereal* symptoms. Stuff just doesn't work all of the time. The PC reboots itself. You get a Blue Screen of Death (BSoD) in the midst of heavy computing, such as right before you smack the villain and rescue the damsel. What can cause such symptoms? If you answered any of the following, you win the prize:

- Faulty component
- Buggy device driver
- Buggy application software
- Slight corruption of the operating system
- Power supply problems

Err … you get the picture.

What a nightmare scenario to troubleshoot! The Way of the Tech knows paths through such perils, though, so let's turn to troubleshooting techniques now.

Techniques

To troubleshoot a potential motherboard failure requires time, patience, and organization. Some problems will certainly be quicker to solve than others. If the hard drive doesn't work as expected, as in the previous example, check the settings on the drive. Try a different drive. Try the same drive with a different motherboard to verify that it's a good drive. Like every other troubleshooting technique, all you try to do with motherboard testing is to isolate the problem by eliminating potential factors.

This three-part system—check, replace, verify good component—works for the simpler and the more complicated motherboard problems. You can even apply the same technique to ethereal-type problems that might be anything, but you should add one more verb: *document*. Take notes on the individual components you test so you don't repeat efforts or waste time. Plus, taking notes can lead to the establishment of patterns. Being able to re-create a system crash by performing certain actions in a specific order can often lead you to the root of the problem. Document your actions. Motherboard testing is time-consuming enough without adding inefficiency.

Options

Once you determine that the motherboard has problems, you have several options for fixing the three types of failures. If you have a catastrophic failure, you must replace the motherboard. Even if it works somewhat, don't mess around. The motherboard should provide bedrock stability for the system. If it's even remotely buggy or problematic, get rid of it!

If you have a component failure, you can often replace the component with an add-on card that will be as good as or better than the failed device. Adaptec, for example, makes fine cards that can replace the built-in SATA ports on the motherboard (Figure 3.38).

If your component failure is more a technology issue than physical damage, you can try upgrading the BIOS on the motherboard.

Finally, if you have an ethereal, ghost-in-the-machine type of problem that you have finally determined to be motherboard related, you have only a couple of options for fixing the problem. You can flash the BIOS in a desperate attempt to correct whatever it is, which sometimes does work and is less expensive than the other option. Or you can replace the motherboard.

 If you've lost components because of ESD or a power surge, you would most likely be better off replacing the motherboard. The damage you *can't* see can definitely sneak up to bite you and create system instability.

Tech Tip

Limits of BIOS Upgrades

Flashing the BIOS for a motherboard can fix a lot of system stability problems and provide better implementation of built-in technology. What it cannot do for your system is improve the hardware. If AMD comes out with a new, improved, lower-voltage Athlon 64, for example, and your motherboard cannot scale down the voltage properly, you cannot use that CPU—even if it fits in your motherboard's Socket AM2. No amount of BIOS flashing can change the hardware built into your motherboard.

• **Figure 3.38**   Adaptec PCIe SATA card

■ Chapter Summary

After reading this chapter and completing the exercises, you should understand the following about motherboards.

Troubleshoot the power-on self test (POST)

■ In addition to the BIOS routines and the CMOS setup program, the system ROM also includes a special program called the power-on self test (POST) that is executed every time the computer boots. POST first has basic devices, up to and including video, run self-diagnostics. If a device detects an error, the computer alerts you with a series of beeps. Different ROM manufacturers have used different beep codes, but your motherboard book should explain them (particularly in older systems). After the basic devices, POST tells the rest of the devices to run tests and displays a text error message on the screen if anything is wrong. Some manufacturers use numeric error codes or combine numeric and text messages.

■ The computer may beep in two situations that are not related to POST beep codes. If the computer beeps constantly until you shut it off, it means RAM is missing or damaged. If the computer beeps after it is booted, it is probably warning you that the system is overheating.

■ If the computer appears dead, with no beeps or screen response, you can place a POST card in an expansion slot to diagnose the problem by using the LED readout on the card. The documentation that comes with the POST card explains the LED codes for your particular BIOS.

■ A beep code, text error message, or POST error may identify a problem, but it does not fix it. After you know which device is causing the problem, you should check the connection for the troublesome device and replace it if possible. If you cannot remove the bad part or if you cannot interpret the error message, you may need to replace the motherboard.

■ When you first power on the PC, the power supply circuitry tests for proper voltage and then sends a signal down a special wire called the power good wire to awaken the CPU. The moment the power good wire wakes it up, the CPU sends a built-in memory address via its address bus. This address is the first line of the POST program on the system ROM, which is how the system starts the POST. After the POST has finished, it passes control to the bootstrap loader function on the system BIOS. This program looks for an operating system, checking the floppy drive, hard drives, or other bootable devices to find the boot sector that identifies the location of the OS. When the BIOS finds a bootable or system disk or device that has a functional operating system, it passes control to that disk or device.

Maintain BIOS and CMOS properly

■ All CMOS setup programs have basically the same main options. On the Standard CMOS Features screen, you can change floppy drive, hard drive, and date/time settings. Today's setup programs have extra CMOS settings that control such items as memory management, password and booting options, diagnostic and error handling, and power management. The Award Modular BIOS enables motherboard manufacturers to add or remove options from the setup program.

■ Among the other things you can configure in CMOS setup are the voltage and multiplier settings for the CPU (the CPU SoftMenu), boot options (check the Advanced BIOS Features menu), power management, password protection, and ports (the Integrated Peripherals menu). All setup programs include options to *Save and Exit* or *Exit Without Saving*. You should not change CMOS settings unless you know exactly what you're doing.

■ On older systems, if the information on the CMOS chip was lost or erased, the computer would not boot. The most common cause was a dead onboard battery, but other factors such as electrical surges, chip creep, or a dirty motherboard could also erase CMOS data. Lost CMOS information produces errors such as *No boot device available* or *CMOS date/time not set*. Making a backup copy of the CMOS data enabled you to restore the information and recover from this catastrophe.

- Unlike earlier ROM chips that you had to replace when you wanted to upgrade the BIOS programs, today's computers use flash ROM chips that you can reprogram without removing. If you install a CPU or other new hardware that the flash ROM chip does not support, you can run a small command-line program combined with an update file to change your BIOS. The exact process varies from one motherboard maker to another. If the flash ROM utility allows you to make a backup of your BIOS, you should always do so. Don't update your BIOS unless you have a good reason. As the old saying goes, "If it ain't broke, don't fix it!"

- Many CMOS setup programs enable you to set a boot password, a password to enter the CMOS setup program itself, or both. These passwords are stored in CMOS. If you forget your password, you simply need to clear the CMOS data. Unplug the AC power from the PC and remove the motherboard battery. This removes the trickle charge that enables CMOS to store information and clears all CMOS data, including the passwords. Reinstall the battery, plug in the power cord, boot up the computer, and re-enter your CMOS settings. Alternatively, many motherboards provide a CMOS-clear jumper you can use to clear the CMOS data without removing the battery. Small padlocks on the system chassis can prevent unauthorized users from accessing the motherboard and clearing CMOS data.

- When you make changes to the CMOS settings, make only as many changes at one time as you can remember. Document the original settings and the changes on a piece of paper so you can reverse any changes that had the wrong effect.

- If you have CMOS settings that keep reverting to defaults or if the clock in Windows resets itself to January 1 every time you reboot the system, the battery on the motherboard is losing its charge and needs to be replaced.

- You can update the firmware in ROM by flashing the BIOS. This process is often done by booting to a bootable floppy diskette after downloading a flashing program and the update BIOS from the manufacturer. Some motherboards enable you to update the BIOS through Windows programs; others come with drivers for USB devices and have a flashing utility built in.

Install expansion cards properly

- There are four basic steps to follow when installing an expansion card: determine that the card is compatible with your system, physically install the card, install the drivers, and verify that the card works.

- Determine that the card is compatible with your system. Many older cards do not work with Windows XP or Windows Vista, and not every card works with older versions of Windows or other operating systems (such as Linux or Macintosh). Read the box before you buy, consult the device manufacturer's Web site, and, if Windows is your operating system, consult the Windows Logo'd Product List (formerly the Hardware Compatibility List).

- Physically install the card without damaging it or other system components. Keep the card in its anti-static bag until you are ready to install it. Power off and unplug the computer. Wear an anti-static wrist strap or use an alternative method of dissipating static electricity.

- Install the correct drivers, which should come on a CD with the device. If you don't have the CD, you may be able to download the drivers from the manufacturer's Web site.

- Some manufacturers use the Microsoft Windows Logo Program to verify and digitally sign their drivers. This means their drivers have been verified by Microsoft to work properly. Other manufacturers skip the certification process and produce unsigned drivers that in most cases work just fine.

- Sometimes driver updates go bad and you find that the new driver just doesn't work. With Windows XP and later, you can roll back to the previous version driver by double-clicking the device in the Device Manager, clicking the Driver tab, and then clicking the Roll Back Driver button.

- Always verify that your newly installed device works. Immediately after installation, open the Device Manager and verify that no error icons are displayed. Next, check the physical device. Finally, test the device's functionality.

Troubleshoot expansion cards

- If you find a device is not working as expected, your first step is to check the Device Manager. If the device is not listed in the Device Manager, verify that you inserted it correctly and it has power. You can also try the Add Hardware Wizard to see if Windows recognizes the device.

- A good tech is familiar with the Device Manager's trouble icons. A black "!" on a yellow circle indicates that the device is missing, the device is not recognized, or there is a problem with the driver. A device may work even when displaying this icon. A red "X" indicates a disabled device and usually means the device has been turned off or is damaged. A device with a red "X" will not work. A blue "i" on a white circle indicates that system resources have been configured manually. This icon is informational and does not imply any error.

- If you encounter the "!" icon, verify the device's connections. Next, try to reinstall the driver by right-clicking the device in the Device Manager and selecting Properties. Click the Driver tab and then click the Update Driver button.

- If a device displays the red "X" icon, right-click the device in the Device Manager and select Enable. If that doesn't work, try rolling back or uninstalling the driver. Shut down the system, verify the device's connections, and repeat the installation procedure. If the device still doesn't work, it is likely the device is either bad or not compatible with your operating system. Return the card to the place of purchase.

Upgrade and install motherboards

- Not all motherboards fit in all cases. If you upgrade a motherboard, make sure the new motherboard fits in the existing case. If you purchase a new motherboard and a new case, make sure you purchase a case that supports the form factor of your motherboard.

- Determine the CPU you or your client wants before purchasing a motherboard. Not all CPUs are supported by, or even fit in, all motherboards.

Make sure your motherboard supports your CPU and, if possible, purchase a motherboard that supports higher speeds than your CPU in case you want to upgrade the processor at a later time.

- To replace a motherboard, first remove all of the expansion cards from the old motherboard. Document the position of all of the little wires before removing them. Unscrew the motherboard and remove it from the case.

- Before installing a new motherboard in the case, attach the CPU, heat sink/fan, and RAM. Check the standouts in the case—you might have to add or remove a few to accommodate the new motherboard. Once installed, boot the system and make sure there are no POST errors and the BIOS information appears on the screen. Then install any expansion cards.

- Cases come with a series of little wires that connect to LEDs on the front of the case. You need to plug these wires into the motherboard for the LEDs to function. LEDs have a positive and a negative side, so the wires must be connected the right way or the LEDs will not work. If you find that the LEDs are not working, turn the connector around to reverse the positive/negative connection. Getting it wrong will not damage your system; it will only cause the LEDs not to light up.

Troubleshoot motherboard problems

- Motherboards and motherboard components can die for many reasons, including time, dust, pet hair, manufacturing defects, ESD, or physical damage. Motherboard failures usually fall into one of three main categories: catastrophic, component, or ethereal.

- Catastrophic failure is typically caused by manufacturing defects (burn-in failure) or ESD. Burn-in failures are uncommon and usually manifest within the first 30 days of use. In the case of a catastrophic failure, replace the motherboard.

- Component failure appears as a flaky connection between a device and the motherboard or as intermittent problems. In the case of a component failure, replace the failed component with an expansion card or peripheral device. Sometimes a BIOS upgrade can fix component failures.

- Ethereal failure is the most difficult to diagnose. Symptoms vary from the PC rebooting itself to Blue Screens of Death and can be caused by a faulty component, buggy device driver, buggy application software, operating system corruption, or power supply problems.

- Use three steps to troubleshoot problems: check, replace, and verify. For example, first check the

settings of the problem device. If the device still fails, replace the device. If the device continues to malfunction, try the device with a different motherboard. Remember to document your troubleshooting steps. Not only will it help you to become an efficient troubleshooter, but it also can lead to the establishment of patterns. Being able to re-create a system crash by performing certain actions in a specific order can often lead you to the root of the problem.

■ Key Terms

- [3] **beep codes** *(41)*
- [8] **bootable disk** *(43)*
- [16] **burn-in failure** *(65)*
- [9] **bootstrap loader** *(43)*
- [17] **catastrophic failure** *(65)*
- [10] **chassis intrusion detection** *(46)*
- [18] **component failure** *(65)*
- [12] **device driver** *(54)*
- [11] **DriveLock** *(48)*
- [13] **Microsoft Windows Logo Program** *(55)*

- [1] **motherboard** *(40)*
- [14] **motherboard book** *(60)*
- [5] **POST card** *(42)*
- [4] **power-on self test (POST)** *(41)*
- [7] **power good** *(43)*
- [15] **standouts** *(62)*
- [6] **system disk** *(43)*
- [2] **traces** *(40)*
- [15] **unsigned driver** *(56)*
- [14] **Windows Hardware Quality Labs** *(55)*

■ Key Term Quiz

Use the Key Terms list to complete the sentences that follow. Not all terms will be used.

1. Loaded when the system boots, a(n) *device driver* is a file that contains instructions to support a hardware device.

2. When the computer starts, it runs a program on the system BIOS called *Power on self test (POST)* that checks the hardware.

3. If the computer appears dead, with no beeps or screen responses, you can insert a(n) *Post Card* in an expansion slot to diagnose what is wrong.

4. Device drivers for devices manufactured by companies not participating in the Windows certification program are reported as *unsigned drivers*.

5. The *Motherboard book* is your primary source for all of the critical information about the motherboard.

6. The motherboard mounts to the case via small connectors called *Standouts* that slide into keyed slots or screw into the bottom of the case.

7. *chassis intrusion detection* lets you know if someone has opened the case of your computer.

■ Multiple-Choice Quiz

1. The nonprofit agency that Sid works for received a half-dozen new motherboards as a donation, but when he tried to install one into a case, it didn't fit at all. The ports and expansion slots seemed to be switched. What's most likely the issue?

   A. Sid's motherboard has a manufacturing defect.

   B. Sid needs to readjust his motherboard standouts.

   C. Sid's case has a manufacturing defect.

   D. The motherboards are the wrong form factor for Sid's cases.

2. In a routine check of a system newly built by her latest intern, Sarah discovers that everything works except the hard drive and power LEDs on the front of the case. What could be the problem? (Select two.)

   A. The intern forgot to connect the LED leads to the motherboard.

   B. The intern reversed the LED leads to the motherboard.

   C. There is no power to the motherboard.

   D. There is no activity on the hard drive.

3. Robert installed a new motherboard, CPU, and RAM into his old case. After he attached the power correctly and pressed the power button, not only did the system not boot up, he also could smell ozone and realized the motherboard had shorted out. What could have been the cause?

   A. Robert installed an ATX motherboard into a BTX case.

   B. Robert installed a BTX motherboard into an ATX case.

   C. Robert used an AT power supply on an ATX motherboard.

   D. Robert left a standout in the wrong place under the motherboard.

4. Which of the following is the testing part of the Windows Logo Program?

   A. ACL

   B. HCL

   C. WHQL

   D. WKRP

5. What should you do *before* installing an expansion card? (Select two.)

   A. Attach an anti-static wrist strap.

   B. Install the drivers.

   C. Plug the PC into a grounded outlet.

   D. Unplug the PC.

6. In a Windows XP workstation, Steven updated the drivers for a network expansion card that worked, but he thought it could be faster. Almost immediately, he discovered that the new drivers not only didn't speed up the NIC but they also made it start dropping data! What his best option?

   A. Download the driver pack from Microsoft.

   B. Reinstall the networking software.

   C. Remove the NIC.

   D. Use the driver rollback feature to return to the previous drivers.

7. Jack decided to go retro and added a second floppy disk drive to his computer. He thinks he has it physically installed correctly, but it doesn't show up in Windows. Which of the following options will most likely lead Jack where he needs to go to resolve the issue?

   A. Reboot the computer and press the F key on the keyboard twice. This signals that the computer has two floppy disk drives.

   B. Reboot the computer and watch for instructions to enter the CMOS setup utility (for example, a message may say to press the DELETE key). Do what it says to go into CMOS setup.

C. In Windows, press the DELETE key twice to enter the CMOS setup utility.

D. In Windows, go to Start | Run and type **floppy**. Click OK to open the Floppy Disk Drive Setup Wizard.

8. Which of the following will result in a POST beep code message?

A. The system is overheating.

B. The video card is not seated properly.

C. The keyboard is unplugged.

D. The hard drive has crashed.

9. Which of the following most typically enables you to upgrade a flash ROM chip?

A. Remove the chip and replace it with a different one.

B. Reboot the computer.

C. Install a different operating system.

D. Run a small command-line program combined with a BIOS update file.

■ Essay Quiz

1. Why do some POST error messages manifest themselves as beep codes while others display as text messages? What should you do if you get a POST error message?

2. Your friend Merrill just called. He bought a new sound card for his computer and tried to install it. It's not working. What should he do now? Using the methodology for card installation that you learned in this chapter, explain the steps he should follow to determine whether he installed the card incorrectly or the card itself is faulty.

3. Prepare a PowerPoint presentation or write a paper that would help your classmates select and replace a bad motherboard. Be sure to walk through all of the necessary steps.

Lab Projects

• Lab Project 3.1

One of the most important skills a PC technician can possess is the ability to read and interpret documentation. No single piece of documentation is as important as the motherboard book. Let's see how well you can understand this documentation. Consult your motherboard book or use one that your instructor provides. (If you do not have the motherboard book, try to download it from the manufacturer's Web site.) Then write a paragraph about your motherboard that includes answers to the following questions:

- What make and model is the motherboard?

- What chipset does it use?

- What kinds of RAM slots does it contain?

- What kinds of expansion slots does your motherboard have and how many of each kind does it have?

- What kinds of onboard ports does it have?

- What kinds of CPUs does it support and what kind of processor slot does it have?

- Does your motherboard use jumpers or dip switches for configuration? If so, what do the jumpers or dip switches control?

- The motherboard book probably contains an illustration of the way the motherboard components are laid out. By examining this illustration, determine what form factor your motherboard uses.

- Does your motherboard have any unusual or proprietary features?

• Lab Project 3.2

Watch closely as your computer boots to see if it displays a message about how to reach the setup program. If it does not, consult your motherboard book to try to locate this information. Then, using the method appropriate for your system BIOS chip, access the setup program and examine the various screens. Do not change anything! Usually, your motherboard book includes default settings for the various setup screens and perhaps includes explanations of the various choices. Compare what you see on the screen with what the book says. Do you see any differences? If so, how do you account for these differences? As you examine the setup program, answer the following questions:

- How do you n
  next? Are ther
  simply jump
  next? Are th
  navigating

- What is th
  In other
  look for a boot

- What is the core voltage of t

- How many SATA drives does the BIOS

When you have finished, choose Exit Without Saving.

Mastering PC Power

"Electricity can be dangerous. My nephew tried to stick a penny into a plug. Whoever said a penny doesn't go far didn't see him shoot across that floor. I told him he was grounded."

—TIM ALLEN

In this chapter, you will learn how to

- **Describe common power supply connectors and features**
- **Install, maintain, and troubleshoot power supplies**

While the CompTIA A+ 220-701 Essentials exam expects you to have a general understanding of how power supplies work, you'll have to have some, well, practical knowledge to pass the Practical Application exam. If you've already taken the 701 exam, you should be familiar with the information in the first section of this chapter, but it's always helpful to review. If you haven't taken the 701 exam, then you're about to learn how to take a power supply, with all its sundry connectors and its potential deadliness, and actually plug it into your computer.

As always when working with electricity, doing this can be dangerous, so be sure to take every possible precaution and don't fool around with power supplies. When working with a power supply, always make sure it's not plugged into the wall, and never, under any circumstances, open up a power supply to work inside it. There are powerful capacitors inside a power supply that hold a charge even when unplugged, and they can hold more than enough voltage for you to get "Here lies Bert, who opened up a power supply" written on your tombstone. Getting electrocuted is no fun, trust me!

■ Power Supplies in Brief

When you've plugged your computer into the wall socket and flipped the power switch, the power supply unit (PSU) takes over, converting high-voltage AC into several DC voltages (notably, 5.0, 12.0, and 3.3 volts) usable by the delicate interior components. Power supplies come in a large number of shapes and sizes, but the most common size by far is the standard 150 mm × 140 mm × 86 mm desktop PSU shown in Figure 4.1.

The PC uses the 12.0-volt current to power motors on devices such as hard drives and CD-ROM drives, and it uses the 5.0-volt and 3.3-volt current for support of onboard electronics. Manufacturers may use these voltages any way they wish, however, and may deviate from these assumptions. Power supplies also come with standard connectors for the motherboard and interior devices.

● **Figure 4.1**   Desktop PSU

Power to the Motherboard

Modern motherboards use a 20- or 24-pin P1 power connector (Figure 4.2).This particular connector has a dongle on the side so the power supply can attach to a 20- or a 24-pin connector on the motherboard. Some motherboards may require special 4-, 6-, or 8-pin connectors to supply extra power. The 4-pin connector that you see is called a P4 power connector and it provides additional 12-volt power to the motherboard. The 6-pin connector is used to power high-end PCIe graphics cards, and the 8-pin connector is an even more powerful version of the P4 for newer motherboards.

● **Figure 4.2**   Motherboard power connectors

Power to Peripherals: Molex, Mini, and SATA

Many devices inside the PC require power. These include hard drives, floppy drives, optical-media drives, Zip drives (for techs who enjoy retro computing), and fans. The typical PC power supply has up to three types of connectors that plug into peripherals: Molex, mini, and SATA.

Molex Connectors

The most common type of power connection for devices that need 5 or 12 volts of power is the Molex connector (Figure 4.3). The Molex connector has notches, called *chamfers*, that guide its installation. The tricky part is that Molex connectors require a firm push to plug in properly, and a strong person can defeat the chamfers, plugging a Molex in upside down. Not a good thing. *Always* check for proper orientation before you push it in!

● **Figure 4.3**   Molex connector

Try This!

Testing DC

A common practice for techs troubleshooting a system is to test the DC voltages coming out of the power supply. Even with good AC, a bad power supply can fail to transform AC to DC at voltages needed by the motherboard and peripherals. So grab your trusty multimeter and Try This! on a powered-up PC with the side cover removed. Note that you must have P1 connected to the motherboard and the system must be running (you don't have to be in Windows, of course).

1. Switch your multimeter to DC, somewhere around 20 V DC if you need to make that choice. Make sure your leads are plugged into the multimeter properly: red to hot, black to ground. The key to testing DC is that which lead you touch to which wire matters. Red goes to hot wires of all colors; black *always* goes to ground.

2. Plug the red lead into the red wire socket of a free Molex connector and plug the black lead into one of the two black wire sockets. You should get a reading of ~5 V. What do you have?

3. Now move the red lead to the yellow socket. What voltage do you get?

4. Testing the P1 connector is a little more complicated. You push the red and black leads into the top of P1, sliding in alongside the wires until you bottom out. Leave the black lead in one of the black wire ground sockets. Move the red lead through all of the colored wire sockets. What voltages do you find?

Mini Connectors

All power supplies have a second type of connector, called a **mini connector** (Figure 4.4), that supplies 5 and 12 volts to peripherals, although only floppy disk drives in modern systems use this connector. Drive manufacturers adopted the mini as the standard connector on 3.5-inch floppy disk drives. Often these mini connectors are referred to as floppy power connectors.

Be extra careful when plugging in a mini connector! Whereas Molex connectors are difficult to plug in backward, you can insert a mini connector incorrectly with very little effort. As with a Molex connector, doing so will almost certainly destroy the floppy drive. Figure 4.5 depicts a correctly

• **Figure 4.4**   Mini connector

⚠️   As with any power connector, plugging a mini connector into a device the wrong way will almost certainly destroy the device. Check twice before you plug one in!

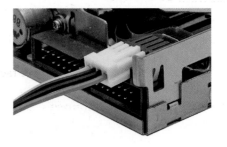

• **Figure 4.5**   Correct orientation of a mini connector

Mike Meyers' CompTIA A+ Guide: Practical Application

oriented mini connection, with the small ridge on the connector away from the body of the data socket.

SATA Power Connectors

Serial ATA (SATA) drives need a special 15-pin **SATA power connector** (Figure 4.6). The larger pin count supports the SATA hot-swappable feature and 3.3-V, 5.0-V, and 12.0-V devices. SATA power connectors are *L* shaped, making it almost impossible to insert one incorrectly into a SATA drive. No other device on your computer uses the SATA power connector.

Splitters and Adapters

You may occasionally find yourself without enough connectors to power all of the devices inside your PC. In this case, you can purchase splitters to create more connections (see Figure 4.7). You might also run into the phenomenon of needing a SATA connector but having only a spare Molex. Because the voltages on the wires are the same, a simple adapter will take care of the problem nicely.

Rails

Generally, all of the PC's power comes from a single transformer that takes the AC current from a wall socket and converts it into DC current that is split into three primary DC voltage rails: 12.0 volts, 5.0 volts, and 3.3 volts. Individual lines run from each of these voltage rails to the various connectors. That means the 12-volt connector on a P4 draws from the same rail as the main 12-volt connector feeding power to the motherboard. This works fine as long as the collective needs of the connectors sharing a rail don't exceed its capacity to feed them power. To avoid this, EPS12V divided the 12-volt supply into two or three separate 12-volt rails, each one providing a separate source of power.

Active PFC

Visualize the AC current coming from the power company as water in a pipe, smoothly moving back and forth, 60 times a second. A PC's power supply, simply due to the process of changing this AC current into DC current, is like a person sucking on a straw on the end of this pipe. It takes gulps only when the current is fully pushing or pulling at the top and bottom of each cycle and creating an electrical phenomena—sort of a back pressure—that's called *harmonics* in the power industry. These harmonics create the humming sound you hear from electrical components. Over time, harmonics damage electrical equipment, causing serious problems with the power supply and other electrical devices on the circuit. Once you put a few thousand PCs with power supplies in the same local area, harmonics can even damage the electrical power supplier's equipment!

Good PC power supplies come with **active power factor correction (active PFC)**, extra circuitry that smooths out the way the power supply takes power from the power company and eliminates harmonics (Figure 4.8). Never buy a power supply that does not have active PFC—all power supplies with active PFC proudly show you on the box.

● **Figure 4.6**   SATA power connector

SATA also supports a slimline connector that has a 6-pin power segment and a micro connector that has a 9-pin power segment.

It's normal and common to have unused power connectors inside your PC case.

● **Figure 4.7**   Molex splitter

[ENGLISH] Model: Neo HE 550

- ATX12V v2.2 and EPS12V compliant.
- Dual CPU and dual core ready.
- **Advanced cable management system** improves internal airflow and reduces system clutter by allowing you to use only the cables that you need.
- **Universal Input** automatically accepts line voltages from 100V to 240V AC.
- **Active PFC** (Power Factor Correction) delivers environmentally-friendlier power.
- **Up to 85% efficiency** reduces heat generation and saves power and money.
- **Dedicated voltage outputs** to deliver more stable power.
- **Voltage feedback** and tight ±3% regulation for improved system stability.
- **Three +12V output circuits** provide maximum stable power for the CPU independently and for other peripherals.
- **Dual PCI Express** graphics card power connectors.
- **Low-speed 80mm fan** delivers whisper-quiet cooling and ensures quiet operation by varying fan speed in response to load and conditions.
- **SATA connectors** for your Serial ATA drives.
- **Industrial grade protection circuitry** prevents damage resulting from short circuits (SCP), power overloads (OPP), excessive current (OCP), excessive voltages (OVP), and under voltage (UVP).
- **Approvals:** UL, CUL, CE, CB, FCC Class B, TÜV, CCC, C-tick.
- **MTBF:** 80,000 hrs.
- **Size:** 5.9" (D) x 5.9" (W) x 3.4" (H)
      15cm (D) x 15cm (W) x 8.6cm (H)
- **AQ3*** – Antec's unbeatable three-year parts and labor warranty.

• **Figure 4.8**   Power supply advertising active PFC

> The CompTIA A+ Practical Application exam doesn't require you to figure precise wattage needs for a particular system. When building a PC for a client, however, you do need to know this stuff!

Wattage Requirements

Every device in a PC requires a certain amount of wattage to function. A typical hard drive draws 15 watts of power when accessed, for example, whereas some Athlon 64 X2 CPUs draw a whopping 110 watts at peak usage—with average usage around 70 watts. The total wattage of all devices combined is the minimum you need the power supply to provide.

If the power supply cannot produce the wattage a system needs, that PC won't work properly. Because most devices in the PC require maximum wattage when first starting, the most common result of insufficient wattage is a paperweight that looks like a PC. This can lead to some embarrassing moments. You might plug in a new hard drive for a client, push the power button on the case, and nothing happens—a dead PC! Eek! You can quickly determine if insufficient wattage is the problem. Unplug the drive and power up the system. If the system boots up, the power supply is a likely suspect.

The only fix for this problem is to replace the power supply with one that provides more wattage (or leave the new drive out—a less-than-ideal solution).

No power supply can turn 100 percent of the AC power coming from the power company into DC current, so all power supplies provide less power to the system than the wattage advertised on the box. ATX12V 2.0 standards require a power supply to be at least 70 percent efficient, but you can find power supplies with better than 80 percent efficiency. More efficiency can tell you how many watts the system puts out to the PC in actual use. Plus, the added efficiency means the power supply uses less power, saving you money.

One common argument these days is that people buy power supplies that provide far more wattage than a system needs and therefore waste power. This is untrue. A power supply provides only the amount of power your system needs. If you put a 1000-watt power supply (yes, they really exist) into a system that needs only 250 watts, that big power supply will put out only 250 watts to the system. So buying an efficient, higher-wattage power supply gives you two benefits. First, running a power supply at less than 100 percent load lets it live longer. Second, you'll have plenty of extra power when adding new components.

As a general recommendation for a new system, use at least a 500-watt power supply. This is a common wattage and gives you plenty of extra power for booting as well as for whatever other components you might add to the system in the future.

Tech Tip

Build in Aging
Don't cut the specifications too tightly for power supplies. All power supplies produce less wattage over time, simply because of wear and tear on the internal components. If you build a system that runs with only a few watts of extra power available from the power supply initially, that system will most likely start causing problems within a year or less. Do yourself or your clients a favor and get a power supply that has more wattage than you need.

Installing, Maintaining, and Troubleshooting Power Supplies

Although installing, maintaining, and troubleshooting power supplies take a little less math than selecting the proper power supply for a system, they remain essential skills for any tech. Installing takes but a moment, and maintaining is almost as simple, but troubleshooting can cause headaches. Let's take a look.

Installing

The typical power supply connects to the PC with four standard computer screws, mounted in the back of the case (Figure 4.9). Unscrew the four screws and the power supply lifts out easily (Figure 4.10). Insert a new power supply that fits the case and attach it by using the same four screws.

Handling ATX power supplies requires special consideration. Understand that an ATX power supply *never turns off*. As long as that power supply stays connected to a power outlet, the power supply will continue to supply 5 volts to the motherboard. Always unplug an ATX system before you do any work! For years, techs bickered about the merits of leaving a PC plugged in or unplugged while you serviced it. ATX settled this issue forever. Many ATX power supplies provide a real on/off

● **Figure 4.9** Mounting screws for power supply

● **Figure 4.10**   Removing power supply from system unit

● **Figure 4.11**   On/off switch for an ATX system

● **Figure 4.12**   Shorting the soft on/off jumpers

● **Figure 4.13**   Power supply fan

switch on the back of the PSU (see Figure 4.11). If you really need the system shut down with no power to the motherboard, use this switch.

When working on an ATX system, you may find using the power button inconvenient because you're not using a case or you haven't bothered to plug the power button's leads into the motherboard. That means there is no power button. One trick when in that situation is to use a set of car keys or a screwdriver to contact the two wires to start and stop the system (see Figure 4.12).

Your first task after acquiring a new power supply is simply making sure it works. Insert the motherboard power connectors before starting the system. If you have video cards with power connectors, plug them in too. Other connectors such as hard drives can wait until you have one successful boot—or if you're cocky, just plug everything in!

Cooling

Heat and computers are not the best of friends. Cooling is therefore a vital consideration when building a computer. Electricity equals heat. Computers, being electrical devices, generate heat as they operate, and too much can seriously damage a computer's internal components.

The **power supply fan** provides the basic cooling for the PC (Figure 4.13). It not only cools the voltage regulator circuits *within* the power supply, but it also provides a constant flow of outside air throughout the interior of the computer case. A dead power supply fan can rapidly cause tremendous problems, even equipment failure. If you ever turn on a computer and it boots just fine but you notice that it seems unusually quiet, check to see if the power supply fan has died. If it has, quickly turn off the PC and replace the power supply.

Some power supplies come with a built-in sensor to help regulate the airflow. If the system gets too hot, the power supply fan spins faster. The 3-pin, 3-wire fan sensor connector plugs into the motherboard directly (Figure 4.14).

Case fans are large, square fans that snap into special brackets on the case or screw directly to the case, providing extra cooling for key components (see Figure 4.15). Most cases come with a case fan, and no modern computer should really be without one or two.

The single biggest issue related to case fans is where to plug them in. Most case fans come with standard Molex connectors, which are easy to plug in, but other case fans come with special three-pronged power connectors that need to connect to the motherboard. You can get adapters to plug three-pronged connectors into Molex connectors or Molex connectors into three-pronged connectors.

• **Figure 4.14**   3-wire fan sensor connector

Maintaining Airflow

A computer is a closed system, and computer cases help the fans keep things cool: everything is inside a box. Although many tech types like to run their systems with the side panel of the case open for easy access to the components, in the end they are cheating themselves. Why? A closed case enables the fans to create airflow. This airflow substantially cools off interior components. When the side of the case is open, you ruin the airflow of the system, and you lose a lot of cooling efficiency.

An important point to remember when implementing good airflow inside your computer case is that hot air rises. Warm air always rises above cold air, and you can use this principle to your advantage in keeping your computer cool.

In the typical layout of case fans for a computer case, an intake fan is located near the bottom of the front bezel of the case. This fan draws cool air in from outside the case and blows it over the components inside the case. Near the top and rear of the case (usually near the power supply), you'll usually find an exhaust fan. This fan works the opposite of the intake fan: it takes the warm air from inside the case and sends it to the outside.

Another important part of maintaining proper airflow inside the case is ensuring that **slot covers** are covering all empty expansion bays (Figure 4.16). To maintain good airflow inside your case, you shouldn't provide too many opportunities for air to escape. Slot covers not only assist in maintaining a steady airflow; they also help keep dust and smoke out of your case.

• **Figure 4.15**   Case fan

Missing slot covers can cause the PC to overheat!

Reducing Fan Noise

Fans generate noise. In an effort to ensure proper cooling, many techs put several high-speed fans into a case, making the PC sound like a jet engine. You can reduce fan noise by using manually adjustable fans, larger fans, or

● **Figure 4.16**   Slot covers

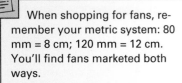

Knob for adjusting
fan speed

● **Figure 4.17**   Manual fan adjustment device

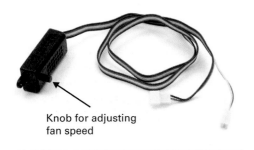

When shopping for fans, remember your metric system: 80
mm = 8 cm; 120 mm = 12 cm.
You'll find fans marketed both
ways.

specialty "quiet" fans. Many motherboards enable you to control fans through software.

Manually adjustable fans have a little knob you can turn to speed up or slow down the fan (Figure 4.17). This kind of fan can reduce some of the noise, but you run the risk of slowing down the fan too much and thus letting the interior of the case heat up. A better solution is to get quieter fans.

Larger fans that spin more slowly are another way to reduce noise while maintaining good airflow. Fan sizes are measured in millimeters (mm) or centimeters (cm). Traditionally the industry used 80-mm power supply and cooling fans, but today you'll find 100-mm, 120-mm, and even larger fans in power supplies and cases.

Many companies manufacture and sell higher-end low-noise fans. The fans have better bearings than run-of-the-mill fans, so they cost a little more, but they're definitely worth it. They market these fans as "quiet" or "silencer" or other similar adjectives. If you run into a PC that sounds like a jet, try swapping out the case fans for a low-decibel fan from Papst, Panasonic, or Cooler Master. Just check the decibel rating to decide which one to get. Lower, of course, is better.

Because the temperature inside a PC changes depending on the load put on the PC, the best solution for noise reduction combines a good set of fans with temperature sensors to speed up or slow down the fans automatically. A PC at rest uses less than half of the power of a PC running a video-intensive computer game and therefore makes a lot less heat. Virtually all modern systems support three fans through three 3-pin fan connectors on the motherboard. The CPU fan uses one of these connectors, and the other two are for system fans or the power supply fan.

Most CMOS setup utilities provide a little control over fans plugged into the motherboard. Figure 4.18 shows a typical CMOS setting for the fans. Note that you can't tell the fans when to come on or off—only when to set off an alarm when they reach a certain temperature.

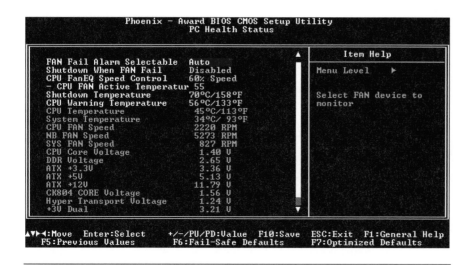

Phoenix - Award BIOS CMOS Setup Utility
PC Health Status

		Item Help
FAN Fail Alarm Selectable	Auto	
Shutdown When FAN Fail	Disabled	Menu Level ▶
CPU FanEQ Speed Control	60% Speed	
- CPU FAN Active Temperatur	55	
Shutdown Temperature	70°C/158°F	Select FAN device to
CPU Warning Temperature	56°C/133°F	monitor
CPU Temperature	45°C/113°F	
System Temperature	34°C/ 93°F	
CPU FAN Speed	2220 RPM	
NB FAN Speed	5273 RPM	
SYS FAN Speed	827 RPM	
CPU Core Voltage	1.40 V	
DDR Voltage	2.65 V	
ATX +3.3V	3.36 V	
ATX +5V	5.13 V	
ATX +12V	11.79 V	
CK804 CORE Voltage	1.56 V	
Hyper Transport Voltage	1.24 V	
+3V Dual	3.21 V	

▲▼▶◀:Move Enter:Select   +/-/PU/PD:Value F10:Save   ESC:Exit F1:General Help
F5:Previous Values   F6:Fail-Safe Defaults   F7:Optimized Defaults

• **Figure 4.18**   CMOS fan options

Software is the best way to control your fans. Some motherboards come with system-monitoring software that enables you to set the temperature at which you want the fans to come on and off. If no program came with your motherboard, and the manufacturer's Web site doesn't offer one for download, try the popular freeware SpeedFan utility (Figure 4.19). Written by Alfredo Milani Comparetti, SpeedFan monitors voltages, fan speeds, and temperatures in computers with hardware monitor chips. SpeedFan can even access S.M.A.R.T. information for hard disks that support this feature and show hard disk temperatures, too, if supported. You can find SpeedFan at www.almico.com/speedfan.php.

Even if you don't want to mess with your fans, always make a point to turn on your temperature alarms in CMOS. If the system gets too hot, an alarm will warn you. There's no way to know if a fan dies other than to have an alarm.

When Power Supplies Die

Power supplies fail in two ways: sudden death and slowly over time. When they die suddenly, the computer will not start and the fan in the power supply will not turn. In this case, verify that electricity is getting to the power supply before you do anything. Avoid the embarrassment of trying to repair a power supply when the only problem is a bad outlet or an extension cord that is not plugged in. Assuming that the system has electricity, the best way to verify that a power supply is working or not working is to use a multimeter to check the voltages coming out of the power supply (see Figure 4.20).

Do not panic if your power supply puts out slightly more or less voltage than its nominal value. The voltages supplied by most PC power supplies can safely vary by as much as ±10 percent of their stated values. This means that the 12-volt line can vary from roughly 10.5 to 12.9 volts without exceeding the tolerance of the various systems in the PC. The 5.0- and 3.3-volt lines offer similar tolerances.

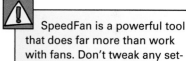

SpeedFan is a powerful tool that does far more than work with fans. Don't tweak any settings you don't understand!

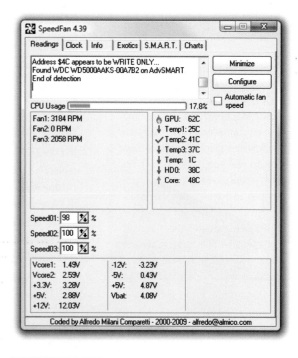

• **Figure 4.19**   SpeedFan

Be sure to test every connection on the power supply—that means every connection on your main power as well as every Molex and mini. Because all voltages are between –20 and +20 VDC, simply set the voltmeter to the 20-V DC setting for everything. If the power supply fails to provide power, throw it into the recycling bin and get a new one—even if you're a component expert and a whiz with a soldering iron. Don't waste your or your company's time; the price of new power supplies makes replacement the obvious way to go.

No Motherboard

Power supplies will not start unless they're connected to a motherboard, so what do you do if you don't have a motherboard you trust to test? First, try an ATX tester. Many companies make these devices. Look for one that supports both 20- and 24-pin motherboard connectors as well as all of the other connectors on your motherboard. Figure 4.21 shows a power supply tester.

Switches

Broken power switches form an occasional source of problems for power supplies that fail to start. The power switch is behind the on/off button on every PC. It is usually secured to the front cover or inside front frame on your PC, making it a rather challenging part to access. To test, try shorting the soft power jumpers as described earlier. A key or screwdriver will do the trick.

When Power Supplies Die Slowly

If all power supplies died suddenly, this would be a much shorter chapter. Unfortunately, the majority of PC problems occur when power supplies die slowly over time. This means that one of the internal electronics of the power supply has begun to fail. The failures are *always* intermittent and tend to cause some of the most difficult to diagnose problems in PC repair. The secret to discovering that a power supply is dying lies in one word: intermittent. Whenever you experience intermittent problems, your first guess should be that the power supply is bad. Here are some other clues you may hear from users:

- "Whenever I start my computer in the morning, it starts to boot and then locks up. If I press CTRL-ALT-DEL two or three times, it will boot up fine."

- "Sometimes when I start my PC, I get an error code. If I reboot, it goes away. Sometimes I get different errors."

- "My computer will run fine for an hour or so. Then it locks up, sometimes once or twice an hour."

Sometimes something bad happens and sometimes it does not. That's the clue for replacing the power supply. And don't bother with the voltmeter; the voltages will show up within tolerances, but only *once in a while* they will spike and sag (far more quickly than your

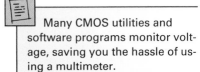

● **Figure 4.20**   Testing one of the 5-volt DC connections

Many CMOS utilities and software programs monitor voltage, saving you the hassle of using a multimeter.

● **Figure 4.21**   ATX power supply tester

voltmeter can measure) and cause these intermittent errors. When in doubt, change the power supply. Power supplies break in computers more often than any other part of the PC except the floppy disk drives. You might choose to keep power supplies on hand for swapping and testing.

Fuses and Fire

Inside every power supply resides a simple fuse. If your power supply simply pops and stops working, you might be tempted to go inside the power supply and check the fuse. This is not a good idea. First off, the capacitors in most power supplies carry high voltage charges that can hurt a lot if you touch them. Second, fuses blow for a reason. If a power supply is malfunctioning inside, you want that fuse to blow, because the alternative is much less desirable.

Failure to respect the power of electricity will eventually result in the most catastrophic of all situations: a fire. Don't think it won't happen to you! Keep a fire extinguisher handy. Every PC workbench needs a fire extinguisher, but make sure you have the right one. The fire prevention industry has divided fire extinguishers into four fire classes:

- **Class A** Ordinary free-burning combustible, such as wood or paper
- **Class B** Flammable liquids, such as gasoline, solvents, or paint
- **Class C** Live electrical equipment
- **Class D** Combustible metals such as titanium or magnesium

As you might expect, you should only use a Class C fire extinguisher on your PC if it should catch fire. All fire extinguishers are required to have their type labeled prominently on them. Many fire extinguishers are multiclass in that they can handle more than one type of fire. The most common fire extinguisher is type ABC—it works on all common types of fires.

Beyond A+

Power supplies provide essential services for the PC, creating DC out of AC and cooling the system, but that utilitarian role does not stop the power supply from being an enthusiast's plaything. Plus, server and high-end workstations have somewhat different needs than more typical systems, so naturally they need a boost in power. Let's take a look Beyond A+ at these issues.

It Glows!

The enthusiast community has been modifying, or *modding*, their PCs for years, cutting holes in the cases, adding fans to make overclocking feasible, and slapping in glowing strips of neon and cold cathode tubes. The power supply escaped the scene for a while, but it's back. A quick visit to a good computer store off- or online, such as http://directron.com, reveals power supplies that light up, sport a fancy color, or have more fans than some rock stars. Figure 4.22 shows a see-through PSU.

• **Figure 4.22**   See-through power supply that glows blue

On the other hand, you also find super-quiet stealth power supplies, with single or double high-end fans that react to the temperature inside your PC—speeding up when necessary but running slowly and silently when not. One of these would make a perfect power supply for a home entertainment PC because it would provide function without adding excessive decibels of noise.

Modular Power Supplies

It's getting more and more popular to make PCs look good on both the inside and the outside. Unused power cables dangling around inside PCs creates a not-so-pretty picture. To help stylish people, manufacturers created power supplies with modular cables (Figure 4.23).

Modular cables are pretty cool, because you add only the lines you need for your system. On the other hand, some techs claim that modular cables hurt efficiency because the modular connectors add resistance to the lines. You make the choice; is a slight reduction in efficiency worth a pretty look?

• **Figure 4.23**   Modular-cable power supply

Rail Power

When you start using more powerful CPUs and video cards, you can run into a problem I call "rail power." Every ATX12V power supply using multiple rails supplies only a certain amount of power, measured in amps (A), on each rail. The problem is with the 12-V rails. The ATX12V standard requires up to 18 A for each 12-V rail—more than enough for the majority of users, but not enough when you're using a powerful CPU and one or more PCIe video cards. If you have a powerful system, get online and read the detailed specs for your power supply. Figure 4.24 shows sample power supply specs. Many power supply makers do not release detailed specs—avoid them!

Look for power supplies that offer about 16 to 18 A per rail. These will be big power supplies—400 W and up. Nothing less will support a big CPU and one or two PCIe video cards.

Watch out for power supplies that list their operating temperature at 25° C—about room temperature. A power supply that provides 500 W at 25° C will supply substantially less in warmer temperatures, and the inside of your PC is usually 15° C warmer than the outside air. Sadly, many power supply makers—even those who make good power supplies—fudge this fact.

Niche-Market Power Supply Form Factors

The demand for smaller and quieter PCs and, to a lesser extent, the emergence of the BTX form factor has led to the development of a number of niche-market power supply form factors. All use standard ATX connectors but differ in size and shape from standard ATX power supplies.

Here are some of the more common specialty power supply types:

- **TFX12V** A small power supply form factor optimized for low-profile ATX systems
- **SFX12V** A small power supply form factor optimized for systems using FlexATX motherboards (see Figure 4.25)
- **CFX12V** An L-shaped power supply optimized for microBTX systems
- **LFX12V** A small power supply form factor optimized for low-profile BTX systems

NeoHE 550

FEATURES	
Switches	ATX Logic on-off Additional power rocker switch
Maximum Power	550W
Transient Response	+12V, +5Vand +3.3V independent output circuitry provides stable power and tighter cross regulation (+/- 3%)
P. G. Signal	100-500ms
Over Voltage Protection recycle AC to reset	+5V trip point < +6.5V +3.3V trip point < +4.1V +12V trip point < +14.3V
Special Connectors	ATX12V/EPS12V Compatible 4 + 4 pin +12V Molex Peripheral Floppy SATA PCI Express
Leakage Current	<3.5mA @ 115VAC

OUTPUT							
Output Voltage	+3.3V	+5V	+12V1	+12V2	+12V3	-12V	+5Vsb
Max. Load	24A	20A	18A	18A	18A	0.8A	2.5A
Min. Load	0.5A	0.3A	1A	1A	1A	0A	0A
Regulation	3%	3%	3%	3%	3%	6%	3%
Ripple & Noise(mV)	50	50	120	120	120	120	50
Available Power	79.2W	100W	504W			9.6W	12.5W
Total Power	550W continuous output @ 50C ambient temperature						

● **Figure 4.24** Sample specs

 You'll commonly find niche-market power supplies bundled with computer cases (and often motherboards as well). These form factors are rarely sold alone.

● **Figure 4.25** SFX power supply

Chapter 4 Review

■ Chapter Summary

After reading this chapter and completing the exercises, you should understand the following about power supplies.

Describe common power supply connectors and features

- The power supply converts AC into several DC voltages (5.0, 12.0, and 3.3 volts). Devices such as hard drives and CD-ROM drives require 12.0 volts, and onboard electronics use 3.3- and 5.0-volt currents.

- The power supply has several standard connectors for the motherboard and interior devices. Today's motherboards have a P1 socket that uses the P1 connector from the power supply. A standard ATX power supply has a 20-pin P1 connector, while the newer ATX12V 2.0 power supplies come with a 24-pin P1 connector. Some motherboards also need a 4-, 6-, or 8-pin connector to provide an additional 12 volts of power.

- Peripherals use two or possibly three different kinds of connectors: the larger Molex connector, the smaller mini connector, and the SATA connector. Used with hard drives and CD- and DVD-media drives, the Molex has chamfers to ensure that it is connected properly. Used today only for floppy drives, the mini connector can easily be inserted incorrectly, thus destroying the floppy drive. The SATA connector is used for SATA drives. If you do not have enough connectors for all of the devices inside your PC, you can create more connections with a splitter. Similarly, if your power supply does not have the connector a device needs, you can purchase adapters to convert one type to another.

- Power supplies are rated in watts. If you know the amount of wattage that every device in the PC needs, you can arrive at the total wattage required for all devices, and that is the minimum wattage your power supply should provide. If the power supply does not provide sufficient wattage, the computer will not work. For a new computer system, you should select at least a 500-watt power supply to have extra power for adding components in the future.

Install, maintain, and troubleshoot power supplies

- Power supplies connect to the PC case via four screws mounted in the rear of the case. Unscrew the four screws and the power supply will lift out. Because an ATX power supply is always on, be sure to unplug it from the wall outlet before working on it.

- Adequate cooling is important to prevent damage to the computer's internal components. The fan inside the power supply itself cools the voltage regulator circuits within the power supply and provides a constant flow of outside air throughout the interior of the computer case. If the fan is not working, turn the computer off before you experience equipment failure. Some power supplies regulate airflow by using a sensor with a three-wire connector that plugs into the motherboard.

- Because power companies supply high-voltage AC, the computer's power supply converts AC to low-voltage DC that is then portioned out to the internal devices. Heat is a byproduct of electricity and must be controlled in the computer.

- To improve cooling, most cases come with a case fan. If the case does not have one, you should add one. Most case fans use standard Molex connectors, but some use a special three-pronged power connector that plugs directly into the motherboard. To enable the fans to create airflow, the case needs to be closed. If slot covers are left off of empty expansion bays, the computer can overheat. Slot covers also help keep dust and smoke out of the case. Beware of "great deals" on cases that come with power supplies, because the included power supply is often substandard.

- Electrical problems range from irregular AC to dying or faulty power supplies. Power supplies may fail suddenly or slowly over time. After you make sure that the wall outlet is providing electricity, checking voltages from the power supply with a voltmeter is the best way to verify whether the power supply is working or has failed. A power supply is functioning properly if the output voltages are within 10 percent over or under the expected voltage. Be sure to check all of the connections on the power supply. If you determine that the power supply is bad, the most economical solution is to throw it away and replace it with a new one.

- Power supplies will not start unless they are connected to a motherboard. If you need to test a power supply but don't have a motherboard, use an ATX tester.

- If one of the internal electrical components in the power supply begins to fail, the result is usually intermittent problems, making diagnosis difficult. If you are experiencing intermittent problems, such as lockups or different error codes that disappear after rebooting, suspect the power supply. Unfortunately, the voltmeter is not good for diagnosing intermittent problems. Because power supply failures rank second behind floppy drive failures, it is a good idea to keep power supplies in stock for swapping and testing.

- Never open a power supply, even to check the fuse; the unit contains capacitors that carry high voltage charges that can hurt you.

- Every PC workbench should have a Class C fire extinguisher handy in case of an electrical fire. Although some fire extinguishers are multi-class, handling all types of fires, use only a Class C fire extinguisher on your PC.

■ Key Terms

active power factor correction (active PFC) *(77)* ✓	**P4 power connector** *(75)* ✓
mini connector *(76)* ✓	**power supply fan** *(80)* ✓
Molex connector *(75)*	**SATA power connector** *(77)*
P1 power connector *(75)* ✓	**slot covers** *(81)* ✓

■ Key Term Quiz

Use the Key Terms list to complete the sentences that follow.

1. The _power supply fan_ provides the basic cooling for the PC.

2. The _P4 power connector_ provides additional 12-volt power to the motherboard.

3. If the _slot covers_ are left off of the expansion slots, the computer may overheat.

4. A(n) _mini connector_ powers a floppy disk drive.

5. Older hard drives and optical drives used _Molex connector_ to hook up to the power supply.

6. _PFC_ circuitry in the power supply smooths out any spikes in the power going into your computer and eliminates harmonics.

7. Newer hard drives and optical drives use _Sata_ to hook up to the power supply.

8. The main connector used to hook a power supply to a hard drive is the 20- or 24-pin _P1_.

■ Multiple-Choice Quiz

1. Which statement is true?

   A. Removing the expansion slot covers on the back of your case will improve cooling by allowing hot air to escape.

   B. Shop around when purchasing a case as you will often find good deals that include a powerful PSU.

   C. Always keep the power supply plugged in to the wall outlet when working on the inside of a computer as this helps to ground it.

   D. An AC testing device is never as accurate as a multimeter.

2. Which of the following problems points to a dying power supply?

   Ⓐ. Intermittent lockups at bootup

   B. A power supply fan that does not turn

   C. A multimeter reading of 11 V for the 12-V power line

   D. A computer that won't start by shorting the soft power jumpers

3. Which kind of fire extinguisher should you use for computer equipment?

   A. Class A

   B. Class B

   Ⓒ. Class C

   D. Class D

4. What should you check first if a computer will not start and the fan in the power supply will not turn?

   A. Check the voltages coming out of the power supply.

   B. Check the motherboard power connector.

   Ⓒ. Check the power coming into the power supply.

   D. Check the power switch.

5. Under what conditions should a PC technician work inside the power supply?

   A. Only when it is unplugged.

   B. Only when the technician is wearing an anti-static wrist strap.

   C. Anytime, because the power supply only has low-energy DC electricity that will not hurt the technician.

   Ⓓ. Never, because the power supply has capacitors that hold electrical charges that may harm the technician.

6. What is the effect of exceeding the wattage capabilities of a power supply by inserting too many devices?

   A. The system will boot normally, but some of the devices will not function properly.

   B. The system will boot normally and all of the devices will work, but only for a limited time. After an hour or so, the system will spontaneously shut down.

   Ⓒ. The system will not boot or turn on at all.

   D. The system will try to boot, but the overloaded power supply will fail, burning up delicate internal capacitors.

7. What kind of case fans should you use in a home theater PC?

   A. High RPM fans to keep the system extra cool.

   B. You shouldn't use fans in a home theater PC.

   C. Small fans to fit inside a small case.

   Ⓓ. Silent fans to keep noise down while watching movies.

8. What sort of power connector does a hard drive typically use?

   Ⓐ. Molex

   B. Mini

   C. Sub-mini

   D. Micro

9. What is a power supply's output rated in?

   Ⓐ. Watts

   B. Joules

   C. Volts

   D. Amps

10. What kind of connector is used to provide additional 12-volt power to the motherboard?

   A. Molex

   B. Mini

   Ⓒ. P4

   D. P1

Essay Quiz

1. Because microprocessors have become more powerful and more devices have been invented for the computer, the wattage demands for the PC have gone up. So has the need for cooling. Discuss the cooling devices that come with today's PCs and what the user needs to know about keeping the PC cool.

2. Helene's computer worked fine last week. Although she has not changed anything since then, today her computer won't even boot. You

suspect that the p
she does not hav
tell her to check
does need to re
she be sure the

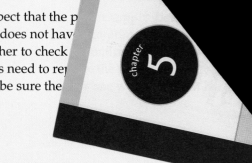

Lab Projects

• Lab Project 4.1

This chapter recommends a 500-watt power supply for a new computer. Is that the wattage that manufacturers usually offer with their computers? Check the following Web sites to see what wattage comes with a new PC:

- www.dell.com

- www.gateway.com
- www.hp.com

Do any of these companies mention a power supply upgrade with a higher wattage rating? If so, what are the wattages and what are the additional costs?

• Lab Project 4.2

If you've got access to a computer that you can disassemble and work on, practice removing and reinstalling the computer's power supply. This may additionally involve removing optical drives, RAM,

and possibly even the CPU, so be careful! Definitely make sure the power supply is unplugged from the wall before starting.

mplementing Hard Drives

"Wisely and slow; they stumble that run fast."

—SHAKESPEARE, *ROMEO AND JULIET*, ACT 2, SCENE 3

In this chapter, you will learn how to

- ■ **Install hard drives**
- ■ **Configure CMOS and install drivers**
- ■ **Troubleshoot hard drive installation**
- ■ **Explain the partitions available in Windows**
- ■ **Discuss hard drive formatting options**
- ■ **Partition and format hard drives**
- ■ **Maintain and troubleshoot hard drives**

You can be dead certain about one thing as you train to be a PC tech: you won't get far if you don't know how to work on hard drives. A computer's hard drive is one of its most fragile parts, and, given enough time, every hard drive in the world will fail eventually. With that in mind, it's imperative that you learn not only how to physically install a hard drive (that's the easy part!), but also how to set up a drive in Windows.

In this chapter, you'll first look at the process for installing a hard drive in a computer system, as well as how to troubleshoot that installation. After that, you'll move on to the heady world of Windows hard drive management, which is honestly much more fun than it may sound.

Installing Drives

Installing a drive is a fairly simple process if you take the time to make sure you have the right drive for your system, configure the drive properly, and do a few quick tests to see if it's running properly. Since PATA, SATA, and SCSI have different cabling requirements, we'll look at each of these separately.

Choosing Your Drive

First, decide where you're going to put the drive. Look for an open ATA connection. Is it PATA or SATA? Is it a dedicated RAID controller? Many motherboards with built-in RAID controllers have a CMOS setting that enables you to turn the RAID on and off (Figure 5.1). Do you have the right controller for a SCSI drive?

Second, make sure you have room for the drive in the case. Where will you place it? Do you have a spare power connector? Will the data and power cables reach the drive? A quick test fit is always a good idea.

Don't worry about PIO modes and DMA—a new drive will support anything your controller wants to do.

Jumpers and Cabling on PATA Drives

If you have only one hard drive, set the drive's jumpers to master or standalone. If you have two drives, set one to master and the other to slave. See Figure 5.2 for a close-up of a PATA hard drive, showing the jumpers.

At first glance, you might notice that the jumpers aren't actually labeled *master* and *slave*. So how do you know how to set them properly? The easiest way is to read the front of the drive; most drives have a diagram on the housing that explains how to set the jumpers properly. Figure 5.3 shows the front of one of these drives so you can see how to set the drive to master or slave.

Hard disk drives may have other jumpers that may or may not concern you during installation. One common set of jumpers is used for diagnostics at the manufacturing plant or for special settings in other kinds of devices that use hard drives. Ignore them; they have no bearing in the PC world. Second, many drives provide a third setting to be used if only one drive connects to a controller. Often, master and single drive are the same setting on the hard drive, although some hard drives require separate settings. Note that the name for

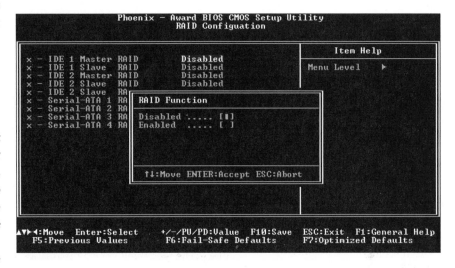

• **Figure 5.1**   Settings for RAID in CMOS

• **Figure 5.2**   Master/slave jumpers on a hard drive

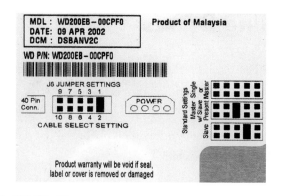

● **Figure 5.3**   Drive label showing master/slave settings

Most of the high-speed ATA/ 66/100/133 cables support cable select—try one and see!

the single drive setting varies among manufacturers. Some use Single; others use 1 Drive or Standalone.

Many current PATA hard drives use a jumper setting called *cable select* rather than master or slave. As the name implies, the position on the cable determines which drive will be master or slave: master on the end, slave in the middle. For cable select to work properly with two drives, you must set both drives as cable select and the cable itself must be a special cable-select cable. If you see a ribbon cable with a pinhole through one wire, watch out! That's a cable-select cable.

If you don't see a label on the drive that tells you how to set the jumpers, you have several options. First, look for the drive maker's Web site. Every drive manufacturer lists its drive jumper settings on the Web, although finding the information you want can take a while. Second, try phoning the hard drive maker directly. Unlike many other PC parts manufacturers, hard drive producers tend to stay in business for a long time and offer great technical support.

Hard drive cables have a colored stripe that corresponds to the number-one pin—called *pin 1*—on the connector. You need to make certain that pin 1 on the controller is on the same wire as pin 1 on the hard drive. Failing to plug in the drive properly will also prevent the PC from recognizing the drive. If you incorrectly set the master/slave jumpers or cable to the hard drives, you won't break anything; it just won't work.

Finally, you need to plug a Molex connector from the power supply into the drive. All modern PATA drives use a Molex connector.

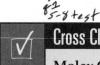

✓	**Cross Check**

Molex Connectors

Hard drives and other internal devices use Molex connectors for power. Refer to Chapter 4, "Mastering PC Power," and check your memory. What voltages go through the four wires on a Molex connector? What should you note about the connector and inserting it into the corresponding socket on the drive?

Mike Meyers' CompTIA A+ Guide: Practical Application

Cabling SATA Drives

Installing SATA hard disk drives is even easier than installing PATA devices because there's no master, slave, or cable-select configuration to mess with. In fact, there are no jumper settings to worry about at all, as SATA supports only a single device per controller channel. Simply connect the power and plug in the controller cable as shown in Figure 5.4—the OS automatically detects the drive and it's ready to go. The keying on SATA controller and power cables makes it impossible to install either incorrectly.

The biggest problem with SATA drives is that many motherboards come with four or more. Sure, the cabling is easy enough, but what do you do when it comes time to start the computer and the system is trying to find the right hard drive to boot up? That's where CMOS comes into play.

● **Figure 5.4** Properly connected SATA cable

Connecting Solid-State Drives

You install a solid-state drive as you would any PATA or SATA drive. Just as with earlier hard drive types, you either connect SSDs correctly and they work, or you connect them incorrectly and they don't. If they fail, nine times out of ten they will need to be replaced.

You're most likely to run into solid-state drives today in portable computers. SSDs are expensive and offer a lot less storage capacity compared to traditional hard drives. Because they require a lot less electricity to run, on the other hand, they make a lot of sense in portable computers where battery life is the Holy Grail. You can often use solid-state drives to replace existing platter-based drives in laptops.

Keep in mind the following considerations before installing or replacing an existing HDD with an SSD:

- Does the system currently use a PATA or SATA interface? You need to make sure your solid-state drive can connect properly.

- Do you have the appropriate drivers and firmware for the SSD? This is especially important if you run Windows XP. Windows Vista, on the other hand, is likely to load most currently implemented SSD drivers. As always, check the manufacturer's specifications before you do anything.

- Do you have everything important backed up? Good! You are ready to turn the system off, unplug the battery, ground yourself, and join the wonderful world of solid state.

SSDs address the many shortcomings of traditional HDDs. With solid-state technology, there are no moving metal parts, less energy is used, they come in smaller form factors, and you can access that fancy PowerPoint presentation you created and saved almost instantaneously. In geek terms, little or no latency is involved in accessing fragmented data with solid-state devices.

Don't have any SATA or eSATA ports in your computer, but want to install a shiny new SATA or eSATA drive? Don't worry! Just buy a SATA or eSATA controller card, install it into the appropriate expansion slot, and then install your SATA or eSATA hard drive.

SSDs are more dependable as well as more expensive than traditional hard drives. They use less energy overall, have smaller form factors, are noiseless, and use either NAND (nonvolatile flash memory) or SDRAM (volatile "RAM drive") technology to store and retrieve data. They can retrieve (read) data much faster than typical HDDs. Their write times, on the other hand, are often slower.

Tech Tip

Don't Defragment SSDs

Don't defragment an SSD! Because solid-state drives access data without having to find that data on the surface of a physical disk first, there's never any reason to defrag one. What's more, SSDs have a limited (albeit massive) number of read/write operations before they turn into expensive paperweights, and the defragmentation process uses those up greedily.

Connecting SCSI Drives

Connecting SCSI drives requires three things. You must use a controller that works with your drive. You need to set unique SCSI IDs on the controller and the drive. You also need to connect the ribbon cable and power connections properly.

With SCSI, you need to attach the data cable correctly. You can reverse a PATA cable, for example, and nothing happens except the drive doesn't work. If you reverse a SCSI cable, however, you can seriously damage the drive. Just as with PATA cables, pin 1 on the SCSI data cable must go to pin 1 on both the drive and the host adapter.

■ BIOS Support: Configuring CMOS and Installing Drivers

Every device in your PC needs BIOS support, and the hard drive controllers are no exception. Motherboards provide support for the ATA hard drive controllers via the system BIOS, but they require configuration in CMOS for the specific hard drives attached. SCSI drives require software drivers or firmware on the host adapter.

In the old days, you had to fire up CMOS and manually enter CHS information whenever you installed a new ATA drive to ensure the system saw the drive. Today, this process takes place, but it's much more automated. Still, there's plenty to do in CMOS when you install a new hard drive.

CMOS settings for hard drives vary a lot among motherboards. The following information provides a generic look at the most common settings, but you'll need to look at your specific motherboard manual to understand all of the options available.

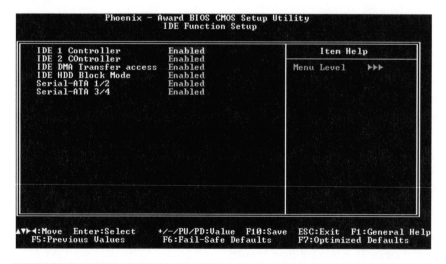

• **Figure 5.5**   Typical controller settings in CMOS

Configuring Controllers

As a first step in configuring controllers, make certain they're enabled. It's easy to turn off controllers in CMOS, and many motherboards turn off secondary ATA controllers by default. Scan through your CMOS settings to locate the controller on/off options (see Figure 5.5 for typical settings). This is also the time to check whether your onboard RAID controllers work in both RAID and non-RAID settings.

Autodetection

If the controllers are enabled and the drive is properly connected, the drive should appear in CMOS through a process called autodetection. Autodetection is a powerful and handy feature, but it seems that every CMOS has a different way to manifest it, and how it is manifested may affect how your computer decides which hard drive to try to boot when you start your PC.

One of your hard drives stores the operating system needed when you boot your computer, and your system needs a way to know where to look for this operating system. The traditional BIOS supported a maximum of only four ATA drives on two controllers, called the *primary controller* and the *secondary controller*. The BIOS looked for the master drive on the primary controller when the system booted up. If you used only one controller, you used the primary controller. The secondary controller was used for CD-ROMs, DVDs, or other nonbootable drives.

Older CMOS made this clear and easy, as shown in Figure 5.6. When you booted up, the CMOS queried the drives through autodetection, and whatever drives the CMOS saw, showed up here. In some even older CMOS, you had to run a special menu option called Autodetect to see the drives in this screen. There are places for up to four devices; notice that not all of them actually have a device.

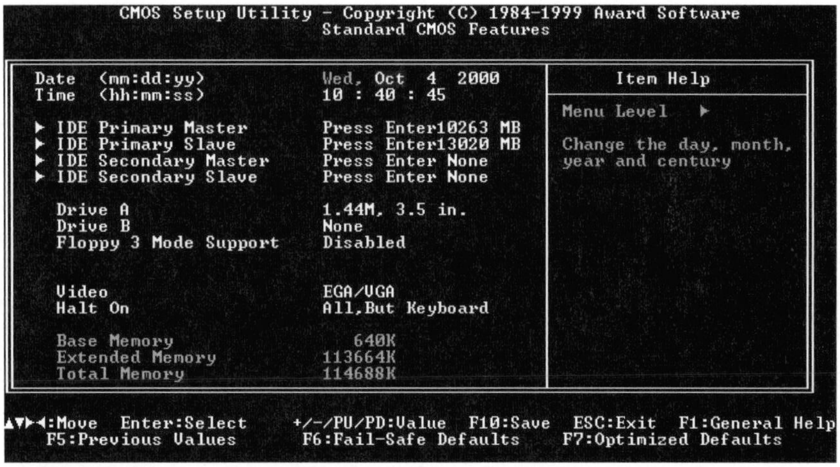

The autodetection screen indicated that you installed a PATA drive correctly. If you installed a hard drive on the primary controller as master but messed up the jumper and set it to slave, it showed up in the autodetection screen as the slave. If you had two drives and set them both to master, one drive or the other (or sometimes both) didn't appear, telling you that something was messed up in the physical installation. If you forgot to plug in the ribbon cable or the power, the drives wouldn't autodetect.

• **Figure 5.6** Old standard CMOS settings

SATA changed the autodetection happiness. The SATA world has no such thing as master, slave, or even primary and secondary controller. To get around this, motherboards with PATA and SATA today use a numbering system—and every motherboard uses its own numbering system! One common numbering method uses the term *channels* for each controller. The first boot device is channel 1, the second is channel 2, and so on. PATA channels may have a master and a slave, but a SATA channel has only a master, because SATA controllers support only one drive. So instead of names of drives, you see numbers. Take a look at Figure 5.7.

Whew! Lots of hard drives! This motherboard supports the traditional four PATA drives, and it also supports four SATA drives. Each controller is assigned a number; note that channel 1 and channel 2 have master/slave settings, and that's how you know channels 1 and 2 are the PATA drives.

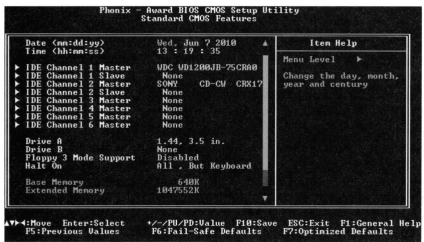

```
         Phonix - Award BIOS CMOS Setup Utility
                  Standard CMOS Features

   Date (mm:dd:yy)        Wed, Jun 7 2010    ▲        Item Help
   Time (hh:mm:ss)        13 : 19 : 35
                                               Menu Level   ▶
 ▶ IDE Channel 1 Master   WDC WD1200JB-75CRA0
 ▶ IDE Channel 1 Slave    None                  Change the day, month,
 ▶ IDE Channel 2 Master   SONY    CD-CW  CRX17   year and century
 ▶ IDE Channel 2 Slave    None
 ▶ IDE Channel 3 Master   None
 ▶ IDE Channel 4 Master   None
 ▶ IDE Channel 5 Master   None
 ▶ IDE Channel 6 Master   None

   Drive A                1.44, 3.5 in.
   Drive B                None
   Floppy 3 Mode Support  Disabled
   Halt On                All , But Keyboard

   Base Memory               640K
   Extended Memory        1047552K              ▼

▲▼►◄:Move  Enter:Select   +/-/PU/PD:Value  F10:Save  ESC:Exit  F1:General Help
   F5:Previous Values      F6:Fail-Safe Defaults   F7:Optimized Defaults
```

• **Figure 5.7**   New standard CMOS features

```
 ▶ Hard Disk Boot Priority    Press Enter
   First Boot Device          Floppy
   Second Boot Device         Hard Disk
   Third Boot Device          CDROM
   Boot Other Device          Enabled
```

• **Figure 5.8**   Boot order

Channels 3 through 6 are SATA, even though the listing says *master*. (SATA is still somewhat new, and a CMOS using incorrect terms such as *master* is common.)

Boot Order

If you want your computer to run, it's going to need an operating system to boot. While the PCs of our forefathers (those of the 1980s and early 1990s) absolutely required you to put the operating system on the primary master, most BIOS makers by 1995 enabled you to put the OS on any of the four drives and then tell the system through CMOS which hard drive to boot. With the many SATA drives available on modern systems, you're not even limited to a mere four choices. Additionally, you may need to boot from an optical disc, a USB thumb drive, or even a floppy disk (if you're feeling retro). CMOS takes care of this by enabling you to set a *boot order*.

Figure 5.8 shows a typical boot-order screen, with a first, second, and third boot option. Many users like to boot first from optical and then from a hard drive. This enables them to put in a bootable optical disc if they're having problems with the system. Of course, you can set it to boot first from your hard drive and then go into CMOS and change it when you need to—it's your choice.

Most modern CMOS setup utilities lump the hard drive boot order onto a second screen. This screen works like an autodetect in that it shows only actual hard drives attached. This beats the heck out of guessing.

Try This!

Working with CMOS

One of the best ways to get your mind around the different drive standards and capabilities is to run benchmarking software on the hard drive to get a baseline of its capabilities. Then, change CMOS settings to alter the performance of the drive and run the diagnostics again. Try This!

1. Get a reliable hard drive benchmarking program. I recommend HD Tach (www.simplisoftware.com) as reliable and rugged.

2. Run the software, and record the scores.

3. Change some or all of the following CMOS settings, and then run the benchmarking utility again: PIO mode, DMA mode, block mode.

4. What were the effects of changing settings?

Enabling AHCI

On motherboards that support AHCI (Advanced Host Controller Interface—a method that some motherboards use to control SATA hard drives), you implement it in CMOS. You'll generally have up to three options: IDE or compatibility mode, AHCI, or RAID. Use compatibility mode to install older operating systems, such as Windows XP. Going to AHCI or RAID enables the AHCI option for the HBA.

Device Drivers

Devices that do not get BIOS via the system BIOS routines naturally require some other source for BIOS. For ATAPI devices and many SATA controllers, the source of choice is software device drivers, but both technologies have a couple of quirks you should know about.

ATAPI Devices and BIOS

ATAPI drives plug into an ATA controller on the motherboard and follow the same conventions on cabling and jumpers used by PATA hard drives. In fact, all current CMOS setup utilities *seem* to autodetect optical-media ATAPI drives. If you go into CMOS after installing a CD-ROM drive as master on the secondary IDE controller, for example, the drive will show up just fine, as in Figure 5.9.

The reporting of installed optical-media drives in CMOS serves two purposes. First, it tells the technician that the ATAPI drive has good connectivity. Second, it shows that you have the option to boot to an optical disc, such as a Windows XP disc. What it *doesn't* do, however, is provide true BIOS support for that drive. That has to come with a driver loaded at boot-up.

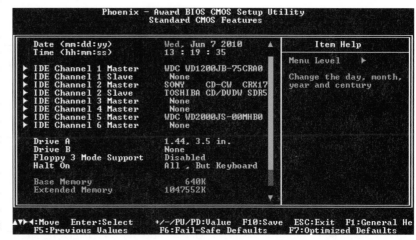

• **Figure 5.9** CMOS screen showing a CD-ROM drive detected

▣ Troubleshooting Hard Drive Installation

The best friend a tech has when it comes to troubleshooting hard drive installation is the autodetection feature of the CMOS setup utility. When a drive doesn't work, the biggest question, especially during installation, is "Did I plug it in correctly?" With autodetection, the answer is simple; if the system doesn't see the drive, something is wrong with the hardware configuration. Either a device has physically failed or, more likely, you didn't give the hard drive power, plugged a cable in backward, or messed up some other connectivity issue.

Getting a drive installed and recognized by the system takes four things: jumpers (PATA only), data cable, power, and the CMOS setup recognizing the drive. If you miss or mess up any of these steps, you have a drive that doesn't exist according to the PC! To troubleshoot hard drives, simply work your way through each step to figure out what went wrong.

First, set the drive to master, slave, standalone, or cable select, depending on where you decide to install it. If a drive is alone on the cable, set it to master or standalone. With two drives, one must be master and the other slave. Alternatively, you can set both drives to cable select and use a cable-select cable.

Second, you must connect the data cable to both the drive and the controller, pin 1 to pin 1. Reversing the data cable at one end is remarkably easy to do, especially with the rounded cables. They obviously don't have a big red stripe down the side to indicate the location of pin 1! If you can't autodetect the drive, check the cabling.

Third, be sure to give the hard drive power. Most hard drives use a standard Molex connector. If you don't hear the whirring of the drive, make certain you plugged in a Molex from the power supply rather than from another source such as an otherwise disconnected fan. You'd be surprised how often I've seen that.

Fourth, you need to provide BIOS for the controller and the drive. This can get tricky because the typical CMOS setup program has a lot of hard drive options. Plus, you have an added level of confusion with RAID settings and nonintegrated controllers that require software drivers.

Once you've checked the physical connections, run through these issues in CMOS. Is the controller enabled? Is the storage technology—LBA, INT13, ATA/ATAPI-6—properly set up? Similarly, can the motherboard support the type of drive you're installing? If not, you have a couple of options. You can flash the BIOS with an upgraded BIOS from the manufacturer or you can get a hard drive controller that goes into an expansion slot.

Finally, with nonintegrated hard drive controllers such as those that come with many SATA drives, make certain that you've installed the proper drivers for the controller. Driver issues can crop up with new, very large drives and with changes in technology. Always check the manufacturer's Web site for new drivers.

■ Working with Installed Drives

From the standpoint of your PC, a new hard drive successfully installed is nothing more than a huge pile of sectors. CMOS sees the drive; it shows up in your autodetect screen and BIOS knows how to talk to the drive, but as far as an operating system is concerned, that drive is unreadable. Your operating system must organize that big pile of sectors so you can create two things: folders and files. The rest of this chapter covers that process.

After you've successfully installed a hard drive, you must perform two more steps to translate a drive's geometry and circuits into something the system can use: partitioning and formatting. **Partitioning** is the process of electronically subdividing the physical hard drive into groups of cylinders called **partitions** (or **volumes**). A hard drive must have at least one partition, and you can create multiple partitions on a single hard drive if you wish. In Windows, each of these partitions typically is assigned a drive letter such as C: or D:. After partitioning, you must *format* the drive. This step installs a file system onto the drive that organizes each partition in such a way that the operating system can store files and folders on the drive. Several types of file systems are used in the Windows world. This chapter will go through them after covering partitioning.

Partitioning and formatting a drive is one of the few areas remaining on the software side of PC assembly that require you to perform a series of fairly complex manual steps. The CompTIA A+ Practical Application exam tests your knowledge of *what* these processes do to make the drive work, as well as the steps needed to partition and format hard drives in Windows 2000, XP, and Vista.

This chapter continues the exploration of hard drive installation by explaining partitioning and formatting and then going through the process of partitioning and formatting hard drives. The chapter wraps with a discussion on hard drive maintenance and troubleshooting issues.

Hard Drive Partitions

Partitions provide tremendous flexibility in hard drive organization. With partitions, you can organize a drive to suit your personal taste. For example, I partitioned my 1.5-TB hard drive into a 250-GB partition where I store Windows Vista and all my programs, a second 250-GB partition for Windows 7, and a 1-TB partition where I store all my personal data. This is a matter of personal choice; in my case, backups are simpler because the data is stored in one partition, and I can back up that partition without including the applications.

You can partition a hard drive to store more than one operating system (OS). Store one OS in one partition and create a second partition for another OS. Granted, most people use only one OS, but if you want the option to boot to Windows or Linux, partitions are the key.

Windows 2000/XP and Windows Vista/7 support two different partitioning methods: the older but more universal master boot record (MBR) partitioning scheme and the newer (but proprietary to Microsoft) dynamic storage partitioning scheme. Microsoft calls a hard drive that uses the MBR partitioning scheme a basic disk and a drive using the dynamic storage partitioning scheme a dynamic disk. A single Windows system with two hard drives may have one of the drives partitioned as a basic disk and the other as a dynamic disk, and the system will run perfectly well. The bottom line? You get to learn about two totally different types of partitioning. Yay! Given that basic disks are much older, we'll start there.

Basic Disks

Basic disk partitioning creates two very small data structures on a drive, the master boot record (MBR) and a partition table, and stores them on the first sector of the hard drive—called the boot sector. The MBR is nothing more than a tiny bit of code that takes control of the boot process from the system BIOS. When the computer boots to a hard drive, the BIOS automatically looks for MBR code on the boot sector. The MBR has only one job: to look in the partition table for a partition with a valid operating system (Figure 5.10).

Only one MBR and one partition table exist per basic disk.

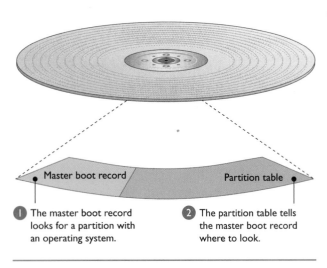

1. The master boot record looks for a partition with an operating system.

2. The partition table tells the master boot record where to look.

• **Figure 5.10**   Functions of the MBR and partition table

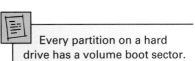

Every partition on a hard drive has a volume boot sector.

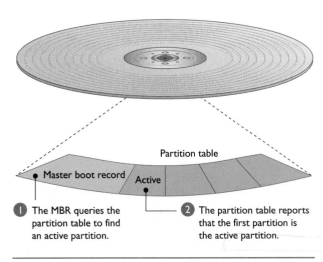

1. The MBR queries the partition table to find an active partition.

2. The partition table reports that the first partition is the active partition.

• **Figure 5.11**   The MBR checks the partition table to find the active partition.

All basic disk partition tables support up to four partitions. The partition table supports two types of partitions: primary partitions and extended partitions. **Primary partitions** are designed to support bootable operating systems. **Extended partitions** are not bootable. A single basic disk may have up to three primary partitions and one extended partition. If you do not have an extended partition, you may have up to four primary partitions.

Each partition must have some unique identifier so users can recognize it as an individual partition. Microsoft operating systems (DOS and Windows) traditionally assign primary partitions a drive letter from C: to Z:. Extended partitions do not get drive letters.

After you create an extended partition, you must create **logical drives** within that extended partition. A logical drive traditionally gets a drive letter from D: to Z:. (The drive letter C: is always reserved for the first primary partition in a Windows PC.)

Windows 2000/XP and Windows Vista/7 partitions are not limited to drive letters. With the exception of the partition that stores the boot files for Windows (which will always be C:), any other primary partitions or logical drives may get either a drive letter or a folder on a primary partition. You'll see how all of this works later in this chapter.

If a primary partition is a bootable partition, why does a basic drive's partition table support up to four primary partitions? Remember when I said that partitioning allows multiple operating systems? This is how it works. You can install up to four different operating systems, each OS installed on its own primary partition, and boot to your choice each time you fire up the computer.

Every primary partition on a single drive has a special setting called *active* stored in the partition table. This setting is either on or off on each primary partition, determining which is the **active partition**. At boot, the MBR uses the active setting in the partition table to determine which primary partition to choose to try to load an OS. Only one partition at a time can be the active partition because you can run only one OS at a time (see Figure 5.11). This restriction refers to a single drive, by the way. You can have active partitions on more than one physical drive; the settings in CMOS will dictate which drive is the current bootable or system drive.

The boot sector at the beginning of the hard drive isn't the only special sector on a hard drive. The first sector of the first cylinder of each partition also has a special sector called the **volume boot sector**. Although the "main" boot sector defines the partitions, the volume boot sector stores information important to its partition, such as the location of the OS boot files. Figure 5.12 shows a hard drive with two partitions. The first partition's volume boot sector contains information about the size of the partition and the code pointing to the boot files on this partition. The second volume boot sector contains information about the size of the partition.

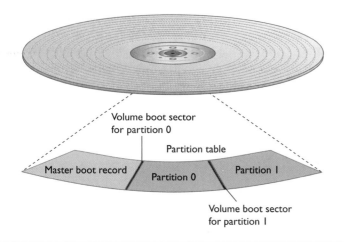

Volume boot sector
for partition 0

Partition table

Master boot record   Partition 0   Partition 1

Volume boot sector
for partition 1

● **Figure 5.12**   Volume boot sector

Primary Partitions   If you want to boot an operating system from a hard drive, that hard drive must have a primary partition. The MBR checks the partition table for the active primary partition (see Figure 5.13). In Windows, the primary partition is C: and that cannot be changed. Even though hard drives support up to four primary partitions, you almost never see four partitions in the Windows world. Windows supports up to four primary partitions on one drive, but how many people (other than nerdy CompTIA A+ people like you and me) really want to boot up more than one OS? We use a number of terms for this function, but dual-boot and multiboot are the most common. The system in my house, for example, uses four primary partitions, each holding one OS: Ubuntu Linux, Windows 2000, Windows XP, and Windows Vista. In other words, I chopped my drive up into four chunks and installed a different OS in each.

To do multiboot, most people use a free, Linux-based boot manager called GRUB (Grand Unified Boot Manager), although some people prefer a third-party tool such as System Commander 9 by VCOM to set up the partitions. Windows 2000 and up come with similar tools that can do this, but they can be messy to use, and GRUB helps simplify the process. When the computer boots, GRUB yanks control from the MBR and asks which OS you wish to boot (see Figure 5.14). You select an OS and it appears.

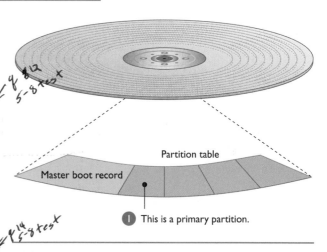

Partition table

Master boot record

1   This is a primary partition.

● **Figure 5.13**   The MBR checks the partition table to find a primary partition.

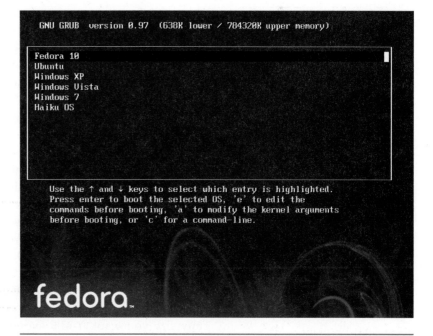

● **Figure 5.14**   GRUB's OS selection menu

Again, few systems use more than one primary partition. You may work on PCs for years and never see a system with more than one primary partition. The CompTIA A+ Practical Application exam certainly doesn't expect you to demonstrate how to create a system with multiple primary partitions, but it assumes that you know you can add more than one primary partition to a hard drive if you so desire. The rest of this book assumes that you want only one primary partition.

Active Partition   When you create a primary partition and decide to place an OS on that partition, you must set that partition as active. You must do this even if you use only a single primary partition. Luckily, this step is automated in the Windows installation process. Consider this: when would you want to go though the steps to define a partition as active? That would be when you install an OS on that partition. So when you install Windows on a new system, the installation program automatically sets up your first primary partition as the active partition. It never actually says this in the installation; it just does it for you.

So if you raise your right hand and promise to use only Microsoft Windows and make only single primary partitions on your hard drives, odds are good you'll never have to mess with manually adjusting your active partitions. Of course, because you're crazy enough to want to get into PCs, that means within a year of reading this text you're going to want to install other operating systems such as Linux on your PC (and that's OK—all techs want to try this at some point). The moment you do, you'll enter the world of boot manager programs of which there are many, many choices. You also might use tools to change the active partition manually—exactly when and how this is done varies tremendously for each situation and is way outside the scope of the Practical Application exam, but make sure you know why you might need to set a partition as active.

When my System Commander boot screen comes up, it essentially asks me, "What primary partition do you want me to make active?"

Extended Partition   Understanding the purpose of extended partitions requires a brief look at the historical PC. The first versions of the old DOS operating system to support hard drives only supported primary partitions up to 32 MB. As hard drives went past 32 MB, Microsoft needed a way to support them. Instead of rewriting DOS to handle larger drives, Microsoft developers created the idea of the extended partition. That way, if you had a hard drive larger than 32 MB, you could make a 32-MB primary partition and the rest of the drive an extended partition. Over the years, DOS and then Windows were rewritten to support large hard drives, but the extended partition is still fully supported.

The beauty of an extended partition is in the way it handles drive letters. When you create a primary partition, it gets a drive letter and that's it. But when you create an extended partition, it does not automatically get a drive letter. Instead, you go through a second step where you divide the extended partition into one or more logical drives. An extended partition may have as many logical drives as you wish. By default, Windows gives each logical drive in an extended partition a drive letter, and most Windows users use drive letters. However, if you'd like, you may even mount the drive letter as a folder on any lettered drive. You can set the size of each logical drive to any size you want. You'll learn how to mount drives later in this chapter—for now, just get the idea that a partition may be mounted with a drive letter or as a folder.

Primary partitions and logical drives on basic disks are also called *basic volumes*.

Extended partitions are completely optional; you do not have to create an extended partition on a hard drive. So, if you can't boot to an extended partition and your hard drive doesn't need an extended partition, why would you want to create one? First of all, the majority of systems do not use extended partitions. Most systems use only one hard drive, and that single drive is partitioned as one big primary partition—nothing wrong with that! Some users like having an extended partition with one or more logical drives, and they use the extended partitions as a way to separate data. For example, I might store all of my movie files on my G: logical drive.

Instead of assigning drive letters, you can mount logical drives as folders on an existing drive. It's easy to make a logical drive and call it C:\STORAGE. If the C:\STORAGE folder fills up, you could add an extra hard drive, make

the entire extra drive an extended partition with one logical drive, un-mount the old C:\STORAGE drive, and then mount the new huge logical drive as C:\STORAGE. It's as though you made your C: drive bigger without replacing it.

 Try This!

Folder Swapping

What steps would you have to go through to add a new drive to a system and remount it as the C:\STORAGE folder without losing any data in the existing C:\STORAGE folder? Don't bother telling me the tools you need, just think about the logical steps you'd need to do this.

Dynamic Disks

With the introduction of Windows 2000, Microsoft defined an entirely new type of partitioning called *dynamic storage partitioning*, better known as dynamic disks. Dynamic disks drop the word *partition* and instead use the term *volume*. There is no dynamic disk equivalent to primary versus extended partitions. A volume is still technically a partition, but it can do things a regular partition cannot do, such as spanning. A spanned volume goes across more than one drive. Windows allows you to span up to 32 drives under a single volume. Dynamic disks also support RAID 0 in Windows 2000 Professional, Windows XP Professional, and Windows Vista Business and Ultimate. Windows 2000, 2003, and 2008 Server editions support RAID 0, 1, and 5.

 Windows XP Home and Windows Media Center do not support dynamic disks, nor do any Vista editions besides Business and Ultimate.

Dynamic disks use an MBR and a partition table, but these older structures are there only for backward compatibility. All of the information about a dynamic disk is stored in a hidden partition that takes up the last 1 MB of the hard drive. Every partition in a partition table holds a 2-byte value that describes the partition. For example, an extended partition gets the number 05. Windows adds a new number, 42, to the first partition on a dynamic disk. When Windows 2000 or XP reads the partition table for a dynamic disk, it sees the number 42 and immediately jumps to the 1-MB hidden partition, ignoring the old-style partition table. By supporting an MBR and partition table, Windows also prevents other disk partitioning programs from messing with a dynamic disk. If you use a third-party partitioning program, it simply sees the entire hard drive as either an unformatted primary partition or a non-readable partition.

 A key thing to understand about dynamic drives is that the technology is *proprietary*. Microsoft has no intention of telling anyone exactly how dynamic disks work. Only fairly recent Microsoft operating systems (Windows 2000 and up) can read a drive configured as a dynamic disk.

You can use five volume types with dynamic disks: simple, spanned, striped, mirrored, and RAID 5. Most folks stick with simple volumes.

Simple volumes work much like primary partitions. If you have a hard drive and you want to make half of it C: and the other half D:, you create two volumes on a dynamic disk. That's it: no choosing between primary and extended partitions. Remember that you were limited to four primary partitions when using basic disks. To make more than four volumes with a basic disk, you first had to create an extended partition and then make logical drives within the extended partition. Dynamic disks simplify the process by treating all partitions as volumes, so you can make as many as you need.

Spanned volumes use unallocated space on multiple drives to create a single volume. Spanned volumes are a bit risky: if any of the spanned drives fails, the entire volume is permanently lost.

Striped volumes are RAID 0 volumes. You may take any two unallocated spaces on two separate hard drives and stripe them. But again, if either drive fails, you lose all of your data.

Mirrored volumes are RAID 1 volumes. You may take any two unallocated spaces on two separate hard drives and mirror them. If one of the two mirrored drives fails, the other keeps running.

RAID 5 volumes, as the name implies, are for RAID 5 arrays. A RAID 5 volume requires three or more dynamic disks with equal-sized unallocated spaces.

> If you want to set up a RAID in your computer, but you don't want to use dynamic disks, buy a PCI or PCIe RAID controller and install it. Now you can set up a hardware RAID without even booting into Windows first!

Other Partitions

The partition types supported by Windows are not the only partition types you may encounter; other types exist. One of the most common is called the *hidden partition*. A hidden partition is really just a primary partition that is hidden from your operating system. Only special BIOS tools may access a hidden partition. Hidden partitions are used by some PC makers to hide a backup copy of an installed OS that you can use to restore your system if you accidentally trash it—by, for example, learning about partitions and using a partitioning program incorrectly.

A *swap partition* is another special type of partition, but swap partitions are only found on Linux and BSD systems. A swap partition's only job is to act like RAM when your system needs more RAM than you have installed. Windows has a similar function called a *page file* that uses a special file instead of a partition. Most OS experts believe a swap partition is a little bit faster than a page file. You'll learn all about page files and swap partitions in Chapter 8, "Maintaining and Troubleshooting Windows."

> Early versions of Windows (3.*x* and 9*x*/Me) called the page file a *swap file*. Most techs use the terms interchangeably today.

When to Partition

Partitioning is not a common task. The two most common situations likely to require partitioning are when you're installing an OS on a new system and when you're adding a second drive to an existing system. When you install a new OS, the installation CD at some point asks you how you would like to partition the drive. When you add a new hard drive to an existing system, every OS has a built-in tool to help you partition it.

Each version of Windows offers a different tool for partitioning hard drives. For more than 20 years, through the days of DOS and early Windows (up to Windows Me), you used a command-line program called FDISK to partition drives. Figure 5.15 shows the FDISK program. Windows 2000, Windows XP, and Windows Vista use a graphical partitioning program called Disk Management (Figure 5.16).

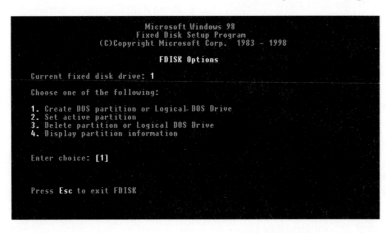

```
                    Microsoft Windows 98
                  Fixed Disk Setup Program
          (C)Copyright Microsoft Corp.  1983 - 1998

                        FDISK Options

Current fixed disk drive: 1

Choose one of the following:

1. Create DOS partition or Logical DOS Drive
2. Set active partition
3. Delete partition or Logical DOS Drive
4. Display partition information

Enter choice: [1]


Press Esc to exit FDISK
```

• **Figure 5.15**   FDISK

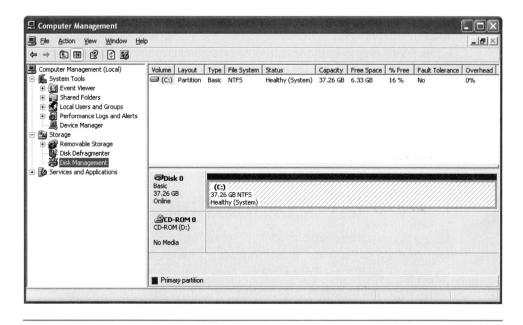

● **Figure 5.16**   Windows XP Disk Management tool in Computer Management

Linux uses a number of different tools for partitioning. The oldest is called FDISK—yup, the exact same name as the DOS/Windows version. However, that's where the similarities end, as Linux FDISK has a totally different command set. Even though every copy of Linux comes with the Linux FDISK, it's rarely used because so many better partitioning tools are available. One of the newer Linux partitioning tools is called GParted. GParted is graphical like Disk Management and is fairly easy to use (Figure 5.17). GParted is also a powerful partition management tool—so powerful that it also works with Windows partitions.

Traditionally, once you make a partition, you cannot change its size or type other than by erasing it. You might, however, want to take a hard drive partitioned as a single primary partition and change it to half primary and half extended. Before Windows 2000, there was no way to do this nondestructively. As a result, a few third-party tools, led by Symantec's now famous Norton PartitionMagic, gave techs the tools to resize partitions without losing the data they held.

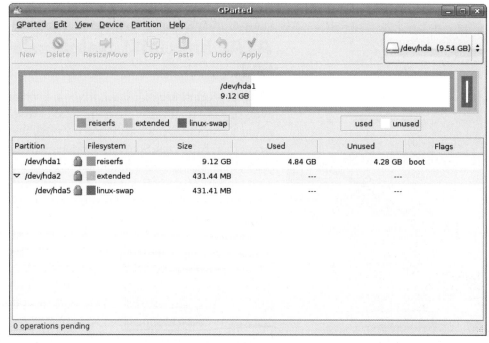

● **Figure 5.17**   GParted in action

Windows 2000 and XP can nondestructively resize a partition to be larger but not smaller.

In Vista, you can nondestructively resize partitions by shrinking or expanding existing partitions with available free space. Although undoubtedly handy, this is sometimes hampered by the presence of unmovable system files, such as the MBR. You can sometimes circumvent this problem by disabling such things as Hibernation mode and System Restore, but that doesn't always work, and third-party tools remain necessary in many cases.

■ Hard Drive Formatting

Once you've partitioned a hard drive, you must perform one more step before your OS can use that drive: formatting. Formatting does two things: it creates a file system—like a library's card catalog—and makes the root directory in that file system. You must format every partition and volume you create so it can hold data that you can easily retrieve. The various versions of Windows you're likely to encounter today can use several different file systems, so we'll look at those in detail next. The *root directory* provides the foundation upon which the OS builds files and folders.

File Systems in Windows

Every version of Windows comes with a built-in formatting utility with which to create one or more file systems on a partition or volume. The versions of Windows in current use support three separate Microsoft file systems: FAT16, FAT32, and NTFS.

The simplest hard drive file system, called FAT or FAT16, provides a good introduction to how file systems work. More complex file systems fix many of the problems inherent in FAT and add extra features as well.

FAT

The base storage area for hard drives is a sector; each sector stores up to 512 bytes of data. If an OS stores a file smaller than 512 bytes in a sector, the rest of the sector goes to waste. We accept this waste because most files are far larger than 512 bytes. So what happens when an OS stores a file larger than 512 bytes? The OS needs a method to fill one sector, find another that's unused, and fill it, continuing to fill sectors until the file is completely stored. Once the OS stores a file, it must remember which sectors hold the file, so it can be retrieved later.

MS-DOS version 2.1 first supported hard drives using a special data structure to keep track of stored data on the hard drive, and Microsoft called this structure the file allocation table (FAT). Think of the FAT as nothing more than a card catalog that keeps track of which sectors store the various parts of a file. The official jargon term for a FAT is data structure, but it is more like a two-column spreadsheet.

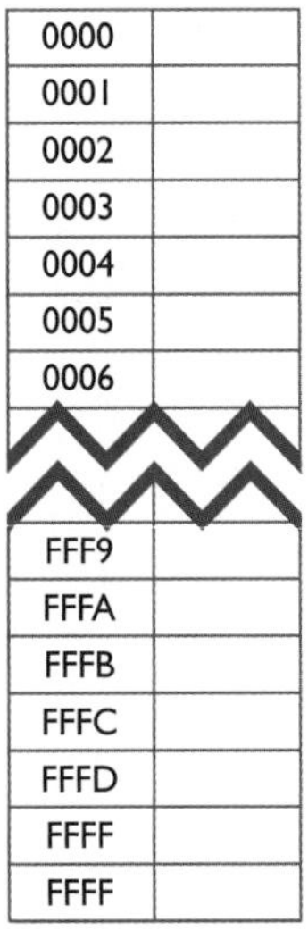

The left column (see Figure 5.18) gives each sector a number from 0000 to FFFF (in hex, of course). This means there are 65,536 (64 K) sectors.

0000	
0001	
0002	
0003	
0004	
0005	
0006	
FFF9	
FFFA	
FFFB	
FFFC	
FFFD	
FFFF	
FFFF	

● **Figure 5.18**   16-bit FAT

Notice that each value in the left column contains 16 bits. (Four hex characters make 16 bits, remember?) We call this type of FAT a *16-bit FAT* or *FAT16*. Not just hard drives have FATs. Some USB thumb drives also use FAT16. Floppy disks use FATs, but their FATs are only 12 bits because they store much less data.

The right column of the FAT contains information on the status of sectors. All hard drives, even brand-new drives fresh from the factory, contain faulty sectors that cannot store data because of imperfections in the construction of the drives. The OS must locate these bad sectors, mark them as unusable, and then prevent any files from being written to them. This mapping of bad sectors is one of the functions of **high-level formatting**. After the format program creates the FAT, it proceeds through the entire partition, writing and attempting to read from each sector sequentially. If it finds a bad sector, it places a special status code (FFF7) in the sector's FAT location, indicating that the sector is unavailable for use. Formatting also marks the good sectors as 0000.

Using the FAT to track sectors, however, creates a problem. The 16-bit FAT addresses a maximum of 64 K (2^{16}) locations. Therefore, the size of a hard drive partition should be limited to 64 K × 512 bytes per sector, or 32 MB. When Microsoft first unveiled FAT16, this 32-MB limit presented no problem because most hard drives were only 5 to 10 MB. As hard drives grew in size, you could use FDISK to break them up into multiple partitions. You could divide a 40-MB hard drive into two partitions, for example, making each partition smaller than 32 MB. But as hard drives started to become much larger, Microsoft realized that the 32-MB limit for drives was unacceptable. We needed an improvement to the 16-bit FAT, a new and improved FAT16 that would support larger drives while still maintaining backward compatibility with the old style 16-bit FAT. This need led to the development of a dramatic improvement in FAT16, called *clustering*, that enabled you to format partitions larger than 32 MB (see Figure 5.19). This new FAT16 appeared way back in the DOS-4 days.

Clustering simply refers to combining a set of contiguous sectors and treating them as a single unit in the FAT. These units are called **file allocation units** or **clusters**. Each row of the FAT addressed a cluster instead of a sector. Unlike sectors, the size of a cluster is not fixed. Clusters improved FAT16, but it still only supported a maximum of 64 K storage units, so the formatting program set the number of sectors in each cluster according to the size of the partition. The larger the partition, the more sectors per cluster. This method kept clustering completely compatible with the 64-K locations in the old 16-bit FAT. The new FAT16 could support partitions up to 2 GB. (The old 16-bit FAT is so old it doesn't really even have a name—if someone says "FAT16," they mean the newer FAT16 that supports clustering.) Table 5.1 shows the number of sectors per cluster for FAT16.

There is such a thing as "low-level formatting," but that's generally done at the factory and doesn't concern techs. This is especially true if you're working with modern hard drives (post-2001).

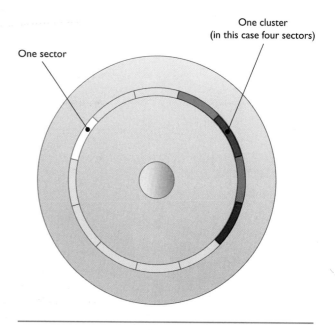

One sector

One cluster (in this case four sectors)

● **Figure 5.19**   Cluster versus sector

Table 5.1	FAT16 Cluster Sizes	
If FDISK makes a partition this big:	**You'll get this many sectors/cluster:**	
16 to 127.9 MB	4	
128 to 255.9 MB	8	
256 to 511.9 MB	16	
512 to 1023.9 MB	32	
1024 to 2048 MB	64	

FAT16 in Action

Assume you have a copy of Windows using FAT16. When an application such as Microsoft Word tells the OS to save a file, Windows starts at the beginning of the FAT, looking for the first space marked "open for use" (0000), and begins to write to that cluster. If the entire file fits within that one cluster, Windows places the code *FFFF* (last cluster) into the cluster's status area in the FAT. That's called the *end-of-file marker*. Windows then goes to the folder storing the file and adds the filename and the cluster's number to the folder list. If the file requires more than one cluster, Windows searches for the next open cluster and places the number of the next cluster in the status area, filling and adding clusters until the entire file is saved. The last cluster then receives the end-of-file marker (FFFF).

Let's run through an example of this process, and start by selecting an arbitrary part of the FAT: from 3ABB to 3AC7. Assume you want to save a file called MOM.TXT. Before saving the file, the FAT looks like Figure 5.20.

Windows finds the first open cluster, 3ABB, and fills it. But not all of the MOM.TXT file fits into that cluster. Needing more space, the OS goes through the FAT to find the next open cluster. It finds cluster 3ABC. Before filling 3ABC, the value *3ABC* is placed in 3ABB's status (see Figure 5.21).

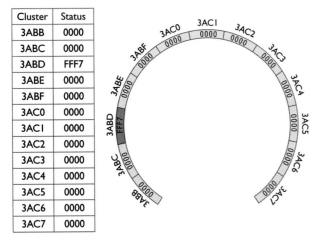

● **Figure 5.20**   The initial FAT

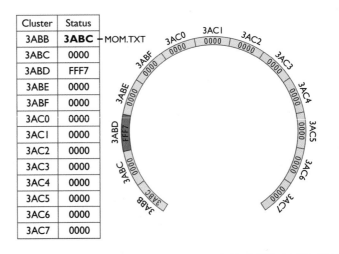

● **Figure 5.21**   The first cluster used

Even after filling two clusters, more of the MOM.TXT file remains, so Windows must find one more cluster. The 3ABD has been marked FFF7 (bad cluster or *bad-sector marker*), so Windows skips over 3ABD, finding 3ABE (see Figure 5.22).

Before filling 3ABE, Windows enters the value *3ABE* in 3ABC's status. Windows does not completely fill 3ABE, signifying that the entire MOM.TXT file has been stored. Windows enters the value *FFFF* in 3ABE's status, indicating the end of file (see Figure 5.23).

After saving all of the clusters, Windows locates the file's folder (yes, folders also are stored on clusters, but they get a different set of clusters, somewhere else on the disk) and records the filename, size, date/time, and starting cluster, like this:

MOM.TXT 19234 05-19-09 2:04p 3ABB

If a program requests that file, the process is reversed. Windows locates the folder containing the file to determine the starting cluster and then pulls a piece of the file from each cluster until it sees the end-of-file cluster. Windows then hands the reassembled file to the requesting application.

Clearly, without the FAT, Windows cannot locate files. FAT16 automatically makes two copies of the FAT. One FAT backs up the other to provide special utilities a way to recover a FAT that gets corrupted—a painfully common occurrence.

Even when FAT works perfectly, over time the files begin to separate in a process called fragmentation.

Fragmentation

Continuing with the example, let's use Microsoft Word to save two more files: a letter to the IRS (IRSROB.DOC) and a letter to IBM (IBMHELP.DOC). IRSROB.DOC takes the next three clusters—3ABF, 3AC0, and 3AC1—and IBMHELP.DOC takes two clusters—3AC2 and 3AC3 (see Figure 5.24).

Now suppose you erase MOM.TXT. Windows does not delete the cluster entries for MOM.TXT when it erases a file. Windows only alters the information in the folder, simply changing the first letter of MOM.TXT to the Greek letter Σ (sigma). This causes the file to "disappear" as far as the OS knows. It won't show up, for example, in Windows Explorer, even though the data still resides on the hard drive for the moment (see Figure 5.25).

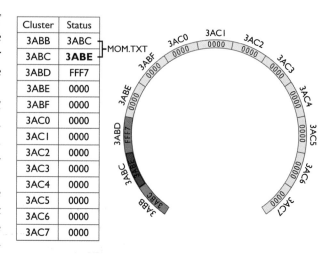

● **Figure 5.22**   The second cluster used

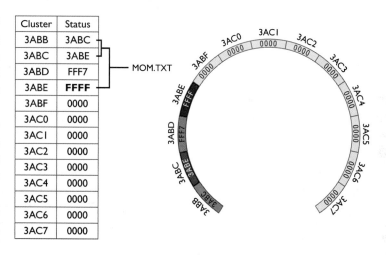

● **Figure 5.23**   End of file reached

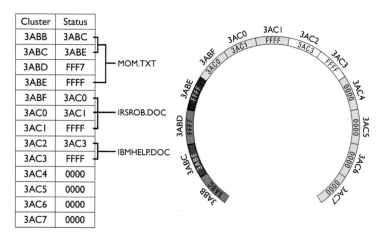

● **Figure 5.24**   Three files saved

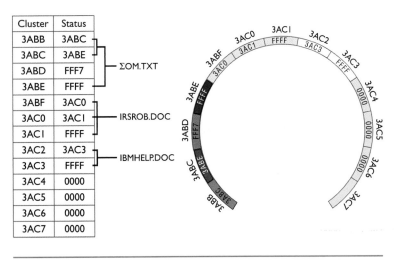

Cluster	Status
3ABB	3ABC
3ABC	3ABE
3ABD	FFF7
3ABE	FFFF
3ABF	3AC0
3AC0	3AC1
3AC1	FFFF
3AC2	3AC3
3AC3	FFFF
3AC4	0000
3AC5	0000
3AC6	0000
3AC7	0000

ΣOM.TXT

IRSROB.DOC

IBMHELP.DOC

• **Figure 5.25**   MOM.TXT erased

Note that under normal circumstances, Windows does not actually delete files when you press the DELETE key. Instead, Windows moves the files to a special hidden directory that you can access via the Recycle Bin. The files themselves are not actually deleted until you empty the Recycle Bin. (You can skip the Recycle Bin entirely if you wish, by highlighting a file and then holding down the SHIFT key when you press DELETE).

Because all of the data for MOM.TXT is intact, you could use some program to change the Σ back into another letter and thus get the document back. A number of third-party undelete tools are available. Figure 5.26 shows one such program at work. Just remember that if you want to use an undelete tool, you must use it quickly. The space allocated to your deleted file may soon be overwritten by a new file.

Let's say you just emptied your Recycle Bin. You now save one more file, TAXREC.XLS, a big spreadsheet that will take six clusters, into the same folder that once held MOM.TXT. As Windows writes the file to the drive, it overwrites the space that MOM.TXT used, but it needs three more clusters. The next three available clusters are 3AC4, 3AC5, and 3AC6 (see Figure 5.27).

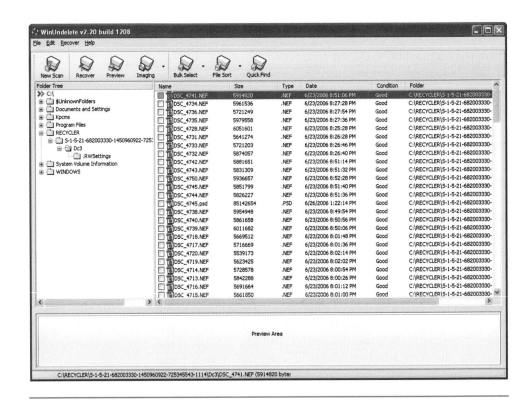

• **Figure 5.26**   WinUndelete in action

Mike Meyers' CompTIA A+ Guide: Practical Application

Notice that TAXREC.XLS is in two pieces, thus *fragmented*. Fragmentation takes place all of the time on FAT16 systems. Although the system easily negotiates a tiny fragmented file split into only two parts, excess fragmentation slows down the system during hard drive reads and writes. This example is fragmented into two pieces; in the real world, a file might fragment into hundreds of pieces, forcing the read/write heads to travel all over the hard drive to retrieve a single file. You can dramatically improve the speed at which the hard drive reads and writes files by eliminating this fragmentation.

Every version of Windows (with the exception of NT) comes with a program called Disk Defragmenter, which can rearrange the files into neat contiguous chunks (see Figure 5.28). Defragmentation is crucial for ensuring the top performance of a hard drive. The "Maintaining and Troubleshooting Hard Drives" section of this chapter gives the details on working with the various Disk Defragmenters in Windows.

Cluster	Status
3ABB	3ABC
3ABC	3ABE
3ABD	FFF7
3ABE	3AC4
3ABF	3AC0
3AC0	3AC1
3AC1	FFFF
3AC2	3AC3
3AC3	FFFF
3AC4	3AC5
3AC5	3AC6
3AC6	FFFF
3AC7	0000

TAXREC.XLS

• **Figure 5.27**   TAXREC.XLS fragmented

You can also start the Disk Defragmenter by typing DEFRAG into a command prompt.

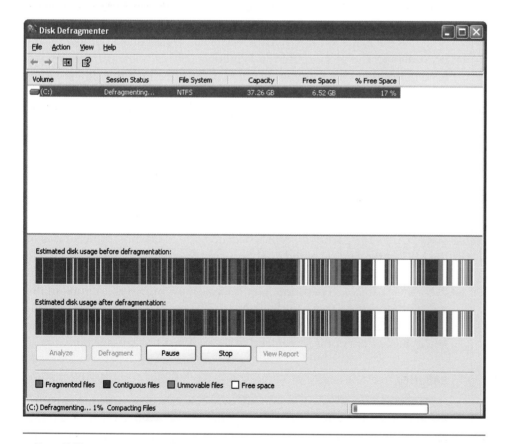

• **Figure 5.28**   Windows Disk Defragmenter

FAT32

When Microsoft introduced Windows 95 OSR2 (OEM Service Release 2), it also unveiled a totally new file format called FAT32 that brought a couple of dramatic improvements. First, FAT32 supports partitions up to 2 terabytes (more than 2 trillion bytes). Second, as its name implies, FAT32 uses 32 bits to describe each cluster, which means clusters can drop to more reasonable sizes. FAT32's use of so many FAT entries gives it the power to use small clusters, making the old "keep your partitions small" rule obsolete. A 2-GB volume using FAT16 would use 32-KB clusters, while the same 2-GB volume using FAT32 would use 4-KB clusters. You get far more efficient use of disk space with FAT32, without the need to make multiple small partitions. FAT32 partitions still need defragmentation, however, just as often as FAT16 partitions.

Table 5.2 shows cluster sizes for FAT32 partitions.

Table 5.2	FAT32 Cluster Sizes
Drive Size	**Cluster Size**
512 MB or 1023 MB	4 KB
1024 MB to 2 GB	4 KB
2 GB to 8 GB	4 KB
8 GB to 16 GB	8 KB
16 GB to 32 GB	16 KB
>32 GB	32 KB

Tech Tip

NTFS Naming Nightmare

Most computer writers, including those at Microsoft (until recently), label the version of NTFS that shipped with a particular version of Windows by the version number of Windows. So the NTFS that shipped with Windows NT 4.0 is frequently called NTFS 4, although that's not technically correct. Similarly, because the NTFS that shipped with Windows 2000 offered great improvements over the earlier versions, it became NTFS 5 in the minds of most techs.

Current Microsoft Knowledge Base articles refer to the NTFS that ships with Windows XP specifically as NTFS 3.1. Windows Vista still technically uses NTFS 3.1, even though it adds a few minor features such as transactional NTFS, which reduces the incidence of data corruption, and self-healing, which is basically a CHKDSK command that runs all of the time.

NTFS

The Windows format of choice these days is the New Technology File System (NTFS). NTFS came out a long time ago with the first version of Windows NT, thus the name. Over the years, NTFS has undergone a number of improvements. The version used in Windows 2000 is NTFS 3.0; the version used in Windows XP and Vista is called NTFS 3.1, although you'll see it referred to as NTFS 5.0/5.1 (Windows 2000 was unofficially Windows NT version 5). NTFS uses clusters and file allocation tables but in a much more complex and powerful way compared to FAT or FAT32. NTFS offers six major improvements and refinements: redundancy, security, compression, encryption, disk quotas, and cluster sizing.

NTFS Structure

NTFS utilizes an enhanced file allocation table called the master file table (MFT). An NTFS partition keeps a backup copy of the most critical parts of the MFT in the middle of the disk, reducing the chance that a serious drive error can wipe out both the MFT and the MFT copy. Whenever you defragment an NTFS partition, you'll see a small, immovable chunk in the middle of the drive; that's the backup MFT (Figure 5.29). It's a little difficult to see in black and white, but the color image shows bright green both in the key at the bottom of the screen and in the estimated disk usage bars.

Security

NTFS views individual files and folders as objects and provides security for those objects through a feature called the *access control list* (*ACL*). Future chapters go into this in much more detail, but a quick example here should make the basic concept clear.

If you have a geeky interest in what version of NTFS you are running, open up a prompt and type this command: **fsutil fsinfo ntfsinfo c:**

The Practical Application exam tests you extensively on NTFS, such as when to use it, what advantages it has over FAT32, and how to lock down information. You'll also be quizzed on the tools, such as Disk Management, in both exams. Don't skip anything in this chapter!

● **Figure 5.29** An NTFS MFT appears in a defragmenter program as an immovable file.

Suppose Bill the IT Guy sets up a Windows XP PC as a workstation for three users: John, Wilma, and Felipe. John logs into the PC with his user name and password (johns and f3f2f1f0, respectively, in case you're curious) and begins to work on his project. The project folder is stored on the C: drive as C:\Projects\JohnSuperSecret. When John saves his work and gets ready to leave, he alters the permissions on his folder to deny access to anyone but him. When curious Wilma logs into the PC after John leaves, she cannot access the C:\Programs\JohnSuperSecret folder contents at all, although she can see the entry in Explorer. Without the ACL provided by NTFS, John would have no security over his files or folders at all.

Microsoft has never released the exact workings of NTFS to the public.

Compression

NTFS enables you to compress individual files and folders to save space on a hard drive. Compression makes access time to the data slower because the OS has to uncompress files every time you use them, but in a space-limited environment, sometimes that's what you have to do.

Encryption

One of the big draws with NTFS is file encryption, the black art of making files unreadable to anybody who doesn't have the right key. You can encrypt a single file, a folder, or a folder full of files. Microsoft calls the encryption utility in NTFS the **encrypting file system (EFS)**, but it's simply an aspect of NTFS, not a standalone file system. To encrypt a file or folder, right-click it in My Computer or Computer and select Properties to open the Properties dialog box (Figure 5.30). Click the Advanced button to open the Advanced

Windows XP Home and Media Center editions do not support EFS.

● **Figure 5.30**   Folder Properties

Attributes dialog box. As you can see in Figure 5.31, encryption (and compression) is simply a selectable checkbox. Click the box next to *Encrypt contents to secure data* and then click the OK button—instantly your file is safe from prying eyes!

Encryption does not hide files; it simply makes them unreadable to other users. Figure 5.32 shows a couple of image files encrypted by another user. Note that in addition to the pale green color of the filenames, the files seem readily accessible. Windows XP can't provide a thumbnail, however, even though it can read the type of image file (JPEG) easily. Further, double-clicking the files opens the Windows Picture and Fax Viewer, but you still can't see the image (Figure 5.33). Better still, you can try to access the files across

● **Figure 5.31**   Options for compression and encryption

● **Figure 5.32**   Encrypted files

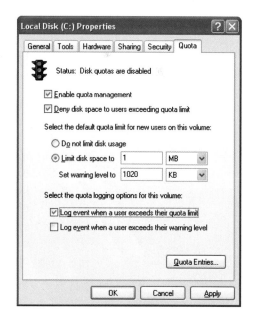

Encryption protects against other users, but only if you log out. It might seem obvious, but I've had lots of users get confused by encryption, thinking that the PC *knows* who's clicking the keyboard. All protections and security are based on user accounts. If someone logs into your computer with a different account, the encrypted files will be unreadable. We'll get to user accounts, permissions, and such in later chapters in detail.

• **Figure 5.33**   Windows Picture and Fax Viewer blocked by file encryption

your network and the encryption does precisely what it's supposed to do: blocks unwanted access to sensitive data.

Remember that encryption is separate from the NTFS file security provided by the ACL—to access encrypted files, you need both permission to access the files based on the ACL and the keys used to encrypt the files. We discuss key management in much more detail in Chapter 7, "Securing Windows Resources."

Disk Quotas

NTFS supports disk quotas, enabling administrators to set limits on drive space usage for users. To set quotas, you must log in as an Administrator, right-click the hard drive name, and select Properties. In the Drive Properties dialog box, select the Quota tab and make changes. Figure 5.34 shows configured quotas for a hard drive. Although rarely used on single-user systems, setting disk quotas on multi-user systems prevents any individual user from monopolizing your hard disk space.

Cluster Sizes

Unlike FAT16 or FAT32, you can adjust the cluster sizes in NTFS, although you'll probably rarely do so. Table 5.3 shows the default cluster sizes for NTFS.

• **Figure 5.34**   Hard drive quotas in Windows XP

Table 5.3	NTFS Cluster Sizes	
Drive Size	Cluster Size	Number of Sectors
512 MB or less	512 bytes	1
513 MB to 1024 MB (1 GB)	1024 bytes (1 KB)	2
1025 MB to 2048 MB (2 GB)	2048 bytes (2 KB)	4
2049 MB and larger	4096 bytes (4 KB)	8

 NTFS supports partitions up to 16 TB by default.

By default, NTFS supports partitions up to ~16 terabytes on a dynamic disk, (though only up to 2 TB on a basic disk). By tweaking the cluster sizes, you can get NTFS to support partitions up to 16 exabytes, or 18,446,744,073,709,551,616 bytes! That might support any and all upcoming hard drive capacities for the next 100 years or so.

With so many file systems, how do you know which one to use? In the case of internal hard drives, you should use the most feature-rich system your OS supports. If you have Windows 2000 or greater, use NTFS. External hard drives still often use FAT32 because NTFS features such as the ACL and encryption can make access difficult when you move the drive between systems, but with that exception, NTFS is your best choice on a Windows-based system.

The Partitioning and Formatting Process

Now that you understand the concepts of formatting and partitioning, let's go through the process of setting up an installed hard drive by using different partitioning and formatting tools. If you have access to a system, try following along with these descriptions. Remember, don't make any changes to a drive you want to keep, because both partitioning and formatting are destructive processes.

Bootable Disks

Imagine you've built a brand-new PC. The hard drive has no OS, so you need to boot up something to set up that hard drive. Any software that can boot up a system is by definition an operating system. You need a floppy disk, optical disk, or USB thumb drive with a bootable OS installed. Any removable media that has a bootable OS is generically called a *boot device* or *boot disk*. Your system boots off of the boot device, which then loads some kind of OS that enables you to partition, format, and install an OS on your new hard drive. Boot devices come from many sources. All Windows OS installation discs are boot devices, as are Linux installation discs. You can make your own bootable devices, and most techs do, because a boot device often has a number of handy tools included to do certain jobs.

Partitioning and Formatting with the Windows XP Installation CD

When you boot up a Windows XP installation CD and the installation program detects a hard drive that is not yet partitioned, it prompts you through a sequence of steps to partition (and format) the hard drive. Even though this example uses the Windows XP installation CD, don't worry, because this part of the Windows 2000 installation is almost identical and the next section discusses Vista in detail.

Single Partition

The most common partitioning scenario involves turning a new blank drive into a single bootable C: drive. To accomplish this goal, you need to make the entire drive a primary partition and then make it active. Let's go through the process of partitioning and formatting a single, brand-new, 200-GB hard drive.

The Windows installation begins by booting from a Windows installation CD-ROM like the one shown in Figure 5.35. The installation program starts automatically from the CD. The installation first loads some needed files but eventually prompts you with the screen shown in Figure 5.36. This is your clue that partitioning is about to start.

Press the ENTER key to start a new Windows installation and accept the license agreement to see the main partitioning screen (Figure 5.37). The bar that says Unpartitioned Space is the drive.

● **Figure 5.35**   Windows installation CD

The Windows installer is pretty smart. If you press ENTER at this point, it partitions the hard drive as a single primary partition, makes it active, and installs Windows for you—but what fun is that? Instead, press C to create a partition. The installer then asks you how large a partition to make (Figure 5.38). You may make the partition any size you want by typing in a number, from a minimum of 8 MB up to the size of the entire drive (in this case, 204789 MB). Let's just make the entire drive a single C: drive by pressing ENTER.

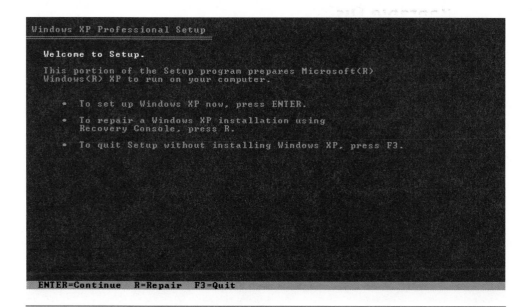

```
Windows XP Professional Setup

    Welcome to Setup.

    This portion of the Setup program prepares Microsoft(R)
    Windows(R) XP to run on your computer.

        •   To set up Windows XP now, press ENTER.

        •   To repair a Windows XP installation using
            Recovery Console, press R.

        •   To quit Setup without installing Windows XP, press F3.

    ENTER=Continue   R=Repair   F3=Quit
```

● **Figure 5.36**   Welcome to Setup

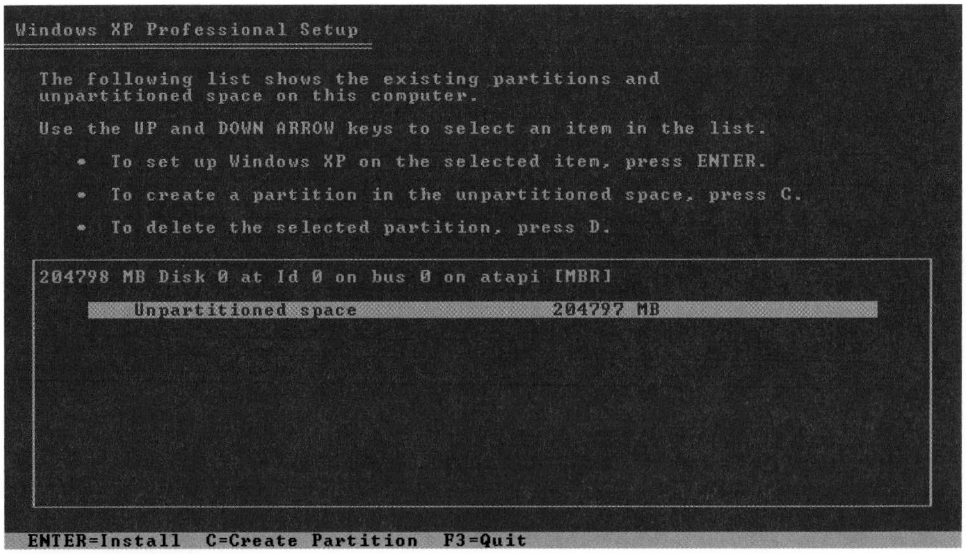

```
Windows XP Professional Setup

The following list shows the existing partitions and
unpartitioned space on this computer.

Use the UP and DOWN ARROW keys to select an item in the list.

    • To set up Windows XP on the selected item, press ENTER.

    • To create a partition in the unpartitioned space, press C.

    • To delete the selected partition, press D.

204798 MB Disk 0 at Id 0 on bus 0 on atapi [MBR]

        Unpartitioned space                    204797 MB




ENTER=Install  C=Create Partition  F3=Quit
```

● **Figure 5.37**   Partitioning screen

Ta-da! You just partitioned the drive! Now Windows asks you how you want to format that drive (Figure 5.39). So you might be asking, where's the basic versus dynamic? Where do you tell Windows to make the partition primary instead of extended? Where do you set it as active?

The Windows installer makes a number of assumptions for you, such as always making the first partition primary and setting it as active. The installer also makes all hard drives basic disks. You'll have to convert it to dynamic later (if you even want to convert it at all).

Select NTFS for the format. Either option—quick or full—will do the job here. (Quick format is quicker, as the name would suggest, but the full option is more thorough and thus safer.) After Windows formats the drive, the installation continues, copying the new Windows installation to the C: drive.

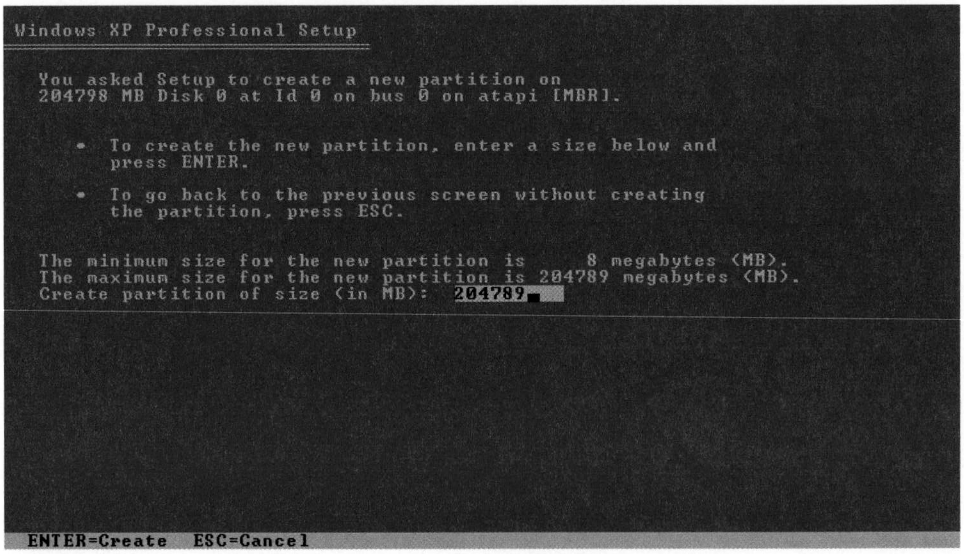

```
Windows XP Professional Setup

You asked Setup to create a new partition on
204798 MB Disk 0 at Id 0 on bus 0 on atapi [MBR].

    • To create the new partition, enter a size below and
      press ENTER.

    • To go back to the previous screen without creating
      the partition, press ESC.

The minimum size for the new partition is       8 megabytes (MB).
The maximum size for the new partition is 204789 megabytes (MB).
Create partition of size (in MB):  204789




ENTER=Create   ESC=Cancel
```

● **Figure 5.38**   Setting partition size

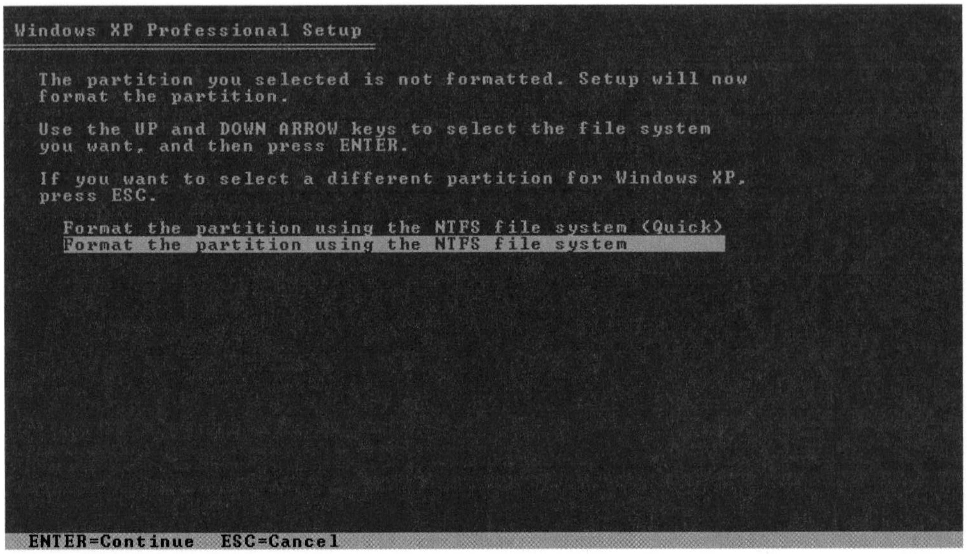

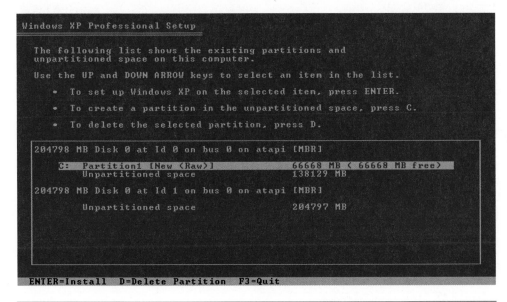

Windows XP Professional Setup

The partition you selected is not formatted. Setup will now
format the partition.

Use the UP and DOWN ARROW keys to select the file system
you want, and then press ENTER.

If you want to select a different partition for Windows XP,
press ESC.

    Format the partition using the NTFS file system (Quick)
    Format the partition using the NTFS file system

ENTER=Continue   ESC=Cancel

● Figure 5.39   Format screen

Two Partitions

Well, that was fun! So much fun that I'd like to do another new Windows installation, with a bit more complex partitioning. This time, you again have
the 200-GB hard drive, but you want to split the drive into three drive letters
of roughly 66 GB each. That means you need to make a single 66-GB primary
partition, then a 133-GB extended partition, and then split that extended
partition into two logical drives of 66 GB each.

Back at the Windows installation main partitioning screen, first press C
to make a new partition, but this time change the 204789 to 66666, which will
give you a partition of about 66 GB. When you press ENTER, the partitioning
screen should look like Figure 5.40. Even though the installation program
doesn't tell you, the partition is primary.

Windows almost always
adjusts the number you type in
for a partition size. In this case,
it changed 66666 to 66668, a
number that makes more sense
when translated to binary. Don't
worry about it!

Windows XP Professional Setup

The following list shows the existing partitions and
unpartitioned space on this computer.

Use the UP and DOWN ARROW keys to select an item in the list.

    ● To set up Windows XP on the selected item, press ENTER.

    ● To create a partition in the unpartitioned space, press C.

    ● To delete the selected partition, press D.

204798 MB Disk 0 at Id 0 on bus 0 on atapi [MBR]
    C: Partition1 [New (Raw)]   66668 MB (66668 MB free)
        Unpartitioned space   138129 MB
204798 MB Disk 0 at Id 1 on bus 0 on atapi [MBR]
        Unpartitioned space   204797 MB

ENTER=Install   D=Delete Partition   F3=Quit

● Figure 5.40   You've created a 66-GB partition.

Chapter 5: Implementing Hard Drives

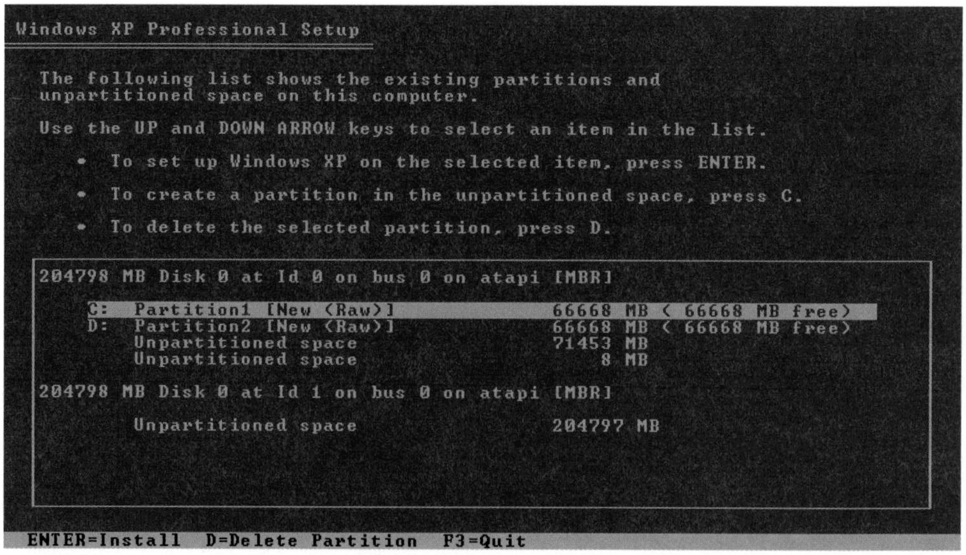

```
Windows XP Professional Setup

The following list shows the existing partitions and
unpartitioned space on this computer.

Use the UP and DOWN ARROW keys to select an item in the list.

    • To set up Windows XP on the selected item, press ENTER.

    • To create a partition in the unpartitioned space, press C.

    • To delete the selected partition, press D.

  204798 MB Disk 0 at Id 0 on bus 0 on atapi [MBR]

    C:  Partition1 [New (Raw)]            66668 MB ( 66668 MB free)
    D:  Partition2 [New (Raw)]            66668 MB ( 66668 MB free)
        Unpartitioned space              71453 MB
        Unpartitioned space                  8 MB

  204798 MB Disk 0 at Id 1 on bus 0 on atapi [MBR]

        Unpartitioned space             204797 MB



ENTER=Install   D=Delete Partition   F3=Quit
```

● **Figure 5.41**   Second partition created

Notice that two-thirds of the drive is still unpartitioned space. Move the selection down to this option and press C to create the next partition. Once again, type **66666** in the partition size screen and press ENTER, and you'll see something similar to Figure 5.41.

Create your last partition exactly as you made the other two to see your almost-completely partitioned drive (Figure 5.42). (Note that the example is not realistic in one respect: you would never leave any unpartitioned space on a drive in a typical PC.)

Even though the Windows installation shows that you've made three partitions, you've really made only two: the primary partition, which is C:,

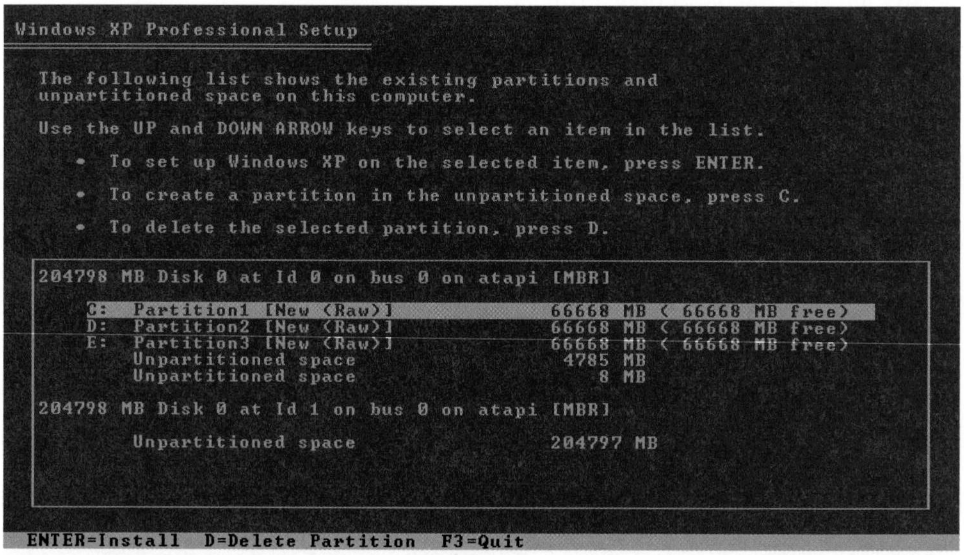

```
Windows XP Professional Setup

The following list shows the existing partitions and
unpartitioned space on this computer.

Use the UP and DOWN ARROW keys to select an item in the list.

    • To set up Windows XP on the selected item, press ENTER.

    • To create a partition in the unpartitioned space, press C.

    • To delete the selected partition, press D.

  204798 MB Disk 0 at Id 0 on bus 0 on atapi [MBR]

    C:  Partition1 [New (Raw)]            66668 MB ( 66668 MB free)
    D:  Partition2 [New (Raw)]            66668 MB ( 66668 MB free)
    E:  Partition3 [New (Raw)]            66668 MB ( 66668 MB free)
        Unpartitioned space               4785 MB
        Unpartitioned space                  8 MB

  204798 MB Disk 0 at Id 1 on bus 0 on atapi [MBR]

        Unpartitioned space             204797 MB



ENTER=Install   D=Delete Partition   F3=Quit
```

● **Figure 5.42**   Fully partitioned drive

and then two logical drives (D: and E:) in an extended partition. Once again, the next step, formatting, is saved for a later section in this chapter.

You've just created three drive letters. Keep in mind that the only drive you must partition during installation is the drive on which you install Windows.

The installation program can delete partitions just as easily as it makes them. If you use a hard drive that already has partitions, for example, you just select the partition you wish to delete and press the letter D. This brings up a dialog box where Windows gives you one last change to change your mind (Figure 5.43). Press L to kill the partition.

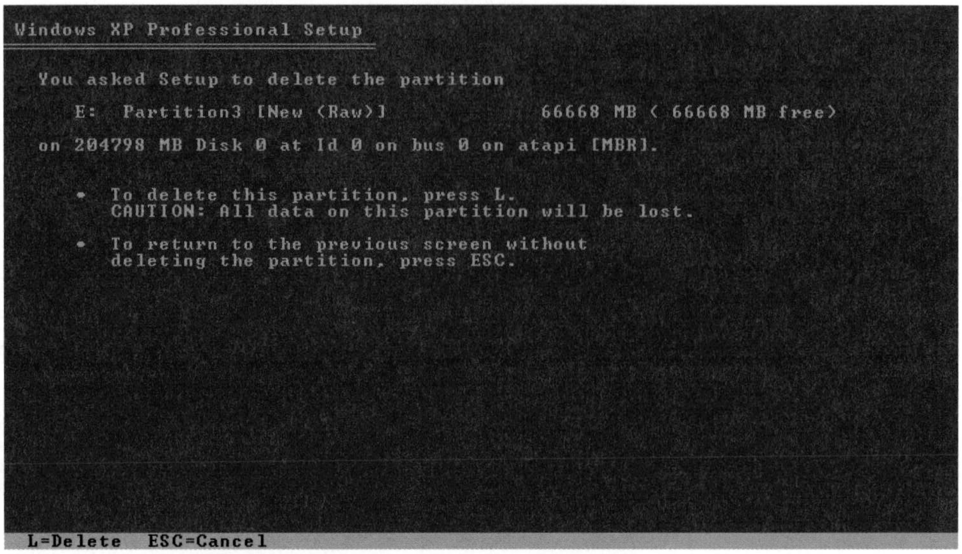

```
Windows XP Professional Setup

    You asked Setup to delete the partition
        E:   Partition3 [New (Raw)]              66668 MB ( 66668 MB free)
    on 204798 MB Disk 0 at Id 0 on bus 0 on atapi [MBR].

        •   To delete this partition, press L.
            CAUTION: All data on this partition will be lost.

        •   To return to the previous screen without
            deleting the partition, press ESC.




    L=Delete    ESC=Cancel
```

• **Figure 5.43**   Option to delete partition

Partitioning and Formatting with the Windows Vista Installation DVD

Among the many changes in Microsoft's newest operating system is a completely revamped installation process, complete with a fancy looking and, more importantly, easy-to-use graphical user interface. A lot of this will seem a little familiar, but just because you've already looked at partitioning in Windows XP doesn't mean you don't have to be familiar with what's changed in Vista.

Single Partition

One thing that definitely hasn't changed with Vista is that the most common installation is on a single active partition, so let's start there. Again, you're going to partition and format a single 200-GB drive.

The Vista installation GUI has a few more steps than XP before you get to the actual formatting page, so let's get through those as quickly as possible to get to the fun stuff. When you boot from the installation DVD, you'll be greeted with a screen asking you for language and regional information (Figure 5.44). Unless you're having this book read to you by a translator, I expect you'll want to keep the language set to English, but set the other entries as needed.

The next page has a large Install Now button, so click that and move on. After that, the installer asks for a product key (Figure 5.45). Don't bother entering one yet—just leave the field blank and click Next to move on to the next page.

● **Figure 5.44**   The Windows Vista language preferences screen

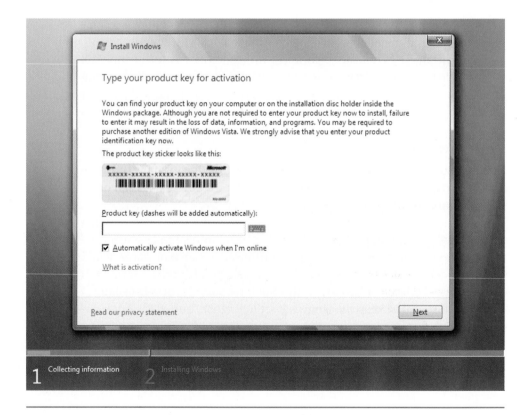

● **Figure 5.45**   The product key page

The next page asks which version of Vista you want to install (Figure 5.46). Every Vista installation DVD contains all editions of the operating system—your product key ultimately determines which edition you can install, so you wouldn't get this page if you entered a product key when first prompted. Select Windows Vista ULTIMATE (in this example) and move on to the next page.

The next page is just a license agreement that you'll need to, ahem, agree with before moving on. Getting impatient to do some formatting? Don't worry—I know this process is a tad longer than on XP, but you're almost there. Click the Custom install button on the next page and you'll be greeted with the partitioning page (Figure 5.47). Whew!

Your hard drive is the bar that says Disk 0 Unallocated Space, which is currently the only thing there. If you just click Next, Windows automatically partitions and formats the drive for you, but I still fail to see any fun in that, so let's once again manually create a partition on the drive. Click the *Drive options (advanced)* button to see the advanced drive features. To create a new partition, click the New button. You could simply click Apply

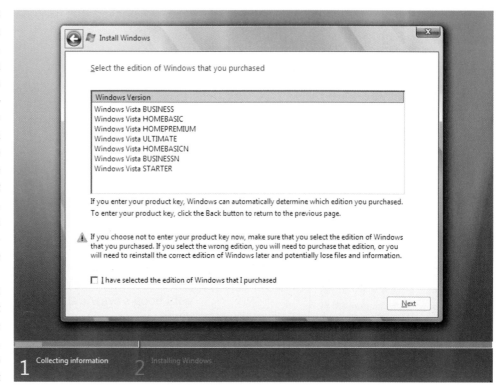

● **Figure 5.46**   Choose your edition

● **Figure 5.47**   The Vista partitioning page

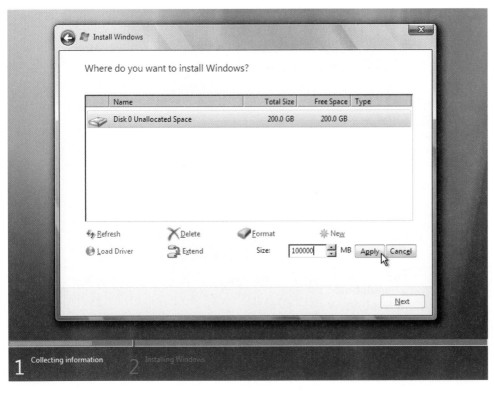

● **Figure 5.48**   Setting partition size

to make a 200-GB partition, but, to demonstrate one of Vista's handy new features, type **100000** and then click Apply (Figure 5.48).

Once you have created your 100-GB partition, click the Format button. Notice that the installer never asks you what file system to use. Vista can read FAT drives, but it will not install itself to one by default. There are, of course, some people on the Internet who have figured out how to install Vista to a FAT32 drive, but why anyone would want to lose all of NTFS's functionality is beyond me.

So now you have set up a 100-GB partition, but what if you want to make it a 200-GB partition? In XP, you would have to delete the partition and start over, but not so in Vista. You can simply click the Extend button and then apply the rest of the unallocated space to your currently formatted partition. The extend function allows you to easily tack unpartitioned space onto an already partitioned drive.

Multiple Partitions

You can format a drive to contain two partitions just as easily as formatting a single drive. Just as in the XP example, you'll be creating three 66-GB partitions. Unlike in Windows XP, this process actually leaves you with three primary partitions, not a primary partition and an extended partition with two logical drives. Vista will not create extended partitions if a user has fewer than four partitions on a drive, so if you're making three partitions, you're actually creating three primary partitions. If you made a fourth, it would manifest itself as a logical drive on an extended partition.

However, you're not going to create four partitions for this exercise, so you don't need to worry about that. You'll start out, again, with a 200-GB drive, but this time, after clicking the New button, type **66666** into the Size box and click Apply. That will give you a 66-GB (more or less) primary partition (Figure 5.49).

Do the same thing to create the next two drives and you're finished. That was pretty easy, wasn't it?

Mike Meyers' CompTIA A+ Guide: Practical Application

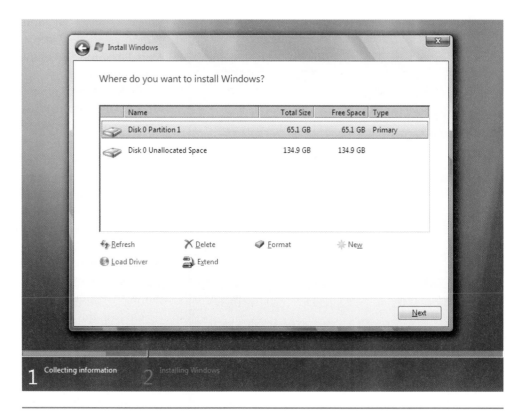

Partitions and Drive Letters

So you have a hard drive, maybe several hard drives, all partitioned up, and you've installed Windows on one of them, but where do those drive letters come from? Older systems assigned drive letters based on some fairly complicated rules having to do with master and slave drives, but things are much simpler on modern systems.

The primary active partition will always be C: and you can't change that, but the rest of the drives are assigned the next available letter, with hard drives taking priority over optical drives. If you have two hard drives and an optical drive in your computer, the hard drives will be C: and D:, and the optical drive will be E:. If, however, you later install another hard drive in the computer, it will become your F: drive. Newly installed drives do not take drive letters from previously installed drives.

You can change the lettering on every drive but your system partition, which you'll find out how to do in the next section.

Disk Management

The real tool for partitioning and formatting is the Disk Management utility. You can use Disk Management to do everything you want to do to a hard drive in one handy tool. You can access Disk Management by going to the Control Panel and opening the Computer Management applet. If you're cool, you can click Start | Run, type in **diskmgmt.msc**, and press ENTER.

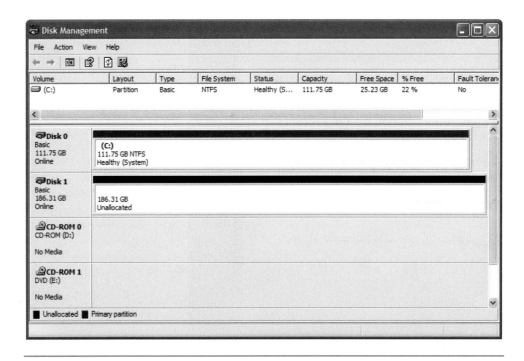

Windows 2000/XP and Windows Vista/7 come with Disk Management (Figure 5.50).

Disk Management works only within Windows, so you can't use Disk Management from a boot device. If you install Windows from an installation disc, in other words, you must use the special partitioning/formatting software built into the installation program you just saw in action.

One of the most interesting parts of Disk Management is disk initialization. Every hard drive in a Windows system has special information placed onto the drive. This initialization information includes identifiers that say "this drive belongs in this system" and other information that defines what this hard drive does in the system. If the hard drive is part of a RAID array, its RAID information is stored in the initialization. If it's part of a spanned volume, this is also stored there. All new drives must be initialized before you can use them. When you install an extra hard drive into a Windows system and start Disk Management, it notices the new drive and starts the Hard Drive Initialization Wizard. If you don't let the wizard run, the drive will be listed as unknown (Figure 5.51).

• **Figure 5.50** Disk Management

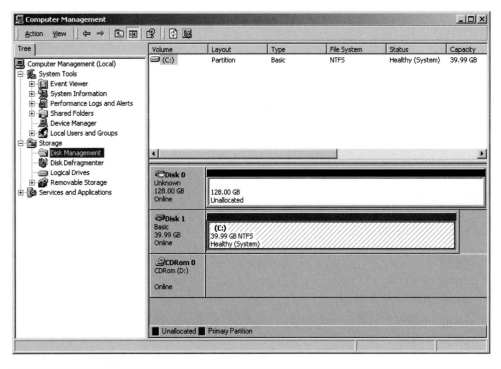

• **Figure 5.51** Unknown drive in Disk Management

To initialize a disk, right-click the disk icon and select Initialize. Once a disk is initialized, you can see the status of the drive—a handy tool for troubleshooting.

Disk Management enables you to view the status of every drive in your system. Hopefully, you'll mostly see the drive listed as Healthy, meaning that nothing is happening to it and things are going along swimmingly. You're also already familiar with the Unallocated and Active statuses, but here are a few more to be familiar with for the test:

- **Foreign drive** You see this when you move a dynamic disk into another computer.

- **Formatting** As you might have guessed, you see this when you're formatting a drive.

- **Failed** Pray you never see this status, because it means that the disk is damaged or corrupt and you've probably lost some data.

- **Online** This is what you see if a disk is healthy and communicating properly with the computer.

- **Offline** The disk is either corrupted or having communication problems.

A newly installed drive is always set as a basic disk. There's nothing wrong with using basic disks, other than that you miss out on some handy features. To create partitions, right-click the unallocated part of the drive and select New Partition. Disk Management runs the New Partition Wizard, with which you can select a primary or extended partition (Figure 5.52). Afterward, you see a screen where you specify the size partition you prefer (Figure 5.53).

If you choose to make a primary partition, the wizard asks if you want to assign a drive letter to the partition, mount it as a folder to an existing partition, or do neither (Figure 5.54). (If you choose to make an extended partition, you just get a confirmation screen and you are returned to Disk Management.) In almost all cases, you'll want to give primary partitions a drive letter.

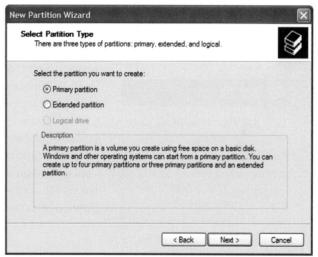

• **Figure 5.52** The New Partition Wizard

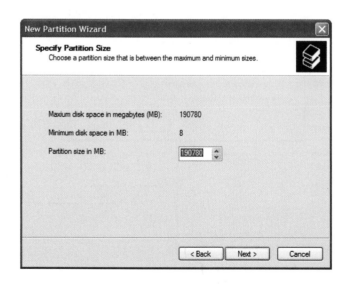

• **Figure 5.53** Specifying the partition size

• **Figure 5.54** Assigning a drive letter to a primary partition

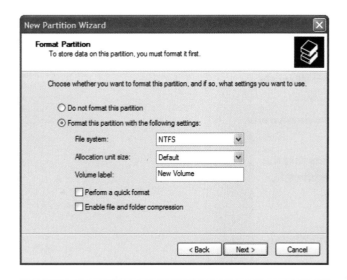

● **Figure 5.55** Choosing a file system type

Tech Tip

Big FAT Partitions
Windows 2000/XP and Windows Vista/7 read and write to FAT32 partitions larger than 32 GB; they just don't allow Disk Management to make them. If you ever stumble across a drive from a system that ran the old Windows 9x/Me that has a FAT32 partition larger than 32 GB, it will work just fine in a modern Windows system.

The last screen of the New Partition Wizard asks for the type of format you want to use for this partition (Figure 5.55). If your partition is 4 GB or less, you may format it as FAT, FAT32, or NTFS. If your partition is greater than 4 GB but less than 32 GB, you can make the drive FAT32 or NTFS. Windows requires NTFS on any partition greater than 32 GB. Although FAT32 supports partitions up to 2 TB, Microsoft wants you to use NTFS on larger partitions and creates this limit. In today's world of big hard drives, there's no good reason to use anything other than NTFS.

You have a few more tasks to complete at this screen. You can add a volume label if you want. You can also choose the size of your clusters (Allocation unit size). There's no reason to change the default cluster size, so leave that alone—but you can sure speed up the format if you select the *Perform a quick format* checkbox. This will format your drive without checking every cluster. It's fast and a bit risky, but new hard drives almost always come from the factory in perfect shape—so you must decide whether to use it or not.

Last, if you chose NTFS, you may enable file and folder compression. If you select this option, you'll be able to right-click any file or folder on this partition and compress it. To compress a file or folder, choose the one you want to compress, right-click, and select Properties. Then click the Advanced button to turn compression on or off (Figure 5.56). Compression is handy for opening up space on a hard drive that's filling up, but it also slows down disk access, so use it only when you need it.

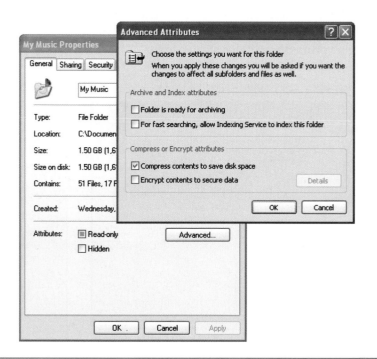

● **Figure 5.56** Turning on compression

After the drive finishes formatting, you'll go back to Disk Management and see a changed hard drive landscape. If you made a primary partition, you will see your new drive letter. If you made an extended partition, things will look a bit different. Figure 5.57 shows the extended partition as free space because it has no logical drive yet. As you can easily guess from Figure 5.58, to create a logical drive, simply right-click in that extended partition and choose New Logical Drive. Disk Management fires up the New Partition Wizard again, this time with the option to create a logical drive.

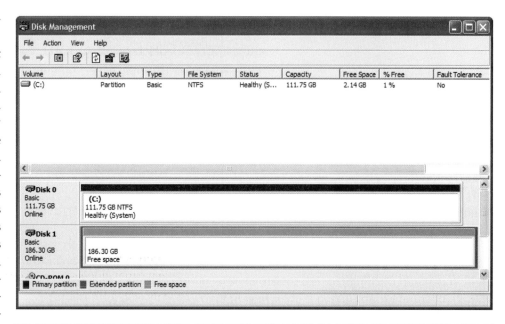

● **Figure 5.57**   Extended partition with no logical drives

When you create a logical drive, the New Partition Wizard automatically gives you the same options to format the partition by using one of the three file systems you saw earlier with primary partitions (Figure 5.59). You get another confirmation screen, and then the Disk Management console shows you the newly created drive.

One interesting aspect of Windows is the tiny (approximately 8 MB) mysterious unallocated partition that shows up on the C: drive. The Windows

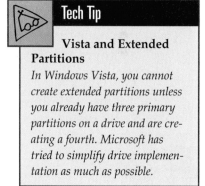

Tech Tip

Vista and Extended Partitions
In Windows Vista, you cannot create extended partitions unless you already have three primary partitions on a drive and are creating a fourth. Microsoft has tried to simplify drive implementation as much as possible.

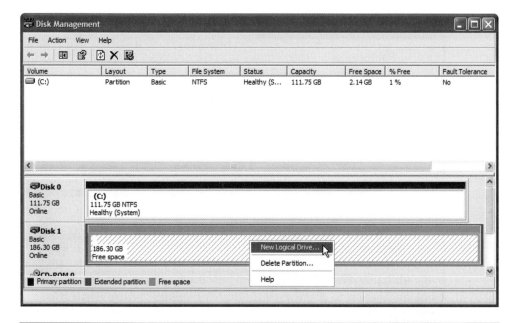

● **Figure 5.58**   Selecting to create a logical drive in the extended (free space) partition

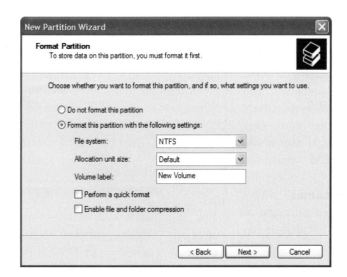

• **Figure 5.59** The New Partition Wizard offering formatting options

installation program does this when you first install Windows on a new system, to reserve a space Windows needs for converting the C: drive to a dynamic disk. It doesn't hurt anything and it's tiny, so just leave it alone. If you want to make a volume and format it, feel free to do so.

Dynamic Disks

You create dynamic disks from basic disks in Disk Management. Once you convert a drive from a basic to a dynamic disk, primary and extended partitions no longer exist; dynamic disks are divided into volumes instead of partitions.

To convert a basic disk to dynamic, just right-click the drive icon and select Convert to Dynamic Disk (Figure 5.60). The process is very quick and

When you move a dynamic disk from one computer to another, it shows up in Disk Management as a foreign drive. You can import a foreign drive into the new system by right-clicking the disk icon and selecting Import Foreign Disks.

The home editions of Windows XP and Windows Vista do not support dynamic disks.

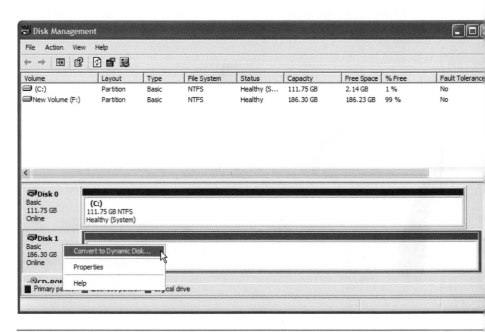

• **Figure 5.60** Converting to a dynamic disk

safe, although the reverse is not true. The conversion from dynamic disk to basic disk first requires you to delete all partitions off of the hard drive.

Once you've converted, no partitions exist, only volumes. You can make five types of volumes on a dynamic disk: simple, spanned, striped, mirrored, and RAID 5, although you'll commonly see only the first three in a Windows 2000/XP Professional or Windows Vista Business environment. You'll next learn how to implement the three most common volume types. The final step involves assigning a drive letter or mounting the volume as a folder.

Simple Volumes

A simple volume acts just like a primary partition. If you have only one dynamic disk in a system, it can have only a simple volume. It's important to note here that a simple volume may act like a traditional primary partition, but it is very different. If you install a hard drive partitioned as a simple volume dynamic disk into any version of Windows prior to Windows 2000, you would see no usable partition.

In Disk Management, right-click any unallocated space on the dynamic disk and choose New Volume (Figure 5.61) to run the New Volume Wizard. You'll see a series of screens that prompt you on size and file system, and then you're finished. Figure 5.62 shows Disk Management with three simple volumes.

Spanning Volumes

You can extend the size of a simple volume to any unallocated space on a dynamic disk. You can also extend the volume to grab extra space on completely different dynamic disks, creating a spanned volume. To extend or span, simply right-click the volume you want to make bigger, and choose Extend Volume from the options (Figure 5.63). This opens the Extend

Tech Tip

Mirrored and Striped with Parity Volumes

Disk Management enables you to create mirrored and striped with parity volumes, but only on Windows Server machines. The cool thing is that you can do this remotely across a network. You can sit at your Windows XP Professional workstation, in other words, and open Disk Management, surf to a Windows Server that you want to work with, and poof!

You have two new options for configuring volumes. By limiting the implementation of mirroring and RAID 5 to server machines, Microsoft clearly meant to encourage small businesses to pony up for a copy of Server rather than using the less-expensive Professional or Business OS for the company server. Both mirrored and striped with parity volumes are included here for completeness and because they show up in the Windows Help Files when you search for dynamic disks. Both are cool, but definitely way beyond CompTIA A+!

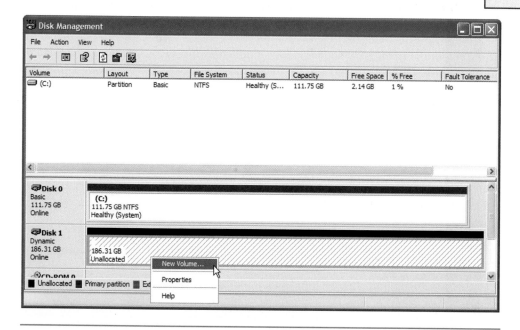

• **Figure 5.61**   Selecting to open the New Volume Wizard

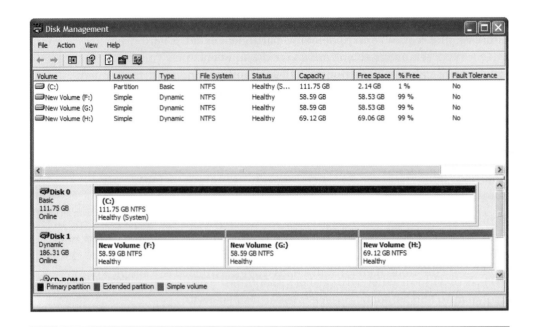

● **Figure 5.62**   Simple volumes

Volume Wizard, which prompts you for the location of free space on a dynamic disk and the increased volume size you want to assign (Figure 5.64). If you have multiple drives, you can span the volume just as easily to one of those drives.

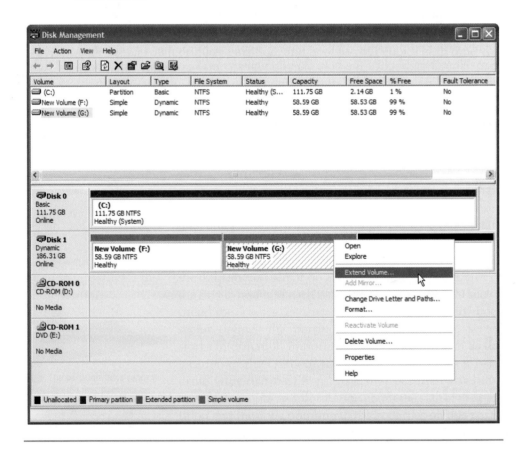

● **Figure 5.63**   Selecting the Extend Volume option

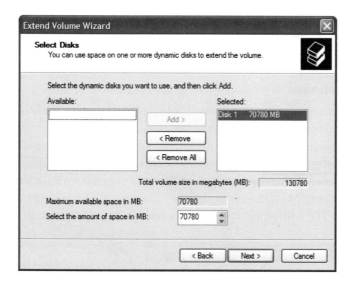

• **Figure 5.64**   The Extend Volume Wizard

The capability to extend and span volumes makes dynamic disks worth their weight in gold. If you start running out of space on a volume, you can simply add another physical hard drive to the system and span the volume to the new drive. This keeps your drive letters consistent and unchanging so your programs don't get confused, yet enables you to expand drive space when needed.

You can extend or span any simple volume on a dynamic disk, not just the "one on the end" in the Disk Management console. You simply select the volume to expand and the total volume increase you want. Figure 5.65 shows a simple 4-GB volume named Extended that has been enlarged an

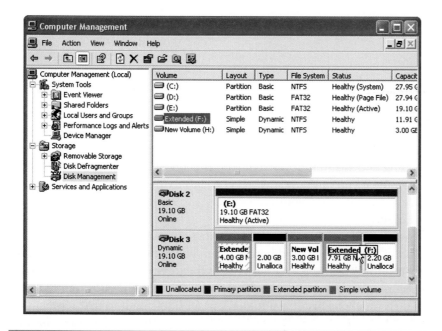

• **Figure 5.65**   Extended volume

Once you convert a drive to dynamic, you cannot revert it to a basic disk without losing all of the data on that drive. Be prepared to back up all data before you convert.

Tech Tip

Extending Hard Drives in Vista
You can extend and shrink hard drives in Vista without using dynamic disks. You can shrink any primary partition with available free space (though you can't always shrink the partition by the whole amount of free space, based on the location of unmovable sectors such as the MBR), and you can expand partitions with unpartitioned space on the drive. Using dynamic disks in Vista still has benefits, however, because you cannot expand a partition by using space on another drive, and the unpartitioned space has to be contiguous with the partition you're expanding.

extra 7.91 GB in a portion of the hard drive, skipping the 2-GB section of unallocated space contiguous to it. This created an 11.91-GB volume. Windows has no problem skipping areas on a drive.

Striped Volumes

If you have two or more dynamic disks in a PC, Disk Management enables you to combine them into a *striped* volume. A striped volume spreads out blocks of each file across multiple disks. Using two or more drives in a group called a stripe set, striping writes data first to a certain number of clusters on one drive, then on the next, and so on. It speeds up data throughput because the system has to wait a much shorter time for a drive to read or write data. The drawback of striping is that if any single drive in the stripe set fails, all data in the stripe set is lost.

To create a striped volume, right-click unused space on a drive and choose New Volume and then Striped. The wizard asks for the other drives you want to add to the stripe, and you need to select two unallocated spaces on other dynamic disks. Select the other unallocated spaces and go through the remaining screens on sizing and formatting until you've created a new striped volume (Figure 5.66). The two stripes in Figure 5.66 appear to have different sizes, but if you look closely you'll see they are both 4 GB. All stripes must be the same size on each drive.

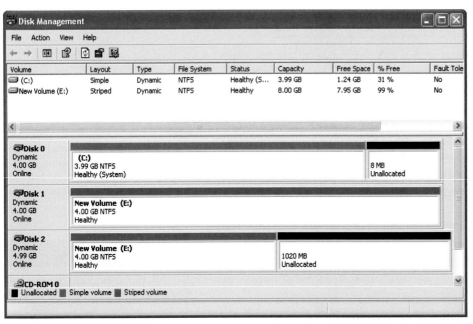

● **Figure 5.66**   Two striped drives

Mount Points

The one drive that can't take full advantage of being dynamic is the drive containing the operating system: your primary master C: drive. You can make it dynamic, but you still can't do all of the cool dynamic things such as extending and spanning. So what good is being able to allocate more space to a volume if you can't use it when you start to fill up your C: drive? If you can't add to that drive, your only option is to replace it with a new, bigger drive, right?

Not at all! Earlier we discussed the idea of mounting a drive as a folder instead of a drive letter, and here's where you get to do it. A *volume mount point* (or simply mount point) is a place in the directory structure of an existing volume that you can point to a volume or partition. The mounted volume then functions just like a folder, but all files stored in that segment of the directory structure will go to the mounted volume. After partitioning and formatting the drive, you don't give it a drive letter; instead, you *mount*

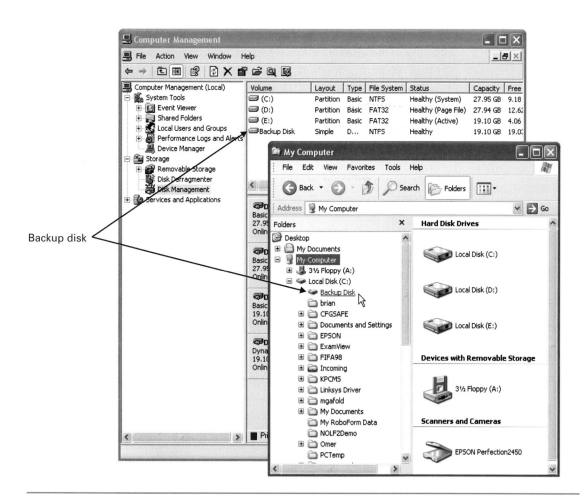

• **Figure 5.67**   A drive volume mounted as a folder of drive C:

the volume to a folder on the C: drive and make it nothing more than just another folder (Figure 5.67). You can load programs to that folder, just as you would to your Program Files folder. You can use it to store data files or backed-up system files. In *function*, therefore, the new hard drive simply extends the capacity of the C: drive, so neither you nor your client need ever trouble yourselves with dealing with multiple drive letters.

To create a mount point, right-click an unallocated section of a dynamic disk and choose New Volume. This opens the New Volume Wizard. In the second screen, you can select a mount point rather than a drive letter (Figure 5.68). Browse to a blank folder on an NTFS-formatted drive or create a new folder and you're in business.

With mount points, Microsoft dramatically changed the way you can work with hard drives. You're no longer stuck in the rut of adding drive letters that mess up Windows' mapping of the optical drive. You don't have to confuse clients with multiple drive letters when they

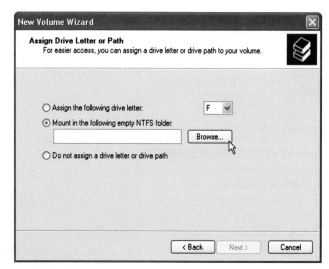

• **Figure 5.68**   Choosing to create a mounted volume

just want a little more space. You can resurrect smaller hard drives, making them a functional part of today's computer. With the Disk Management console in Windows 2000/XP and Windows Vista/7, Microsoft got it right.

Formatting a Partition

You can format any Windows partition/volume in My Computer/Computer. Just right-click the drive name and choose Format (Figure 5.69). You'll see a dialog box that asks for the type of file system you want to use and the cluster size, provides a place to put a volume label, and lists two other options. The Quick Format option tells Windows not to test the clusters and is a handy option when you're in a hurry—and feeling lucky. The Enable Compression option tells Windows to give users the capability to compress folders or files. It works well but slows down your hard drive.

Disk Management is today's preferred formatting tool for Windows 2000, XP, and Vista. When you create a new volume on a dynamic disk or a new partition on a basic disk, the New Volume Wizard also asks you what type of format you want to use. Always use NTFS unless you're that rare and strange person who wants to dual-boot Windows XP or Windows Vista with some ancient version of Windows.

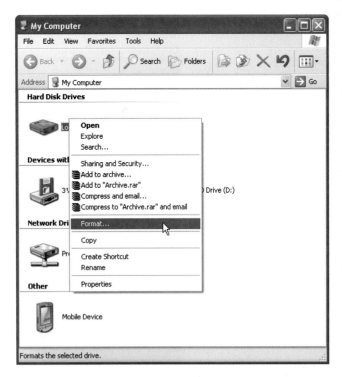

● **Figure 5.69**   Choosing Format in My Computer

All OS installation discs partition and format as part of the OS installation. Windows simply prompts you to partition and then format the drive. Read the screens and you'll do great.

Maintaining and Troubleshooting Hard Drives in Windows

Hard drives are complex mechanical and electrical devices. With platters spinning at thousands of rotations per minute, they also generate heat and vibration. All of these factors make hard drives susceptible to failure. In this section, you will learn some basic maintenance tasks that will keep your hard drives healthy, and for those inevitable instances when a hard drive fails, you will also learn what you can do to repair them.

Maintenance

Hard drive maintenance can be broken down into two distinct functions: checking the disk occasionally for failed clusters, and keeping data organized on the drive so it can be accessed quickly.

Error-Checking

Individual clusters on hard drives sometimes go bad. There's nothing you can do to prevent this from happening, so it's important that you check occasionally for bad clusters on drives. The tools used to perform this checking are generically called error-checking utilities, although the terms for two older Microsoft tools—ScanDisk and CHKDSK (pronounced "Checkdisk")—are often used. Microsoft calls the tool Error-checking in Windows XP/ Vista/7. Whatever the name of the utility, each does the same job: when the tool finds bad clusters, it puts the electronic equivalent of orange cones around them so the system won't try to place data in those bad clusters.

Most error-checking tools do far more than just check for bad clusters. They go through all of the drive's filenames, looking for invalid names and attempting to fix them. They look for clusters that have no filenames associated with them (we call these *lost chains*) and erase them. From time to time, the underlying links between parent and child folders are lost, so a good error-checking tool checks every parent and child folder. With a folder such as C:\TEST\DATA, for example, they make sure that the folder DATA is properly associated with its parent folder, C:\TEST, and that C:\TEST is properly associated with its child folder, C:\TEST\DATA.

To access Error-checking on a Windows 2000/XP or Windows Vista/7 system, open My Computer/Computer, right-click the drive you want to check, and choose Properties to open the drive's Properties dialog box. Select the Tools tab and click the Check Now button (Figure 5.70) to display the Check Disk dialog box, which has two options (Figure 5.71). Check the box next to *Automatically fix file system errors*, but save the option to *Scan for and attempt recovery of bad sectors* for

CompTIA A+ uses the term CHKDSK rather than Error-checking.

• **Figure 5.70** The Tools tab in the Properties dialog box in Windows XP

● **Figure 5.71**   Options

times when you actually suspect a problem, because it takes a while on bigger hard drives.

Now that you know how to run Error-checking, your next question should be, "How often do I run it?" A reasonable maintenance plan would include running it about once a week. Error-checking is fast (unless you use the *Scan for and attempt recovery* option), and it's a great tool for keeping your system in top shape.

Defragmentation

Fragmentation of clusters can increase your drive access times dramatically. It's a good idea to defragment—or *defrag*—your drives as part of monthly maintenance. You access the defrag tool that runs with Windows 2000, XP, Vista, and 7, called Disk Defragmenter, the same way you access Error-checking—right-click a drive in My Computer/Computer and choose Properties—except you click the Defragment Now button on the Tools tab to open the Defragmenter (Figure 5.72).

Defragmentation is interesting to watch—once. From then on, schedule it to run late at night. You should defragment your drives about once a month, although you could run it every week, and if you run it every night, it takes only a few minutes. The longer you go between defrags, the longer it takes. If you don't run Disk Defragmenter, your system will run slower. If you don't run Error-checking, you may lose data.

Disk Cleanup

Did you know that the average hard drive is full of trash? Not the junk you intentionally put in your hard drive such as the 23,000 e-mail messages that you refuse to delete from your e-mail program. This kind of trash is all of the files that you never see that Windows keeps for you. Here are a few examples:

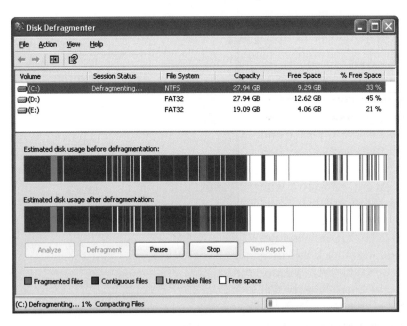

● **Figure 5.72**   Disk Defragmenter in Windows XP

- **Files in the Recycle Bin**   When you delete a file, it isn't really deleted. It's placed in the Recycle Bin in case you decide you need the file later. I just checked my Recycle Bin and found 3 GB worth of files (Figure 5.73). That's a lot of trash!

- **Temporary Internet files**   When you go to a Web site, Windows keeps copies of the graphics and other items so the page will load more quickly the next time you access it. You can see these files by opening the Internet Options applet on the Control Panel. Figure 5.74 shows my temporary Internet files.

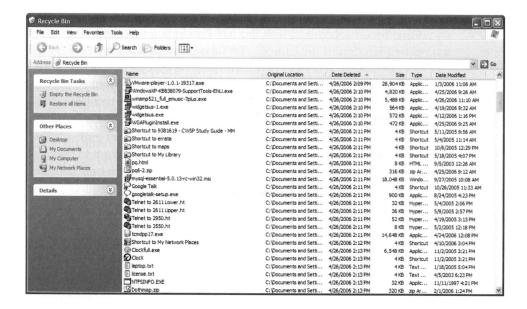

● **Figure 5.73** Mike's Recycle Bin

■ **Downloaded program files** Your system always keeps a copy of any Java or ActiveX applets it downloads. You can see these in the Internet Options applet. You'll generally find only a few tiny files here.

■ **Temporary files** Many applications create temporary files that are supposed to be deleted when the application is closed. For one reason or another, these temporary files sometimes aren't deleted. The location of these files varies with the version of Windows, but they always reside in a folder called TEMP.

Every hard drive eventually becomes filled with lots of unnecessary trash. All versions of Windows tend to act erratically when the drives run out of unused space. Fortunately, all versions of Windows have a powerful tool called Disk Cleanup (Figure 5.75). You can access Disk Cleanup in all versions of Windows by choosing Start | All Programs | Accessories | System Tools | Disk Cleanup.

Disk Cleanup gets rid of the four types of files just described (and a few others). Run Disk Cleanup once a month or so to keep plenty of space available on your hard drive.

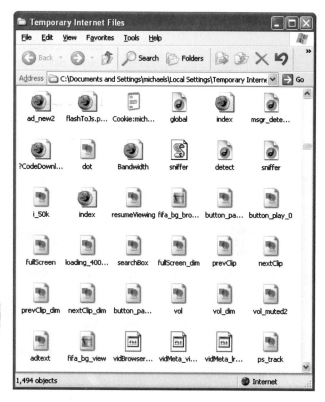

● **Figure 5.74** Lots of temporary Internet files

Troubleshooting Hard Drive Implementation

There's no scarier computer problem than an error that points to trouble with a hard drive. This section looks at some of the more common problems

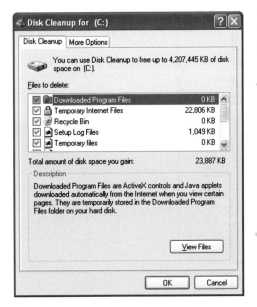

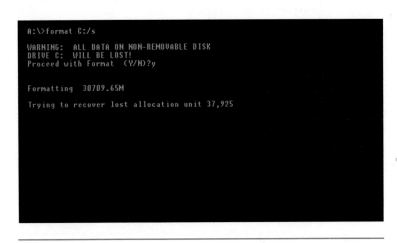

that occur with hard drives and how to fix them. These issues fall into three broad categories: installation, data corruption, and dying hard drives.

Installation Errors

Installing a drive and getting to the point where it can hold data requires four distinct steps: connectivity, CMOS, partitioning, and formatting. If you make a mistake at any point on any of these steps, the drive won't work. The beauty of this is that if you make an error, you can walk back through each step and check for problems. You covered physical connections and CMOS earlier in this chapter, so this section concentrates on the latter two issues.

Partitioning   Partitioning errors generally fall into two groups: failing to partition at all and making the wrong size or type of partition. You'll recognize the former type of error the first time you open My Computer/Computer after installing a drive. If you forgot to partition it, the drive won't even show up in My Computer, only in Disk Management. If you made the partition too small, that'll become painfully obvious when you start filling it up with files.

The fix for partitioning errors is simply to open Disk Management and do the partitioning correctly. If you've added files to the wrongly sized drive, don't forget to back them up before you repartition.

Formatting   Failing to format a drive makes the drive unable to hold data. Accessing the drive in Windows results in a drive "is not accessible" error, and from a C:\ prompt, you'll get the famous "Invalid media" type error. Format the drive unless you're certain that the drive has a format already. Corrupted files can create the invalid media error. Check one of the sections on corrupted data later in this chapter for the fix.

Most of the time, formatting is a slow, boring process. But sometimes the drive makes "bad sounds" and you start seeing errors like the one shown in Figure 5.76 at the bottom of the screen.

An *allocation unit* is FORMAT's term for a cluster. The drive has run across a bad cluster and is trying to fix it. For years, I've told techs that seeing this error a few (610) times doesn't mean anything; every drive comes with a few bad spots. This is no longer true. Modern drives actually hide a significant number of extra sectors that they use to replace bad sectors automatically. If a new drive gets a lot of "Trying to recover lost allocation unit" errors, you can bet that the drive is dying and needs to be replaced. Get the hard drive maker's diagnostic to be sure. Bad clusters are reported by S.M.A.R.T.

Mental Reinstallation   Focus on the fact that all of these errors share a common thread—you just installed a drive! Installation errors don't show up on a system that has been running correctly for three weeks; they show up the moment you try to do something with the drive you just installed. If a newly installed drive fails to work, do a "mental reinstallation." Does the drive show up in the CMOS autodetect? No? Then recheck the cables, master/slave settings, and power. If it does show up, did you remember to partition and format the drive? Did it need to be set to active? These are common-sense questions that come to mind as you march through your mental reinstallation. Even if you've installed thousands of drives over the years, you'll be amazed at how often you do things such as forget to plug in power to a drive, forget CMOS, or install a cable backward. Do the mental reinstallation—it really works!

Data Corruption

All hard drives occasionally get corrupted data in individual sectors. Power surges, accidental shutdowns, corrupted installation media, and viruses, along with hundreds of other problems, can cause this corruption. In most cases, this type of error shows up while Windows is running. Figure 5.77 shows a classic example.

You may also see Windows error messages saying one of the following:

- "The following file is missing or corrupt"
- "The download location information is damaged"
- "Unable to load file"

Winamp: winamp.exe - Unable To Locate Component

This application has failed to start because libsndfile.dll was not found. Re-installing the application may fix this problem.

OK

• **Figure 5.77**   A corrupted data error

If core boot files become corrupted, you may see text errors at boot, such as the following:

- "Cannot find COMMAND.COM"
- "Error loading operating system"
- "Invalid BOOT.INI"
- "NTLDR is missing or corrupt"

On older programs, you may see a command prompt open with errors such as this one:

```
Sector not found reading drive C: Abort, Retry, Fail?
```

The first fix for any of these problems is to run the Error-checking utility. Error-checking will go through and mark bad clusters and hopefully move your data to a good cluster.

Windows 2000/XP Extract/Expand   If Error-checking fails to move a critically important file—such as a file Windows needs so it can load—on pre-Vista systems you can always resort to the command line and try to extract the file from the Windows cabinet files. Most Windows programs store all files in a compressed format called CAB (which is short for cabinet file). One CAB file contains many files, and most installation discs have lots of CAB files (see Figure 5.78).

To replace a single corrupt file this way, you need to know two things: the location of the CAB file that contains the file you need, and how to get

Chapter 6, "Mastering the Windows Command Line," goes into a lot of detail on using the command line.

• **Figure 5.78**   CAB files

the file out so you can copy it back to its original spot. Microsoft supplies the **EXPAND** program to enable you to get a new copy of the missing file from the CAB files on the installation CD-ROM. Also notice how they are numbered—that's the secret to understanding these programs.

In most cases, all of the CAB files for a program are piled into some folder, as shown in Figure 5.78. Let's say you need a file called OLEPRO32.DLL. (I have no idea what this file does. I only know that Windows can't find it and you need to put it back.) Get to a command prompt within Windows and tell EXPAND to check *all* of the CAB files on your installation CD (drive E: in this example) with this command:

```
EXPAND e:\I386\*.CAB -F:OLEPRO32.DLL
```

EXPAND goes through all of the CAB files and finds the file. If you want to see details on the EXPAND command, use Windows Help or type **EXPAND /?** at a command prompt.

Corrupted Data on Bad Sectors   If the same errors continue to appear after you run the disk-checking utility, there's a chance that the drive has bad sectors.

Almost all drives today take advantage of built-in **error correction code (ECC)** that constantly checks the drive for bad sectors. If the ECC detects a bad sector, it marks the sector as bad in the drive's internal error map. Don't confuse this error map with a FAT. The partitioning program creates the FAT. The drive's internal error map was created at the factory on reserved drive heads and is invisible to the system. If the ECC finds a bad sector, you will get a corrupted data error as the computer attempts to read the bad sector. Disk-checking utilities fix this problem most of the time.

Many times, the ECC thinks a bad sector is good, however, and fails to update the internal error map. In this case, you need a program that goes back into the drive and marks the sectors as bad. That's where the powerful SpinRite utility from Gibson Research comes into play. SpinRite marks sectors as bad or good more accurately than ECC and does not disturb the data, enabling you to run SpinRite without fear of losing anything. And if it finds a bad sector with data in it, SpinRite has powerful algorithms that usually recover the data on all but the most badly damaged sectors (see Figure 5.79).

Without SpinRite, you must use a low-level format program supplied by the hard drive maker, assuming you can get one (not all are willing to distribute these). These programs work like SpinRite in that they aggressively check the hard drive's sectors and update the internal error map. Unfortunately, all of them wipe out all data on the drive. At least you can use the drive, even if it means repartitioning, formatting, and reinstalling everything.

Dying Hard Drive

Physical problems are rare, but devastating when they happen. If a hard drive is truly damaged physically, there is nothing that you or any service technician can do to fix it. Fortunately, hard drives are designed to take a phenomenal amount of punishment without failing. Physical problems manifest themselves in two ways: either the drive works properly but makes a lot of noise, or the drive seems to disappear.

All hard drives make noise—the hum as the platters spin and the occasional slight scratching noise as the read/write heads access sectors are normal. However, if your drive begins to make any of the following sounds, it is about to die:

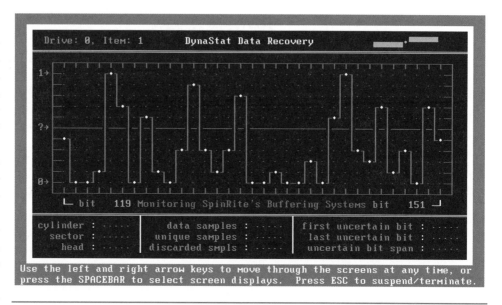

• **Figure 5.79**   SpinRite at work

- Continuous high-pitched squeal

- Series of clacks, a short pause, and then another series of clacks

- Continuous grinding or rumbling

Back up your critical data and replace the drive. Windows comes with great tools for backing up data.

You'll know when a drive simply disappears. If it's the drive that contains your operating system, the system will lock up. When you try to restart the computer, you'll see this error message or something similar to it:

`No Boot Device Present`

If it's a second drive, it will simply stop showing up in My Computer/Computer. The first thing to do in this case is to fire up the System Setup program and see if autodetect sees the drive. If it does, you do not have a physical problem with the drive. If autodetect fails, shut off the system and remove the ribbon cable, but leave the power cable attached. Restart the system and listen to the drive. If the drive spins up, you know it is getting good power. This is usually a clue that the drive is probably good. In that case, you need to look for more mundane problems such as an unplugged power cord or jumpers incorrectly set. If the drive doesn't spin up, try another power connector. If it still doesn't spin up and you've triple-checked the jumpers and ribbon cable, you have a problem with the onboard electronics, and the drive is dead.

Tech Tip

Long Warranties

Most hard drives have three-year warranties. Before you throw away a dead drive, check the hard drive maker's Web site or call them to see if the drive is still under warranty. Ask for a return material authorization (RMA). You'll be amazed how many times you get a newer, usually larger, hard drive for free. It never hurts to check!

Tech Tip

Data Rescue Specialists

If you ever lose a hard drive that contains absolutely critical information, you can turn to a company that specializes in hard drive data recovery. The job will be expensive—prices usually start around $1000 (U.S.)—but when you have to have the data, such companies are your only hope. Do a Web search for "data recovery" or check the Yellow Pages for companies in this line of business.

Beyond A+

Modern hard drives have many other features that are worth knowing about but that rarely impact beginning techs. A couple of the more interesting ones are spindle speed and third-party hard drive tools. If you have a burning desire to dive into hard drives in all their glory, you need not go any farther than the Storage Review, an excellent site dedicated solely to hard drives. Here's the link: www.storagereview.com.

Third-Party Partition Tools

Disk Management is a good tool, but it's limited for some situations. Some really great third-party tools on the market can give you incredible flexibility and power to structure and restructure your hard drive storage to meet your changing needs. They each have interesting unique features, but in general they enable you to create, change, and delete partitions on a hard drive *without* destroying any of the programs or data stored there. Slick! These programs aren't on the CompTIA A+ Practical Application exam, but all PC techs use at least one of them, so let's explore three of the most well-known examples: Symantec's Norton PartitionMagic, Avanquest Partition Commander Professional, and the open source Linux tool, GParted.

Probably the most well-known third-party partition tool is PartitionMagic, although it's quite dated at this point. It supports older versions of Windows but has problems with Windows Vista/7. With it, you can create, resize, split, merge, delete, undelete, and convert partitions without destroying your data. Among the additional features it advertises are the capabilities to browse, copy, or move files and folders between supported partitions; to expand an NTFS partition—even if it's a system partition—without rebooting; to change NTFS cluster sizes; and to add new partitions for multiple OSs by using a simple wizard.

Avanquest offers a variety of related products, one of which is the very useful Partition Commander Professional. Unlike PartitionMagic, it supports all versions of Windows and enables you to play with your partitions without destroying your data. Among its niftier features are the capabilities to convert a dynamic disk to a basic disk nondestructively (which you can't do with the Microsoft-supplied Windows tools); to defrag the master file table on an NTFS partition; and to move unused space from one partition to another on the same physical drive, automatically resizing the partitions based on the amount of space you tell it to move. Figure 5.80 shows the Partition Commander dialog box for moving unused space between partitions.

The only problem with PartitionMagic and Partition Commander is that they cost money. There's nothing wrong with spending money on

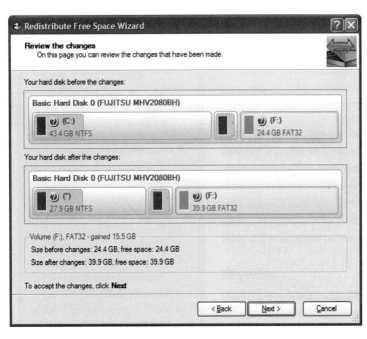

• **Figure 5.80** Partition Commander

a good product, but if you can find something that does the job for free, why not try it? If you think like I do, check out the Gnome Partition Editor, better known as GParted. You can find it at http://sourceforge.net/.

GParted is an incredibly powerful partition editor and does almost everything the for-pay partition editors do, but it's free. It's still in beta—which means it's constantly changing and it has a few bugs (that are constantly being fixed)—but I use it all of the time and love it. If you look closely at Figure 5.81, you'll notice that it uses strange names for the partitions, such as HDA1 or HDB3. These are Linux conventions and are well documented in GParted's Help screens. Take a little time and you'll love GParted too.

The one downside to GParted is that it is a Linux program—because no Windows version exists, you need Linux to run it. So how do you run Linux on a Windows system without actually installing Linux on your hard drive? The answer is easy—the folks at GParted will give you the tools to burn a live CD that boots Linux so you can run GParted!

A live CD is a complete OS on a CD. Understand this is not an installation CD like your Windows installation disc. The OS is already installed on the CD. You boot from the live CD and the OS loads into RAM, just like the OS on your hard drive loads into RAM at boot. As the live CD boots, it recognizes your hardware and loads the proper drivers into RAM so everything works. You get everything you'd expect from an OS with one big exception: a live CD does not touch your hard drive. Of course you may run programs (such as GParted) that work on your hard drive, which makes live

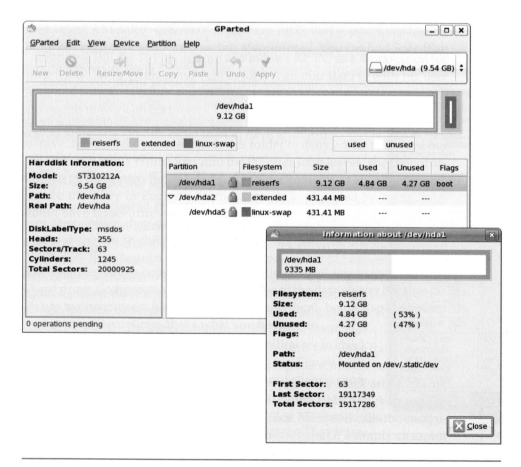

• **Figure 5.81**   GParted in action

CDs popular with PC techs, because you can toss them into a cranky system and run utilities.

The truly intrepid might want to consider using The Ultimate Boot CD (UBCD), basically a huge pile of useful freeware utilities compiled by frustrated technician Ben Burrows, who couldn't find a boot disk when he needed one. His Web site is www.ultimatebootcd.com. The UBCD has more than 100 different tools, all placed on a single live CD. It has all of the low-level diagnostic tools for all of the hard drive makers, four or five different partitioning tools, S.M.A.R.T. viewers, hard drive wiping utilities, and hard drive cloning tools (nice for when you want to replace a hard drive with a larger one). Little documentation is provided, however, and many of the tools require experience way beyond the scope of the Practical Application exam. I will tell you that I have a copy and I use it.

Chapter 5 Review

■ Chapter Summary

After reading this chapter and completing the exercises, you should understand the following about implementing hard drives.

Install hard drives

- Older PATA drives use a 40-wire cable, while the newer Ultra DMA drives use an 80-wire cable. Either round or flat and containing no twists, each ribbon cable supports two drives. A diagram on the hard drive's housing shows how to set its jumpers to identify it as master, slave, standalone (on some drives), or cable select (cable position determines whether the drive will be master or slave). Two devices on one cable must both be set to cable select, and the cable itself must also be cable select, as indicated with a pinhole through one wire. Align the colored stripe on the cable with pin 1 on the controller and the drive. Use a Molex connector to provide power to the drive.

- SATA supports only a single device per controller channel, so there are no master, slave, or cable-select jumpers. SATA controller and power cables are keyed to prevent incorrect insertion. You can connect a PATA device to a SATA motherboard controller by way of a SATA bridge.

- Solid-state drives are PATA, SATA, eSATA, SCSI, or USB. Before upgrading or installing an SSD, you should verify that the new drive uses the same interface as the old drive or that you have the proper connection type available. As for any hardware device, it is also important to ensure you have the appropriate SSD drivers and firmware before installation.

Configure CMOS and install drivers

- While system BIOS supports built-in PATA controllers, hard drives require configuration in CMOS. ATAPI devices require software drivers to provide BIOS support. Built-in SATA controllers on a motherboard also require software drivers, as does a SATA controller on a separate expansion card. All SATA devices get BIOS support from the SATA controller, but some drives require additional configuration. In particular, with RAID systems, you may also have to configure controller

Flash ROM settings for the specific drives you install.

- When the hard drive type is set to Auto, PATA devices can be queried directly by BIOS routines, resulting in the correct CMOS settings for up to four ATA devices. Autodetection made hard drive types obsolete. Because PATA drives have CHS values stored inside them, the BIOS routine, when set to Auto, updates the CMOS each time the computer boots. An alternative is to run the autodetection option from the CMOS screen.

- Even if the autodetect feature indicates that an optical-media ATAPI drive has been installed, this merely shows that the drive is connected properly and has the option to function as a boot device. This autodetection does *not* provide true BIOS support. You must still install drivers to provide the BIOS.

- If the autodetection feature of the CMOS utility does not detect a drive, it is installed incorrectly or the drive itself is bad. Check the master/slave jumper settings. Make sure that the ribbon cable aligns pin 1 with pin 1, and that the Molex connector is supplying power to the drive.

- Once you've checked the physical connections, run through these issues in CMOS. Is the controller enabled? Is the storage technology—LBA, Large, INT13, ATA/ATAPI-6—properly set up? What about the data-transfer settings for PIO and DMA modes? Similarly, can the motherboard support the type of drive you're installing? If not, you can flash the BIOS or get a hard drive controller that goes into an expansion slot. With nonintegrated hard drive controllers, such as those that come with many SATA drives, make sure that you've installed the proper drivers for the controller. Always check the manufacturer's Web site for new drivers.

Troubleshoot hard drive installation

- Getting a drive installed and recognized by the system takes four things: jumpers (PATA only), data cable, power, and CMOS setup recognizing the drive. If you miss or mess up any of these steps, you have a drive that doesn't exist according to the PC! To troubleshoot hard drives, simply work your way through each step to figure out what went wrong.

- Once you've checked the physical connections, run through these issues in CMOS. Is the controller enabled? Is the storage technology—LBA, INT13, ATA/ATAPI- 6—properly set up? Similarly, can the motherboard support the type of drive you're installing? If not, you have a couple of options. You can flash the BIOS with an upgraded BIOS from the manufacturer or you can get a hard drive controller that goes into an expansion slot.

Explain the partitions available in Windows

- Partitions are electronic subdivisions of physical hard drives into groups of cylinders. After partitioning, each partition must be formatted before it can be used to store files. Every hard drive must contain at least one partition, but many users choose to create multiple partitions on a single hard drive to make backups easier or to install another operating system for dual-boot or multiboot environments. Windows 2000/XP and Windows Vista/7 support two partitioning schemes: master boot record (MBR) and dynamic storage partitioning.

- Basic disks use the master boot record (MBR) partitioning scheme. The MBR, a tiny bit of code in the first sector of a hard drive, looks for a partition in the partition table with a valid operating system. Every basic disk has one and only one MBR.

- Basic disks support primary and extended partitions. Windows limits each basic-disk hard drive to a maximum of four partitions, with no more than one extended partition. Primary partitions can receive drive letters and support bootable operating systems. Extended partitions, which do not receive drive letters, house logical drives, which can receive drive letters. In Windows 2000/XP and Windows Vista/7, both primary partitions and logical drives may use folder mount points instead of drive letters.

- Every partition contains a volume boot sector in its first sector. During boot-up, a hard drive's MBR finds the active partition and loads the boot record code from the partition's volume boot sector. The boot record code finds and loads the operating system. Only active primary partitions can boot an operating system. Only one primary partition per hard drive can be marked as active.

- Primary partitions and logical drives may be accessed via a folder mount point rather than a drive letter. Use the administrative tool Disk Management to create mount points and change drive letters.

- Hard drives that use the dynamic storage partitioning scheme instead of an MBR are called dynamic disks by Microsoft. Dynamic disks use volumes rather than partitions and are accessible only in Windows 2000 and later. There are no primary or extended volumes—a volume is simply a volume. Dynamic disks and volumes offer capabilities not possible with partitions, namely spanning, striping, and RAID.

- Dynamic disks support a total of five types of volumes: simple, spanned, striped, mirrored, and RAID 5. A simple volume is similar to a primary partition in that it can store files and can receive a drive letter or be mounted to a folder. Spanned volumes combine space from several volumes and treat them as a single volume. After one volume is full, files are written to the next volume in the span. Striped volumes are similar to spanned volumes, but files are deliberately split across volumes to increase read/write access time. Neither spanned nor striped volumes are fault tolerant. RAID 1, or mirrored volumes, use exactly two volumes that are exact duplicates of each other. You suffer a slight performance hit but make up for it with fault tolerance. RAID 5, or striping with parity, requires at least three same-size volumes, enjoys the speed boost of striping, and is fault tolerant.

- Other partition types are hidden and swap partitions. Hidden partitions are not visible to the operating system and are often used by PC manufacturers to store emergency restore images of the system partition. Swap partitions are used by Linux and BSD systems for virtual memory and function much the same as Windows page files.

- Most operating systems allow you to create partitions during the installation process. To create partitions at other times, you use a dedicated partitioning tool. Older versions of Windows shipped with the command-line program FDISK (fdisk.exe) for this purpose. Windows 2000 and later versions ship with a graphical tool called Disk

Management to manage partitions, convert basic disks to dynamic disks, and manage volumes. Linux uses several partitioning tools, such as FDISK (same name, but different from the Windows version) and GParted.

Discuss hard drive formatting options

■ After a disk has been partitioned, it must be formatted before it can be used. Formatting creates a file system and root directory. You can use the Windows command-line program FORMAT (format.com) or the GUI tool Disk Management to format a partition or volume. Current versions of Windows support three file systems: FAT16, FAT32, and NTFS.

■ The base storage area for hard drives is a sector, which can store up to 512 bytes of data. If a file is smaller than 512 bytes and does not fill a sector, the rest of the sector remains unused because only one file can reside in any one sector. If a file is more than 512 bytes, the file is split into pieces, with each piece residing in a different sector. If the sectors containing all of the pieces of a single file are not contiguous, the file is said to be fragmented.

■ MS-DOS version 2.1 first supported the file allocation table (FAT). The FAT is a data structure similar to a two-column spreadsheet that tracks where data is stored on a hard drive.

■ FAT comes in several variations: FAT12, FAT16, and FAT32. The number indicates how many bits are available in the "left side of the FAT spreadsheet." Floppy disks use FAT12, while hard drives can use FAT16 or FAT32.

■ Every version of Windows fully supports FAT16, which uses only 16 bits to address sector locations. This translates to 2^{16}, or 64 K locations. With 64 K locations of 512-byte sectors, 64 K × 512 bytes hits the ceiling at 32 MB. For this reason, FAT16 partitions were initially limited to 32 MB. FAT16 later added a feature called clustering that treats a set of contiguous sectors as a single FAT unit. These clusters (also called file allocation units) allow a maximum partition size of 2 GB.

■ Since FAT16, a cluster rather than a sector is the basic unit of storage. Unlike sectors, the size of a cluster is not fixed but changes with the size of the partition. Because FAT16 still supported only a maximum of 64 K storage units, the formatting

program set the number of sectors in each cluster according to the size of the partition.

■ After the format program creates the FAT, it tests each sector and places a special status code (FFF7) in the FAT for any bad sectors so they won't be used. Good sectors are marked with 0000. When an application saves a file, the OS starts writing the file to the first available cluster marked as good. If the entire file fits in the cluster, the OS places the end-of-file marker (FFFF) in the cluster's status area. If the file does not fit entirely in a single cluster, the OS searches for the next available cluster. Once found, its location is written to the status area of the preceding cluster holding a piece of the file, and the OS writes the next 512 bytes of the file in the available cluster. This continues until the file has been completely written and the final cluster in the chain receives the status code FFFF in the FAT. After saving the entire file, the OS lists the filename and starting cluster in the file's folder.

■ As a file is split across multiple noncontiguous clusters, the file becomes fragmented. Fragmentation slows read/write access because the OS has to piece together the many fragments of the file. Every version of Windows, except NT, comes with a Disk Defragmenter program that reorganizes the clusters of hard drive data so files are stored wherever possible in contiguous clusters.

■ FAT32 was introduced with Windows 95 OS2. FAT32, which uses 32 bits to describe each cluster, supports partitions up to 2 terabytes. FAT32 creates smaller clusters and therefore stores files more efficiently than FAT16.

■ The New Technology File System (NTFS) was introduced with Windows NT and has gone through several versions. The most recent version, used since Windows 2000, is referred to as NTFS 5. NTFS does not use a FAT such as FAT16 or FAT32, but instead uses a master file table (MFT).

■ NTFS offers several major improvements over FAT, including redundancy, security, compression, encryption, disk quotas, and cluster sizing. A backup copy of the most critical parts of the MFT is stored in the middle of the disk, where it is less likely to become damaged.

■ With NTFS, you can protect individual files and folders by allowing only certain users or groups access to them. You can compress individual files or folders to save hard drive space and can encrypt files or folders so they are unreadable to anyone but you. You can also limit the amount of disk space per user by enforcing disk quotas. Finally, you can adjust cluster sizes to allow support of partitions up to 16 exabytes.

Partition and format hard drives

- Any software that can boot up a system is called an operating system, and any removable media that contains a bootable operating system is generically called a boot device or boot disc. All Windows and Linux operating system installation CD/DVDs are boot devices. You can also make your own boot device, complete with handy tech tools.

- Windows 2000/XP installation discs walk you through the process of partitioning and formatting your hard drive. After accepting the license agreement, you can simply press ENTER and Windows partitions and formats your drive as one large primary partition. If you prefer to partition only a portion of the hard drive, you can do so manually by pressing the letter C to create a partition, entering the desired size in MB, and pressing ENTER. Finally, you are offered several options for formatting before the installation continues. It is recommended that you choose NTFS. Note that the disk is partitioned and formatted as a basic disk. Once Windows is installed, you can convert basic disks to dynamic disks with the Disk Management tool.

- Windows Vista installation discs also walk you through the partitioning and formatting process but use a graphical user interface, thus greatly simplifying the process. When you click the Custom install button, you're taken to the partitioning screen, where you can create, delete, edit, and format partitions. You can only format partitions as NTFS off of the Vista installation disc, and you can't create extended partitions unless you create more than three partitions on a single disk.

- You can change or remove drive letters with the Disk Management tool. Only the C: drive cannot be changed. Drive letters are assigned by going down the list of drives and assigning the next available drive letter, with hard drives taking precedence over optical drives.

- All new disk drives must be initialized by Disk Management before you can use them.

The initialization process places information on the drive identifying it as part of a particular system. New drives are always initialized as basic disks but can be converted to dynamic disks by right-clicking and choosing Convert to Dynamic Disk. Creating a partition or volume is just as simple. Right-click the drive and choose Create Partition or New Volume. Remember that you must create logical drives inside an extended partition before you can format and use it to store files.

- Once a disk has been initialized and partitioned, you can format it. Microsoft requires using NTFS for any partition larger than 32 GB. Performing a Quick Format skips the checking of clusters, which results in a faster format but is risky.

- The Windows installation program creates a tiny partition on the C: drive, which is used to later convert the disk to a dynamic disk. Although you can format and use that space for file storage, it is recommended that you leave it as is.

- A mount point is a folder on an NTFS drive that provides access to another drive that may or may not have a drive letter. The new drive extends the capacity of the drive providing the folder mount point. Although the files in the mount point folder appear to be stored on the first drive, they are actually stored on the additional drive. Create a mount point by first creating a folder on an NTFS drive. Then launch Disk Management, select the additional partition/volume, right-click, and choose Change Drive Letter and Paths. From there, choose Add and browse to the mount point folder you created earlier.

- You can format any partition/volume in My Computer/Computer by right-clicking and choosing Format. Alternatively, you can format partitions/volumes from the Disk Management tool. Both methods offer you options to perform a Quick Format and enable compression.

Maintain and troubleshoot hard drives

- Hard drive maintenance can be broken down into two distinct functions: checking the disk occasionally for failed clusters and keeping data organized on the drive so it can be accessed quickly.

- Microsoft offers Error-checking for scanning hard drives. It checks for bad clusters and, if found, marks them as bad so no data gets written to those areas of the hard drive. Additionally, it looks for invalid filenames and attempts to fix them, and it searches for and erases lost cluster chains.

- To run Error-checking in Windows, right-click a drive to view its Properties window, choose the Tools tab, and click the Check Now button. Check the box next to *Automatically fix file system errors*, but save the option to *Scan for and attempt recovery of bad sectors* for times when you actually suspect a problem.

- You should run Error-checking and Disk Defragmenter once a month as preventive maintenance to keep your system running smoothly. Both are available on the Tools tab of the drive's Properties window.

- The Disk Cleanup utility deletes files from the Recycle Bin, temporary Internet files, copies of downloaded Java or ActiveX applets, and other temporary files on your hard drive. You can access Disk Cleanup in all versions of Windows by choosing Start | All Programs | Accessories | System Tools | Disk Cleanup. Run Disk Cleanup once a month.

- Hard drive problems fall into three broad categories: installation, data corruption, and dying hard drives. Installation errors can happen at any of the four steps: connectivity, CMOS, partitioning, or formatting. When troubleshooting, you should always walk back through each step and check for problems.

- Usually showing up at boot time, a connectivity error indicates that something isn't plugged in correctly or something has become unplugged. Some connectivity errors are harmless, such as plugging in the data cable backward for a PATA drive, while others, such as installing the power cable backward, will destroy your drive. The autodetect function of your BIOS will not detect a drive unless it is installed correctly, making it a great connectivity verifier. Some PATA drives simply will not work on the same controller.

- If autodetect fails to see the drive in question, it's probably a connectivity problem.

- Partitioning errors generally fall into two groups: failing to partition at all and making the wrong size/type of partition. If you try to access a nonpartitioned drive, you'll get an "Invalid Drive Specifications" error and you can't see the drive in anything but CMOS, FDISK, and Disk Management.

- If you try to access a drive that's not formatted, Windows displays a drive "is not accessible" error, while you'll get an "Invalid media" error from a C:\ prompt. Format the drive unless you're certain that the drive has already been formatted. Corrupted files can also create the "Invalid media" error.

- The "Trying to recover lost allocation unit" error means the drive has bad sectors. Time to replace the drive.

- If a newly installed drive fails to work, do a "mental reinstall." If the drive does not show in CMOS autodetect, recheck the cables, master/slave jumper settings, and power. If it shows up, make sure you remembered to partition and format it. Remember the drive must be marked as Active to be bootable.

- Power surges, accidental shutdowns, corrupted installation media, and viruses are among the causes of corrupted data in individual sectors. These errors usually show while Windows is running. If core boot files become corrupted, you may see text errors such as "NTLDR is missing or corrupt," "Error loading operating system," or "Invalid BOOT.INI." Older systems may generate a "sector not found" error. The first fix for any of these problems is to run an error-checking utility.

- To replace a single corrupt file on a Windows XP or earlier, you must know the location of the numbered Windows CAB (cabinet) file that contains the file you need and how to extract the file from the CAB file. Use the EXPAND program with Windows 2000/XP to get a new copy of the desired file from the CAB file on the installation disc. EXPAND searches all CAB files to find the file you specify, and then expands it and places it in the C:\ folder.

- Almost all drives today have built-in error correction code (ECC) that constantly checks the drive for bad sectors. If it detects a bad sector, it marks the sector as bad in the drive's internal error map so it's invisible to the system. If the ECC finds a bad sector, however, you will get a corrupted data error when the computer attempts to read the bad sector.

- The powerful SpinRite utility from Gibson Research marks sectors as bad or good more accurately than ECC and does not disturb the data. When it finds a bad sector with data in it, SpinRite uses powerful algorithms that usually recover the data on all but the most badly damaged sectors. Without SpinRite, you must use a low-level formatting program supplied by the hard drive manufacturer, which will wipe out all data on the drive.

- If a hard drive is truly physically damaged, it cannot be fixed. Physical problems manifest themselves in two ways: either the drive works properly but makes a lot of noise, or the drive seems to disappear. If you hear a continuous high-pitched squeal; a series of clacks, a short pause, and then another series of clacks; or a continuous grinding or rumbling, your hard drive is about to die. Back up your critical data and replace the drive. If the drive that contains your operating system disappears, the system locks up or you get the error message "No Boot Device Present" when you try to reboot. If the problem is with a second

drive, it simply stops showing up in My Computer/Computer.

- If your drive makes noise or disappears, first run the System Setup program to see if autodetect sees the drive. If it does, the drive doesn't have a physical problem. If autodetect fails, shut down the system and remove the ribbon cable, but leave the power cable attached. Restart the system and listen to the drive. If the drive spins up, the drive is getting good power, which usually means the drive is good. Next, check for an unplugged power cord or incorrectly set jumpers. If the drive doesn't spin up, try another power connector. If it still doesn't spin up and you've triple-checked the jumpers and ribbon cable, you have a problem with the onboard electronics and the drive is dead.

■ Key Terms

active partition (102)
autodetection (97)
basic disk (101)
boot sector (101)
CHKDSK (139)
cluster (109)
data structure (108)
defragment (140)
Disk Cleanup (141)
Disk Management (106)
disk quota (117)
dual-boot (103)
dynamic disk (101)
encrypting file system (EFS) (115)
Error-checking (139)
error correction code (ECC) (144)
extended partition (102)
EXPAND (144)
FAT32 (114)
FDISK (106)
file allocation table (FAT) (108)
file allocation unit (109)

file system (101)
formatting (108)
fragmentation (111)
high-level formatting (109)
logical drive (102)
master boot record (MBR) (101)
master file table (MFT) (114)
mirrored volume (106)
mount point (136)
multiboot (103)
New Technology File System (NTFS) (114)
operating system (OS) (101)
partition (100)
partition table (101)
partitioning (100)
primary partition (102)
RAID 5 volume (106)
simple volume (105)
spanned volume (105)
stripe set (136)
volume (100)
volume boot sector (102)

■ Key Term Quiz

Use the Key Terms list to complete the sentences that follow. Not all terms will be used.

1. The MBR checks the partition table to find the _active_ or bootable partition.

2. If a file is not stored in contiguous clusters, you can improve hard drive performance by using the _defragment_ tool.

3. Instead of using a FAT, NTFS uses a(n) _Master File Table (MFT)_ with a backup copy placed in the middle of the disk for better security.

4. If you are installing Windows 2000/XP or Windows Vista/7, the best file system to choose is _NTFS_.

5. The Windows tool that attempts to fix invalid filenames, erases lost clusters, and seals off bad clusters is called _Error checking_ (or *CHKDSK*).

6. A great way to verify that a drive is installed correctly is to use _autodetect_.

7. If an XP or earlier operating system file has become corrupted or is missing, you can replace it by using _Expand_ to extract a specific file from a CAB file.

8. Only a single _primary partition_ may be set to active on one drive.

9. The _Disk Cleanup_ utility is useful for purging your system of unnecessary temporary files.

10. A(n) _mirror volume_ requires exactly two volumes and is extremely fault tolerant.

■ Multiple-Choice Quiz

1. Which is the most complete list of file systems Windows 2000/XP and Vista/7 can use?

   A. FAT16, FAT32, NTFS

   B. FAT16, FAT32, FAT64, NTFS

   C. FAT16, FAT32

   D. FAT16, NTFS

2. The Disk Cleanup utility removes which types of unneeded files?

   A. Temporary Internet files

   B. Temporary files that remain when an application is closed

   C. Programs no longer in use

   D. Both A and B

3. Which of the following correctly identifies the four possible entries in a file allocation table?

   A. Filename, date, time, size

   B. Number of the starting cluster, number of the ending cluster, number of used clusters, number of available clusters

   C. An end-of-file marker, a bad-sector marker, code indicating the cluster is available, the number of the cluster where the next part of the file is stored

   D. Filename, folder location, starting cluster number, ending cluster number

4. You receive an "Invalid media" error when trying to access a hard drive. What is the most likely cause of the error?

   A. The drive has not been partitioned.

   B. The drive has not been set to active.

   C. The drive has not been formatted.

   D. The drive has died.

5. Which of the following is an advantage of partitioning a hard drive into more than one partition?

   A. It enables a single hard drive to store more than one operating system.

   B. It protects against boot sector viruses.

   C. It uses less power.

   D. It allows for dynamic disk RAID 5.

6. If you install two IDE drives on the same cable, how will the computer differentiate them?

   A. The CMOS setup allows you to configure them.

   B. You must set jumpers to determine which drive functions as master and which functions as slave.

   C. You will set jumpers so each drive has a unique ID number.

   D. The drives will be differentiated by whether you place them before or after the twist in the ribbon cable.

7. What does NTFS use to provide security for individual files and folders?

   A. Dynamic disks

   B. ECC

   C. Access control list

   D. MFT

8. Which of the following statements is true about extended partitions?

    Ⓐ. They are optional.

    B. They are assigned drive letters when they are created.

    C. They may be set to active.

    D. Each drive must have at least one extended partition.

9. Adam wants to create a new simple volume in some unallocated space on his hard drive, but when he right-clicks the space in Disk Management he sees only an option to create a new partition. What is the problem?

    A. The drive has developed bad sectors.

    Ⓑ. The drive is a basic disk and not a dynamic disk.

    C. The drive has less than 32 GB of unallocated space.

    D. The drive is jumpered as a slave.

10. Jaime wishes to check her hard drive for errors. What tool should she use?

    A. FDISK

    B. Format

    C. Disk Management

    Ⓓ. Error-checking

11. To make your files unreadable by others, what should you use?

    A. Clustering

    B. Compression

    C. Disk quotas

    Ⓓ. Encryption

12. Which of the following utilities should you run once a month to maintain the speed of your PC?

    Ⓐ. Disk Defragmenter

    B. FDISK

    C. Disk Management

    D. System Commander

13. Which two terms identify a bootable partition?

    A. Master, FAT

    B. Slave, FAT

    Ⓒ. Primary, Active

    D. Primary, NTFS

14. For what purpose can you use disk quotas?

    A. Limit users to a specific drive.

    B. Extend the capacity of a volume.

    C. Manage dual-boot environments.

    Ⓓ. Limit users' space on a drive.

15. What is the capacity of a single sector?

    A. 256 bytes

    B. 512 bits

    Ⓒ. 512 bytes

    D. 4 kilobytes

■ Essay Quiz

1. Your new boss is pretty old-school, having cut his teeth on Windows 3.11 and Windows 95. Accordingly, you discover that all of the Windows XP computers in the office use only FAT32 for their hard drives. Write a two- to three-paragraph memo that (gently) extols the virtues and benefits of NTFS over FAT32.

2. You've been tasked by your supervisor to teach basic hard drive partitioning to a couple of new hires. Write a short essay describing the difference between simple volumes, spanned volumes, and striped volumes. What's better? When would you use one and not the other?

3. One of your employees doesn't quite get it when it comes to computers and keeps complaining that his hard drive is stopped up, by which he most likely means "full." He installed a second hard drive by using some steps he found on the Internet, but he claims it doesn't work. On closer examination, you determine that the drive shows up in CMOS but not in Windows—he didn't partition or format the drive! Write a short essay describing partitioning and formatting, including the tools used to accomplish this task on a second hard drive.

4. Your office has a PC shared by four people to do intensive graphics work. The hard drive has about 400 GB of free space. Write a memo on how you could use disk quotas to make certain that each user takes no more than 25 percent of the free space.

5. Your office has sev
GB drives in the
Write a short e
use spannin
extra driv

Lab Projects

• Lab Project 5.1

Grab a test system with multiple drives and experiment with the partitioning tools in Windows Disk Management. Create various partition combinations, such as all primary or all extended

with logical drives. Change basic disks into dynami disks and create volumes that span multiple drives. Add to them. You get the idea—experiment and have fun!

• Lab Project 5.2

Partitioning gets all the glory and exposure in tech classes because, frankly, it's cool to be able to do some of the things possible with the Disk Management console. But the experienced tech does not forget about the other half of drive preparation: formatting. Windows offers you at least two different file systems. In this lab, you'll put them through their paces.

In at least one OS, partition a drive with two equal partitions and format one as FAT32 and the other as NTFS. Then get a couple of monster files (larger than 50 MB) and move them to those partitions. Did you notice any difference in transfer speed? Examine the drives in My Computer. Do they show the same amount of used space?

• Lab Project 5.3

If your lab has the equipment, install a second hard drive in your system. Install it on the same cable as the existing drive and jumper it as the slave. (You may need to jumper the existing drive as master.) Reboot, enter CMOS, and verify that both drives

are detected. Boot into your operating system and verify that both drives are accessible. (You may need to partition and format the second drive before it is actually usable.)

Mastering the Windows Command Line

*...u wanted to know who I am,
...ero Cool? Well, let me explain
the New World Order.
Governments and corporations
need people like you and me. We
are Samurai...the Keyboard
Cowboys...and all those other
people who have no idea what's
going on are the cattle....
Moooo."*

—THE PLAGUE, *HACKERS*

In this chapter, you will learn how to

- **Explain the operation of the command-line interface**
- **Execute fundamental commands from the command line**
- **Manipulate files from the command line**

Whenever I teach a class of new techs and we get to the section on working with the command line, I'm invariably met with a chorus of moans and a barrage of questions and statements. "Why do we need to learn this old stuff?" "We're running Windows Vista, not Windows 3.1!" "Is this ritualistic hazing appropriate in an IT class?"

For techs who master the interface, the command line provides a powerful, quick, and elegant tool for working on a PC. Learning that interface and understanding how to make it work is not only useful, but also necessary for all techs who want to go beyond baby-tech status. You simply cannot work on all PCs without knowing the command line! I'm not the only one who thinks this way. The CompTIA A+ Practical Application exam tests you on a variety of command-line commands for doing everything from renaming a file to rebuilding a system file.

If you're interested in moving beyond Windows and into other operating systems such as Linux, you'll find that pretty much all of the serious work is done at a command prompt. Even the Apple Macintosh operating system (OS), for years a purely graphical operating system, now supports a command prompt. Why is the command prompt so popular? Well, for three reasons: First, if you know what you're doing, you can do most jobs more quickly by typing a text command than by clicking through a graphical user interface (GUI). Second, a command-line interface doesn't take much operating system firepower, so it's the natural choice for jobs where you don't need or don't want (or can't get to, in the case of Linux) a full-blown GUI for your OS. Third, text commands take very little bandwidth when sent across the network to another system.

So, are you sold on the idea of the command prompt? Good! This chapter gives you a tour of the Windows command-line interface, explaining how it works and what's happening behind the scenes. You'll learn the concepts and master essential commands, and then you'll work with files and folders throughout your drives. The chapter wraps up with a brief section on encryption and file compression in the "Beyond A+" section. A good tactic for absorbing the material in this chapter is to try out each command or bit of information as it is presented. If you have some experience working with a command prompt, many of these commands should be familiar to you. If the command line is completely new to you, please take the red pill and join me as we step into the matrix.

Historical/Conceptual

Operating systems existed long before PCs were invented. Ancient, massive computers called *mainframes* and *minicomputers* employed sophisticated operating systems. It wasn't until the late 1970s that IBM went looking for an OS for a new *microcomputer*—the official name for the PC—the company was developing, called the IBM Personal Computer, better known as the PC. After being rebuffed by a company called Digital Research, IBM went to a tiny company that had written a popular new version of the programming language called BASIC. They asked the company president if he could create an OS for the IBM PC. Although his company had never actually written an OS, he brazenly said "Sure!" That man was Bill Gates, and the tiny company was Microsoft.

After shaking hands with IBM representatives, Bill Gates hurriedly began to search for an OS based on the Intel 8086 processor. He found a primitive OS called *Quick-and-Dirty Operating System* (QDOS), which was written by a one-man shop, and he purchased it for a few thousand dollars. After several minor changes, Microsoft released it as MS-DOS (Microsoft Disk Operating System) version 1.1. Although primitive by today's standards, MS-DOS 1.1 could provide all of the functions an OS needed. Over the years, MS-DOS went through version after version until the last Microsoft version, MS-DOS 6.22, was released in 1994. Microsoft licensed MS-DOS to PC makers so they could add their own changes and then rename the program. IBM called its version PC-DOS.

DOS used a command-line interface. You typed a command at a prompt, and DOS responded to that command. When Microsoft introduced Windows 95 and Windows NT, many computer users and techs thought that the command-line interface would go away, but techs not only continued to use the command line, they also *needed it* to troubleshoot and fix problems. With Windows 2000, it seemed once again that the command line would die, but again, that just didn't turn out to be the case.

Finally recognizing the importance of the command-line interface, Microsoft beefed it up in Windows XP and then again in Windows Vista. The command line in Windows XP and in Vista offers commands and options for those commands that go well beyond anything seen in previous Microsoft operating systems. This chapter starts with some essential concepts of the command line and then turns to more specific commands.

■ Deciphering the Command-line Interface

So how does a command-line interface work? It's a little like having an Instant Message conversation with your computer. The computer tells you it's ready to receive commands by displaying a specific set of characters called a **prompt**.

```
Computer: Want to play a game?
Mike: _
```

You type a command and press ENTER to send it.

```
Mike: What kind of game?
Computer: _
```

The PC goes off and executes the command, and when it's finished, it displays a new prompt, often along with some information about what it did.

```
Computer: A very fun game...
Mike: _
```

Once you get a new prompt, it means the computer is ready for your next instruction. You can give the computer commands in the graphical user interface (GUI) of Windows as well, just in a different way, by clicking buttons and menu options with your mouse instead of typing on the keyboard. The results are basically the same: you tell the computer to do something and it responds.

When you type in a command from the command line, you cause the computer to respond. As an example, suppose you want to find out the contents of a particular folder. From the command line, you'd type a command (in this case **DIR**, but more on that in a minute), and the computer would respond by displaying a screen like the one in Figure 6.1.

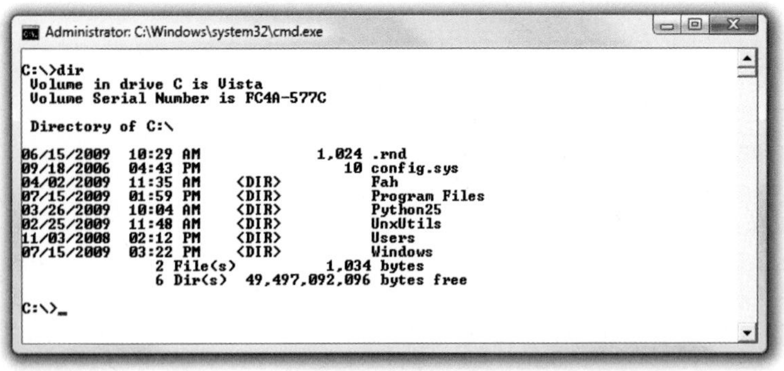

• **Figure 6.1**   Contents of C: directory from the command line

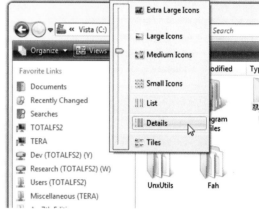

• **Figure 6.2**   Contents of C: in Computer—Icon view

• **Figure 6.3**   Selecting Details view in Computer

In the Windows GUI, you would open My Computer or Computer and click the C: drive icon to see the contents of that directory. The results might look like Figure 6.2, which at first glance isn't much like the command-line screen; however, simply by choosing a different view (Figure 6.3), you can make the results look quite a bit like the command-line version, albeit much prettier (Figure 6.4). The point here is that whichever interface you use, the information available to you is essentially the same.

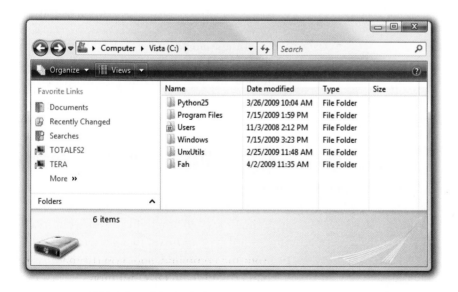

• **Figure 6.4**   Contents of C: in Computer—Details view

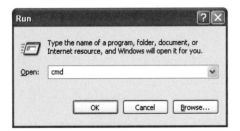

● **Figure 6.5** Type **CMD** in the Run dialog box to open a command-line window.

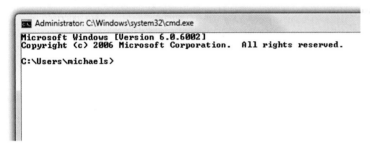

● **Figure 6.6** The command-line-interface window with a C:\prompt

Accessing the Command Line

Before you can use the command-line interface, you have to open it. You can use various methods to do this, depending on the flavor of Windows you are using. Some methods are simpler than others; just make sure that you know at least one, or you'll never get off the starting line!

One easy way to access the command-line interface in Windows 2000 or XP is by using the **Run dialog box**. Click the Start button, and then select Run. If you're using Windows 2000 or Windows XP, type **CMD** or **COMMAND** and press the ENTER key (Figure 6.5). If you are using Vista, you access the command-line interface through the Start menu Search box with the same two commands. A window pops up on your screen with a black background and white text—this is the command-line interface. Alternatively, buried in the Start menu of *most* computers, under Programs | Accessories, is a link to the command-line interface. In Windows 2000, XP, and Vista, it's called command prompt. These links, just like the Run dialog box, pull up a nice command-line-interface window (Figure 6.6). If you are displaying the command-line-interface in Windows Vista, notice that it uses a newer version number and copyright date. Also notice that the default user profile directory is C:\Users*User name* rather than C:\Documents and Settings*User name* as in previous operating systems (shown in Figure 6.7). To close the command-line-interface window, you can either click the Close box, as on any other window, or simply type **EXIT** at any command prompt and press ENTER.

If you attempt to enter a command at the Windows Vista command prompt that requires elevated or administrative privileges, you receive a UAC "Windows needs your permission to continue" dialog box (you'll learn more about UAC in the next chapter, "Securing Windows Resources"). You can also "manually" run a command with elevated privileges by right-clicking a command-prompt shortcut and then selecting *Run as administrator*. If you are prompted for administrator password or credentials, enter them as needed.

● **Figure 6.7** The Windows Vista command-line-interface window

You can also create an administrator shortcut to the Windows Vista command prompt by right-clicking on the desktop and selecting New | Shortcut. Then for the location of the item, type **CMD** and click Next. Type **CMD** to name the shortcut and click Finish. Your shortcut appears on the desktop. Next, right-click the shortcut and select the Advanced button. In the Advanced Properties dialog box, check the *Run as administrator* box and click OK. You have now created a Windows Vista command-prompt shortcut that will always run with administrative privileges.

Try This!

Accessing the Command Line

This chapter will be much more fun if you follow along with your own command line, so Try This! Using one of the methods outlined in this section, access a command prompt in Windows. Just remember that everything you do at the prompt can affect the functioning of your PC. So don't delete stuff if you don't know what it's for.

The Command Prompt

The command prompt is always *focused* on a specific folder. This is important because any commands you issue are performed *on the files in the folder* on which the prompt is focused. For example, if you see a prompt that looks like the following line, you know that the focus is on the root directory of the C: drive:

```
C:\>
```

If you see a prompt that looks like Figure 6.8, you know that the focus is on the C:\Diploma\APLUS\ folder of the C: drive. The trick to using a command line is first to focus the prompt on the drive and folder where you want to work.

Filenames and File Formats

Windows manifests each program and piece of data as an individual file. Each file has a name, which is stored with the file on the drive. Windows inherits the idea of files from older operating systems—namely DOS—so a quick review of the old-style DOS filenames helps in understanding how Windows filenames work. Names are broken down into two parts: the filename and the extension. In true DOS, the filename could be no longer than eight characters, so you'll often see oddly named files on older systems. The extension, which is optional, could be up to three characters long in true DOS, and most computer programs and users continue to honor that old limit, even though it does not apply to modern PCs. No spaces or other illegal characters (/ \ [ ] | ÷ + = ; , * ?) could be used in the filename or extension. The filename and extension are separated by a period, or *dot*. This naming system was known as the 8.3 (eight-dot-three) naming system.

Here are some examples of acceptable true DOS filenames:

FRED.EXE	SYSTEM.INI	FILE1.DOC
DRIVER3.SYS	JANET	CODE33.H

Here are some unacceptable true DOS filenames:

4CHAREXT.EXEC   WAYTOOLONG.FIL   BAD÷CHAR.BAT   .NO

I mention the true DOS limitations for a simple reason: *backward compatibility*. Starting with *9x*, Windows versions did not suffer from the 8.3 filename limitation. Instead they supported filenames of up to 255 characters (but still with the three-character extension) by using a trick called long filenames (LFN). Windows systems using LFN retained complete backward compatibility by automatically creating two names for every file, an 8.3 filename and a long filename. Modern Windows using NTFS works almost exactly the same way as LFNs.

Tech Tip

Booting Directly to a Prompt

Early versions of Windows (3.x, 9x—though not Me) enabled you to boot directly to the command-line interface, not loading the GUI at all. Windows 2000 and Windows XP do not have that option, as the graphical portion of the OS is the OS. You can simulate the old user interface, if you're feeling brave, by altering the way the shortcut to a command prompt works.

In Windows 2000 or Windows XP (this won't work for Vista), go to Start | All Programs | Accessories (or Start | Programs | Accessories, depending on the configuration of your Start menu). Right-click the Command Prompt icon and select Properties to open the Command Prompt Properties dialog box. Select the Options tab, where you'll find four option boxes. The one you want is Display Options. By default, the command prompt displays in a window. Click the radio button for Full Screen, click OK, and you're good to go. The next time you open the command-line interface—from the shortcut only—it'll be full screen.

*At about this time, a lot of users who have been following along are staring at a screen with no buttons to click, and ESC doesn't do anything! No worries; remember that you can type **EXIT** and press ENTER to get out of the command-line interface.*

• **Figure 6.8**   Command prompt indicating focus on the C:\ Diploma\APLUS\ folder

You can hold down the F5 or F8 key during boot-up to access the Windows 2000, Windows XP, or Windows Vista Advanced Boot Options menu. This has an option to boot to Safe Mode with Command Prompt, which loads the GUI into Safe Mode and then overlays that with a command-line interface for rapid access to a prompt. This saves you the step of going to Start | Run and typing CMD. This is not the old-style command prompt–only interface!

• **Figure 6.9**   What kind of file is the one on the lower right?

```
Administrator: C:\Windows\system32\cmd.exe

C:\Photos>dir
 Volume in drive C is Vista
 Volume Serial Number is FC4A-577C

 Directory of C:\Photos

07/23/2009  10:44 AM    <DIR>          .
07/23/2009  10:44 AM    <DIR>          ..
07/23/2009  10:43 AM         6,903,739 Squirrel
07/23/2009  10:43 AM         6,903,739 Squirrel.psd
               2 File(s)     13,807,478 bytes
               2 Dir(s)  49,308,864,512 bytes free

C:\Photos>
```

• **Figure 6.10**   One file has no extension.

000 (nul)	032 sp	064 @	096 `	128 Ç	160 á	192 └	224 α
001 (soh)	033 !	065 A	097 a	129 ü	161 í	193 ┴	225 ß
002 (stx)	034 "	066 B	098 b	130 é	162 ó	194 ┬	226 Γ
003 (etx)	035 #	067 C	099 c	131 â	163 ú	195 ├	227 π
004 (eot)	036 $	068 D	100 d	132 ä	164 ñ	196 ─	228 Σ
005 (enq)	037 %	069 E	101 e	133 à	165 Ñ	197 ┼	229 σ
006 (ack)	038 &	070 F	102 f	134 å	166 ª	198 ╞	230 µ
007 (bel)	039 '	071 G	103 g	135 ç	167 º	199 ╟	231 τ
008 (bs)	040 (	072 H	104 h	136 ê	168 ¿	200 ╚	232 Φ
009 (tab)	041)	073 I	105 i	137 ë	169 ⌐	201 ╔	233 Θ
010 (lf)	042 *	074 J	106 j	138 è	170 ¬	202 ╩	234 Ω
011 (vt)	043 +	075 K	107 k	139 ï	171 ½	203 ╦	235 δ
012 (np)	044 ,	076 L	108 l	140 î	172 ¼	204 ╠	236 ∞
013 (cr)	045 -	077 M	109 m	141 ì	173 ¡	205 ═	237 φ
014 (so)	046 .	078 N	110 n	142 Ä	174 «	206 ╬	238 ε
015 (si)	047 /	079 O	111 o	143 Å	175 »	207 ╧	239 ∩
016 (dle)	048 0	080 P	112 p	144 É	176 ░	208 ╨	240 ≡
017 (dc1)	049 1	081 Q	113 q	145 æ	177 ▒	209 ╤	241 ±
018 (dc2)	050 2	082 R	114 r	146 Æ	178 ▓	210 ╥	242 ≥
019 (dc3)	051 3	083 S	115 s	147 ô	179 │	211 ╙	243 ≤
020 (dc4)	052 4	084 T	116 t	148 ö	180 ┤	212 ╘	244 ⌠
021 (nak)	053 5	085 U	117 u	149 ò	181 ╡	213 ╒	245 ⌡
022 (syn)	054 6	086 V	118 v	150 û	182 ╢	214 ╓	246 ÷
023 (etb)	055 7	087 W	119 w	151 ù	183 ╖	215 ╫	247 ≈
024 (can)	056 8	088 X	120 x	152 ÿ	184 ╕	216 ╪	248 °
025 (em)	057 9	089 Y	121 y	153 Ö	185 ╣	217 ┘	249 ·
026 (eof)	058 :	090 Z	122 z	154 Ü	186 ║	218 ┌	250 ·
027 (esc)	059 ;	091 [	123 {	155 ¢	187 ╗	219 █	251 √
028 (fs)	060 <	092 \	124 |	156 £	188 ╝	220 ▄	252 ⁿ
029 (gs)	061 =	093]	125 }	157 ¥	189 ╜	221 ▌	253 ²
030 (rs)	062 >	094 ^	126 ~	158 ₧	190 ╛	222 ▐	254 ■
031 (us)	063 ?	095 _	127 ⌂	159 ƒ	191 ┐	223 ▀	255

• **Figure 6.11**   ASCII characters

Whether you're running an ancient DOS system or the latest version of Windows Vista, the extension is very important, because the extension part of the filename tells the computer the type or function of the file. Program files use the extension .EXE (for executable) or .COM (for command). Anything that is not a program is some form of data to support a program. Different programs use different types of data files. The extension usually indicates which program uses that particular data file. For example, Microsoft Word uses the extension .DOC (.DOCX for Microsoft Office Word 2007), while WordPerfect uses .WPD and PowerPoint uses .PPT (.PPTX for Microsoft Office PowerPoint 2007). Graphics file extensions, in contrast, often reflect the graphics standard used to render the image, such as .GIF for CompuServe's Graphics Interchange Format or .JPG for the JPEG (Joint Photographic Experts Group) format.

Changing the extension of a data file does not affect its contents, but without the proper extension, Windows won't know which program uses it. You can see this clearly in My Computer. Figure 6.9 shows a folder with two identical image files. The one on top shows the Photoshop icon, which is the program Windows will use to open that file; the one on the bottom shows a generic icon because I deleted the extension. Windows GUI doesn't show file extensions by default. Figure 6.10 shows the contents of that same folder from the command line.

All files are stored on the hard drive in binary format, but every program has its own way of reading and writing this binary data. Each unique method of binary organization is called a file *format*. One program cannot read another program's files unless it can convert the other program's format into its format. In the early days of DOS, no programs were capable of performing this type of conversion, yet people wanted to exchange files. They wanted some type of common format that any program could read. The answer was a special format called American Standard Code for Information Interchange (ASCII).

The ASCII standard defines 256 eight-bit characters. These characters include all of the letters of the alphabet (uppercase and lowercase), numbers, punctuation, many foreign characters (such as accented letters for French and Spanish—é, ñ, ô—and other typical non-English characters), box-drawing characters, and a series of special characters for commands such as a carriage return, bell, and end of file (Figure 6.11). ASCII files, more commonly known as *text files*, store all data in ASCII format. The ASCII standard, however, is for more than just files. For example, when you press a key, the keyboard sends the letter of that key to the PC in ASCII code. Even the monitor outputs in ASCII when you are running DOS.

ASCII was the first universal file format. Virtually every type of program—word processors, spreadsheets, databases, presentation programs—can read and write text files. However, text files have severe limitations. A text file can't store important information such as shapes, colors, margins, or text attributes (bold, underline, font, and so on). Therefore, even though text files are fairly universal, they are also limited to the 256 ASCII characters.

Try This!

Make Some Unicode!

A lot of e-mail programs can use Unicode characters, as can Internet message boards such as my Tech Forums. You can use Unicode characters to accent your writing or simply to spell a person's name correctly—Martin *Acuña*—when you address him. Working with Unicode is fun, so Try This!

1. Open a text editing program such as Notepad in the Windows GUI.

2. Hold down the ALT key on your keyboard and, referring to Figure 6.11, press numbers on your keyboard's number pad to enter special characters. For example, pressing ALT-164 should display an *ñ*, whereas ALT-168 shows a *¿*.

3. If you have access to the Internet, surf over to the Tech Forums (www.totalsem.com/techforum/index.php) and say howdy. Include some Unicode in your post, of course!

Even in the most basic text, you need to perform a number of actions beyond just printing simple characters. For example, how does the program reading the text file know when to start a new line? This is where the first 32 ASCII characters come into play. These first 32 characters are special commands (actually, some of them are both commands and characters). For example, the ASCII value 7 can be either a large dot or a command to play a note (bell) on the PC speaker. ASCII value 9 is a Tab. ASCII value 27 is an Escape.

ASCII worked well for years, but as computers became used worldwide, the industry began to run into a problem: there are a lot more than 256 characters used all over the world! Nobody could use Arabic, Greek, Hebrew, or even Braille! In 1991, the Unicode Consortium, an international standards group, introduced Unicode. Basic Unicode is a 16-bit code that covers every character for the most common languages, plus a few thousand symbols. With Unicode you can make just about any character or symbol you might imagine—plus a few thousand more you'd never even think of. The first 256 Unicode characters are exactly the same as ASCII characters, making for easy backward compatibility.

Drives and Folders

When working from the command line, you need to be able to focus the prompt at the specific drive and folder that contains the files or programs with which you want to work. This can be a little more complicated than it seems, especially in Windows 2000, Windows XP, and Windows Vista.

At boot, Windows assigns a drive letter (or name) to each hard drive partition and to each floppy or other disk drive. The first floppy drive is called A:, and the second, if installed, is called B:. Hard drives usually start with the letter C: and can continue to Z: if necessary. Optical drives by default get the next available drive letter after the last hard drive. Windows 2000, XP, and Vista enable you to change the default lettering for drives, so you're likely to see all sorts of lettering schemes. On top of that, Windows 2000, XP, and Vista let you mount a hard drive as a volume in another drive.

Whatever the names of the drives, Windows uses a hierarchical directory tree to organize the contents of these drives. All files are put into groups Windows calls *folders*, although you'll often hear techs use the term *directory* rather than *folder*, a holdover from the true DOS days. Any file not in a folder *within* the tree—that is, any file in the folder at the root of the directory tree—is said to be in the root directory. A folder inside another folder is called a *subfolder*. Any folder can have multiple subfolders. Two or more files with the same name can exist in different folders on a PC, but two files in the same folder cannot have the same name. In the same way, no two subfolders under the same folder can have the same name, but two subfolders under different folders can have the same name.

When describing a drive, you use its letter and a colon. For example, the hard drive would be represented by C:. To describe the root directory, put a backslash (\) after the C:, as in C:\. To describe a particular directory, add the name of the directory. For example, if a PC has a directory in the root directory called TEST, it is C:\TEST. Subdirectories in a directory are displayed by adding backslashes and names. If the TEST directory has a subdirectory called SYSTEM, it is shown like this: C:\TEST\SYSTEM. This naming convention provides for a complete description of the location and name of any file. If the C:\TEST\SYSTEM directory includes a file called TEST2.TXT, it is C:\TEST\SYSTEM\TEST2.TXT.

The exact location of a file is called its path. The path for the TEST2.TXT file is C:\TEST\SYSTEM. Here are some examples of possible paths:

```
C:\PROGRAM FILES
C:\WINNT\system32\1025
F:\FRUSCH3\CLEAR
A:\REPORTS
D:\
```

Here are a few items to remember about folder names and filenames:

- Folders and files may have spaces in their names.
- The only disallowed characters are the following eleven: * " / \ [ ] : ; | = ,
- Files aren't required to have extensions, but Windows won't know the file type without an extension.
- Folder names may have extensions—but they are not commonly used.

■ Mastering Fundamental Commands

It's time to try using the command line, but before you begin, a note of warning is in order: the command-line interface is picky and unforgiving. It will do what you *say*, not what you *mean*, so it always pays to double-check that those are one and the same before you press ENTER and commit the command. One careless keystroke can result in the loss of crucial data, with no warning and no going back. In this section, you'll explore the structure of commands and then play with four commands built into all versions of Microsoft's command-line interface: DIR, CD, MD, and RD.

Structure: Syntax and Switches

All commands in the Windows command-line interface use a similar structure and execute in the same way. You type the name of the command, followed by the target of that command and any modifications of that command that you want to apply. You can call up a modification by using an extra letter or number, called a switch or *option*, which may follow either the command or the target, depending on the command. The proper way to write a command is called its syntax. The key with commands is that you can't spell anything incorrectly or use a \ when the syntax calls for a /. The command line is completely inflexible, so you have to learn the correct syntax for each command.

```
command] [target (if any)] [switches]
```

or

```
command] [switches] [target (if any)]
```

How do you know what switches are allowed? How do you know whether the switches come before or after the target? If you want to find out the syntax and switches used by a particular command, always type the command followed by a **/?** to get help.

DIR Command

The DIR command shows you the contents of the directory where the prompt is focused. DIR is used more often than any other command at the command prompt. When you open a command-line window in Windows, it opens focused on your user folder. You will know this because the prompt in 2000/XP will look like this: C:\Documents and Settings\username>. By typing in **DIR** and then pressing the ENTER key (remember that you must always press ENTER to execute a command from the command line), you will see something like Figure 6.12.

If you are following along on a PC, remember that different computers contain different files and programs, so you will absolutely see something different from what's shown in Figure 6.12! If a lot of text scrolls quickly down the screen, try typing **DIR /P** (pause). Don't forget to press ENTER.

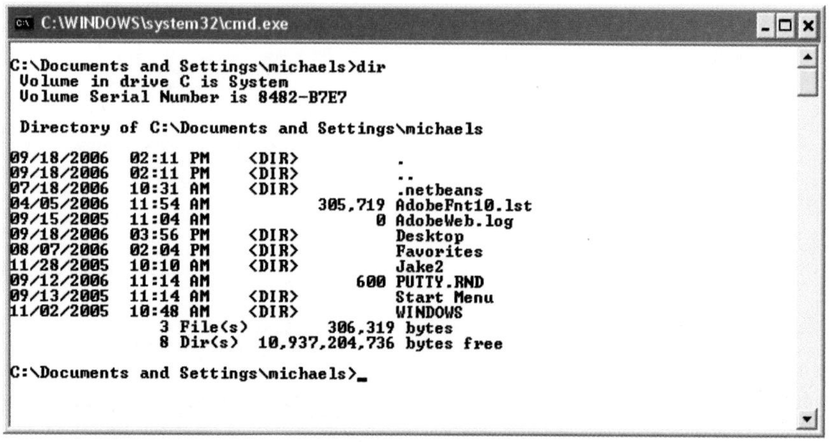

```
C:\WINDOWS\system32\cmd.exe

C:\Documents and Settings\michaels>dir
 Volume in drive C is System
 Volume Serial Number is 8482-B7E7

 Directory of C:\Documents and Settings\michaels

09/18/2006  02:11 PM    <DIR>          .
09/18/2006  02:11 PM    <DIR>          ..
07/18/2006  10:31 AM    <DIR>          .netbeans
04/05/2006  11:54 AM           305,719 AdobeFnt10.lst
09/15/2005  11:04 AM                 0 AdobeWeb.log
09/18/2006  03:56 PM    <DIR>          Desktop
08/07/2006  02:04 PM    <DIR>          Favorites
11/28/2005  10:10 AM    <DIR>          Jake2
09/12/2006  11:14 AM               600 PUTTY.RND
09/13/2005  11:14 AM    <DIR>          Start Menu
11/02/2005  10:48 AM    <DIR>          WINDOWS
               3 File(s)        306,319 bytes
               8 Dir(s)  10,937,204,736 bytes free

C:\Documents and Settings\michaels>_
```

• **Figure 6.12**   DIR in a user's folder

Tech Tip:

Do You Need Spaces?

Some commands give you the same result whether you include spaces or not. DIR/P and DIR /P, for example, provide the same output. Some commands, however, require spaces between the command and switches. In general, get into the habit of putting spaces between your command and switches and you won't run into problems.

The DIR /P command is a lifesaver when you're looking for something in a large directory.

When you type a simple DIR command, you will see that some of the entries look like this:

```
09/04/2008    05:51 PM            63,664 bambi.jpg
```

All of these entries are files. The DIR command lists the creation date, creation time, file size in bytes, filename, and extension. Any entries that look like this are folders:

```
12/31/2009  10:18 AM    <DIR>          WINDOWS
```

The DIR command lists the creation date, creation time, *<DIR>* to tell you it is a folder, and the folder name. If you ever see a listing with *<JUNCTION>* instead of *<DIR>*, you're looking at a hard drive partition that's been mounted as a folder instead of a drive letter:

```
08/06/2008  02:28 PM    <JUNCTION>     Other Drive
```

Extra text typed after a command to modify its operation, such as the /W or /P after DIR, is called a *switch*. Almost all switches can be used simultaneously to modify a command. For example, try typing **DIR /W /P**.

Now type the **DIR /W** command. Note that the DIR /W command shows only the filenames, but they are arranged in five columns across your screen. Finally, type **DIR /?** to see the screen shown in Figure 6.13, which lists all possible switches for the command.

Typing any command followed by a **/?** brings up a help screen for that particular command. Although these help screens can sometimes seem a little cryptic, they're useful when you're not too familiar with a command or you can't figure out how to get a command to do what you need. Even though I have almost every command memorized, I still refer to these help screens; you should use them as well. If you're really lost, type **HELP** at the command prompt for a list of commands you may type. Once you find one, type **HELP** and then the name of the command. For example, if you type **HELP DIR**, you'll see the screen shown in Figure 6.13.

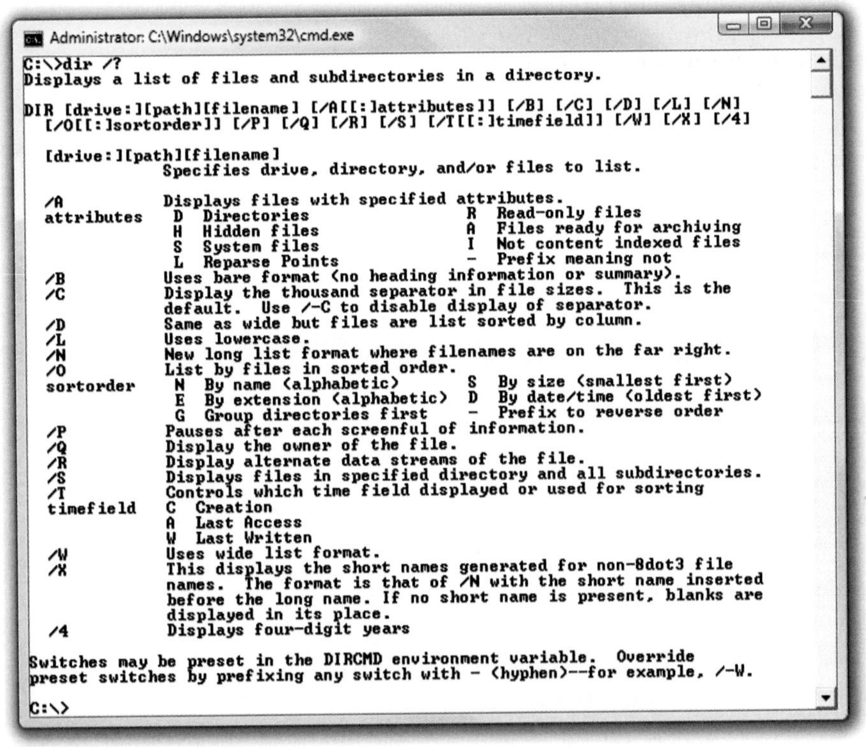

Administrator: C:\Windows\system32\cmd.exe

```
C:\>dir /?
Displays a list of files and subdirectories in a directory.

DIR [drive:][path][filename] [/A[[:]attributes]] [/B] [/C] [/D] [/L] [/N]
  [/O[[:]sortorder]] [/P] [/Q] [/R] [/S] [/T[[:]timefield]] [/W] [/X] [/4]

  [drive:][path][filename]
              Specifies drive, directory, and/or files to list.

  /A          Displays files with specified attributes.
  attributes   D  Directories                R  Read-only files
               H  Hidden files               A  Files ready for archiving
               S  System files               I  Not content indexed files
               L  Reparse Points             -  Prefix meaning not
  /B          Uses bare format (no heading information or summary).
  /C          Display the thousand separator in file sizes.  This is the
              default.  Use /-C to disable display of separator.
  /D          Same as wide but files are list sorted by column.
  /L          Uses lowercase.
  /N          New long list format where filenames are on the far right.
  /O          List by files in sorted order.
  sortorder    N  By name (alphabetic)       S  By size (smallest first)
               E  By extension (alphabetic)  D  By date/time (oldest first)
               G  Group directories first    -  Prefix to reverse order
  /P          Pauses after each screenful of information.
  /Q          Display the owner of the file.
  /R          Display alternate data streams of the file.
  /S          Displays files in specified directory and all subdirectories.
  /T          Controls which time field displayed or used for sorting
  timefield   C  Creation
              A  Last Access
              W  Last Written
  /W          Uses wide list format.
  /X          This displays the short names generated for non-8dot3 file
              names.  The format is that of /N with the short name inserted
              before the long name. If no short name is present, blanks are
              displayed in its place.
  /4          Displays four-digit years

Switches may be preset in the DIRCMD environment variable.  Override
preset switches by prefixing any switch with - (hyphen)--for example, /-W.

C:\>
```

• **Figure 6.13** Typing **DIR /?** lists all possible switches for DIR command.

Directories: The CD Command

You can use the **CD (or CHDIR) command** to change the focus of the command prompt to a different directory. To use the CD command, type **CD** followed by the name of the directory on which you want the prompt to focus. For example, to go to the C:\OBIWAN directory, you type

CD\OBIWAN and then press ENTER. If the system has an OBIWAN directory, the prompt changes focus to that directory and appears as C:\OBIWAN>. If no OBIWAN directory exists or if you accidentally type something like **OBIWAM**, you get the error "The system cannot find the path specified." If only I had a dollar for every time I've seen that error! I usually get it because I've typed too fast. If you get this error, check what you typed and try again.

To return to the root directory, type **CD** and press ENTER. You can use the CD command to point the command prompt to any directory. For example, you could type **CD\FRED\BACKUP\TEST** from a C:\ prompt, and the prompt would change to C:\FRED\BACKUP\TEST\>—assuming, of course, that your system *has* a directory called C:\FRED\BACKUP\TEST.

Once the prompt has changed, type **DIR** again. You should see a different list of files and directories. Every directory holds different files and subdirectories, so when you point the command prompt to different directories, the DIR command shows you different contents.

The CD command allows you to use a space instead of a backslash, a convenient shortcut. For example, you could go to the C:\WINDOWS directory from the root directory simply by typing **CD WINDOWS** at the C:\ prompt. You can use the CD [space] command to move one level at a time, like this:

```
C:\>CD FRED
C:\FRED\>CD BACKUP
C:\FRED\BACKUP>CD TEST
```

Or you can jump multiple directory levels in one step, like this:

```
C:\>CD FRED\BACKUP\TEST
C:\FRED\BACKUP\TEST>
```

A final trick: If you want to go *up* a single directory level, you can type **CD** followed immediately by two periods. So, for example, if you're in the C:\FRED\BACKUP directory and you want to move up to the C:\FRED directory, you can simply type **CD..** and you'll be there:

```
C:\FRED\BACKUP>CD..
C:\FRED>
```

Take some time to move the command prompt focus around the directories of your PC, using the CD and DIR commands. Use DIR to find a directory, and then use CD to move the focus to that directory. Remember, CD\ always gets you back to the root directory.

Moving Between Drives

The CD command is *not* used to move between drives. To get the prompt to point to another drive ("point" is command-line geekspeak for "switch its focus"), just type the drive letter and a colon. If the prompt points at the C:\ Sierra directory and you want to see what is on the USB thumb drive (E:), just type **E:** and the command prompt will point to the USB drive. You'll see the following on the screen:

```
C:\Sierra>E:
E:\>
```

Tech Tip

Errors Are Good!

Consider errors in general for a moment—not just command-prompt errors such as "Invalid directory," but any error, including Windows errors. Many new computer users freeze in horror when they see an error message. Do not fear error messages. Error messages are good! Love them. Worship them. They will save you.

Seriously, think how confusing it would be if the computer didn't tell you when you messed up. Error messages tell you what you did wrong so you can fix it. You absolutely cannot hurt your PC in any way by typing the DIR or CD command incorrectly. Take advantage of this knowledge and experiment. Intentionally make mistakes to familiarize yourself with the error messages. Have fun and learn from errors!

To return to the C: drive, just type **C:** and you'll see the following:

```
E:\>C:
C:\Sierra>
```

Note that you return to the same directory you left. Just for fun, try typing in a drive letter that you know doesn't exist. For example, I know that my system doesn't have a W: drive. If I type in a nonexistent drive on a Windows system, I get the following error:

```
The system cannot find the drive specified.
```

Try inserting a floppy disk and using the CD command to point to its drive. Do the same with an optical disc. Type **DIR** to see the contents of the floppy or optical disc. Type **CD** to move the focus to any folders on the floppy or optical disc. Now return focus to the C: drive.

Using the DIR, CD, and drive letter commands, you can access any folder on any storage device on your system. Make sure you can use these commands comfortably to navigate inside your computer.

Making Directories

Now that you have learned how to navigate in a command-prompt world, it's time to start making stuff, beginning with a new directory.

To make a directory, use the **MD (or MKDIR) command**. To create a directory called STEAM under the root directory C:, for example, first type **CD** to ensure that you are in the root directory. You should see the prompt

```
C:\>
```

Now that the prompt points to the root directory, type **MD STEAM** to create the directory:

```
C:\>MD STEAM
```

Once you press ENTER, Windows executes the command, but it won't volunteer any information about what it did. You must use the DIR command to see that you have, in fact, created a new directory. Note that the STEAM directory in this example is not listed last, as you might expect.

```
C:\>DIR
 Volume in Drive C is
 Volume Serial Number is 1734-3234
 Directory of C:\

07/12/2009  04:46 AM    <DIR>          Documents and Settings
06/04/2008  10:22 PM    <DIR>          STEAM
09/11/2009  11:32 AM    <DIR>          NVIDIA
08/06/2007  02:28 PM    <JUNCTION>     Other Drive
09/14/2008  11:11 AM    <DIR>          Program Files
09/12/2009  08:32 PM                21 statusclient.log
07/31/2008  10:40 PM               153 systemscandata.txt
03/13/2008  09:54 AM         1,111,040 t3h0
04/21/2008  04:19 PM    <DIR>          temp
07/12/2008  10:18 AM    <DIR>          WINDOWS
               3 file(s)      1,111,214 bytes
                          294,182,881,834   bytes free
```

What about uppercase and lowercase? Windows supports both, but it interprets all commands as uppercase. Use the MD command to make a folder called steam (note the lowercase) and see what happens. This also happens in the graphical Windows. Go to your desktop and try to make two folders, one called STEAM and the other called steam, and see what Windows tells you.

To create a FILES subdirectory in the STEAM directory, first use the CD\ command to point the prompt to the STEAM directory:

```
CD\STEAM
```

Then run the MD command to make the FILES directory:

```
MD FILES
```

Make sure that the prompt points to the directory in which you want to make the new subdirectory before you execute the MD command. When you're finished, type **DIR** to see the new FILES subdirectory. Just for fun, try the process again and add a GAMES directory under the STEAM directory. Type **DIR** to verify success.

Removing Directories

Removing subdirectories works exactly like making them. First, get to the directory that contains the subdirectory you want to delete, and then execute the RD (or RMDIR) command. In this example, let's delete the FILES subdirectory in the C:\STEAM directory. First, get to where the FILES directory is located—C:\STEAM—by typing **CD\STEAM**. Then type **RD FILES**. If you received no response from Windows, you probably did it right! Type **DIR** to check that the FILES subdirectory is gone.

The plain RD command will not delete a directory in Windows if the directory contains files or subdirectories. If you want to delete a directory that contains files or subdirectories, you must first empty that directory by using the DEL (for files) or RD (for subdirectories) command. You can use the RD command followed by the /S switch to delete a directory as well as all files and subdirectories. RD followed by the /S switch is handy but dangerous, because it's easy to delete more than you want. When deleting, always follow the maxim "Check twice and delete once."

Let's delete the STEAM and GAMES directories with RD followed by the /S switch. Because the STEAM directory is in the root directory, point to the root directory with CD\. Now execute the command **RD C:\STEAM /S**. In a rare display of mercy, Windows responds with the following:

```
C:\>rd steam /s
steam, Are you sure (Y/N)?
```

Press the Y key and both C:\STEAM and C:\STEAM\GAMES are eliminated.

Working with Directories

PC techs should be comfortable creating and deleting directories. To get some practice, try this:

1. Create a new directory in the root directory by using the make directory command (MD). Type **CD** to return to the root directory. At the command prompt, make a directory called JEDI:

   ```
   C:\>MD JEDI
   ```

2. As usual, the prompt tells you nothing; it just presents a fresh prompt. Do a DIR (that is, type the **DIR** command) to see your new directory. Windows creates the new directory wherever it is pointing when you issue the command, whether or not that's where you meant to put it. To demonstrate, point the prompt to your new directory by using the CD command:

   ```
   C:\>CD JEDI
   ```

3. Now use the make directory command again to create a directory called YODA:

   ```
   C:\JEDI>MD YODA
   ```

   Do a DIR again, and you should see that your JEDI directory now contains a YODA directory.

4. Type **CD** to return to the root directory so you can delete your new directories by using the remove directory command (RD):

   ```
   C:\>RD /S JEDI
   ```

   In another rare display of mercy, Windows responds with the following:

   ```
   jedi, Are you sure <Y/N>?
   ```

5. Press Y to eliminate both C:\JEDI and C:\JEDI\YODA.

Windows includes a lot of command-line tools for specific jobs such as starting and stopping services, viewing computers on a network, converting hard drive file systems, and more. The book discusses these task-specific tools in the chapters that reflect their task. Chapter 13, "Mastering Local Area Networking," goes into detail on the versatile and powerful NET command, for example. You'll read about the CONVERT command in Chapter 16, "Mastering Computer Security." I couldn't resist throwing in two of the more interesting tools, COMPACT and CIPHER, in the Beyond A+ section of this chapter.

Running a Program

To run a program from the command line, simply change the prompt focus to the folder where the program is located, type the name of the program, and then press the ENTER key on your keyboard. Try this safe example. Go to the C:\WINNT\System32 or C:\WINDOWS\System32 folder—the exact name of this folder varies by system. Type **DIR /P** to see the files one page at a time. You should see a file called MEM.EXE (Figure 6.14).

As mentioned earlier, all files with extensions .EXE and .COM are programs, so MEM.EXE is a program. To run the MEM.EXE program, just type the filename, in this case **MEM**, and press ENTER (Figure 6.15). Note that you do not have to type the .EXE extension, although you can. Congratulations! You have just run your first program from the command line.

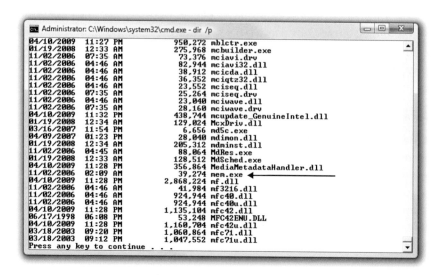

● **Figure 6.14**   MEM.EXE displayed in the System32 folder

■ Working with Files

This section deals with basic file manipulation. You will learn how to look at, copy, move, rename, and delete files. You'll look at the ins and outs of batch files. The examples in this section are based on a C: root directory with the following files and directories:

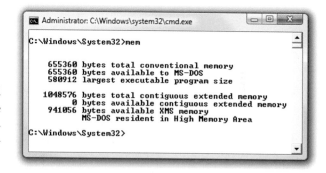

● **Figure 6.15**   Running MEM in Windows Vista

```
C:\>dir
 Volume in drive C has no label.
 Volume Serial Number is 4C62-1572

 Directory of C:\

05/26/2009  11:37 PM                 0 AILog.txt
05/29/2009  05:33 PM             5,776 aoedoppl.txt
05/29/2009  05:33 PM             2,238 aoeWVlog.txt
07/12/2009  10:38 AM    <DIR>          books
07/15/2009  02:45 PM             1,708 CtDrvStp.log
07/12/2008  04:46 AM    <DIR>          Documents and Settings
06/04/2009  10:22 PM    <DIR>          Impressions Games
09/11/2008  11:32 AM    <DIR>          NVIDIA
08/06/2009  02:28 PM    <JUNCTION>     Other Drive
01/03/2009  01:12 PM    <DIR>          pers-drv
09/14/2008  11:11 AM    <DIR>          Program Files
09/12/2009  08:32 PM                21 statusclient.log
07/31/2009  10:40 PM               153 systemscandata.txt
03/13/2009  09:54 AM         1,111,040 t3h0
04/21/2009  04:19 PM    <DIR>          temp
01/10/2008  07:07 PM    <DIR>          WebCam
12/31/2007  10:18 AM    <DIR>          WINDOWS
09/14/2008  12:48 PM    <DIR>          WINNT
01/03/2008  09:06 AM    <DIR>          WUTemp
               7 File(s)      1,120,936 bytes
              12 Dir(s)  94,630,002,688 bytes free
```

Because you probably don't have a PC with these files and directories, follow the examples but use what's on your drive. In other words, create your own folders and copy files to them from various folders currently on your system.

Attributes

All files have four special values, or attributes, that determine how programs (such as My Computer in Windows XP or Computer in Windows Vista) treat the file in special situations. The first attribute is the hidden attribute. If a file is hidden, it is not displayed when you issue the DIR command. Next is the read-only attribute. A file with a read-only attribute cannot be modified or deleted. Third is the system attribute, which is used only for system files such as NTLDR and BOOT.INI. In reality, it does nothing more than provide an easy identifier for these files. Fourth is the archive attribute, which is used by backup software to identify files that have been changed since their last backup.

ATTRIB.EXE is an external command-line program you can use to inspect and change file attributes. To inspect a file's attributes, type the **ATTRIB** command followed by the name of the file. To see the attributes of the file AILog.txt, type **ATTRIB AILOG.TXT**. The result is

```
A       AILog.txt
```

The letter *A* stands for archive, the only attribute of AILog.txt.

Go to the C:\ directory and type **ATTRIB** by itself. You'll see a result similar to the following:

```
C:\>attrib
A               C:\AILog.txt
A               C:\aoedoppl.txt
A               C:\aoeWVlog.txt
A    H          C:\AUTOEXEC.BAT
A    SH         C:\boot.ini
A    H          C:\CONFIG.SYS
A               C:\CtDrvStp.log
A    SH         C:\hiberfil.sys
A    SHR        C:\IO.SYS
A    SHR        C:\MSDOS.SYS
A    SHR        C:\NTDETECT.COM
A    SHR        C:\ntldr
A    SH         C:\pagefile.sys
A               C:\statusclient.log
A               C:\systemscandata.txt
A               C:\t3h0
```

The letter *R* means read-only, *H* is hidden, and *S* is system. Hey! There are some new files there. That's right, some were hidden. Don't panic if you see a number of files different from those just listed. No two C:\ directories are ever the same. In most cases, you'll see many more files than just these.

Notice that important files such as NTLDR and NTDETECT.COM have the system, hidden, and read-only attributes set. Microsoft does this to protect them from accidental deletion.

You also use the ATTRIB command to change a file's attributes. To add an attribute to a file, type the attribute letter preceded by a plus sign (+) as an option, and then type the filename. To delete an attribute, use a minus sign (–). For example, to add the read-only attribute to the file AILog.txt, type this:

```
ATTRIB +R AILOG.TXT
```

To remove the archive attribute, type this:

```
ATTRIB -A AILOG.TXT
```

Try This!

Working with Attributes

It's important for you to know that everything you do at the command line affects the same files at the GUI level, so Try This!

1. In Windows XP, go to My Computer and create a folder in the root directory of your C: drive called TEST.

2. Copy a couple of files into that folder and then right-click one to see its properties.

3. Open a command-line window and navigate to the C:\TEST folder. Type **DIR** to see that the contents match what you see in My Computer.

4. From the command line, change the attributes of one or both files. Make one a hidden file, for example, and the other read-only.

5. Now go back to My Computer and access the properties of each file. Any changes?

You can add or remove multiple attributes in one command. Here's an example of removing three attributes from the NTDETECT.COM file:

```
ATTRIB -R -S -H NTDETECT.COM
```

You can also automatically apply ATTRIB to matching files in subdirectories by using the /s switch at the end of the statement. For example, if you have lots of files in your My Music folder that you want to hide, but they are neatly organized in many subdirectories, you could readily use ATTRIB to change all of them with a simple command. Change directories from the prompt until you're at the My Music folder and then type the following:

```
ATTRIB +H *.MP3 /S
```

When you press the ENTER key, all your music files in My Music and any My Music subdirectories will become hidden files.

Wildcards

Visualize having 273 files in one directory. A few of these files have the extension .DOC, but most do not. You are looking only for files with the .DOC extension. Wouldn't it be nice to type the DIR command so that only the .DOC files come up? You can do this by using wildcards.

A wildcard is one of two special characters—asterisk (*) and question mark (?)—that you can use in place of all or part of a filename, often so that a command-line command will act on more than one file at a time. Wildcards work with all command-line commands that take filenames. A great example is the DIR command. When you execute a plain DIR command, it finds and displays all of the files and folders in the specified directory; however, you can also narrow its search by adding a filename. For example, if you type the command **DIR AILOG.TXT** while in your root (C:\) directory, you get the following result:

```
C:\>dir AILOG.TXT
 Volume in drive C has no label.
 Volume Serial Number is 4C62-1572
 Directory of C:\
05/26/2009  11:37 PM                    0 AILog.txt
               1 File(s)               0 bytes
               0 Dir(s)  94,630,195,200 bytes free
```

If you just want to confirm the presence of a particular file in a particular place, this is very convenient. But suppose you want to see all files with the extension .TXT. In that case, you use the * wildcard, like this: **DIR *.TXT**. A good way to think of the * wildcard is *"I don't care."* Replace the part of the filename that you don't care about with an asterisk (*). The result of DIR *.TXT would look like this:

```
 Volume in drive C has no label.
 Volume Serial Number is 4C62-1572

 Directory of C:\

05/26/2009  11:37 PM                    0 AILog.txt
05/29/2009  05:33 PM                5,776 aoedoppl.txt
05/29/2009  05:33 PM                2,238 aoeWVlog.txt
07/31/2008  10:40 PM                  153 systemscandata.txt
               4 File(s)            8,167 bytes
               0 Dir(s)  94,630,002,688 bytes free
```

Wildcards also substitute for parts of filenames. This DIR command will find every file that starts with the letter *a:*

```
C:\>dir a*.*
 Volume in drive C has no label.
 Volume Serial Number is 4C62-1572

 Directory of C:\

05/26/2009  11:37 PM                    0 AILog.txt
05/29/2009  05:33 PM                5,776 aoedoppl.txt
05/29/2009  05:33 PM                2,238 aoeWVlog.txt
               3 File(s)            8,014 bytes
               0 Dir(s)  94,629,675,008 bytes free
```

We've used wildcards only with the DIR command, but virtually every command that deals with files will take wildcards. Let's examine the REN and DEL commands and see how they use wildcards.

Renaming Files

To rename files, you use the **REN (or RENAME) command**, which seems pretty straightforward. To rename the file IMG033.jpg to park.jpg, type the following followed by the ENTER key:

```
ren img033.jpg park.jpg
```

"That's great," you might be thinking, "but what about using a more complex and descriptive filename, such as Sunny day in the park.jpg?" Type what should work, like this:

```
ren img033.jpg Sunny day in the park.jpg
```

But you'll get an error message (Figure 6.16). Even the tried-and-true method of seeking help by typing the command followed by /? doesn't give you the answer.

You can use more complicated names by putting them in quotation marks. Figure 6.17 shows the same command that failed but now succeeds because of the quotation marks.

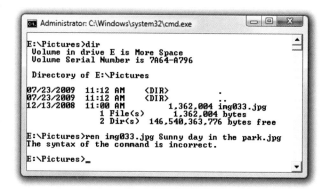

• **Figure 6.16**   Rename failed me.

Deleting Files

To delete files, you use the **DEL (or ERASE) command.** DEL and ERASE are identical commands that you can use interchangeably. Deleting files is simple—maybe too simple. Windows users enjoy the luxury of retrieving deleted files from the Recycle Bin on those "Oops, I didn't mean to delete that" occasions everyone encounters at one time or another. The command line, however, shows no such mercy to the careless user. It has no function equivalent to the Windows Recycle Bin. Once you have erased a file, you can recover it only by using a special recovery utility such as Norton's UNERASE. Again, the rule here is to *check twice and delete once.*

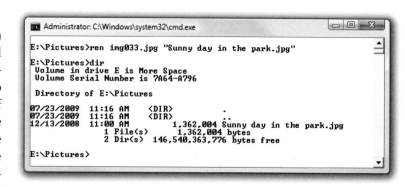

• **Figure 6.17**   Success at last.

To delete a single file, type the **DEL** command followed by the name of the file to delete. To delete the file AILOG.TXT, for example, type this:

```
DEL AILOG.TXT
```

Although nothing appears on the screen to confirm it, the file is now gone. To confirm that the AILOG.TXT file is no longer listed, use the DIR command.

As with the DIR command, you can use wildcards with the DEL and ERASE commands to delete multiple files. For example, to delete all files with the extension .TXT in a directory, you would type this:

```
DEL *.TXT
```

To delete all files with the filename CONFIG in a directory, type **DEL CONFIG.***. To delete all of the files in a directory, you can use the popular *.* wildcard (often pronounced "star-dot-star"), like this:

```
DEL *.*
```

This is one of the few command-line commands that elicits a response. Upon receiving the DEL *.* command, Windows responds with "Are you sure? (Y/N)," to which you respond with a *Y* or *N*. Pressing Y erases every file in the directory, so use *.* with care!

Don't confuse deleting *files* with deleting *directories*. DEL deletes files, but it will not remove directories. Use RD to delete directories.

Copying and Moving Files

Being able to copy and move files in a command line is crucial to all technicians. Because of its finicky nature and many options, the COPY command is also rather painful to learn, especially if you're used to dragging icons in Windows. The following tried-and-true, five-step process makes it easier, but the real secret is to get in front of a C:\ prompt and just copy and move files around until you're comfortable. Keep in mind that the only difference between copying and moving is whether the original is left behind (COPY) or not (MOVE). Once you've learned the COPY command, you've also learned the MOVE command!

Mike's Five-Step COPY/MOVE Process

I've been teaching folks how to copy and move files for years by using this handy process. Keep in mind that hundreds of variations on this process exist. As you become more confident with these commands, try doing a COPY /? or MOVE /? at any handy prompt to see the real power of the commands. But first, follow this process step by step:

1. Point the command prompt to the directory containing the files you want to copy or move.

2. Type **COPY** or **MOVE** and a space.

3. Type the *name(s)* of the file(s) to be copied/moved (with or without wildcards) and a space.

4. Type the *path* of the new location for the files.

5. Press ENTER.

Let's try an example. The directory C:\STEAM contains the file README.TXT. Copy this file to a USB thumb drive (E:).

1. Type **CD\STEAM** to point the command prompt to the STEAM directory.

   ```
   C:\>CD\STEAM
   ```

2. Type **COPY** and a space.

   ```
   C:\STEAM>COPY
   ```

3. Type **README.TXT** and a space.

   ```
   C:\STEAM>COPY README.TXT
   ```

4. Type **E:**.

   ```
   C:\STEAM>COPY README.TXT E:\
   ```

5. Press ENTER.

The entire command and response would look like this:

```
C:\STEAM>COPY README.TXT E:\
1 file(s) copied
```

If you point the command prompt to the E: drive and type **DIR**, the README.TXT file will be visible. Let's try another example. Suppose 100 files are in the C:\DOCS directory, 30 of which have the .DOC extension, and suppose you want to move those files to the C:\STEAM directory. Follow these steps:

1. Type **CD\DOCS** to point the command prompt to the DOCS directory.

   ```
   C:\>CD\DOCS
   ```

2. Type **MOVE** and a space.

   ```
   C:\DOCS>MOVE
   ```

3. Type *.**DOC** and a space.

   ```
   C:\DOCS>MOVE *.DOC
   ```

4. Type **C:\STEAM**.

   ```
   C:\DOCS>MOVE *.DOC C:\STEAM
   ```

5. Press ENTER.

   ```
   C:\DOCS>MOVE *.DOC C:\STEAM
   30 file(s) copied
   ```

The power of the COPY/MOVE command makes it rather dangerous. The COPY/MOVE command not only lets you put a file in a new location; it also lets you change the name of the file at the same time. Suppose you want to copy a file called AUTOEXEC.BAT from your C:\ folder to a thumb drive, for example, but you want the name of the copy on the thumb drive to be AUTO1.BAT. You can do both things with one COPY command, like this:

```
COPY C:\AUTOEXEC.BAT E:\AUTO1.BAT
```

Not only does the AUTOEXEC.BAT file get copied to the thumb drive, but the copy also gets the new name AUTO1.BAT.

As another example, move all of the files with the extension .DOC from the C:\DOCS directory to the C:\BACK directory and simultaneously change the .DOC extension to .SAV. Here is the command:

```
MOVE C:\DOCS\*.DOC C:\BACK\*.SAV
```

This says, "Move all files that have the extension .DOC from the directory C:\DOCS into the directory C:\BACK, and while you're at it, change their file extensions to .SAV." This is very handy, but very dangerous!

Let's say, for example, that I made one tiny typo. Here I typed a semicolon instead of a colon after the second C:

```
MOVE C:\DOCS\*.DOC C;\BACK\*.SAV
```

The command line understands the semicolon to mean "end of command" and therefore ignores both the semicolon and anything I type after it. As far as the command line is concerned, I typed this:

```
MOVE C:\DOCS\*.DOC C
```

This, unfortunately for me, means "take all of the files with the extension .DOC in the directory C:\DOCS and copy them back into that same directory, but squish them all together into a single file called C." If I run this command, Windows gives me only one clue that something went wrong:

```
MOVE C:\DOCS\*.DOC C
1 file(s) copied
```

See "1 file(s) copied"? Feeling the chilly hand of fate slide down my spine, I do a DIR of the directory, and I now see a single file called C, where there used to be 30 files with the extension .DOC. All of my DOC files are gone, completely unrecoverable.

XCOPY

The standard COPY and MOVE commands can work only in one directory at a time, making them a poor choice for copying or moving files in multiple directories. To help with these multi-directory jobs, Microsoft added the XCOPY command. (Note that there is no XMOVE, only XCOPY.)

XCOPY works similar to COPY, but XCOPY has extra switches that give it the power to work with multiple directories. Here's how it works. Let's say I have a directory on my C: drive called \DATA. The \DATA directory has three subdirectories: \JAN, \FEB, and \MAR. All of these directories, including the \DATA directory, contain about 50 files. If I wanted to copy all of these files to my D: drive in one command, I would use XCOPY in the following manner:

```
XCOPY C:\DATA D:\DATA /S
```

Because XCOPY works on directories, you don't have to use filenames as you would in COPY, although XCOPY certainly accepts filenames and wildcards. The /S switch, the most commonly used of all of the many switches that come with XCOPY, tells XCOPY to copy all subdirectories except for empty ones. The /E switch tells XCOPY to copy empty subdirectories. When you have a lot of copying to do over many directories, XCOPY is the tool to use.

Their power and utility make the DEL, COPY/MOVE, and XCOPY commands indispensable for a PC technician, but that same power and utility can cause disaster. Only a trained Jedi, with The Force as his ally...well, wrong book, but the principle remains: Beware of the quick and easy keystroke, for it may spell your doom. Think twice and execute the command once. The data you save may be yours!

Working with Batch Files

Batch files are nothing more than text files that store a series of commands, one command per line. The only thing that differentiates a batch file from any other text file is the .BAT extension. Take a look at Figure 6.18, and note

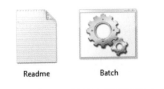

Readme   Batch

● **Figure 6.18** Text and batch file icons

the unique icon used for a batch file compared to the icon for a regular text file.

You can create and edit batch files by using any text editor program—good old Notepad is often the tool of choice. This is the command-line chapter, though, so let's dust off the ancient but still important Edit program—it comes with every version of Windows—and use it to create and edit batch files.

Get to a command prompt on any Windows system and use the CD\ command to get to the root directory (use C: to get to the C: drive if you're not on the C: drive by default). From there, type **EDIT** at the command prompt to see the Edit program's interface (Figure 6.19).

Now that you've started Edit, type in the two commands as shown in Figure 6.20. Make sure they look exactly the same as the lines in Figure 6.20.

Great! You have just made your first batch file. All you need to do now is save it with some name—the name doesn't matter, but this example uses FIRST as the filename. It is imperative, however, that you use the extension .BAT. Even though you could probably figure this out on your own later, do it now. Hold down the ALT key to activate the menu. Press the F (File) key. Then press S (Save). Type in the name **FIRST.BAT** as shown in Figure 6.21. Press ENTER and the file is now saved.

Now that you've saved the file, exit the Edit program by pressing ALT-F and then pressing X (Exit). You're back at the command prompt. Go ahead and run the program by typing **FIRST** and pressing ENTER. Your results should look something like Figure 6.22.

Super! The batch file created a folder and moved the prompt to

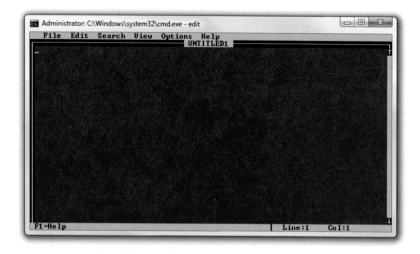

• **Figure 6.19**   Edit interface

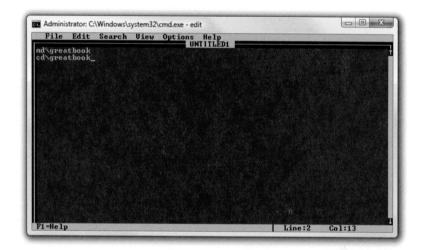

• **Figure 6.20**   Edit with two commands

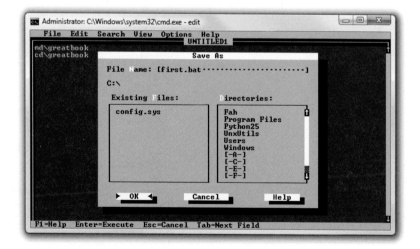

• **Figure 6.21**   Saving the batch file

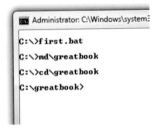

● **Figure 6.22**   Running the batch file

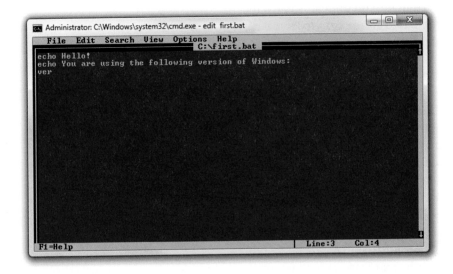

● **Figure 6.23**   New version of FIRST.BAT

focus on that folder. Don't run the First batch file again or you'll create another folder inside the first one.

Let's now get back to the root directory of C: and edit the FIRST.BAT file again. This time type **EDIT FIRST.BAT** and press ENTER. The batch file will come up, ready to edit. Now change the batch file to look like Figure 6.23. Use the ARROW keys to move your cursor and the DELETE key to delete.

The VER command shows the current version of Windows. The ECHO command tells the batch file to put text on the screen. Run the batch file, and it should look like Figure 6.24.

Gee, that's kind of ugly. Try editing the FIRST.BAT file one more time and add the following line as the first line of the batch file:

```
@echo off
```

Run FIRST.BAT again. It should look quite a bit nicer. The @echo off command tells the system not to show the command, just the result.

> Most of the keyboard short-cuts used in WordPad, Word, and so on, were first used in the Edit program. If you know keyboard shortcuts for WordPad or Word, many will work in Edit.

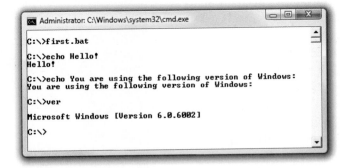

● **Figure 6.24**   Running FIRST.BAT

Mike Meyers' CompTIA A+ Guide: Practical Application

Sometimes you just want to look at a batch file. The TYPE command displays the contents of a text file on the screen, as shown in Figure 6.25.

One of the more irritating aspects to batch files is that sometimes they don't work unless you run them in the folder in which they are stored. This is because of the path setting. Every time you open a command prompt, Windows loads a number of settings by default. You can see all of these settings by running the SET command. Figure 6.26 shows the results of running the SET command.

Don't worry about understanding everything the SET command shows you, but do notice a line that starts with `Path=`. This line tells Windows where to look for a program (or batch file) if you run a program that's not in your current folder. For example, let's say I make a folder called C:\batch to store all of my batch files. I can run the PATH command from the command prompt to see my current path (Figure 6.27).

I can then run the PATH command again, this time adding **%PATH%;C:\batch** (Figure 6.28). The %PATH% bit is a variable that represents what is currently in the path. By placing it before my batch folder, I am telling the path command to keep what is there and just add c:\batch. I can now place all of my batch files in this folder, and they will always work, no matter where I am in the system.

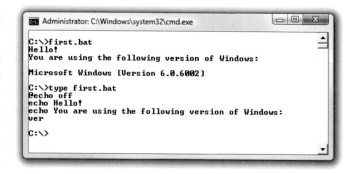

• **Figure 6.25**   Using the TYPE command to see file contents

 Don't try using the TYPE command on anything other than a text file—the results will be unpredictable.

• **Figure 6.26**   Using the SET command to see settings

In Windows 2000 and XP, you can edit the BOOT.INI file by using the Edit program. Just make sure you use ATTRIB first to turn off the System and Hidden attributes! In Windows Vista, the boot configuration data (BCD) store contains boot configuration parameters and objects that control how the operating system starts. You use the bcdedit.exe command-line tool to add, delete, and edit the objects and entries stored in the BCD store.

• **Figure 6.27**   Using the PATH command to see the current path

• **Figure 6.28**   Using PATH to add a folder

Cross Check

Command Line versus GUI

Now that you've become familiar with the command-line interface, you should be able to switch between the Windows GUI and the command line with relative ease. Check to make sure you can explain how to do the basic tasks covered in this chapter in both the Windows GUI and the command line.

1. How do you delete a folder in Windows?

2. How do you delete a directory from the command line?

3. What advantage do wildcards give the command line over the GUI when you're working with files?

And Even More Tools, Utilities, and Commands

As a proficient IT technician in the field, you need to be familiar with a whole slew of command-line tools and other important utilities. The CompTIA 220-702 exam focuses in on several of them, and although many have been discussed in detail in previous chapters, it is extremely important that you understand and practice with CHKDSK, FORMAT, and SFC.

CHKDSK (/f /r)

The **CHKDSK (Checkdisk) command** scans, detects, and repairs hard drive– and volume-related issues and errors. You can run the CHKDSK utility from a command prompt with the switches /f and /r. The /f switch attempts to fix volume-related errors, while the /r switch attempts to locate and repair bad sectors. To run successfully, CHKDSK needs direct access to a drive. In other words, the drive needs to be "unlocked." For example, if you run CHKDSK /f /r and CHKDSK does not consider your drive unlocked, you will receive a "cannot lock current drive" message, meaning that another process has the drive locked and is preventing CHKDSK from locking the drive itself. After this, CHKDSK presents you with the option to run it the next time the system restarts (Figure 6.29).

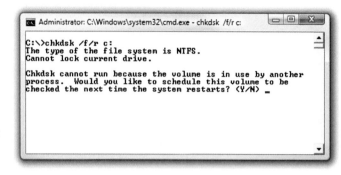

• **Figure 6.29**   The CHKDSK /f /r utility and switches on a locked drive

Cross Check

Error-checking

You've seen the graphical version of CHKDSK back in Chapter 5, "Implementing Hard Drives," but how about refreshing your memory? How do you get to the Error-checking utility in Windows' graphical user interface? Does it have the same functionality as the command-line version's switches?

FORMAT

After the previous chapter, you should have an expert-level knowledge of (or, at the very least, a passing familiarity with) formatting and partitioning hard drives. Formatting, you may remember, is the process of wiping or preparing a disk to be partitioned so it can hold an operating system or data. We have already discussed the various built-in Windows utilities available to provide the formatting of drives, and you no doubt know that a myriad of third-party formatting tools are out there. In this chapter, you just need to become familiar with the FORMAT command and its switches.

The **FORMAT command**, you may have guessed, enables you to format disks from the command line. The very best way to familiarize yourself with FORMAT and its available switches is simply to enter **FORMAT /?** from the command prompt. Your results should be similar to those displayed in Figure 6.30.

Although the new Practical Application exam focuses primarily on operating system formatting utilities and options, you should familiarize yourself with the FORMAT command and its switches by practicing them on a test system you are literally not afraid to wipe out. Besides, you never know what skeletons CompTIA may pull out of the closet.

SFC (System File Checker)

The Windows **SFC (System File Checker)**, or simply SFC.exe, scans, detects, and restores important Windows system files, folders, and paths. Techs often use the SFC utility from within a working version of Windows or from a Windows installation disc to restore a corrupt Windows environment. If you run SFC and it finds issues, it attempts to replace corrupted or missing files from cached DLLs located in the %WinDir%\System32\Dllcache\ directory. Without getting very deep into the mad science involved, just

● Figure 6.30   Using Format /? at the command prompt

know that you can use SFC to correct corruption. To run SFC from a command prompt, enter **SFC /SCANNOW**. To familiarize yourself with SFC's switches, enter **SFC /?** (Figure 6.31).

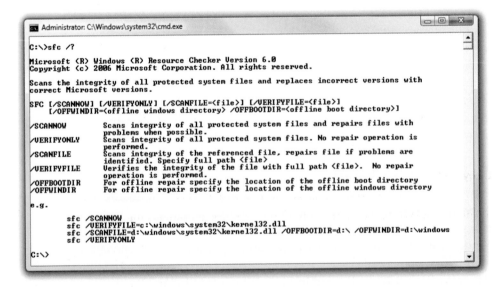

● Figure 6.31   Checking SFC options with SFC /? at a command prompt

Beyond A+

Using Special Keys

You might find yourself repeatedly typing the same commands, or at least very similar commands, when working at a prompt. Microsoft has provided a number of ways to access previously typed commands. Type the **DIR** command at a command prompt. When you get back to a prompt, press F1, and the letter *D* appears. Press F1 again. Now the letter *I* appears after the *D*. Do you see what is happening? The F1 key brings back the previous command one letter at a time. Pressing F3 brings back the entire command at once. Now try running these three commands:

    DIR /W

    ATTRIB

    MD FRED

Now press the UP ARROW key. Keep pressing it till you see your original DIR command—it's a history of all your old commands. Now use the RIGHT ARROW key to add /W to the end of your DIR command. Windows command history is very handy.

Compact and Cipher

Windows XP and Vista offer two cool commands at the command-line interface: COMPACT and CIPHER. COMPACT displays or alters the compression of files on NTFS partitions. CIPHER displays or alters the encryption of folders and files on NTFS partitions. If you type just the command with no added parameters, COMPACT and CIPHER display the compression state and the encryption state, respectively, of the current directory and any files it contains. You may specify multiple directory names, and you may use wildcards, as you learned earlier in the chapter. You must add parameters to make the commands change things. For example, you add /C to compress and /U to uncompress directories and/or files with the COMPACT command, and you add /E to encrypt and /D to decrypt directories and/or files with the CIPHER command. When you do these operations, you also mark the directories involved so that any files you add to them in the future will take on their encryption or compression characteristics. In other words, if you encrypt a directory and all its files, any files you add later will also be encrypted. Same thing if you compress a directory. I'll run through a quick example of each.

COMPACT

First let's try the COMPACT command. Figure 6.32 shows the result of entering the COMPACT command with no switches. It displays the compression status of the contents of a directory called compact on a system's C: drive. Notice that after the file listing, COMPACT helpfully tells you that 0 files are compressed and 6 files (all of them) are not compressed, with a total compression ratio of 1.0 to 1.

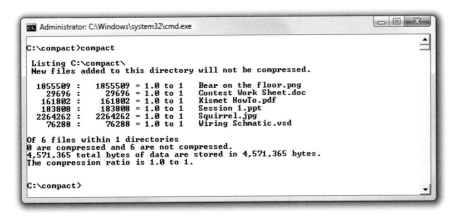

Figure 6.32 The COMPACT command with no switches

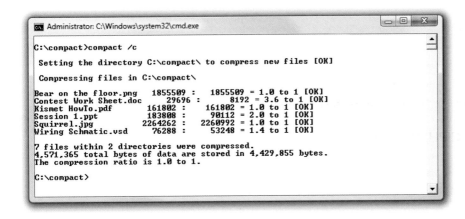

Figure 6.33 Typing **COMPACT /C** compresses the contents of the directory.

If you enter the COMPACT command with the /C switch, it compresses all of the files in the directory, as shown in Figure 6.33. Look closely at the listing. Notice that it includes the original and compressed file sizes and calculates the compression ratio for you. Notice also that the JPG and PNG files (both compressed graphics files) didn't compress at all, while the Word file and the PowerPoint file compressed down to around a third of their original sizes. Also, can you spot what's different in the text at the bottom of the screen? COMPACT claims to have compressed *seven* files in *two* directories! How can this be? The secret is that when it compresses all of the files in a directory, it must also compress the directory file itself, which is "in" the C: directory above it. Thus it correctly reports that it compressed seven files: six in the compact directory, and one in the C: directory.

Typing **COMPACT** again shows you the directory listing, and now there's a C next to each filename, indicating that the file is compressed (Figure 6.34).

Okay, now suppose you want to uncompress a file—say a PowerPoint file, Session 1.ppt. To do this, you must specify the decompression operation, using the /U switch and the name of the file you want decompressed,

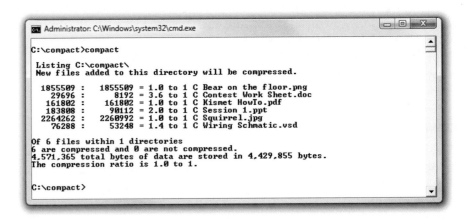

Figure 6.34 The contents of C:\COMPACT have been compressed.

● Figure 6.35 Typing **COMPACT /U "Session 1.ppt"** decompresses only that file.

as shown in Figure 6.35. Note that COMPACT reports the successful decompression of one file only: Session 1.ppt. You could do the same thing in reverse, using the /C switch and a filename to compress an individual file.

CIPHER

The CIPHER command is a bit complex, but in its most basic implementation, it's pretty straightforward. Figure 6.36 shows two steps in the process. Like the COMPACT command, the CIPHER command simply displays the current state of affairs when entered with no switches. In this case, it

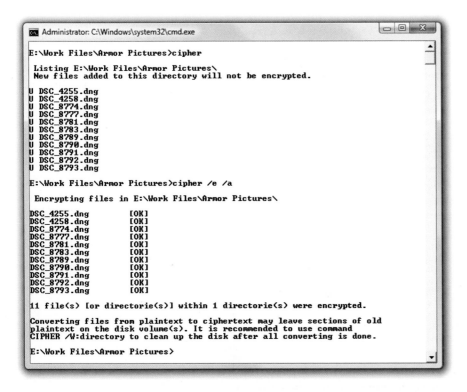

● Figure 6.36 Typing **CIPHER /E /A** encrypts the contents of the directory.

displays the encryption state of the files in the E:\Work Files\Armor Pictures directory. Notice the letter *U* to the left of the filenames, which tells you they are unencrypted. The second command you can see on the screen in Figure 6.36 is this:

```
E:\Work Files\Armor Pictures>cipher /E /A
```

This time the CIPHER command carries two switches: /E specifies the encryption operation, and /A says to apply it to the *files* in the directory, not just the directory itself. As you can see, the command-line interface is actually pretty chatty in this case. It reports that it's doing the encryption and then tells you what it's done, and it even warns you that you should clean up any stray unencrypted bits that may have been left in the directory.

To confirm the results of the cipher operation, enter the **CIPHER** command again, as shown in Figure 6.37. Note that the *U* to the left of each filename has been replaced with an *E*, indicating an encrypted file. The other indication that this directory has been encrypted is the statement above the file listing:

• **Figure 6.37** CIPHER command confirms that the files were encrypted.

```
New files added to this directory will not be encrypted.
```

Remember that the CIPHER command works on directories first and foremost, and it works on individual files only when you specifically tell it to do so.

That's great, but suppose you want to decrypt just *one* of the files in the Armor Pictures directory. Can you guess how you need to alter the command? Simply add the filename of the file you want to decrypt after the command and the relevant switches. Figure 6.38 shows the CIPHER command being used to decipher DSC_4255.dng, a single file.

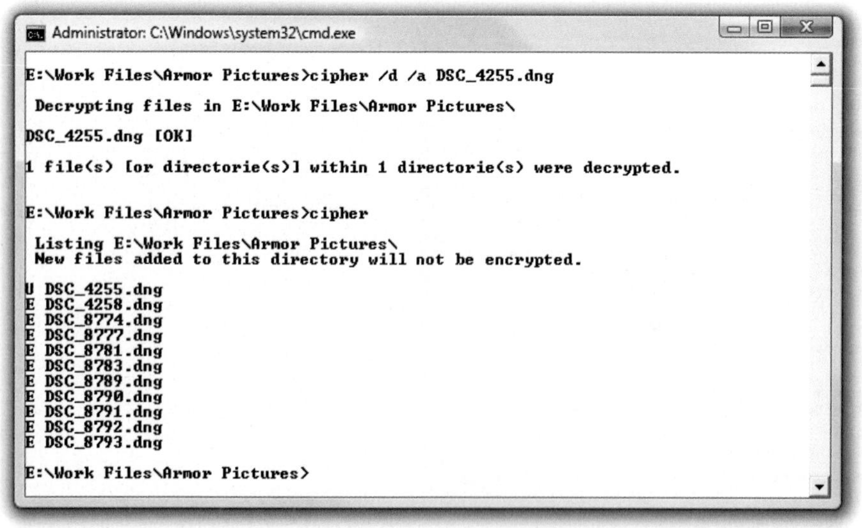

• **Figure 6.38** Typing **CIPHER /D /A DSC_4255.dng** decrypts only that file.

Chapter 6 Review

■ Chapter Summary

After reading this chapter and completing the exercises, you should understand the following about the command-line interface.

Explain the operation of the command-line interface

■ The text-based DOS-like user interface, now known as the command-line interface, still functions as a basic installation and troubleshooting tool for techs in Windows 2000, XP, and Vista. Windows comes with a text editor called EDIT that enables technicians to manipulate text files from within the command prompt.

■ When you use a command-line interface, the computer tells you it's ready to receive commands by displaying a specific set of characters called a prompt. You type a command and press ENTER to send it. The OS goes off and executes the command, and when it's finished, it displays a new prompt, often along with some information about what it did. The new prompt means the computer is ready for your next instruction.

■ You can access the command-line interface in Windows 2000 or XP by clicking Start | Run to open the Run dialog box, and then typing **CMD** or **Command** and pressing ENTER. In Windows Vista, you enter **CMD** in the Start menu Search box. You can also click Start | Programs | Accessories | Command Prompt in Windows 2000, XP, and Vista. To close the command-line-interface window, either click the Close box in the upper-right corner of the window or type **EXIT** at the prompt and press ENTER.

■ The command prompt is always focused on some directory, and any commands you issue are performed *on the files in the directory* on which the prompt is focused. Make sure you focus the prompt's attention on the drive and directory in which you want to work.

■ Windows manifests each program and piece of data as an individual *file*. Each file has a name, which is stored with the file on the drive. Names are broken down into two parts: the filename and the extension. In true DOS, the filename could be no longer than eight characters. The extension, which is optional, could be up to three characters long. No spaces or other illegal characters (/ \ [ ] | ÷ + = ; , * ?) could be used in the filename or extension. The filename and extension are separated by a period, or dot. This naming system is known as the "eight-dot-three" (8.3) naming system. All versions of Windows starting with 9*x* allow filenames of up to 255 characters.

■ The filename extension tells the computer the type or function of the file. Program files use the extension .EXE (for executable) or .COM (for command). If the file is data, the extension indicates which program uses that particular data file. Graphics files most often reflect the graphics standard used to render the image, such as .GIF or .JPG. Changing the file extension does not change the data in the file. The Windows GUI doesn't show the file extensions by default.

■ All files are stored on the hard drive in binary format, but every program has a unique method of binary organization, called a file format. One program cannot read another program's files unless it can convert the other program's file format into its file format.

■ ASCII (American Standard Code for Information Interchange) was the first universal file format. The ASCII standard defines 256 eight-bit characters, including all of the letters of the alphabet (uppercase and lowercase), numbers, punctuation, many foreign characters, box-drawing characters, and a series of special characters for commands, such as a carriage return, bell, and end of file. ASCII files, often called text files, store all data in ASCII format. The keyboard sends the characters you press on the keyboard to the PC in ASCII code. Even the monitor outputs in ASCII when you are running a command line.

■ As a rule, the OS treats the first 32 ASCII values as commands. Some of them are both commands and characters. How these first 32 values are treated depends on the program that reads them.

■ Unicode supports thousands of 16-bit characters. The first 256 Unicode characters are the same as the complete 256 ASCII character set, which maintains backward compatibility.

- At boot, the OS assigns a drive letter to each hard drive partition and to each floppy or other disk drive. The first floppy drive is called A:, and the second, if installed, is called B:. Hard drives start with the letter C: and can continue to Z: if necessary. Optical drives usually get the next available drive letter after the last hard drive.

- Windows uses a hierarchical directory tree to organize the contents of these drives. All files are put into groups called directories. Windows also uses directories, but it calls them folders. Any file not in a directory *within* the tree—which is to say, any file in the directory at the root of the directory tree—is said to be in the root directory. Directories inside directories are called subdirectories. Any directory can have multiple subdirectories. Two or more files or subdirectories with the same name can exist in different directories on a PC, but two files or subdirectories in the same directory cannot have the same name.

- When describing a drive, you use its assigned letter, such as C: for the hard drive. To describe the root directory, add a backslash (\), as in C:\. To describe a particular directory, add the name of the directory after the backslash. To add a subdirectory after the directory, add another backslash and then the subdirectory's name. This naming convention provides for a complete description of the location and name of any file. The exact location of a file is called its path.

Execute fundamental commands from the command line

- The command-line interface will do what you *say*, not what you *mean*, so it always pays to double-check that those are the same before you press ENTER. One careless keystroke can result in the loss of crucial data, with no warning and no going back.

- The DIR command shows you the contents of the directory on which the prompt is focused. The DIR command lists the filename, extension, file size in bytes, and creation date/time. The DIR /P command pauses after displaying a screen's worth of the directory contents; press the SPACEBAR to display the next screen. The DIR /W command shows you filenames only, arranged in columns, with directory names in square brackets.

- Extra text typed after a command to modify its operation, such as the /W or /P after DIR, is called a switch. Almost all switches can be used simultaneously to modify a command. Typing any command followed by a /? brings up a help screen for that particular command.

- You can use the CD command to change the focus of the command prompt to a different directory. Type **CD** followed by the name of the directory on which you want to focus the prompt, and press ENTER. If no such directory exists or if you mistyped the name, Windows will report "The system cannot find the path specified." To return to the root directory, type **CD** and press ENTER. The CD command also allows you to use a space instead of a backslash. The CD command is not used to move between drives; to point the prompt to another drive, type the drive letter and a colon.

- To make a directory, use the MD (or MKDIR) command. Once you press ENTER, the OS executes the command, but it won't volunteer any information about what it did. You must use the DIR command to see that you have, in fact, created a new directory. Make sure that the prompt points to the directory in which you want to make the new subdirectory before you execute the MD command.

- To remove a directory, first point the prompt at the directory that contains the subdirectory you want to delete, and then execute the RD (or RMDIR) command. If you get no response, you probably did it right, but use the DIR command to be sure. The RD command will not delete a directory if it contains files or subdirectories; you must first empty that directory by using the DEL (for files) or RD (for subdirectories) command. The RD command followed by the /S switch deletes the directory as well as all files and subdirectories.

Manipulate files from the command line

- All files have four special values, or attributes, that determine how they will act in special situations: hidden, read-only, system, and archive. You can set these attributes through software. If a file is hidden, it will not be displayed when the DIR command is performed. A read-only file cannot be modified or deleted. The system attribute, which is used only for system files such as NTLDR and

NTDETECT.COM, provides an easy identifier for these files. The archive attribute is used by backup software to identify files that have been changed since their last backup.

- ATTRIB.EXE is an external program with which you can inspect and change file attributes. Type the **ATTRIB** command followed by the name of the file and press ENTER. In the resulting list of files, letter codes indicate each file's attributes, if any: A stands for archive, R means read-only, H is hidden, and S is system. The ATTRIB command can change a file's attributes. To add an attribute to a file, type the attribute letter preceded by a plus sign (+), and then the filename. To delete an attribute, use a minus sign (−). Multiple attributes can be added or removed in one command.

- Wildcards are two special characters, asterisk (*) and question mark (?), that you can use in place of all or part of a filename to make a command act on more than one file at a time. Wildcards work with all command-line commands that take filenames. The asterisk (*) wildcard replaces any part of a filename, before and/or after the period. The ? wildcard replaces any single character. Virtually every command that deals with files will take wildcards.

- Use the REN (or RENAME) command to rename files and folders. If the new name contains spaces, enclose the name in quotation marks.

- To delete files, you use the DEL or ERASE command. DEL and ERASE are identical commands and can be used interchangeably. DEL will not erase directories. To delete a single file, type the **DEL** command followed by the name of the file. No confirmation will appear on the screen. To delete all of the files in a directory, you can use the *.* (star-dot-star) wildcard. Upon receiving the DEL *.* command, Windows responds with "Are you sure? (Y/N)," to which you respond with a Y or N. Pressing Y erases every file in the directory. It pays to check twice before you delete, because the command line has no function equivalent to the Windows Recycle Bin that allows you to retrieve an accidentally deleted file; once a file has been erased, you can recover it only by using a special recovery utility.

- The COPY and MOVE commands are used to copy and move files. The only difference between them is whether the original is left behind (COPY) or not (MOVE). Type **COPY** or **MOVE** and a space. Point the prompt to the directory containing the files to be copied or moved. Type the *name(s)* of the file(s) to be copied/moved (with or without wildcards) and a space. Type the *path* of the new location for the files. Press ENTER. The COPY/MOVE command not only lets you put a file in a new location; it also lets you change the name of the file at the same time.

- Check for the common typo of substituting a semicolon for a colon, because the semicolon means "end of command" and therefore ignores both the semicolon and anything you type after it.

- XCOPY works similarly to COPY but has extra switches that give XCOPY the power to work with multiple directories. Because XCOPY works on directories, you don't have to use filenames as you would in COPY, although you can use filenames and wildcards. The /S switch tells XCOPY to copy all subdirectories except empty ones. The /E switch tells it to copy empty subdirectories.

- Batch files are text files that contain a series of commands, with one command per line. Batch files must end with the .BAT file extension. To create batch files, you can use the Edit program within the command line or a text editor from the Windows GUI such as Notepad.

- The TYPE command displays the contents of a file on the screen. Don't use TYPE on binary files, as the results are unpredictable.

- Every time you open a command prompt, Windows loads a number of settings by default. You can see all of these settings by running the SET command.

- Storing batch files in a folder included in a Windows path ensures that your batch files will run no matter where your command prompt is focused. Use the PATH command to see the current path. To add a folder to the Windows path, type **PATH** followed by that folder.

- A plethora of tools, utilities, and commands are available to prepare, maintain, detect, and/or correct operating system file structures. Many of these, including CHKDSK, FORMAT, and SFC, can be started or run from a command prompt and/or from the Windows GUI.

Key Terms

8.3 naming system *(163)*

American Standard Code for Information Interchange (ASCII) *(164)*

ATTRIB.EXE *(174)*

attributes *(174)*

CD (CHDIR) command *(168)*

CHKDSK (Checkdisk) command *(185)*

COPY command *(178)*

DEL (ERASE) command *(177)*

DIR command *(167)*

FORMAT command *(185)*

MD (MKDIR) command *(170)*

MOVE command *(178)*

path *(166)*

prompt *(160)* ✓

read-only attribute *(174)*

RD (RMDIR) command *(171)*

REN (RENAME) command *(176)* ✓

root directory *(166)*

Run dialog box *(162)*

SFC (System File Checker) *(185)*

switch *(167)*

syntax *(167)*

Unicode *(165)*

wildcard *(175)*

XCOPY command *(180)*

Key Term Quiz

Use the Key Terms list to complete the sentences that follow. Not all terms will be used.

1. The _Command-line Interface_ tells you it's ready to receive commands by displaying a specific set of characters called a(n) _prompt_.

2. Extra text you type after a command to modify its operation is called a(n) _switch_.

3. The first universal file format was called _ASCII_.

4. The _DIR command_ shows you the contents of the directory that currently has focus.

5. Each file's _attributes_ determine how programs (such as My Computer or Computer) treat the file in special situations.

6. The exact location of a file is called its _Path_.

7. An external program that enables you to inspect and change file attributes is _Attrib.exe_.

8. The asterisk is a special character called a(n) _wildcard_ that you can use in place of part of a filename when executing a DOS command.

9. Use the _Ren (Rename) Command_ to rename a file.

10. To move a file from the root directory into a subfolder, use the _Move command_.

Multiple-Choice Quiz

1. Which of the following is an illegal character in a Windows filename?

   A. * (asterisk) ⟵ circled

   B. . (dot)

   C. – (dash)

   D. _ (underscore)

2. Which command pauses after displaying a screen's worth of directory contents?

   A. DIR P

   B. PDIR

   C. PD

   D. DIR /P ⟵ circled

3. Which of the following commands will delete all of the files in a directory?

   A. DEL *.* ⟵ circled

   B. DEL ALL

   C. DEL ?.?

   D. DEL *.?

4. Which command do you use to change the focus of the command prompt to a different directory?

   A. DIR /N

   B. CDDIR

   C. CD

   D. DIR /C

5. Which attribute keeps a file from being displayed when the DIR command is performed?

   A. Hidden

   B. Archive

   C. Read-only

   D. Protected

6. What command enables you to make a new directory in a Windows XP Professional system?

   A. MF

   B. MKFOL

   C. MD

   D. MAKEDIR

7. What is the name of the command-line text editor that comes with Windows?

   A. Text

   B. Edit

   C. DOStxt

   D. DOSedt

8. What commands can you type at the Run dialog box to access the command-line interface in Windows XP? (Select two.)

   A. CMD

   B. COMMAND

   C. MSDOS

   D. PROMPT

9. Joey wants to change the name of a file from START.BAT to HAMMER.BAT. Which of the following commands would accomplish this feat?

   A. REN HAMMER.BAT START.BAT

   B. REN START.BAT HAMMER.BAT

   C. RENAME /S START.BAT HAMMER.BAT

   D. RENAME /S HAMMER.BAT START.BAT

10. What is the name for the rules for typing a command correctly?

    A. Protocol

    B. Syntax

    C. Legacy

    D. Instruction set

11. What is the command to make MYFILE.TXT read-only?

    A. ATTRIB MYFILE.TXT +R

    B. ATTRIB MYFILE.TXT –R

    C. READONLY MYFILE.TXT

    D. MYFILE.TXT /READONLY

12. What is the maximum number of characters in a Windows 2000/XP/Vista filename?

    A. 8

    B. 255

    C. 65,536

    D. No limit

13. What user profile directory is displayed at a Windows Vista command prompt by default?

    A. C:\All Users*User name*

    B. C:\Users*User name*

    C. C:\ Documents and Settings*User name*

    D. C:\Windows\system32\drivers\etc

14. How do you run a command at the Windows Vista command prompt with elevated or administrative privileges?

    A. Enter an elevated user name and password at the command prompt.

    B. Right-click a command-prompt shortcut and then select Run as PowerUser.

    C. Right-click a command-prompt shortcut and then select Run as administrator.

    D. When prompted, enter a valid root or supervisor password.

15. What tool would you use at a Windows Vista command prompt to edit operating system startup parameters located in the data store?

    A. SFC /runnow

    B. Msconfig

    C. Msinfo32

    D. Bcdedit.exe

■ Essay Quiz

1. You've been tasked to teach some newbie techs, whose only computer experience involves Windows, about the beauty and power of the command line. For their first lesson, write a short essay explaining how the command-line interface works, including the directory structure, filename limitations, and interaction with the command prompt.

2. You work the help desk at a college computing center. Some applications that the students must use are run from a command line. Write a memo for the help desk personnel explaining how to use the DIR, CD, MD, DEL, and RD commands, including any appropriate cautions.

3. Your coworker needs to remove the hidden attribute from a file called PAYROLL.XLS that is stored in the EMPLOYEE directory on the D: drive. Write an e-mail explaining how to open a command-line window, navigate to the file, verify its presence, and remove the hidden attribute.

4. You've been tasked to teach some newbie techs, whose only computer experience involves Windows, about the beauty and power of the command line. For their second lesson, write a short essay explaining how wildcards work.

5. Write a brief essay explaining in your own words how to use Mike's Five-Step COPY/MOVE process. Give an example.

Lab Projects

• Lab Project 6.1

For each of the following files, translate the location into a path you can type at a command prompt.

- A file named BEACH.JPG in the subdirectory PICTURES in the directory EZIBA on the primary floppy drive:

  _____

- A file named BLACKDOG.WAV in the subdirectory LEDZEP in the subdirectory ROCK in the directory MUSIC on the C: drive:

  _____

- A file named WEAPON.PCX in the subdirectory BOBAFETT in the subdirectory PLAYERS in the subdirectory BASEQ2 in the directory QUAKE2 on the D: drive:

  _____

- A file named AUTOEXEC.BAT in the root directory on a standard PC with a single hard drive:

  _____

- A file named MEYERS.DOC in the subdirectory CONTRACTS in the subdirectory LEGAL in the directory ACCOUNTS on a CD-ROM on a system with one hard drive, one CD-ROM drive, and one floppy drive:

  _____

• Lab Project 6.2

To practice making/removing directories and copying/moving files, do the following:

① Open a command-line window and point to the root directory, C:.

② Use the MD command to create a directory called WHALES. Use the CD command to point to the new directory. Use the MD command again to create a subdirectory of WHALES called MOBYDICK. Use the CD command to point to the new subdirectory.

③ Populate the MOBYDICK subdirectory with files by opening Notepad and creating a "dummy" file called AHAB.TXT. Save it in the MOBYDICK subdirectory.

④ Use the MOV
AHAB.TX
DIR com
success
copy
subd
Again use

⑤ Use the RD com
MOBYDICK subdirec
not? Use the RD command
to solve the problem.

Securing Windows Resources

"Only the insecure strive for security."

—WAYNE DYER

In this chapter, you will learn how to

- **Create and administer Windows users and groups**
- **Define and utilize NTFS permissions for authorization**
- **Describe how to share a Windows computer securely**

You might ask me, "What's the single greatest aspect that keeps Microsoft Windows the number one operating system in the world?" My answer is "Windows is the easiest operating system for securing resources, individual computers, and entire networks." Windows really gets it right when it comes to protection. Windows uses a combination of user accounts and groups that tie into the NTFS file system to provide incredibly powerful file and folder protection. This user/group/NTFS combo scales down to just a single computer and scales up to a network of computers that can span the world. Windows doesn't just stop at files and folders, either.

The only serious challenge to all this great security is that Windows blurs the line between protecting just a single computer versus protecting a single computer over a network. In this chapter you will see Windows security from the aspect of a single, or *standalone*, machine. You will look more at network security in Chapter 16, "Mastering Computer Security."

Authentication with Users and Groups

The key to protecting your data is based on two related processes: authentication and authorization. Authentication is the process by which you determine a person at your computer is who he says he is. The most common way to authenticate is by using a user name and password. Once a user is authenticated, he needs authorization, the process that states what a user can and cannot do on that system. Authorization, at least for files and folders, is controlled by the NTFS file system, so we'll tackle that in the second section of this chapter.

Microsoft's answer to the authentication/authorization process is amazing. Inside every Windows computer is a list of names of users who are allowed access to the system. When Windows starts, it presents some form of logon screen where you enter (or select) your user name and then enter something secret (usually a password) that confirms you are the person assigned to that user name. Each of these individual records is called a local user account. If you don't have a local user account created on a particular system, you won't be able to log on to that computer (Figure 7.1).

Each version of Windows has a similar application for creating user accounts. But each one differs enough that it's useful to view them individually. Then we'll look at using passwords and groups to manage users, tasks that all Windows versions share.

Tech Tip

Principle of Least Privilege

A good security practice to determine what type of user account to give to a specific person is the principle of least privilege. In essence, you want to give users just enough—but no more—permissions to accomplish their tasks. Giving more than needed begs for problems or accidents and should be avoided.

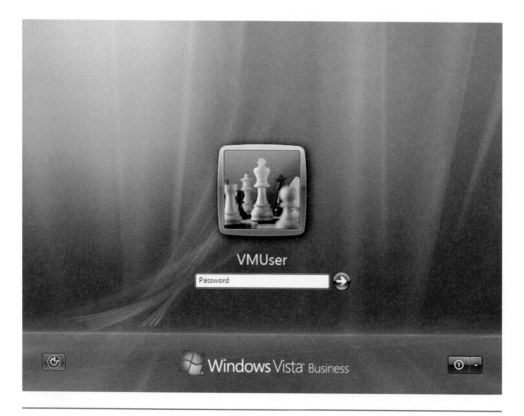

• **Figure 7.1** Windows Logon screen

Managing Users in Windows 2000

One handy tool for managing users in Windows 2000 is called the **Users and Passwords applet** (Figure 7.2). You access this tool from the Control Panel.

When you install Windows 2000, by default you add two user accounts to the computer: administrator and guest. You can also choose to let the operating system assume that you are the sole user of the computer and not prompt you for a password for logging into Windows. As you might imagine, this severely limits any security on that Windows machine.

You can check this setting after installation by opening the Users and Passwords applet in Control Panel to see the setting for *Users must enter a user name and password to use this computer*. Figure 7.3 shows this choice selected, which means you will see a logon box every time you restart your computer. Also notice that the only user is administrator. That's the account used to log on when no other user is assumed.

Using the administrator account is just fine when you're doing administrative tasks such as installing updates, adding printers, adding and removing programs and Windows components, updating device drivers, and creating users and groups. Best practice for the workplace is to create one or more user accounts and only log in with the user accounts, not the administrator account. This gives you a lot more control over who or what happens to the computer.

For the sake of security, a wise administrator also enables the setting on the Advanced tab of Users and Passwords under Secure Boot Settings. If checked, as shown in Figure 7.4, it requires users to press CTRL-ALT-DELETE before logging on. This setting is a defense against certain viruses that try to capture your user name and password, sometimes by presenting a fake logon prompt. Pressing CTRL-ALT-DELETE removes such programs from memory and allows the actual logon dialog box to appear.

Creating a new user account enables that user to log on with a user name and password. The administrator can set the rights and permissions for the user and audit the user's access to certain network resources. For that reason, it is good practice to create users on a desktop computer. You are working with the same concepts on a small scale that an administrator must work with in a domain. Let's review the steps in this procedure for Windows 2000.

If you're logged on in Windows 2000 as the administrator or a member of the local Administrators group, open the Users and Passwords applet

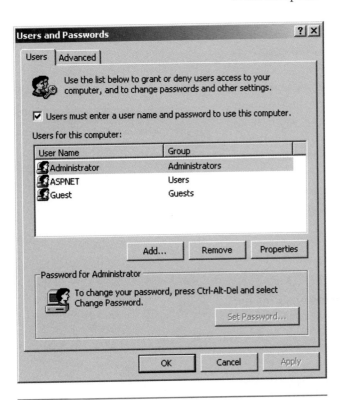

• **Figure 7.2**   Users and Passwords

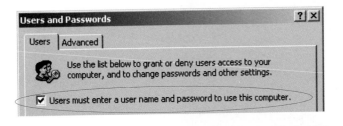

• **Figure 7.3**   Security begins with turning on *Users must enter a user name and password to use this computer.*

When you install Windows, assuming your computer is not made a member of a domain, you may choose to let the OS assume that you are the only user of the computer and do not want to see the logon dialog box.

Try This!

Turning On Logon Requirements and Secure Boot Settings

Security is all the rage in today's world, so having a computer with wonderful built-in security features sitting there with those features disabled makes little sense. Try This! Turn on the option to require a logon.

To complete this, you need a computer running Windows 2000 Professional.

1. Go to Control Panel and open Users and Passwords.

2. Make sure the box by *Users must enter a user name and password to use this computer* is checked.

3. Click the Advanced tab and make sure the box under Secure Boot Settings is checked.

4. Click OK to close the dialog box.

The next time anyone logs on to this computer, they will first have to press CTRL-ALT-DELETE to open a logon dialog box. Then they will be required to provide a user name and password.

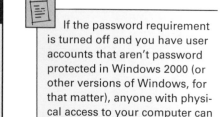

If the password requirement is turned off and you have user accounts that aren't password protected in Windows 2000 (or other versions of Windows, for that matter), anyone with physical access to your computer can turn it on and use it by pressing the power button. This is potentially a very bad thing!

To create and manage users, you must be logged on as the administrator, be a member of the Administrators group, or have an administrator account. Assign a password to the administrator account so that only authorized users can access this all-powerful account.

from Control Panel and click the Add button. This opens the Add New User Wizard (Figure 7.5). Enter the user name that the user will use to log on. Enter the user's first and last names in the Full name field, and if you wish, enter some text that describes this person in the Description field. If this is at work, enter a job description in this field. The Full name and Description fields are optional.

Blank passwords or those that are easily visible on a sticky note provide *no security*. Always insist on non-blank passwords, and do not let anyone leave a password sitting out in the open. See the section on passwords later in the chapter.

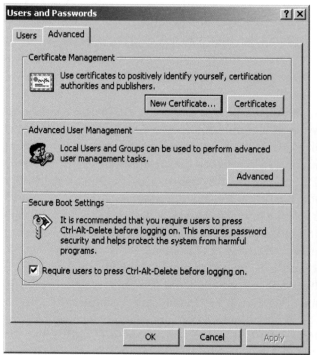

• **Figure 7.4** Make your computer more secure by enabling Secure Boot Settings.

• **Figure 7.5** Adding a new user

● Figure 7.6   Create user password

After entering the user information, click the Next button to continue. This opens a password dialog box where you can enter and confirm the initial password for this new user (Figure 7.6). Click the Next button to continue.

Now you get to decide what groups the new user should belong to. Select one of the two suggested options—standard user or restricted user—or select the Other option button and choose a group from the drop-down list. Select **Standard User**, which on a Windows 2000 Professional desktop makes this person a member of the local Power Users group as well as the Local Users group. Click the Finish button to close the dialog box. You should see your new user listed in the Users and Passwords dialog box. While you're there, note how easy it is for an administrator to change a user's password. Simply select a user from the list and then click on the Set Password button. Enter and confirm the new password in the Set Password dialog box. Figure 7.7 shows the Set Password dialog box with the Users and Passwords dialog box in the background.

Now let's say you want to change a password. Select the new user in the *Users for this computer* list on the Users page. Then click the Set Password button on the Users page. Enter and confirm the new password and then click the OK button to apply the changes.

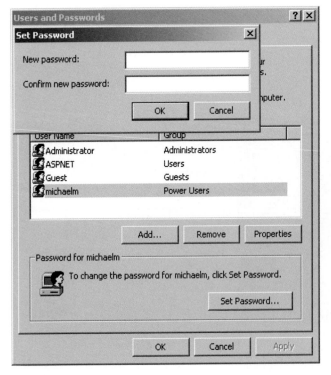

● Figure 7.7   Set Password dialog box

Managing Users in Windows XP

Although Windows XP has essentially the same type of accounts database as Windows 2000, the **User Accounts applet** in the Control Panel replaces the Users and Passwords applet and further simplifies user management tasks.

Windows XP has two very different ways to deal with user accounts and how you log on to a system: the blank user name and password text boxes, reminiscent of Windows 2000, and the Windows XP **Welcome screen** (Figure 7.8). If your Windows XP computer is a member of a Windows domain, your system automatically uses the Windows Classic style, including the requirement to press CTRL-ALT-DEL to get to the user name and password text boxes, just as in Windows 2000. If your Windows XP computer is not a member of a domain, you may use either method, although the Welcome screen is the default. Windows XP Home and Windows XP Media Center cannot join a domain, so these versions of Windows only use the Welcome screen. Windows Tablet PC Edition functions just as Windows XP Professional.

• **Figure 7.8**   Windows XP Welcome screen

Assuming that your Windows XP system is *not* a member of a domain, I'll concentrate on the XP Welcome screen and some of the options you'll see in the User Accounts Control Panel applet.

The User Accounts applet is very different from the old Users and Passwords applet in Windows 2000. User Accounts hides the complete list of users, using a simplistic reference to account types that is actually a reference to its group membership. An account that is a member of the local administrators group is said to be a **computer administrator**; an account that only belongs to the Local Users group is said to be a **limited user** account. Which users the applet displays depends on which type of user is currently logged on (see Figure 7.9). When an administrator is logged on, the administrator sees both types of accounts and the guest account. Limited users see only their own account in User Accounts.

Windows XP requires you to create a second account that is a member of the administrators group during the initial Windows installation. This is for simple redundancy—if one administrator is not available or is not able to log on to the computer, another one can.

Creating users is a straightforward process. You need to provide a user name (a password can be added later), and you need to know which type of account to create: computer administrator or limited. To create a new user in Windows XP, open the User Accounts applet from the Control Panel and

203

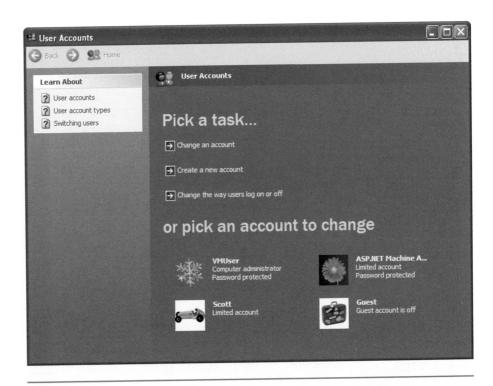

● **Figure 7.9**   User Accounts dialog box showing a computer administrator, a couple of limited accounts, and the guest account (disabled)

click *Create a new account*. On the *Pick an account type* page, you can create either type of account (Figure 7.10). Simply follow the prompts on the screen. After you create your local accounts, you'll see them listed when you open the User Accounts applet.

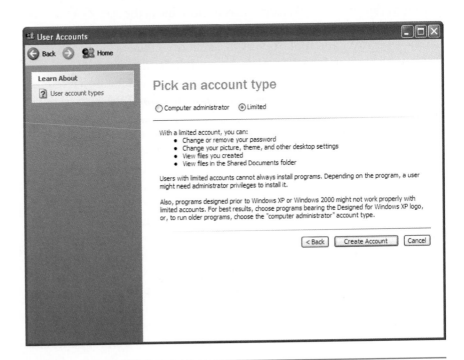

● **Figure 7.10**   The *Pick an account type* page showing both options available

Head back to the User Accounts applet and look at the *Change the way users log on and off* option. Select it to see two checkboxes (Figure 7.11). If you select the *Use the Welcome screen* checkbox, Windows brings up the friendly Welcome screen shown in Figure 7.12 each time users log in. If this box is unchecked, you'll get the classic login screen (Figure 7.13).

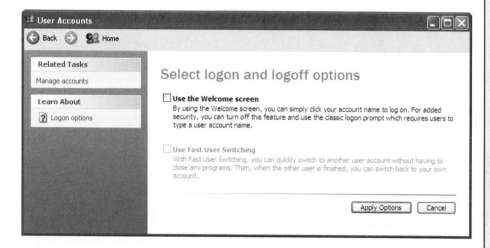

Tech Tip

Going Retro

The old Users and Passwords Control Panel applet is still in every version of Windows XP. If you're on a Windows XP Professional or Windows XP Tablet PC Edition system and your system is part of a domain, the old program comes up automatically when you click the User Accounts applet. If you're running Window XP Professional or Windows XP Tablet PC Edition but not on a domain, or if you're running XP Home or Media Center, go to Start | Run and type the following:

`control userpasswords2`

This brings up the old applet, which is the best way to change the administrator password on a system.

• **Figure 7.11**   Select logon and logoff options

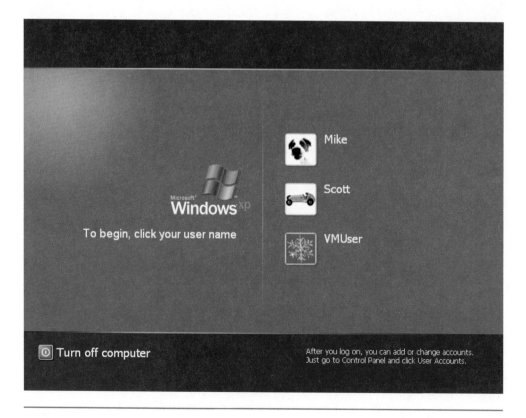

• **Figure 7.12**   Welcome screen with three accounts

The second option, Use Fast User Switching, enables you to switch to another user without logging off of the currently running user, a feature appropriately called *Fast User Switching*. This option is handy when two people actively share a system, or when someone wants to borrow your system for a moment but you don't want to close all of your programs. This option is only active if you have the *Use the Welcome screen* checkbox enabled. If Fast User Switching is enabled, when you click the Log Off button on the Start menu, you get the option to switch users, as shown in Figure 7.14.

● **Figure 7.13**   Classic Logon screen, XP style

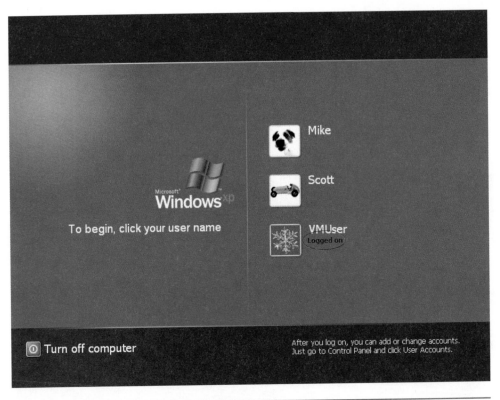

● **Figure 7.14**   Switching users on the Welcome screen

Managing Users in Windows Vista

Microsoft made some major changes in the transition to Windows Vista, including to the user accounts and the applet used to create and modify them. Just as with Windows XP, you create three accounts when you set up a computer: guest, administrator, and a local account that's a member of the Administrators group. That's about where the similarities end.

To add or modify a user account, you have numerous options depending on which Control Panel view you select and which version and update of Vista you have installed. Windows Vista Business and Ultimate, for example, in the default Control Panel Home view, offer the User Accounts

applet (Figure 7.15). Windows Home Premium, in contrast, gives you the User Accounts and Family Safety applet (Figure 7.16). The options under each applet differ as well, as you can see in the screenshots.

Most techs almost immediately change the Control Panel view to Classic, but even there the different versions of Windows—and whether you're logged into a workgroup or a domain—give you different versions of the User Accounts applet. Figure 7.17 shows the User Accounts applet in

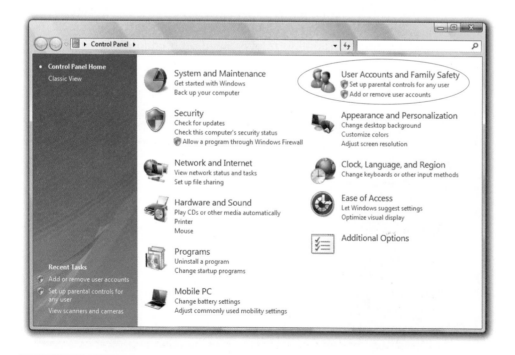

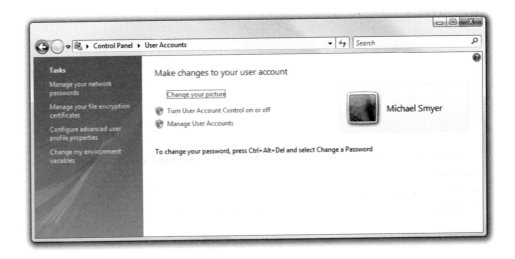

• **Figure 7.17** User Accounts applet in Windows Vista Business

Windows Vista Business in a domain environment. Figure 7.18 shows the applet in Windows Vista Home Premium.

The Tasks options on the left are similar, with the addition of Parental Controls in the Home Premium edition, but the main options differ a lot. This chapter assumes a standalone machine, so we'll look more closely at the options with Vista Home Premium.

Windows Vista Home Premium uses Vista's version of the Welcome screen for logging in, so each user account has a picture associated with it. You can change the picture from the User Accounts applet. You can also change the name of the user account here and alter the account type, demoting an account from administrator to standard user, for example.

 You must have one account as an administrator. If you try to demote the sole administrator account, you'll find the option dimmed.

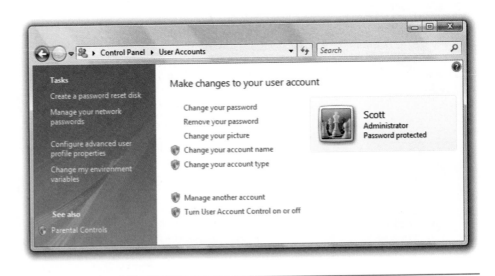

• **Figure 7.18** User Accounts applet in Windows Vista Home Premium

User Account Control

Windows XP made it too easy—and, in fact, almost necessary—to make your primary account on a computer an administrator account. Because limited users can't do common tasks, such as running certain programs, installing applications, updating applications, updating Windows, and so on, most users simply created an administrator-level account and logged in. Because such accounts have full control over the computer, malware that slipped in with that account could do a lot more harm.

Microsoft addressed this problem with the User Account Control (UAC), a feature that enables standard users to do common tasks and provides a permissions dialog (Figure 7.19) when standard users *and* administrators do certain things that could potentially harm the computer (such as attempt to install a program). Vista user accounts now function much more like user accounts in Linux and Macintosh OS X, with programs asking for administrative permission before making changes to the computer.

Parental Controls

With Parental Controls, you can monitor and limit the activities of any Standard User in Windows Vista, a feature that gives parents and managers an excellent level of control over the content their children and employees can access (Figure 7.20). Activity Reporting logs applications run or attempted to run, Web sites visited or attempted to visit, any kind of files downloaded, and more. You can block various Web sites by type or specific URL, or you can allow only certain Web sites, a far more powerful option.

Parental Controls enable you to limit the time that standard users can spend logged in. You can specify acceptable and unacceptable times of day when standard users can log in. You can restrict access both to types of games and to specific applications. If you like playing rather gruesome games filled with monsters and blood that you don't want your kids to play, for example, you can simply block any games with

• **Figure 7.19** Prompting for permission

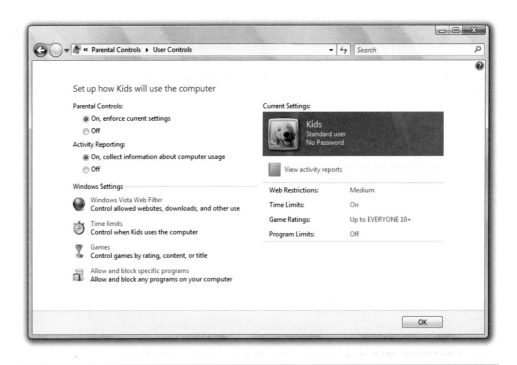

● **Figure 7.20**   Parental Controls

certain ESRB (Entertainment Software Rating Board) ratings, such as E for Everyone, T for Teen, or M for Mature or Mature 17+.

Managing Users in General

Aside from the specific aspects of managing users in each particular version of Windows, there are a few security considerations that apply to every version of Windows, such as using appropriate passwords and creating user groups.

Passwords

Passwords are the ultimate key to protecting your computers. A user account with a valid password gets you into any system. Even if the user account only has limited permissions, you still have a security breach. Remember: for a hacker, just getting into the network is half the battle.

Protect your passwords. Never give out passwords over the phone. If a user forgets a password, an administrator should reset the password to a complex combination of letters and numbers, and then allow the user to change the password to something the user wants, according to the parameters set by the administrator.

Make your users choose good passwords. I once attended a security seminar, and the speaker had everyone stand up. She then began to ask questions about our passwords—if we responded yes to the question, we were to sit down. She began to ask questions such as

"Do you use the name of your spouse as a password?" and

"Do you use your pet's name?"

Using non-alphanumeric characters makes any password much more difficult to crack, for two reasons. First, adding non-alphanumeric characters forces the hacker to consider many more possible characters than just letters and numbers. Second, most password crackers use combinations of common words and numbers to try to hack a password.

Because non-alphanumeric characters don't fit into common words or numbers, including a character such as an exclamation point defeats these common-word hacks. Not all serving systems allow you to use characters such as @, $, %, or \, however, so you need to experiment to see if a particular server will accept them.

By the time she had asked about 15 questions, only 6 people out of some 300 were still standing! The reality is that most of us choose passwords that are amazingly easy to hack. Make sure you use a **strong password**: at least eight characters in length, including letters, numbers, and punctuation symbols. *test question*

Once you've forced your users to choose strong passwords, you should make them change passwords at regular intervals. Although this concept sounds good on paper, in the real world it is a hard policy to maintain. For starters, users tend to forget passwords when they change a lot. This can lead to an even bigger security problem because users start writing passwords down!

If your organization forces you to change passwords often, one way to remember the password is to use a numbering system. I worked at a company that required me to change my password at the beginning of each month, so I did something very simple. I took a root password—let's say it was "m3y3rs5"—and simply added a number to the end representing the current month. So when June rolled around, for example, I would change my password to "m3y3rs56." It worked pretty well!

Windows XP and Windows Vista enable currently logged-on users to create a **password reset disk** they can use if they forget a password. This is very important to have. If an administrator resets the password by using User Accounts or Local Users and Groups, and you then log on with the new password, you will discover that you cannot access some items, including files you encrypted when logged on with the forgotten password. When you reset a password with a password reset disk, you can log on with the new password and still have access to previously encrypted files.

Best of all, with the password reset disk, users have the power to fix their own passwords. Encourage your users to create this disk; they only have this power if they create a password reset disk *before* they forget the password! If you need to create a password reset disk for a computer on a network (domain), search the Help system for "password reset disk" and follow the instructions for password reset disks for a computer on a domain.

Windows Vista has an obvious option in the Tasks list to *Create a password reset disk*. You'll need to have a floppy disk inserted or a USB flash drive to create the disk.

Groups

A **group** is simply a collection of accounts that share the same access capabilities. A single account can be a member of multiple groups. Groups are essential for managing a network of computers but also can come in handy on a single computer with multiple users.

Groups make Windows administration much easier in two ways. First, you can assign a certain level of access for a file or folder to a group instead of to just a single user account. For example, you can make a group called Accounting and put all of the accounting user accounts in that group. If a person quits, you don't need to worry about assigning all of the proper access levels when you create a new account for his or her replacement. After you make an account for the new person, you just add the new account to the appropriate access group! Second, Windows provides numerous built-in groups with various access levels already predetermined. As you might imagine, there are differences among the versions.

Every secure organization sets up various security policies and procedures to ensure that security is maintained. Windows has various mechanisms to implement such things as requiring a strong password, for example.

See the last section of this chapter, "Protecting Data with Encryption," for the scoop on the ultimate in security.

Groups in Windows 2000 Windows 2000 provides seven built-in groups: Administrators, Power Users, Users, Backup Operators, Replicator, Everyone, and Guests. These built-in groups have a number of preset capabilities. You cannot delete these groups.

- **Administrators** Any account that is a member of the Administrators group has complete administrator privileges. It is common for the primary user of a Windows system to have her account in the Administrators group.

- **Power Users** Members of the Power Users group are almost as powerful as Administrators, but they cannot install new devices or access other users' files or folders unless the files or folders specifically provide them access.

- **Users** Members of the Users group cannot edit the Registry or access critical system files. They can create groups but can manage only those they create.

- **Backup Operators** Backup operators have the same rights as users, except that they can run backup programs that access any file or folder—for backup purposes only.

- **Replicator** Members of the Replicator group can replicate files and folders in a domain.

- **Everyone** This group applies to any user who can log on to the system. You cannot edit this group.

- **Guests** Enabling the Guests group allows someone who does not have an account on the system to log on by using a guest account. You might use this feature at a party, for example, to provide casual Internet access to guests, or at a library terminal. Most often, the guest account remains disabled for every version of Windows.

Groups in Windows XP Windows XP diverges a lot from Windows 2000 on user accounts. If you're running XP Professional and you are on a Windows domain, XP offers all of the accounts listed previously, but it adds other specialized groups, including HelpServicesGroup and Remote Desktop Users. Windows XP Home and XP Professional, when installed on standalone PCs or PCs that are connected to a workgroup but not a domain, run in a specialized networking mode called *simple file sharing*. A Windows XP system running simple file sharing has only three account types: computer administrator, limited user, and guest. Computer administrators can do anything, as you might suspect. Limited users can access only certain things and have limits on where they can save files on the PC. The guest account is disabled by default but works the same way as in Windows 2000.

Groups in Windows Vista The professional editions of Windows Vista (Business, Ultimate, and Enterprise) offer the same groups found in Windows XP Professional and throw in a lot more. Some of the default groups, such as Distributed COM Users, target specific roles in certain industries and mean little for the average user or tech. Other specific group types enable people to check on the performance and reliability of a computer, but without gaining access to any of the documents on the computer. These groups include Event Log Readers, Performance Log Users, and Performance

Monitor Users. These groups provide excellent levels of access for technicians to help keep busy Vista machines healthy.

Like Windows XP, the home editions of Windows Vista (Home Basic and Home Premium) offer only three groups: administrators, users, and guests. Administrators and guests function as they do in all of the other versions of Windows. Members of the Users group, on the other hand, are called standard users and differ significantly from the limited users of Windows XP infamy. Standard users are prevented from harming the computer or uninstalling applications but can run most applications. Technicians don't have to run over to standard user accounts to enable access to common tasks such as printing or doing e-mail.

● **Figure 7.21**   Local Users and Groups in Windows Vista

Adding Groups and Changing Group Membership

The professional versions of Windows—including Windows 2000, XP, and Vista—enable you to add new groups to your computer by using the **Local Users and Groups** tool, found in the Computer Management applet of the Administrative Tools. This tool also enables you to create user accounts and change group membership for users. Figure 7.21 shows the Local Users and Groups in Windows Vista with the Groups selected.

To add a group, simply right-click on a blank spot in the Groups folder and select New Group. This opens the New Group dialog box, where you can type in a group name and description in their respective fields (Figure 7.22).

To add users to this group, click the Add button. The dialog box that opens varies a little in name among the three operating systems. In Vista it's called the Se-

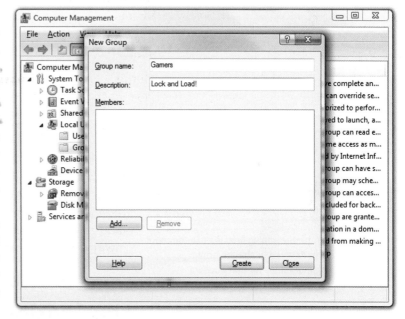

● **Figure 7.22**   New Group dialog box in Windows Vista

lect Users, Computers, or Groups dialog box (Figure 7.23). The Windows 2000 dialog box presents a list of user accounts. Windows XP and Vista add some complexity to the tool.

A user account, a group, a computer; these are all object types in Microsoft lingo. To give you a lot of control over what you do or how you select various objects, Microsoft beefed up this dialog box. The short story of how to select a user account is to click the Advanced button to expand the dialog box and then click the Find Now button (Figure 7.24).

Figure 7.23 Select Users, Computers, or Groups dialog box

Figure 7.25 Properties dialog box of a user account, where you can change group memberships for that account

Figure 7.24 Select Users, Computers, or Groups dialog box with Advanced options expanded to show user accounts

You can add or remove user accounts from groups with the Local Users and Groups tool. You select the Users folder, right-click a user account you want to change, and select Properties from the context menu. Then select the Member Of tab on the user account's Properties dialog box (Figure 7.25). Click Add to add group membership. Select a group and click Remove to take away a group membership. It's a clean, well-designed tool.

■ Authorization Through NTFS

User accounts and passwords provide the foundation for securing a Windows computer, enabling users to authenticate onto that PC. The essential next step in security is authorization, determining what a legitimate user can do with the resources—files, folders, applications, and so on—on that computer. Windows uses the NT file system and permissions to protect its resources.

NTFS Permissions

In Windows 2000, XP, Vista, and 7, every folder and file on an NTFS partition has a list that contains two sets of data. First, the list details every user and group that has access to that file or folder. Second, the list specifies the level of access that each user or group has to that file or folder. The level of access is defined by a set of restrictions called NTFS permissions.

NTFS permissions define exactly what a particular account can or cannot do to the file or folder and are thus quite detailed and powerful. You can make it possible, for example, for a person to edit a file but not delete it. You can let someone create a folder and not allow other people to make subfolders. NTFS file and folder permissions are so complicated that entire books have been written on them! Fortunately, the CompTIA A+ Practical Application exam tests your understanding of only a few basic concepts of NTFS permissions: Ownership, Take Ownership permission, Change permission, Folder permissions, and File permissions.

- **Ownership** When you create a new file or folder on an NTFS partition, you become the *owner* of that file or folder. A newly created file or folder by default gives everyone full permission to access, delete, and otherwise manipulate that file or folder. Owners can do anything they want to the files or folders they own, including changing the permissions to prevent anybody, even administrators, from accessing them.

- **Take Ownership permission** With the Take Ownership special permission, anyone with the permission can seize control of a file or folder. Administrator accounts have Take Ownership permission for everything. Note the difference here between owning a file and accessing a file. If you own a file, you can prevent anyone from accessing that file. An administrator whom you have blocked, however, can take that ownership away from you and *then* access that file!

- **Change permission** Another important permission for all NTFS files and folders is the Change permission. An account with this permission can give or take away permissions for other accounts.

- **Folder permissions** Let's look at a typical folder in my Windows XP system to see how this one works. My E: drive is formatted as NTFS, and on it I created a folder called E:\MIKE. I set the permissions for the E:\MIKE folder by right-clicking on the folder, selecting Properties, and clicking the Security tab (see Figure 7.26).

- **File permissions** File permissions are similar to Folder permissions. We'll talk about File permissions right after we cover Folder permissions.

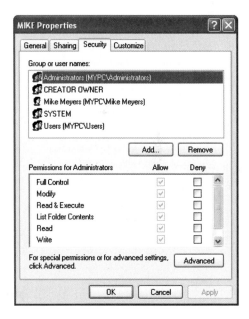

● **Figure 7.26** The Security tab lets you set permissions.

In Windows, just about everything in the computer has a Security tab in its properties, and every Security tab contains two main areas. The top area shows the list of accounts that have permissions for that resource. The lower area shows exactly what permissions have been assigned to the selected account.

Here are the standard permissions for a folder:

- **Full Control** Enables you to do anything you want.
- **Modify** Enables you to do anything except delete files or subfolders.
- **Read & Execute** Enables you to see the contents of the folder and any subfolders.
- **List Folder Contents** Enables you to see the contents of the folder and any subfolders. (This permission seems the same as the Read & Execute permission, but it is only inherited by folders.)
- **Read** Enables you to read any file in the folder.
- **Write** Enables you to write to files and create new files and folders.

File permissions are quite similar to folder permissions, with the main difference being the Special Permissions option, which I'll talk about a bit later in the chapter.

- **Full Control** Enables you to do anything you want.
- **Modify** Enables you to do anything except take ownership or change permissions on the file.
- **Read & Execute** If the file is a program, you can run it.
- **Read** If the file is data, you can read it.
- **Write** Enables you to write to the file.

Take some time to think about these permissions. Why would Microsoft create them? Think of situations where you might want to give a group Modify permission. Also, you can assign more than one permission. In many situations, we like to give users both the Read as well as the Write permission.

Permissions are cumulative. If you have Full Control on a folder and only Read permission on a file in the folder, you get Full Control permission on the file.

Permission Propagation

Permissions present an interesting challenge when you're moving and copying files. Techs need to understand what happens to permissions in several circumstances:

- Copying data within one NTFS-based partition
- Moving data within one NTFS-based partition
- Copying data between two NTFS-based partitions
- Moving data between two NTFS-based partitions

Windows versions for home use have only a limited set of permissions you can assign. As far as folder permissions go, you can assign only one: Make This Folder Private. To see this in action, right-click a file or folder and select Sharing and Security from the options. Note that you can't just select the properties and see a Security tab as you can in the professional-oriented versions of Windows. Windows Home versions do not have file-level permissions.

- Copying data from an NTFS-based partition to a FAT- or FAT32-based partition

- Moving data from an NTFS-based partition to a FAT- or FAT32-based partition

Do the permissions stay as they were on the original resource? Do they change to something else? Microsoft would describe the questions as such: Do inheritable permissions propagate? Ugh. CompTIA describes the process with the term **permission propagation**, which I take to mean "what happens to permissions on an object when you move or copy that object."

If you look at the bottom of the Security tab in Windows 2000, you'll see a little checkbox that says *Allow Inheritable Permissions from Parent to Propagate to This Object*. In other words, any files or subfolders created in this folder get the same permissions for the same users/groups that the folder has, a feature called **inheritance**. Deselecting this option enables you to stop users from getting a specific permission via inheritance. Windows XP and Windows Vista have the same feature, only it's accessed through the Advanced button in the Security tab. Windows also provides explicit Deny functions for each option (Figure 7.27). Deny overrules inheritance.

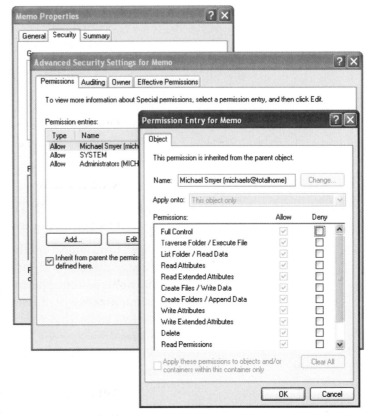

• **Figure 7.27**   Special permissions

Let's look at our list of six things techs need to know to see what happens when you copy or move an object, such as a file or folder.

1. Copying within a partition creates two copies of the object. The object in the original location *retains* its permissions, unchanged. The copy of the object in the new location *inherits* the permissions from that new location. So the new copy can have different permissions than the original.

2. Moving within a partition creates one copy of the object. That object *retains* its permissions, unchanged.

3. Copying from one NTFS partition to another creates two copies of the object. The object in the original location *retains* its permissions, unchanged. The copy of the object in the new location *inherits* the permissions from that new location. So the new copy can have different permissions than the original.

4. Moving from one NTFS partition to another creates one copy of the object. The object in the new location *inherits* the permissions from that new location. So the newly moved file can have different permissions than the original.

5. Copying from an NTFS-based partition to a FAT- or FAT32-based partition creates two copies of the object. The object in the original location *retains* its permissions, unchanged. The copy of the object in the new location has no permissions at all.

Don't panic about memorizing special permissions; just appreciate that they exist and that the permissions you see in the Security tab cover the vast majority of our needs.

6. Moving from an NTFS-based partition to a FAT- or FAT32-based partition creates one copy of the object. That object has no permissions at all.

From a tech's standpoint, you simply need to be aware of how permissions can change when you move or copy files and, if in doubt about a sensitive file, check it before you sign off to a client. Having a top secret document totally locked down on a hard drive doesn't do you a lot of good if you put that document on a thumb drive to transport it and the thumb drive is FAT32!

Techs and Permissions

Techs, as a rule, hate NTFS permissions. You must have administrative privileges to do almost anything on a Windows machine, such as install updates, change drivers, and install applications; most administrators hate giving out administrative permissions (for obvious reasons). If one does give you administrative permission for a PC, and something goes wrong with that system while you're working on it, you immediately become the primary suspect!

If you're working on a Windows system administered by someone else, make sure he understands what you are doing and how long you think it will take. Have the administrator create a new account for you that's a member of the Administrators group. Never ask for the password for a permanent administrator account! That way, you won't be blamed if anything goes wrong on that system: "Well, I told Janet the password when she installed the new hard drive…maybe she did it!" When you have fixed the system, *make sure the administrator deletes the account you used*.

This "protect yourself from passwords" attitude applies to areas other than just doing tech support on Windows. PC support folks get lots of passwords, scan cards, keys, and ID tags. New techs tend to get an "I can go anywhere and access anything" attitude, and this is dangerous. I've seen many jobs lost and friendships ruined when a tape backup suddenly disappears or a critical file gets erased. Everybody points to the support tech in these situations. In physical security situations, make other people unlock doors for you. In some cases, I've literally asked the administrator or system owner to sit behind me, read a magazine, and be ready to punch in passwords as needed. What you don't have access to can't hurt you.

■ Sharing a Windows PC Securely

User accounts, groups, and NTFS work together to enable you to share a Windows PC securely with multiple user accounts. You can readily share files, folders, programs, and more. More to the point, you can share only what should be shared, locking access to files and folders that you want to make private. Each version of Windows handles multiple user accounts and sharing among those accounts differently, so let's look at Windows 2000, Windows XP, and Windows Vista separately and then finish with a look at a few other sharing and security issues involving sharing.

Sharing in Windows 2000

Every user account on a Windows 2000 computer gets a My Documents folder, the default storage area for personal documents. That sounds great, but every account that's a member of the Administrators group can view the contents of everybody's My Documents folder, by default.

A typical way to create a secure shared Windows 2000 computer is to change the permissions on your My Documents folder to give yourself full control, but take away the permissions that allow other accounts access. You also should not create user accounts that go beyond Power Users or even Standard Users.

Finally, make a folder for people to share so that moving files to and from accounts is easy. A typical example would be to create a folder on the C: drive called Shared and then alter the permissions, giving full control to everyone.

To make changes to the permissions on folders, right-click and select Sharing to open the Properties dialog box with the Sharing tab already selected (Figure 7.28). Select *Share this folder* and change the options to what you want.

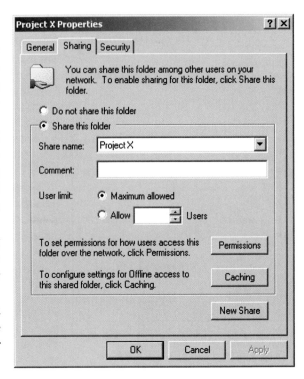

• **Figure 7.28**   Sharing tab on Properties for the Shared folder

Sharing in Windows XP

Microsoft tried to make Windows XP secure sharing easier than previous versions of Windows. To this end, they included several features. First, just as with Windows 2000, each user account gets a series of folders in My Documents that the user can share and administrators can access. But Windows XP also comes with a set of pre-made folders called Shared Documents accessible by all of the users on the computer. Also, Windows XP comes with simple file sharing enabled by default, which makes the option to share or not pretty easy. Finally, Windows XP Professional provides the option to use the full NTFS permissions and make customized shares possible.

Making Personal Documents Secure

The fact that most users of Windows XP computers will be computer administrators rather than limited users creates a bit of an issue with computers shared by many users. By default, administrators can see all of the contents of Documents and Settings, where the My Documents folder for each user account resides. You can override this option in the My Documents Properties dialog box. Selecting the option to *Make this folder private* blocks the contents from anyone accessing them (Figure 7.29).

Note that an administrator can take ownership of anything, so the only true way to lock down your data is to encrypt it. In the My Documents Properties dialog box, select the General tab and then click the Advanced button to open the Advanced Attributes dialog box. Click the checkbox next to *Encrypt contents to secure data* and that'll handle the encryption. Just make sure you have a password reset disk if you're going to use encryption to secure your files.

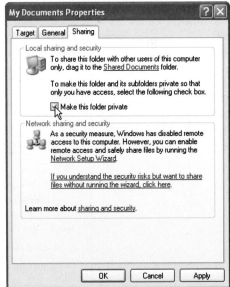

• **Figure 7.29**   Making personal documents secure from prying eyes

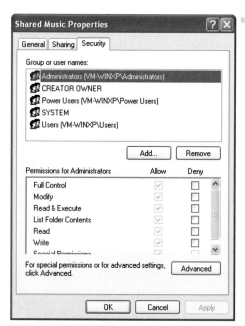

● Figure 7.30 Shared Music Properties dialog box

When you join Windows XP Professional to a domain, simple file sharing is disabled. You must use the full power of NTFS.

Shared Documents

You can use the Shared Documents folders to move files and folders among many users of a single machine. Every account can access the Shared Documents and the sub-folders within, such as Shared Music and Shared Pictures (Figure 7.30). Because new folders inherit the permissions of parent folders, by default any new subfolder you create in Shared Folders can be accessed by any account.

Simple File Sharing

With simple file sharing, you essentially have one local sharing option, and that's to put anything you want to share into the Shared Documents. To share a folder over a network, you only have a couple of options as well, such as to share or not and, if so, to give full control to everybody. Note that the sharing option is enabled in Figure 7.31. It's pretty much all or nothing.

Windows XP Home and Media Center only give you the simple file sharing, so the sharing of files and folders is straightforward. Windows XP Professional, on the other hand, enables you to turn off simple file sharing and unlock the true power of NTFS and permissions. To turn off simple file sharing, in some form of Windows Explorer, such as My Documents, go to Tools | Folder Options and select the View tab. The very last option on the View tab is *Use simple file sharing (Recommended)*. Deselect that option, as in Figure 7.32, and then click OK.

When you access sharing and security now, you'll see a more fully formed security dialog box reminiscent of the one you saw with Windows 2000 (Figure 7.33).

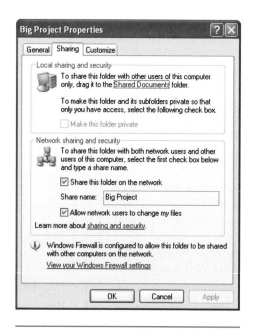

● Figure 7.31 Folder shared, but seriously not secure

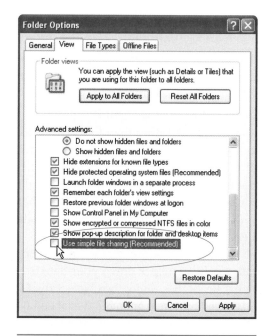

● Figure 7.32 Turning off simple file sharing

Sharing in Windows Vista

Microsoft tweaked the settings for sharing a single PC with multiple users in Windows Vista to fix the all-or-nothing approach offered by simple file sharing; for example, enabling you to target shared files and folders to specific user accounts. They beefed up the Standard User account (as you read about earlier in the chapter) so users could access what they needed to get meaningful work done. Plus they expanded the concept of the Shared Documents into the Public folder.

Targeted Sharing

To share a folder or file with specific users—or to everyone, for that matter—you simply right-click on it and select Share. This opens the File Sharing dialog box where you can select specific user accounts from a drop-down list (Figure 7.34).

Once you select a user account, you can then choose what permission level to give that user. You have three choices: Reader, Contributor, or Co-owner (Figure 7.35). *Reader* simply means the user has read-only permissions. *Contributor* gives the user read and write permissions and the permission to delete any file the user contributed to the folder. (Contributor only works at the folder level.) A *co-owner* can do anything.

Public Folder

The **Public folder** offers another way to share files and folders. Anything you want to share with all other users on the local machine—or if on a network, throughout the network—simply place in the Public folder or one of the

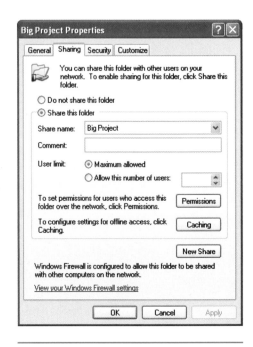

• **Figure 7.33** Full sharing and security options in Windows XP

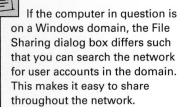

If the computer in question is on a Windows domain, the File Sharing dialog box differs such that you can search the network for user accounts in the domain. This makes it easy to share throughout the network.

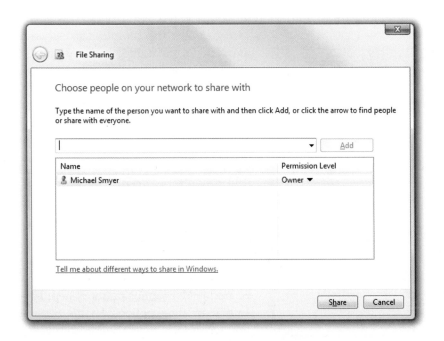

• **Figure 7.34** File Sharing dialog box on a standalone machine

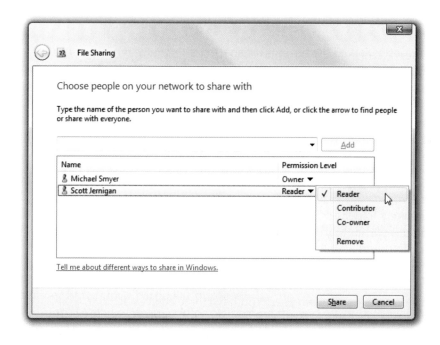

● **Figure 7.35**   Permissions options

many subfolders, such as Public Documents or Public Pictures (Figure 7.36). Note that the Public folder does not give you any control over what someone accessing the files contained within can do with those files.

Locating Shared Folders

Before you walk away from a computer, you should check for any unnecessary or unknown (to you) shared folders on the hard drives. This enables you to make the computer as secure as possible for the user. When you open My Computer or Computer, shared folders don't just jump out at you, especially if they're buried deep within the file system. A shared C: drive is obvious, but a shared folder all the way down in D:\temp\ backup\Simon\secret share would not be obvious, especially if none of the parent folders were shared.

Windows comes with a handy tool for locating all of the shared folders on a computer, regardless of where they reside on the drives. The Computer Management console in the Administrative Tools has a Shared Folders option under System Tools. In that are three options: Shares, Sessions, and Open Files. Select Shares to reveal all of the shared folders (Figure 7.37).

● **Figure 7.36**   Shared folders in the Public folder

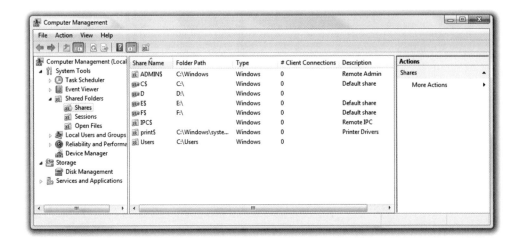

● Figure 7.37   Shared Folders tool in Computer Management

You can double-click on any share to open the Properties dialog box for that folder. At that point, you can make changes to the share—such as users and permissions—just as you would from any other sharing dialog.

Administrative Shares

A close glance at the screenshot in Figure 7.37 might have left some of you with raised eyebrows and quizzical looks. What kind of share is ADMIN$ or F$?

Every version of Windows since Windows NT comes with several default shares, notably all hard drives—not optical drives or removable devices, such as thumb drives—plus the %systemroot% folder—usually C:\Windows or C:\WINNT—and a couple of others, depending on the system. These administrative shares give local administrators administrative access to these resources, whether they log in locally or remotely. (In contrast, shares added manually are called *local shares*.)

Administrative shares are odd ducks. You cannot change the default permissions on them. You can delete them, but Windows will re-create them automatically every time you reboot. They're hidden, so they don't appear when you browse a machine over the network, though you can map them by name. Keep the administrator password safe, and these default shares won't affect the overall security of the computer.

Administrative shares have been exploited by malware programs, especially because many users who set up their computers never give the administrator account a password. Starting with Windows XP Home, Microsoft changed the remote access permissions for such machines. If you log into a computer remotely as administrator with no password, you get guest access rather than administrator access. That neatly nips potential exploits in the bud.

Protecting Data with Encryption

The scrambling of data through encryption techniques provides the only true way to secure your data from access by any other user. Administrators can use the Take Ownership permission to seize any file or folder on a computer, even those you don't actively share. Thus you need to implement other security measures for that data that needs to be ultra secure. Depending on the version of Windows, you have between zero and three encryptions tools: Windows Home versions have basically no security features; Windows XP Professional uses the Encrypting File System to, well,

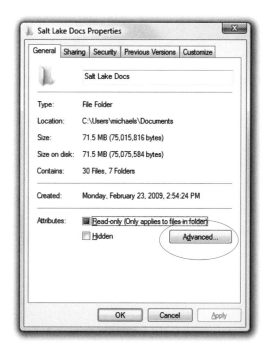

• **Figure 7.38** Click the Advanced button on the
Properties, General tab

• **Figure 7.39** Selecting encryption

encrypt files; and Windows Vista Ultimate and Enterprise add
an encryption system that can encrypt entire hard drives.

Encrypting File System

The professional versions of Windows offer a feature called the
Encrypting File System (EFS), an encryption scheme that any user
can use to encrypt individual files or folders on a computer. The
home versions of Windows do not enable encryption through
the built-in tools, though you have the option to use third-party
encryption methods, such as TrueCrypt, to lock down data.

To encrypt a file or folder takes but a moment. You right-
click the file or folder you want to encrypt and select Properties.
In the Properties for that object, General tab, click the Advanced
button (Figure 7.38) to open the Advanced Attributes dialog
box. Click the checkbox next to *Encrypt contents to secure data*
(Figure 7.39). Click OK to close the Advanced Attributes dialog
box and then click OK again on the Properties dialog box, and
you've locked that file or folder from any user account aside
from your own.

As long as you maintain the integrity of your password, any
data you encrypt by using EFS is secure from prying. That security comes at a potential price, though, and your password is the
key. The Windows security database stores the password (securely, not plain text, so no worries there), but that means access
to your encrypted files is based on that specific installation of Windows. If
you lose your password or an administrator resets your password, you're
locked out of your encrypted files permanently. There's no recovery. Also, if
the computer dies and you try to retrieve your data by installing the hard
drive in another system, you're likewise out of luck. Even if you
have an identical user name on the new system, the security ID
that defines that user account will differ from what you had on
the old system. You're out of luck.

Remember the password reset disk we discussed earlier in
the chapter? If you use EFS, you simply must have a valid password reset disk in the event of some horrible catastrophe.

And one last caveat. If you copy an encrypted file to a disk
formatted as anything but NTFS, you'll get a prompt saying
that the copied file will not be encrypted. If you copy to a disk
with NTFS, the encryption stays. The encrypted file—even if on
a removable disk—will only be readable on your system with
your login.

BitLocker Drive Encryption

Windows Vista Ultimate and Enterprise editions offer full drive
encryption through BitLocker Drive Encryption. BitLocker does
the whole drive, including every user's files, so it's not dependent on any one account. The beauty of BitLocker is that if your
hard drive is stolen, such as in the case of a stolen portable computer, all of the data on the hard drive is safe. The thief can't get

access, even if you have a user on that laptop that failed to secure his or her data through EFS.

BitLocker requires a special Trusted Platform Module (TPM) chip on the motherboard to function. The TPM chip validates on boot that the Vista computer has not changed, that you still have the same operating system installed, for example, and that the computer wasn't hacked by some malevolent program. The TPM also works in cases where you move the BitLocker drive from one system to another.

If you have a legitimate BitLocker failure (rather than a theft) because of tampering or moving the drive to another system, you need to have a properly created and accessible recovery key or recovery password. The key or password is generally created at the time you enable BitLocker and should be kept somewhere secure, such as a printed copy in a safe or a file on a network server accessible only to administrators.

To enable BitLocker, double-click the BitLocker Drive Encryption icon in the Classic Control Panel, or select Security in Control Panel Home view and then click *Protect your computer by encrypting data on your disk* (Figure 7.40).

Tech Tip

TrueCrypt

TrueCrypt is an open-source disk encryption application with versions available for just about every operating system. You can use TrueCrypt to encrypt an entire partition or you can create an encrypted volume into which you can securely store data. The beauty of the encrypted volume is that it acts like a folder that you can move around or toss on a USB flash drive. You can take the volume to another system and, as long as you have the password and TrueCrypt installed on the other system, you can read the contents of the encrypted volume. If the thumb drive is big enough, you can even put a copy of TrueCrypt on it and run the program directly from the thumb drive, enabling you to read the contents of the encrypted volume—as long as you know the proper password.

TrueCrypt has some limitations, such as a lack of support for dynamic disks and some problems with multi-boot systems, but considering the price—free, though donations are cheerfully accepted—and the amazing power, it's hard not to love the program. This discussion of TrueCrypt barely scratches the surface of what the application can do, so check it out at www.truecrypt.org. If you're running Windows XP Home or Windows Vista Home Premium, you can't get a better tool for securing your data.

• **Figure 7.40** Enabling BitLocker Drive Encryption

Chapter 7 Review

Chapter Summary

After reading this chapter and completing the exercises, you should understand the following about securing Windows resources.

Create and administer Windows users and groups

- The key to protecting your data is based on two related processes: authentication and authorization. Authentication is the process by which you determine a person at your computer is who he says he is. The most common way to authenticate is by using a user name and password. Once a user is authenticated, he needs authorization, the process that states what a user can and cannot do on that system. Authorization, at least for files and folders, is controlled by the NTFS file system.

- The tool for managing users in Windows 2000 is the Users and Passwords Control Panel applet. You can use the applet to create accounts and control password use, such as require a user to type in a password at logon. You can also require users to press CTRL-ALT-DELETE to make logon even more secure.

- Administrators can create new users and then assign the users to a specific group. Selecting Standard User makes that user a member of both the Power Users group and the Local Users group.

- Windows XP uses the User Accounts applet in Control Panel to create and manage user accounts. Windows XP has two very different ways to deal with user accounts and how you log on to a system: the blank user name and password text boxes, reminiscent of Windows 2000, and the Windows XP Welcome screen.

- User Accounts hides the complete list of users, using a simplistic reference to account types that is actually a reference to its group membership. An account that is a member of the local Administrators group is said to be a computer administrator; an account that only belongs to the Local Users group is said to be a limited account.

- Creating users is a straightforward process. You need to provide a user name (a password can be added later), and you need to know which type of account to create: computer administrator or limited.

- You can option out of the Welcome screen and thus require a user to type both a user name and a password. You can also enable or disable Fast User Switching—a feature that enables you to switch to another user account without logging out and thus having to close open programs.

- To add or modify a user account in Windows Vista, you have numerous options depending on which Control Panel view you select and which edition and update of Vista you have installed. Windows Vista Business and Ultimate, for example, in the default Control Panel Home view, offer the User Accounts applet. Windows Home Premium, in contrast, gives you the User Accounts and Family Safety applet. The Tasks options on the left are similar, with the addition of Parental Controls in the Home Premium edition, but the main options differ a lot.

- Windows Vista Home Premium uses Vista's version of the Welcome screen for logging in, so each user account has a picture associated with it. You can change the picture from the User Accounts applet. You can also change the name of the user account here and alter the account type.

- Passwords are the ultimate key to protecting your computers. A user account with a valid password will get you into any system. Protect your passwords. Never give out passwords over the phone. If a user forgets or loses a password, an administrator should reset the password to a complex combination of letters and numbers, and then allow the user to change the password to something they want.

- Make sure you use strong passwords: at least eight characters in length, including letters, numbers, and punctuation symbols.

- Windows XP and Windows Vista enable currently logged-on users to create a password reset disk they can use if they forget a password. This is very important to have. If an administrator resets the password by using User Accounts or Local Users and Groups, and you then log on with the new password, you will discover that you cannot access some items, including files that you encrypted when logged on with the forgotten password. When you reset a password with a password reset disk, you can log on with the new password and still have access to previously encrypted files.

- A group is simply a collection of accounts that share the same access capabilities. A single account can be a member of multiple groups. Groups are essential for managing a network of computers but also can come in handy on a single computer with multiple users.

- Windows 2000 provides seven built-in groups: Administrators, Power Users, Users, Backup Operators, Replicator, Everyone, and Guests. These built-in groups have a number of preset capabilities. You cannot delete these groups.

- If you're running XP Professional and you are on a Windows domain, XP offers all of the accounts Windows 2000 has, but it adds other specialized types, such as HelpServicesGroup and Remote Desktop Users. Windows XP Home and XP Professional, when installed on standalone PCs or PCs that are connected to a workgroup but not a domain, run in a specialized networking mode called simple file sharing. A Windows XP system running simple file sharing has only three account types: computer administrator, limited user, and guest.

- The professional editions of Windows Vista (Business, Ultimate, and Enterprise) offer the groups found in Windows XP Professional and throw in a lot more. Some group types enable people to check on the performance and reliability of a computer but without gaining access to any of the documents on the computer. These groups include Event Log Readers, Performance Log Users, and Performance Monitor Users and provide excellent levels of access for technicians to help keep busy Vista machines healthy.

- The professional versions of Windows—including Windows 2000, XP, and Vista—enable you to add new groups to your computer by using the Local Users and Groups tool, found in the Computer Management applet of the Administrative Tools. This tool also enables you to create user accounts and change group membership for users.

- Windows XP made it almost necessary to make your primary account on a computer an administrator account, because limited users can't do common

tasks such as installing applications or updating Windows. In Vista, Microsoft rolled out User Account Control, a feature where a standard user account is prompted for the login information for an administrator account when trying to do something potentially nefarious, such as uninstall an application.

- With Parental Controls, you can monitor and limit the activities of any standard user in Windows Vista, a feature that gives parents and managers an excellent level of control over the content their children and employees can access. Parental Controls enable you to limit the time that standard users can spend logged in, for example. You can specify acceptable and unacceptable times of day when standard users can log in. Parental Controls offer a lot of control.

Define and utilize NTFS permissions for authorization

- In Windows, every folder and file on an NTFS partition has a list that contains two sets of data: every user and group that has access to that file or folder, and the level of access each user or group has to that file or folder. A set of detailed and powerful restrictions called permissions define exactly what a particular account can or cannot do to the file or folder.

- When you create a new file or folder on an NTFS partition, you become the owner of that file or folder, which means you can do anything you want to it, including changing the permissions to prevent anybody, even administrators, from accessing it. The special Take Ownership permission enables an account to seize control of a file or folder. Administrator accounts have Take Ownership permission for everything. Change permission–equipped accounts can give or take away permissions for other accounts.

- In Windows, just about everything in the computer has a Security tab in its properties (provided the hard drive is NTFS). Every Security tab contains a list of accounts that have permissions for that resource, and the permissions assigned to those accounts. The standard permissions for a folder are Full Control, Modify, Read & Execute, List Folder Contents, Read, and Write. The standard file permissions are Full Control, Modify, Read & Execute, Read, and Write. Permissions are cumulative.

- Moving or copying objects such as files and folders can have an effect on the permissions of those objects, something that techs need to understand. If you copy or move an object from one NTFS partition to another, the new object inherits the permissions associated with the new location. If you copy an object within a partition, the newly created copy inherits the permissions associated with the new location, but the original copy retains its permissions. Any object that you put on a FAT or FAT32 partition loses any permissions because FAT and FAT32 don't support NTFS permissions.

Describe how to share a Windows computer securely

- User accounts, groups, and NTFS work together to enable you to share a Windows PC securely with multiple user accounts. You can readily share files, folders, programs, and more. You can share only what should be shared, locking access to files and folders that you want to make private.

- Every user account on a Windows 2000 computer gets a My Documents folder, the default storage area for personal documents. Every account that's a member of the Administrators group can view the contents of everybody's My Documents folder, by default. A typical way to create a secure shared Windows 2000 computer is to change the permissions on your My Documents folder to give yourself Full Control but take away the permissions that allow other accounts access.

- Make a folder for people to share so that moving files to and from accounts is easy. A typical example would be to create a folder on the C: drive called Shared and then alter the permissions, giving full control to everyone.

- The fact that most users of Windows XP computers will be computer administrators rather than limited users creates a bit of an issue with a computer shared by many users. By default, administrators can see all of the contents of Documents and Settings, where

the My Documents folders for each user account reside. Selecting the option to *Make this folder private* in the My Documents Properties dialog box blocks anyone from accessing the contents.

- Use the Shared Documents folders to move files and folders among many users of a single machine. Every account can access the Shared Documents and the sub-folders within.

- With simple file sharing, you essentially have one local sharing option, and that's to put anything you want to share into the Shared Documents. To share a folder over a network, you only have a couple of options as well, such as to share or not and, if so, to give full control to everybody. Windows XP Professional enables you to disable simple file sharing and have full control over sharing and permissions.

- Windows Vista enables you to permit specific user accounts to access shared resources and to set the level of access permitted, such as reader, contributor, or co-owner. Vista also has an expanded default shares, called the Public folder, which contains multiple shared folders. Any user account can access the Public folder.

- The scrambling of data through encryption techniques provides the only true way to secure your data from access by any other user. The professional versions of Windows enable a feature called the Encrypting File System (EFS), an encryption scheme that any user can use to encrypt individual files or folders on a computer. The home versions of Windows do not enable encryption.

- Windows Vista Ultimate and Enterprise editions offer full drive encryption through BitLocker Drive Encryption. BitLocker encrypts the whole drive, including every user's files, so it's not dependent on any one account. BitLocker requires a special Trusted Platform Module (TPM) chip on the motherboard to function. The TPM chip validates on boot that the Vista computer hasn't changed and that you still have the same operating system installed.

■ Key Terms

administrative shares *(223)*
Administrators group *(212)*
authentication *(199)*
authorization *(199)*
BitLocker Drive Encryption *(224)*
computer administrator *(203)*

Encrypting File System (EFS) *(224)*
encryption *(223)*
Fast User Switching *(206)*
group *(211)*
Guests group *(212)*
inheritance *(217)*

limited user *(203)*

local user account *(199)*

Local Users and Groups *(213)*

NTFS permissions *(215)*

Parental Controls *(209)*

password reset disk *(211)*

permission propagation *(217)*

Power Users group *(212)*

Public folder *(221)*

Shared Documents *(219)*

simple file sharing *(220)*

standard user *(202)*

strong password *(211)*

Take Ownership *(215)*

User Account Control (UAC) *(209)*

User Accounts applet *(202)*

Users and Passwords applet *(200)*

Users group *(212)*

Welcome screen *(202)*

■ Key Term Quiz

Use the Key Terms list to complete the sentences that follow. Not all terms will be used.

1. The ___user and Password applet___ enables you to manage user accounts in Windows 2000.

2. To log on to a standalone Windows PC, you need a(n) ___local user account___

3. An account that belongs only to the Local Users group in Windows XP is called a(n) ___limited user___.

4. On the ___Welcome screen___ in Windows XP and Vista, you can click on an icon and type a password to log into the computer.

5. A(n) ___group___ is a collection of user accounts that share the same access capabilities.

6. The ___User account control___ enables standard users to perform common tasks and provides a permissions dialog when standard users and administrators do certain things that could potentially harm the computer.

7. By default, any file you drop into a folder on an NTFS drive gets the same permissions as those assigned to the folder, a feature called ___Inheritance___.

8. The ___Simple File sharing___ feature of Windows XP Home means you can share or not share a folder. You don't have any finer control than that.

9. The ___Encrypting File System (EFS)___ enables you to scramble a file or folder and thus hide the contents from anyone, even an administrator.

■ Multiple-Choice Quiz

1. What process determines the identity of a user?

   A. Authentication

   B. Authorization

   C. Identification

   D. Indemnification

2. Which of the following user account types can create other user accounts?

   A. Administrator

   B. Limited User

   C. Restricted User

   D. Standard User

3. To which of the following groups does a standard user in Windows 2000 belong by default? (Select two.)

   A. Limited Users

   B. Power Users

   C. Restricted Users

   D. Local Users

4. Which utility enables you to add a user account in Windows XP?

   A. User Account Control

   B. User Accounts applet

   C. Users and Groups applet

   D. Users and Passwords applet

5. Which of the following is the strongest password?

    A. 5551212

    B. Spot01

    C. 43*xv

    D. 479love*

6. Which tool would enable a user to recover his encrypted files if he forgets his password?

    A. BitLocker

    B. Encrypting File System

    C. Password reset disk

    D. Password restore disk

7. Which of the following groups can you assign a user to in Windows Vista Home Premium? (Select two.)

    A. Administrators

    B. Power Users

    C. Replicators

    D. Users

8. Which tool in Windows Vista enables an administrator to create a log that shows all of the applications a user runs or attempts to run?

    A. Create Log

    B. NTFS

    C. Parental Controls

    D. User Account Control

9. As a member of the accounting group, John has Write permission to the Database folder; as a member of the technicians group, John has Read permission to the Database folder. What permission or permissions does John have to the Database folder?

    A. Read only

    B. Write only

    C. Read and Write

    D. Full Control

10. In a Windows XP Professional computer, where can you place files that other users can access easily?

    A. Public Documents

    B. Public folder

    C. Shared Documents

    D. Shared folder

11. John wants to share a folder in Windows Vista with Liz but wants to make sure she can only delete files she creates in that folder, not the ones he creates. What permission level should he use?

    A. Contributor

    B. Co-owner

    C. Full Control

    D. Reader

12. Which of the following is a safe way to deal with your new password?

    A. Memorize it

    B. Put a note in your wallet

    C. Tape it under your keyboard

    D. E-mail it to yourself

Essay Quiz

1. Your boss has tasked you with setting up five Windows Vista workstations, each to be used by three different users. Write a short essay on procedures or policies that should be implemented at each workstation to ensure that each user can share files that need to be shared but can also keep private files that need to be private.

2. Your company has a shared database in Windows Vista. Management must have full access to the database. The salespeople need to be able to access the database and make changes, but can't delete the database. All other employees should be able to read the contents of the database, but not make any changes. Write a short essay describing what groups and permissions you would need to set to make this work.

3. You have a computer with three users, plus an administrator. The three users need to be able to add documents to a folder, but only the administrator should be allowed to see the contents of those documents. Write a short essay describing how you would set up the folder, user accounts, groups, and permissions to make this work.

Lab Projects

Lab Project 7.1

Take a single computer and create multiple user accounts and groups. Create some shared folders and change permissions on those folders to vary

what different
Try to make
can make.

Lab Project 7.2

Experiment with permission propagation. On a computer with two hard drives, both formatted as NTFS, go through the process of copying and moving files and folders—with differing

permissions—between folders on
and between the two drives. Note care
permissions change or do not change with

Lab Project 7.3

On a computer with multiple user accounts, experiment with encryption. Encrypt files with one user account and then place those files into shared folders. What happens? Can other accounts access

those files? Can they see the filenames? What about the administrator account? Go through the process of taking ownership to see if you can recover the contents of the encrypted files.

Lab Project 7.4

On a Windows Vista Ultimate computer, experiment with BitLocker on a second hard drive. Make note of what happens when you remove the drive and put it

into another computer. How can you access the data that's been encrypted?

Using and Troubleshooting Windows

In this chapter, you will learn how to

- **Identify the operating system folders of Windows 2000, XP, and Vista**
- **Describe the utilities in Windows essential to techs**
- **Troubleshoot Windows**

Every computer running a Windows operating system requires occasional optimization to keep the system running snappily, ongoing maintenance to make sure nothing goes wrong, and troubleshooting when the system doesn't work correctly. Not that long ago, Windows had a bad rap as being difficult to maintain and challenging when troubleshooting problems. That's no longer true. Microsoft used its decades of experience with operating systems to search for ways to make the tasks of maintaining and troubleshooting less onerous. They've done such a good job with the latest versions of Windows that, out of the box, they are easy to optimize and maintain, although troubleshooting—and all operating systems share this—is still a bit of a challenge.

The chapter starts with maintenance and optimization, so let's make sure you know what these two terms mean. *Maintenance* means jobs you do from time to time to keep Windows running well, such as running hard drive utilities. CompTIA sees *optimization* as jobs you do to your Windows system to make it better—a good example is adding RAM. This chapter covers the location of the operating system folders in Windows (it's tough to maintain an operating system if you don't understand its basic structure, after all), standard maintenance and optimization activities performed on Windows, and the tools techs use to perform them.

The last part of this chapter dives into *troubleshooting* Windows, examining steps you can take to bring a system back from the brink of disaster. You'll learn techniques for recovering a PC that won't boot and a PC that almost boots into Windows but fails.

Operating System Folders

The modern versions of Windows organize essential files and folders in a relatively similar fashion. All have a primary system folder for storing most Windows internal tools and files. All have a set of folders for programs and user files. All use a special grouping of files called the Registry to keep track of all the hardware loaded and the drivers that enable you to use that hardware. Finally, every version has a page file, enabling more robust access to programs and utilities. Yet once you start to get into details, you'll find some very large differences. It's very important for you to know in some detail the location and function of many common folders and their contents.

 The CompTIA A+ Practical Application exam loves to ask detailed questions about the locations of certain folders. Make sure you know this section!

System Folder

SystemRoot is the tech name given to the folder in which Windows has been installed. SystemRoot by default is C:\WINNT in Windows 2000, while Windows XP and Vista's SystemRoot defaults to C:\WINDOWS. Be warned, these are defaults but not always the case; during the installation process, you can change where Windows is installed.

It's handy to know about SystemRoot. You'll find it cropping up in many other tech publications, and you can specify it when adjusting certain Windows settings to make sure they work under all circumstances. When used as part of a Windows configuration setting, add percent signs (%) to the beginning and end like so: %SystemRoot%.

If you don't know where Windows is installed on a particular system, here's a handy trick. Get to a command prompt, type **cd %systemroot%**, and press ENTER. The prompt changes to the directory in which the Windows OS files are stored. Slick! See Chapter 6, "Mastering the Windows Command Line" for details on how to use the command prompt in Windows.

The system folder contains many subfolders, too numerous to mention here, but CompTIA wants you to know the names of some of these subfolders as well as what goes in them. Let's run through the subfolders you should recognize and define (these folders are in all versions of Windows):

- **%SystemRoot%\FONTS**   All of the fonts installed in Windows live here.

Getting to a Command Prompt

Each version of Windows gives you several ways to access a command prompt, so depending on your version, try the steps below.

- In Windows 2000 or Windows XP, go to Start | Run to open the Run dialog box.

- Type **cmd** and press ENTER to open a command prompt.

- Alternatively, go to Start | All Programs | Accessories | System Tools and select Command Prompt.

- In Windows Vista, go to Start and type **cmd** into the Start Search text area. Press ENTER to open a command line.

- Alternatively, go to Start | All Programs | Accessories and select Command Prompt.

- **%SystemRoot%\Offline Files**
  When you tell your Web browser to save Web pages for offline viewing, they are stored in this folder. This is another folder that Windows automatically deletes if it needs the space.

- **%SystemRoot%\SYSTEM32**
  This is the *real* Windows! All of the most critical programs that make Windows run are stored here.

- **%SystemRoot%\Temp**
  Anytime Windows or an application running on Windows needs to create temporary files, they are placed here. Windows deletes these files automatically as needed, so never place an important file in this folder.

Program and Personal Document Folders

Windows has a number of important folders that help organize your programs and documents. They sit in the root directory at the same level as the system folder, and of course they have variations in name depending on the version of Windows. We'll assume that your computer is using a C: drive—a pretty safe assumption, although there actually is a way to install all of Windows on a second hard drive partition.

C:\Program Files (All Versions)

By default, most programs install some or all of their essential files into a subfolder of the Program Files folder. If you installed a program, it should have its own folder in here. Individual companies decide how to label their subfolders. Installing Photoshop made by Adobe, for example, creates the Adobe subfolder and then an Adobe Photoshop subfolder within it. Installing Silverlight from Microsoft, on the other hand, only creates a Microsoft Silverlight folder with the program files within it. (Some programmers choose to create a folder at the root of the C: drive, bypassing Program Files altogether, but that's becoming increasingly rare.)

C:\Program Files (x86)

The 64-bit versions of Windows Vista and Windows 7 create two directory structures for program files. The 64-bit applications go into the C:\Program Files folder. The 32-bit applications, in contrast, go into the C:\Program Files (×86) folder. The separation makes it easy to find the proper version of whatever application you seek.

Personal Documents

As you might expect, given the differences among the desktop names for personal document locations outlined earlier in the chapter, the personal folders for Windows 2000/XP and Windows Vista differ in location and name. Windows 2000 and Windows XP place personal folders in the Documents and Settings folder, whereas Windows Vista uses the Users folder. From there, they differ even more.

C:\Documents and Settings (2000 and XP)   All of the personal settings for each user are stored here. All users have their own subfolders in Documents and Settings. In each user folder, you'll find another level of folders with familiar names such as Desktop, My Documents, and Start Menu. These folders hold the actual contents of these items. Let's dive through these to see the ones you need to know for the Practical Application exam.

- **\Documents and Settings\Default User (hidden)**   All of the default settings for a user. For example, if the user doesn't specify a screensaver to use, Windows refers to this folder's settings to determine what screensaver it should use if needed.

- **\Documents and Settings\All Users**   You can make settings for anyone who uses the computer. This is especially handy for applications: some applications are installed so all users may use them and some might be restricted to certain users. This folder stores information for any setting or application that's defined for all users on the PC.

- **\Documents and Settings\Shared Documents (XP Only)**   If you're using XP's Simple File Sharing, this is the only folder on the computer that's shared.

- **\Documents and Settings\<User Name>**   This folder stores all settings defined for a particular user (Figure 8.1).

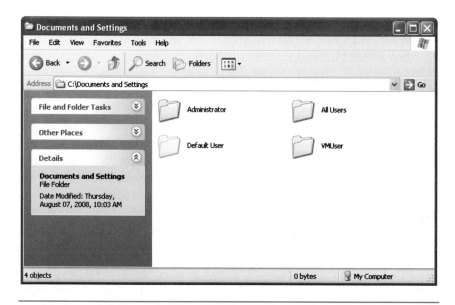

● **Figure 8.1**   Contents of a typical \Documents and Settings folder in XP

Opening any user's folder reveals a number of even lower folders. Each of these stores very specific information about the user.

- **\Documents and Settings\\<User Name>\\Desktop** This folder stores the files on the user's desktop. If you delete this folder, you delete all the files placed on the desktop.

- **\Documents and Settings\\<User Name>\\<User name's> Documents** This is the My Documents folder for that user.

- **\Documents and Settings\\<User Name>\\Application Data (hidden)** This folder stores information and settings used by various programs that the user has installed.

- **\Documents and Settings\\<User Name>\\Start Menu** This folder stores any customizations the user made to the Start menu.

C:\Users (Vista) Vista dumps the old Documents and Settings for the Users folder. Functionally similar to Documents and Settings, there are a number of subfolders here that you need to know to pass the CompTIA A+ Practical Application exam.

Let's repeat the process, locating the same functions in their new locations.

- **\Users\Default (hidden), \Users\All Users, \Users\\<User Name>** All of these folders retain the same functions as in 2000/XP.

- **\Users\\<user name>** The big change takes place under each of the \Users\\<user name> folders. This folder still stores all settings defined for a particular user; however, this folder in Vista/7 is much more detailed than in 2000/XP (Figure 8.2). Luckily, you only need to know a few folders for the exams.

- **\Users\\<User Name>\\Desktop** Same as 2000/XP.

- **\Users\\<User Name>\\Documents** This is the Documents folder for that user. Compare the name of this folder to the one in Windows 2000/XP and know which is which.

- **\Users\\<User Name>\\Downloads** Microsoft's preferred download folder for applications to use. Most applications use this folder, but some do not.

- **\Users\\<User Name>\\Start Menu** Same as 2000/XP.

Any good tech knows the name and function of all the folders just listed. As a tech, you will find yourself manually drilling into these folders for a number of reasons. Users rarely go directly into any of these folders with Windows Explorer. That's a good thing since, as a technician, you need to appreciate how dangerous it is for them to do so. Imagine a user going into a \Users\\<User Name>\\Desktop folder and wiping out someone's desktop folders. Luckily, Windows protects these folders by using NTFS permissions, making it very difficult for users to destroy anything other than their own work.

When you're looking at your own account folders, you'll see My Documents rather than <User name's> Documents in the \Documents and Settings\\<User Name> folder.

Vista and 7 make a special hidden folder called "Default User" that points to the User folder to support older applications.

Be very careful here. Some of the folder name differences between 2000/XP and Vista/7 are subtle. Make sure you know the difference.

● **Figure 8.2** Contents of a typical \Users\<User Name>\ folder in Vista

Tech Utilities

Windows offers a huge number of utilities that enable techs to configure the OS, optimize and tweak settings, install hardware, and more. The trick is to know where to go to find them. This section shows the six most common locations in Windows where you can access utilities: right-click, Control Panel, System Tools, command line, Administrative Tools, and the Microsoft Management Console. Note that these are locations for tools, not tools themselves, and you can access many tools from more than one of these locations. However, you'll see some of the utilities in many of these locations. Stay sharp in this section, as you'll need to access utilities to understand the inner workings of Windows in the next section.

Right-Click

Windows, being a graphical user interface OS, covers your monitor with windows, menus, icons, file lists—all kinds of pretty things you click on to do work. Any single thing you see on your desktop is called an **object**. If you want to open any object in Windows, you double-click on it. If you want to change something about an object, you right-click on it.

Right-clicking on an object brings up a small menu called the **context** *test question?* **menu**, and it works on everything in Windows. In fact, try to place your mouse somewhere in Windows where right-clicking does *not* bring up a menu (there are a few places, but they're not easy to find). What you see on

Figure 8.3 Right-clicking on a program

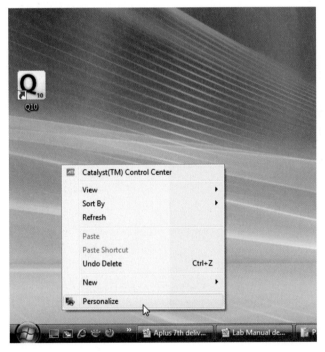

Figure 8.4 Right-clicking on the desktop

Figure 8.5 Right-clicking on My Computer

the little menu when you right-click varies dramatically depending on the item you decide to right-click. If you right-click a running program in the running program area on the taskbar, you'll see items that relate to a window, such as move, resize, and so on (Figure 8.3). If you right-click on your desktop, you get options for changing the appearance of the desktop (Figure 8.4). Even different types of files show different results when you right-click on them. Right-clicking is something techs do often.

One menu item you'll see almost anywhere you right-click is Properties. Every object in Windows has properties. When you right-click on something and can't find what you're looking for, select Properties. Figure 8.5 shows the results of right-clicking on My Computer—not very exciting. But if you select Properties, you'll get a dialog box like the one shown in Figure 8.6.

Control Panel

The **Control Panel** handles most of the maintenance, upgrade, and configuration aspects of Windows. As such, the Control Panel is the first set of tools for every tech to explore. Select Start | Settings | Control Panel to open the Control Panel in Windows 2000 and Windows Vista. In Windows XP, the Control Panel is directly on the Start menu by default.

The Control Panel in Windows 2000 opens in the traditional icon-littered view. In Windows XP and Vista, the Control Panel opens in the Category view, in which all of the icons are grouped into broad categories such as "Printers and Other Hardware." This view requires an additional click (and sometimes a guess about which category includes the icon you need), so most techs use the Switch to Classic View link to get back to the icons. Figure 8.7 shows the Windows XP Control Panel in both Category and Classic views.

A large number of programs, called **applets**, populate the Control Panel. The names and selection of applets vary depending on the version of Windows and whether any installed programs have added applets. But all versions of Windows share many of the same applets, including Display/Personalization, Add or Remove Programs/Programs and Features, and System (all versions)—what I call the *Big Three* applets for techs. With Display/Personalization, you can make changes to the look and feel of your Windows desktop and tweak your video settings. Add or Remove Programs/Programs and Features enables you to add or remove programs. The System applet gives you access to essential system information and tools, such as the Device Manager, although Microsoft wisely added Device Manager right on the Control Panel starting with Vista.

Every icon you see in the Control Panel is actually a file with the extension .cpl. Any time you get an error opening the Control Panel, you can bet

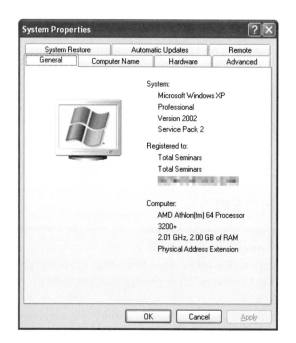

• **Figure 8.6** My Computer properties

you have a corrupted CPL file. These are a pain to fix. You have to rename all of your CPL files with another extension (I use .cpb) and then rename them back to .cpl one at a time, each time reopening the Control Panel, until you find the CPL file that's causing the lockup.

You can use the Control Panel applets to do an amazing array of things to a Windows system, and each applet displays text that helps explain its functions. The Add Hardware applet in Windows XP, for example, says quite clearly, "Installs and troubleshoots hardware" (Figure 8.8). They are all like that. Figure 8.9 shows the User Accounts applet. Can you determine its use? Don't bother trying to memorize all these applets. Each Control Panel applet relevant to the Practical Application exam is discussed in detail in the relevant chapters throughout the rest of the book. For now, just make sure you can get to the Control Panel and appreciate why it exists.

Tech Tip

Classic View Goodness

All the cool, hip techs use Classic view in the Control Panel. It's messier, but everything is visible on one page. You do want to be cool and hip, right?

Even these common applets vary slightly among Windows versions. The CompTIA A+ Practical Application exam doesn't test you on every little variance among the same applets in different versions—just know what each applet does.

• **Figure 8.7** Windows XP Control Panel in two views: Category (left) and Classic (right)

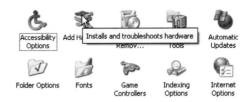

● **Figure 8.8**   Add Hardware Wizard of the Add Hardware applet

Device Manager

With the **Device Manager**, you can examine and configure all of the hardware and drivers in a Windows PC. As you might suspect from that description, every tech spends a lot of time with this tool! You'll work with the Device Manager many more times during the course of this book and your career as a PC tech.

There are many ways to get to the Device Manager—make sure you know all of them! The first way is to open the Control Panel and double-click the System applet icon. This brings up the System Properties dialog box. In 2000/XP, you access the Device Manager by selecting the Hardware tab and then clicking the Device Manager button. Figure 8.10 shows the Hardware tab of the System Properties dialog box in Windows XP. In Vista/7, the System dialog box has a direct connection to Device Manager (Figure 8.11).

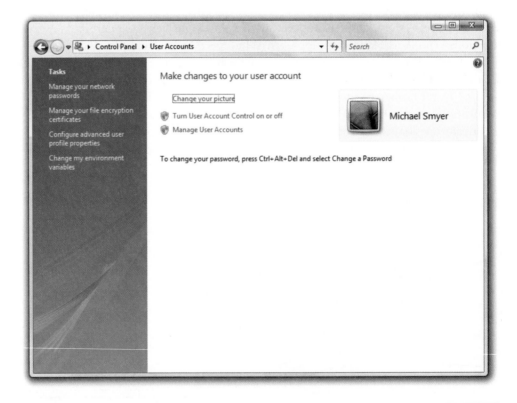

● **Figure 8.9**   User Accounts window of the User Accounts applet

You can also get to the System Properties dialog box in all versions of Windows by right-clicking My Computer/Computer and selecting Properties. From there, the path to the Device Manager is the same as when you access this dialog box from the Control Panel.

The second (and more streamlined) method is to right-click My Computer/Computer and select Manage. This opens a window called Computer Management, where you'll see Device Manager listed on the left side of the screen, under System Tools. Just click on Device Manager and it opens. You can also access Computer Management by opening the Administrative Tools applet in the Control Panel and then selecting Computer Management (Figure 8.12).

Why are there so many ways to open Device Manager? Well, remember that we're only looking at locations in Windows from which to open utilities, not at the actual utilities themselves. Microsoft wants you to get to the tools you need when you need them, and it's better to have multiple paths to a utility rather than just one.

The Device Manager displays every device that Windows recognizes, organized in special groups called *types*. All devices of the same type are grouped under the same type heading. To see

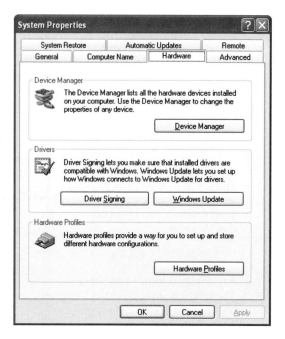

● **Figure 8.10** Windows XP System applet with the Hardware tab selected

● **Figure 8.11** Windows Vista System applet with the Device Manager menu option circled

• **Figure 8.12** Device Manager in Computer Management

the devices of a particular type, you must open that type's group. Figure 8.12 shows a Windows Vista Device Manager screen with all installed devices in good order—which makes us techs happy. If Windows detects a problem, the device has a red *X* or a black exclamation point on a yellow field, as in the case of the device in Figure 8.13.

A red *X* in Windows 2000 or XP means Windows (or you) disabled the device—right-click on the device to enable it. The tough one is the black exclamation point. If you see this, right-click on the device and select Properties. Read the error code in the Device Status pane, and then look up Microsoft Knowledge Base article 310123 to see what to do. There are around 40 different errors—nobody bothers to memorize them! (The knowledge base article is for Windows XP, but these error codes are the same in all versions of Windows.)

Vista and Windows 7 use the same icons and add one very handy one. If a device is working but you manually disable it, you get a down-arrow (Figure 8.14). Just as in previous versions, right-click the down-arrow and select Properties. You'll see a nice dialog box explaining the issue (Figure 8.15).

The Device Manager isn't just for dealing with problems. It also enables you to update drivers with a simple click of the mouse (assuming you have a replacement driver on your computer). Right-click a device and select Update Driver from the menu to get the process started. Figure 8.16 shows the options in Windows Vista.

Make sure you can get to Device Manager! You will come back to it again and again in subsequent chapters, because it is the first tool you should access when you have a hardware problem.

● Figure 8.13   Problem device

● Figure 8.14   Hmm…could be a problem.

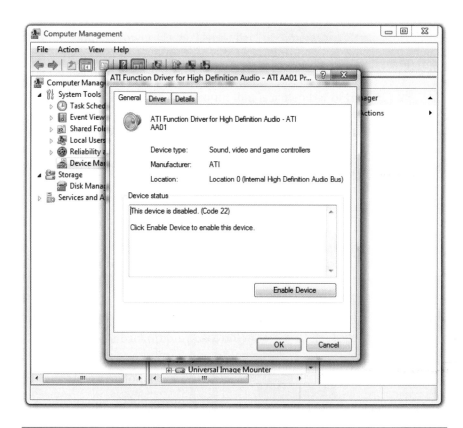

● **Figure 8.15**   Problem device properties

● **Figure 8.16**   Selecting Update Driver Software in the Windows Vista Device Manager

System Tools

The Start menu offers a variety of tech utilities collected in one place: select Start | Programs | Accessories | System Tools. In the **System Tools** menu, you'll find commonly accessed tools such as System Information and Disk Defragmenter (Figure 8.17).

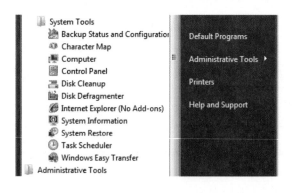

● **Figure 8.17**   System Tools menu options

Mike Meyers' CompTIA A+ Guide: Practical Application

Many techs overlook memorizing how to find the appropriate Windows tool to diagnose problems, but nothing hurts your credibility with a client like fumbling around, clicking a variety of menus and applets, while mumbling, "I know it's around here somewhere." The CompTIA A+ Practical Application exam therefore tests you on a variety of paths to appropriate tools. One of those paths is Start | Programs | Accessories | System Tools. Windows XP has all the same tools as Windows 2000, plus a few more. Vista adds a few beyond XP. I'll say what version of Windows has the particular system tool.

Activate Windows (XP, Vista)

Windows XP unveiled a copy-protection scheme called **activation**. Activation is a process where your computer sends Microsoft a unique code generated on your machine based on the Install CD/DVD's product key and a number of hardware features, such as the amount of RAM, the CPU processor model, and other ones and zeros in your PC. Normally, activation is done at install time, but if you choose not to activate at install or if you make "substantial" changes to the hardware, you'll need to use the Activate Windows utility (Figure 8.18). With the Activate Windows utility, you can activate over the Internet or over the telephone.

Backup (2000, XP)

The Backup utility enables you to back up selected files and folders to removable media such as tape drives.

Once you've activated Windows, this applet goes away.

Neither Windows XP Home nor Windows XP Media Center Edition includes Backup during installation. You must install the Backup program from the Windows installation CD by running the \Valueadd\MSFT\Ntbackup\ NTbackup.msi program.

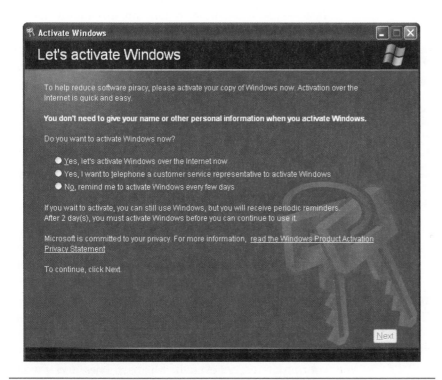

● **Figure 8.18**   Activate Windows

Backup Status and Configuration (Vista, 7)

Vista and 7 do not enable you to back up files on your computer selectively. You can only back up personal data with the Backup Status and Configuration Tool or, if you have Vista Business, Ultimate, or Enterprise, perform a complete PC backup by using Windows Complete PC Backup. If you want to pick and choose the file to back up, you need to buy a third-party tool. Also, this tool only allows you to back up to optical media, a hard drive, or a networked drive.

Character Map (All)

Ever been using a program only to discover you need to enter a strange character such as the euro character (ε) but your word processor doesn't support it? That's when you need the Character Map. It enables you to copy any Unicode character into the Clipboard (Figure 8.19).

Disk Cleanup (All)

Disk Cleanup looks for unneeded files on your computer, which is handy when your hard drive starts to get full and you need space. You must run Disk Cleanup manually in Windows 2000, but Windows XP and Windows Vista start this program whenever your hard drive gets below 200 MB of free disk space.

Disk Defragmenter (All)

You use Disk Defragmenter to make your hard drive run faster—you'll see more details on this handy tool in Chapter 5, "Implementing Hard Drives." You can access this utility in the same way you access the Device Manager; you also find Disk Defragmenter in the Computer Management Console. A simpler method is to select Start | All Programs | Accessories | System Tools—you'll find Disk Defragmenter listed there. You can also right-click on any drive in My Computer or Computer, select Properties, and click the Tools tab, where you'll find a convenient Defragment Now button.

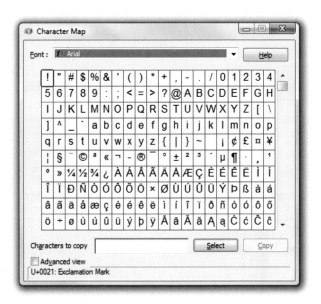

• **Figure 8.19**   Character Map

• **Figure 8.20**   Files and Settings Transfer Wizard

Files and Settings Transfer Wizard (Windows XP)

Suppose you have an old computer full of files and settings, and you just bought yourself a brand-new computer. You want to copy everything from your old computer onto your new computer—what to do? Microsoft touts the Files and Settings Transfer Wizard as just the tool you need (Figure 8.20). This utility copies your desktop files and folders and, most conveniently, your settings from Internet Explorer and Outlook Express; however, it won't copy over your programs, not even the Microsoft ones, and it won't copy settings for any programs other than IE and Outlook Express. If you need to copy everything from an old computer to a new one, you'll probably want to use a disk-imaging tool such as Norton Ghost.

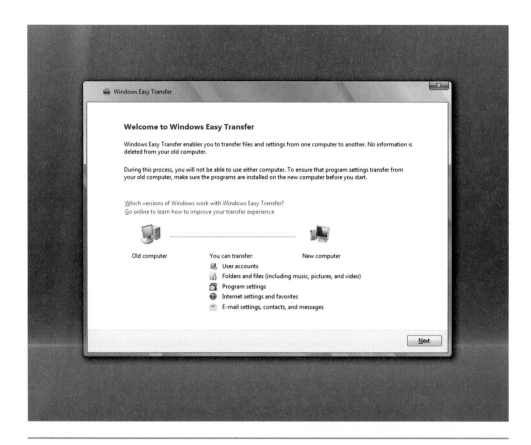

● **Figure 8.21**   Windows Easy Transfer

Windows Easy Transfer (Windows Vista)

Vista's Windows Easy Transfer is an aggressively updated version of the Files and Settings Transfer Wizard. It does everything the older version does and adds the capability to copy user accounts and other settings (Figure 8.21).

Scheduled Tasks (All)

With the Scheduled Tasks utility, you can schedule any program to start and stop any time you wish. The only trick to this utility is that you must enter the program you want to run as a command on the command line, with all the proper switches. Figure 8.22 shows the configuration line for running the Disk Defragmenter program.

Security Center (Windows XP)

The Security Center is a one-stop location for configuring many security features on your computer. This tool is also in the Control Panel. Vista removes Security Center from System Tools. All of these security features, and many more, are discussed in detail in their related chapters.

● **Figure 8.22**   Task Scheduler

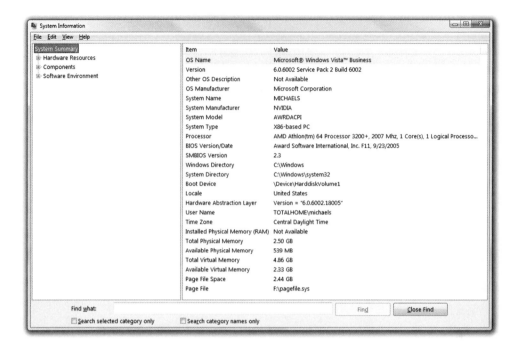

Item	Value
OS Name	Microsoft® Windows Vista™ Business
Version	6.0.6002 Service Pack 2 Build 6002
Other OS Description	Not Available
OS Manufacturer	Microsoft Corporation
System Name	MICHAELS
System Manufacturer	NVIDIA
System Model	AWRDACPI
System Type	X86-based PC
Processor	AMD Athlon(tm) 64 Processor 3200+, 2007 Mhz, 1 Core(s), 1 Logical Processo...
BIOS Version/Date	Award Software International, Inc. F11, 9/23/2005
SMBIOS Version	2.3
Windows Directory	C:\Windows
System Directory	C:\Windows\system32
Boot Device	\Device\HarddiskVolume1
Locale	United States
Hardware Abstraction Layer	Version = "6.0.6002.18005"
User Name	TOTALHOME\michaels
Time Zone	Central Daylight Time
Installed Physical Memory (RAM)	Not Available
Total Physical Memory	2.50 GB
Available Physical Memory	539 MB
Total Virtual Memory	4.86 GB
Available Virtual Memory	2.33 GB
Page File Space	2.44 GB
Page File	F:\pagefile.sys

• **Figure 8.23**   System Information

System Information (All)

System Information is one of those tools that everyone (including the CompTIA A+ exams) likes to talk about, but it's uncommon to meet techs who say they actually use this tool. System Information shows tons of information about the hardware and software on your PC (Figure 8.23). You can also click on the Tools menu to use it as a launch point for a number of programs.

System Restore (XP, Vista)

System Restore is not only handy, it's also arguably the most important single utility you'll ever use in Windows when it comes to fixing a broken system. System Restore enables you to take a "snapshot"—a copy of a number of critical files and settings—and return to that state later (Figure 8.24). System Restore holds multiple snapshots, any of which you may restore to in the future.

Imagine you're installing some new device in your PC, or maybe a piece of software. Before you actually install, you take a snapshot and call it "Before Install." You install the device, and now something starts acting weird. You go back into System Restore and reload the previous snapshot, and the problem goes away.

System Restore isn't perfect. It only backs up a few critical items, and it's useless if the computer won't boot, but it's usually the first thing to try when something goes wrong—assuming, of course, you made a snapshot!

BitLocker (Vista Enterprise and Ultimate)

BitLocker is a tool to encrypt files, folders, or entire hard drives. It's a great way to make sure other people can't read your stuff, but it also makes data recovery risky. If you really want security, use BitLocker.

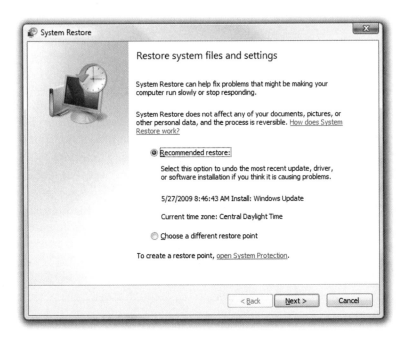

● **Figure 8.24**   System Restore

Command Line

The Windows command-line interface is a throwback to how Microsoft operating systems worked a long, long time ago when text commands were entered at a command prompt. Figure 8.25 shows the command prompt from DOS, the first operating system commonly used in PCs.

> The command-line interface goes back to the early days of computing, but it continues to be an essential tool in all modern operating systems, including Linux, Mac OS X, and all versions of Windows. Chapter 6, "Mastering the Windows Command Line," goes into the command line in detail.

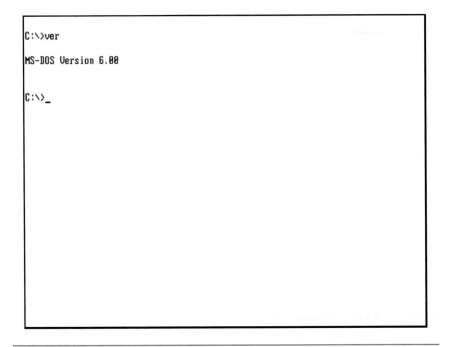

```
C:\>ver

MS-DOS Version 6.00

C:\>_
```

● **Figure 8.25**   DOS command prompt

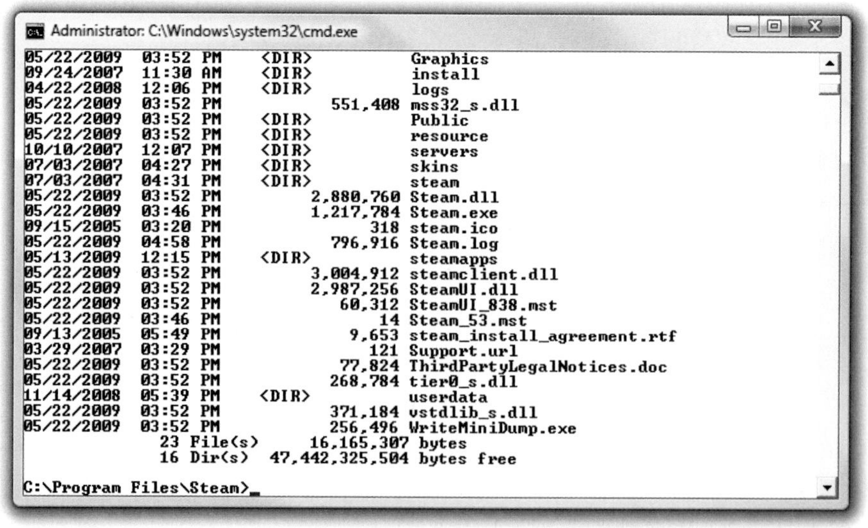

```
 Administrator: C:\Windows\system32\cmd.exe
05/22/2009  03:52 PM    <DIR>          Graphics
09/24/2007  11:30 AM    <DIR>          install
04/22/2008  12:06 PM    <DIR>          logs
05/22/2009  03:52 PM           551,408 mss32_s.dll
05/22/2009  03:52 PM    <DIR>          Public
05/22/2009  03:52 PM    <DIR>          resource
10/10/2007  12:07 PM    <DIR>          servers
07/03/2007  04:27 PM    <DIR>          skins
07/03/2007  04:31 PM    <DIR>          steam
05/22/2009  03:52 PM         2,880,760 Steam.dll
05/22/2009  03:46 PM         1,217,784 Steam.exe
09/15/2005  03:20 PM               318 steam.ico
05/22/2009  04:58 PM           796,916 Steam.log
05/13/2009  12:15 PM    <DIR>          steamapps
05/22/2009  03:52 PM         3,004,912 steamclient.dll
05/22/2009  03:52 PM         2,987,256 SteamUI.dll
05/22/2009  03:52 PM            60,312 SteamUI_838.mst
05/22/2009  03:46 PM                14 Steam_53.mst
09/13/2005  05:49 PM             9,653 steam_install_agreement.rtf
03/29/2007  03:29 PM               121 Support.url
05/22/2009  03:52 PM            77,824 ThirdPartyLegalNotices.doc
05/22/2009  03:52 PM           268,784 tier0_s.dll
11/14/2008  05:39 PM    <DIR>          userdata
05/22/2009  03:52 PM           371,184 vstdlib_s.dll
05/22/2009  03:52 PM           256,496 WriteMiniDump.exe
              23 File(s)     16,165,307 bytes
              16 Dir(s)  47,442,325,504 bytes free

C:\Program Files\Steam>_
```

• **Figure 8.26**   Command prompt in Windows Vista

DOS is dead, but the command-line interface is alive and well in every version of Windows—including Windows 7. Every good tech knows how to access and use the command-line interface. It is a lifesaver when the graphical part of Windows doesn't work, and it is often faster than using a mouse if you're skilled at using it. An entire chapter is devoted to the command line, but let's look at one example of what the command line can do. First, you need to get there. In Windows XP, select Start | Run, and type **cmd** in the dialog box. Click OK and you get to a command prompt. In Windows Vista, you type the same thing in the Start | Start Search dialog box. Figure 8.26 shows a command prompt in Windows Vista.

Once at a command prompt, type **dir** and press ENTER on your keyboard. This command displays all the files and folders in a specific directory—probably your user folder for this exercise—and gives sizes and other information. DIR is just one of many useful command-line tools you'll learn about in this book.

Computer Management

The **Computer Management** applet is a tech's best buddy, or at least a place where you'll spend a lot of time when building or maintaining a system (Figure 8.27). You've already spent considerable time with two of its components: System Tools and Storage. Depending on the version of Windows, System Tools also offers System Information, Performance Logs and Alerts, Reliability and Performance, Device Manager, and more. Storage is where you'll find Disk Management.

Event Viewer

Event Viewer shows you at a glance what has happened in the last day, week, or more, including when people logged in and when the PC had problems (Figure 8.28). You'll see more of Event Viewer in Chapter 16, "Mastering Computer Security."

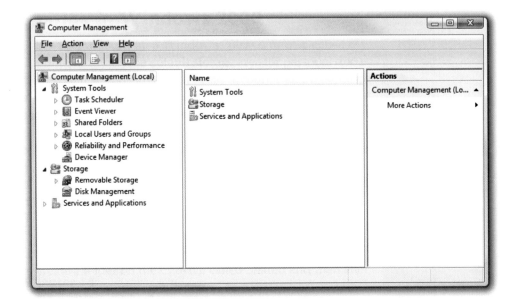

● **Figure 8.27**   Computer Management applet

Performance (Windows 2000/XP)

The Performance console consists of two snap-ins: System Monitor and Performance Logs and Alerts. You can use these for reading *logs*—files that record information over time. The System Monitor can also monitor real-time data (Figure 8.29).

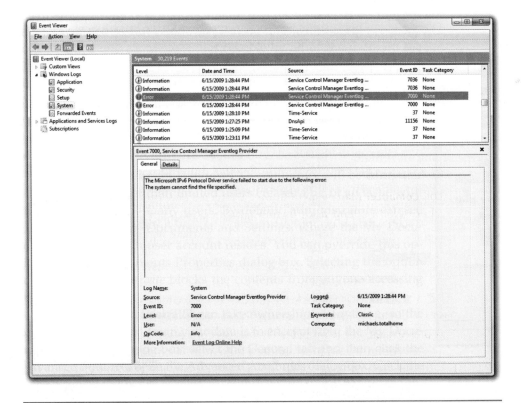

● **Figure 8.28**   Event Viewer reporting system errors

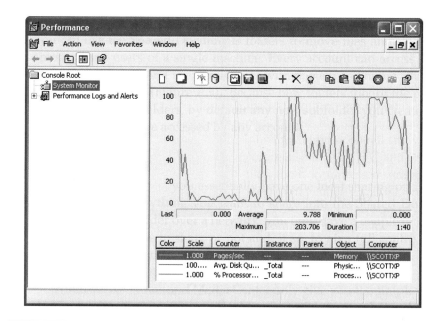

● **Figure 8.29**   System Monitor in action

Suppose you are adding a new cable modem and you want to know just how fast you can download data. Click the plus sign (+) on the toolbar to add a counter. Click the *Use local computer counters* radio button, and then choose Network Interface from the Performance Object pull-down menu. Make sure the *Select counters from list* radio button is selected. Last, select Bytes Received/sec. The dialog box should look like Figure 8.30.

Click Add, and then click Close; probably not much is happening. Go to a Web site, preferably one where you can download a huge file. Start downloading and watch the chart jump; that's the real throughput (Figure 8.31).

Reliability and Performance Monitor (Windows Vista)

The Reliability and Performance Monitor in Windows Vista offers just about everything you can find in the Performance applet of older versions of Windows—although everything is monitored by default, so there's no need to add anything. In addition, it includes the Reliability Monitor. The Reliability Monitor enables you to see at a glance what's been done to the computer over a period of time, including software installations and uninstallations, failures of hardware or applications, and general uptime (Figure 8.32). It's a nice starting tool for checking a Vista machine that's new to you.

Services

Windows runs a large number of separate programs called services. The best way to visualize a service is to think of it as something that runs, yet is invisible. Windows comes with about 100 services by default, and they handle a huge number of tasks, from application support to network functions. You can use the Services applet to see the status of all services on the system, including services that are not running (Figure 8.33).

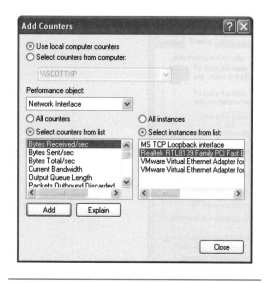

● **Figure 8.30**   Setting up a throughput test

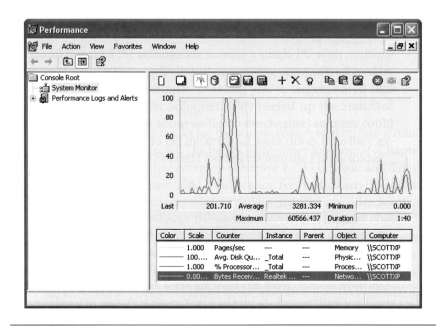

● **Figure 8.31**   Downloading with blazing speed

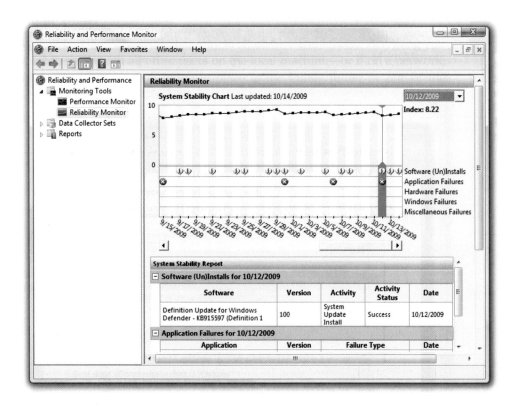

● **Figure 8.32**   The Reliability and Performance Monitor open to the Reliability Monitor screen

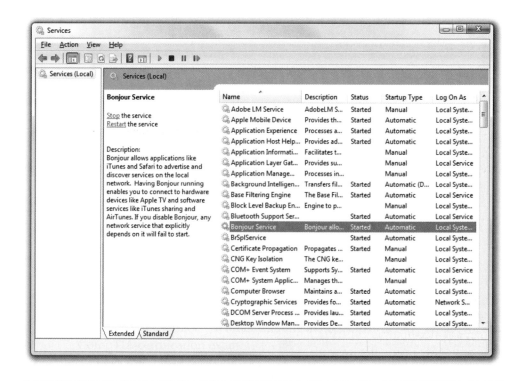

● Figure 8.33   Services applet

Right-click a service and select Properties to modify its settings. Figure 8.34 shows the properties for the Bluetooth support service. See the Startup type pull-down menu? It shows three options: Automatic, Manual, and Disabled. Automatic means it starts when the system starts, Manual means you

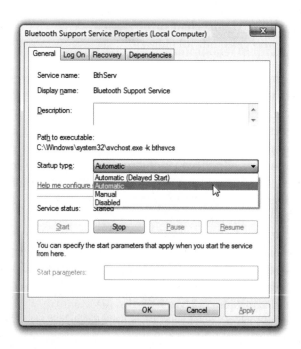

● Figure 8.34   Bluetooth support service properties

have to come to this tab to start it, and Disabled prevents anything from starting it. Make sure you know these three settings, and also make sure you understand how to start, stop, pause, and resume services (note the four buttons below Startup Type).

Windows Sidebar

Windows Vista comes with a UI feature called the Windows Sidebar, a tool that sits on the desktop and enables small helper applications—called Microsoft Gadgets—to run. You can display a clock, for example, or a dynamic weather update. Vista comes with a handful of Gadgets, but developers have gone crazy with them, enabling you to add all sorts of useful tools, such as Twitter feeds and World of Warcraft search and realm status Gadgets.

 The CompTIA A+ Practical Application exam isn't interested in having you memorize all of these services—just make sure you can manipulate them.

 To change the settings for Windows Sidebar, go to Start | All Programs | Acessories and then select Windows Sidebar.

■ Troubleshooting Windows

This section looks at Windows problems from the ground up. It starts with catastrophic failure—a PC that won't boot—and then discusses ways to get past that problem. The next section covers the causes and work-arounds when the Windows GUI fails to load. Once you can access the GUI, the world of Windows diagnostic and troubleshooting tools that you've spent so much time learning about comes to your fingertips. First, though, you have to get there.

Failure to Boot

Windows boot errors take place in those short moments between the time the POST ends and the Loading Windows screen begins. For Windows 2000/XP to start loading the main operating system, the critical system files NTLDR, NTDETECT.COM, and BOOT.INI must reside in the root directory of the C: drive, and BOOT.INI must point to the Windows boot files. If any of these requirements isn't in place, the system won't get past this step. Here are some of the common errors you see at this point:

No Boot Device Present\Inaccessible Boot Device

NTLDR Bad or Missing

Invalid BOOT.INI\ Invalid Boot Disk

Windows Vista or 7 no longer use these files, so you need to look for an entirely new set of errors to tell you that there's a boot failure. Luckily, the only truly critical file that has any hope of corruption is the BOOTMGR file, and Windows Vista normally restores this on the fly if it detects an error. In all but the rarest cases, the Windows Boot Manager detects a problem and brings up a Windows Boot Manager error like the one shown in Figure 8.35.

Note that these text errors take place very early in the startup process. That's your big clue that you have a boot issue. If you get to the Windows splash screen and then lock up, that's a whole different game, so know the difference.

If you get one of the catastrophic error messages and you're running Windows 2000 or XP, you have a three-level process to get back up and

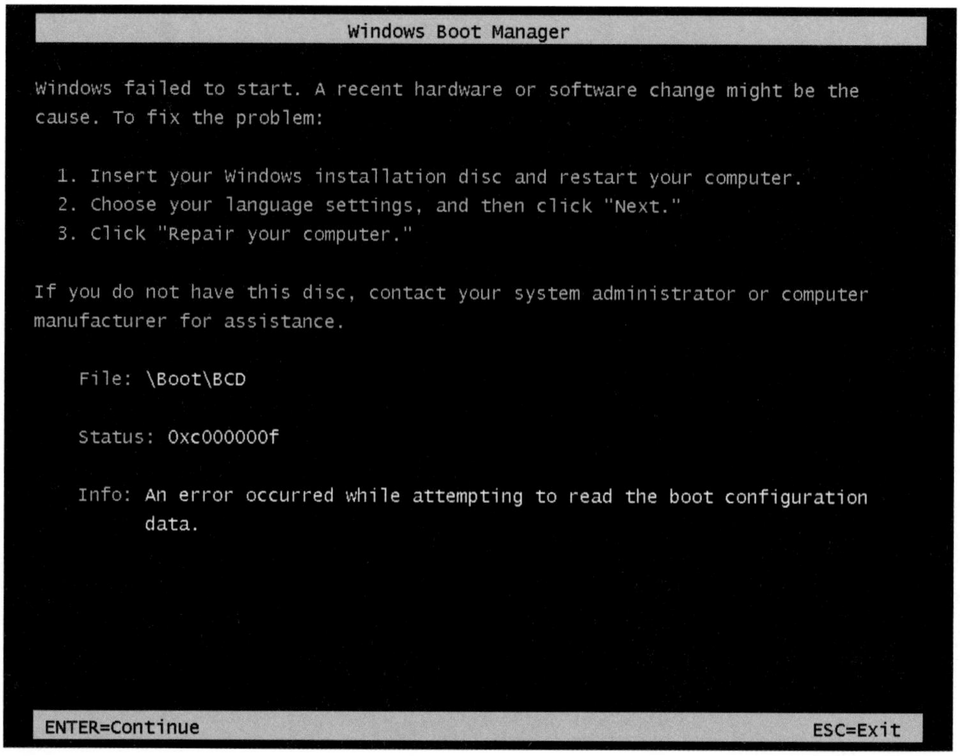

```
┌─────────────────────────────────────────────────────────────────────┐
│                        Windows Boot Manager                          │
├─────────────────────────────────────────────────────────────────────┤
│                                                                       │
│ Windows failed to start. A recent hardware or software change might be the │
│ cause. To fix the problem:                                            │
│                                                                       │
│   1. Insert your Windows installation disc and restart your computer. │
│   2. Choose your language settings, and then click "Next."            │
│   3. Click "Repair your computer."                                    │
│                                                                       │
│ If you do not have this disc, contact your system administrator or computer │
│ manufacturer for assistance.                                          │
│                                                                       │
│     File: \Boot\BCD                                                   │
│                                                                       │
│     Status: 0xc000000f                                                │
│                                                                       │
│     Info: An error occurred while attempting to read the boot configuration │
│           data.                                                       │
│                                                                       │
│                                                                       │
├─────────────────────────────────────────────────────────────────────┤
│ ENTER=Continue                                                ESC=Exit │
└─────────────────────────────────────────────────────────────────────┘
```

● **Figure 8.35**   Boot Manager error

running. You first should attempt to repair. If that fails, attempt to restore from a backup copy of Windows. If restore is either not available or fails, your only recourse is to rebuild. You will lose data at the restore and rebuild phases, so you definitely want to spend a lot of energy on the repair effort first! If you're running Vista, the repair process for boot failures is exactly the same as a failure to load the GUI. Read about the System Recovery Options in the next section to see what you need to do.

Attempt to Repair by Using Recovery Console (2000/XP)

To begin troubleshooting one of these errors, boot from the installation CD-ROM and have Windows do a repair of an existing installation. Windows prompts you if you want to use the Recovery Console or the emergency repair process (ASR/ERD). Start with the Recovery Console.

If you followed the instructions in the sidebar to the left, you've installed the Recovery Console onto your system and have it as an option when you boot the system. If not, start it by booting to the Windows 2000 or XP install disc and pressing the R key when prompted. When you select the Recovery Console, you will see a message about NTDETECT and another one that the Recovery Console is starting up, and then you are greeted with the following message and command prompt:

```
Microsoft Windows XP<TM> Recovery Console.
The Recovery Console provides system repair and recovery
functionality.
```

Many techs find it useful to install the Recovery Console as a boot option. To do this, you first need to log into the system with the Administrator account. Grab your Windows 2000 or XP installation CD-ROM and drop it in your system. If the Autorun function kicks in, just click the No button. After that, click the Start button, select Run, and type the following:

`d:\i386\winnt32 /cmdcons`

If your CD-ROM drive uses a different drive letter, substitute it for the D: drive. Then just follow the instructions on the screen. If you are connected to the Internet, allow the Setup program to download updated files. From now on, every time the system boots, the OS selection menu will show your Windows OS (Windows 2000 Professional or Windows XP) and the Microsoft Windows Recovery Console.

```
Type Exit to quit the Recovery Console and restart the
computer.
```

```
1: C:\WINDOWS
Which Windows XP installation would you like to log onto
<To cancel, press ENTER>?
```

The cursor is a small white rectangle sitting to the right of the question mark on the last line. If you are not accustomed to working at the command prompt, this may be disorienting. If there is only one installation of Windows XP on your computer, type the number **1** at the prompt and press the ENTER key. If you press ENTER before typing in a valid selection, the Recovery Console will cancel and the computer will reboot. The only choice you can make in this example is 1. Having made that choice, the screen displays a new line, followed by the cursor:

```
Type the Administrator password:
```

Enter the Administrator password for that computer and press ENTER. The password does not display on the screen; you see asterisks in place of the password. The screen still shows everything that has happened so far, unless something has happened to cause an error message. It now looks like this:

```
Microsoft Windows XP<TM> Recovery Console.
The Recovery Console provides system repair and recovery
functionality.
Type Exit to quit the Recovery Console and restart the
computer.

1: C:\WINDOWS
Which Windows XP installation would you like to log onto
<To cancel, press ENTER>? 1
Type the Administrator password: ********
C:\Windows>
```

By now, you've caught on and know that there is a rectangular prompt immediately after the last line. Now what do you do? Use the Recovery Console commands, of course. Recovery Console uses many of the commands that worked in the Windows command-line interface that you explored in Chapter 6, "Mastering the Windows Command Line," as well as some uniquely its own. Table 8.1 lists the common Recovery Console commands.

The Recovery Console shines in the business of manually restoring Registries, stopping problem services, rebuilding partitions (other than the system partition), and using the EXPAND program to extract copies of corrupted files from a CD-ROM or floppy disk.

Using the Recovery Console, you can reconfigure a service so that it starts with different settings, format drives on the hard disk, read and write on local FAT or NTFS volumes, and copy replacement files from a floppy or CD-ROM. The Recovery Console enables you to access the file system and is still constrained by the file and folder security of NTFS, which makes it a more secure tool to use than some third-party solutions.

The Recovery Console is best at fixing three items: repairing the MBR, reinstalling the boot files, and rebuilding BOOT.INI. Let's look at each of these.

Table 8.1	Common Recovery Console Commands
Command	**Description**
attrib	Changes attributes of selected file or folder.
cd (or chdir)	Displays current directory or changes directories.
chkdsk	Runs CheckDisk utility.
cls	Clears screen.
copy	Copies from removable media to system folders on hard disk. No wildcards.
del (or delete)	Deletes service or folder.
dir	Lists contents of selected directory on system partition only.
disable	Disables service or driver.
diskpart	Replaces FDISK—creates/deletes partitions.
enable	Enables service or driver.
extract	Extracts components from .CAB files.
fixboot	Writes new partition boot sector on system partition.
fixmbr	Writes new Master Boot Record for partition boot sector.
format	Formats selected disk.
listsvc	Lists all services on system.
logon	Lets you choose which Windows installation to log on to if you have more than one.
map	Displays current drive letter mappings.
md (or mkdir)	Creates a directory.
more (or type)	Displays contents of text file.
rd (or rmdir)	Removes a directory.
ren (or rename)	Renames a single file.
systemroot	Makes current directory system root of drive you're logged into.
type	Displays a text file.

A bad boot sector usually shows up as a No Boot Device error. If it turns out that this isn't the problem, the Recovery Console command to fix it won't hurt anything. At the Recovery Console prompt, just type:

```
fixmbr
```

This fixes the master boot record.

The second problem the Recovery Console is best at fixing is missing system files, usually indicated by the error *NTLDR bad or missing*. Odds are good that if NTLDR is missing, so are the rest of the system files. To fix this, get to the root directory (CD\—remember that from Chapter 6, "Mastering the Windows Command Line"?) and type the following line:

```
copy d:\i386\ntldr
```

Then type this line:

```
copy d:\i386\ntdetect.com
```

This takes care of two of the big three and leads us to the last issue, rebuilding BOOT.INI. If the BOOT.INI file is gone or corrupted, run this command from the Recovery Console:

```
bootcfg /rebuild
```

The Recovery Console will then try to locate all installed copies of Windows and ask you if you want to add them to the new BOOT.INI file it's about to create. Say yes to the ones you want.

If all goes well with the Recovery Console, do a thorough backup as soon as possible (just in case something else goes wrong). If the Recovery Console does not do the trick, the next step is to restore Windows XP.

To use the Windows XP System Restore, you need to be able to get into Windows. "Restore" in the context used here means to give you an option to get into Windows.

Attempt to Restore

If you've been diligent about backing up, you can attempt to restore to an earlier, working copy of Windows. You have two basic choices, depending on your OS. In Windows 2000, you can try the ERD. Windows XP limits you to the ASR.

If you elected to create an ERD in Windows 2000, you can attempt to restore your system with it. Boot your system to the Windows 2000 installation CD-ROM and select *repair a Windows 2000 installation*, but in this case opt for the ERD. Follow the steps outlined earlier in the chapter and you might have some success.

ASR can restore your system to a previously installed state, but you should use it as a last resort. You lose everything on the system that was installed or added after you created the ASR disk. If that's the best option, though, just do what you have to do.

Rebuild

If faced with a full system rebuild, you have several options, depending on the particular system. You could simply reboot to the Windows CD-ROM and install right on top of the existing system, but that's usually not the optimal solution. To avoid losing anything important, you'd be better off swapping the C: drive for a blank hard drive and installing a clean version of Windows.

Most OEM systems come with a misleadingly named *Recover CD* or *recovery partition*. The Recover CD is a CD-ROM that you boot to and run. The recovery partition is a hidden partition on the hard drive that you activate at boot by holding down a key combination specific to the manufacturer of that system. (See the motherboard manual or users' guide for the key combination and other details.) Both "recover" options do the same thing—restore your computer to the factory-installed state. If you run one of these tools, you will wipe everything off your system—all personal files, folders, and programs will go away! Before running either tool, make sure all important files and folders are backed up on an optical disc or spare hard drive.

Failure to Load the GUI

Assuming that Windows gets past the boot part of the startup, it then begins to load the real Windows OS. You will see the Windows startup image on the screen, hiding everything until Windows loads the desktop (Figure 8.36).

● **Figure 8.36**   GUI time!

Several issues can cause Windows to hang during the GUI-loading phase, such as buggy device drivers or Registry problems. Even autoloading programs can cause the GUI to hang on load. The first step in troubleshooting these issues is to use one of the Advanced Startup options (covered later in the chapter) to try to get past the hang spot and into Windows.

If you're running Vista or 7 and you think the GUI looks a little off, the first thing you should do is to make sure that Aero is turned on. To turn on Aero, right-click on your desktop and then select the Personalize menu option. Next, select Window Color and Appearance. If you see a screen that looks like Figure 8.37, you already have Aero running. If you see a screen that looks like Figure 8.38, select the Windows Aero color scheme to activate the Aero desktop.

Device Drivers

Device driver problems that stop Windows GUI from loading look pretty scary. Figure 8.39 shows the infamous Windows *Stop error*, better known as the Blue Screen of Death (BSoD). The BSoD only appears when something causes an error from which Windows cannot recover. The BSoD is not limited to device driver problems, but device drivers are one of the reasons you'll see the BSoD.

Whenever you get a BSoD, take a moment and read what it says. Windows BSoDs tell you the name of the file that caused the problem and usually suggests a recommended action. Once in a while these are helpful—but not often.

BSoD problems due to device drivers almost always take place immediately after you've installed a new device and rebooted. Take out the device and reboot. If Windows loads properly, head over to the manufacturer's Web site. A new device producing this type of problem is a serious issue

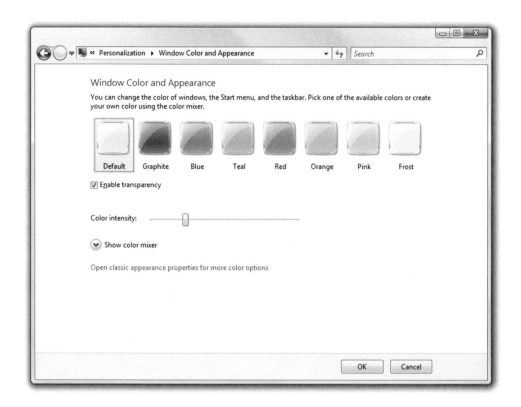

● **Figure 8.37**   You've got Aero!

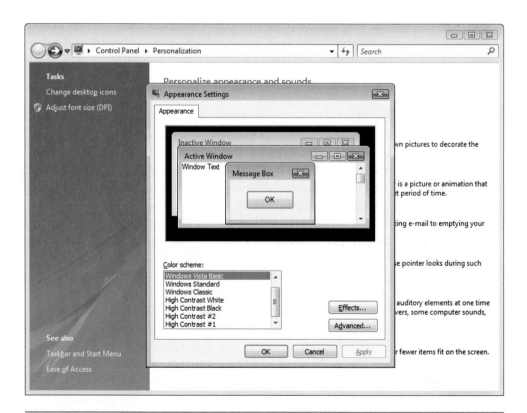

● **Figure 8.38**   The lack of transparency and the flat window with no drop shadow shows that Aero is not activated.

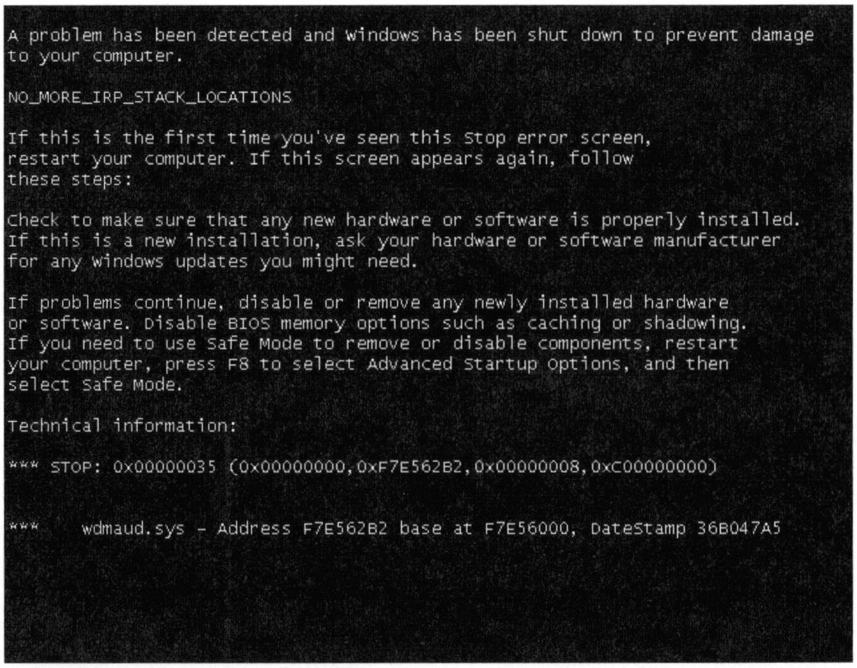

```
A problem has been detected and windows has been shut down to prevent damage
to your computer.

NO_MORE_IRP_STACK_LOCATIONS

If this is the first time you've seen this stop error screen,
restart your computer. If this screen appears again, follow
these steps:

Check to make sure that any new hardware or software is properly installed.
If this is a new installation, ask your hardware or software manufacturer
for any windows updates you might need.

If problems continue, disable or remove any newly installed hardware
or software. Disable BIOS memory options such as caching or shadowing.
If you need to use Safe Mode to remove or disable components, restart
your computer, press F8 to select Advanced Startup Options, and then
select Safe Mode.

Technical information:

*** STOP: 0x00000035 (0x00000000,0xF7E562B2,0x00000008,0xC00000000)

***     wdmaud.sys - Address F7E562B2 base at F7E56000, DateStamp 36B047A5
```

• **Figure 8.39** BSoD

the manufacturer will have updated drivers available for download or will recommend a replacement device.

The second indication of a device problem that shows up during the GUI part of startup is a freeze-up: the Windows startup screen just stays there and you never get a chance to log on. If this happens, try one of the Advanced Startup Options, covered later.

Registry

Your Registry files load every time the computer boots. Windows does a pretty good job of protecting your Registry files from corruption, but from time to time something may slip by Windows and it will attempt to load a bad Registry. These errors may show up as BSoDs that say "Registry File Failure" or text errors that say "Windows could not start." Whatever the case, you need to restore a good Registry copy. The best way to do this is the Last Known Good Configuration boot option (see the upcoming section). If that fails, you can restore an earlier version of the Registry through the Recovery Console.

Boot to the Windows installation CD-ROM, select the repair installation to get to the Recovery Console, and type the following commands to restore a Registry. Notice I didn't say "your" Registry in the previous sentence. Your Registry is corrupted and gone, so you need to rebuild.

```
delete c:\windows\system32\config\system
delete c:\windows\system32\config\software
delete c:\windows\system32\config\sam
delete c:\windows\system32\config\security
delete c:\windows\system32\config\default
```

```
copy c:\windows\repair\system c:\windows\system32\config\system
copy c:\windows\repair\software c:\windows\system32\config\software
copy c:\windows\repair\sam c:\windows\system32\config\sam
copy c:\windows\repair\security c:\windows\system32\config\security
copy c:\windows\repair\default c:\windows\system32\config\default
```

Advanced Startup Options

If Windows fails to start up, use the Windows **Advanced Startup Options** menu to discover the cause. To get to this menu, restart the computer and press F8 after the POST messages but before the Windows logo screen appears. Windows 2000 and Windows XP have similar menus. Vista's is just a tad different. Central to these advanced options are Safe Mode and Last Known Good Configuration. Here's a rundown of the menu options.

 Windows 9*x* had an option for step-by-step confirmation, but that is not a choice in Windows 2000/XP/Vista. Look for it as a wrong answer on the exams!

Safe Mode (All Versions)   **Safe Mode** starts up Windows but loads only very basic, non–vendor-specific drivers for mouse, VGA monitor (not in Vista), keyboard, mass storage, and system services (see Figure 8.40).

Once in Safe Mode, you can use tools such as Device Manager to locate and correct the source of the problem. When you use Device Manager in Safe Mode, you can access the properties for all the devices, even those that are not working in Safe Mode. The status displayed for the device is the status for a normal startup. Even the network card will show as enabled. You can disable any suspect device or perform other tasks, such as removing or updating drivers. If a problem with a device driver is preventing the

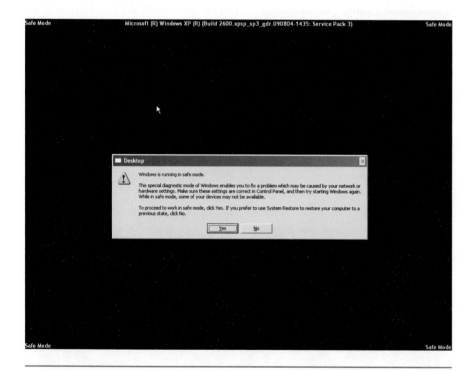

• **Figure 8.40**   Safe Mode

operating system from starting normally, check the Device Manager for warning icons that indicate an unknown device.

Safe Mode with Networking (All Versions)   This mode is identical to plain Safe Mode except that you get network support. I use this mode to test for a problem with network drivers. If Windows won't start up normally but does start up in Safe Mode, I reboot into Safe Mode with Networking. If it fails to start up with Networking, the problem is a network driver. I reboot back to Safe Mode, open Device Manager, and start disabling network components, beginning with the network adapter.

Safe Mode with Command Prompt (All Versions)   When you start Windows in this mode, rather than loading the GUI desktop, it loads the command prompt (CMD.EXE) as the shell to the operating system after you log on, as shown in Figure 8.41. This is a handy option to remember if the desktop does not display at all, which, after you have eliminated video drivers, can be caused by corruption of the EXPLORER.EXE program. From the command prompt, you can delete the corrupted version of EXPLORER.EXE and copy in an undamaged version. This requires knowing the command-line commands for navigating the directory structure, as well as knowing the location of the file you are replacing. Although Explorer is not loaded, you can load other GUI tools that don't depend on Explorer. All you have to do is enter the correct command. For instance, to load Event Viewer, type **eventvwr.msc** at the command line and press ENTER.

Enable Boot Logging (All Versions)   This option starts Windows normally and creates a log file of the drivers as they load into memory. The file is named Ntbtlog.txt and is saved in the %SystemRoot% folder. If the startup failed because of a bad driver, the last entry in this file may be the driver the OS was initializing when it failed.

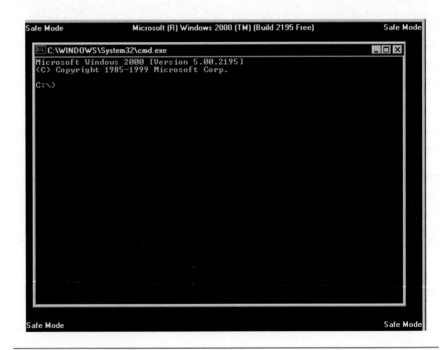

• **Figure 8.41**   Safe Mode with command prompt

Reboot and go into the Recovery Console. Use the Recovery Console tools to read the boot log (type **ntbtlog.txt**) and disable or enable problematic devices or services.

Enable VGA Mode (2000/XP)/Enable Low-Resolution Mode (Vista)   Enable VGA Mode/Enable Low-resolution Mode starts Windows normally but only loads a default VGA driver. If this mode works, it may mean you have a bad driver, or it may mean you are using the correct video driver but it is configured incorrectly (perhaps with the wrong refresh rate and/or resolution). Whereas Safe Mode loads a generic VGA driver, this mode loads the driver Windows is configured to use but starts it up in standard VGA mode rather than using the settings for which it is configured. After successfully starting in this mode, open the Display Properties and change the settings.

Last Known Good Configuration (All Versions)   When Windows' startup fails immediately after installing a new driver but before you have logged on again, you may want to try the Last Known Good Configuration option. This can be a rather fickle and limited tool, but it never hurts to try it.

Directory Services Restore Mode (All Versions)   The title says it all here; this option only applies to Active Directory domain controllers, and only Windows Server versions can be domain controllers. I have no idea why Microsoft includes this option. If you choose it, you simply boot into Safe Mode.

Debugging Mode (All Versions)   If you select this choice, Windows starts in kernel debug mode. It's a super-techie thing to do, and I doubt that even über techs do debug mode anymore. To do this, you have to connect the computer you are debugging to another computer via a serial connection, and as Windows starts up, a debug of the kernel is sent to the second computer, which must also be running a debugger program. I remember running debug for an early version of Windows 2000. My coworkers and I did it back then simply because we were studying for the MCSE exams and expected to be tested on it! We all decided it was an experience that we didn't need to repeat.

Disable Automatic Restart on System Failure (All Versions)   Sometimes a BSoD will appear at startup, causing your computer to spontaneously reboot. That's all well and good, but if it happens too quickly, you might not be able to read the BSoD to see what caused the problem. Selecting *Disable automatic restart on system failure* from the Advanced Startup Options menu stops the computer from rebooting on Stop errors. This gives you the opportunity to write down the error and hopefully find a fix.

Disable Driver Signature Enforcement (Vista)   Windows Vista (and 7) requires that all very low-level drivers (kernel drivers) must have a Microsoft driver signature. If you are using an older driver to connect to your hard drive controller or some other low-level feature, you must use this option to get Windows to load the driver. Hopefully you will always check your motherboard and hard drives for Vista compatibility and never have to use this option.

Start Windows Normally (All Versions)   This choice will simply start Windows normally, without rebooting. You already rebooted to get to this menu. Select this if you changed your mind about using any of the other exotic choices.

Reboot (All Versions)   This choice will actually do a soft reboot of the computer.

Return to OS Choices Menu (All Versions)   On computers with multiple operating systems, you get an OS Choices menu to select which OS to load. If you load Windows and press F8 to get the Advanced Startup Options menu, you'll see this option. Choosing it returns you to the OS Choices menu, from which you can select the operating system to load.

Troubleshooting Tools in the GUI

Once you're able to load into Windows, whether through Safe Mode or one of the other options, the whole gamut of Windows tools is available for you. If a bad device driver caused the startup problems, for example, you can open Device Manager and begin troubleshooting just as you've learned in previous chapters. If you suspect some service or Registry issue caused the problem, head on over to Event Viewer and see what sort of logon events have happened recently.

Event Viewer might reveal problems with applications failing to load, a big cause of Windows loading problems (Figure 8.42). It might also reveal problems with services failing to start. Finally, Windows might run into problems loading DLLs. You can troubleshoot these issues individually or you can use System Restore in Windows XP to load a restore point that predates the bugginess.

Startup Programs

Windows loves to autoload programs so they start at boot. Most of the time this is an incredibly handy option, used by every Windows PC in existence. The problem with autoloading programs is that when one of them starts behaving badly, you need to shut off that program! Use the System Configuration utility to stop programs from autoloading.

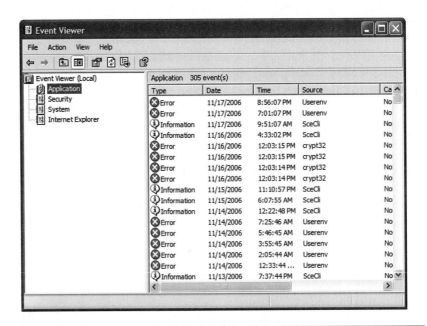

• **Figure 8.42**   Event Viewer showing some serious application errors!

Mike Meyers' CompTIA A+ Guide: Practical Application

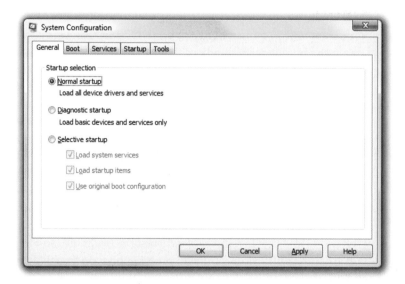

• **Figure 8.43**   The Windows Vista System Configuration utility

Techs use the **System Configuration utility** to edit and troubleshoot operating system and program startup processes and services. It has been available in all Windows operating systems except Windows 95 and Windows 2000. Prior to Windows Vista, the System Configuration utility offered quick access to troubleshoot and edit the boot.ini file. It still offers some of these features in Vista, such as the capability to disable or enable troublesome or unwanted services and startup items. The BCD data store is used in place of the boot.ini in Windows Vista, however, so you obviously cannot use the System Configuration utility to edit the boot.ini in Vista.

To start the System Configuration utility, go to Start | Run or Start | Start Search, enter **msconfig**, and click OK or press ENTER (Figure 8.43). The program will run automatically in Windows XP; in Vista you may need to provide the necessary credentials or response, depending on the User Account Control (UAC) setup.

Services

Windows loads a number of services as it starts. If any critical service fails to start, Windows tells you at this point with an error message. The important word here is *critical*. Windows will not report *all* service failures at this point. If a service that is less than critical in Windows' eyes doesn't start, Windows usually waits until you actually try to use a program that needs that service before it prompts you with an error message (Figure 8.44).

To work with your system's services, go to the Control Panel | Administrative Tools | Services and verify that the service you need is running. If not, turn it on. Also notice that each service has a Startup Type—Automatic, Manual, or Disabled—that defines when it starts. It's very common to find that a service has been set to Manual when it needs to be set to Automatic so that it starts when Windows boots (Figure 8.45).

You should remember that you can configure the System Configuration utility with startup selections for troubleshooting. After using the System Configuration utility to change your startup programs, you can choose Normal startup to load all drivers and services. A Diagnostic startup loads basic services only, and a Selective startup enables you to select which system services and startup items to load on startup.

Many services require other services, called dependency services, to start before they can start. If your target service needs a dependency service, you'll get an error when you try to start your target service, telling you which dependency service needs to start first.

• **Figure 8.44**   Service error

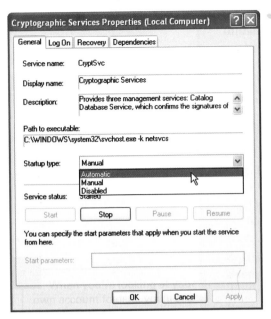

● **Figure 8.45**   Autostarting a service

Windows Indexing Service (XP and Vista) is designed to help you find files quickly on your system but it can slow down your system as it builds these indexes. To turn off Indexing, in XP go to Services and shut down the Index service. In Vista, turn off the Windows Search service.

Remember that you need local administrator privileges to install applications in all versions of Windows.

System Files

Windows lives on dynamic link library (DLL) files. Almost every program used by Windows—and certainly all of the important ones—call to DLL files to do most of the heavy lifting that makes Windows work. Windows protects all of the critical DLL files very carefully, but once in a while you may get an error saying Windows can't load a particular DLL. Although rare, the core system files that make up Windows itself may become corrupted, preventing Windows from starting properly. You usually see something like "Error loading XXXX.DLL," or sometimes a program you need simply won't start when you double-click its icon. In these cases, the tool you need is the System File Checker. The System File Checker is a command prompt program (SFC.EXE) you can use to check a number of critical files, including the ever-important DLL cache. SFC takes a number of switches, but by far the most important is /scannow. Go to a command prompt and type the following to start the program:

```
SFC /scannow
```

SFC automatically checks all critical files and replaces any it sees as corrupted. During this process, it may ask for the Windows installation CD-ROM, so keep it handy!

System Restore

With Windows XP and Vista systems, you can recover from a bad device or application installation by using System Restore to load a restore point. Follow the process explained earlier in the chapter. System Restore is the final step in recovering from a major Windows meltdown.

Application Problems

Almost all Windows programs come with some form of handy installer. You run the installer and the program runs. It almost couldn't be simpler.

A well-behaved program should always make itself easy to uninstall as well. In most cases, you should see an uninstallation option in the program's Start menu area; and in all cases (unless you have an application with a badly configured installer), the application should appear in either the Add/Remove Programs or Programs and Features Control Panel applet (Figure 8.46).

Despite Microsoft's best efforts, you can run into trouble with applications. Although these errors come in hundreds of varieties, the overwhelming majority of problems can be broken down into three categories: installation problems, compatibility problems, or uninstallation problems.

Installation Problems

Programs that fail to install usually aren't to blame in and of themselves. In most cases, a problem with Windows prevents them from installing, most notably the lack of some other program that the application needs so it can operate. One of the best examples of this is the popular .Net Framework. .Net is an extension to the Windows operating system that includes support for a number of powerful features, particularly more powerful interface

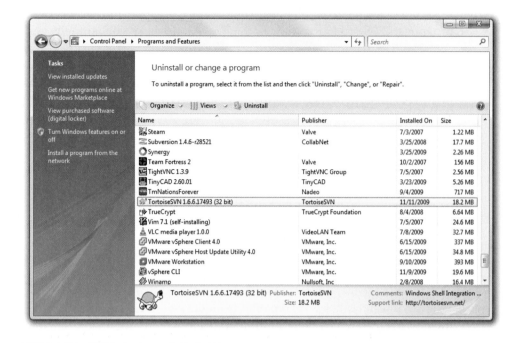

● **Figure 8.46** Programs and Features Control Panel applet

tools and much more flexible database access. If a program is written to take advantage of .Net, .Net must itself be installed. In most cases, if .Net is missing, the application should try to install it at the same time it is installed, but you can't count on this. If .Net is missing or if the version of .Net you are using is too old (there have been a number of .Net versions since it came out in 2002), you can get some of the most indecipherable errors in the history of Windows applications.

Figure 8.47 shows one such example in Windows 7 where the popular VMware vSphere client fails due to the wrong .Net version. Too bad the error doesn't give you any clues!

These types of errors invariably require you to go online and do Web searches, using the application name and the error. No matter how bad the error, someone else has already suffered from the same problem. The trick is to find out what they did to get around it.

● **Figure 8.47** .Net error

Compatibility

Most applications are written with the most recent version of Windows in mind, but as you know, Windows versions change over time. In some cases, such as the jump from Windows 2000 to Windows XP, the changes are minor enough to cause few if any compatibility problems when running an application designed for an earlier version of Windows. In other cases, especially the jump from Windows XP to Vista (and beyond), the underpinnings of the OS differ so much that you have to perform certain steps to ensure that the older programs run. Windows 2000, XP, and Vista provide different forms of **compatibility modes** to support older applications.

Windows 2000 only provides compatibility support for ancient DOS programs. DOS programs know nothing of Windows, so you normally just copy the EXE file to your computer. In Windows 2000, right-clicking on a DOS program shows two tabs: Memory and Program. The memory tab enables you to adjust the amount of memory used by the DOS program. Back in the year 2000, RAM was still precious and you could save a few kilobytes by some careful adjustments. More interesting was the Advanced button under the Program tab (Figure 8.48). This enabled you to let the DOS program load a custom AUTOEXEC.BAT or CONFIG.SYS file.

Windows XP took the idea of compatibility a step further by adding another tab called Compatibility (Figure 8.49). This tab enabled you to configure older Windows programs to work in XP by introducing the concept of compatibility modes. You can also set specific video settings on the Compatibility tab.

Windows Vista takes the Compatibility tab one step further by adding two important features: Windows XP mode and *Run this program as an administrator* (Figure 8.50).

The secret to using compatibility mode isn't much of a secret at all: if the program doesn't run, try a compatibility mode! If you want to be really careful, do a Web search on your application before you try to run it. Compatibility mode is a handy tool to get older applications running.

One error common on older systems but largely absent or invisible on modern systems is a *general protection fault* (*GPF*). A GPF occurs when a program tries to do something not permitted, such as writing to protected memory or something else Windows doesn't like. This can cause an error message to appear or even crash the computer. You are very unlikely to encounter a GPF today.

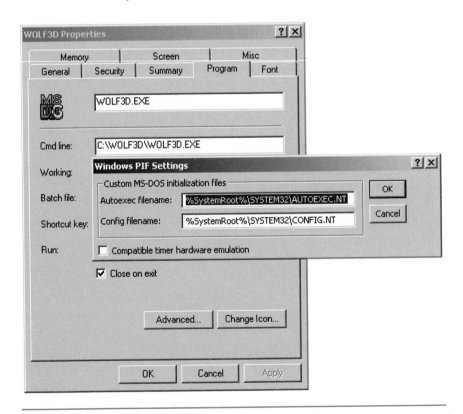

• **Figure 8.48** Windows 2000 Program tab for DOS program

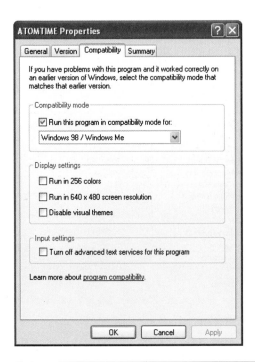

● **Figure 8.49**   XP compatibility mode

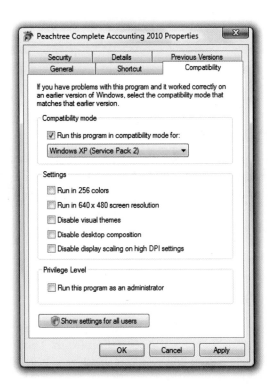

● **Figure 8.50**   Vista compatibility mode

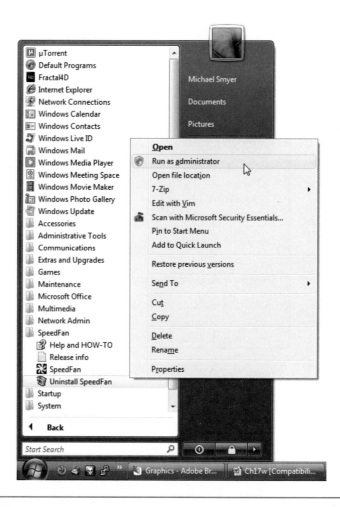

● **Figure 8.51**   Selecting *Run as administrator* from context menu

Problems with Uninstalling

The single biggest problem with uninstalling is that people try to uninstall without administrator privileges. If you try to uninstall and get an error, log back in as an administrator and you should be fine. Don't forget you can right-click on most uninstallation menu options on the Programs menu and select *Run as administrator* to switch to administrator privileges (Figure 8.51).

Beyond A+

The majority of the tools and utilities discussed in this chapter are in direct correlation with the 2009 Practical Application exam. There are also many others you should check out for your personal use. With that said, these commands available at the Windows Vista command prompt deserve mention:

CHOICE   A batch file command that allows users to select from a set of options.

CLIP   Redirects the output of another command to the Windows Clipboard.

CMDKEY Creates, lists, and deletes stored user names, passwords, and other credentials.

FORFILES Selects files in a particular folder for batch processing.

ICACLS Displays, modifies, backs up, or restores ACLs for files and directories.

FSUTIL Increases the file system memory cache.

MKLINK Creates symbolic links and hard links.

TAKEOWN Allows an administrator to take ownership of a file.

TIMEOUT Pauses the command processor for the specified number of seconds.

VSP1CLN Cleans up after a Windows Vista SP1 installation.

VSSADMIN Volume Shadow Copy Service administration tool.

WHERE Displays the location of files that match a search pattern.

Other Windows Versions

Microsoft adds or tweaks utilities from one version of its flagship operating system to the next. Plus, tools often move from version to version. The Performance applet in Windows XP, for example, became the Reliability and Performance Monitor in Windows Vista. With Windows 7, Microsoft shifted things again, with Reliability going into a new Control Panel applet called Action Center. Go figure. Half the fun in migrating to a new OS is hunting down your favorite tools!

This Beyond A+ section addresses the several versions of Windows not on the CompTIA A+ Practical Application exam: Windows 7, Windows Mobile, Windows XP Tablet PC, and Windows Embedded.

Windows 7

Windows 7 came out just a few months after CompTIA announced the 220-701 and 220-702 exams, so it's not on those exams. However, the differences between Vista and 7 are so minor "under the hood" that it's safe to say if you know Vista, you know Windows 7 (Figure 8.52).

Windows Mobile

Windows Mobile is a very small version of Windows designed for PDAs and phones. Windows Mobile is only available as an Original Equipment Manufacturer (OEM) product, which means you buy the device and it comes with Windows Mobile—you can't buy some PDA or phone and then buy Windows Mobile separately.

Windows XP Tablet PC

A tablet PC is a laptop with a built-in touch screen. The idea behind a tablet PC is to drastically reduce, if not totally eliminate, the use of a keyboard (Figure 8.53). In some situations, tablet PCs have started to become popular. Windows XP Tablet PC edition is Microsoft's operating solution for tablet PCs. Tablet PC is still Windows XP, but it adds special drivers and applications to support the tablet.

● **Figure 8.52**   Windows 7

Windows Vista comes with the Tablet PC features built in, so there's no need for a special tablet-version of Vista (or Windows 7, for that matter).

Windows Embedded

You'll see more of Windows XP Tablet PC Edition in Chapter 11, "Mastering Portable Computing."

The world is filled with PCs in the most unlikely places. Everything from cash registers to the F-22 Raptor fighter plane contains some number of tiny PCs. These aren't the PCs you're used to seeing, though. They almost never have mice, monitors, keyboards, and the usual I/O you'd expect to see, but they are truly PCs, with a CPU, RAM, BIOS, and storage.

These tiny PCs need operating systems just like any other PC, and a number of companies make specialized OSs for embedded PCs. Microsoft makes Windows Embedded just for these specialized embedded PCs.

● **Figure 8.53**   Tablet PC

Chapter 8 Review

■ Chapter Summary

After reading this chapter and completing the exercises, you should understand the following about using and troubleshooting Windows.

Identify the operating system folders of Windows 2000, XP, and Vista

- SystemRoot is the tech name given to the folder in which Windows has been installed. SystemRoot by default is C:\WINNT in Windows 2000, while Windows XP and Vista's SystemRoot defaults to C:\WINDOWS.

- Most programs install some or all of their essential files into a subfolder of the Program Files folder. This folder is found almost always in the root of the same drive where you find the Windows system folder. Windows Vista 64-bit versions have a separate Program Files (x86) folder for 32-bit applications.

- Personal documents are stored by default in the Documents and Settings folder (Windows 2000 and Windows XP) or the Users folder in Windows Vista. Within the folder structure, you'll find folders for each user account and, within those user account folders, folders such as Desktop, Start Menu, and so on. Just as with Program Files, the Documents and Settings/Users folder will be on the same drive as the Windows system folder.

- The Registry is a database that stores everything about your PC, including information on all of the hardware in the PC, network information, user preferences, file types, and virtually anything else you might run into with Windows.

- You can access the Registry Editor by typing **regedt32** or **regedit** at the Start | Run menu or at the Start | Start Search dialog box, depending on the version of Windows.

Describe the utilities in Windows essential to techs

- Windows offers many utilities that enable techs to configure the operating system, optimize and tweak settings, install hardware, and more. Six that techs use frequently are right-click, Control Panel, System Tools, command line, Administrative Tools, and the Microsoft Management Console.

- Right-clicking an object brings up the context menu for the object so you can act on it. One common right-click option is Properties.

- The Control Panel handles most of the maintenance, upgrade, and configuration aspects of Windows. The Control Panel contains many applets that are displayed either as a set or in categories in Windows XP or Windows Vista.

- The Device Manager enables techs to examine and configure all the hardware and drivers in a Windows PC. The Device Manager displays every device that Windows recognizes, organized in special groups called types. You can see resources used by devices and update drivers directly in Device Manager. Device Manager places an icon on top of any hardware device that's not functioning properly or is manually disabled. Device Manager is the first tool you should access when you have a hardware problem.

- The System Tools menu in the Start menu offers techs a one-stop shop for many handy utilities. You'll find Disk Defragmenter and Disk Cleanup here, for example. The Files and Settings Transfer Wizard in Windows XP or the Windows Easy Transfer tool in Windows Vista appears in this menu as well.

- The command-line interface enables you to type commands to the operating system. This can give you access to utilities and tools that often provide quicker results than graphical tools.

- The Microsoft Management Console (MMC) is simply a shell program in Windows that holds individual utilities called snap-ins. These snap-ins enable you to accomplish varying tech tasks. You can create custom MMCs or use ones preconfigured by Microsoft.

- The Administrative Tools in the Control Panel are preconfigured MMCs, such as Computer Management and Event Viewer. Users rarely need to access these MMCs, but techs know their Administrative Tools.

Troubleshoot Windows

- If you see a "No Boot Device Present," "NTLDR Bad or Missing," or "Invalid BOOT.INI" error on startup, you first should attempt to repair. If that fails, attempt to restore from a backup copy of Windows. If restore is either not available or fails, your only recourse is to rebuild. Note that Vista has different error messages but almost always just automatically fixes the problem.

- The Recovery Console works as a command-line utility. Many of its commands are those familiar to DOS users, but some new commands have been added. Because the file for the Recovery Console is on the system partition in a folder called CMDCONS, this program is useless for system partition crashes, but it is excellent for restoring Registries, stopping problem services, or using EXPAND to extract copies of files from the CD-ROM. You can also use it to format hard drives and read and write on local FAT or NTFS volumes.

- The Recovery Console is best at fixing three items: repairing the MBR, reinstalling the boot files, and rebuilding BOOT.INI.

- A bad boot sector usually shows up as a No Boot Device error. If it turns out that this isn't the problem, the Recovery Console command to fix it won't hurt anything. At the Recovery Console prompt, just type **fixmbr**, which fixes the master boot record.

- The second problem the Recovery Console is best at fixing is missing system files, usually indicated by the error NTLDR bad or missing. To fix this, get to the root directory (CD\) and type the following line: **copy d:\i386\ntldr**. Then type **copy d:\i386\ntdetect.com**.

- Automated System Recovery can restore your system to a previously installed state, but you should use it as a last resort. You lose everything on the system that was installed or added after you created the ASR disk.

- When rebuilding your Windows installation, you're best off swapping the C: drive for a blank hard drive and installing a clean version of Windows.

- Several issues can cause Windows to hang during the GUI-loading phase, such as buggy device drivers, Registry problems, and even autoloading programs. The first step in troubleshooting these issues is to use one of the Advanced Startup options to try to get past the hang spot and into Windows.

- The System Configuration utility enables techs to edit and troubleshoot operating system and program startup processes and services. Prior to Windows Vista, the System Configuration utility also offered quick access to troubleshoot and edit the boot.ini file.

- The Blue Screen of Death is not limited to device driver problems, but device drivers are one of the reasons you'll see the BSoD. BSoD problems due to device drivers almost always take place immediately after you've installed a new device and rebooted. Take out the device and reboot. In many cases, the manufacturer will have updated drivers available for download or will recommend a replacement device.

- If the Windows startup screen just stays there and you never get a chance to log on, try starting up with the Last Known Good Configuration boot option. If that fails, you can restore an earlier version of the Registry through the Recovery Console.

- To get to the Advanced Startup Options menu, restart the computer and press F8 after the POST messages but before the Windows logo screen appears. From here, you can start your computer into Safe Mode or into the Last Known Good Configuration.

- Safe Mode starts up Windows but loads only very basic, non–vendor-specific drivers for mouse, VGA monitor (not in Vista), keyboard, mass storage, and system services.

- Safe Mode with Networking is identical to plain Safe Mode except that you get network support.

- When you start Windows in Safe Mode with Command Prompt, rather than loading the GUI desktop, it loads the command prompt (CMD.EXE) as the shell to the operating system after you log on. Use this if the desktop does not display at all, which can be caused by the corruption of the EXPLORER.EXE program. From the command prompt, you can delete the corrupted version of EXPLORER.EXE and copy in an undamaged version.

- The Enable Boot Logging option starts Windows normally and creates a log file of the drivers as they load into memory. The file is named Ntbtlog.txt and is saved in the %SystemRoot% folder. If the startup failed because of a bad driver, the last entry in this file may be the driver the OS was initializing when it failed.

- Enable VGA Mode/Enable Low-resolution Mode starts Windows normally but only loads a default VGA driver. If this mode works, it may mean that you have a bad driver, or it may mean that you are using the correct video driver but it is configured incorrectly. This mode loads the graphics driver Windows is configured to use but starts it up in standard VGA mode rather than using the settings for which it is configured.

- Selecting *Disable automatic restart on system failure* from the Advanced Startup Options menu stops the computer from rebooting on Stop errors. This gives you the opportunity to write down the error and hopefully find a fix.

- Windows Vista (and 7) requires that all very low-level drivers (kernel drivers) must have a Microsoft driver signature. You can disable this by using the Disable Driver Signature Enforcement mode.

- The System Configuration utility enables you to keep individual programs and services from autoloading, but it does not actually remove the programs/services.

- Windows loads a number of services as it starts. If any critical service fails to load, Windows will tell you at this point with an error message.

- Windows protects all of its critical DLL files very carefully, but once in a while you may get an error saying Windows can't load a particular DLL. In these cases, the tool you need is the System File Checker, a command prompt program (SFC.EXE) that is used to check a number of critical files, including the ever-important DLL cache. SFC automatically checks all critical files and replaces any it sees as corrupted.

- Programs that fail to install usually aren't to blame in and of themselves. In most cases, a problem with Windows prevents them from installing, most notably the lack of some other program that the application needs so it can operate.

- Trying to run older programs in newer operating systems can cause compatibility errors that prevent the programs from running. Every Windows OS since 2000 has a compatibility mode that can often help older programs run.

■ Key Terms

activation *(245)*	**object** *(237)*
Advanced Startup Options *(263)*	**Performance** *(251)*
applet *(238)*	**Reliability and Performance Monitor** *(252)*
Blue Screen of Death (BSoD) *(260)*	**Safe Mode** *(263)*
compatibility mode *(269)*	**service** *(252)*
Computer Management *(250)*	**SystemRoot** *(233)*
context menu *(237)*	**System Configuration utility (MSCONFIG.EXE)** *(267)*
Control Panel *(238)*	**System Tools** *(244)*
Device Manager *(240)*	**Windows Sidebar** *(255)*
Last Known Good Configuration *(265)*	

■ Key Term Quiz

Use the Key Terms list to complete the sentences that follow. Not all terms will be used.

1. A(n) _Object_ is a system component with a set of characteristics that is managed by the OS as a single entity.

2. If Windows fails but you have *not* logged on, you can select _Last Known Configuration_ to restore the computer to the way it was the last time a user logged on.

3. To start Windows using only the most basic and essential drivers and services, use _Safe Mode_.

4. To change what programs and services start with Windows, you would use the _System Configuration utility_.

5. If installing a new driver causes problems in your system, the _Device Manager_ enables you to roll back the driver to a previously installed version.

6. The *Control Panel* houses many useful tech utilities, called *applets*, that control a wide variety of setup and maintenance tasks for Windows, such as managing user accounts, viewing performance information, and even changing mouse pointers.

■ Multiple-Choice Quiz

1. Mark loaded a new video card on his system, but now everything looks very bad. What should he do first?

   A. Go to Event Viewer and check the log.

   B. Go to Device Manager.

   C. Go to the printed manual.

   D. Call tech support.

2. What command should you run to check and fix corrupt system files, DLLs, and other critical files?

   A. CMDCONS /FIXBOOT

   B. SFC /SCANNOW

   C. CHKDSK /R

   D. DEFRAG –A

3. Pam needs to connect a hard drive controller to her new Windows Vista/7 computer but is unable to because of the older, unsigned driver. What can she do to make Windows load her driver?

   A. Start the computer in Disable Driver Signature Enforcement mode.

   B. Install the driver in Windows XP compatibility mode.

   C. She's plain out of luck.

   D. Use the Legacy Driver option in Device Manager.

4. Diane complains that her system seems sluggish and she keeps running out of disk space. What tool can you use to get rid of unnecessary files and compress older files? Select the best answer.

   A. Disk Cleanup

   B. Disk Doctor

   C. File Manager

   D. Registry Cleaner

5. Alberto installs a video card into a Windows XP computer and it seems to work just fine until he tries to run a game. Then he gets low-end graphics and it just doesn't look right.

   What might he try to fix the problem? Select the best answer.

   A. Check the video card manufacturer's Web site and download updated drivers.

   B. Check the video card manufacturer's Web site and download the FAQ.

   C. Run the Driver Update utility.

   D. Reinstall Windows.

6. You get a tech call from a distraught Windows XP user who can't get into Windows. He says he has a Recover CD from the manufacturer and plans to run it. What would you suggest?

   A. Run the Recover CD to restore the system.

   B. Run the Recover CD to return the system to the factory-installed state.

   C. Try to get the computer to boot into Safe Mode.

   D. Reinstall Windows by using a Windows XP disc.

7. The folder in which Windows is installed is known generically as what?

   A. RootFolder

   B. WinRoot

   C. SystemRoot

   D. System32

8. For a user account called "Ethan," where would you expect to find the personal documents folder in a Windows Vista computer?

   A. C:\Ethan

   B. C:\Users\Ethan

   C. C:\Documents and Settings\Ethan

   D. C:\Windows\Ethan

9. What applet can you use to view the status of all services on a system?

   A. Character Map

   B. Performance Monitor

   C. Services

   D. System Information

1. A fellow tech sends a message crying for help. He has a Windows 2000 system that has crashed hard and he's never worked with 2000 before. He's afraid to try to boot up the machine until he hears back from you. He found a copy of the OS disc and a hand-labeled diskette called Emergency Repair Disk. What advice do you give him to try to get the system back up and running quickly?

Lab Project

• Lab Project 8.1

In a couple of places in the chapter, you got a taste of working with some of the more complex tools in Windows, such as the Event Viewer and Performance console. Go back through the text and reread those sections, and then do an Internet search for a how-to article. Then work with the tools.

Mastering Input/Output

"Windows 2000 already contains features such as the human discipline component, where the PC can send an electric shock through the keyboard if the human does something that does not please Windows."

—BILL GATES

In this chapter, you will learn how to

- **Support common input/output ports**
- **Install optical drives**
- **Install floppy disk drives**
- **Troubleshoot optical drives and removable media**

If you're a PC tech, it's a good thing to know how to replace a motherboard. You're doing great if you know how to service a dying hard drive or a malfunctioning video card. If you can install a CPU, you will make a great tech. But as important as all of that stuff is, knowing how to fix the parts of the computer that users directly interact with is golden.

I can't tell you how many times I've had to repair a malfunctioning USB port, or make sure someone's FireWire port was functioning properly so they could transfer home movies from their camcorder. People heap all kinds of abuse on their input/output ports, so you absolutely must know how to get broken ports up and running again if you want to be a tech.

Once you've got a handle on input/output ports, you'll take a look at installing and troubleshooting optical drives. You'll learn not only how to physically install a drive—a process that should be at least somewhat familiar from Chapter 5, "Implementing Hard Drives"—but also how to choose the right drive for your needs. You'll also take a look at troubleshooting other types of removable media, which has become a major focus since the advent of digital cameras and thumb drives.

Supporting Common I/O Ports

Whenever you're dealing with an I/O device that isn't playing nice, you need to remember that you're never dealing with just a device—you're dealing with a device and the port to which it is connected. Before you start looking at I/O devices, you need to take a look into the issues and technologies of some of the more common I/O ports and see what needs to be done to keep them running well.

Serial Ports

Finding a new PC with a real serial port is difficult, because devices that traditionally used serial ports have for the most part moved on to better interfaces, in particular, USB. Physical serial ports may be hard to find on new PC cases, but many devices—in particular, the modems many people still use to access the Internet—continue to use built-in serial ports.

In Chapter 3, "Mastering Motherboards," you learned that COM ports are nothing more than preset I/O addresses and interrupt request lines (IRQs) for serial ports. Want to see a built-in serial port? Open Device Manager on a system and see if you have an icon for Ports (COM and LPT). If you do, click the plus (+) sign to the left of the icon to open it and see the ports on your system—don't be surprised if you have COM ports on your PC. Even if you don't see any physical serial ports on your PC, the serial ports are there; they're simply built into some other device, probably a modem.

Your PC's expansion bus uses parallel communication: multiple data wires, each one sending one bit of data at a time between your devices. Many I/O devices use serial communication: one wire to send data and another wire to receive data. The job of a serial port is to convert data moving between parallel and serial devices. A traditional serial port consists of two pieces: the physical, 9-pin DB connector (Figure 9.1) and a chip that actually does the conversion between the serial data and parallel data, called the **universal asynchronous receiver/transmitter (UART)** chip. If you want to be

 Having trouble finding a PC with serial ports? Try a laptop—almost all laptops come with built-in modems.

> **Tech Tip**
>
> **Serial Ports Are RS-232 Ports**
> *Speaking of standardization, all serial ports on PCs use the RS-232 standard. Many old techs will look at a serial port and say "That's an RS-232 port!" Because all physical serial ports are standardized on RS-232, they're right.*

● **Figure 9.1**   Serial port

completely accurate, the UART *is* the serial port. The port on the back of your PC is nothing more than a standardized connector that enables different serial devices to use the serial port. The UART holds all of the smarts that make the true serial port.

RS-232 is a very old standard that defines everything about serial ports: how fast they communicate, the language they use, even how the connectors should look. The RS-232 standard specifies that two serial devices must talk to each other in 8-bit chunks of data, but it also allows flexibility in other areas, such as speed and error-checking. Serial came out back in the days when devices were configured manually, and the RS-232 standard has never been updated for automatic configuration. Serial ports are a throwback to the old days of computer maintenance (though they're still very prevalent in some hardware, such as high-end routers) and are the last manually configured port you'll find on a PC.

So what type of settings do you need to configure on a serial port? Find a PC with a real serial port (a real 9-pin connector on the back of the PC). Right-click the COM port and choose Properties to see the properties of that port in Device Manager. Open the Port Settings tab and click the Advanced button to see a dialog box that looks like Figure 9.2.

Devices such as modems that have built-in serial ports don't have COM port icons in Device Manager, because there's nothing to change. Can you see why? Even though these devices are using a COM port, that port is never going to connect to anything other than the device it's soldered onto, so all of the settings are fixed and unchangeable—thank goodness!

When you are configuring a serial port, you will have a lot of different settings to configure, many of which may or may not make sense. The convenient part about all this is that when you get a new serial device to plug into your serial port, the instructions will tell you what settings to use. Figure 9.3 shows an instruction sheet for a Cisco switch.

USB Ports

You should be familiar with the concept of USB, USB connectors, and USB hubs from the discussion of those concepts in the 220-701 exam guide. If you haven't yet run through that book, here's an in-depth look at USB and some of the issues involved with using USB devices.

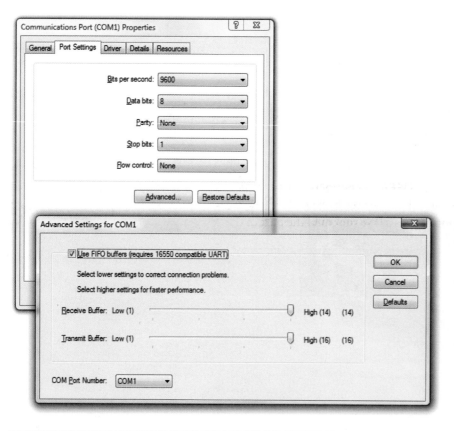

• **Figure 9.2**   Serial port settings

Connecting a PC or Terminal to the Console Port

To connect a PC to the console port, use the supplied RJ-45-to-DB-9 adapter cable. To connect the switch console port to a terminal, you need to provide a RJ-45-to-DB-25 female DTE adapter. You can order a kit (part number ACS-DSBUASYN=) containing that adapter from Cisco. For console port and adapter pinout information, see the "Cable and Adapter Specifications" section.

The PC or terminal must support VT100 terminal emulation. The terminal-emulation software—frequently a PC application such as Hyperterminal or Procomm Plus—makes communication between the switch and your PC or terminal possible during the setup program.

Follow these steps to connect the PC or terminal to the switch:

Step 1 Configure the baud rate and character format of the PC or terminal to match these console port default characteristics:

- ♦ 9600 baud

- ♦ 8 data bits

- ♦ 1 stop bit

- ♦ No parity

After you have gained access to the switch, you can change the console baud rate through the **Administration > Console Baud Rate** window in the Cluster Management Suite (CMS).

Step 2 Using the supplied RJ-45-to-DB-9 adapter cable, insert the RJ-45 connector into the console port, as shown in Figure 2-1.

Step 3 Attach the DB-9 female DTE adapter of the RJ-45-to-DB-9 adapter cable to a PC, or attach an appropriate adapter to the terminal.

Step 4 Start the terminal-emulation program if you are using a PC or terminal.

Figure 2-1: Connecting to the Console Port

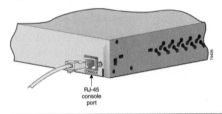

RJ-45
console
port

● **Figure 9.3**   Serial port instructions

Understanding USB

The cornerstone of a USB connection is the **USB host controller**, an integrated circuit that is usually built into the chipset and controls every USB device that connects to it. Inside the host controller is a **USB root hub**: the part of the host controller that makes the physical connection to the USB ports. Every USB root hub is really just a bus—similar in many ways to an expansion bus. Figure 9.4 shows a diagram of the relationship between the host controller, root hub, and USB ports.

No rule says how many USB ports a single host adapter may use. Early USB host adapters had two USB ports. The most recent ones support up to ten. Even if a host adapter supports a certain number of ports, there's no guarantee that

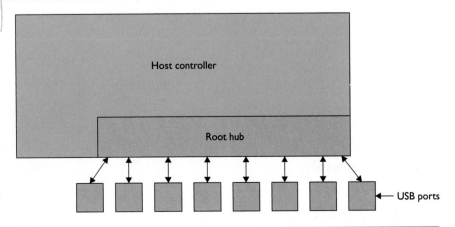

Host controller

Root hub

USB ports

● **Figure 9.4**   Host controller, root hub, and USB ports

the motherboard maker will supply that many ports. To give a common example, a host adapter might support eight ports while the motherboard maker only supplies four adapters.

The most important point to remember about this is that every USB device connected to a single host adapter/root hub *shares* that USB bus with every other device connected to it. The more devices you place on a single host adapter, the more the total USB bus slows down and the more power they use. These issues are two of the biggest headaches that take place with USB devices in the real world.

USB devices, like any electrical device, need power to run, but not all take care of their own power needs. A powered USB device comes with its own electrical cord that is usually connected in turn to an AC adapter. *Bus-powered* USB devices take power from the USB bus itself; they don't bring any AC or DC power with them. When too many bus-powered devices take too much power from the USB bus, bad things happen: devices that work only some of the time and devices that lock up. You'll also often get a simple message from Windows saying that the hub power has been exceeded and it just won't work.

Every USB device is designed to run at one of three speeds. The first USB standard, version 1.1, defined two speeds: Low-Speed USB, running at a maximum of 1.5 Mbps (plenty for keyboards and mice), and Full-Speed USB, running up to 12 Mbps. Later, the USB 2.0 standard introduced Hi-Speed USB running at a whopping 480 Mbps. The industry sometimes refers to Low-Speed and Full-Speed USB as USB 1.1 and Hi-Speed as USB 2.0.

In addition to a much faster transfer rate, Hi-Speed USB is fully backward compatible with devices that operate under the slower USB standards. Those old devices won't run any faster than they used to, however. To take advantage of the fastest USB speed, you must connect Hi-Speed USB devices to Hi-Speed USB ports by using Hi-Speed USB cables. Hi-Speed USB devices function when plugged into Full-Speed USB ports, but at only 12 Mbps. Although backward compatibility at least allows you to use the newer USB device with an older port, a quick bit of math tells you how much time you're sacrificing when you're transferring a 240-MB file at 12 Mbps instead of 480 Mbps!

When USB 2.0 came out in 2001, folks scrambled to buy USB 2.0 controllers so their new hi-speed devices would work at their designed speeds. Of the variety of solutions people came up with, the most popular early on was to add a USB 2.0 adapter card like the one shown in Figure 9.5.

USB 2.0 defined more than just a new speed. Many Low-Speed and Full-Speed USB devices are also under the USB 2.0 standard.

The USB Implementers Forum (USB-IF) does not officially use "low-speed" and "full-speed" to describe 1.5 Mbps and 12 Mbps devices, calling both of them simply "USB." On the CompTIA A+ Practical Application exam, though, you'll see the marketplace-standard nomenclature used here.

USB 2.0 enables you to hook up media card readers in order to view files stored on flash memory cards, such as the ones used in digital cameras.

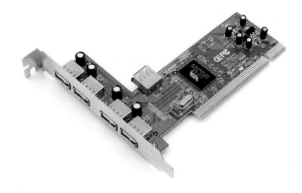

• **Figure 9.5**   USB adapter card

Motherboard makers quickly added a second USB 2.0 host controller—and they did it in a clever way. Instead of making the USB 2.0 host controller separate from the USB 1.1 host controller, they designed things so that both controllers share all of the connected USB ports (Figure 9.6). That way, no matter which USB port you choose, if you plug in a low-speed or full-speed device, the 1.1 host controller takes over, and if you plug in a hi-speed device, the USB 2.0 host controller takes over. Clever, and convenient!

USB 2.0 has remained the standard for quite a while, but as of this writing, the future of USB is nigh! USB 3.0 (also called SuperSpeed) devices are set to appear on the market sometime in 2010, with massively increased speed (up to 4.8 Gbps), increased power to peripherals, and full backward compatibility with older devices. USB 3.0 probably won't show up on the Practical Application exam until it becomes widely adopted, but you should definitely be aware of it, because if it retains the popularity USB has enjoyed up to this point, it's going to be huge.

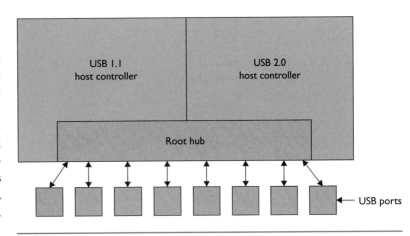

● **Figure 9.6**   Shared USB ports

Try This!

What Speed Is Your USB?

Using a PC running Windows 2000 or later, open the Device Manager and locate two controllers under the Universal Serial Bus icon. The one named Standard Enhanced Host Controller is the hi-speed controller. The Standard OpenHCD Host Controller is the low- and full-speed controller.

USB Hubs and Cables

Each USB host controller supports up to 127 USB devices, but as mentioned earlier, most motherboard makers provide only six to eight real USB ports. So what do you do when you need to add more USB devices than the motherboard provides ports? You can add more host controllers (in the form of internal cards), or you can use a USB hub. A **USB hub** is a device that extends a single USB connection to two or more USB ports, almost always directly from one of the USB ports connected to the root hub. Figure 9.7 shows a typical USB hub. USB hubs are sometimes embedded into peripherals. The keyboard in Figure 9.8 comes with a built-in USB hub—very handy!

USB hubs are one of those parts of a PC that tend not to work nearly as well in the real world as they do on paper. (Sorry, USB folks, but it's true!) USB hubs have a speed just like any other USB device; for example, the hub in the keyboard in Figure 9.8 runs at full speed. This becomes a problem when someone decides to insert a Hi-Speed USB device into one of those ports, as it forces the hi-speed device to crawl along at only 12 Mbps. Windows XP and Windows Vista are nice enough to warn you of this problem with a bubble over the system tray like the one shown in Figure 9.9.

● **Figure 9.7**   USB hub

● **Figure 9.8**   USB keyboard with built-in hub

Hubs also come in powered and bus-powered versions. If you choose to use a general purpose USB hub like the one shown in Figure 9.7, try to find a powered one, as too many devices on a single USB root hub will draw too much power and create problems.

Cable length is an important limitation to keep in mind with USB. ~~USB specifications allow for a maximum cable length of 5 meters~~, although you may add a powered USB hub every 5 meters to extend this distance. Although most USB devices never get near this maximum, some devices, such as digital cameras, can come with cables at or near the maximum 5-meter cable length. Because USB is a two-way (bidirectional) connection, as the cable grows longer, even a standard, well-shielded, 20-gauge, twisted-pair USB cable begins to suffer from electrical interference. To avoid these problems, I stick to cables that are no more than about 2 meters long.

If you really want to play it safe, spend a few extra dollars and get a high-quality USB 2.0 cable like the one shown in Figure 9.10. These cables come with extra shielding and improved electrical performance to make sure your USB data gets from the device to your computer safely.

USB Configuration

The biggest troubleshooting challenge you encounter with USB is a direct result of its widespread adoption and ease of use. Pretty much every modern PC comes with multiple USB ports, and anyone can easily pick up a cool new USB device at the local computer store. The problems arise when all of this USB installation activity gets out of control, with too many devices using the wrong types of ports or pulling too much power. Happily, by following a few easy steps, you can avoid or eliminate these issues.

The first and often-ignored rule of USB installation is this: always install the device driver for a new USB device *before* you plug it into the USB port. Once you've installed the device and you know the ports are active (running properly in Device Manager), feel free to plug in the new device and hot-swap to your heart's content. USB device installation really is a breeze as long as you follow this rule!

Windows 2000, XP, and Vista have a large number of built-in drivers for USB devices. You can count on Windows 2000,

● **Figure 9.10**   USB 2.0 cable

Windows XP, and Windows Vista to recognize keyboards, mice, and other basic devices with their built-in drivers. Just be aware that if your new mouse or keyboard has some extras, the default USB drivers will probably not support them. To be sure I'm not missing any added functionality, I always install the driver that comes with the device or an updated one downloaded from the manufacturer's Web site.

When looking to add a new USB device to a system, first make sure your machine has a USB port that supports the speed you need for the USB device. On more modern PCs, this is likely to be a nonissue. Even then, if you start adding hubs and such, you can end up with devices that either won't run at all or, worse yet, exhibit strange behaviors.

The last and toughest issue is power. A mismatch between available and required power for USB devices can result in nonfunctioning or malfunctioning USB devices. If you're pulling too much power, you must take devices off that root hub until the error goes away. Buy an add-in USB hub card if you need to use more devices than your current USB hub supports.

To check the USB power usage in Windows, open Device Manager and locate any USB hub under the Universal Serial Bus Controller icon. Right-click the hub and select Properties, and then select the Power tab. This shows you the current use for each of the devices connected to that root hub (Figure 9.11).

Most root hubs provide 500 mA per port—more than enough for any USB device. Most power problems take place when you start adding hubs, especially bus-powered hubs, and then you add too many devices to them. Figure 9.12

• **Figure 9.11**   USB hub Power tab

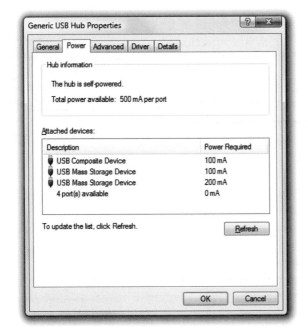

• **Figure 9.12**   General purpose bus-powered hub

Tech Tip

Refresh the Tab
The USB Hub Power Properties tab shows you the power usage only for a given moment, so to ensure you keep getting accurate readings, you must click the Refresh button to update its display. Make sure your USB device works, and then refresh to see the maximum power used.

shows the Power tab for a bus-powered hub; note that it provides a maximum of 200 mA per port.

There's one more problem with USB power: sometimes USB devices go to sleep and don't wake up. Actually, the system is telling them to sleep, to save power. You can suspect this problem if you try to access a USB device that was working earlier but that suddenly no longer appears in Device Manager. To fix this, head back into Device Manager to inspect the hub's Properties, but this time open the Power Management tab and deselect *Allow the computer to turn off this device to save power*, as shown in Figure 9.13.

FireWire Ports

At first glance, FireWire, also known as IEEE 1394, looks and acts much like USB. FireWire has all of the features of USB, but it uses different connectors and is actually the older of the two technologies. For years, FireWire had the upper hand when it came to moving data quickly to and from external devices. The onset of Hi-Speed USB changed that, and FireWire has lost ground to USB in many areas. One area where FireWire still dominates is editing digital video. Most modern digital video cameras use the IEEE 1394 interface for transferring video from camera to PC for editing. The high transfer speed of FireWire makes transferring large video files quick and easy.

Understanding FireWire

FireWire has two distinct types of connectors, both of which are commonly found on PCs. The first is a 6-pin *powered* connector, the type you see on many desktop PCs. Like USB, a FireWire port is capable of providing power to a device, and it carries the same cautions about powering high-power devices through the port. The other type of connector is a 4-pin *bus-powered* connector, which you see on portable computers and such FireWire devices as cameras. This type of connector does not provide power to a device, so you need to find another method of powering the external device.

FireWire comes in two speeds: IEEE 1394a, which runs at 400 Mbps, and IEEE 1394b, which runs at 800 Mbps. FireWire devices can also take advantage of bus mastering, enabling two FireWire devices—such as a digital video camera and an external FireWire hard drive—to communicate directly with each other. When it comes to raw speed, FireWire 800—that would be 1394b, naturally—is much faster than Hi-Speed USB.

FireWire does have differences from USB other than just speed and a different-looking connector. First, a USB device must connect directly to a hub, but a FireWire device may use either a hub or daisy chaining. Figure 9.14 shows the difference between hubbed connections and daisy chaining. Second, FireWire supports a maximum of 63 devices, compared to USB's 127. Third, each cable in a FireWire daisy chain has a maximum length of 4.5 meters, as opposed to USB's 5 meters.

• **Figure 9.13** Power Management tab

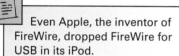

Even Apple, the inventor of FireWire, dropped FireWire for USB in its iPod.

Mike Meyers' CompTIA A+ Guide: Practical Application

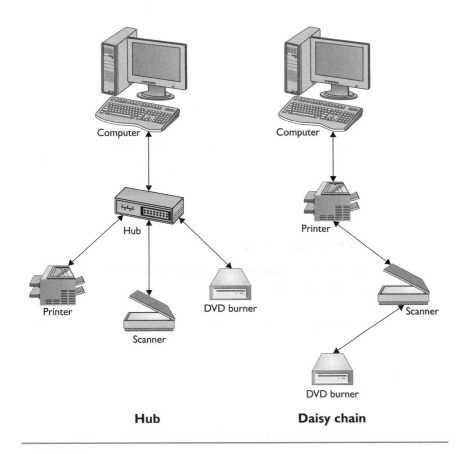

Hub **Daisy chain**

● Figure 9.14 Hubbed versus daisy chain connections

Configuring FireWire

FireWire was invented by and still controlled to a degree by Apple Computer. This single source of control makes FireWire more stable and more interchangeable than USB—in plain language, FireWire is ridiculously easy to use. In a Windows environment, FireWire is subject to many of the same issues as USB, such as the need to preinstall drivers, verify that onboard devices are active, and so on. But none of these issues is nearly as crucial with a FireWire connection. For example, as with USB, you really should install a FireWire device driver before attaching the device, but given that 95 percent of the FireWire devices used in PCs are either external hard drives or digital video connections, the preinstalled Windows drivers almost always work perfectly. FireWire devices do use much more power than USB devices, but the FireWire controllers are designed to handle higher voltages, and they'll warn you on the rare chance that your FireWire devices pull too much power.

General Port Issues

No matter what type of port you use, if it's not working, you should always check out a few issues. First of all, make sure you can tell a port problem from a device problem. Your best bet here is to try a second "known good" device in the same port to see if that device works. If it does *not*, you can assume the port is the problem. It's not a bad idea to reverse this and plug the device into a known good port.

 A "known good" device is simply a device that you know is in good working order. All techs count heavily on the use of known good devices to check other devices. For example, if you think a PC has a bad keyboard, borrow one from the PC next door and see if that keyboard works on the broken machine.

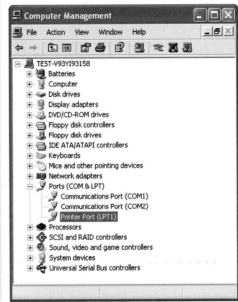

● **Figure 9.15** Disabled parallel port in Device Manager in both Vista and XP

If you're pretty sure the port's not working, you can check three things: First, make sure the port is turned on. Almost any I/O port on a motherboard can be turned off in CMOS. Reboot the system and find the device and see if the port's been turned off. You can also use Windows Device Manager to disable most ports. Figure 9.15 shows a disabled parallel port in Device Manager—you'll see a small down-pointing arrow in Windows Vista/7 or a red *X* over the device icon if you are using Windows 2000/XP. To turn the port back on, right-click the device's icon and choose Enable.

Being able to turn off a port in Device Manager points to another not-so-obvious fact: ports need drivers just as devices need drivers. Windows has excellent built-in drivers for all common ports, so if you fail to see a port in Device Manager (and you know the port is turned on in CMOS), you can bet the port itself has a physical problem.

Because ports have connectors inserted and removed from them repeatedly, eventually they can physically break. Figure 9.16 shows the back of a USB port that's been pushed on too hard for too long and has physically separated from the motherboard. Unless you're an expert solderer, you either must stop using those ports or replace the entire motherboard.

Many ports (or the plugs that fit into those ports) use tiny pins or relatively delicate metal casings that are susceptible to damage. PS/2 plugs are some of the worst for bent pins or misshaped casings. Figure 9.17 shows what happened to a PS/2 plug when I was in a hurry and thought

● **Figure 9.16** Broken USB port

• **Figure 9.17**   Badly bent PS/2 plug

force was an alternative to lining up the plug properly. Replacement plugs are available—but again, unless you're excellent at soldering, they're not a viable alternative. Still, if you're patient, you might be able to save the plug. Using needle-nose pliers and a pair of scissors, I was able to reshape the plug so that it once again fit in the PS/2 port.

■ Installing Optical Drives

Now that you're familiar with the process involved in supporting various common I/O ports, it's time to look at installing optical drives. Almost every modern PC has an optical drive of some description, so it's important as a tech to know how to install these drives when putting together a computer. Additionally, there are concerns such as region codes and burning capability that must be addressed when picking out hardware for a PC.

From ten feet away, optical drives of all flavors look absolutely identical. Figure 9.18 shows CD-RW, DVD, and BD-R drives. Can you tell them apart just by a glance? In case you were wondering, the CD-RW is on the bottom, the DVD is next, and finally the BD-R is on the top. If you look closely at an optical drive, you will normally see its function either stamped on the front of the case or printed on a label somewhere less obvious (see Figure 9.19).

Connections

Most internal optical drives use PATA or SATA connections and support the ATAPI standard. (Other connections, such as SCSI and USB, are possible but less common.) External optical drives often use USB, FireWire, or eSATA connections. ATAPI treats an optical drive exactly as though it were an ATA drive. PATA optical drives have regular 40-pin IDE connectors and master/slave jumpers. SATA optical drives use standard SATA or eSATA cables. You install them the same way you would install any ATA hard drive. Figure 9.20 shows a typical DVD installation using PATA. The DVD is configured as slave with a master hard drive on a system's primary IDE controller.

• **Figure 9.18**   CD-RW, DVD, and BD-R drives

Tech Tip

External Optical Drives

Almost all new PCs have one, two, or three external expansion buses—USB, FireWire, or eSATA—and the makers of optical drives have quickly taken this fact to heart. Many manufacturers have released external versions of CD, DVD, and Blu-ray Disc drives, both readers and burners. Of the two most common expansion options, I prefer FireWire simply because it's the standard for most digital video cameras, and its 400 Mbps sustained data transfer rate easily trumps the Hi-Speed USB 480 Mbps burst rate for transferring huge files.

The only benefit to the USB versions is that USB is still more common than FireWire, particularly on portable computers. In fact, quite a few super-light laptops don't have an optical drive built in; the only way to load an OS on them is through an external drive. If you can't decide which expansion type to use, several manufacturers have taken pity on you.

You won't find any CD or DVD drives with eSATA—they just can't take advantage of the blazing speed offered by the best of the external ports. Blu-ray Disc drive manufacturers, on the other hand, have released several drives with both eSATA and Hi-Speed USB connections. If you have the choice, there is no choice. Choose eSATA every time.

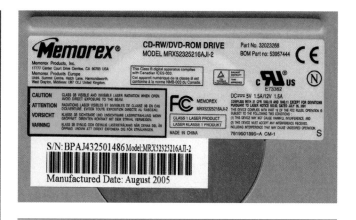

• **Figure 9.19**   Label on optical drive indicating its type and speeds

ATAPI drives require no CMOS changes as part of the installation process. When the industry first introduced ATAPI drives, techs familiar with hard-drive installations swamped the CD-ROM makers' service departments asking how to set up the drives in CMOS. To reduce these calls, BIOS makers added a CD-ROM option in many CMOS setup utilities, just to give the techs something to do! You can find this option in many older CMOS setup utilities. This setting actually didn't do anything at all; it just kept users from bothering the CD-ROM makers with silly support calls. Modern motherboards report the actual model numbers of optical drives, giving techs a degree of assurance that they configured and installed the drive correctly (Figure 9.21).

Device Manager

When you install a new optical drive, such as a DVD drive, into an existing system, the first question to ask is "Does Windows recognize my DVD drive?" You can determine this by opening the My Computer icon and verifying that a DVD drive is present (see Figure 9.22). When you want to know more, go to Device Manager.

• **Figure 9.20**   Typical DVD installation

• **Figure 9.21**   Autodetect settings for two optical drives

The Device Manager contains most of the information about the DVD drive. The General tab tells you about the current status of the DVD drive, basically saying whether the device is working properly or not—rather less useful than actually trying the device. Other tabs, such as the Driver tab, provide other pertinent information about the drive.

Auto Insert Notification

Another setting of note is the Auto Insert Notification option, often referred to as **AutoPlay** in Windows 2000/XP/Vista. This set-

• Figure 9.22   DVD drive letter in My Computer

ting enables Windows to detect automatically the presence of audio or data optical discs when they are placed in the drive.

Windows 2000, Windows XP, and Windows Vista all have very different ways of dealing with AutoPlay. In Windows 2000, if the CD is an audio disc, track 1 plays automatically. If the CD-ROM is a data disc, Windows searches the disc's root directory for a special text file called AUTORUN.INF.

Although handy, the AutoPlay option can sometimes be annoying and unproductive. Windows 2000 does not provide a simple method to turn off AutoPlay. The only way to turn it off is to edit the Registry. You can use the REGEDT32 version of the Registry Editor and do it directly. In REGEDT32, access this subkey:

HKEY_LOCAL_MACHINE\SYSTEM\CurrentControlSet\Services\Cdrom

Change Autorun 0 x 1 to 0 x 0.

Most techs use Group Policy to make the change because it gives you much more control in multiple optical drive situations. With Group Policy, you can turn off AutoPlay on your CD-RW drive, for example, but leave it enabled for your DVD drive. Group Policy is a powerful tool that goes well beyond CompTIA A+, so be careful with what you're about to do. To run Group Policy, go to Start | Run and type **gpedit.msc** in the Run dialog box; or in Vista, just go to Start and type **gpedit.msc** in the Start Search text box. Click OK to open the MMC. To turn off AutoPlay, navigate down in the menu to the left as follows: Local Computer Policy | Computer Configuration | Administrative Templates. Select the System option and you'll see the *Turn off Autoplay* option in the Setting section on the right pane of the MMC (Figure 9.23).

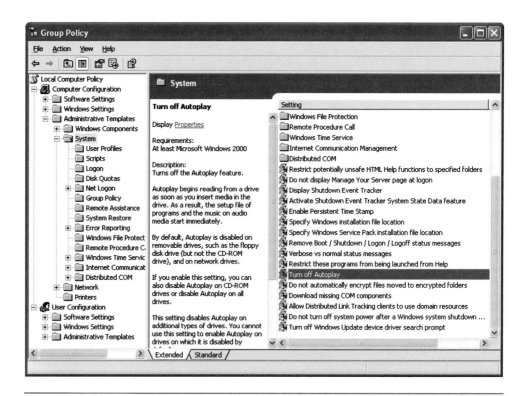

• **Figure 9.23** Group Policy MMC with *Turn off Autoplay* selected

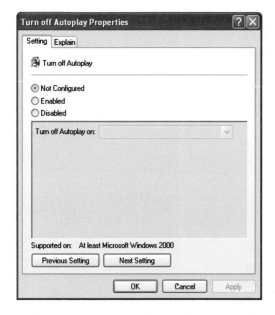

• **Figure 9.24**   Turn off Autoplay Properties
                    dialog box

Double-click or right-click *Turn off Autoplay* to open the Properties. Note in Figure 9.24 that the default option is Not Configured, but you can enable or disable it here. The words are messy here, so make sure you know what you're doing. *Enabling* Turn off Autoplay gives you the option to stop an optical-media device from automatically playing a disc. *Disabling* Turn off Autoplay prevents you or any other user from stopping any optical-media device from automatically playing a disc. Got the distinction?

Windows XP provides a much more sophisticated and simpler approach to AutoPlay. By default, when you insert a CD- or DVD-media disc that doesn't have an AUTORUN.INF file, XP asks you what you want to do (Figure 9.25). You can change the default behavior simply by accessing the properties for a particular drive in My Computer and making your selection on the AutoPlay tab. Figure 9.26 shows some of the options for a typical Windows XP machine.

AutoPlay in Windows Vista is much more robust and offers many more options than in Windows 2000 or Windows XP. For example, you can choose to enable or disable AutoPlay for all media and devices. (Using AutoPlay for all media and devices is the default.) But what's more interesting is that you can enable very specific actions for Windows to take when digital media or devices are inserted or detected. For an audio CD, for example, you can specify that Windows should use Windows Media Player. If a DVD movie is detected, you can tell AutoPlay to play the DVD by using PowerDVD 8 or some other program. You can adjust AutoPlay options in Windows Vista through Control Panel | Hardware and Sound | AutoPlay.

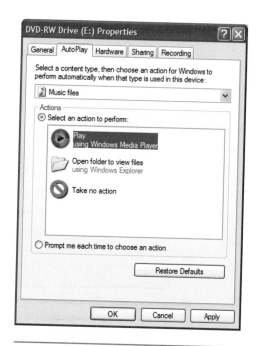

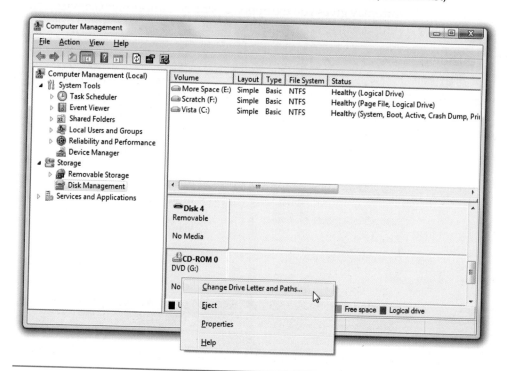

Figure 9.25 XP prompting user for action

As a final note, in Windows 2000, XP, and Vista, you can change the drive letter for an optical drive just as you can change the letter of a hard drive. You'll find that option in Disk Management (Figure 9.27).

Figure 9.26 AutoPlay tab for a CD-RW drive

Applications

A regular CD-ROM drive installation involves no applications. You install it, Windows sees it, and you're finished. CD-R and CD-RW drives, in contrast,

Figure 9.27 Change CD drive letter option in Disk Management

require applications to enable their burning features. DVD and Blu-ray Disc drives need software to enable you to watch movies, burn DVDs and Blu-ray Discs, and so on. As of this writing, Nero (www.nero.com) and Roxio Creator (www.roxio.com) share the reins as the most popular CD-burning software programs. CyberLink PowerDVD and Corel WinDVD fight for Blu-ray Disc burning supremacy rights. If you're looking for a free burner, try CDBurnerXP Pro, pictured in Figure 9.28 (www.cdburnerxp.se). Windows XP contains basic CD-burning capabilities built into the operating system. With XP, you can readily drag and drop files to your CD-R or CD-RW drive and move those files from PC to PC. Almost all optical drives will read the discs burned in an XP system.

Windows Media Player makes an excellent DVD-watching application, but for DVD burning you need to turn to a third-party tool. Nero and Roxio make great software that handles every DVD recordable standard your drive can use (as well as CD-R and CD-RW).

Ever wanted to make a perfect copy of a CD so you can keep your original in a safe place? You can do so by using a special file type called an ISO file. An ISO file is a complete copy—an ISO image as we say—of a CD or DVD. As you might imagine, they are huge files, but they are also very important to techs. Techs use ISO images to send each other copies of bootable utility CDs. For example, if you want a copy of the Ultimate Boot CD, you go to their Web site and download an ISO image. You then take your third-party burning program (Windows XP/Vista built-in burning software can't do this) and go through a special process called burning an ISO image. Learn how to burn ISO images with your burning program; you'll use it all the time.

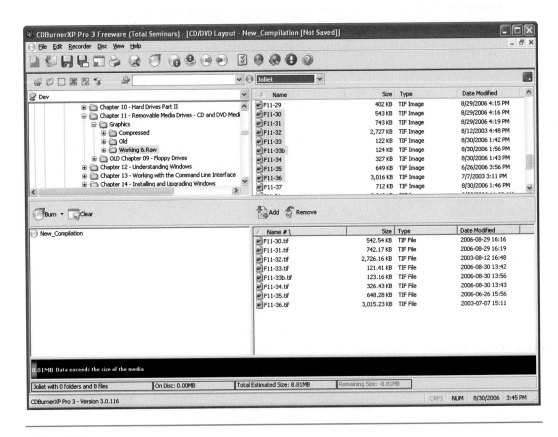

• **Figure 9.28** Typical third-party CD-burning program

Burning Digital Music Files to a CD

Almost all computers and many portable CD players now can play recordable CDs loaded with MP3 files. This enables you to mix songs from your music collection and fit a lot of songs on a disc (MP3s are smaller than CD-audio files). That's a great feature—but where do digital audio files come from and how do you put them on a CD?

You can create MP3s from your favorite CDs by using a *ripper*. A ripper is a piece of software that takes standard CD-audio files and compresses them, using specialized algorithms, into much smaller files while maintaining most of the audio qualities of the original file. One legal note, however: you should only make MP3s from CDs that you have purchased. Borrowing a CD from a friend and ripping MP3s from it is illegal! Likewise, downloading MP3s from unauthorized sources on the Internet is also illegal. You don't want to go to jail because you just had to listen to the latest, greatest single from your favorite artist, right?

Now that I've taken care of the legal disclaimer, get ready to burn your MP3s. You need three things: a recordable/rewritable optical drive, some CD authoring software, and, of course, a blank disc. I recommend a CD-R. (Audio-only devices stand a much better chance of playing a CD-R successfully rather than a CD-RW.)

1. Confirm that you have a CD-R/RW drive installed in your computer. You don't have to have a drive like this to rip audio files *from* a CD, but you must have one to burn digital audio to a CD-R.

2. Launch your favorite CD authoring software. Popular titles in this category include Nero Burning ROM and Roxio Creator.

3. Most CD authoring programs use a simple drag-and-drop interface, similar to the Windows Explorer interface. Browse to the location of the audio files and select them. Then drag them into the appropriate area—this is often called the *queue*.

4. After you've selected all the files you want to have on your CD, it's time to burn. The procedure for initiating the CD-burning sequence is different for each program. You should always make sure to *close* the CD after you've burned it. Most standalone CD players (even ones that play MP3s) won't play CD-Rs that haven't been closed.

Once you've keyed in all of the configuration information, just sit back and watch the fireworks. Always be sure to use CD-media that is rated appropriately for your drive, for both speed and media type. In no time at all, you'll be listening to MP3s while jogging around the park.

Blu-ray Disc Drive Considerations

Physically installing, attaching, and maintaining optical drives is pretty straightforward, but a Blu-ray Disc drive installation requires some special considerations. If you plan to use your Blu-ray Disc drive primarily for storage purposes, for example, system requirements are minimal. If you plan on watching Blu-ray Disc movies in HD resolution (720p, 1080i, or 1080p), on the other hand, the requirements are quite hefty. Here's a list of recommended minimum specs.

- **Processor** At the very least, a Pentium 4, Pentium D, or dual or multicore processor or an AMD Athlon 64 X2 or Phenom multicore processor.

- **System Memory** At least 1 GB RAM for Windows XP, 2 GB RAM for Windows Vista.

- **Video** You need an HDCP-compliant (either DVI or HDMI) video card and drivers. That's a lot of initials in one sentence! Here's the scoop: The High-Bandwidth Digital Content Protection (HDCP) is a standard developed by Intel to ensure copyright protection on behalf of the Motion Picture Association of America. The Digital Video Interface (DVI) and High-Definition Multimedia Interface (HDMI) standards enable fast uncompressed connections between an HDTV, PC, and any other DVI/HDMI component. HDMI, which transmits both video and audio signals, has all but replaced the older DVI standard that only supports video. ATI and NVIDIA both offer Blu-ray Disc-compliant PCIe video cards with enough horsepower to get the job done.

CyberLink provides an awesome tool called BD Advisor that will tell you if your system meets the requirements to play Blu-ray Discs. You can get it at www.cyberlink.com/prog/bd-support/diagnosis.do.

Region Codes

Production movies on DVD and Blu-ray Disc can feature a region code, encoding that enables you to play those movies only on a player that shares the same region code. This was instituted to try to stop piracy of movies, though it didn't manage to accomplish that goal.

Can you play a DVD or Blu-ray Disc encoded to play in the geographical region location of Somalia on your system manufactured in the U.S.A.? Why, sure you can. To do so, however, you have to change the region code on your DVD or Blu-ray Disc player to match Somalia (5 or B, respectively, in case you're curious). You can only change the region code on your player four times. After that, you get stuck with whatever was the last-used region code. Today, most optical discs are sold *region free*, meaning you can play them anywhere. Many optical-media devices are set to play only discs encoded for the region in which they were sold or manufactured. You can easily check and set your device's current region code under the hardware properties of your optical device in any version of Windows. As either a technician or home enthusiast, you should be familiar with the following optical device and media region codes.

DVD Region Codes:

- **REGION 0** All regions
- **REGION 1** USA, Canada
- **REGION 2** Europe, Japan, Middle East, South Africa, Greenland
- **REGION 3** South Korea, Taiwan, Hong Kong, Areas of Southeast Asia

Be sure you are familiar with the Blu-ray Disc requirements discussed in this section, especially the stringent requirements for supporting high-definition video and audio. Also, be aware that CompTIA expects you to be somewhat knowledgeable of DVD/BD region codes, so pay attention to those as well.

- **REGION 4**   Australia, New Zealand, Central and South America
- **REGION 5**   Eastern Europe, Russia, India, Africa
- **REGION 6**   China
- **REGION 7**   Reserved for special and future use
- **REGION 8**   Reserved for cruise ships and airlines

Blu-ray Disc Region Codes:

- **A**   East Asia (China and Mongolia excluded), Southeast Asia, Americas, and their dependencies
- **B**   Africa, Southwest Asia, Europe (except Russia), Oceania, and their dependencies
- **C**   Central Asia, East Asia (China and Mongolia only), South Asia, central Eurasia, and their dependencies

■ Installing Floppy Drives

All Windows systems reserve the drive letters A: and B: for floppy drives. You cannot name them anything other than A: or B:, but you can configure a floppy to get either drive letter. However, convention dictates that if you have only one floppy drive, you should call it A:. The second floppy drive is then called B:.

Floppy drives connect to the computer via a **34-pin ribbon cable**. If the cable supports two floppy drives, it has a seven-wire twist in the middle to differentiate electronically between the A: and B: drives. Given that the majority of users do not want two floppy drives, many system makers have dropped the twist and saved a couple of pennies on a simpler cable (Figure 9.29).

By default, almost all PCs (well, the ones that still support floppy drives) first try to boot to a floppy before any other boot device, looking for an operating system. This process enables technicians to insert a floppy disk into a sick computer to run programs when the hard drives fail. It also means hackers can insert bootable floppy disks into servers and do bad things. You do have a choice, however, because most systems have special CMOS settings with which you can change this default boot order to something other than the default drive A: and then C:; I'll show you how in a minute.

Inserting Ribbon Cables

Look at the floppy cable in Figure 9.29. Notice the connector on the left side. This connector, identical to the other connector on the same cable, plugs into the floppy controller on the motherboard, as shown in Figure 9.30. Notice how clearly the motherboard has pin 1 marked in Figure 9.30. Not all motherboards are so clear. Make sure to orient the cable so that the colored stripe on the side of the cable is aligned with pin 1.

● **Figure 9.29**   Floppy cable for only one drive

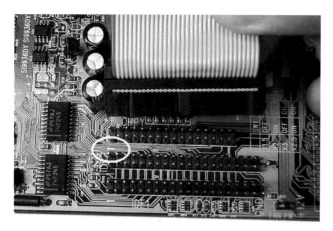

Here are a few tips on cable orientation. (By the way, these rules work for all ribbon cables, not just floppy cables.) Ribbon cable connectors usually have a distinct orientation notch in the middle. If your cable connector has an orientation notch and the controller socket has a slot in which the orientation notch fits, your job is easy (Figure 9.31).

Unfortunately, not all connectors use the orientation notch. Try looking in the motherboard book. All motherboard books provide a graphic of the motherboard, showing the proper orientation position. Look at other ribbon cables on the motherboard. In almost all motherboards, all plugs orient the same way. Last of all, just guess! You will not destroy anything by inserting the cable backward. When you boot up, the floppy drive will not work. This is not a big deal; turn off the system and try again.

* **Figure 9.30** Plugging a floppy cable into a controller, pin 1 labeled at left

After you insert the floppy ribbon cable into the floppy controller, you need to insert the ribbon cable into the floppy drive. Watch out here! You still need to orient the cable by pin 1—all the rules of ribbon cable insertion apply here, too. Before you plug in the floppy ribbon cable to the floppy drive, you need to know which connector on the cable to use; it makes a big difference. The specific connector that you insert into the floppy drive determines its drive letter.

If the floppy drive is installed on the end connector, it becomes the A: drive; if the drive is installed on the middle connector, it is the B: drive (Figure 9.32). If you're installing only one floppy, make sure you install it in the A: drive position.

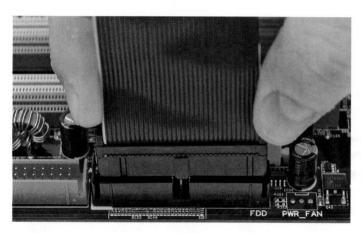

* **Figure 9.31** Floppy controller with notch

Power

Floppy drives need electricity to work, just like every other device in the PC. Modern 3½-inch floppy drives use the small mini power connector. Be careful! Inserting a mini connector incorrectly is easy, and if you install it incorrectly, you'll destroy the floppy drive and make what we call "The Nasty Smell." Look at Figure 9.33, a bottom view of a properly installed mini connector—note the chamfers (beveled edges) that show correct orientation. The problem lies in the plastic used to make the connector. The plastic connector bends easily, so even the least brawny techs can put the plug in a mini backward or hit only three of the four pins.

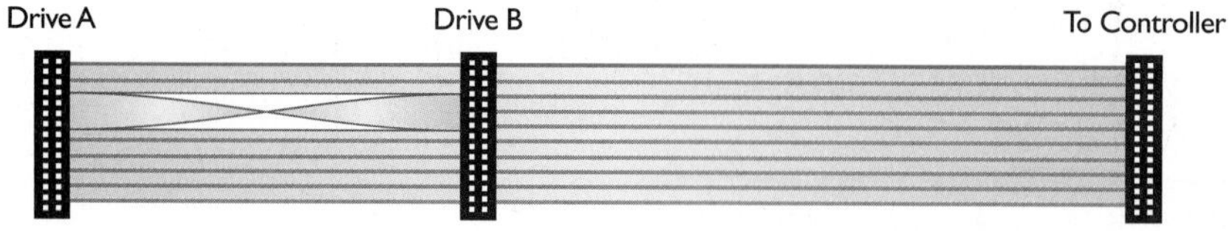

Great! You have installed a floppy drive! Once you have physically installed the floppy drive, it's time to go into CMOS.

> In the past, the CompTIA A+ Practical Application exam has been very focused on the pins on cables! Know the number (34) and orientation (pin 1 to pin 1) for the pins on the floppy drive ribbon cable.

```
Drive A          Drive B                          To Controller
```

* **Figure 9.32** Cable placement determines the drive letter.

• **Figure 9.33**   Properly installed mini connector

CMOS

After the floppy drive is installed, you need to configure the CMOS settings, which must correspond to the capacities of the drives. Look in your CMOS for a menu called "Standard CMOS Features" (or something similar to that) to see your floppy settings. Most CMOS setups configure the A: drive by default as a 3½-inch, 1.44 MB drive, so in most cases the floppy is already configured. Simply double-check the setting in CMOS; if it's okay, exit without changing anything. Figure 9.34 shows a typical CMOS setting for a single floppy drive. On the rare occasion that you require a setting other than the typical 3½-inch, 1.44-MB A: drive, simply select the drive (A: or B:) and enter the correct capacity.

Disabling the Boot Up Floppy Seek option tells the PC not to check the floppy disk during the POST, which isn't very handy except for slightly speeding up the boot process (Figure 9.35).

Many CMOS setup utilities have an option called Floppy 3 Mode Support. Refer to Figure 9.34 to see an example of a CMOS with this option. A Mode 3 floppy is a special 1.2-MB format used outside the United States, primarily in Japan. Unless you live in Japan and use Mode 3 floppy disks, ignore this option.

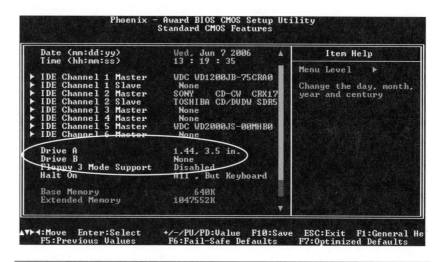

• **Figure 9.34**   CMOS setting for one standard floppy drive

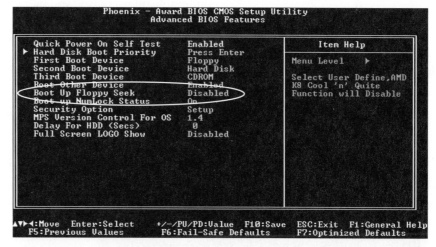

• **Figure 9.35**   CMOS Boot Up Floppy Seek option

Troubleshooting Removable Media

Floppy disk drives, flash memory, and optical drives are fairly robust devices that rarely require troubleshooting due to an actual hardware failure. Most problems with removable media stem from lack of knowledge, improper installation, abuse, and incorrect use of associated applications. There's no way to repair a truly broken flash memory—once a flash card dies you replace it—so let's concentrate on troubleshooting floppy drives and optical drives.

Floppy Drive Maintenance and Troubleshooting

No single component fails more often than the floppy drive. This is not really that surprising because floppy drives have more exposure to the outside environment than anything but the keyboard. Only a small door (or in the case of 5¼-inch drives, not even a door) divides the read/write heads from dust and grime. Floppy drives are also exposed to the threat of mechanical damage. Many folks destroy floppy drives by accidentally inserting inverted disks, paper clips, and other foreign objects. Life is tough for floppy drives.

In the face of this abuse, the key preventive maintenance performed on floppy drives is cleaning. You can find floppy drive cleaning kits at some electronics stores, or you can use a cotton swab and some denatured alcohol to scour gently inside the drive for dust and other particles.

If cleaning the drive doesn't help, try replacing the suspect disk with another one to see if the floppy drive itself is bad. If it turns out that your floppy drive won't read any disks, it's time to replace the drive.

Troubleshooting Optical Drives and Discs

Optical drives are extremely reliable and durable PC components. At times, however, a reliable and durable device decides to turn into an unreliable, nondurable pile of plastic and metal frustration. This section covers a few of the more common problems with optical drives and discs—installation issues, burning issues, and firmware updates—and how to fix them.

Installation Issues

The single biggest problem with optical drives, especially in a new installation, is the connection. Your first guess should be that the drive has not been properly installed in some way. A few of the common culprits are forgetting to plug in a power connector, inserting a cable backward, and misconfiguring jumpers/switches. Although you need to know the type of drive, the test for an improper physical connection is always the same: using BIOS to see whether the system can see the optical drive.

How BIOS detects an optical drive depends on the system. Most BIOS makers have created intelligent BIOS software that can see an installed CD-media drive. Figure 9.36 shows a modern Award Software, Inc. BIOS recognizing a CD-RW during startup.

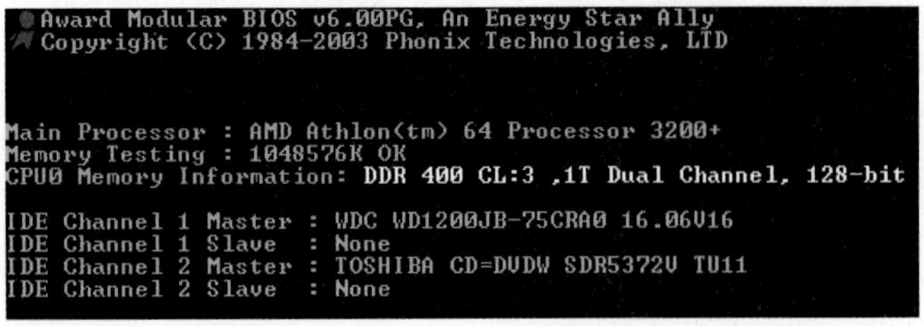

```
Award Modular BIOS v6.00PG, An Energy Star Ally
Copyright (C) 1984-2003 Phonix Technologies, LTD


Main Processor : AMD Athlon(tm) 64 Processor 3200+
Memory Testing : 1048576K OK
CPU0 Memory Information: DDR 400 CL:3 ,1T Dual Channel, 128-bit

IDE Channel 1 Master : WDC WD1200JB-75CRA0 16.06V16
IDE Channel 1 Slave  : None
IDE Channel 2 Master : TOSHIBA CD=DVDW SDR5372V IV11
IDE Channel 2 Slave  : None
```

• **Figure 9.36** BIOS recognizing an optical drive at boot

If BIOS detects the device, Windows recognizes the drive and you'll see it in My Computer or Computer and Device Manager.

If the drive won't read a CD-R or CD-RW disc, first try a commercial CD-ROM disc that is in good condition. CD-R and CD-RW discs sometimes have compatibility issues with CD-ROM drives. The same goes for DVD-RWs or any other writable DVD discs in your DVD drive or writable Blu-ray Discs in your Blu-ray Disc drive. Also, no optical drive will read badly scratched discs.

If the drive still does not see a disc, try cleaning the drive. Most modern optical drives have built-in cleaning mechanisms, but from time to time, you need to use a commercial optical-drive cleaning kit (see Figure 9.37).

Optical drives are not cleaned too often, but the discs are. Although a number of fine optical disc cleaning kits are available, you can clean most discs quite well with nothing more than a damp soft cloth. Occasionally, you can add a mild detergent. Always wipe from the center of the optical disc to the edge—never use a circular motion when cleaning a CD, DVD, or Blu-ray Disc! A common old tech's tale about cleaning optical discs is that you can wash them in a dishwasher. Although this may seem laughable, the tale has become so common that it requires a serious response. This is *not true* for two reasons: First, the water in most dishwashers is too hot and can cause the discs to warp. Second, the water pushes the discs around, causing them to hit other objects and get scratched. Don't do it!

The final problem with optical drives—stuck discs—comes from *technician* error and is not actually the fault of the drives. I can't tell you the number of times I've pulled an optical drive out of a system to replace it, only to discover that I or my customer left an essential disc inside the now-powerless drive. Luckily, most optical drives have a small hole in the front, usually just below the drive opening, into which you can insert a wire—an unbent paper clip is the standard tool for this purpose—and push on an internal release lever that ejects the disc. Try it!

● **Figure 9.37**   Optical-drive cleaning kit

Burning Issues

The tremendous growth of the CD-R and CD-RW industry—and to a lesser extent, the recordable DVD industry—has led to a substantial number of incompatibility issues between discs and drives. Some of these incompatibilities trace back to serious IO (Ignorant Operator) problems; people try to make these discs do jobs they aren't designed to do. Even when people read the manuals and jump through the proper hoops, real problems do arise, many of which you can easily solve with a few checks.

Know What It Can Do   Most mistakes take place at the point of purchase, when someone buys a drive without completely understanding its capabilities. Don't just assume that the device will do everything. Before I purchase a CD-RW or DVD-RW drive, for example, I make it a point to get my hands on every technical document the maker provides to verify exactly what capabilities the drive possesses. I make sure the drive has a good reputation; just use any search engine and type in **review** and the model number of the drive to get several people's opinions.

Media Issues   The optical disc standards committees refused to mandate the types of materials used in the construction of discs. As a result, you see substantial quality differences among CD-R and CD-RW discs of different brands and sources (they are made in several different countries). In order to write data,

CD-R discs use organic inks as part of the burning process. Fellow techs love to talk about which color to use or which color gives the best results. Ignore them; the color itself means nothing. Instead, try several brands of CD-R discs when you first get your drive to determine what works best for you. If you have a particular reason for burning CDs, such as music recording, you may want to ask for opinions and recommendations among folks in online communities with the same focus. They're usually happy to share their hard-won knowledge about what works.

In general, two items can affect media quality: speed and inks. Most CD-R and CD-RW media makers certify their CDs to work up to a certain speed multiplier. A media maker often has two product lines: a quality line guaranteed to work at a certain speed, and a generic line where you take your chances. As a rule, I buy both. I primarily use cheap discs, but I always stash five to ten good-quality discs in case I run into a problem. Again, this in large part depends on what you want them for: you may want to pull out the cheapies for temporary backups but stick with the high-end discs for archiving musical performances.

All of this discussion about CD-Rs and CD-RWs definitely holds true for recordable DVD and Blu-ray Discs and drives as well. Factor in the incompatibility of standards and you're looking at a fine mess. Do your homework before you buy or advise a client to buy a DVD/BD-writable or rewritable drive.

Buffer Underrun   Every CD, DVD, and Blu-ray Disc burner comes with onboard RAM, called *buffer RAM*—usually just called the buffer—that stores the incoming data from the recording source. Buffer underrun, the inability of the source device to keep the burner loaded with data, creates more *coasters*—that is, improperly burned and therefore useless CDs, DVDs, and Blu-ray Discs—than any other single problem. Buffer underrun most often occurs when copying from CD-ROM to CD-R/RW or from DVD-ROM to DVD-writable of all stripes. Many factors contribute to buffer underrun, but two stand out as the most important. The first factor is buffer size. Make sure you purchase drives with large buffers, a minimum of 2 MB. Unlike with system RAM, you can't get a buffer upgrade. Second is multitasking. Most systems won't enable you to run any other programs while the burner is running.

One trick to reduce underrun is using an ISO. Unlike some optical drives, *any* hard drive can keep up with an optical burner. Doing a bit-by-bit copy from disc to disc dramatically reduces the chances that a buffer underrun will add to your coaster collection.

All current optical disc burners include the BURN-Proof technology developed by Sanyo, which has eliminated the underrun issue. These drives can literally turn off the burning process if the buffer runs out of information and automatically restart as soon as the buffer refills. I love this feature, as I can now burn CDs in the background and run other programs without fear of underrun. If you're buying a new burner, make sure you get one that uses the BURN-Proof technology.

Firmware Updates

Almost all optical drives come with an upgradeable flash ROM chip. If your drive doesn't read a particular type of media, or if any other nonintermittent reading/writing problems develop, check the manufacturer's Web site to see if it offers a firmware upgrade. Almost every optical drive seems to get one or two firmware updates during its production cycle.

The majority of problems that occur with CD, DVD, and Blu-ray Disc drives are usually a direct result of incorrectly installed or updated device drivers, disconnected cables, or incompatible or just plain bad media. Also, keep in mind that DVD and Blu-ray Disc drives use specific region codes that are often misconfigured. Blu-ray Disc drives have very specific hardware and driver specifications that must be met for trouble-free end-user experiences. CompTIA is likely to target these areas specifically on the 220-702 exam, so make sure you understand this information.

Chapter 9 Review

■ Chapter Summary

After reading this chapter and completing the exercises, you should understand the following about input/output.

Support common input/output ports

- Many new computers do not come with serial ports, as other high-speed ports such as USB have replaced them. You can tell if you have serial ports by checking for the Ports (COM and LPT) icon in Device Manager.

- The UART chip that comprises the serial port converts data moving between the parallel expansion bus on a PC and the serial bus used by many I/O devices. Most serial port connectors consist of a 9-pin DB style connector. The connector on the PC or device itself (not the cable) is male. Serial ports are also known as RS-232, which is the standard that describes how serial ports work.

- The USB host controller (sometimes called a host adapter) controls every USB device connected to it. The host controller includes a root hub that provides the physical connection for devices. Host controllers support many ports, but the number of USB ports a system has is usually dependent on what the motherboard manufacturer decided to supply. The host controller is shared by every device plugged into it, so speed and power are reduced with each new device.

- Powered USB devices require their own power cord, in which case they do not pull power from the USB bus itself. Bus-powered devices draw their power directly from the USB bus and do not require a separate power cord. Too many bus-powered devices may result in system lockups, device lockups, or devices that just don't work. To solve the power problem, unplugging a device or two will lower the demand for bus power. Alternatively, you can purchase and install a USB expansion card, which will provide another USB host controller with its own set of connection ports.

- Three flavors of USB are in use today, and one is just around the bend: Low-Speed USB that runs at 1.5 Mbps, Full-Speed USB that runs at 12 Mbps, Hi-Speed USB that runs at 480 Mbps, and SuperSpeed USB that will run at up to 4.8 Gbps when it comes out in 2010. Many people refer to the low-speed and full-speed devices as USB 1.1, although that's not correct; all three speeds are part of the USB 2.0 specification. You can plug a hi-speed device into a low-speed host—or *vice versa*—and the device will work just fine, but at the lower speed.

- In theory, the USB interface can support up to 127 devices on a single USB port; in reality, too many devices on a single USB chain will overtax its power capabilities. USB specifications allow for a maximum cable length of 5 meters, although you may add a powered USB hub every 5 meters to extend this distance.

- USB hubs extend the number of USB devices you can connect to a single port. Make sure you get a powered Hi-Speed USB hub so it will support the fastest speed and not draw power away from other devices.

- Normally, you will install the device driver before connecting the USB device to the system. Although this is the norm, it is not carved in stone. Be sure to read the manual that came with your device for instructions on installation. For example, many USB devices, such as flash drives, do not need a separate driver installed and work fine if simply plugged in (they can use the generic driver provided by Windows 2000/XP/Vista).

- The high transfer speed of FireWire makes transferring large video files quick and easy. Most modern digital video cameras use the IEEE 1394 interface for transferring video from camera to PC for editing. FireWire has two distinct types of connectors: a 6-pin powered connector and a 4-pin bus-powered connector. IEEE 1394a runs at 400 Mbps and IEEE 1394b runs at 800 Mbps.

- FireWire devices must connect directly to a root hub but may be daisy chained to support up to 63 devices. Similar to USB devices, you should install the drivers before connecting the FireWire device, but most devices can use the generic Windows driver and thus can be plugged in immediately.

- When troubleshooting problems, first determine if the issue is a port problem or a device problem. Swap out the troubled device for a known good device (one that works in another computer). If a known good device fails, you can safely assume you have a port problem. If a known good device functions properly, you most likely have a device problem. For device problems, replace the device. For port problems, verify that the port is enabled, make sure you have the drive installed for the port itself, and check the condition of the cables and physical connectors.

Install optical drives

- Most optical drives use PATA or SATA connections and support the ATAPI standard. PATA drives use a regular 40-pin IDE connector; SATA drives use a standard SATA or eSATA (for external use) connector. You install them just as you would any ATA hard drive. After installing a new optical drive, check My Computer or Device Manager to confirm that Windows sees the drive.

- The Windows feature Auto Insert Notification (or AutoPlay) causes Windows to automatically begin an action when an optical disc is inserted in the drive. In Windows 2000, if an audio CD is inserted, track 1 plays automatically. If a data CD or DVD is inserted, AutoPlay scans the root of the disc for the AUTORUN.INF file and executes the commands in that file. In Windows 2000, the only way to disable AutoPlay is to manually edit the Registry. Windows XP can be configured by accessing the AutoPlay tab in the drive's Properties window. AutoPlay options in Windows Vista can be adjusted through Control Panel | Hardware and Sound | AutoPlay.

- An ISO file is a complete copy of an entire CD, DVD, or BD disc. Windows 2000/XP/Vista can't burn an ISO back to disc, but third-party programs such as Nero or Roxio Creator can.

Install floppy disk drives

- Floppy disk drives are becoming a thing of the past as Microsoft and Intel push for legacy-free computing. The small, 1.44-MB capacity floppy disks are being replaced by higher-capacity removable media.

- Floppy disks are constructed of a flexible magnetic disc housed inside a square plastic case. The case has a sliding protective cover that opens to reveal a portion of the magnetic media when inside a floppy drive. Read/write heads inside the floppy disk drive move back and forth across the media, reading or writing data as necessary.

- During disk access, an LED on the front of the drive lights up. Never eject a floppy disk when this light is on.

- Floppy disks have gone through several stages of improvement, becoming smaller with each phase. Pre-PC computers used an 8-inch floppy. Early PCs used a 5¼-inch floppy. Modern floppy disks, which appeared around 1986, are 3½ inches.

- You may have a maximum of two floppy disk drives in a system, and they must use either the drive letter A: or B:; however, a single floppy disk drive can be configured to use either drive letter. By convention, if your system has only one floppy disk drive, you should configure it as drive A:. A 34-pin ribbon data cable is used to connect the floppy disk drive to the motherboard; a 4-pin mini connector supplies power. Attaching the data cable backward won't damage anything, but the drive won't work. If you attach the power connector incorrectly, you risk damaging the drive.

- Most floppy ribbon cables have three connectors and a twist. The end without the twist connects to the motherboard, matching the red stripe on the cable with pin 1 of the motherboard connector. The drive attached to the middle connector on the cable receives the drive letter B:. The drive attached to the other end of the cable (after the twist) is assigned the drive letter A:.

- After connecting a floppy disk drive, configure the CMOS settings. Make sure the CMOS setting matches your floppy disk drive size/capacity; for example, 3½ inches and 1.44 MB.

Troubleshoot optical drives and removable media

- The key preventive maintenance for floppy drives is cleaning. If your floppy drive won't read a disk, try another. If your floppy drive won't read any disks, replace the drive.

- If your optical drive doesn't work, first check the installation. Specifically, look at the master/slave jumper settings, data cable, and power cable. If the drive is seen by Windows but can't read a particular disc, try a commercial disc. It's also possible that your drive doesn't support your media type; for example, your DVD-R drive may not be able to read your DVD+RW disc. Clean the disc with a soft damp cloth, wiping from the center toward the edge. Never clean an optical disc in the dishwasher!

- If an optical disc becomes stuck in a drive, or if the drive has no power and you need to eject the disc, straighten a paper clip and look for the small hole on the front of the drive. Insert the paper clip in the hole and push the internal release lever to eject the disc.

- Not all media brands are created equally, and not all drives play nicely with all brands of media. Experiment and try several brands of media until you find one that works reliably with your drive.

- DVD and Blu-ray Disc drives have very specific hardware and driver specifications that must be met and use specific region codes that are often misconfigured. If a user is experiencing problems with a Blu-ray Disc device, it is likely to be associated with a video adapter, driver, or noncompliant media issue.

- A buffer underrun is caused when the source device fails to keep the recording device loaded with data. Buffer underruns are the leading cause of improperly burned, and therefore useless, CDs and DVDs. Purchase a drive with a large buffer— at least 2 MB. Some drives protect against buffer underrun with a technology called BURN-Proof. Purchase a BURN-Proof drive and your buffer underruns will be eliminated.

- Most optical drives come with an upgradeable flash ROM chip. If your drive is suffering read/write problems, check the manufacturer's Web site for a firmware upgrade.

■ Key Terms

34-pin ribbon cable *(299)*
AutoPlay *(293)*
AUTORUN.INF *(293)*
buffer underrun *(304)*
cleaning kit *(302)*
FireWire *(288)*
Full-Speed USB *(284)*
Hi-Speed USB *(284)*
IEEE 1394a *(288)*
IEEE 1394b *(288)*
ISO file *(296)*

Low-Speed USB *(284)*
mini power connector *(300)*
pin I *(299)*
region code *(298)*
RS-232 *(282)*
serial port *(281)*
universal asynchronous receiver/transmitter (UART) *(281)*
USB host controller *(283)*
USB hub *(285)*
USB root hub *(283)*

■ Key Term Quiz

1. Serial ports are defined by the ___RS-232___ standard.

2. A(n) ___Full-speed USB___ device transfers data at up to 12 Mbps on the universal serial bus.

3. A(n) ___Ieee 1394b___ FireWire device transfers data at up to 800 Mbps.

4. The ___UART___ contains the logic to convert data moving between parallel and serial devices.

5. A(n) ___USB hub___ enables users to connect multiple USB devices to a single USB port.

6. The common name for IEEE 1394 devices is ___Firewire___.

7. Drives with BURN-Proof technology were designed to eliminate the problem of ___buffe Underrun___.

■ Multiple-Choice Quiz

1. List these technologies in order from slowest to fastest.

    A. Serial, Full-Speed USB, Hi-Speed USB, IEEE 1394a, IEEE 1394b

    B. Serial, Full-Speed USB, IEEE 1394a, Hi-Speed USB, IEEE 1394b

    C. Full-Speed USB, serial, Hi-Speed USB, IEEE 1394a, IEEE 1394b

    D. Low-Speed USB, serial, IEEE 1394a, Hi-Speed USB, IEEE 1394b

2. What do serial ports use to ensure that the sending device doesn't overload the receiving device with data?

    A. Flow control

    B. Parity

    C. Stop bits

    D. 7-bit chunking

3. How many devices can a single USB host controller support?

    A. 2

    B. 4

    C. 63

    D. 127

4. What is the maximum USB cable length as defined by the USB specifications?

    A. 4.5 feet

    B. 4.5 meters

    C. 5 feet

    D. 5 meters

5. Malfunctioning USB devices may be caused by which of the following?

    A. Too many USB devices attached to the host controller

    B. Improper IRQ settings for the device

    C. Device plugged in upside down

    D. USB 1.1 device plugged into USB 2.0 port

6. FireWire dominates USB in which area?

    A. Keyboards and mice

    B. Digital video editing

    C. MP3 players

    D. Biometric devices

7. Which FireWire standard is properly matched with its speed?

    A. IEEE 1394a, 400 Mbps

    B. IEEE 1394a, 480 Mbps

    C. IEEE 1394b, 400 Mbps

    D. IEEE 1394b, 480 Mbps

8. FireWire supports a maximum of how many devices?

    A. 2

    B. 4

    C. 63

    D. 127

9. While studying abroad, you purchased brand-new Blu-ray Discs produced in China. After returning to the United States, you find they will not work in your Blu-ray Disc player. What is most likely the problem?

    A. The Blu-ray Discs have a C region code.

    B. The Blu-ray Discs have a 6 region code.

    C. The Blu-ray Discs have a B region code.

    D. The Blu-ray Discs have an A region code.

10. You just installed a floppy drive and you notice that the floppy drive LED stays on. What is most likely the problem?

    A. You attached the floppy drive to the wrong connector on the ribbon cable.

    B. You forgot to configure the floppy drive through the CMOS setup.

    C. You did not attach the colored stripe on the ribbon cable to pin 1 at the drive or at the controller.

    D. You forgot to attach the power cable to the floppy drive.

11. AutoPlay reads which of the following files when an optical disc is inserted?

    A. AUTOPLAY.INF

    B. AUTORUN.INF

    C. AUTORUN.INI

    D. AUTORUN.EXE

Essay Quiz

1. Dylan is excited because he just got a new USB digital camera. He tried to install it on his laptop, but the computer doesn't recognize it. He's called you for help. What will you tell him?

2. Sandra is having
suspects her por
vaguely remem
the stop bit sho
where she can

Lab Projects

• Lab Project 9.1

Many personal computers do not normally include FireWire ports. Check the following three Web sites: www.dell.com, www.hp.com, and www.apple.com. Is a FireWire port standard built-in equipment on their new computers? If so, how many FireWire ports are included? If not, do the sites offer FireWire as an optional add-on?

• Lab Project 9.2

If your lab PC has a floppy disk drive, install a second floppy disk drive. How does your system determine which is drive A: and which is drive B:? Reverse the ribbon cable on the A: drive so the red stripe no longer aligns with pin 1. What happens when you boot the system back up? Can the drive read disks in this condition?

• Lab Project 9.3

Adding a second optical drive to a PC enables you to do some fun things, from making your own music CDs to watching movies. Assuming you want to install an ATAPI drive, you then need to face some issues. Which controller should you use, primary or secondary? Should both optical drives be on the same controller or on different controllers? Why?

Most techs would install a burner as secondary master and put a read-only drive on the primary as slave, but different drives require different considerations. If you don't plan to copy CD to CD, there's no reason the read-only CD shouldn't be secondary slave. The key is you have to experiment.

Install a second optical drive—preferably a burner—and run it through its paces. Copy files and burn discs to and from the optical and hard drives. Then change the configuration of your drives (such as having both optical drives on the same controller) and run through the testing process again. Do you notice any differences?

Mastering Video and Multimedia

In this chapter, you will learn how to

- **Install and configure video**
- **Describe how to implement sound in a PC**
- **Troubleshoot multimedia problems**

In the world of tech support, certain problems get noticed more quickly than others. If a user has a USB port go bad, he might not notice for days, or even weeks. If a printer breaks, no one will care until someone tries to use that printer, which could be a while. A dead optical drive could elicit no complaints for weeks until someone tries to use it. However, you'll hear about a bad video card the second something fishy happens.

Troubleshooting multimedia devices—video cards in particular—will save your clients a lot of grief. Not being able to get any video or hear any sound can cripple someone's productivity (or entertainment, as the case may be). In this chapter, you'll first learn to install a video card, then a sound card, and then you'll figure out how to troubleshoot all these devices when they go haywire.

Installing and Configuring Video

Once you've decided on the features and price for a new video card or monitor, you need to install them into your system. As long as you have the right connection to your video card, installing a monitor is straightforward. The challenge comes when installing the video card.

During the physical installation of a video card, watch out for two possible issues: long cards and proximity of the nearest PCI card. Some high-end video cards simply won't fit in certain cases or block access to needed motherboard connectors such as the IDE sockets. There's no clean fix for such a problem—you simply have to change at least one of the components (video card, motherboard, or case). Because high-end video cards run very hot, you don't want them sitting right next to another card; make sure the fan on the video card has plenty of ventilation space. A good practice is to leave the slot next to the video card empty to allow better airflow (Figure 10.1).

Once you've properly installed the video card and connected it to the monitor, you've conquered half the territory for making the video process work properly. You're ready to tackle the drivers and tweak the operating system, so let's go!

● **Figure 10.1**   Installing a video card

(15 Pin D-Shape test)

Software

Configuring your video software is usually a two-step process. First you need to load drivers for the video card. Then you need to open the Control Panel and go to the Display applet (Windows 2000/XP) or Personalization applet (Windows Vista/7) to make your adjustments. Let's explore how to make the video card and monitor work in Windows.

> ### Try This!
>
> **Install a Video Card**
>
> You know how to install an expansion card from your reading in earlier chapters. Installing a video card is pretty much the same, so Try This!
>
> 1. Refer to Chapter 3, "Mastering Motherboards," for steps on installing a new card.
>
> 2. Plug the monitor cable into the video card port on the back of the PC and power up the system. If your PC seems dead after you install a video card, or if the screen is blank but you hear fans whirring and the internal speaker sounding off *long-short-short-short*, your video card likely did not get properly seated. Unplug the PC, remove the card, and try again.

Drivers

Just like any other piece of hardware, your video card needs a driver to function. Video card drivers install pretty much the same way as all of the other drivers we've discussed thus far: either the driver is already built into Windows or you must use the installation CD that comes with the video card.

Video card makers are constantly updating their drivers. Odds are good that any video card more than a few months old has at least one driver update. If possible, check the manufacturer's Web site and use the driver located there, if there is one. If the Web site doesn't offer a driver, it's usually best to use the installation CD. Always avoid using the built-in Windows driver as it tends to be the most dated.

We'll explore driver issues in more detail after we discuss the Display applet. Like so many things about video, you can't fully understand one topic without understanding at least one other!

Using the Display/Personalization Applet

With the driver installed, you're ready to configure your display settings. The Display applet or Personalization applet on the Control Panel is your next stop. The Display applet and Personalization applet provide convenient, central locations for all of your display settings, including resolution, refresh rate, driver information, and color depth.

The default Display applet window in Windows XP, called the Display Properties dialog box (Figure 10.2), has five tabs: Themes, Desktop, Screen Saver, Appearance, and Settings. Earlier versions of Windows have a subset of these tabs. The first four tabs have options you can choose to change the look and feel of Windows and set up a screensaver; the fifth tab is where you make adjustments that relate directly to your monitor and video card.

The Personalization applet in Windows Vista offers functions similar to the Display applet, but each function manifests as a clickable option rather than as a separate tab (Figure 10.3). Four of the seven options mirror the look and feel options of earlier versions of Windows, such as Window Color and Appearance, Desktop Background,

• **Figure 10.2** Display Properties dialog box in Windows XP

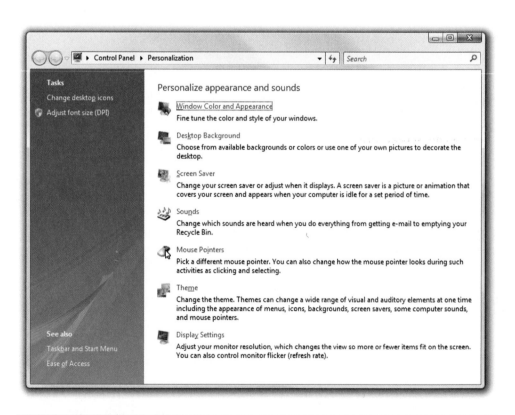

• **Figure 10.3** Personalization applet in Windows Vista

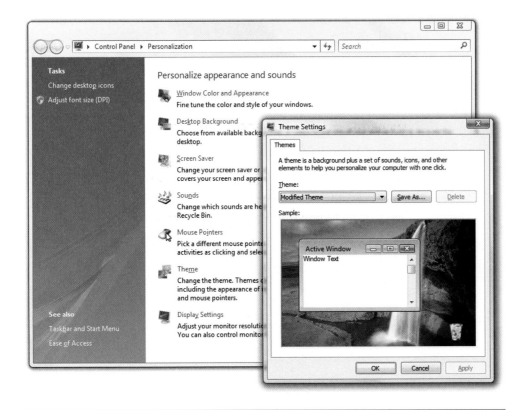

● **Figure 10.4**   Theme option in the Personalization applet

Screen Saver, and Theme. The last option, Display Settings, is where you make adjustments to your monitor and video card. Two options, Sounds and Mouse Pointers, don't concern us at all at this time.

Whether discussing tabs or options, the functions on both applets are pretty much the same, so let's do this in one discussion. I'll point out any serious differences among the versions.

Making the Screen Pretty

Three tabs/options in the Display/Personalization applet have the job of adjusting the appearance of the screen: Themes/Theme, Desktop/Desktop Background, and Appearance/ Windows Color and Appearance. Windows themes are preset configurations of the look and feel of the entire Windows environment (Figure 10.4).

The Desktop tab/option (Figure 10.5) defines the background color or image. In Windows XP, it also includes the handy Customize Desktop button that enables you to define the icons as well as any Web pages you want to appear on the Desktop. Windows Vista/7 give you the option to position the image on the screen (Figure 10.6), and the *Change desktop icons* option on the Tasks list in the Personalization applet enables you to choose which system icons (such as Computer, Recycle Bin, and Network) show up on your desktop, as well as which graphical icons they use.

The last of the tabs for the look and feel of the desktop in Windows 2000/XP is the Appearance tab. Think of the Appearance tab as the

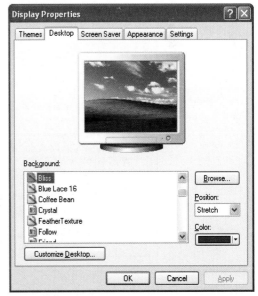

● **Figure 10.5**   Desktop tab on Display Properties dialog box

● **Figure 10.6**   Desktop Background options in Windows Vista

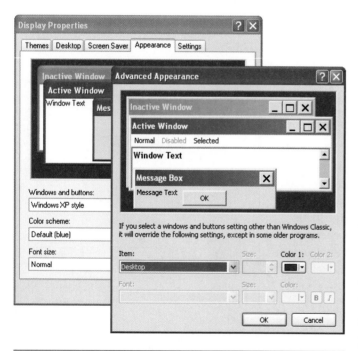

● **Figure 10.7**   Advanced Appearance dialog box

way to fine-tune the theme to your liking. The main screen gives only a few options—the real power is when you click the Advanced button (Figure 10.7). Using this dialog box, you may adjust almost everything about the desktop, including the types of fonts and colors of every part of a window.

The Window Color and Appearance option in Windows Vista/7 is a little simpler on the surface, enabling you to change the color scheme, intensity, and transparency (Figure 10.8). You can unlock the full gamut of options, though, by clicking the *Open classic appearance properties for more color options* link.

Screen Saver

At first glance, the Screen Saver tab/option seems to do nothing but set the Windows screensaver—no big deal; just about everyone has set a screensaver. But another option on the Screen Saver tab gets you to one of the most important settings of your system: power management. Click on the Power button or *Change power settings* option to get to the Power Options Properties dialog box or Power Options applet (Figure 10.9).

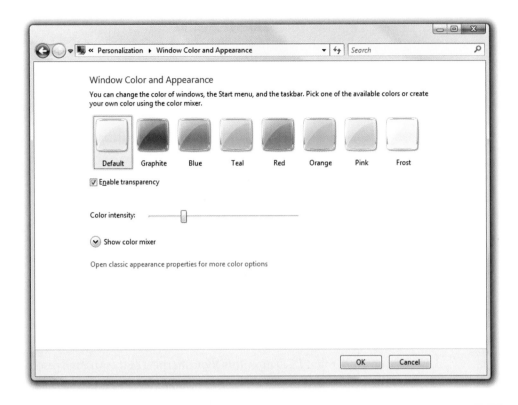

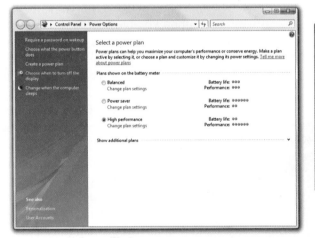

Figure 10.8   Window Color and Appearance option

The tabs and options define all of the power management of the system. Power management is a fairly involved process, and it's not really covered on the Practical Application exam, so don't worry about it too much for this test.

Settings Tab/Display Settings Applet

The Settings tab or Display Settings applet (Figure 10.10) is the centralized location for configuring all of your video settings. From the main screen you can adjust both the resolution and the color depth. Windows only displays resolutions and color depths that your video card/monitor combination can accept and that are suitable for most situations. Everyone has a favorite resolution, and higher isn't always better. Especially for those with trouble seeing small screen elements, higher resolutions can present a difficulty—already small icons are *much* smaller at 1280 × 1024 than at 800 × 600. Try all of the resolutions to see which you

Figure 10.9   Power Options Properties dialog box

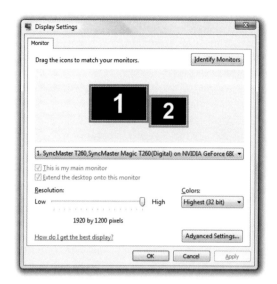
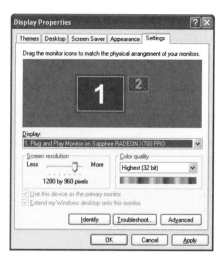

• **Figure 10.10** Monitor/Settings tab

Windows supports *DualView* technology, enabling you to use multiple monitors.

like—just remember that LCD monitors look sharpest at their native resolution (usually the highest listed).

The color quality is the number of colors displayed on the screen. You can change the screen resolution with a simple slider, adjusting the color depth from 4-bit all of the way up to 32-bit color. Unless you have an older video card or a significant video speed issue, you'll probably set your system for 32-bit color and never touch this setting again.

Another option you may see in the Settings tab is dual monitors. Windows supports the use of two (or more) monitors. These monitors may work together like two halves of one large monitor, or the second monitor might simply show a duplicate of what's happening on the first monitor. Dual monitors are handy if you need lots of screen space but don't want to buy a really large, expensive monitor (Figure 10.11). Microsoft calls this feature DualView.

There are two ways to set up dual monitors: plug in two video cards or use a single video card that supports two monitors (a "dual-head" video card). Both methods are quite common and work well. Dual monitors are easy to configure: just plug in the monitors and Windows should detect them. Windows will show both monitors in the Monitor/Settings tab, as shown in Figure 10.12. By default, the second monitor is not enabled. To use the second monitor, just select *Extend the desktop onto this monitor*.

If you need to see more advanced settings, click on… that's right, the Advanced or Advanced Settings button (Figure 10.13). The title of this dialog box reflects the monitor and video card. As you can see in the screen shot, this particular monitor is a Samsung SyncMaster T220 running off of an ATI Radeon 3850 video card.

• **Figure 10.11** My editor hard at work with dual monitors

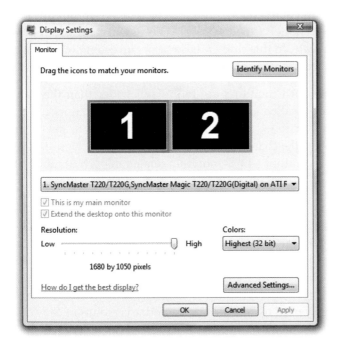

• **Figure 10.12** Enabling dual monitors

• **Figure 10.13** Advanced video settings

The two tabs you're most likely to use are the Adapter and Monitor tabs. The Adapter tab gives detailed information about the video card, including the amount of video memory available, the graphics processor, and the BIOS information (yup, your video card has a BIOS, too!). You can also click on the List All Modes button to change the current mode of the video card—although any mode you may set here you can also set in the sliders on the main screen.

If you're still using a CRT, you'll find the Monitor tab a handy place. This is where you can set the refresh rate (Figure 10.14). Windows only shows refresh rates that the monitor says it can handle, but many monitors can take a faster—and therefore easier on the eyes—refresh rate. To see all of the modes the video card can support, uncheck the *Hide modes that this monitor cannot display* option.

If you try this, always increase the refresh rate in small increments. If the screen looks better, use it. If the screen seems distorted or disappears, wait a moment and Windows will reset to the original refresh rate. Be careful when using modes that Windows says the monitor cannot display. Pushing a CRT past its fastest refresh rate for more than a minute or two can damage it.

Most video cards add their own tab to the Advanced dialog box, such as the one shown in Figure 10.15. This tab adjusts all of the specialized settings for that video card. What you see here varies by model of card and version of driver, but here's a list of some of the more interesting settings you might see.

All LCD monitors have a fixed refresh rate.

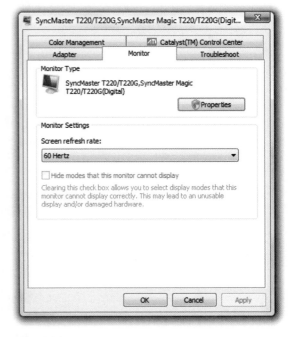

• **Figure 10.14** Monitor tab

Color Correction Sometimes the colors on your monitor are not close enough for your tastes to the actual color you're trying to create. In this case you use color correction to fine-tune the colors on the screen to get the look you want.

Rotation All monitors are by default wider than they are tall. This is called *landscape mode*. Some LCD monitors can be physically rotated to facilitate users who like to see their desktops taller than they are wide (*portrait mode*). Figure 10.16 shows the author's LCD monitors rotated in portrait mode. If you want to rotate your screen, you must tell the system you're rotating it.

Modes Most video cards add very advanced settings to enable you to finely tweak your monitor. These very dangerous settings have names such as "sync polarity" or "front porch" and are outside the scope of both CompTIA A+ certification and the needs of all but the most geeky techs. These settings are mostly used to display a non-standard resolution. Stay out of these settings!

• **Figure 10.15** Third-party video tab

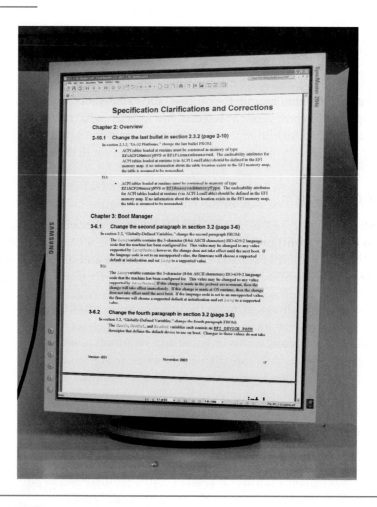

• **Figure 10.16** Portrait mode

Working with Drivers

Now that you know the locations of the primary video tools within the operating system, it's time to learn about fine-tuning your video. You need to know how to work with video drivers from within the Display/Personalization applet, including how to update them, roll back updates, and uninstall them.

Windows is very persnickety when it comes to video card drivers. You can crash Windows and force a reinstallation simply by installing a new video card and not uninstalling the old card's drivers. This doesn't happen every time, but it certainly can happen. As a basic rule, always uninstall the old card's drivers before you install drivers for a new card.

When you update the drivers for a card, you have a choice of uninstalling the outdated drivers and then installing new drivers—which makes the process the same as for installing a new card—or you can let Windows flex some digital muscle and install the new ones right over the older drivers.

To update your drivers, go to the Control Panel and double-click the Display applet or Personalization applet. In the Display Properties/Display Settings dialog box, select the Settings tab/Monitor tab and click the Advanced or Advanced Settings button. In the Advanced button dialog box, click the Adapter tab and then click the Properties button. In the Properties dialog box for your adapter (Figure 10.17), select the Driver tab and then click the Update Driver button to run the Hardware Update wizard.

Once you're familiar with the process of installing and configuring a video card, it might interest you to learn what that fancy GPU is doing inside your computer while you're playing the latest computer games.

• **Figure 10.17** Adapter Properties dialog box

3-D Graphics

No other area of the PC world reflects the amazing acceleration of technological improvements more than **3-D graphics**—in particular, 3-D gaming—that attempt to create images with the same depth and texture as objects seen in the real world. We are spectators to an amazing new world where software and hardware race to produce new levels of realism and complexity displayed on the computer screen. Powered by the wallets of tens of millions of PC gamers always demanding more and better, the video industry constantly introduces new video cards and new software titles that make today's games so incredibly realistic and fun. Although the gaming world certainly leads the PC industry in 3-D technologies, many other PC applications—such as *Computer Aided Design (CAD)* programs—quickly snatch up these technologies, making 3-D more useful in many ways other than just games. In this section, we'll add to the many bits and pieces of 3-D video encountered over previous chapters in the book and put together an understanding of the function and configuration of 3-D graphics.

Before the early 1990s, PCs did not mix well with 3-D graphics. Certainly, many 3-D applications existed, primarily 3-D design programs such

• **Figure 10.18**   Wolfenstein 3D

• **Figure 10.19**   Each figure had a limited number of sprites.

• **Figure 10.20**   Vertices for a 3-D airplane

as AutoCAD and Intergraph, but these applications would often run only on expensive, specialized hardware—not so great for casual users.

The big change took place in 1992 when a small company called id Software created a new game called Wolfenstein 3D (see Figure 10.18). They launched an entirely new genre of games, now called *first-person shooters* (*FPSs*), in which the player looks out into a 3-D world, interacting with walls, doors, and other items, and shoots whatever bad guys the game provides.

Wolfenstein 3D shook the PC gaming world to its foundations. That this innovative format came from an upstart little company made Wolfenstein 3D and id Software into overnight sensations. Even though their game was demanding on hardware, they gambled that enough people could run it to make it a success. The gamble paid off for John Carmack and John Romero, the creators of id Software, making them the fathers of 3-D gaming.

Early 3-D games used fixed 3-D images called **sprites** to create the 3-D world. A sprite is nothing more than a bitmapped graphic such as a BMP file. These early first-person shooters would calculate the position of an object from the player's perspective and place a sprite to represent the object. Any single object had only a fixed number of sprites—if you walked around an object, you noticed an obvious jerk as the game replaced the current sprite with a new one to represent the new position. Figure 10.19 shows different sprites for the same bad guy in Wolfenstein 3D. Sprites weren't pretty, but they worked without seriously taxing the 486s and early Pentiums of the time.

The second generation of 3-D began to replace sprites with true 3-D objects, which are drastically more complex than sprites. A true 3-D object is composed of a group of points called **vertices**. Each vertex has a defined X, Y, and Z position in a 3-D world. Figure 10.20 shows the vertices for an airplane in a 3-D world.

The computer must track all of the vertices of all of the objects in the 3-D world, including the ones you cannot currently see. Keep in mind that objects may be motionless in the 3-D world (a wall, for example), may have animation (such as a door opening and closing), or may be moving (like bad monsters trying to spray you with evil alien goo). This calculation process is called *transformation* and, as you might imagine, is extremely taxing to most CPUs. Intel's SIMD and AMD's 3DNow! processor extensions were expressly designed to perform transformations.

Once the CPU has determined the positions of all vertices, the system begins to fill in the 3-D object. The process begins by drawing lines (the 3-D term is *edges*) between vertices to build the 3-D object into many triangles. Why triangles? Well, mainly by consensus of game developers. Any shape works, but triangles make the most sense from a mathematical standpoint. I could go into more depth here, but that would require talking about trigonometry, and I'm gambling you'd rather not read that detailed a description! All 3-D games use triangles to connect vertices. The 3-D process then groups triangles into various shapes called polygons. Figure 10.21 shows the same model as Figure 10.20, now displaying all of the connected vertices to create a large number of polygons.

Originally, the CPU handled these calculations to create triangles, but now special 3-D video cards do the job, greatly speeding up the process.

The last step in second-generation games was texturing. Every 3-D game stores a number of image files called textures. The program wraps textures around an object to give it a surface. Textures work well to provide dramatic detail without using a lot of triangles. A single object may take one texture or many textures, applied to single triangles or groups of triangles (polygons). Figure 10.22 shows the finished airplane.

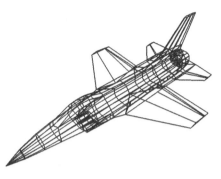

• **Figure 10.21** Connected vertices forming polygons on a 3-D

True 3-D objects, more often referred to as *rendered*, immediately created the need for massively powerful video cards and much wider data buses. Intel's primary motivation for creating AGP was to provide a big enough pipe for massive data pumping between the video card and the CPU. Intel gave AGP the ability to read system RAM to support textures. If it weren't for 3-D games, AGP (and probably even PCIe) would almost certainly not exist.

• **Figure 10.22** 3-D airplane with textures added

3-D Video Cards

No CPU of the mid-1990s could ever hope to handle the massive processes required to render 3-D worlds. Keep in mind that to create realistic movement, the 3-D world must refresh at least 24 times per second. That means that this entire process, from transformation to texturing, must repeat once every 1/24th of a second! Furthermore, although the game re-creates each screen, it must also keep score, track the positions of all of the objects in the game, provide some type of intelligence to the bad guys, and so on. Something had to happen to take the workload off the CPU. The answer came from video cards.

Video cards were developed with smart onboard graphics processing units (GPUs). The GPU helped the CPU by taking over some, and eventually all, of the 3-D rendering duties. These video cards not only have GPUs, but also have massive amounts of RAM to store textures.

But a problem exists with this setup: how do we talk to these cards? This is done by means of a device driver, of course, but wouldn't it be great if we could create standard commands to speed up the process? The best thing to do would be to create a standardized set of instructions that any 3-D program could send to a video card to do all of the basic work, such as "make a cone" or "lay texture 237 on the cone you just made."

The video card instructions standards manifested themselves into a series of application programming interfaces (APIs). In essence, an API is a library of commands that people who make 3-D games must use in their programs. The program currently using the video card sends API commands directly to the device driver. Device drivers must know how to understand the API commands. If you were to picture the graphics system of your computer as a layer cake, the top layer would be the program making a call to the video card driver that then directs the graphics hardware. The next layer is the API. The device driver comes next, and way down at the base of the cake is the actual graphics hardware: RAM, graphics processor, and RAMDAC. OpenGL and DirectX are the most popular APIs.

Several APIs have been developed over the years, with two clear winners among all of them: OpenGL and DirectX. The OpenGL standard was developed for UNIX systems but has since been *ported to*, or made compatible with, a wide variety of computer systems, including Windows and Apple computers. As the demand for 3-D video became increasingly strong, Microsoft decided to throw its hat into the 3-D graphics ring with its own API, called DirectX. We look at DirectX in depth in the next section.

Although they might accomplish the same task (for instance, translating instructions and passing them on to the video driver), every API handles things just a little bit differently. In some 3-D games, the OpenGL standard might produce more precise images with less CPU overhead than the DirectX standard. In general, however, you won't notice a large difference between the images produced by using OpenGL and DirectX.

DirectX and Video Cards

In the old days, many applications communicated directly with much of the PC hardware and, as a result, could crash your computer if not written well enough. Microsoft tried to fix this problem by placing all hardware under the control of Windows, but programmers balked because Windows added too much work for the video process and slowed down everything. For the most demanding programs, such as games, only direct access of hardware would work.

This need to "get around Windows" motivated Microsoft to unveil a new set of protocols called DirectX. Programmers use DirectX to take control of certain pieces of hardware and to talk directly to that hardware; it provides the speed necessary to play the advanced games so popular today. The primary impetus for DirectX was to build a series of products to enable Windows to run 3-D games. That's not to say that you couldn't run 3-D games in Windows *before* DirectX; rather, it's just that Microsoft wasn't involved in the API rat race at the time and wanted to be. Microsoft's goal in developing DirectX was to create a 100-percent stable environment, with direct hardware access, for running 3-D applications and games within Windows.

DirectX is not only for video; it also supports sound, network connections, input devices, and other parts of your PC. Each of these subsets of DirectX has a name, such as DirectDraw, Direct3D, or DirectSound.

- **DirectDraw** Supports direct access to the hardware for 2-D graphics.
- **Direct3D** Supports direct access to the hardware for 3-D graphics—the most important part of DirectX.
- **DirectInput** Supports direct access to the hardware for joysticks and other game controllers.
- **DirectSound** Supports direct access to the hardware for waveforms.
- **DirectMusic** Supports direct access to the hardware for MIDI devices.
- **DirectPlay** Supports direct access to network devices for multiplayer games.
- **DirectShow** Supports direct access to video and presentation devices.

Microsoft constantly adds to and tweaks this list. As almost all games need DirectX and all video cards have drivers to support DirectX, you need to verify that DirectX is installed and working properly on your system. To do this, use the DirectX Diagnostic Tool. In Windows 2000/XP, you can find it in the System Information program. After you open System Information (it usually lives in the Accessories | System Tools area of the Start menu), click the Tools menu and select DirectX Diagnostic Tool (see Figure 10.23).

For Windows Vista/7, go to Start and type **dxdiag** in the Start search box. Press ENTER to run the program.

The System tab gives the version of DirectX. The system pictured in Figure 10.23 runs DirectX 10. You may then test the separate DirectX functions by running through the other tabs and running the tests.

So, what does DirectX do for video cards? Back in the bad old days before DirectX became popular with the game makers, many GPU makers created their own chip-specific APIs. 3dfx had Glide, for example, and S3 had ViRGE. This made buying 3-D games a mess. There would often be multiple versions of the same game for each card. Even worse, many games never used 3-D acceleration because it was just too much work to support all of the different cards.

That all changed when Microsoft beefed up DirectX and got more GPU makers to support it. That in turn enabled the game companies to write games by using DirectX and have them run on any card out there. The bottom line: when Microsoft comes out with a new version of DirectX, all of the GPU companies hurry to support it or they will be left behind.

Trying to decide what video card to buy gives me the shakes—too many options! One good way to narrow down your buying decision is to see what

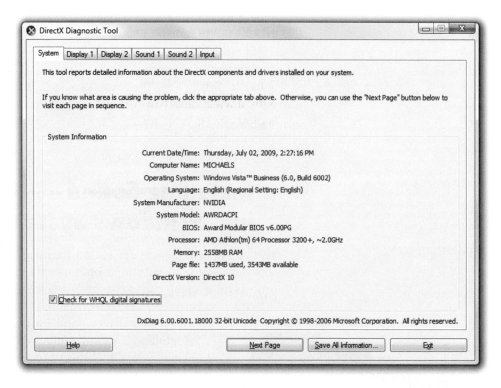

• **Figure 10.23**   The DirectX Diagnostic Tool

Try This!

Testing Your Video

Your client needs to know right now whether his system will run the latest game, so turn to the DirectX Diagnostic Tool and give it a go. Although you can open the tool in System Information, you can also run it directly from the Start menu. Go to Start | Run, type in **dxdiag**, and click OK. Or in Vista/7, just Start, type **dxdiag**, and press ENTER.

1. Select the Display tab and then click the Test DirectDraw button.

2. After the DirectDraw test runs, click the Test Direct3D button.

3. How did your system handle the test? If anything failed, you might think about replacing the card!

GPU is hot at the moment. I make a point to check out these Web sites whenever I'm getting ready to buy, so I can see what everyone says is the best.

- www.arstechnica.com
- www.hardocp.com
- www.tomshardware.com
- www.sharkyextreme.com

Installing Sound in a Windows System

You've got two choices for sound hardware on today's PCs: a separate sound card or onboard sound built into the motherboard. The installation process for a sound card is basically the same as the process for any other card. You snap the card into a slot, plug some speakers into the card, load a driver—and for the most part, you're finished. With onboard sound, you need to make sure the sound is enabled in your CMOS and then load the driver. As with most of the devices discussed in this book, sound card installation consists of three major parts: physical installation, device driver installation, and configuration.

• **Figure 10.24**   Typical sound card

Physical Installation

Physical installation is easy. Onboard sound is already physically installed and most sound cards are run-of-the-mill PCI cards (Figure 10.24), although you can find PCIe and USB versions too. The real trick to physical installation is deciding where to plug in the speakers, microphone, and so on. The surround sound devices so common today feature a variety of jacks, so you will probably want to refer to your sound card documentation for details, but here are a few guidelines:

- The typical stereo or 2.1 speaker system will use only a single jack. Look for the jack labeled Speaker or Speaker 1.
- Surround speakers either use a single digital (S/PDIF) connection, which in most cases runs from the sound card to the subwoofer, or they need three separate cables: one for the front two speakers that runs to the Speaker 1 connector, one for the back two speakers that runs to the Speaker 2 connector, and a third cable for the center channel and subwoofer that runs to the digital/audio out or Speaker 3 connector.

Here's a quick look at sound card installation. As with any expansion card, you'll need a Phillips-head screwdriver to install a sound card, as well as your electrostatic discharge (ESD) prevention equipment. Of course, you'll also need the sound card itself, a set of speakers, an audio cable if it's an older system, and a microphone if you want to be able to record sounds.

1. Shut down your computer, unplug it, and open the case.

2. Find an open PCI or PCIe slot and snap in the sound card. Remember to handle the card with tender loving care—especially if you're installing an expensive, high-end card! Make sure the card is securely seated, and secure it to the chassis with a hex screw.

Installing Drivers

Once the sound card is installed, start the system and let Windows install the card's drivers. This applies to expansion cards and onboard sound. As you might expect by now, you'll probably have a choice between the built-in Windows drivers and the driver that comes on a CD-ROM with your sound card. Just as with other cards, it's always best to install the driver that comes with the card. All sound devices have easy-to-use autorun-enabled installation CD-ROMs that step you through the process (Figure 10.25).

You might run into one of the USB sound cards out on the market (Figure 10.26), in which case the installation process is reversed. The only secret to these devices is to follow the important rule of all USB devices: *install the drivers before you plug in the device.* Windows, especially Windows XP and Vista, probably have basic drivers for these USB sound cards, but don't take a chance—always install the drivers first.

• **Figure 10.25** Typical autorun screen for a sound card

After your sound card and driver are installed, make a quick trip to the Device Manager to ensure that the driver was installed correctly, and you're two-thirds of the way there. Installing the driver is never the last step for a sound card. Your final step is to configure the sound card by using configuration programs and test it by using an application. Most sound cards come with both special configuration programs and a few sound applications on the same CD-ROM that supplies the drivers. Take a look at these extra bits of software that I call *sound programs*.

Sound card drivers are updated occasionally. Take a moment to check the manufacturer's Web site to see whether your sound card has any driver updates.

Installing Sound Programs

There are many programs available that will play sounds on your PC: Windows Media Player, Winamp, or something similar. But several other classes of sound programs also reside on your computer: programs for the configuration of your sound card—tools built into Windows as well as proprietary tools—and special applications that may or may not come with your sound card.

Windows Configuration Applications Every Windows computer comes with at least one important sound configuration program built right into the operating system: the Control Panel applet called Sound in Windows Vista, Sounds and Audio Devices in Windows XP, or Sounds and Multimedia in Windows 2000. Whatever the name, this

• **Figure 10.26** USB sound card

applet (or applets) performs the same job: it provides a location for performing most or all of the configuration you need for your sound card. Consider the Sounds and Audio Devices applet in Windows XP, for example; the Sounds and Multimedia applet in Windows 2000 works roughly the same, although it may have one control or another in a different place.

The Sounds and Audio Devices applet has five tabs: Volume, Sounds, Audio, Voice, and Hardware. The Volume tab is the most interesting. This tab adjusts the volume for the speakers, and it allows you to set up the type of speaker system you have, as shown in Figure 10.27.

The Sounds tab allows you to add customized sounds to Windows events, such as the startup of a program or Windows shutdown. The Audio tab (Figure 10.28) and Voice tab do roughly the same thing: they allow you to specify the device used for input and output of general sounds (Audio tab) and voice (Voice tab). These settings are handy for folks like me who have a regular microphone and speakers but also use a headset with microphone for voice recognition or Internet telephone software. By telling Windows to use the microphone for normal sounds and to use the headset for voice recognition, I don't have to make any manual changes when I switch from listening to an MP3 to listening to my brother when he calls me over the Internet.

• **Figure 10.27**   Advanced Audio Properties dialog box

The Hardware tab isn't used very often, but it does have one interesting feature: it shows you all of the audio and video codecs installed in your system. (See the section on "Missing Codecs" later in this chapter for more details on codecs.)

Microsoft changed a few things between Windows XP and Windows Vista when it comes to configuring sound. The Sound applet offers better support for multiple speaker setup, for example, and integration with television via HDMI configuration options.

To configure speakers, go to Control Panel and click Hardware and Sound; then click Sound if in Category View or double-click the Sound applet if in Classic View. Either route opens the Sound applet (Figure 10.29).

Select the Speakers option and click the Configure button to open the Speaker Setup dialog box (Figure 10.30). Select the audio channel option that's appropriate for your setup, such as the stereo system selected for my setup at the office and shown in Figure 10.30. You can click on individual speaker icons to test if the speakers are set up properly, or click the Test button to cycle through the whole range of speakers.

• **Figure 10.28**   Audio tab

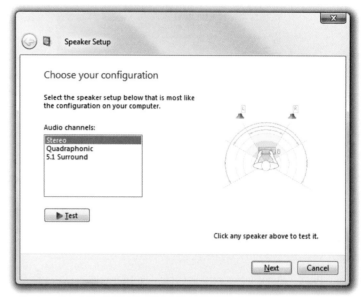

• **Figure 10.30** Speaker Setup dialog box in Windows Vista

• **Figure 10.29** Sound applet in Windows Vista

Proprietary Configuration Applications ~~Many sound cards install propri-~~ ~~etary software to support configuration features not provided by Windows.~~ Figure 10.31 shows one such application. This special configuration application comes with Creative Labs sound cards to add a few tweaks to the speaker setup that the Sounds and Audio Devices applet doesn't support.

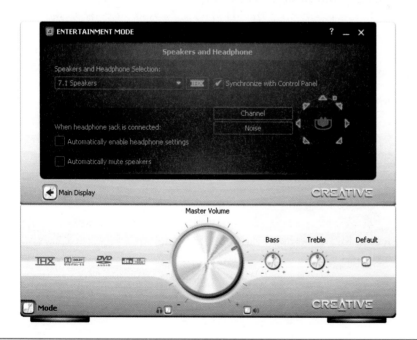

• **Figure 10.31** Creative Labs Speakers and Headphone panel

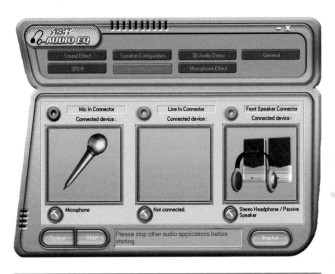

● **Figure 10.32** Autosensing software detecting connected devices

Most sound cards come with some form of configuration program that works with the Control Panel applet to tweak the sound the way you want it. Figure 10.32 shows the applet that came with my motherboard. One of its many interesting features is to detect what types of devices are installed into the sound ports and adjust the system to use them. In other words, I don't even have to look where I'm plugging in anything! If I plug a microphone into the front speaker port, the system just adjusts the outputs—very cool. Software and sound cards that can do this are called **autosensing.**

Take some time to experiment with the program that comes with your sound card—this is a great way to learn about some of the card's features that you might otherwise not even know are there!

Specialized Applications Some sound cards—Creative Labs sound cards are by far the most infamous for this—install one or more applications, ostensibly to improve your sound experience. These are not the configuration programs just described. These applications enable you to do anything from composing music to organizing your sound files. Personally, I don't have much use for an application such as the 3DMIDI Player (Figure 10.33)—but you might be just the type of person who loves it. Be sure at least to install the applications that come with your card. If you don't like them, you can easily uninstall them.

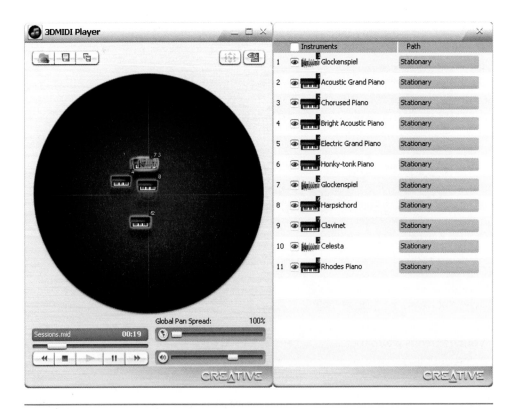

● **Figure 10.33** Creative Labs 3DMIDI Player program

▪ Troubleshooting Multimedia

People tend to notice when their monitors or speakers stop working, making multimedia problems a big issue for technicians. This section will look at the various things you can do as a tech to restore function to your clients' multimedia adapters.

Troubleshooting Video Cards/Drivers

Video cards rarely go bad, so the vast majority of video card/driver problems are bad or incompatible drivers or incorrect settings. Always make sure you have the correct driver installed. If you're using an incompatible driver, Windows defaults to good old 640 × 480, 16-color VGA. A driver that is suddenly corrupted usually doesn't show the problem until the next reboot. If you reboot a system with a corrupted driver, Windows will do one of the following: go into VGA mode, blank the monitor, lock up, or display a garbled screen. Whatever the output, reboot into Safe mode and roll back or delete the driver. Keep in mind that more advanced video cards tend to show their drivers as installed programs under Add or Remove Programs, so always check there first before you try deleting a driver by using Device Manager. Download the latest driver and reinstall.

Video cards are pretty durable but they have two components that do go bad: the fan and the RAM. Lucky for you, if either of these goes out, it tends to show the same error—bizarre screen outputs followed shortly by a screen lockup. Usually Windows keeps running; you may see your mouse pointer moving around and windows refreshing, but the screen turns into a huge mess (Figure 10.34).

Bad drivers sometimes also make this error, so always first try going into Safe mode to see if the problem suddenly clears up. If it does, you do not have a problem with the video card!

The last and probably most common problem is nothing more than improperly configured video settings. Identifying the problem is just common sense—if your monitor is showing everything sideways, someone messed with your rotation settings; if your gorgeous wallpaper of a mountain pass looks like an ugly four-color cartoon, someone lowered the

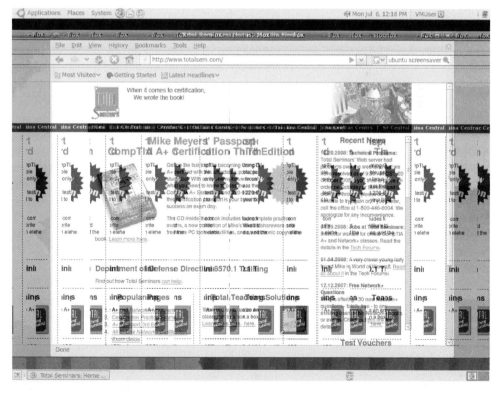

● **Figure 10.34**   Serious video problem

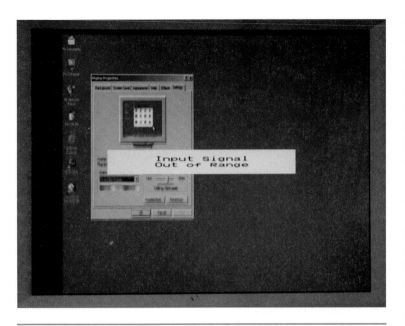

• **Figure 10.35** Pushing a monitor too hard

color depth. Go into your Display Properties and reset them to a setting that works! The one serious configuration issue is pushing the resolution too high. If you adjust your resolution and then your monitor displays an error message such as "Input Signal Out of Range" (Figure 10.35), you need to set your resolution back to something that works for your video card/monitor combination!

Troubleshooting Monitors

Because of the inherent dangers of the high-frequency and high-voltage power required by monitors, and because proper adjustment requires specialized training, this section concentrates on giving a support person the information necessary to decide whether a trouble call is warranted. Virtually no monitor manufacturers make schematics of their monitors available to the public because of liability issues regarding possible electrocution. To simplify troubleshooting, look at the process as three separate parts: common monitor problems, external adjustments, and internal adjustments.

Common Monitor Problems

Although I'm not super comfortable diving into the guts of a monitor, you can fix a substantial percentage of monitor problems yourself. The following list describes the most common monitor problems and tells you what to do—even when that means sending it to someone else.

- Almost all CRT and LCD monitors have replaceable controls. If the Brightness knob or Menu button stops working or seems loose, check with the manufacturer for replacement controls. They usually come as a complete package.

- For problems with ghosting, streaking, and/or fuzzy vertical edges, check the cable connections and the cable itself. These problems rarely apply to monitors; more commonly, they point to the video card.

- If one color is missing, check cables for breaks or bent pins. Check the front controls for that color. If the color adjustment is already maxed out, the monitor will require internal service.

- As monitors age, they lose brightness. If the brightness control is turned all of the way up and the picture seems dim, the monitor will require internal adjustment. This is a good argument for power-management functions. Use the power switch or the power-management options in Windows to turn off the monitor after a certain amount of time.

Common Problems Specific to CRTs

The complexity of CRTs compared to LCDs requires us to look at a number of monitor problems unique to CRTs. Most of these problems require opening the monitor, so be careful! When in doubt, take it to a repair shop.

- Most out-of-focus monitors can be fixed. Focus adjustments are usually on the inside, somewhere close to the flyback transformer. This is the transformer that provides power to the high-voltage anode.

- Hissing or sparking sounds are often indicative of an insulation rupture on the flyback transformer. This sound is usually accompanied by the smell of ozone. If your monitor has these symptoms, it definitely needs a qualified technician. Having replaced a flyback transformer once myself, I can say it is not worth the hassle and potential loss of life and limb.

- Big color blotches on the display are an easy and cheap repair. Find the Degauss button and use it. If your monitor doesn't have a Degauss button, you can purchase a special tool called a degaussing coil at any electronics store.

- Bird-like chirping sounds occurring at regular intervals usually indicate a problem with the monitor's power supply.

- Suppose you got a good deal on a used 19-inch monitor, but the display is kind of dark, even though you have the brightness turned up all the way. This points to a dying CRT. So, how about replacing the CRT? Forget it. Even if the monitor was free, it just isn't worth it; a replacement tube runs into the hundreds of dollars. Nobody ever sold a monitor because it was too bright and too sharp. Save your money and buy a new monitor.

- If the monitor displays only a single horizontal or vertical line, the problem is probably between the main circuit board and the yoke, or a blown yoke coil. This definitely requires a service call.

- A single white dot on an otherwise black screen means the high-voltage flyback transformer is most likely shot. Take it into the repair shop.

External Adjustments

Monitor adjustments range from the simplest—brightness and contrast—to the more sophisticated—pincushioning and trapezoidal adjustments. The external controls provide users with the opportunity to fine-tune the monitor's image. Many monitors have controls for changing the tint and saturation of color, although plenty of monitors put those controls inside the monitor. Better monitors enable you to square up the visible portion of the screen with the monitor housing.

Finally, most monitors have the ability to degauss themselves with the push of a button. Over time, the shadow mask picks up a weak magnetic charge that interferes with the focus of the electron beams. This magnetic field makes the image look slightly fuzzy and streaked. Most monitors have a special built-in circuit called a *degaussing coil* to eliminate this magnetic buildup. When the degaussing circuit is used, an alternating current is sent through a coil of wire surrounding the CRT, and this current generates an alternating magnetic field that demagnetizes the shadow mask. You activate the degaussing coil by using the Degauss button or menu selection on the monitor. Degaussing usually makes a rather nasty thunk sound and the screen goes crazy for a moment—don't worry, that's normal. Whenever a user calls me with a fuzzy monitor problem, I always have them degauss first.

Troubleshooting CRTs

As shipped, most monitors do not produce an image out to the limits of the screen because of poor convergence at the outer display edges. Convergence defines how closely the red, green, and blue colors can meet at a single point on the display. At the point of convergence, the three colors combine to form a single white dot. With misconvergence, a noticeable halo of one or more colors appears around the outside of the white point. The farther away the colors are from the center of the screen, the more likely the chance for misconvergence. Low-end monitors are especially susceptible to this problem. Even though adjusting the convergence of a monitor is not difficult, it does require getting inside the monitor case and having a copy of the schematic, which shows the location of the variable resistors. For this reason, it is a good idea to leave this adjustment to a trained specialist.

I don't like opening a CRT monitor. I avoid doing this for two reasons: (1) I know very little about electronic circuits, and (2) I once almost electrocuted myself. At any rate, the CompTIA A+ Practical Application exam expects you to have a passing understanding of adjustments you might need to perform inside a monitor. Before we go any further, let me remind you about a little issue with CRT monitors (see Figure 10.36).

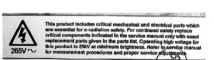

The CRT monitor contains a wire called a **high-voltage anode,** covered with a suction cup. If you lift that suction cup, you will almost certainly be seriously electrocuted. The anode wire leads to the flyback transformer and produces up to 25,000 volts. Don't worry about what they do; just worry about what they can do to *you!* That charge is stored in a capacitor, which holds that charge even if the monitor is turned off. It will hold the charge even if the monitor is unplugged. That capacitor (depending on the system) can hold a charge for days, weeks, months, or even years. Knowing this, you should learn how to discharge a CRT.

• **Figure 10.36** Hey! That's 25,000 volts! *Be careful!*

Discharging a CRT There are 75,000 opinions on how to discharge a CRT properly. Although my procedure may not follow the steps outlined in someone's official handbook on electrical code, I know this works. Read the rules, and then look at Figure 10.37.

1. Make sure everything is unplugged.

2. If possible, let the monitor sit for a couple of hours. Most good monitors discharge themselves in two to three hours, and many new monitors discharge in just a few moments.

3. Get a heavy, well-insulated, flat-head screwdriver.

4. Get a heavy-gauge wire with alligator clips on each end.

5. Do not let yourself be grounded in any way. Wear rubber-soled shoes, and no rings or watches.

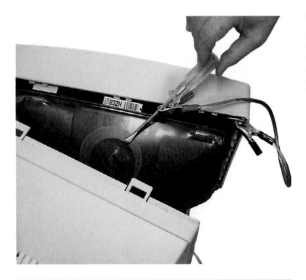

• **Figure 10.37** Discharging a CRT

6. Wear safety goggles to protect yourself in the very rare case that the CRT implodes.

7. Remove the monitor's case. Remember where the screw went in.

8. Attach one alligator clip to an unpainted part of the metal frame of the monitor.

9. Clip the other clip to the metal shaft of the screwdriver.

10. Slide the screwdriver blade under the suction cup. Make triple-sure that neither you nor the screwdriver is in any incidental contact with anything metal.

11. Slide the blade under until you hear a loud pop—you'll also see a nice blue flash.

12. If anyone is in the building, they will hear the pop and come running. Tell them everything's okay.

13. Wait about 15 minutes and repeat.

The main controls that require you to remove the monitor case to make adjustments include those for convergence, gain for each of the color guns, and sometimes the focus control. A technician with either informal or formal training in component-level repair can usually figure out which controls do what. In some cases, you can also readily spot and repair bad solder connections inside the monitor case and thus fix a dead or dying CRT. Still, balance the cost of repairing the monitor against the cost of death or serious injury—is it worth it? Finally, before making adjustments to the display image, especially with the internal controls, give the monitor at least 15 to 30 minutes of warm-up time. This is necessary both for the components on the printed circuit boards and for the CRT itself.

Troubleshooting LCDs

With the proliferation of LCD panels in the computing world, PC techs need to have some understanding of what to do when they break. Some of the components you can fix, including replacing some of the internal components. I tend to use monitor repair shops for most LCD issues, but let's take a look.

An LCD monitor may have bad pixels. A bad pixel is any single pixel that does not react the way it should. A pixel that never lights up is a dead pixel, a pixel that is stuck on pure white is a lit pixel, and a pixel on a certain color is a stuck pixel. You cannot repair bad pixels; the panel must be replaced. All LCD panel makers allow a certain number of bad pixels, even on a brand-new LCD monitor! You need to check the warranty for your monitor and see how many they allow before you may return the monitor.

- If your LCD monitor cracks, it is not repairable and must be replaced.

- If the LCD goes dark but you can still barely see the image under bright lights, you lost either the lamp or the inverter. In many cases, especially with super-thin panels, you'll replace the entire panel and lamp as a unit. On the other hand, an inverter can be on a separate circuit board that you can replace, such as the one pictured in Figure 10.38.

- If your LCD makes a distinct hissing noise, an inverter is about to fail. Again, you can replace the inverter if need be.

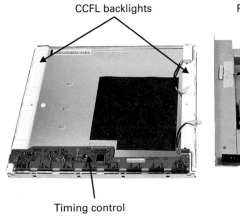

CCFL backlights

Timing control

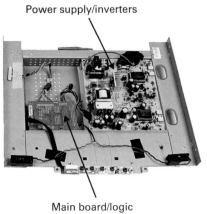

Power supply/inverters

Main board/logic

● **Figure 10.38** LCD components labeled

Be careful if you open an LCD to work on the inside. ~~The inverter can bite you in several ways. First, it's powered by a high-voltage electrical circuit that can give you a nasty shock.~~ Worse, the inverter will retain a charge for a few minutes after you unplug it, so unplug and wait for a bit. Second, inverters get very hot and present a very real danger of burning you at a touch. Again, wait for a while after you unplug it to try to replace. Finally, if you shock an inverter, you might irreparably damage it. So use proper ESD-avoidance techniques.

Bottom line on fixing LCD monitors? You can find companies that sell replacement parts for LCDs, but repairing an LCD is difficult, and there are folks who will do it for you faster and cheaper than you can. Search for a specialty LCD repair company. Hundreds of these companies exist all over the world.

Cleaning Monitors

Cleaning monitors is easy. ~~Always use anti-static monitor wipes or at least a general anti-static cloth.~~ Some LCD monitors may require special cleaning equipment. Never use window cleaners that contain ammonia or any liquid, because getting liquid into the monitor may create a shocking experience! Many commercial cleaning solutions will also melt older LCD screens, which is never a good thing.

Troubleshooting Sound

The problems you'll run into with sound seem to fall into one of two camps: those that are embarrassingly simple to repair and those that defy any possible logic and are seemingly impossible to fix. This section divides sound problems into three groups—hardware, configuration, and application problems—and gives you some ideas on how to fix these problems.

Hardware Problems

Hardware problems are by far the most common sound problems, especially if your sound card has worked for some amount of time already. Properly installed and configured sound cards almost never suddenly stop making sounds.

Volume ~~The absolute first item to check when a sound dies is the volume controls.~~ Remember that you can set the volume in two places: in software and on the speakers. I can't tell you the number of times I've lost sound only to discover that my wife turned down the volume on the speakers. If the speaker volume is okay, open the volume controls in Windows by clicking the little speaker icon on the system tray, and make sure that both the master volume and the volume of the other controls are turned up (Figure 10.39).

If your system tray (i.e., the *notification area*) is cluttered and the little speaker icon hard to find, you can access the Play Control dialog box by opening the Sounds and Audio Devices applet in the Control Panel. On the Volume tab—the one that's on top by default—click the Advanced button under Device volume.

If you don't have a little speaker in your system tray at all in Windows XP, you can add it. Just check the box next to the *Place volume icon in the taskbar* option in the Sounds and Audio Devices Properties dialog box, Volume tab. Presto!

Speakers   The second place to look for sound problems is the speakers. Make sure the speakers are turned on and are getting good power. Then make sure the speakers are plugged into the proper connection on the back of the sound card. If this all checks out, try playing a sound, using any sound program. If the sound program *looks* like it is playing—maybe the application has an equalizer that is moving or a status marker that shows that the application is playing the sound— you may have blown speakers. Try another pair and see if the sound returns.

Configuration Problems

Configuration errors occur when the sound card is physically good but some setting hasn't been properly configured. I also include driver problems in this category. These errors happen almost exclusively at installation, but they can appear on a working system too.

The first place to check is the Device Manager. If the driver has a problem, you'll see it right there. Try reinstalling the driver. If the driver doesn't show any problems, again try playing a sound and see if the player acts as though the sound is playing. If that's the case, you need to start touring the Sound applet or Sounds and Audio Devices applet to see if you've made a configuration error—perhaps you have the system configured for 5.1 when you have a stereo setup, or maybe you set the default sound output device to some other device. Take your time and look—configuration errors always show themselves.

Application Problems

Application problems are always the hardest to fix and tend to occur on a system that was previously playing sounds without trouble.

First, look for an error message (Figure 10.40). If an error code appears, write it down *exactly* as you see it and head to the program's support site. Odds are very good that if you have the error text, you'll get the fix right away from the support site. Of course, you can always hope the built-in help has some support, but help systems tend to be a little light in providing real fixes.

Don't always blame the sound application—remember that any sound file might be corrupted. Most sound players will display a clear error message, but not always. Try playing the sound file with a different application.

Last, a good approach almost always is to reinstall the application.

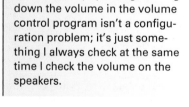

• **Figure 10.39**   Volume controls in Windows XP

> **Tech Tip**
>
> **Sound Quality**
>
> *Most of the time, speakers come in a matched set—whether it's a 2.1, 4.1, 5.1, or other system—and the manufacturer includes adequate connecting wires for the whole set. On occasion, you might run into a system in which the user has connected pairs of speakers from different sets or rigged a surround-sound system by replacing the stock wires with much longer wires. Either option can create a perfectly functional surround-sound system that works for a specific room, but you should make sure that all the speakers require the same wattage and that high-quality wire is used to connect them.*
>
> *If you troubleshoot a system in which two of the speakers are very quiet and two are very loud, the wattages are probably different between the two pairs. A simple check of the labels should suffice to troubleshoot, or you can swap out one pair for a different pair and see if that affects the volume issues. Cheap wire, on the other hand, simply degrades the sound quality. If the speakers sounded good before being strung on long wires but they now have a lot of low-grade noise, blame the wires.*

Technically speaking, turning down the volume in the volume control program isn't a configuration problem; it's just something I always check at the same time I check the volume on the speakers.

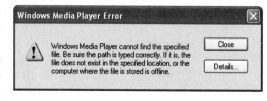

• **Figure 10.40**   Sample error message

Troubleshooting Video Capture

Video capture and playback suffer from several quirks. On the capture side, you'll find dropped frames, problems synchronizing video and audio when capturing content from an analog device, and generally poor-quality captures. On the playback side, the only real issue is missing codecs.

Dropped Frames

Many things cause an initial capture to drop frames, the end result of which is loss of video information and choppy playback. This happens with both analog and digital sources, so it's not necessarily a conversion issue, and it's maddeningly common.

The most common fix for dropped frames is to *turn stuff off*. Some of this is obvious. If you're surfing the Web or doing instant messaging while trying to capture video, you'll drop frames with wild abandon. Don't do it. In fact, disconnect the computer completely from the Internet so no traffic happens in the background. Only do video capture on that machine and use another computer if you need to multitask.

Often the viewing of content you're capturing—while in the capture process—causes dropped frames. Best practice is to know what you're importing, turn off the playback or preview feature, and then start the capture. But the obvious programs aren't necessarily the primary cause of dropped frames.

Windows is a wildly extensible operating system, and programmers love to dump helper applications to run in the background to optimize their specific application. Install Apple's iTunes, for example, and you'll get more than you bargained for in programs installed. To go along with the iTunes player, the installation puts in automatic update-checking tools, iPod helpers, a quick-launch for QuickTime, and more.

The best solution is to have a machine dedicated to video capture. If you have a machine with multiple functions, however, you can turn off some of the automatically loading helper applications before you start the video capture process. You do this by stopping processes and services through the Task Manager.

In Windows Vista, get to the Task Manager by pressing CTRL + SHIFT + ESC or by pressing CTRL + ALT + DELETE and clicking the Start Task Manager option. The Processes tab shows your running processes. You can right-click any unnecessary process and close it by selecting *End process* or *End process tree* from the context menu (Figure 10.41). I generally go for the latter option, just in case some other process is running only because of the unnecessary process. That gets them all.

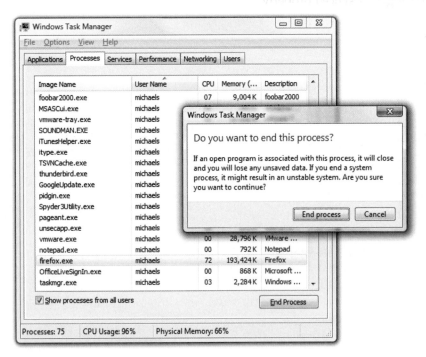

• **Figure 10.41**   Ending a process

Once you've stopped processes, click over to the Services tab. You can quickly see what's running, by sorting services by status. Just click the Status column heading to sort. Right-click any unnecessary service and select Stop Service from the context menu (Figure 10.42). Couldn't be easier!

If you find you've stopped a necessary service, you can simply right-click it again and select Start Service from the context menu. Or, if the system has become unstable, a simple reboot will reload everything.

Sync Problems

Capturing a video and audio stream simultaneously can be tough, because it takes the computer a lot longer to encode the video than the audio stream. This can lead to significant disconnection between the video and audio streams so they become desynchronized. It's surprisingly easy to create a movie that's very badly lip-synced! The process of synchronizing audio and video is called A/V sync.

You can fix this problem sometimes by changing software or even versions of software. Alternatively, if you're having problems with an analog capture, you can record the analog signal into a digital video camcorder and then try to capture from the digital device. A bit clunky, perhaps, but it can work. Finally, you do the last solution in processing, where you manually separate the audio and video streams and then put the whole thing back together synced properly.

Dealing with video capture can be difficult and time consuming, especially in the analog-to-digital process. A good resource to start learning the detailed ins and outs is with the folks at the Digital FAQ: www.digitalfaq.com.

Poor Capture Quality

Numerous factors can degrade the quality of a video capture, including background programs, marginal hardware for the job, and poor-quality source materials. For the background program issue, follow the same procedures as you did earlier with the dropped frames. If the computer or the capture components can't do the job, the only fix is to upgrade. The best things to upgrade are the capture hardware and the CPU. It goes almost without saying that you'll need gobs of RAM, too.

There's very little you can do if your source material, such as an old video cassette, has degraded. You're simply not going to get a pristine capture from a damaged source. You can sometimes get better quality by having the heads on the camcorder or player cleaned or by using the camcorder on which the tape was initially recorded.

Missing Codecs

All versions of Windows come with some audio and video codecs installed. The default audio codecs will handle most common music formats, though

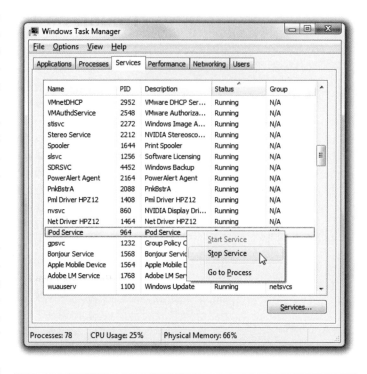

● **Figure 10.42** Stopping a service

You can disable services in the Services applet in Administrative Tools, but it's usually better to stop a service first through Task Manager, just to see if it's truly unnecessary for system stability or function.

There's also a common problem of video and audio going out of sync in the process of burning from a hard drive to a DVD, but that's a distinctly different problem than a lack of A/V sync in the capture process.

A dedicated A/V computer should have a fast processor and a lot of RAM. You'll want plenty of hard drive storage space too.

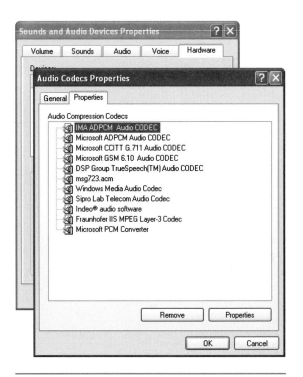

● **Figure 10.43** Default audio codecs in Windows XP SP2

you'll need to download the Vorbis codec if you want to use that format. Video codecs are a different animal.

The first clue you might have that your computer doesn't have the codec to process a video file properly is that the sound will play but no picture will appear. Occasionally, whatever media player you use will tell you that it's missing a video codec and attempt to go out onto the Internet to download a codec automatically. You can also download a codec or set of codecs manually.

Windows XP makes it easy to see the installed codecs. In Control Panel, open the Sounds and Audio Devices applet. Select the Hardware tab | Audio Codecs and click the Properties button. In the Audio Codec Properties dialog box, select the Properties tab and you'll see all the installed audio codecs (Figure 10.43).

Similarly, you can see the video codecs by choosing the Video Codecs option on the Hardware tab. Click through to the Properties tab. Figure 10.44 shows the default video codecs in Windows XP.

Microsoft made the codecs a bit more difficult to find in Windows Vista. In Vista, open Windows Media Player. Press CTRL-M to show the classic menus. Select Help | About Windows Media Player to open the About Windows Media Player dialog box (Figure 10.45).

Click the link for Technical Support Information and Windows will open your default Web browser with a long page showing various multimedia settings. Scroll down the page and you'll find the audio and video codecs installed (Figure 10.46).

If you don't have a codec that you need, you can download that specific codec. A great site for codec information is www.fourcc.org.

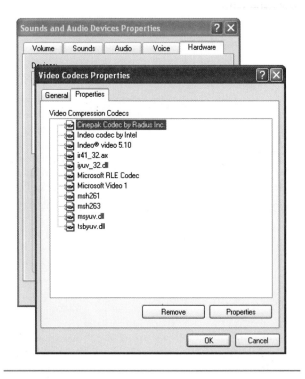

● **Figure 10.44** Default video codecs in Windows XP SP2

● **Figure 10.45** About Windows Media Player dialog box in Windows Vista

You can also download codec packs, such as the Vista Codec Package available at www.afreecodec.com. The packs contain just about everything you need to view and hear content found on the Internet.

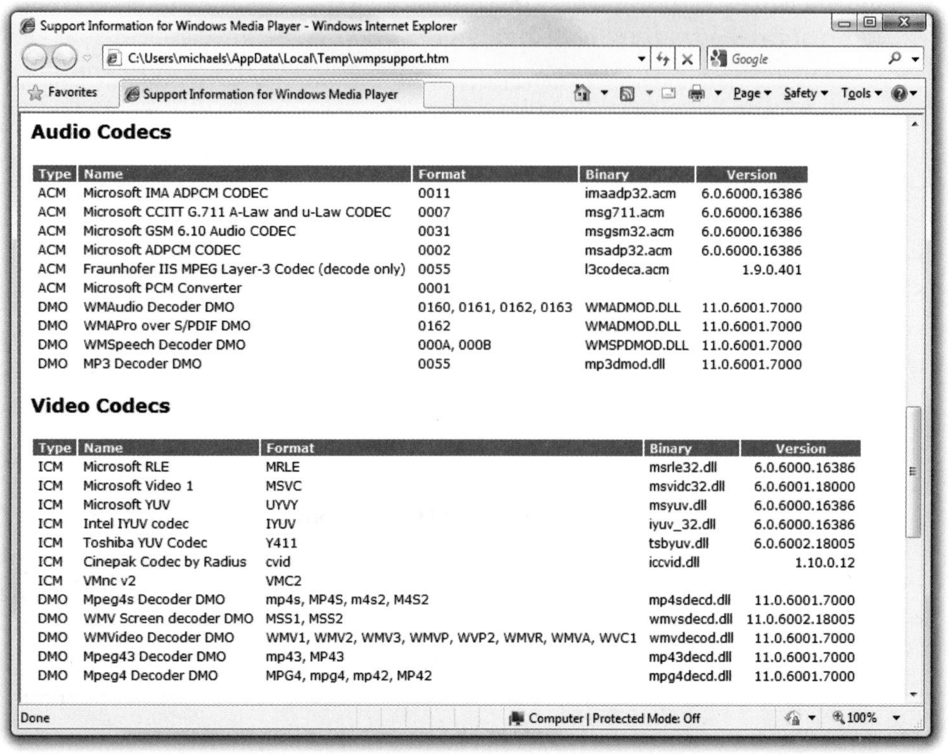

Audio Codecs

Type	Name	Format	Binary	Version
ACM	Microsoft IMA ADPCM CODEC	0011	imaadp32.acm	6.0.6000.16386
ACM	Microsoft CCITT G.711 A-Law and u-Law CODEC	0007	msg711.acm	6.0.6000.16386
ACM	Microsoft GSM 6.10 Audio CODEC	0031	msgsm32.acm	6.0.6000.16386
ACM	Microsoft ADPCM CODEC	0002	msadp32.acm	6.0.6000.16386
ACM	Fraunhofer IIS MPEG Layer-3 Codec (decode only)	0055	l3codeca.acm	1.9.0.401
ACM	Microsoft PCM Converter	0001		
DMO	WMAudio Decoder DMO	0160, 0161, 0162, 0163	WMADMOD.DLL	11.0.6001.7000
DMO	WMAPro over S/PDIF DMO	0162	WMADMOD.DLL	11.0.6001.7000
DMO	WMSpeech Decoder DMO	000A, 000B	WMSPDMOD.DLL	11.0.6001.7000
DMO	MP3 Decoder DMO	0055	mp3dmod.dll	11.0.6001.7000

Video Codecs

Type	Name	Format	Binary	Version
ICM	Microsoft RLE	MRLE	msrle32.dll	6.0.6000.16386
ICM	Microsoft Video 1	MSVC	msvidc32.dll	6.0.6001.18000
ICM	Microsoft YUV	UYVY	msyuv.dll	6.0.6000.16386
ICM	Intel IYUV codec	IYUV	iyuv_32.dll	6.0.6000.16386
ICM	Toshiba YUV Codec	Y411	tsbyuv.dll	6.0.6002.18005
ICM	Cinepak Codec by Radius	cvid	iccvid.dll	1.10.0.12
ICM	VMnc v2	VMC2		
DMO	Mpeg4s Decoder DMO	mp4s, MP4S, m4s2, M4S2	mp4sdecd.dll	11.0.6001.7000
DMO	WMV Screen decoder DMO	MSS1, MSS2	wmvsdecd.dll	11.0.6002.18005
DMO	WMVideo Decoder DMO	WMV1, WMV2, WMV3, WMVP, WVP2, WMVR, WMVA, WVC1	wmvdecod.dll	11.0.6001.7000
DMO	Mpeg43 Decoder DMO	mp43, MP43	mp43decd.dll	11.0.6001.7000
DMO	Mpeg4 Decoder DMO	MPG4, mpg4, mp42, MP42	mpg4decd.dll	11.0.6001.7000

• **Figure 10.46** Viewing audio and video codecs installed in Windows Vista

Tuner Troubleshooting

The two biggest issues with TV tuner devices are operating system compatibility and poor reception. Some cards simply don't work with Windows Vista, due to driver incompatibility or some other issue. The only fix for this problem is to use one that does work.

The antenna that comes with your tuner should enable you to pick up TV broadcasts in most places, certainly around cities. But a small sliver of metal can only do so well, so you'll experience stuttering, essentially lost frames that may or may not make the program you're viewing viewable. So an antenna used primarily for portable computing is great, but if you install a tuner in a static computer, consider investing in a proper outdoor antenna.

Beyond A+

Video and CMOS

I'm always impressed by the number of video options provided in CMOS, especially in some of the more advanced CMOS options. I'm equally impressed by the amount of disinformation provided on these settings. In this section, I'll touch on some of the most common CMOS settings that deal with video. You may notice that no power-management video options have been included.

Video

Every standard CMOS setup shows an option for video support. The default setting is invariably EGA/VGA. Many years ago, this setting told the BIOS what type of card was installed on the system, enabling it to know how to talk to that card. Today, this setting has no meaning. No matter what you put there, the system will ignore it and boot normally.

Init Display First

This CMOS setting usually resides in an advanced options or BIOS options screen. In multi-monitor systems, Init Display First enables you to decide between PCIe and PCI as to which monitor initializes at boot. This also determines the initial primary monitor for Windows.

Assign IRQ for VGA

Many video cards do not need an **interrupt request (IRQ)**. This option gives you the ability to choose whether your video card gets an IRQ. In general, lower-end cards that do not provide input to the system do not need an IRQ. Most advanced cards will need one; try it both ways. If you need it, your system will freeze up without an IRQ assigned. If you don't need it, you get an extra IRQ.

VGA Palette Snoop

True-VGA devices only show 16 out of a possible 262,000 colors at a time. The 16 current colors are called the *palette*. VGA Palette Snoop opens a video card's palette to other devices that may need to read or temporarily change the palette. I am unaware of any device made today that still needs this option.

Video Shadowing Enabled

As mentioned in previous chapters, this setting enables you to shadow the Video ROM. In most cases, this option is ignored as today's video cards perform their own automatic shadowing. A few cards require this setting to be off, so I generally leave it off now, after years of leaving it on.

Other Display Technologies

A few other screen technologies exist, but not so much for computer monitors. Plasma and DLP screens grace many a household's media room as the primary television display.

Plasma

Plasma display panels (*PDPs*) are a very popular technology for displaying movies. Unfortunately, plasma TVs have two issues that make them a bad choice for PC use. First, they have strange native resolutions (such as 1366 × 768) that are hard to get your video card to accept. Second is *burn-in*—the tendency for a screen to "ghost" an image even after the image is off the screen. Plasma TV makers have virtually eliminated burn-in, but even the latest plasma displays are subject to burn-in when used with PC displays.

DLP

Digital Light Processing (*DLP*) displays use a chip covered in microscopically small mirrors (Figure 10.47).

These individual mirrors move thousands of times per second toward and away from a light source. The more times per second they move toward a light source, the whiter the image; the fewer times they move, the grayer the image. See Figure 10.48 for a diagram of how the mirrors would appear in a microscopic close-up of the chip.

• **Figure 10.47**   DLP chip (*photo courtesy of Texas Instruments*)

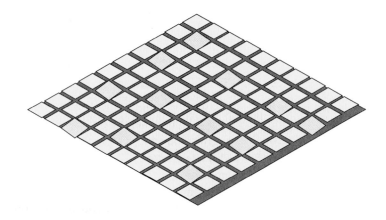

• **Figure 10.48**   Microscopic close-up of DLP showing tiny mirrors—note that some are tilted.

Figure 10.49 shows a diagram of a typical DLP system. The lamp projects through a color wheel onto the DLP chip. The DLP chip creates the image by moving the tiny mirrors, which in turn reflect onto the screen.

DLP was very popular for a time in home theater systems, as it makes an amazingly rich image. DLP has had very little impact on PC monitors but has had great success for projectors. DLP projectors are much more expensive than LCD projectors, but many customers feel the extra expense is worth the image quality.

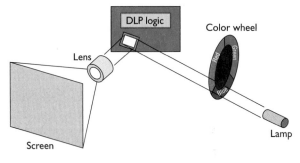

• **Figure 10.49**   DLP in action

Sound Card Benchmarking

Sound cards can demand a huge share of system resources—particularly CPU time—during intense work (such as gaming). Most techs who find an otherwise serviceable PC stuttering during games will immediately blame the video card or the video card drivers. What they don't realize is that sound cards can be the cause of the problem. A test of a client's built-in audio, for example, revealed that at peak usage the sound card took more than 30 percent of the CPU cycles. Thirty percent? Holy smokes! And he wondered why his system bogged down on yesterday's games! He could just forget about playing Crysis.

The folks at http://audio.rightmark.org make an excellent suite of sound card benchmarking utilities that helps you analyze the particulars of any sound card: RightMark 3DSound (Figure 10.50). It will run a system through fairly serious tests, from regular sound to 3-D positional audio, and reveal whether or not the sound processor—built-in or expansion card—is causing a problem with resource use. You can find the utility at http://audio.rightmark.org.

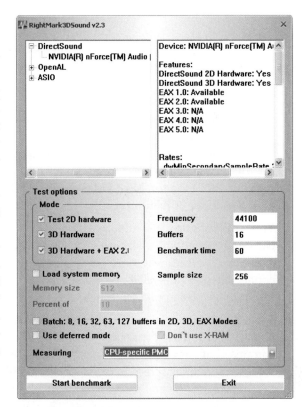

• **Figure 10.50**   RightMark 3DSound

Chapter 10: Mastering Video and Multimedia

■ Chapter Summary

After reading this chapter and completing the exercises, you should understand the following about video and multimedia.

Install and configure video

■ During the physical install of a video card, be conscious of long cards and proximity to other PCI cards. Long cards simply don't fit in some cases, and close proximity to other expansion cards can cause overheating.

■ Video card drivers install pretty much the same as all other drivers: either the driver is already built into Windows or you must use the installation CD that comes with the video card.

■ As a basic rule, always uninstall an old video card's drivers before you install drivers for a new card.

■ The Display applet (Windows 2000/XP) in the Control Panel or Personalization applet (Windows Vista/7) provides a convenient central location for adjusting all of your display settings, including resolution, refresh rate, driver information, and color depth. The Screen Saver tab provides access to the power-management settings. The Settings tab provides access for configuring all of your video settings, such as resolution, color depth, and dual monitor configuration. The Settings tab also provides an Advanced button for access to the Monitor and Adapter tabs. The Adapter tab displays information about your video adapter and the Monitor tab allows you to set the refresh rate for your CRT monitor. Most video cards add their own tabs to the Advanced section.

■ You can configure dual monitors by using a video card with two monitor connectors or by using two video cards. Either way, once both monitors are connected, you can enable the second monitor from the Display applet's Settings tab.

■ Early 3-D games used sprites to create a 3-D world. Later games replaced sprites with true 3-D objects composed of vertices. Bitmap textures are used to tile a section of the screen to provide a surface in the 3-D world.

■ Video cards use a series of APIs to translate instructions for the video device driver. If you were to picture the graphics system of your computer as a layer cake, the top layer would be the program making a call to the graphics hardware. The next layer is the API. The device driver comes next, and way down at the base of the cake is the actual graphics hardware: RAM, graphics processor, and RAMDAC. OpenGL and DirectX are the most popular APIs.

■ DirectX includes several subsets, including DirectDraw, Direct3D, DirectInput, DirectSound, DirectMusic, DirectPlay, and DirectShow. You can verify your DirectX installation via the DirectX Diagnostics Tool found under the Tools menu of the System Information utility.

Describe how to implement sound in a PC

■ Sound card installation can be divided into three major steps: physical installation, device driver installation, and configuration.

■ Although the physical installation of a sound card is straightforward, knowing where to plug in multiple speakers can be a bit of a challenge.

■ It is preferable to use the driver that comes with the sound card as opposed to the Windows built-in drivers.

■ Look for configuration programs in the Control Panel applet for audio, such as the Sounds and Audio Devices applet in Windows XP, and in any proprietary applications that are installed with the sound card.

Troubleshoot multimedia problems

■ Video problems may be divided into two categories: video cards/drivers and monitors.

■ If your screen is black or garbled, or if Windows freezes after you install a video card driver, reboot into Safe mode and roll back or delete the driver. Check Add or Remove Programs first, as many video card drivers show up there. If Safe mode doesn't fix the problem, you may have a bad video card that needs to be replaced.

■ All monitors have replaceable hardware controls (knobs and buttons). Check with the manufacturer for replacement parts. Ghosting, streaking, or fuzzy images may mean a bad or improperly connected video cable, or the video card may be the cause.

- Because monitors have high-voltage power that can harm or kill you, always leave it to the trained professional to work inside the monitor. Monitor troubleshooting falls into two categories: external and internal adjustments.

- Many CRT monitors have a button to degauss themselves. When the shadow mask picks up a weak magnetic charge, it interferes with the focus of the electron beams, making the monitor appear fuzzy or streaked. A built-in circuit called a degaussing coil generates an alternating magnetic field that eliminates the magnetic buildup on the shadow mask.

- Convergence defines how closely the red, green, and blue colors meet at a single point on the display. With misconvergence, one or more of the colors appear to have a halo outside the white point, with the problem more severe toward the outside of the screen.

- Clean CRT monitors with an anti-static monitor wipe. Never use window cleaners or other liquids. LCD monitors need special cleaning equipment or a soft, damp cloth.

- Common monitor problems are often related to cable breaks or bent pins. Monitors also lose brightness over time, especially if you are not using the power-management functions.

- For best performance, keep the screen clean and the cables tightened, use power management, don't block the ventilation slots or place magnetic objects close to the monitor, and don't leave the monitor on all of the time, even with a screensaver. If the monitor is dead, use proper disposal methods.

- A cracked LCD monitor must be replaced. If the LCD screen goes dark, starts to hiss, or develops bad pixels, it is best to either replace the monitor or find a company specializing in LCD repair.

- You can divide sound problems into three groups: hardware, configuration, and application problems. The two first places to check when you suspect a hardware problem are the volume controls and speaker connectivity. Configuration errors almost always take place at installation of the sound card. Application problems are often the most challenging of all sound problems. Your best hope is an error message; you can then check the program's Web site for help.

- Troubleshooting video capture generally falls into three categories: dropped frames, synchronization problems with audio and video, and general picture quality issues. The simplest solution for dropped frames is to turn off any unnecessary program running, including processes and services. Sync problems generally require better software or additional hardware to solve. Poor-quality captures can be helped with better equipment or turning off unnecessary programs, though a poor-quality source cannot be overcome.

- If you're missing a codec to play a video, you can download codec packs from a variety of sources. The place to start is www.fourcc.org.

- About the only issues you'll run into with tuner devices is software incompatibility (older cards, for example, might not have drivers for Windows Vista or Windows 7, or for any 64-bit operating system) and poor source. A small antenna simply can't capture the same quality or quantity of signal that a large, multi-tined traditional outdoor antenna can get.

■ Key Terms

3-D graphics *(319)*	**graphics processing unit (GPU)** *(321)*
A/V sync *(337)*	**high-voltage anode** *(332)*
application programming interface (API) *(321)*	**interrupt request (IRQ)** *(340)*
autosensing *(328)*	**OpenGL** *(322)*
convergence *(332)*	**Personalization applet** *(312)*
degauss *(331)*	**polygons** *(321)*
DirectX *(322)*	**sprite** *(320)*
Display applet *(312)*	**texture** *(321)*
DualView *(316)*	**vertices** *(320)*

Key Term Quiz

Use the Key Terms list to complete the sentences that follow. Not all terms will be used.

1. Better sound cards that can detect a device plugged into a port and adapt the features of that port are called *autosensing* sound cards.

2. DirectX is a(n) _*API*_, one of a number of programs that translate instructions for the video device driver.

3. The term that defines how closely the red, green, and blue colors meet at a single point on the display is *Convergence*.

4. A 3-D model is made up of individual points called *vertics*.

5. The direct competitor to DirectX for the GPU API crown is *OpenGL*.

6. The *Personalization applet* in Windows Vista enables you to change the color and transparency of your window borders.

7. You should never open up a CRT monitor, because there's a(n) *high-voltage anode* that can kill you if you're not careful.

Multiple-Choice Quiz

1. If one of the colors is missing on the monitor and you cannot fix the problem by adjusting the front controls, you should then check for _____.

   A. A refresh rate that is set higher than that recommended by the manufacturer

   B. A corrupted video driver

   C. A broken cable or bent pins

   D. Misconvergence

2. Which of the following problems would make it impossible to repair an LCD monitor?

   A. A blown yoke coil

   B. A broken LCD panel

   C. A bad flyback transformer

   D. Misconvergence

3. If the monitor displays only a single horizontal or vertical line, the problem is likely to be caused by a _____.

   A. Bad flyback transformer

   B. Blown yoke coil

   C. Bad monitor power supply

   D. Bad electron gun

4. Only specially trained technicians should work inside a monitor because the _____ produces over 25,000 V that may harm or kill a person.

   A. Flyback transformer

   B. Yoke

   C. Anode

   D. Electron gun

5. What is the most popular API used by 3-D game developers?

   A. DirectX

   B. OpenGL

   C. DigitalDirector

   D. RAMDAC

6. Jane's sound card is suddenly not making any sound. She suspects that the volume is turned down. She checks the speaker volume and sees that it is turned up. What should she check next?

   A. The volume control program

   B. The application

   C. The speaker power

   D. The Device Manager

7. A Windows XP user calls in complaining that her monitor is too small. Upon further questioning, you find out that it's not the monitor that's small, but the font and icon size are too small! What would you do to help the user fix the problem?

   A. In the Control Panel, open the Display applet. Select the Settings tab and increase the screen resolution.

   B. In the Control Panel, open the Display applet. Select the Settings tab and decrease the screen resolution.

C. In the Control Panel, open the Monitor applet. Select the Settings tab and increase the screen resolution.

D. In the Control Panel, open the Monitor applet. Select the Settings tab and decrease the screen resolution.

8. The same user calls back almost immediately and complains that the icons and screen elements are bigger, but now everything is fuzzy. What's most likely the problem?

A. She has an LCD and set the resolution lower than the native resolution.

B. She has an LCD and set the resolution higher than the native resolution.

C. She has a CRT and set the resolution lower than the native resolution.

D. She has a CRT and set the resolution higher than the native resolution.

■ Essay Quiz

1. The editor of your company's newsletter has asked you to prepare a short article for next month's edition that explains how to care for monitors to extend their lifespan. Explain at least four things that the average user can do.

2. Dave and Shannon disagree about whether the monitor should stay on all of the time or not. Dave says it's okay to leave the monitor on as long as you have a screensaver. Shannon disagrees, saying the monitor will become dim and burn out sooner if you leave it on. Dave thinks that leaving it on actually extends its life because turning the monitor on and off is bad for it. They've called you to save their monitor and their marriage. What will you tell them?

3. Your clients have been having trouble with dropped frames on video capture. Write a memo describing the things they should check before calling for a technician.

Lab Projects

• Lab Project 10.1

Uninstall and reinstall the audio drivers on your system. First, check your sound card manufacturer's Web site for an updated driver. Reinstall, using the most recent driver you can find. Do any problems crop up during the process? After you get the new driver installed and working, do you notice an improvement in performance?

• Lab Project 10.2

If you've got a lab computer that you can work on, try uninstalling and reinstalling the video card. How well does the card fit inside your case? Do you have to remove any other components to get the card out? Does it still work correctly after reinstalling it?

chapter

11

Mastering Portable Computing

"*I work on a laptop specifically so I can work in cafes and pretend I'm part of the human world.*"

—JONATHAN LETHEM

In this chapter, you will learn how to

- ■ **Enhance and upgrade portable computers**
- ■ **Manage and maintain portable computers**
- ■ **Troubleshoot portable computers**

The era of the desktop PC has, for the most part, come and gone. Portable computers are now powerful enough, sophisticated enough, and, quite frankly, hip enough that no one wants to buy a boring old desktop anymore.

This is great for consumers, because laptops and other portable computing devices are incredibly convenient. However, as a tech, it means that you're tasked with upgrading and troubleshooting devices that are more difficult to work on and much, much more prone to failure than their desktop counterparts. Heat and physical wear and tear affect laptops much more than desktops, so you had better know how to fix them if you want to be a tech.

Enhancing and Upgrading Portable Computers

In the dark ages of mobile computing, you had to shell out top dollar for any device that would unplug, and what you purchased was what you got. Upgrade a laptop? Add functions to your desktop replacement? You had few if any options, so you simply paid for a device that would be way behind the technology curve within a year and functionally obsolete within two.

Portable PCs today offer many ways to enhance their capabilities. Internal and external expansion buses enable you to add completely new functions to portables, such as attaching a scanner or mobile printer or both. You can take advantage of the latest wireless technology breakthrough simply by slipping a card into the appropriate slot on the laptop. Further, modern portables offer a modular interior. You can add or change RAM, for example—the first upgrade that almost every laptop owner wants to make. You can increase the hard drive storage space and, at least with some models, swap out the CPU, video card, sound card, and more. Gone forever are the days of buying guaranteed obsolescence! Let's look at four specific areas of technology that laptops use to enhance functions and upgrade components: PC Cards, single- and multiple-function expansion ports, and modular components.

With fully 1 in 5 questions covering laptops and portables, pay attention to this chapter when studying for the CompTIA A+ certification!

PC Cards

The *Personal Computer Memory Card International Association* (*PCMCIA*) establishes standards involving portable computers, especially when it comes to expansion cards, which are generically called PC Cards. PC Cards are roughly credit-card-sized devices that enhance and extend the functions of a portable PC. PC Cards are as standard on today's mobile computers as the hard drive. PC Cards are easy to use, inexpensive, and convenient. Figure 11.1 shows a typical PC Card.

Almost every portable PC has one or two PC Card slots, into which you insert a PC Card. Each card has at least one function, but many have two, three, or more! You can buy a PC Card that offers connections for removable

CompTIA uses the older term *PCMCIA cards* to describe PC Cards. Don't be shocked if you get that as an option on your exam! You'll hear many techs use the phrase as well, though the PCMCIA trade group has not used it for many years.

Many manufacturers use the term *hot-pluggable* rather than hot-swappable to describe the ability to plug in and replace PC Cards on the fly. Look for either term on the exam.

• **Figure 11.1** PC Card

media, for example, such as combination SD and CF card readers. You can also find PC Cards that enable you to plug into multiple types of networks. All PC Cards are hot-swappable, meaning you can plug them in without powering down the PC.

The PCMCIA has established two versions of PC Cards, one using a parallel bus and the other using a serial bus. Each version, in turn, offers two technology variations as well as several physical varieties. This might sound complicated at first, but here's the map to sort it all out.

Parallel PC Cards

Parallel PC Cards come in two flavors, 16-bit and CardBus, and each flavor comes in three physical sizes, called Type I, Type II, and Type III. The 16-bit PC Cards, as the name suggests, are 16-bit 5-V cards that can have up to two distinct functions or devices, such as a modem/network card combination. CardBus PC Cards are 32-bit 3.3-V cards that can have up to eight (!) functions on a single card. Regular PC Cards fit into and work in CardBus slots, but the reverse is not true. CardBus totally dominates the current PC Card landscape, but you might still run into older 16-bit PC Cards.

Type I, II, and III cards differ only in the thickness of the card (Type I being the thinnest, and Type III the thickest). All PC Cards share the same 68-pin interface, so any PC Card will work in any slot that accepts that card type. Type II cards are by far the most common of PC Cards. Therefore, most laptops have two Type II slots, one above the other, so the computer can accept two Type I or II cards or one Type III card (Figure 11.2).

Although PCMCIA doesn't require that certain sizes perform certain functions, most PC Cards follow their recommendations. Table 11.1 lists the sizes and typical uses of each type of PC Card.

ExpressCard

ExpressCard, the high-performance serial version of the PC Card, has begun to replace PC Card slots on newer laptop PCs. Although ExpressCard offers significant performance benefits, keep in mind that ExpressCard and PC Cards are incompatible. You cannot use your PC Card in your new laptop's ExpressCard socket. The PC Card has had a remarkably long life in portable PCs, and you can still find it on some new laptops, but get ready to replace all of your PC Card devices. ExpressCard comes in two widths: 54 mm and 34 mm. Figure 11.3 shows a 34-mm and a 54-mm ExpressCard. Both cards are 75 mm long and 5 mm thick, which makes them shorter than all previous PC Cards and the same thickness as a Type II PC Card.

ExpressCards connect to either the Hi-Speed USB 2.0 bus or a PCI Express bus. These differ phenomenally in speed. The amazingly slow-in-comparison USB version has a maximum throughput of 480 Mbps. The PCIe version, in contrast, roars in at 2.5 Gbps in unidirectional communication. Very nice!

● **Figure 11.2**   PC Card slots

Table 11.1	PC Card Types and Their Typical Uses			
Type	**Length**	**Width**	**Thickness**	**Typical Use**
Type I	85.6 mm	54.0 mm	3.3 mm	Flash memory
Type II	85.6 mm	54.0 mm	5.0 mm	I/O (Modem, NIC, and so on)
Type III	85.6 mm	54.0 mm	10.5 mm	Hard drives

• **Figure 11.3**   34-mm and 54-mm ExpressCards

Table 11.2 shows the throughput and variations for the parallel and serial PC Cards currently or soon to be on the market.

Software Support for PC Cards

The PCMCIA standard defines two levels of software drivers to support PC Cards. The first and lower level is known as **socket services**. Socket services are device drivers that support the PC Card socket, enabling the system to detect when a PC Card has been inserted or removed, and providing the necessary I/O to the device. The second and higher level is known as **card services**. The card services level recognizes the function of a particular PC Card and provides the specialized drivers necessary to make the card work.

In today's laptops, the socket services are standardized and are handled by the system BIOS. Windows itself handles all card services and has a large preinstalled base of PC Card device drivers, although most PC Cards come with their own drivers.

Table 11.2	PC Card Speeds
Standard	**Maximum Theoretical Throughput**
PC Card using 16-bit bus	160 Mbps
CardBus PC Card using PCI bus	1056 Mbps
ExpressCard using USB 2.0 bus	480 Mbps
ExpressCard using PCIe bus	2.5 Gbps

ExpressCards don't require either socket or card services, at least not in the way PC Cards do. The ExpressCard modules automatically configure the software on your computer, which makes them truly plug and play.

Single-Function Ports

All portable PCs and many PDAs come with one or more ports. You'd have a hard time finding a portable computing device that doesn't have a speaker port, and this includes modern PDAs. My Apple iPhone functions as an excellent MP3 player, by the way, a feature now included with most PDAs and smartphones. Some portables have line-in and microphone jacks as well. Laptops invariably provide a video port such as a VGA or DVI connection for hooking up an external monitor and a PS/2 port for a keyboard or mouse. Finally, most current portable PCs come with built-in NICs or modems for networking support. (See the section on "The Modular Laptop" later in this chapter for more on networking capabilities.)

Ports work the same way on portable PCs as they do on desktop models. You plug in a device to a particular port and, as long as Windows has the proper drivers, you will have a functioning device when you boot. The only port that requires any extra effort is the video port.

Most laptops support a second monitor via an analog VGA port or a digital DVI, HDMI, or DisplayPort port in the back of the box. With a second monitor attached, you can display Windows on only the laptop LCD, only the external monitor, or both simultaneously. Not all portables can do all variations, but they're more common than not. Most portables have a special Function (FN) key on the keyboard that, when pressed, adds an additional option to certain keys on the keyboard. Figure 11.4 shows a close-up of a typical keyboard with the Function key; note the other options you can access with the Function key, such as indicated on the F2 key. To engage the second monitor or to cycle through the modes, hold the Function key and press F2.

• **Figure 11.4**   Laptop keyboard showing Function (FN) key that enables you to access additional key options, as on the F2 key

General-Purpose Ports

Laptops rarely come with all of the hardware you want. PC Cards/Express cards certainly help, but today's laptops usually include at least USB ports to give you the option to add more hardware. Some laptops still provide legacy general-purpose expansion ports (PS/2, RS-232 serial ports, and so on) for installing peripheral hardware. If you're lucky, you might even get a FireWire port so you can plug in your fancy new digital video camera. If you're really lucky, you will have a docking station or port replicator so you don't have to plug in all of your peripheral devices one at a time.

USB, FireWire, and eSATA

Universal serial bus (USB), FireWire (or more properly, IEEE 1394), and eSATA feature easy-to-use connectors and give users the ability to connect or insert a device into a system while the PC is running—you won't have to reboot a system to install a new peripheral. With USB, FireWire, and eSATA, just plug the device in and go! Because portable PCs don't have a desktop's multiple internal expansion capabilities, USB, FireWire, and eSATA are three of the more popular methods for attaching peripherals to laptops (see Figure 11.5).

Port Replicators

A **port replicator** plugs into a single port on the portable computer—often a USB port but sometimes a proprietary port—and offers common PC

• **Figure 11.5**   Devices attached to USB connectors on a portable PC

Mike Meyers' CompTIA A+ Guide: Practical Application

● **Figure 11.6**   Port replicator for a Dell portable computer

ports, such as serial, parallel, USB, network, and PS/2. By plugging the port replicator into your notebook computer, you can instantly connect the computer to nonportable components such as a printer, scanner, monitor, or full-sized keyboard. Port replicators are typically used at home or in the office with the nonportable equipment already connected. Figure 11.6 shows a Dell Inspiron laptop connected to a port replicator.

The computer can access any devices attached to the port replicator; you don't need to connect each individual device to the PC. As a side bonus, port replicators enable you to attach legacy devices, such as parallel printers, to a new laptop that only has modern multifunction ports such as USB and FireWire and not parallel or serial ports.

Although portable PCs most often connect to port replicators via USB ports, some manufacturers have proprietary connections for proprietary port replicators. As long as such a portable PC has a USB port, you can use either the proprietary hardware or the more flexible USB devices.

Docking Stations

A **docking station** resembles a port replicator in many ways, offering legacy and modern single- and multifunction ports (see Figure 11.7). The typical docking station uses a proprietary connection but has extra features built in, such as a DVD drive or PC Card slot for extra enhancements. You can find docking stations for most laptop models, but you'll find them used most frequently with the desktop extenders. A docking station makes an excellent companion to such portables.

● **Figure 11.7**   Docking station

The Modular Laptop

For years, portable PC makers required completely proprietary components for each system model they developed. For the most part, this proprietary attitude prevails, but manufacturers have added some modularity to today's portable PCs so you can make basic replacements and upgrades without going back to the manufacturer for expensive proprietary components. You need to surf the Web for companies that sell the components, because very few storefronts stock them. The most common modular components are RAM, hard drives, CPUs, video cards, optical drives, and network cards.

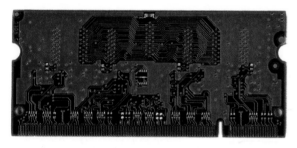

• **Figure 11.8** 200-pin SO-DIMM stick (front and back)

RAM

Stock factory portable PCs almost always come with a minimal amount of RAM, so one of the first laptop upgrades you'll be called on to do is to add more RAM. Economy laptops running Windows XP Home routinely sit on store shelves and go home to consumers with as little as 256 MB of RAM, an amount guaranteed to limit the use and performance of the laptop. The OS alone will consume more than half of the RAM! Luckily, every decent laptop has upgradeable RAM slots. Most older laptops use either 72-pin or 144-pin SO-DIMMs with SDRAM technology. DDR, DDR2, and DDR3 systems primarily use 200-pin SO-DIMMs, although some laptops use micro-DIMMs (Figure 11.8).

How to Add or Replace RAM Upgrading the RAM in a portable PC requires a couple of steps. First, you need to get the correct RAM. Many older portable PCs use proprietary RAM solutions, which means you need to order directly from Dell, HP, or Sony and pay exorbitant prices for the precious extra megabytes. Most manufacturers have taken pity on consumers in recent years and use standard SO-DIMMs or micro-DIMMs. Refer to the manufacturer's Web site or to the manual (if any) that came with the portable for the specific RAM needed.

Second, every portable PC offers a unique challenge to the tech who wants to upgrade the RAM, because there's no standard for RAM placement in portables. More often than not, you need to unscrew or pop open a panel on the underside of the portable (Figure 11.9). Then you press out on the restraining clips and the RAM stick pops up (Figure 11.10). Gently remove the old stick of RAM and insert the new one by reversing the steps.

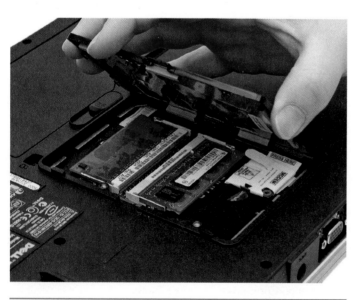

• **Figure 11.9** Removing a RAM panel

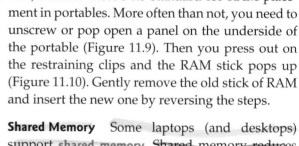

Shared Memory Some laptops (and desktops) support shared memory. Shared memory reduces the cost of video cards by reducing the amount of memory on the video card itself. Instead of having 256 MB of RAM, the video card might have only 64 MB of RAM but be able to borrow 192 MB of RAM from the system. This equates to a 256-MB video card. The video card uses regular system RAM to make up for the loss.

The obvious benefit of shared memory is a less expensive video card (and a less expensive laptop!) with performance comparable to its mega-memory alternative. The downside is that your overall system performance will suffer because a portion of the system RAM is no longer available to programs. (The term *shared* is a bit misleading because the video card takes control of a portion of RAM. The video portion of system RAM is *not* shared back and forth between the video card processor and the CPU.) Shared memory technologies include TurboCache (developed by NVIDIA) and HyperMemory (developed by ATI).

Some systems give you control over the amount of shared memory, while others simply allow you to turn shared memory on or off. The settings are found in CMOS setup and only on systems that support shared memory. Shared memory is not reported to Windows, so don't panic if you have 1 GB of RAM in your laptop but Windows only sees 924 MB—the missing memory is used for video.

Adding more system RAM to a laptop with shared memory will improve laptop performance. Although it might appear to improve video performance, that doesn't tell the true story. It'll improve overall performance because the OS and CPU get more usable RAM. On some laptops, you can improve video performance as well, but that depends on the CMOS setup. If the shared memory is not set to maximum by default, increasing the overall memory and upping the portion reserved for video will improve video performance specifically.

• **Figure 11.10**   Releasing the RAM

Hard Drives

SATA drives in the 2.5-inch drive format now rule in all laptops. Although much smaller than regular 3.5-inch hard drives, they use all the same features and configurations. These smaller hard drives have suffered, however, from diminished storage capacity as compared to their 3.5-inch brothers. Currently, large 2.5-inch hard drives hold up to 1 TB, while the 3.5-inch hard drives can hold more than 2 TB of data! Some PATA drive manufacturers may require you to set the drive to use a cable-select setting as opposed to master or slave, so check with the laptop maker for any special issues. Otherwise, no difference exists between 2.5-inch drives and their larger 3.5-inch brethren (Figure 11.11).

Modular CPUs

Both AMD and Intel make specialized laptop CPUs that produce less heat and consume less power, yet only now are folks realizing that they can sometimes upgrade their laptops by removing the old CPU and replacing it with a new one. Be very careful to follow manufacturer's specifications! You should keep in mind, however, that replacing the CPU in a laptop often requires you to disassemble the entire machine. This can be a daunting task, even for professionals. If you want to upgrade the CPU in your laptop, it's often best to let the professionals take care of it.

• **Figure 11.11**   The 2.5-inch and 3.5-inch drives are mostly the same.

Video Cards

Some video card makers make modular video cards for laptops. Although no single standard works in all systems, a quick phone call to the tech support department of the laptop maker often reveals upgrade options (if any). Modular video cards are the least standardized of all modular components, but as manufacturers adopt more industry-wide standards, we'll be able to replace video cards in laptops more readily.

Modular Drives

To add functionality to laptops, many manufacturers include "modular drives" with their portable machines. CD, DVD, and Blu-ray Disc drives are most common. The beauty of modular drives is that you can swap back and forth easily between different types of drives. Need more storage space? Pull out the DVD drive and put in another hard drive. Many laptops enable you to replace a drive with a second battery, which obviously can extend the time you can go before you have to plug the laptop into an AC outlet.

I have a laptop that allows me to swap out my CD/DVD drive for a second battery. If I don't need to access any CDs and don't need super-extended battery life, I just take out the component that's currently installed and put a blank faceplate into the empty slot. Traveling with an empty bay makes my hefty laptop weigh a little bit less, and every little bit helps!

Most modular drives are truly hot-swappable, enabling you to remove and insert devices without any special software. Many still require you to use the Hardware Removal Tool (also known as Safely Remove Hardware) located in the system tray or notification area (Figure 11.12). When in doubt, always remove modular devices by using this tool. Figure 11.13 shows the Safely Remove Hardware dialog box. To remove a device, highlight it and click the Stop button. Windows will shut down the device and tell you when it's safe to remove the device.

See Chapter 13, "Mastering Local Area Networking," for the scoop on dial-up networking and Ethernet.

● **Figure 11.12** Hardware Removal Tool in system tray

● **Figure 11.13** Safely Remove Hardware dialog box

Mobile NICs and Mini PCI

Every laptop made in the past few years comes with networking capabilities built in. They have Ethernet ports for plugging into a wired network, Wi-Fi for wireless networking, and some even have Cellular WAN radios so you can access the Internet over a cell phone network. Laptops run Windows just like a desktop system, so they have all the networking software ready to go.

Many of these integrated network cards are installed in a Mini PCI slot on the laptop motherboard. The Mini PCI bus is an adaptation of the standard PCI bus and was developed specifically for integrated communications peripherals such as modems and network adapters. Built-in networking support means you don't need an additional PC Card to provide a network adapter. The Mini PCI bus also provides support for other integrated devices, such as Bluetooth, modems, audio, or hard drive controllers. One great aspect of Mini PCI is that if some new technology eclipses the current wireless technology or some other technology that uses the bus, you can upgrade by swapping a card.

Officially released in 1999, Mini PCI is a 32-bit 33-MHz bus and is basically PCI v2.2 with a different form factor. Like PCI, it supports bus mastering and DMA. Mini PCI cards are about a quarter the size of regular PCI cards and can be as small as 2.75 inches by 1.81 inches by .22 inches. They can be found in small products such as laptops, printers, and set-top boxes.

To extend battery life, you can toggle built-in communication devices such as Wi-Fi and Bluetooth adapters on and off without powering down the computer. Many laptops come with a physical switch along the front or side edge allowing you to power the communications adapter on or off. Similarly, you can often use a keyboard shortcut for this, generally by pressing the Function (FN) key along with some other key.

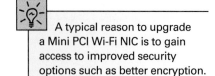
A typical reason to upgrade a Mini PCI Wi-Fi NIC is to gain access to improved security options such as better encryption.

Chapter 14, "Mastering Wireless," covers wireless networking in great detail.

Managing and Maintaining Portable Computers

Most portable PCs come from the factory solidly built and configured. Manufacturers know that few techs outside their factories know enough to work on them, so they don't cut corners. From a tech's standpoint, your most common work on managing and maintaining portables involves taking care of the batteries and extending the battery life through proper power management, keeping the machine clean, and avoiding excessive heat.

Everything you normally do to maintain a PC applies to portable PCs. You need to keep current on Windows patches and Service Packs and use stable, recent drivers. Run Check Disk with some frequency, and definitely defragment the hard drive. Disk Cleanup is a must if the laptop runs Windows XP or Windows Vista. That said, let's look at issues specifically involving portables.

Batteries

Manufacturers use three types of batteries for portable PCs and each battery type has its own special needs and quirks. Once you have a clear understanding of the quirks, you can *usually* spot and fix battery problems. The three types of batteries commonly used in mobile PCs are Nickel-Cadmium (Ni-Cd), Nickel-Metal Hydride (Ni-MH), and Lithium-Ion (Li-Ion) batteries. Manufacturers have also started working with fuel cell batteries, although most of that work is experimental at this writing.

Frist one out

Nickel-Cadmium

Ni-Cds were the first batteries commonly used in mobile PCs, which means the technology was full of little problems. Probably most irritating was a little thing called battery memory, or the tendency of a Ni-Cd battery to lose a significant amount of its rechargeability if it was charged repeatedly without being totally discharged. A battery that originally kept a laptop running

• Figure 11.14   Ni-Cd battery

You *must* use disposal companies or battery recycling services to dispose of the highly toxic Ni-Cd batteries.

• Figure 11.15   Ni-MH battery

for two hours would eventually only keep that same laptop going for 30 minutes or less. Figure 11.14 shows a typical Ni-Cd battery.

To prevent memory problems, a Ni-Cd battery had to be discharged completely before each recharging. Recharging was tricky as well, because Ni-Cd batteries disliked being overcharged. Unfortunately, there was no way to verify when a battery was fully charged without an expensive charging machine, which none of us had. As a result, most Ni-Cd batteries lasted an extremely short time before having to be replaced. A quick fix was to purchase a conditioning charger. These chargers would first totally discharge the Ni-Cd battery and then generate a special "reverse" current that, in a way, cleaned internal parts of the battery so it could be recharged more often and would run longer on each recharge. Ni-Cd batteries would, at best, last for 1,000 charges, and far fewer with poor treatment. Ni-Cds were extremely susceptible to heat and would self-discharge over time if not used. Leaving a Ni-Cd in the car in the summer was guaranteed to result in a fully discharged battery in next to no time!

But Ni-Cd batteries didn't stop causing trouble after they died. The highly toxic metals inside the batteries made it unacceptable simply to throw them in the trash. Ni-Cd batteries should be disposed of via specialized disposal companies. This is very important! Even though Ni-Cd batteries aren't used in PCs very often anymore, many devices, such as cellular and cordless phones, still use Ni-Cd batteries. Don't trash the environment by tossing Ni-Cds in a landfill. Turn them in at the closest special disposal site; most recycling centers are glad to take them. Also, many battery manufacturers/distributors will take them. The environment you help preserve just might be yours—or your kids'!

Nickel-Metal Hydride

Ni-MH batteries were the next generation of mobile PC batteries and are still quite common today. Basically, Ni-MH batteries are Ni-Cd batteries without most of the headaches. Ni-MH batteries are much less susceptible to memory problems, can tolerate overcharging better, can take more recharging, and can last longer between rechargings. Like Ni-Cds, Ni-MH batteries are susceptible to heat, but at least they are considered less toxic to the environment. A special disposal is still a good idea. Unlike Ni-Cds, it's usually better to recharge an Ni-MH with shallow recharges as opposed to a complete discharge/recharge. Ni-MH is a popular replacement battery for Ni-Cd systems (Figure 11.15).

Lithium-Ion

The most common battery used today is Li-Ion. Li-Ion batteries are powerful, completely immune to memory problems, and last at least twice as long as comparable Ni-MH batteries on one charge. Sadly, they can't handle as many charges as Ni-MH types, but today's users are usually more than glad to give up total battery lifespan in return for longer periods between charges. Li-Ion batteries will explode if they are overcharged, so all Li-Ion batteries sold with PCs have built-in circuitry to prevent accidental overcharging. Lithium batteries can only be used on systems designed to use them. They can't be used as replacement batteries (Figure 11.16).

Other Portable Power Sources

In an attempt to provide better maintenance for laptop batteries, manufacturers have developed a new type of battery called the **smart battery**. Smart batteries tell the computer when they need to be charged, conditioned, or replaced.

The Care and Feeding of Batteries

In general, keep in mind the following basics. First, always store batteries in a cool place. Although a freezer is in concept an excellent storage place, the moisture, metal racks, and food make it a bad idea. Second, use a charger for your Ni-Cd and Ni-MH batteries that also conditions the batteries; they'll last longer. Third, keep battery contacts clean with a little alcohol or just a dry cloth. Fourth, *never* handle a battery that has ruptured or broken; battery chemicals are very dangerous. Finally, always recycle old batteries.

● **Figure 11.16**   Li-Ion battery

Power Management

Many different parts are included in the typical laptop, and each part uses power. The problem with early laptops was that every one of these parts used power continuously, whether or not the system needed that device at that time. For example, the hard drive continued to spin even when it was not being accessed, and the LCD panel continued to display, even when the user walked away from the machine.

Try This!

Recycling Old Portable PC Batteries

Got an old portable PC battery lying around? Well, you need to get rid of it, and there are some pretty nasty chemicals in that battery, so you can't just throw it in the trash. Sooner or later, you'll probably need to deal with such a battery, so Try This!

1. Do an online search to find the battery recycling center nearest to you.

2. Sometimes, you can take old laptop batteries to an auto parts store that disposes of old car batteries—I know it sounds odd, but it's true! See if you can find one in your area that will do this.

3. Many cities offer a hazardous materials disposal or recycling service. Check to see if and how your local government will help you dispose of your old batteries.

The optimal situation would be a system where the user could instruct the PC to shut down unused devices selectively, preferably by defining a maximum period of inactivity that, when reached, would trigger the PC to shut down the inactive device. Longer periods of inactivity would eventually enable the entire system to shut itself down, leaving critical information loaded in RAM, ready to restart if a wake-up event (such as moving the mouse or pressing a key) told the system to restart. The system would have to be sensitive to potential hazards, such as shutting down in the middle of writing to a drive, and so on. Also, this feature could not add significantly to the cost of the PC. Clearly, a machine that could perform these functions would need specialized hardware, BIOS, and operating system to operate properly. This process of cooperation among the hardware, the BIOS, and the OS to reduce power use is known generically as *power management*.

System Management Mode

Intel began the process of power management with a series of new features built into the 386SX CPU. These new features enabled the CPU to slow down or stop its clock without erasing the register information, as well as enabling power saving in peripherals. These features were collectively called **System Management Mode (SMM)**. All modern CPUs have SMM. Although a power-saving CPU was okay, power management was relegated to special "sleep" or "doze" buttons that would stop the CPU and all of the peripherals on the laptop. To take real advantage of SMM, the system needed a specialized BIOS and OS to go with the SMM CPU. To this end, Intel put forward the **Advanced Power Management (APM)** specification in 1992 and the **Advanced Configuration and Power Interface (ACPI)** standard in 1996.

Requirements for APM/ACPI

To function fully, APM and ACPI require a number of items. First is an SMM-capable CPU. As virtually all CPUs are SMM-capable, this is easy. Second is an APM-compliant BIOS that enables the CPU to shut off the peripherals when desired. The third requirement is devices that will accept being shut off. These devices are usually called Energy Star devices, which signals their compliance with the EPA's Energy Star standard. To be an Energy Star device, a peripheral must be able to shut down without actually turning off and show that they use much less power than the non–Energy Star equivalent. Last, the system's OS must know how to request that a particular device be shut down, and the CPU's clock must be slowed down or stopped.

ACPI goes beyond the APM standard by supplying support for hot-swappable devices—always a huge problem with APM. This feature aside, it is a challenge to tell the difference between an APM system and an ACPI system at first glance.

APM/ACPI Levels

APM defined four power-usage operating levels for a system. These levels are intentionally fuzzy to give manufacturers considerable leeway in their use; the only real difference among them is the amount of time each takes to return to normal usage. These levels are as follows:

- **Full On** Everything in the system is running at full power. There is no power management.

- **APM Enabled** CPU and RAM are running at full power. Power management is enabled. An unused device may or may not be shut down.

- **APM Standby** CPU is stopped. RAM still stores all programs. All peripherals are shut down, although configuration options are still stored. (In other words, to get back to APM Enabled, you won't have to reinitialize the devices.)

- **APM Suspend** Everything in the PC is shut down or at its lowest power-consumption setting. Many systems use a special type of Suspend called **hibernation**, where critical configuration information is written to the hard drive. Upon a wake-up event, the system is reinitialized, and the data is read from the drive to return the system to the APM Enabled mode. Clearly, the recovery time between Suspend and Enabled will be much longer than the time between Standby and Enabled.

Don't limit your perception of APM, ACPI, and Energy Star just to laptops. Virtually all desktop systems and many appliances also use the power management functions.

ACPI, the successor to APM, handles all these levels plus a few more, such as "soft power on/off" that enables you to define the function of the power button. ~~You should familiarize yourself with the following ACPI global (G) and sleeping (S) system power state specifications for both the A+ exam and your own practical application:~~

- **G0 (S0)**   Working state

- **G1**   Sleeping state mode. Further subdivided into four *S* states.

  - **S1**   CPU stops processing. Power to CPU and memory (RAM) is maintained.

  - **S2**   CPU is powered down.

  - **S3**   Sleep or Standby mode. Power to RAM still on.

  - **S4**   Hibernation mode. Information in RAM is stored to nonvolatile memory or drive and powered off.

- **G2 (S5)**   Soft power off mode. Certain devices used to wake a system—such as keyboard, LAN, USB, and other devices—remain on, while most other components are powered to a mechanical off state (G3).

- **G3**   Mechanical off mode. The system and all components, with the exception of the real-time clock (RTC), are completely powered down.

Configuration of APM/ACPI

~~You configure APM/ACPI via CMOS settings or through Windows.~~ Windows settings override CMOS settings. Although the APM/ACPI standards permit a great deal of flexibility, which can create some confusion among different implementations, certain settings apply generally to CMOS configuration. First is the ability to initialize power management; this enables the system to enter the APM Enabled mode. Often CMOS then presents time frames for entering Standby and Suspend modes, as well as settings to determine which events take place in each of these modes.

Many CMOS versions present settings to determine wake-up events, such as directing the system to monitor a modem or a NIC (Figure 11.17). You'll see this feature as *Wake on LAN* or something similar. A true ACPI-compliant CMOS provides an ACPI setup option. Figure 11.18 shows a typical modern BIOS that provides this setting.

APM/ACPI settings can be found in the Windows 2000/XP/Vista Control Panel applet Power Options. In Windows XP, the Power Options applet has several built-in *power schemes* such as Home/Office and Max Battery that put the system into Standby or Suspend after a certain interval (Figure 11.19). You can also require the system to go into Standby after a set period of time or to turn off the monitor or hard drive

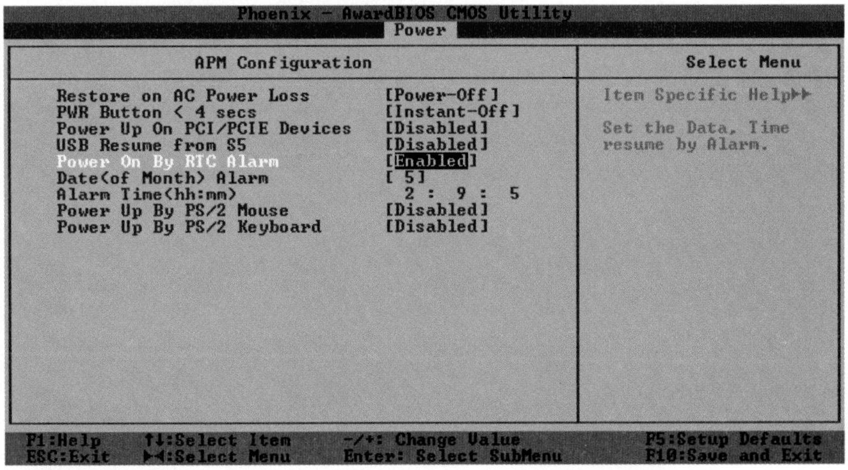

• **Figure 11.17**   Setting a wake-up event in CMOS

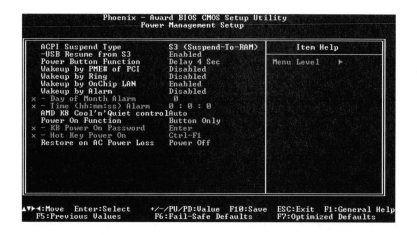

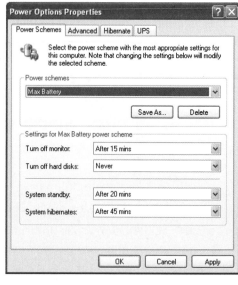

● **Figure 11.18** CMOS with ACPI setup option

In Windows XP you can also access your power options by right-clicking on the desktop, selecting Properties, and then clicking the Power button in the Monitor power section of the Screen Saver tab. In Windows Vista, right-click the Desktop, select Personalize, select Screen Saver, and then click on the *Change power settings* link.

after a time, thus creating your own custom power scheme. This is technically called adjusting the **sleep timers**.

● **Figure 11.19** The Windows XP Power Options applet's Power Schemes tab

Windows Vista's built-in power schemes are similar to Windows XP, though you can better control power utilization by customizing a Balanced, Power saver, or High performance power plan (Figure 11.20). You can customize a power saver plan for your laptop, for example, and configure it to

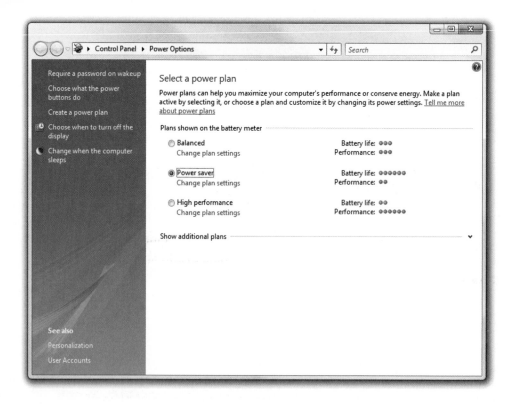

● **Figure 11.20** Windows Vista Balanced, Power saver, or High performance power plans

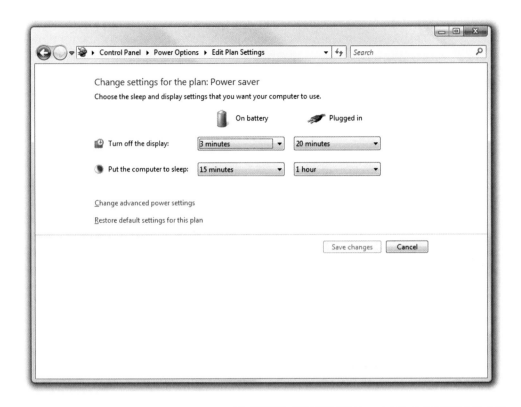

Figure 11.21 Customizing a laptop power plan in Windows Vista

turn off the display at a certain time interval while on battery or plugged in and configure it to put the computer to sleep as desired (Figure 11.21).

Another feature, Hibernate mode, takes everything in active memory and stores it on the hard drive just before the system powers down. When the PC comes out of hibernation, Windows reloads all the files and applications into RAM. Figure 11.22 shows the Power Options Properties applet in Windows XP.

> **Try This!**
>
> **Adjusting Your System's Power Management**
>
> Go into the Power Options applet and take a look at the various settings. What is the current power scheme for your computer? If you're using a laptop with Windows XP, is your system still using the Home/Office Desktop power scheme? If this is the case, change the power scheme to Portable/Laptop. If you're using a laptop with Windows Vista, check to see if you are running a Balanced or High performance power plan. If you are, change the power plan to Power saver and familiarize yourself with some of the advanced power settings (click on the *Change advanced power settings* link).
>
> Try changing the individual settings for each power scheme. For instance, set a new value for the System Standby setting—try making your computer go into standby after five minutes. Don't worry; you aren't going to hurt anything if you fiddle with these settings.

Cleaning

Most portable PCs take substantially more abuse than a corresponding desktop model. Constant handling, travel, airport food on the run, and so on can radically shorten the life of a portable if you don't take action. One of the most important things you should do is clean the laptop regularly. Use an appropriate screen cleaner (not a glass cleaner!) to remove fingerprints and dust from the fragile LCD panel. (Refer to Chapter 10, "Mastering Video and Multimedia," for specifics.)

 Laptop cooling fans tend to get dirty over time. Clean them occasionally using an-anti-static vacuum. Never use canned air!

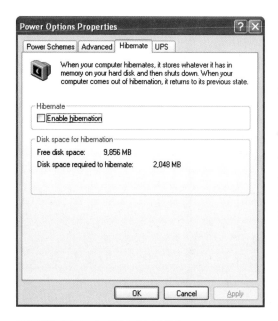

● **Figure 11.22** Windows XP hibernation settings in the Power Options applet

If you've had the laptop in a smoky or dusty environment, try compressed air for cleaning. Compressed air works great for blowing out the dust and crumbs from the keyboard and for keeping PC Card sockets clear. Don't use water on your keyboard! Even a minor amount of moisture inside the portable can toast a component.

Heat

To manage and maintain a healthy portable PC, you need to deal with issues of heat. Every portable has a stack of electronic components crammed into a very small space. Unlike their desktop brethren, portables don't have lots of freely moving air space that enables fans to cool everything down. Even with lots of low-power-consumption devices inside, portable PCs crank out a good deal of heat. Excessive heat can cause system lockups and hardware failures, so you should handle the issue wisely. Try this as a starter guide.

- Use power management, even if you're plugged into the AC outlet. This is especially important if you're working in a warm (more than 80 degrees Fahrenheit) room.

- Keep air space between the bottom of the laptop and the surface on which it rests. Putting a laptop on a soft surface, such as a pillow on your lap, creates a great heat-retention system—not a good thing! Always use a hard, flat surface.

- Don't use a keyboard protector for extended amounts of time.

- Listen to your fan, assuming the laptop has one. If it's often running very fast—you can tell by the high-pitched whirring sound— examine your power management settings and your environment, and change whatever is causing heat retention.

- Speaking of fans, be alert to a fan that suddenly goes silent. Fans do fail on laptops, causing overheating and failure. All laptop fans can be replaced easily.

Protect the Machine

Although prices continue to drop for basic laptops, a fully loaded system is still pricey. To protect your investment, you'll want to adhere to certain best practices. You've already read tips in this chapter to deal with cleaning and heat, so let's look at the "portable" part of portable computers.

Tripping

Pay attention to where you run the power cord when you plug in a laptop. One of the primary causes of laptop destruction is people tripping over the power cord and knocking the laptop off of a desk. This is especially true if you plug in at a public place such as a café or airport. Remember, the life you save could be your portable PC's!

Storage

If you aren't going to use your laptop or PDA for a while, storing it safely will go a long way toward keeping it operable when you do power it up again. Investing in a quality case is worth the extra few dollars—preferably one with ample padding. Smaller devices such as PDAs are well protected inside small shock-resistant aluminum cases that clip onto your belt, while laptops do fine in well-padded cases or backpacks. Not only will this protect your system on a daily basis when transporting it from home to office, but it will keep dust and pet hair away as well. Lastly, protect from battery leakage by removing the battery if you'll be storing your device for an extended time.

Travel

If traveling with a laptop, take care to protect yourself from theft. If possible, use a case that doesn't look like a computer case. A well-padded backpack makes a great travel bag for a laptop and appears less tempting to would-be thieves. Don't forget to pack any accessories you might need, like modular devices, spare batteries, and AC adapters. Make sure to remove any disks, such as CD/DVD or floppies, from their drives. Most importantly—back up any important data before you leave!

Make sure to have at least a little battery power available. Heightened security at airports means you might have to power on your system to prove it's really a computer and not a transport case for questionable materials. And never let your laptop out of your sight. If going through an x-ray machine, request a manual search. The x-ray won't harm your computer like a metal detector would, but if the laptop gets through the line at security before you do, someone else might walk away with it. If flying, stow your laptop under the seat in front of you where you can keep an eye on it.

If you travel to a foreign country, be very careful about the electricity. North America uses ~115-V power outlets, but the most of the rest of the world uses ~230-V outlets. Many portable computers have **auto-switching power supplies**, meaning they detect the voltage at the outlet and adjust accordingly. For these portables, a simple plug converter will do the trick. Other portable computers, however, have fixed-input power supplies, which means they run only on ~115-V or ~230-V power. For these portables, you need a full-blown electricity converting device, either a step-down or step-up transformer. You can find converters and transformers at electrical parts stores, such as Radio Shack in the United States.

Shipping

Much of the storage and travel advice can be applied to shipping. Remove batteries and optical discs from their drives. Pack the laptop well and disguise the container as best you can. Back up any data and verify the warranty coverage. Ship with a reputable carrier and always request a tracking number and, if possible, delivery signature. It's also worth the extra couple of bucks to pay for the shipping insurance. And when the clerk asks what's in the box, it's safer to say "electronics" rather than "a new 20-inch laptop computer."

 Be sure to remove all thumb drives and PC Cards before shipping a laptop.

Security

The fact is, if someone really wants to steal your laptop, they'll find a way. There are, however, some things you can do to make yourself, and your equipment, less desirable targets. As you've already learned, disguise is a good idea. Although you don't need to camouflage your laptop or carry it in a brown grocery bag on a daily basis, an inconspicuous carrying case will draw less attention.

Another physical deterrent is a laptop lock. Similar to a steel bicycle cable, there is a loop on one end and a lock on the other. The idea is to loop the cable around a solid object, such as a bed frame, and secure the lock to the small security hole on the side of the laptop. Again, if someone really wants to steal your computer, they'll find a way. They'll dismantle the bed frame if they're desperate. The best protection is to be vigilant and not let the computer out of your sight.

An alternative to physically securing a laptop with a lock is to use a software tracking system. Software makers, such as Computer Security Products, Inc., at www.computersecurity.com, offer tracking software that transmits a signal to a central office if the computer is stolen and connected to a phone line or the Internet. The location of the stolen PC can be tracked, and sensitive files can even be deleted automatically with the aid of the stealth signal.

■ Troubleshooting Portable Computers

Many of the troubleshooting techniques you learned about for desktop systems can be applied to laptops. For example, take the proper precautions before and during disassembly. Use the proper hand tools, and document, label, and organize each plastic part and screw location for reassembly. Additionally, here are some laptop-specific procedures to try.

Laptop Won't Power On

- Verify AC power by plugging another electronic device into the wall outlet. If the other device receives power, the outlet is good.

- If the outlet is good, connect the laptop to the wall outlet and try to power on. If no LEDs light up, you may have a bad AC adapter. Swap it out with a known good power adapter.

- A faulty peripheral device might keep the laptop from powering up. Remove any peripherals such as USB or FireWire devices.

Screen Doesn't Come On Properly

- If the laptop is booting (you hear the beeps and the drives), first make sure the display is turned on. Press the FN key and the key to activate the screen a number of times until the laptop display comes on. If that doesn't work, check the LCD cutoff switch—on many laptops, this is the small nub somewhere near the screen hinge that shuts the monitor off when you close the laptop—and make sure it isn't stuck in the down position.

Tech Tip

Battery Won't Charge

If you have a laptop with a battery that won't charge up, it could be one of two things: the battery might be cooked or the AC adapter isn't doing its job. To troubleshoot, replace the battery with a known good battery. If the new battery works, you've found the problem. Just replace the battery. Alternatively, remove the battery and run the laptop on AC only. If that works, you know the AC adapter is good. If it doesn't, replace the AC adapter.

- If the laptop display is very dim, you may have lost an inverter. The clue here is that inverters never go quietly. They can make a nasty hum as they are about to die and an equally nasty popping noise when they actually fail. Failure often occurs when you plug in the laptop's AC adapter, as the inverters take power directly from the AC adapter. It's also possible that the backlights in the LCD panel have died, though this is much less common than a bad inverter.

- If the screen won't come on or is cracked, most laptops have a port for plugging in an external monitor, which you can use to log into your laptop.

Wireless Networking Doesn't Work

- Check along the front, rear, or side edges of the laptop for a physical switch that toggles the internal wireless adapter on and off.

- Try the special key combination for your laptop to toggle the wireless adapter. You usually press the FN key in combination with another key.

- You might simply be out of range. Physically walk the laptop over to the wireless router or access point to ensure there are no out-of-range issues.

Handwriting Is Not Recognized

- If your PDA or tablet PC no longer recognizes your handwriting or stylus, you may need to retrain the digitizer. Look for an option in your PDA OS settings to align the screen. On Windows-based tablet PCs, you will find a similar option under Start | Settings | Control Panel.

Keypad Doesn't Work

- If none of the keys work on your laptop, there's a good chance you've unseated the keypad connector. These connectors are quite fragile and are prone to unseating from any physical stress on the laptop. Check the manufacturer's disassembly procedures in your laptop's documentation or on the manufacturer's Web site to locate and reseat the keypad.

- If you're getting numbers when you're expecting to get letters, the number lock (NUMLOCK) function key is turned on. Turn it off.

Touchpad Doesn't Work

- A shot of compressed air does wonders for cleaning pet hair out of the touchpad sensors. You'll get a cleaner shot if you remove the keyboard before using the compressed air. Remember to be gentle when lifting off the keyboard and make sure to follow the manufacturer's instructions.

- The touchpad driver might need to be reconfigured. Try the various options in the Control Panel | Mouse applet.

Chapter 11 Review

■ Chapter Summary

After reading this chapter and completing the exercises, you should understand the following about portable computers.

Enhance and upgrade portable computers

- PC Cards are roughly credit-card-sized devices that enhance and extend the functions of a portable PC. Still commonly known by their older name, PCMCIA cards, PC Cards are as standard on today's mobile computers as the hard drive. Almost every portable PC has one or two PC Card slots. All PC Cards are hot-swappable.

- Parallel PC Cards come in two flavors, 16-bit and CardBus, and each flavor comes in three different physical sizes, called Type I, Type II, and Type III. Type I, II, and III cards differ only in the thickness of the card (Type I being the thinnest and Type III the thickest). Type II cards are by far the most common. All parallel PC Cards share the same 68-pin interface. The 16-bit PC Cards are 16-bit 5-V cards that can have up to two distinct functions or devices, such as a modem/network card combination. CardBus PC Cards are 32-bit 3.3-V cards that can have up to eight different functions on a single card. The 16-bit PC Cards will fit into and work in CardBus slots, but the reverse is not true.

- The serial ExpressCard comes in two widths: 54 mm and 34 mm. Both cards are 75 mm long and 5 mm thick, which makes them shorter than all previous PC Cards and the same thickness as a Type II PC Card. ExpressCards connect to either a Hi-Speed USB 2.0 bus (480 Mbps) or a PCI Express bus (2.5 Gbps).

- The PCMCIA standard defines two levels of software drivers to support PC Cards. The first and lower level is known as socket services. Socket services are device drivers that support the PC Card socket, enabling the system to detect when a PC Card has been inserted or removed and providing the necessary I/O to the device. The second and higher level is known as card services. The card services level recognizes the function of a particular PC Card and provides the specialized drivers necessary to make the card work. In today's laptops, the socket services are standardized and are handled by the system BIOS. Windows itself

handles all card services and has a large preinstalled base of PC Card device drivers, although most PC Cards come with their own drivers.

- Every portable PC and many PDAs come with one or more single-function ports, such as an analog VGA connection for hooking up an external monitor and a PS/2 and/or USB port for a keyboard or mouse. The single PS/2 port on most laptops supports both keyboards and pointing devices. Most portable computing devices have a speaker port, and some have line-in and microphone jacks as well. Most current portable PCs come with built-in NICs or modems for networking support. Simply plug in a device to a particular port and, as long as Windows has the proper drivers, you will have a functioning device when you boot. The only port that requires any extra effort is the video port.

- Most laptops support a second monitor, giving the user the option to display Windows on the laptop only, the external monitor only, or both simultaneously. Usually a special function key on the keyboard will cycle through the monitor configurations.

- Most portable PCs have one or more general-purpose expansion ports that enable you to plug in many types of devices. Older portables sport RS-232 serial and IEEE 1284 parallel ports for mice, modems, printers, scanners, external optical drives, and more. USB, FireWire, and eSATA are popular and widespread methods for attaching peripherals to laptops. All have easy-to-use connectors and can be hot-swapped.

- Port replicators are devices that plug into a single port (usually USB but sometimes proprietary) and offer common PC ports, such as serial, parallel, USB, network, and PS/2. Docking stations resemble port replicators in many ways, offering legacy and modern single- and multifunction ports, but have extra features built in, such as DVD drives or PC Card slots.

- Although earlier portable PCs used proprietary components, we're starting to see some modularity in today's portable PCs, making it possible to do basic replacements and upgrades without buying expensive proprietary components from the manufacturer. These replaceable components include RAM, hard drives, video cards, floppy drives, and CD/DVD-media devices. Modular video cards are the least standardized of all modular components, but manufacturers are beginning to adopt industry-wide standards. Many manufacturers use modular floppy disk drives and CD media devices, even allowing users to swap easily between different types of drives.

- Laptops use one of four types of RAM. Most older laptops use either 72-pin or 144-pin SO-DIMMs with SDRAM technology. DDR SDRAM systems primarily use 200-pin SO-DIMMs, although you'll also find 172-pin micro-DIMMs. Every decent laptop has upgradeable RAM slots. Get the correct RAM; many portable PC makers use proprietary RAM solutions. No standard exists for RAM placement in portables. More often than not, you need to unscrew or pop open a panel on the underside of the portable and press out on the restraining clips to make the RAM stick pop up so you can remove and replace it.

- Laptops that support shared memory benefit from more affordable video cards. The video card has less built-in RAM and uses a portion of the computer's system RAM to make up the difference. Although this results in a lower cost, system performance suffers because RAM that is shared with the video card is not available to programs. NVIDIA calls their shared memory technology TurboCache and ATI calls theirs HyperMemory.

- SATA drives in the 2.5-inch drive format now rule in all laptops. Currently, the larger 2.5-inch hard drives hold up to 500 GB, while the larger 3.5-inch hard drives hold more than 2 TB.

- Both Intel and AMD have long sold specialized, modular CPUs for laptops; however, replacing the CPU in a laptop often requires disassembling the entire machine.

- To add functionality to laptops, manufacturers include modular drives with their machines. Modular drive bays can accommodate various optical drives, hard drives, or batteries. Most modular drives are truly hot-swappable, enabling you to remove and insert devices without any special software.

- Most laptops now come with integrated wireless networking support by way of a built-in Wi-Fi

adapter usually installed in a Mini PCI slot on the laptop motherboard. The Mini PCI bus is an adaptation of the standard PCI bus and was developed specifically for integrated communications peripherals such as modems and network adapters. To extend battery life, built-in communication devices such as Wi-Fi and Bluetooth adapters can be toggled on and off without powering down the computer.

Manage and maintain portable computers

- Portable computers use three types of batteries: Nickel-Cadmium (Ni-Cd), Nickel-Metal Hydride (Ni-MH), and Lithium-Ion (Li-Ion).

- The first batteries used in mobile PCs were Nickel-Cadmium (Ni-Cd). If a Ni-Cd battery was not completely discharged before each recharge, it lost a significant amount of its rechargeability, a condition referred to as battery memory. At best, Ni-Cd batteries would last for 1,000 charges, but they were very susceptible to heat. Because of the toxic metals inside these batteries, they had to be disposed of via specialty disposal companies. Although no longer used in PCs, Ni-Cd batteries are still found in cellular and cordless phones.

- The second generation of mobile PC batteries, the Nickel-Metal Hydride (Ni-MH) batteries are less susceptible to memory problems, tolerate overcharging better, take more recharging, and last longer between rechargings, but they are still susceptible to heat.

- Although some portable PCs still use Ni-MH batteries, Lithium-Ion (Li-Ion) is more common today. This third-generation battery takes fewer charges than Ni-MH, but it lasts longer between charges. Because Li-Ion batteries can explode if they are overcharged, they have circuitry to prevent overcharging.

- A new type of battery called the smart battery tells the computer when it needs to be charged, conditioned, or replaced.

- Batteries should be stored in a cool place, but not in the freezer because of moisture, metal racks, and food. Condition Ni-Cd and Ni-MH batteries to make them last longer. You can clean battery contacts with alcohol or a dry cloth. Because batteries contain dangerous chemicals, never handle one that has ruptured. Always recycle old batteries rather than disposing of them in the trash.

- The process of cooperation among the hardware, the BIOS, and the OS to reduce power use is known generically as power management. Early laptops used power continuously, regardless of whether the system was using the device at the time. With power management features, today's laptops can automatically turn off unused devices or can shut down the entire system, leaving the information in RAM ready for a restart. To perform these power management functions requires specialized hardware, BIOS, and operating system that support power management.

- Starting with the 386SX, Intel introduced System Management Mode (SMM), a power management system that would make the CPU and all peripherals go to "sleep." In 1992, Intel introduced the improved Advanced Power Management (APM) specification, followed by the Advanced Configuration and Power Interface (ACPI) standard in 1996.

- To use APM or ACPI, the computer must have an SMM-capable CPU, an APM-compliant BIOS, and devices that can be shut off. Referred to as Energy Star devices, these peripherals can shut down without actually turning off. The OS must also know how to request that a particular device be shut down. ACPI extends power-saving to include hot-swappable devices.

- Virtually all laptops and desktops use power management functions. APM defines four power-usage levels, including Full On, APM Enabled, APM Standby, and APM Suspend. ACPI, the successor to APM, handles all these levels plus a few more, totaling four Global (G) and seven total (S) states. Support for APM has been discontinued in Windows Vista, which uses ACPI.

- Configure APM/ACPI through CMOS or through the Power Options Control Panel applet in Windows 2000/XP/Vista, with Windows settings overriding CMOS settings. Many CMOS versions allow configuration of wake-up events, such as having the system monitor a modem or particular IRQ.

- Hibernation writes information from RAM to the hard drive. Upon waking up, the data is returned to RAM, and programs and files are in the same state they were in when the computer entered hibernation.

- Use an appropriate screen cleaner (not glass cleaner) to clean the LCD screen. Use compressed air around the keyboard and PC Card sockets. Never use water around the keyboard.

- To combat the inevitable heat produced by a portable computer, always use power management, keep an air space between the bottom of the laptop and the surface on which it rests, don't use a keyboard protector for an extended period of time, and be aware of your fan.

- Store your portable computer in a quality case when traveling. Laptops benefit from a cushy carrying case, while hard aluminum cases keep your PDA from getting banged up. Well-padded backpacks not only keep your laptop protected but also make your system less appealing to would-be thieves. When traveling, don't forget accessories such as AC power cords, additional batteries, or modular devices. Remove all discs from drives and make sure you have enough battery power to boot up for security personnel. If shipping your computer, go with a reputable carrier, keep your tracking number, and request a delivery signature. Use a laptop lock or a software tracking system to protect your laptop when traveling.

Troubleshoot portable computers

- If your laptop won't power on, try a different wall outlet. If it still fails to power up, remove all peripheral devices and try again.

- If the screen doesn't come on properly, verify that the laptop is configured to use the built-in LCD screen by pressing the appropriate key to cycle through the internal and external monitors. If you hear a popping sound, you may have blown an inverter. If the screen is definitely broken, you may use an external monitor to access the laptop.

- If wireless networking is not working, check for the physical switch on the front or side of the laptop that toggles power to the internal network card. If your laptop doesn't have a switch, check for a key combination or function key that toggles power. You also may be out of range. Physically walk the laptop closer to the wireless router or access point.

- If your PDA or tablet PC fails to recognize handwriting, retrain the digitizer. PDAs often have a setting to "align the screen," while tablet PC users can check the Control Panel for the appropriate applet.

- If the keypad or touchpad doesn't work, try a shot of compressed air, reseat the physical internal connection, or reconfigure the driver settings through the Control Panel Keyboard or Mouse applets.

Key Terms

Key Term Quiz

Use the Key Terms list to complete the sentences that follow. Not all terms will be used.

1. With the 386SX, Intel introduced __Smm__, the first power management system with the ability to make the CPU and all peripherals go to sleep.

2. Using a chemical reaction between hydrogen and oxygen, a(n) _____ may in a few years be able to provide a laptop with electrical power for up to 40 hours.

3. Most new laptops and portable devices use _____ batteries.

4. Lower-end laptop graphics cards use _____ to keep the price of the laptop down.

5. Using a(n) _____ often makes a laptop a more viable desktop replacement by giving the laptop more ports than are commonly found on laptops.

6. PC Cards require two levels of software drivers: __6A__ to allow the laptop to detect when a PC Card has been inserted or removed and __6B__ to provide drivers to make the card work.

Multiple-Choice Quiz

1. Which of the following statements best describes hard drives typically found in laptops?

    (A) They are 2.5-inch SATA drives, but they do not hold as much data as the 3.5-inch hard drives found in desktop PCs.

    B. They are 3.5-inch ATA drives just like those found in desktop PCs, but they usually require "cable select" settings rather than master or slave.

    C. They are 3.5-inch SATA drives that hold more data than the 2.5-inch hard drives found in desktop PCs.

    D. They are 2.5-inch PCMCIA drives, while desktops usually have 3.5-inch SCSI drives.

2. Portable PCs typically use which of the following kinds of upgradeable RAM?

    A. 68-pin and 72-pin RIMMs

    B. 30-pin and 72-pin SIMMs

    (C) 72-pin and 144-pin SO-DIMMs

    D. 30-pin and 72-pin SO-RIMMs

3. Which of the following kinds of PC Cards is the most commonly used, especially for I/O functions?

    A. Type I

    (B) Type II

    C. Type III

    D. Type IV

4. Juanita plugged in a new USB mouse, but her laptop does not recognize that a device has been added. What is the most likely cause for this problem?

   A. The device was plugged in while the system was running.

   B. The device was plugged in while the system was off, and then booted.

   C. The system is running Windows XP.

   D. The system does not yet have the proper drivers loaded.

5. How should you remove a modular drive?

   A. Use the Hardware Removal Tool in the system tray.

   B. Shut down, remove the drive, and power back on.

   C. Simply remove the drive with no additional actions.

   D. Use Device Manager to uninstall the device.

6. If wireless networking is not working, what should you check?

   A. Check the switch on the front or side of the laptop that toggles power to the network card.

   B. Make sure the Ethernet cable is plugged into the laptop.

   C. Make sure the digitizer has been trained.

   D. Make sure Power Management is enabled.

7. Which bus was developed specifically for integrated communications peripherals such as modems and network adapters?

   A. FireWire

   B. Mini PCI

   C. PCI

   D. USB

8. Erin has an older laptop with a switch on the back that says 115/230. What does this indicate?

   A. The laptop has an auto-switching power supply.

   B. The laptop has a fixed-input power supply.

   C. The laptop has a step-down transforming power supply.

   D. The laptop has a step-up transforming power supply.

9. John's PDA suddenly stopped recognizing his handwriting. What's a likely fix for this problem?

   A. Replace the stylus.

   B. Retrain the digitizer.

   C. Replace the digitizer.

   D. Retrain the stylus.

■ Essay Quiz

1. Norm wants to upgrade his laptop's hard drive, CPU, and RAM. Because he's upgraded all of these components on his desktop, he doesn't think he'll run into much trouble. What advice will you give him about selecting the components and upgrading the laptop?

2. Monica just received her aunt's old laptop. It uses a Ni-Cd battery, but no matter how long she charges it, it only runs her PC for about 30 minutes before it dies. She can't understand why the battery runs out so fast, but she figures she needs a new battery. The local computer store has two kinds of batteries, Ni-MH and Li-Ion, both of which will physically fit into her computer. She's not sure which of these to buy or whether either of them will work with her PC. She's asked you whether her old battery is indeed bad and to help her select a new battery. What will you tell her?

Lab Project

• Lab Project 11.1

A local company just donated 10 laptops to your school library. They are IBM ThinkPad 600x PIII 500-Mhz laptops with 128 MB of RAM and two Type II PC slots. The school would like to let distance-education students check out these computers, but the laptops do not have modems. Your hardware class has been [...] these laptops [...] selecting the [...] computer store or [...] modem cards you will re[...]

Mastering Printing

In this chapter, you will learn how to

- **Explain the laser printing process**
- **Install a printer on a Windows PC**
- **Recognize and fix basic printer problems**

I can't tell you how many geeks I've met who—despite being able to take apart and reassemble a PC from parts in mere minutes—refuse to install a printer on their machines because they're too much of a hassle. There's no reason things should be this way! Printers are incredibly useful devices that provide much-needed functionality to the PC, and no tech should be afraid of dealing with them. This chapter seeks to alleviate any printer anxiety you may have by showing you how to install and troubleshoot printers, but first, you're going to learn how laser printers work.

The Laser Printing Process

The laser printing process can be broken down into six steps, and the CompTIA A+ Practical Application exam expects you to know them all. As a tech, you should be familiar with these steps, as this can help you troubleshoot printing problems. For example, if an odd line is printed down the middle of every page, you know there's a problem with the photosensitive drum or cleaning mechanism and the toner cartridge needs to be replaced.

You'll look into the physical steps that occur each time a laser printer revs up and prints a page; then you'll see what happens electronically to ensure that the data is processed properly into flawless smooth text and graphics.

The Physical Side of the Process

Most laser printers perform the printing process in a series of six steps. Keep in mind that some brands of laser printers may depart somewhat from this process, although most work in exactly this order:

1. Clean
2. Charge
3. Write
4. Develop
5. Transfer
6. Fuse

Clean the Drum

The printing process begins with the physical and electrical cleaning of the photosensitive drum (Figure 12.1). Before printing each new page, the drum must be returned to a clean, fresh condition. All residual toner left over from printing the previous page must be removed, usually by scraping the surface of the drum with a rubber cleaning blade. If residual particles remain on the drum, they will appear as random black spots and streaks on the next page. The physical cleaning mechanism either deposits the residual toner in a debris cavity or recycles it by returning it to the toner supply in the toner cartridge. The physical cleaning must be done carefully. Damage to the drum will cause a permanent mark to be printed on every page.

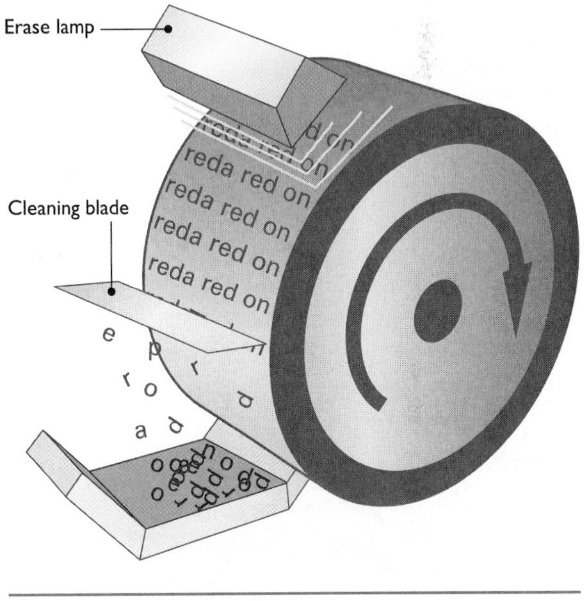

The printer must also be electrically cleaned. One or more **erase lamps** bombard the surface of the drum with the appropriate wavelengths of light, causing the surface particles to discharge into the grounded drum. After the cleaning process, the drum should be completely free of toner and have a neutral charge.

Erase lamp

Cleaning blade

• **Figure 12.1**   Cleaning and erasing the drum

Fax mechine it was invented In 1960

Charge the Drum

To make the drum receptive to new images, it must be charged (Figure 12.2). Using the primary corona wire, a uniform negative charge is applied to the entire surface of the drum (usually between ~600 and ~1000 volts).

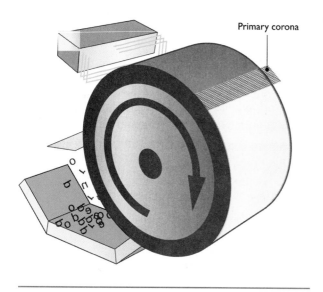

• **Figure 12.2** Charging the drum with a uniform negative charge

⚠ The heated roller produces enough heat to melt some types of plastic media, particularly overhead transparency materials. This could damage your laser printer (and void your warranty), so make sure you're printing on transparencies designed for laser printers!

Write and Develop the Image

A laser is used to write a positive image on the surface of the drum. Every particle on the drum hit by the laser releases most of its negative charge into the drum. Those particles with a lesser negative charge are positively charged relative to the toner particles and attract them, creating a developed image (Figure 12.3).

Transfer the Image

The printer must transfer the image from the drum onto the paper. The transfer corona gives the paper a positive charge; then the negatively charged toner particles leap from the drum to the paper. At this point, the particles are merely resting on the paper and must still be permanently fused to the paper.

Fuse the Image

The particles have been attracted to the paper because of the paper's positive charge, but if the process stopped here, the toner particles would fall off the page as soon as you lift it. Because the toner particles are mostly composed of plastic, they can be melted to the page. Two rollers—a heated roller coated in a nonstick material and a pressure roller—melt the toner to the paper, permanently affixing it. Finally, a static charge eliminator removes the paper's positive charge (Figure 12.4). Once the page is complete, the printer ejects the printed copy and the process begins again with the physical and electrical cleaning of the printer.

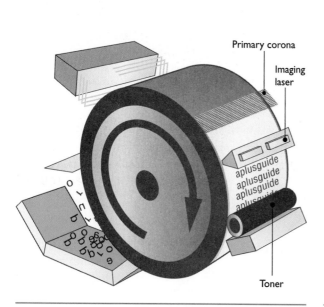

• **Figure 12.3** Writing the image and applying the toner

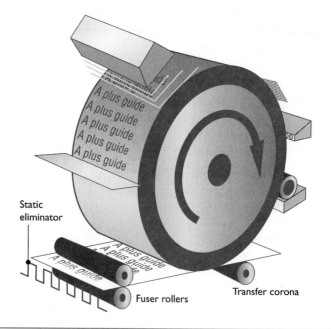

• **Figure 12.4** Transferring the image to the paper and fusing the final image

The Electronic Side of the Process

When you click the Print button in an application, several things happen. First, the CPU processes your request and sends a print job to an area of memory called the print spooler. The **print spooler** enables you to queue up multiple print jobs that the printer will handle sequentially. Next, Windows sends the first print job to the printer. That's your first potential bottleneck—if it's a big job, the OS has to dole out a piece at a time and you'll see the little printer icon in the notification area at the bottom right of your screen. Once the printer icon goes away, you know the print queue is empty—all jobs have gone to the printer.

Once the printer receives some or all of a print job, the hardware of the printer takes over and processes the image. That's your second potential bottleneck and has multiple components.

Raster Images

Impact printers transfer data to the printer one character or one line at a time, whereas laser printers transfer entire pages at a time to the printer. A laser printer generates a **raster image** (a pattern of dots) of the page, representing what the final product should look like. It uses a device (the laser) to "paint" a raster image on the photosensitive drum. Because a laser printer has to paint the entire surface of the photosensitive drum before it can begin to transfer the image to paper, it processes the image one page at a time.

A laser printer uses a chip called the **raster image processor (RIP)** to translate the raster image into commands to the laser. The RIP takes the digital information about fonts and graphics and converts it to a rasterized image made up of dots that can then be printed. An inkjet printer also has a RIP, but it's part of the software driver instead of onboard hardware circuitry. The RIP needs memory (RAM) to store the data that it must process. A laser printer must have enough memory to process an entire page. Some images that require high resolutions require more memory. Insufficient memory to process the image will usually be indicated by a memory overflow (MEM OVERFLOW) error. If you get a memory overflow error, try reducing the resolution, printing smaller graphics, or turning off RET (see the following section for the last option). Of course, the best solution to a memory overflow error is simply to add more RAM to the laser printer.

Do not assume that every error with the word *memory* in it can be fixed simply by adding more RAM to the printer. Just as adding more RAM chips will not solve every conventional PC memory problem, adding more RAM will not solve every laser printer memory problem. The message "21 ERROR" on an HP LaserJet, for example, indicates that "the printer is unable to process very complex data fast enough for the print engine." This means that the data is simply too complex for the RIP to handle. Adding more memory would *not* solve this problem; it would only make your wallet lighter. The only answer in this case is to reduce the complexity of the page image (that is, fewer fonts, less formatting, reduced graphics resolution, and so on).

Resolution

Laser printers can print at different resolutions, just as monitors can display different resolutions. The maximum resolution that a laser printer can handle is determined by its physical characteristics. Laser printer resolution is

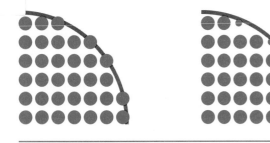

• **Figure 12.5** RET fills in gaps with smaller dots to smooth out jagged characters.

expressed in dots per inch (dpi). Common resolutions are 600 × 600 dpi or 1200 × 1200 dpi. The first number, the horizontal resolution, is determined by how fine a focus can be achieved by the laser. The second number is determined by the smallest increment by which the drum can be turned. Higher resolutions produce higher-quality output, but keep in mind that higher resolutions also require more memory. In some instances, complex images can be printed only at lower resolutions because of their high memory demands. Even printing at 300 dpi, laser printers produce far better quality than dot-matrix printers because of **resolution enhancement technology (RET)**.

RET enables the printer to insert smaller dots among the characters, smoothing out the jagged curves that are typical of printers that do not use RET (Figure 12.5). Using RET enables laser printers to output high-quality print jobs, but it also requires a portion of the printer's RAM. If you get a MEM OVERFLOW error, sometimes disabling RET will free up enough memory to complete the print job.

■ Installing a Printer in Windows

> The CompTIA A+ Practical Application exam tests you on installing and troubleshooting printers, so read these sections carefully!

You need to take a moment to understand how Windows handles printing, and then you'll see how to install, configure, and troubleshoot printers in these operating systems.

To Windows 2000, XP, and Vista/7, a printer is not a physical device; it is a *program* that controls one or more physical printers. The *physical* printer is called a print device to Windows (although I continue to use the term "printer" for most purposes, just like almost every tech on the planet). Printer drivers and a spooler are still present in Windows 2000/XP and Vista/7, but they are integrated into the printer itself (Figure 12.6). This arrangement gives Windows amazing flexibility. For example, one printer can support multiple print devices, enabling a system to act as a print server. If one print device goes down, the printer automatically redirects the output to a working print device.

The general installation, configuration, and troubleshooting issues are basically identical in all modern versions of Windows. Here's a review of a typical Windows printer installation. I'll mention the trivial differences among Windows 2000, XP, and Vista as I go along.

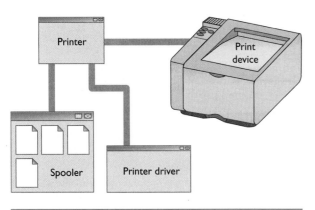

• **Figure 12.6** Printer driver and spooler in Windows

Setting Up Printers

Setting up a printer is so easy that it's almost scary. Most printers are plug and play, so installing a printer is reduced to simply plugging it in and loading the driver if needed. If the system does not detect the printer or if the printer is not plug and play, click Start | Printers and Faxes in Windows XP to open the Printers applet; in Windows 2000, click Start | Settings | Printers. For Windows Vista, you need to open up the Control Panel and find the Printer menu item—it is either by itself or, in the categorized view, under Hardware. You can also find the icon for this applet in the Control Panel of Windows 2000/XP.

As you might guess, you install a new printer by clicking the Add a Printer icon (somehow Microsoft has managed to leave the name of this applet unchanged through all Windows versions since 9x). This starts the Add Printer Wizard. After a pleasant intro screen, you must choose to install either a printer plugged directly into your system or a network printer (Figure 12.7). You also have the *Automatically detect and install My Plug and Play printer* option, which you can use in many cases when installing a USB printer.

If you choose a local printer (see Chapter 13, "Mastering Local Area Networking," for a discussion of networked printers), the applet next asks you to select a port; select the one where you installed the new printer (Figure 12.8). Once you select the port, Windows asks you to specify the type of printer, either by selecting the type from the list or by using the Have Disk option, just as you would for any other device (Figure 12.9). Note the handy Windows Update button, which you can use to get the latest printer driver from the Internet. When you click Next on this screen, Windows installs the printer.

Figure 12.10 shows a typical Windows XP Printers and Faxes screen on a system with one printer installed. Note the small checkmark in the icon's corner; this shows that the device is the default printer. If you have multiple printers, you can change the default printer by selecting the printer's properties and checking Make Default Printer.

In addition to the regular driver installation outlined previously, some installations use printer emulation. *Printer emulation* simply means using a substitute printer driver for a printer, as opposed to using one made exclusively for that printer. You'll run into printer emulation in two circumstances. First, some new printers do not come with their own drivers. They instead emulate a well-known printer (such as an HP LaserJet 4) and run perfectly well on that printer driver. Second, you may see emulation in the "I don't have the right driver!" scenario. I keep about three different HP LaserJet and Epson inkjet printers installed on my PC because I know that with these printer drivers, I can print to almost any printer. Some printers may require you to set them into an *emulation mode* to handle a driver other than their native one.

Optimizing Print Performance

Although a quality printer is the first step toward quality output, your output relies on factors other than the printer itself. What you see on the screen may not match what comes out of the printer, so calibration is important. Using the wrong type of paper can result in less than acceptable printed documents. Configuring the printer driver and spool settings can also affect your print jobs.

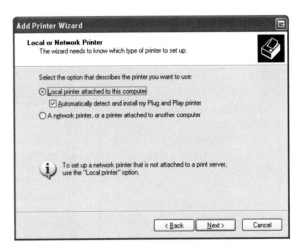

● **Figure 12.7** Choosing local or network printer in Windows XP

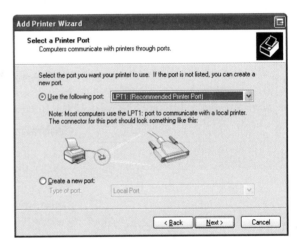

● **Figure 12.8** Selecting a port in Windows XP

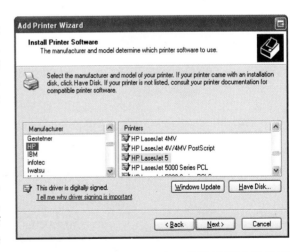

● **Figure 12.9** Selecting a printer model/driver in Windows XP

Tech Tip

Readme Files

You've seen how to get your system to recognize a printer, but what do you do when you add a brand-new printer? Like most peripherals, the printer will include an installation CD-ROM that contains various useful files. One of the most important but least used tools on this CD-ROM is the Readme file. This file, generally in TXT format, contains the absolute latest information on any idiosyncrasies, problems, or incompatibilities related to your printer or printer driver.

Usually, you can find it in the root folder of the installation CD-ROM, although many printer drivers install the Readme file on your hard drive so you can access it from the Start menu. The rule here is read first to avoid a headache later!

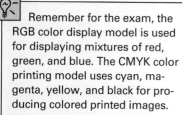

Remember for the exam, the RGB color display model is used for displaying mixtures of red, green, and blue. The CMYK color printing model uses cyan, magenta, yellow, and black for producing colored printed images.

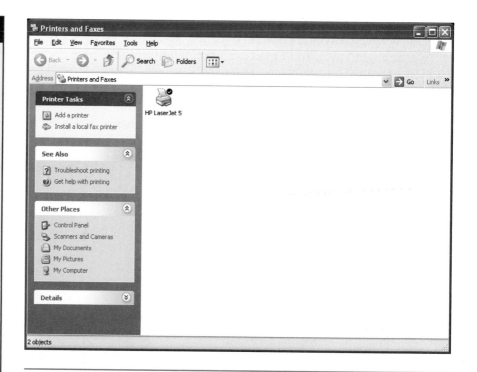

• **Figure 12.10**   Installed default printer in the Printers and Faxes applet

Calibration

If you've ever tweaked that digital photograph so it looks perfect on screen, only to discover that the final printout was darker than you had hoped, consider calibrating your monitor. **Calibration** matches the print output of your printer to the visual output on your monitor and governs that through software. All three parts need to be set up properly for you to print what you see consistently.

Computer monitors output in RGB—that is, they compose colors using red, green, and blue pixels, as discussed in Chapter 10, "Mastering Video and Multimedia"—while printers mix their colors differently to arrive at their output. As mentioned earlier, the CMYK method composes colors from cyan (blue), magenta (red), yellow, and black.

The upshot of all this is that the printer tries to output—by using CMYK (or another technique)—what you see on the screen using RGB. Because the two color modes do not create color the same way, you see color shifts and not-so-subtle differences between the onscreen image and the printed image. By calibrating your monitor, you can adjust the setting to match the output of your printer. You can do this manually through "eyeballing" it or automatically by using calibration hardware.

To calibrate your monitor manually, obtain a test image from the Web (try sites such as www.DigitalDog.net) and print it out. If you have a good eye, you can compare this printout to what you see on the screen and make the adjustments manually through your monitor's controls or display settings.

Another option is to calibrate your printer by using an International Color Consortium (ICC) color profile, a preference file that instructs your printer to print colors a certain way—for example, to match what is on your screen. Loading a different color profile results in a different color output.

Color profiles are sometimes included on the installation CD-ROM with a printer, but you can create or purchase custom profiles as well. The use of ICC profiles is not limited to printers; you can also use them to control the output of monitors, scanners, or even digital cameras. Windows Vista includes *Windows Color System* (*WCS*) to help build color profiles for use across devices. WCS is based on a new standard Microsoft calls *color infrastructure and translation engine* (*CITE*).

■ Troubleshooting Printers

As easy as printers are to set up, they are equally robust at running, assuming that you install the proper drivers and keep the printer well maintained. But printer errors do occasionally develop. Take a look at the most common print problems with Windows, as well as problems that crop up with specific printer types.

General Troubleshooting Issues

Printers of all stripes share some common problems, such as print jobs that don't go, strangely sized prints, and misalignment. Other issues include consumables, sharing multiple printers, and crashing on power-up. Let's take a look at these general troubleshooting issues, but start with a recap of the tools of the trade.

Tools of the Trade

Before you jump in and start to work on a printer that's giving you fits, you'll need some tools. You can use the standard computer tech tools in your toolkit, plus a couple of printer-specific devices. Here are some that will come in handy:

- A multimeter for troubleshooting electrical problems such as faulty wall outlets
- Various cleaning solutions, such as denatured alcohol
- An extension magnet for grabbing loose screws in tight spaces and cleaning up iron-based toner
- An optical disc or USB thumb drive with test patterns for checking print quality
- Your trusty screwdriver—both a Phillips-head and flat-head, because if you bring just one kind, it's a sure bet that you'll need the other

Print Job Never Prints

If you click Print but nothing comes out of the printer, first check all the obvious things. Is the printer on? Is it connected? Is it online? Does it have paper? Assuming the printer is in good order, it's time to look at the spooler. You can see the spooler status either by double-clicking the printer's icon in the Printers applet or by double-clicking the tiny printer icon in the notification area if it's present. If you're having a problem, the printer icon will almost always be there. Figure 12.11 shows the print spooler open.

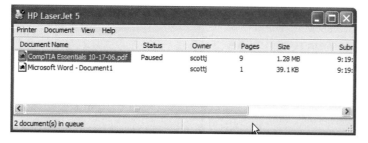

● **Figure 12.11**   Print spooler

Print spoolers can easily overflow or become corrupt due to a lack of disk space, too many print jobs, or one of a thousand other factors. The status window shows all of the pending print jobs and enables you to delete, start, or pause jobs. I usually just delete the affected print job(s) and try again.

Print spoolers are handy. If the printer goes down, you can just leave the print jobs in the spooler until the printer comes back online. Some versions of Windows require you to select Resume Printing manually, but others automatically continue the print job(s). If you have a printer that isn't coming on anytime soon, you can simply delete the print job in the spooler window and try another printer.

If you have problems with the print spooler, you can get around them by changing your print spool settings. Go into the Printers and Faxes applet, right-click the icon of the printer in question, and choose Properties. In the resulting Properties window (see Figure 12.12), choose the *Print directly to the printer* radio button and click OK; then try sending your print job again. Note that this window also offers you the choice of printing immediately—that is, starting to print pages as soon as the spooler has enough information to feed to the printer—or holding off on printing until the entire job is spooled.

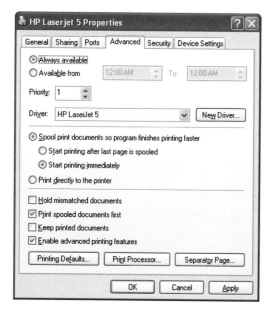

● **Figure 12.12**   Print spool settings

> If you try all this and you still can't print, double-check your connections and make sure the printer is still plugged in. If it's plugged in, try turning the printer off and then back on. CompTIA calls this *power cycling*.

Another possible cause for a stalled print job is that the printer is simply waiting for the correct paper! Laser printers in particular have settings that tell them what size paper is in their standard paper tray or trays. If the application sending a print job specifies a different paper size—for example, it wants to print a standard No. 10 envelope, or perhaps a legal sheet, but the standard paper tray holds only 8.5 × 11 letter paper—the printer usually pauses and holds up the queue until someone switches out the tray or manually feeds the type of paper that this print job requires. You can usually override this pause, even without having the specified paper, by pressing the OK or GO button on the printer.

The printer's default paper tray and paper size options will differ greatly depending on the printer type and model. To find these settings, go into the printer's Properties window from the Printers and Faxes applet, and then select the Device Settings tab. This list of settings includes Form To Tray Assignment, where you can specify which tray (in the case of a printer with multiple paper trays) holds which size paper.

Strange Sizes

A print job that comes out a strange size usually points to a user mistake in setting up the print job. All applications have a Print command and a Page Setup interface. The Page Setup interface enables you to define a number of print options, which vary from application to application. Figure 12.13 shows the Page Setup options for Microsoft Word. Make sure the page is set up properly before you blame the printer for a problem.

If you know the page is set up correctly, recheck the printer drivers. If necessary, uninstall and reinstall the printer drivers. If the problem persists, you may have a serious problem with the printer's print engine, but that comes up as a likely answer only when you continually get the same strangely sized printouts when using a variety of applications.

Misaligned or Garbage Prints

Misaligned or garbage printouts invariably point to a corrupted or incorrect driver. Make sure you're using the right driver (it's hard to mess this up, but not impossible) and then uninstall and reinstall the printer driver. If the problem persists, you may be asking the printer to do something it cannot do. For example, you may be printing to a PostScript printer with a PCL driver. Check the printer type to verify that you haven't installed the wrong type of driver for that printer!

Dealing with Consumables

All printers tend to generate a lot of trash in the form of **consumables**. Impact printers use paper and ribbons, inkjet printers use paper and ink cartridges, and laser printers use paper and toner cartridges. In today's environmentally sensitive world, many laws regulate the proper disposal of most printer components. Be sure to check with the local sanitation department or disposal services company before throwing away any component. Of course, you should never throw away toner cartridges—certain companies will *pay* for used cartridges!

Problems Sharing Multiple Printers

If you want to use multiple printers attached to the same parallel port, you have to use a switch box. Laser printers should never be used with mechanical switch boxes. Mechanical switch boxes create power surges that can damage your printer. If you must use a switch box, use a box that switches between printers electronically and has built-in surge protection.

Crashes on Power-up

Both laser printers and PCs require more power during their initial power-up (the POST on a PC and the warm-up on a laser printer) than once they are running. Hewlett-Packard recommends a *reverse power-up*. Turn on the laser printer first and allow it to finish its warm-up before turning on the PC. This avoids having two devices drawing their peak loads simultaneously.

Troubleshooting Dot-Matrix Printers

Impact printers require regular maintenance but will run forever as long as you're diligent. Keep the platen (the roller or plate on which the pins impact) clean and the printhead clean with denatured alcohol. Be sure to lubricate gears and pulleys according to the manufacturer's specifications. Never lubricate the printhead, however, because the lubricant will smear and stain the paper.

Bad-looking Text

White bars going through the text point to a dirty or damaged printhead. Try cleaning the printhead with a little denatured alcohol. If the problem persists, replace the printhead. Printheads for most printers are readily available from the manufacturer or from companies that rebuild them. If the characters look

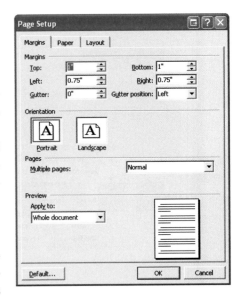

• **Figure 12.13** Page Setup options for Microsoft Word

MSDSs contain important information regarding hazardous materials such as safe use procedures and emergency response instructions. An MSDS is typically posted anywhere a hazardous chemical is used.

~~chopped off at the top or bottom, the printhead probably needs to be adjusted.~~ Refer to the manufacturer's instructions for proper adjustment.

Bad-looking Page

If the page is covered with dots and small smudges—the "pepper look"—the platen is dirty. Clean the platen with denatured alcohol. If the image is faded, and you know the ribbon is good, try adjusting the printhead closer to the platen. If the image is okay on one side of the paper but fades as you move to the other, the platen is out of adjustment. Platens are generally difficult to adjust, so your best plan is to take it to the manufacturer's local warranty/repair center.

Troubleshooting Inkjet Printers

Inkjet printers are reliable devices that require little maintenance as long as they are used within their design parameters (high-use machines will require more intensive maintenance). Because of the low price of these printers, manufacturers know that people don't want to spend a lot of money keeping them running. If you perform even the most basic maintenance tasks, they will soldier on for years without a whimper. Inkjets generally have built-in maintenance programs that you should run from time to time to keep your inkjet in good operating order.

• **Figure 12.14**   Inkjet printer maintenance screen

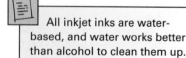

All inkjet inks are water-based, and water works better than alcohol to clean them up.

Inkjet Printer Maintenance

Inkjet printers don't get nearly as dirty as laser printers, and most manufacturers do not recommend periodic cleaning. Unless your manufacturer explicitly tells you to do so, don't vacuum an inkjet. Inkjets generally do not have maintenance kits, but most inkjet printers come with extensive maintenance software (Figure 12.14). Usually, the hardest part of using this software is finding it in the first place. Look for an option in Printing Preferences, a selection on the Start menu, or an icon on your desktop. Don't worry—it's there!

When you first set up an inkjet printer, it normally instructs you to perform a routine to align the printheads properly, wherein you print out a page and select from sets of numbered lines. If this isn't done, the print quality will show it, but the good news is that you can perform this procedure at any time. If a printer is moved or dropped or it's just been working away untended for a while, it's often worth running the alignment routine.

Inkjet Problems

Did I say that you never should clean an inkjet? Well, that may be true for the printer itself, but there is one part of your printer that will benefit from an occasional cleaning: the inkjet's printhead nozzles. The nozzles are the tiny pipes that squirt the ink onto the paper. A common problem with inkjet printers is the tendency for the ink inside the nozzles to dry out when not used even for a relatively short time, blocking any ink from exiting. If your printer is telling Windows that it's printing and it's feeding paper through, but either nothing is coming out (usually the case if you're just printing black text) or only certain colors are printing, the culprit is almost certainly dried ink clogging the nozzles.

Every inkjet has a different procedure for cleaning the printhead nozzles. On older inkjets, you usually have to press buttons on the printer to start a maintenance program. On more modern inkjets, you can access the head-cleaning maintenance program from Windows.

Another problem that sometimes arises is the dreaded multisheet paper grab. This is often not actually your printer's fault—humidity can cause sheets of paper to cling to each other—but sometimes the culprit is an overheated printer, so if you've been cranking out a lot of documents without stopping, try giving the printer a bit of a coffee break. Also, fan the sheets of the paper stack before inserting it into the paper tray.

Finally, check to see if excess ink overflow is a problem. In the area where the printheads park, look for a small tank or tray that catches excess ink from the cleaning process. If the printer has one, check to see how full it is. If this tray overflows onto the main board or even the power supply, it will kill your printer. If you discover that the tray is about to overflow, you can remove excess ink by inserting a twisted paper towel into the tank to soak up some of the ink. It is advisable to wear latex or vinyl gloves while doing this. Clean up any spilled ink with a paper towel dampened with distilled water.

> Cleaning the heads on an inkjet printer is sometimes necessary, but I don't recommend that you do it on a regular basis as preventive maintenance. The head-cleaning process uses up a lot of that very expensive inkjet ink—so do this only when a printing problem seems to indicate clogged or dirty printheads!

Troubleshooting Laser Printers

Quite a few problems can arise with laser printers, but before getting into those details, you need to review some recommended procedures for *avoiding* those problems.

> Before you service a laser printer, always, *always* turn it off and unplug it! Don't expose yourself to the very dangerous high voltages found inside these machines.

Laser Printer Maintenance

Unlike PC maintenance, laser printer maintenance follows a fairly well established procedure. Follow these steps to ensure a long, healthy life for your system.

Keep It Clean   Laser printers are quite robust as a rule. A good cleaning every time you replace the toner cartridge will help that printer last for many years. I know of many examples of original HP LaserJet I printers continuing to run perfectly after a dozen or more years of operation. The secret is that they were kept immaculately clean.

Your laser printer gets dirty in two ways: Excess toner, over time, will slowly coat the entire printer. Paper dust, sometimes called *paper dander*, tends to build up where the paper is bent around rollers or where pickup rollers grab paper. Unlike (black) toner, paper dust is easy to see and is usually a good indicator that a printer needs to be cleaned. Usually, a thorough cleaning using a can of pressurized air to blow out the printer is the best cleaning you can do. It's best to do this outdoors, or you may end up looking like one of those chimney sweeps from *Mary Poppins*! If you must clean a printer indoors, use a special low-static vacuum designed especially for electronic components (Figure 12.15).

Every laser printer has its own unique cleaning method, but the cleaning instructions tend to skip one little area. Every laser printer has a number of rubber guide rollers through which the paper is run during the print process. These little rollers tend to pick up dirt and paper dust over time, making them slip and jam paper. They are easily cleaned with a small amount of 90-percent or better alcohol on a

• **Figure 12.15**   Low-static vacuum

fibrous cleaning towel. The alcohol will remove the debris and any dead rubber. You can also give the rollers and separator pads a textured surface that will restore their feeding properties by rubbing them with a little alcohol on a nonmetallic scouring pad.

If you're ready to get specific, get the printer's service manual. Almost every printer manufacturer sells these; they are a key source for information on how to keep a printer clean and running. Sadly, not all printer manufacturers provide these, but most do. While you're at it, see if the manufacturer has a Quick Reference Guide; these can be very handy for most printer problems!

Finally, be aware that Hewlett-Packard sells maintenance kits for most of its laser printers. These are sets of replacement parts for the parts most likely to wear out on each particular type of HP LaserJet. Although their use is not required to maintain warranty coverage, using these kits when prescribed by HP helps assure the continuing reliability of your LaserJet.

Periodic Maintenance   Although keeping the printer clean is critical to its health and well-being, every laser printer has certain components that you need to replace periodically. Your ultimate source for determining the parts that need to be replaced (and when to replace them) is the printer manufacturer. Following the manufacturer's maintenance guidelines will help to ensure years of trouble-free, dependable printing from your laser printer.

Many manufacturers provide kits that contain components you should replace on a regular schedule. These **maintenance kits** often include a fuser as well as one or more rollers or pads. Typically, you need to reset the page counter after installing a maintenance kit so the printer can remind you to perform maintenance again after a certain number of pages have been printed.

Some ozone filters can be cleaned with a vacuum and some can only be replaced—follow the manufacturer's recommendation. You can clean the fuser assembly with 90-percent or better denatured alcohol. Check the heat roller (the Teflon-coated one with the light bulb inside) for pits and scratches. If you see surface damage on the rollers, replace the fuser unit.

Most printers will give you an error code when the fuser is damaged or overheating and needs to be replaced; others will produce the error code at a preset copy count as a preventive maintenance measure. Again, follow the manufacturer's recommendations.

The transfer corona can be cleaned with a 90-percent denatured alcohol solution on a cotton swab. If the wire is broken, you can replace it; many just snap in or are held in by a couple of screws. Paper guides can also be cleaned with alcohol on a fibrous towel.

Laser Printer Problems

Laser printers usually manifest problems by creating poor output. One of the most important tests you can do on any printer, not just a laser printer, is called a *diagnostic print page* or an *engine test page*. You do this by either holding down the On Line button as the printer is started or using the printer's maintenance software.

Blank Paper   Blank sheets of paper usually mean the printer is out of toner. If the printer does have toner and nothing prints, print a diagnostic print page. If that is also blank, remove the toner cartridge and look at the imaging drum inside. If the image is still there, you know the transfer corona or the high-voltage power supply has failed. Check the printer's maintenance guide to see how to focus on the bad part and replace it.

Dirty Printouts　If the fusing mechanism gets dirty in a laser printer, it will leave a light dusting of toner all over the paper, particularly on the back of the page. When you see toner speckles on your printouts, you should get the printer cleaned.

Ghosting　Ghost images sometimes appear at regular intervals on the printed page. This happens when the imaging drum has not fully discharged and is picking up toner from a previous image or when a previous image has used up so much toner that either the supply of charged toner is insufficient or the toner has not been adequately charged. Sometimes it can also be caused by a worn-out cleaning blade that isn't removing the toner from the drum.

Light Ghosting versus Dark Ghosting　A variety of problems can cause both light and dark ghosting, but the most common source of light ghosting is "developer starvation." If you ask a laser printer to print an extremely dark or complex image, it can use up so much toner that the toner cartridge will not be able to charge enough toner to print the next image. The proper solution is to use less toner. You can fix ghosting problems in the following ways:

- Lower the resolution of the page (print at 300 dpi instead of 600 dpi).
- Use a different pattern.
- Avoid 50-percent grayscale and "dot-on/dot-off patterns."
- Change the layout so that grayscale patterns do not follow black areas.
- Make dark patterns lighter and light patterns darker.
- Print in landscape orientation.
- Adjust print density and RET settings.
- Print a completely blank page immediately prior to the page with the ghosting image, as part of the same print job.

In addition to these possibilities, low temperature and low humidity can aggravate ghosting problems. Check your users' manual for environmental recommendations. Dark ghosting can sometimes be caused by a damaged drum. It may be fixed by replacing the toner cartridge. Light ghosting would *not* be solved in this way. Switching other components will not usually affect ghosting problems, because they are a side effect of the entire printing process.

Vertical White Lines　Vertical white lines usually happen when the toner is clogged, preventing the proper dispersion of toner on the drum. Try shaking the toner cartridge to dislodge the clog. If that doesn't work, replace the toner cartridge.

Blotchy Print　Blotches are commonly a result of uneven dispersion of toner, especially if the toner is low. Shake the toner from side to side and then try to print. Also be sure that the printer is sitting level. Finally, make sure the paper is not wet in spots. If the blotches are in a regular order, check the fusing rollers and the photosensitive drum for any foreign objects.

Spotty Print　If the spots appear at regular intervals, the drum may be damaged or some toner may be stuck to the fuser rollers. Try wiping off the fuser rollers. Check the drum for damage. If the drum is damaged, get a new toner cartridge.

Embossed Effect   If your prints are getting an embossed effect (like putting a penny under a piece of paper and rubbing it with a lead pencil), there is almost certainly a foreign object on a roller. Use 90-percent denatured alcohol or regular water with a soft cloth to try to remove it. If the foreign object is on the photosensitive drum, you're going to have to use a new toner cartridge. An embossed effect can also be caused by the contrast control being set too high. The contrast control is actually a knob on the inside of the unit (sometimes accessible from the outside, on older models). Check your manual for the specific location.

Incomplete Characters   You can sometimes correct incompletely printed characters on laser-printed transparencies by adjusting the print density. Be extremely careful to use only materials approved for use in laser printers.

Creased Pages   Laser printers have up to four rollers. In addition to the heat and pressure rollers of the fuser assembly, other rollers move the paper from the source tray to the output tray. These rollers crease the paper to avoid curling that would cause paper jams in the printer. If the creases are noticeable, try using a different paper type. Cotton bond paper is usually more susceptible to noticeable creasing than other bonds. You might also try sending the output to the face-up tray, which avoids one roller. There is no hardware solution to this problem; it is simply a side effect of the process.

Paper Jams   Every printer jams now and then. If you get a jam, always refer first to the manufacturer's jam removal procedure. It is simply too easy to damage a printer by pulling on the jammed paper! If the printer reports a jam but there's no paper inside, you've almost certainly got a problem with one of the many jam sensors or paper feed sensors inside the printer, and you'll need to take it to a repair center.

Pulling Multiple Sheets   If the printer grabs multiple sheets at a time, first try opening a new ream of paper and loading that in the printer. If that works, you have a humidity problem. If the new paper angle doesn't work, check the separation pad on the printer. The separation pad is a small piece of cork or rubber that separates the sheets as they are pulled from the paper feed tray. A worn separation pad looks shiny and, well, *worn*! Most separation pads are easy to replace. Check out www.printerworks.com to see if you can replace yours.

Warped, Overprinted, or Poorly Formed Characters   Poorly formed characters can indicate either a problem with the paper (or other media) or a problem with the hardware.

Incorrect media cause a number of these types of problems. Avoid paper that is too rough or too smooth. Paper that is too rough interferes with the fusing of characters and their initial definition. If the paper is too smooth (like some coated papers, for example), it may feed improperly, causing distorted or overwritten characters. Even though you can purchase laser printer–specific paper, all laser printers print acceptably on standard photocopy paper. Try to keep the paper from becoming too wet. Don't open a ream of paper until it is time to load it into the printer. Always fan the paper before loading it into the printer, especially if the paper has been left out of the package for more than just a few days.

The durability of a well-maintained laser printer makes hardware a much rarer source of character printing problems, but you should be aware of the possibility. Fortunately, it is fairly easy to check the hardware. Most laser printers have a self-test function—often combined with a diagnostic printout but sometimes as a separate process. This self-test shows whether the laser printer can properly develop an image without actually having to send print commands from the PC. The self-test is quite handy to verify the question "Is it the printer or is it the computer?" Run the self-test to check for connectivity and configuration problems.

Possible solutions include replacing the toner cartridge, especially if you hear popping noises; checking the cabling; and replacing the data cable, especially if it has bends or crimps or if objects are resting on the cable. If you have a front menu panel, turn off advanced functions and high-speed settings to determine whether the advanced functions are either not working properly or not supported by your current software configuration (check your manuals for configuration information). If these solutions do not work, the problem may not be user serviceable. Contact an authorized service center.

Beyond A+

DOT4

The IEEE 1284.4 standard, commonly known as DOT4, was created for multifunction peripherals (MFPs)—those nifty gadgets that combine the functions of printer, fax, and scanner in one big piece of equipment (Figure 12.16). The DOT4 protocol enables the individual devices within the MFP to send and receive multiple data packets simultaneously across a single physical channel. All data exchanges are independent of one another, so you can cancel one—for example, a print job—without affecting the others. DOT4 is an enhancement of the IEEE 1284 protocol for parallel printing; look for products that use it the next time you find yourself in a computer superstore.

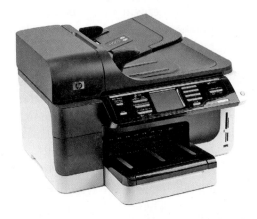

• **Figure 12.16**   All-in-one printer/scanner/fax machine/copier/coffee maker/iPod dock

Chapter 12 Review

■ Chapter Summary

After reading this chapter and completing the exercises, you should understand the following aspects of printers.

Explain the laser printing process

■ Laser printing is a six-step process: clean, charge, write, develop, transfer, and fuse.

■ The printing process begins with the physical and electrical cleaning of the photosensitive drum. All residual toner left over from printing the previous page must be removed, usually by scraping the surface of the drum with a rubber cleaning blade. One or more erase lamps bombard the surface of the drum with the appropriate wavelengths of light, causing the surface particles to discharge completely into the grounded drum.

■ Using the primary corona wire, a uniform negative charge is applied to the entire surface of the drum (usually between ~600 and ~1,000 volts) to make the drum receptive to new images. A laser is used to write a positive image relative to the toner particles on the surface of the drum, attracting them and creating a developed image. The transfer corona gives the paper a positive charge, making the negatively charged toner particles leap from the drum to the paper. The toner particles are mostly composed of plastic, so they can be melted to the page. Two rollers, a heated roller coated in a nonstick material and a pressure roller, melt the toner to the paper, permanently affixing it. Finally, a static charge eliminator removes the paper's positive charge. Once the page is complete, the printer ejects the printed copy and the process begins again with the physical and electrical cleaning of the printer.

■ Laser printers generate a pattern of dots, called a raster image, representing what each page should look like. Laser printers use the laser to "paint" the raster image on the photosensitive drum. Laser printers use a chip called the RIP to translate the raster image sent to the printer into commands to the laser.

■ Laser printer resolution is expressed in dots per inch (dpi). Common resolutions are 600 dpi × 600 dpi or 1200 dpi × 1200 dpi. The first number, the horizontal resolution, is determined by how fine a focus can be achieved by the laser. The second number is determined by the smallest increment by which the drum can be turned. Higher resolutions produce higher-quality output but also require more memory. Even printing at 300 dpi, laser printers produce far better quality than dot-matrix printers, because RET enables the printer to insert smaller dots among the characters, smoothing out the jagged curves that are typical of printers that do not use RET.

Install a printer on a Windows PC

■ In Windows 2000/XP/Vista, a printer is not a physical device; it is a program that controls one or more physical printers. The physical printer is called a print device. Print drivers and a spooler are still present in 2000/XP/Vista, but they are integrated into the printer itself.

■ Select Start | Printers and Faxes in Windows XP to open the Printers applet; in Windows 2000, select Start | Settings | Printers. In Windows Vista, select the Printers item from the Control Panel. This applet can also be found in the Control Panel of Windows 2000/XP. You install a new printer by clicking the Add Printer icon to start the Add Printer Wizard. You must choose to install a local or a network printer, and you must select a port for a local printer. You must specify the printer type from the wizard's list, or use the Have Disk option. Windows XP and Vista's applet features a Windows Update button you can use to get the latest printer driver from the Internet.

■ One printer will always be the default printer. If you have more than one printer installed, you can make any printer the default printer. The icon for the default printer has a small checkmark in the corner. If you have multiple printers, you can change the default printer by selecting the printer's properties and checking Make Default Printer.

■ Printer emulation means to use a substitute printer driver for a printer, as opposed to one made exclusively for that printer. Some printers are designed to emulate other, more widely supported models. If you don't have the specific driver for a printer, you can often use the driver from a similar model.

■ Your monitor creates colors by using RGB, while a printer outputs in CMYK. This difference can lead to a printed page differing greatly in color and tone from what you see on the monitor. Calibrating your monitor to your printer is an important step in printing the colors you see on your screen. Manually calibrate your monitor by eyeballing it, use ICC color profiles to instruct the printer to output colors a certain way, or use calibration hardware and software to automate the process. Windows Vista includes Windows Color System to help build color profiles for use across devices.

Recognize and fix basic printer problems

- When troubleshooting a printer, first check all the obvious things. Is the printer on? Is it connected? Is it online? Does it have paper? Then check the spooler status either by double-clicking the printer's icon in the Printers applet or by double-clicking the tiny printer icon in the system tray, if it's present. You may be able to bypass spooler problems by changing the printer properties setting to *Print directly to the printer*.

- A print job that comes out a strange size usually points to a user mistake in setting up the print job. Use the program's Page Setup feature to fix these problems. If you know the page is set up correctly, recheck the printer drivers. Misaligned or garbage printouts invariably point to a corrupted or incorrect driver.

- Printer manufacturers will supply an MSDS for each of their products; they provide detailed information about the potential environmental hazards associated with different components and proper disposal methods. This isn't just a printer issue—you can find an MSDS for most PC components.

- Turn on the laser printer first and allow it to finish its warm-up before turning on the PC (a reverse power-up). This avoids having two devices drawing their peak loads simultaneously.

- With regular maintenance, impact printers run forever. White bars going through the text point to a dirty or damaged printhead. Try cleaning the printhead with a little 90-percent or better denatured alcohol. If the characters look chopped off at the top or bottom, you probably need to adjust the printhead.

- Inkjet printers generally have built-in maintenance programs that you should run from time to time to keep your inkjet in good operating order. A common problem with inkjet printers is the tendency for the ink inside the nozzles to dry out when not used even for a relatively short time, blocking any ink from exiting. To clean the nozzles on older inkjets, you usually have to press buttons on the printer

to start a maintenance program. On more modern inkjets, you can access the head-cleaning maintenance program from Windows.

- One of the most important tests you can do on any printer, not just a laser printer, is called a diagnostic print page or an engine test page. There are two types of printer tests: the Windows test in which you print a test page, and the printer self-test that runs from the printer itself.

- Over time, excess toner will slowly coat the entire printer. Paper dander will build up where the paper is bent around rollers or where pickup rollers grab paper. Use a small amount of 90-percent or better alcohol on a fibrous cleaning towel to remove the debris and any dead rubber.

- Blank sheets of paper usually mean the printer is out of toner. If the printer has toner and nothing prints, print a diagnostic print page. If that is also blank, remove the toner cartridge and look at the imaging drum inside. If the image is still there, you know the transfer corona or the high-voltage power supply has failed. Blotchy print is most commonly due to uneven dispersion of toner, especially if the toner is low; also check that the printer is level and the paper completely dry.

- Ghost images can be caused either because the imaging drum has not fully discharged (and is picking up toner from a previous image) or because a previous image has used up so much toner that either the supply of charged toner is insufficient or the toner has not been adequately charged. Dark ghosting can sometimes be caused by a damaged drum. It may be fixed by replacing the toner cartridge. Light ghosting would *not* be solved in this way.

- The rollers that move the paper from the source tray to the output tray crease the paper to avoid curling that would cause paper jams in the printer. If the creases are noticeable, try using a different paper type. If the printer reports a jam but there's no paper inside, you've almost certainly got a problem with one of the many jam sensors or paper feed sensors. If the printer grabs multiple sheets at a time, it may be humidity or a worn separation pad. Hardware problems are a much rarer source of character printing problems. Most laser printers have a self-test function that shows whether the laser printer can properly develop an image without having to send print commands from the PC. Run the self-test to check for connectivity and configuration problems.

Key Terms

calibration *(378)* 2
consumables *(381)* 7
erase lamp *(373)* 1
maintenance kit *(384)* 6
material safety data sheet (MSDS) *(381)* 4

print spooler *(375)* 5
raster image *(375)* 3
raster image processor (RIP) *(375)*
resolution enhancement technology (RET) *(376)*

Key Term Quiz

Use the Key Terms list to complete the sentences that follow. Not all terms will be used.

1. The _____ is responsible for cleaning the photosensitive drum of electrical charge.

2. _____ matches the print output of your printer to the visual output on your monitor and governs that through software.

3. A laser printer generates a pattern of dots on the page called a(n) _____.

4. A(n) _____ provides information about the disposal of potential environmental hazards such as toner or ink cartridges.

5. The _____ enables you to queue up multiple print jobs that the printer will handle sequentially.

6. _____ often include a fuser as well as one or more rollers or pads.

7. The items used by printers (for example, paper, toner, and ink) are called _____.

Multiple-Choice Quiz

1. Which part of a laser printer applies a positive charge to the paper that attracts the toner particles to it?

   A. Erase lamp

   B. Transfer corona

   C. Laser

   D. Primary corona

2. Frank's color inkjet printer no longer prints the color yellow, though it prints all the other colors just fine. The printer worked fine last month, the last time he printed in color. Which of the following is the most likely problem?

   A. He turned off the yellow nozzle.

   B. He has run out of yellow ink.

   C. He has a corrupt printer driver.

   D. His printer is set to monochrome mode.

3. Beth's laser printer is printing tiny specks on the paper. What should she do first?

   A. Wipe the paper with bleach.

   B. Run the printer maintenance program.

   C. Clean the nozzles.

   D. Vacuum the printer.

4. Ursula's laser printer has stopped working and is displaying this error message: "Error 81 – Service." What should she do first?

   A. Update the printer's firmware.

   B. Reinstall the printer driver.

   C. Try to find the error in the user's guide or maintenance program or online.

   D. Turn off the printer and call the manufacturer's help line.

5. Kevin's inkjet printer isn't printing blue (cyan). He checks the ink levels and sees that there's plenty of ink. What should he consider next?

   A. A printhead is jammed.

   B. A laser is blocked.

   C. A nozzle is clogged.

   D. An ink cartridge is missing.

6. The output from Diane's laser printer is fading evenly. What should she suspect first?

   A. A laser is blocked.

   B. The printer is out of toner.

   C. A nozzle is clogged.

   D. Her printer is dirty.

7. Sheila in accounting needs to print receipts in duplicate. The white copy stays with accounting and the pink copy goes to the customer. What type of printer should you install?

   A. Inkjet

   B. Impact

   C. Laser Jet

   D. Thermal wax transfer

8. Your laser printer fails to print your print jobs and instead displays a MEM OVERFLOW error. What can you do to rectify the problem? (Select two.)

   A. Install more printer RAM

   B. Install more PC RAM

   C. Upgrade the RIP

   D. Disable RET

9. What is the proper order of the laser printing process?

   A. Clean, charge, write, develop, transfer, and fuse

   B. Charge, write, transfer, fuse, develop, and clean

   C. Clean, write, develop, transfer, fuse, and charge

   D. Clean, charge, write, develop, fuse, and transfer

■ Essay Quiz

1. Your boss is fascinated by the laser printing process. Write a short memo that outlines how it works, in the proper order.

2. Any tech worth his salt can reliably perform basic troubleshooting on all kinds of printers. Write an essay describing some of the standard methods for troubleshooting printers in general and give at least one tip for each type of printer listed in this chapter: laser, inkjet, and dot matrix.

Lab Project

• Lab Project 12.1

Laser printers often have rather complex maintenance procedures and schedules. Select a laser printer—preferably one that you actually have on hand—and answer the following questions.

   1 Using the user's guide or online sources, determine the exact cleaning procedures for your laser printer. How often should it be vacuumed? Do any parts need to be removed for cleaning? Does the manufacturer recommend any specialized cleaning steps? Does your printer come with any specialized cleaning tools? Does the manufacturer have any recommended cleaning tools you should purchase?

   2 Based on the information you gathered, create a cleaning toolkit for your laser printer. Be sure to include a vacuum. Locate sources for these products and determine the cost of the toolkit.

   3 Determine the model number of the toner cartridge. Locate an online company that sells name-brand (such as Hewlett-Packard) toner cartridges. Locate an equivalent third-party toner cartridge. Assuming that the printer uses a toner cartridge every three months, what is your per system annual cost savings if using third-party toner cartridges?

   4 All toner cartridges have a material safety data sheet (MSDS). Locate the MSDS for your model of toner cartridge and read it. Note any potential hazards of the toner cartridges.

   5 Print out the description of the cleaning kit you created as well as the manufacturer's cleaning instructions.

13

Mastering Local Area Networking

"Networking is an essential part of building wealth."

—Armstrong Williams

In this chapter, you will learn how to

- **Explain network operating systems**
- **Install and configure wired networks**

The invention of the first computer was nothing compared to the invention of the first computer network. You've spent this entire book so far learning about all the amazing things that individual computers can do, but it's only when you get multiple computers together in a network that you can truly see the fantastic potential of the personal computer.

Without computer networks, modern life would, quite simply, not exist. This is great news for PC techs, because it means that there will always be work installing and repairing computer networks—at least until we all get Internet access implanted in our brains. That said, this chapter introduces you to the exciting, complex world of network troubleshooting.

■ Network Operating Systems

The CompTIA A+ Practical Application exam assumes that you are already familiar with two of the four main requirements for making a network work. Through Ethernet, you have a NIC for the PC that handles splitting data into packets and putting the packets back together at the destination PC. You've got a cabling standard to connect the NIC to a hub or switch, thus making that data transfer possible. Now it's time to dive into the third and fourth requirements for a network. You need an operating system that can communicate with the hardware and with other networked PCs, and you need some sort of server machine to give out data or services. The third and fourth requirements are handled by a network operating system.

 The CompTIA A+ Practical Application exam assumes you have a working knowledge of network operating systems.

In a classic sense, a **network operating system (NOS)** is a portion of your operating system that communicates with the PC hardware and makes the connections among multiple machines on a network. The NOS enables one or more PCs to act as server machines and share data and services over a network—to share **resources**, in other words. You then need to run software on client computers so those computers can access the shared resources on the server machine.

Before you can share resources across a network, you must answer a number of questions. How do you make a resource available to share? Can everyone share his or her hard drives with everyone else? Should you place limits on sharing? If everyone needs access to a particular file, where will it be stored? What about security? Can anyone access the file? What if someone erases it accidentally? How are backups to be handled? Different versions of Windows answer these questions differently. Let's look at network organization and then turn to protocols, client software, and server software.

Network Organization

All NOSs can be broken into three basic organizational groups: client/server, peer-to-peer, and domain-based. Let's take a look at traditional network organization.

Client/Server

In a **client/server network**, one machine is dedicated as a resource to be shared over the network. This machine will have a dedicated NOS, optimized for sharing files. This special OS includes powerful caching software that enables high-speed file access. It will have extremely high levels of protection and an organization that permits extensive control of the data. This machine is called a *dedicated server*. All of the other machines that use the data are called *clients* (because it's what they usually are) or *workstations*.

The terms *client* and *server* are, to say the least, freely used in the Windows world. Keep in mind that a *client* generally refers to any process (or in this context, computer system) that can request a resource or service, and a *server* is any process (or system) that can fulfill the request.

The client/server system dedicates one machine to act as a server, whose purpose is to serve up resources to the other machines on the network. These servers do not run Windows XP or Vista. They use highly sophisticated and expensive NOSs that are optimized for the sharing and administration of network resources. Dedicated server operating systems include Windows Server 2008, big UNIX systems such as IBM AIX and HP-UX, and some versions of Linux.

Peer-to-Peer

Some networks do not require dedicated servers—every computer can perform both server and client functions. A **peer-to-peer network** enables any or all of the machines on the network to act as servers. Peer-to-peer networks are much cheaper than client/server networks because the software costs less and does not require that you purchase a high-end machine to act as the dedicated server. The most popular peer-to-peer NOSs today are the various versions of Windows and Mac OS X.

The biggest limiting factor to peer-to-peer networking is that it's simply not designed for a large number of computers. Windows has a built-in limit (10) to the number of users who can concurrently access a shared file or folder. Microsoft recommends that peer-to-peer workgroups not exceed 15 PCs. Beyond that, creating a domain-based network makes more sense (see the following section).

Security is the other big weakness of peer-to-peer networks. Each system on a peer-to-peer network maintains its own security.

With the Windows Professional/Business versions, you can tighten security by setting NTFS permissions locally, but you are still required to place a local account on every system for any user who's going to access resources. So even though you get better security in a Windows Professional/Business peer-to-peer network, system administration entails a lot of running around to individual systems to create and delete local users every time someone joins or leaves the workgroup. In a word: bleh.

• **Figure 13.1**   Multiple workgroups in a network

Peer-to-peer workgroups are little more than a pretty way to organize systems to make navigating through Windows networks a little easier (Figure 13.1). In reality, workgroups have no security value. Still, if your networking needs are limited—such as a small home network—peer-to-peer networking is an easy and cheap solution.

Domain-Based

One of the similarities between the client/server network model and peer-to-peer networks is that each PC in the network maintains its own list of user accounts. If you want to access a server, you must log on. When only one server exists, the logon process takes only a second and works very well.

The trouble comes when your network contains multiple servers. In that case, every time you access a different server, you must repeat the logon process (Figure 13.2). In larger networks containing many servers, this becomes a time-consuming nightmare, not only for the user but also for the network administrator.

A **domain-based network** provides an excellent solution for the problem of multiple logins. In a domain-based environment, one or more dedicated servers called *domain controllers* hold the security database for all systems. This database holds a list of all users and passwords in the domain. When you log on to your computer or to any computer, the logon request goes to an available domain controller to verify the account and password (Figure 13.3).

Modern domain-based networks use what is called a **directory service** to store user and computer account information. Large Microsoft-based networks use the *Active Directory* (*AD*) directory service. Think of a directory service as a big, centralized index, similar to a telephone book, that each PC accesses to locate resources in the domain.

Server versions of Microsoft Windows look and act similar to the workstation versions, but they come

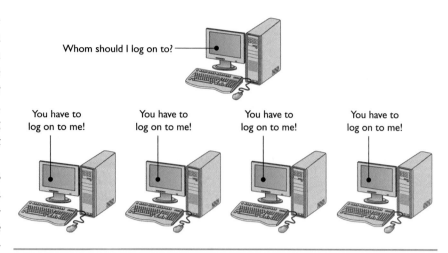

• **Figure 13.2**   Multiple logins in a peer-to-peer network

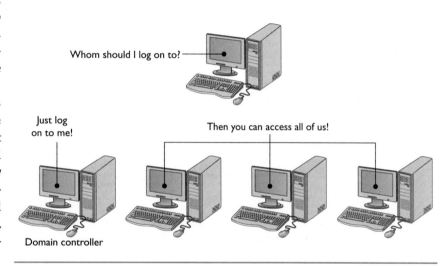

• **Figure 13.3**   A domain controller eliminates the need for multiple logins.

with extra networking capabilities, services, and tools so they can take on the role of domain controller, file server, *remote access services* (*RAS*) server, application server, Web server, and so on. A quick glance at the options you have in Administrative Tools shows how much more full-featured the server versions are compared to the workstation versions of Windows. Figure 13.4 shows the Administrative Tools options on a typical Windows Vista workstation. These should be familiar to you. Figure 13.5 shows the many extra tools you need to work with Windows 2008 Server.

Every Windows system contains a special account called the **administrator account.** This one account has complete and absolute power over the entire system. When you install Windows, you must create a password for the administrator account. Anyone who knows the administrator password can install/delete any program, read/change/delete any file, run any program, and change any system setting. As you might imagine, you should protect the administrator password carefully. Without it, you cannot create additional accounts (including additional accounts with administrative

• Figure 13.4   Administrative Tools in Windows Vista Business

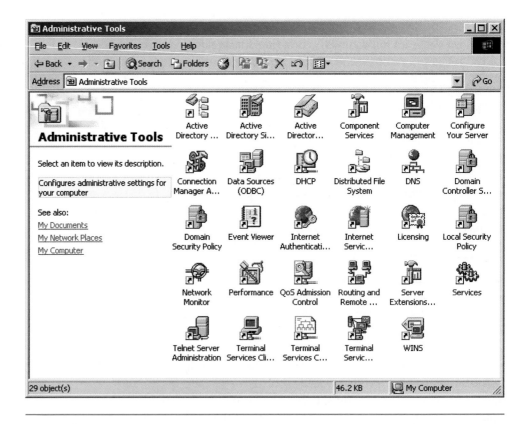

• Figure 13.5   Administrative Tools in Windows Server 2008

Mike Meyers' CompTIA A+ Guide: Practical Application

privileges) or change system settings. If you lose the administrator password (and no other account with administrative privileges exists), you have to reinstall Windows completely to create a new administrator account—so don't lose it!

In Windows XP, open the Properties window for My Computer, and select the Computer Name tab, as shown in Figure 13.6. This shows your current selection. Windows Vista and 7 show the computer name right on the System Properties dialog box and give you a link to the 2000/XP-style dialog box (Figure 13.7). Clicking the Network ID button opens the Network Identification Wizard, but most techs just use the Change button, which brings up the Computer Name/Domain Changes dialog box (Figure 13.8). Clicking the Change button does the same thing as clicking the Network ID button except that the wizard does a lot of explaining that you don't need if you know what you want to do. Make sure you have a valid domain account or you won't be able to log into a domain.

At this point, you've prepared the OS to network in general, but now you need to talk to the specific hardware. For that, you need to load protocols.

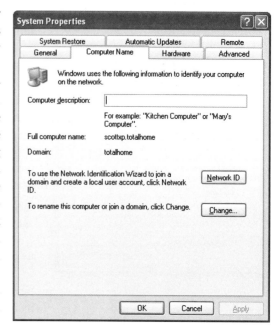

• **Figure 13.6**   Computer Name tab in Windows XP

Protocols

Simply moving data from one machine to another is hardly sufficient to make a complete network; many other functions need to be handled. For

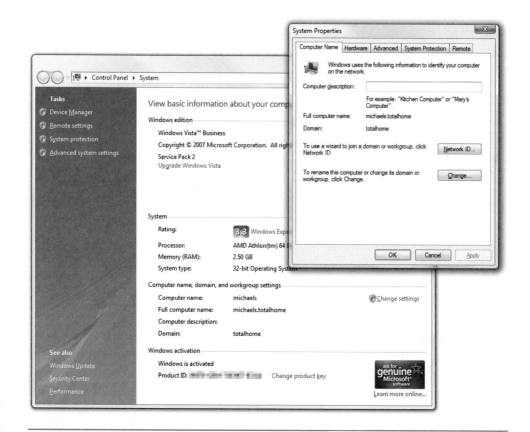

• **Figure 13.7**   Computer Name location in Vista

• **Figure 13.8**   Using the Change button

A *node* is any device that has a network connection—usually this means a PC, but other devices can be nodes. For example, many printers now connect directly to a network and can therefore be deemed nodes. I use the term *node* extensively in the rest of the chapter in place of *PC* or *networked computer*. This is especially true when I talk about wireless technologies, because that's the term the manufacturers use.

Novell developed the *Internetwork Packet Exchange/ Sequenced Packet Exchange (IPX/SPX)* protocol exclusively for its NetWare products. The IPX/SPX protocol is speedy, works well with routers, and takes up relatively little RAM when loaded. Although once popular, it has all but disappeared in favor of TCP/IP. Microsoft implements a version of IPX/SPX called *NWLink*.

example, if a file is being copied from one machine to another, something must keep track of all of the packets so the file can be properly reassembled. If many machines are talking to the same machine at once, that machine must somehow keep track of which packets it sends to or receives from each of the other PCs.

Another issue arises if one of the machines in the network has its network card replaced. Up to this point, the only way to distinguish one machine from another was by the MAC address on the network card. To solve this, each machine must have a name, an identifier for the network, which is "above" the MAC address. Each machine, or at least one of them, needs to keep a list of all of the MAC addresses on the network and the names of the machines, so packets and names can be correlated. That way, if a PC's network card is replaced, the network, after some special queries, can update the list to associate the name of the PC with its new network card's MAC address.

Network protocol software takes the incoming data received by the network card, keeps it organized, sends it to the application that needs it, and then takes outgoing data from the application and hands it to the NIC to be sent out over the network. All networks use some protocol. Although many protocols exist, one dominates the world of PCs: TCP/IP.

NetBEUI/NetBIOS

Before we talk about TCP/IP, we need to discuss a little history. During the 1980s, IBM developed **NetBIOS Extended User Interface (NetBEUI)**, the default protocol for Windows for Workgroups, LANtastic, and Windows 95. NetBEUI offers small size, easy configuration, and a relatively high speed, but it can't be used for routing. Its inability to handle routing limits NetBEUI to networks smaller than about 200 nodes.

You can connect multiple smaller networks into a bigger network, turning a group of LANs into one big WAN, but this raises a couple of issues with network traffic. A computer needs to be able to address a packet so that it goes to a computer within its own LAN or to a computer in another LAN in the WAN. If every computer saw every packet, the network traffic would quickly spin out of control! Plus, the machines that connect the LANs— called **routers**—need to be able to sort those packets and send them along to the proper LAN. This process, called *routing*, requires routers and a routing-capable protocol to function correctly.

NetBEUI was great for a LAN, but it lacked the extra addressing capabilities needed for a WAN. A new protocol was needed, one that could handle routing.

TCP/IP

Transmission Control Protocol/Internet Protocol (**TCP/IP**) was originally developed for the Internet's progenitor, the *Advanced Research Projects Agency Network* (*ARPANET*) of the U.S. Department of Defense. In 1983, TCP/IP became the built-in protocol for the popular BSD (Berkeley Software Distribution) UNIX, and other flavors of UNIX quickly adopted it as well. TCP/IP is the best protocol for larger networks with more than 200 nodes. The biggest network of all, the Internet, uses TCP/IP as its protocol. Windows also uses TCP/IP as its default protocol.

Client Software

To access data or resources across a network, Windows needs to have client software installed for every kind of server you want to access. When you install a network card and drivers, Windows installs at least one set of client software, called Client for Microsoft Networks (Figure 13.9). This client enables your machine to do the obvious: connect to a Microsoft network! Internet-based services work the same way. You need a Web client (such as Mozilla Firefox) to access a Web server. Windows PCs don't just access shared data magically but require that client software be installed.

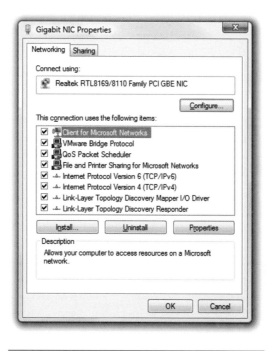

• **Figure 13.9**   LAN Properties window showing Client for Microsoft Networks installed (along with other network software)

Server Software

You can turn any Windows PC into a server simply by enabling the sharing of files, folders, and printers. Windows has file and printer sharing installed but not activated by default (though a simpler form of file sharing, creatively named Simple File Sharing, is enabled by default in Windows XP Home to make sharing media over a home network easier). In Windows Vista, activating file and printer sharing requires nothing more than a click on a checkbox, as you can see in Figure 13.10.

Try This!

Discovering Protocols and Clients

If you have a network card installed in your PC, chances are extremely high that you already have one or more protocols or clients installed. Try This!

1. Right-click My Network Places and select Properties. Then right-click on the Local Area Connection icon and select Properties once more. If you're using Vista, you'll do this by right-clicking Network and selecting Properties. After that, select *Manage network connections*, right-click on the Local Area Connection icon, and select Properties.

2. Which protocols or clients are loaded? If you have a classmate running through the same exercise, compare protocols. Can your two machines connect and swap data?

Tech Tip

Vista's Network and Sharing Center

If you right-click on the Network button in Windows Vista/7, you're taken to the Network and Sharing Center. In the Network and Sharing Center, you can view the status of your network connection and easily enable or disable various network settings, such as file sharing, network discovery, and printer sharing. You can also see what type of network you're on: Public, Private, or Domain. Windows Vista lets you select which type of network you're on, either Public or Private, the first time you join a particular network and modifies your network settings based on the type of network you select. Public networks are assumed not to be secure; as such, Windows automatically turns off all of the network sharing options so that do-bads can't access your computer. Private networks are assumed safe, so all of the file-sharing options are turned on. If your computer is on a domain, your network administrator will control your network options.

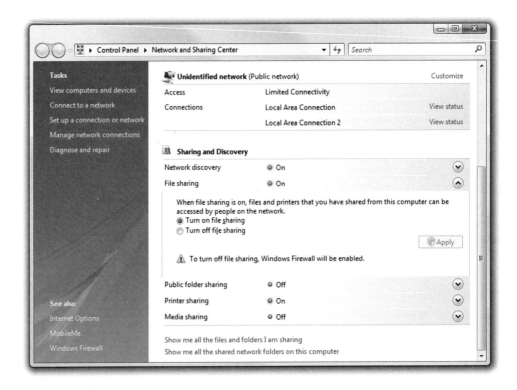

● **Figure 13.10** Enabling file and printer sharing in Windows Vista

Tech Tip

Windows Firewall

Every version of Windows since Windows XP SP 2 has included a built-in firewall that blocks out harmful Internet traffic. Windows Firewall functions slightly differently in each version of Windows, but you should be aware of one quirk in Windows XP: namely, that the Firewall will block file and printer sharing by default. So if you find that you can't access shared folders or printers, you can check to make sure Windows Firewall isn't blocking them. You can do this by going into Control Panel and opening the Windows Firewall applet. Once that's open, click the Exceptions tab and make sure that the checkbox next to File and Printer Sharing is checked. If it isn't, that's your problem!

■ Installing and Configuring a Wired Network

To have network connectivity, you need to have three things in place:

■ **NIC** The physical hardware that connects the computer system to the network media.

■ **Protocol** The language that the computer systems use to communicate.

■ **Network client** The interface that allows the computer system to speak to the protocol.

If you want to share resources on your PC with other network users, you also need to enable Microsoft's File and Printer Sharing. Plus, of course, you need to connect the PC to the network hub or switch via some sort of cable (preferably CAT 6 with Gigabit Ethernet cranking through the wires, but that's just me!). When you install a NIC, by default Windows installs the TCP/IP protocol, the Client for Microsoft Networks, and File and Printer Sharing for Microsoft Networks upon setup.

Installing a NIC = Network Inter Face Card

The NIC is your computer system's link to the network, and installing one is the first step required to connect to a network. NICs are manufactured to operate on specific media and network types, such as 1000BaseT Ethernet.

Follow the manufacturer's instructions for installation. If your NIC is of recent vintage, it will be detected, installed, and configured automatically by Windows. You might need a driver disc or a driver download from the manufacturer's Web site if you install that funky PC Card or gamer NIC.

The Add Hardware Wizard automates installation of non–plug-and-play devices or plug-and-play devices that were not detected correctly. Start the wizard by clicking Start | Settings | Control Panel (2000 or classic Start menu) or Start | Control Panel (XP – 7) and then double-clicking the icon for the Add Hardware applet. (Note that Windows 2000 calls this the Add/Remove Hardware applet.) Click the Next button to select the hardware task you wish to perform, and follow the prompts to complete the wizard.

 If you have the option, you should save yourself potential headaches and troubleshooting woes by acquiring new, name-brand NICs for your Windows installation.

Configuring a Network Client

To establish network connectivity, you need a network client installed and configured properly. You need a client for every type of server NOS to which you plan to connect on the network. Let's look at Microsoft's client.

Installed as part of the OS installation, the Client for Microsoft Networks rarely needs configuration, and, in fact, few configuration options are available. To start it in Windows Vista/7, click Start; then right-click Network and select Properties. Then click *Manage network connections* on the left. In Windows XP, click Start, and then right-click My Network Places and select Properties. In Windows 2000, click Start | Settings | Network and Dial-up Connections.

In all versions of Windows, your next step is to double-click the Local Area Connection icon, click the Properties button, highlight Client for Microsoft Networks, and click the Properties button. Note that there's not much to do here. Unless told to do something by a network administrator, just leave this alone.

Configuring TCP/IP

This final section on protocols covers TCP/IP, the primary protocol of most modern networks, including the Internet. For a PC to access the Internet, it must have TCP/IP loaded and configured properly. TCP/IP has become so predominant that most network folks use it even on networks that do not connect to the Internet. Although TCP/IP is powerful, it is also a bit of a challenge to set up. So whether you are installing a modem for a dial-up connection to the Internet or setting up 500 computers on their own private *intranet*, you must understand some TCP/IP basics. You'll go through the following basic sections of the protocol and then you'll look at specific steps to install and configure TCP/IP.

 Network printers need IP addresses, too! When installing a network printer, refer to the documentation for instructions about assigning the printer an IP address.

Network Addressing

Any network address must provide two pieces of information: it must uniquely identify the machine and it must locate that machine within the larger network. In a TCP/IP network, the IP address identifies the PC and the network on which it resides.

IP Addresses In a TCP/IP network, the systems don't have names but rather use IP addresses. The **IP address** is the unique identification number for your system on the network. Part of the address identifies the network, and part identifies the local computer (host) address on the network. IP addresses consist of four sets of eight binary numbers (octets), each set separated by a period. This is called *dotted-decimal notation*. So, instead of a computer being called SERVER1, it gets an address like so:

```
202.34.16.11
```

Written in binary form, the address would look like this:

```
11001010.00100010.00010000.00001011
```

To make the addresses more comprehensible to users, the TCP/IP folks decided to write the decimal equivalents:

```
00000000 = 0
00000001 = 1
00000010 = 2
...
11111111 = 255
```

IP addresses are divided into class licenses that correspond with the potential size of the network: Class A, Class B, and Class C. Class A licenses were intended for huge companies and organizations, such as major multinational corporations, universities, and governmental agencies. Class B licenses were assigned to medium-size companies, and Class C licenses were designated for smaller LANs. Class A networks use the first octet to identify the network address and the remaining three octets to identify the host. Class B networks use the first two octets to identify the network address and the remaining two octets to identify the host. Class C networks use the first three octets to identify the network address and the last octet to identify the host. Table 13.1 lists range (class) assignments.

You'll note that the IP address ranges listed above skip from 126.x.x.x to 128.x.x.x. That's because the 127 address range (i.e., 127.0.0.1–127.255.255.255) is reserved for network testing (loopback) operations. (We usually just use the address 127.0.0.1 for loopback purposes and call it the *localhost* address, but any address that starts off with *127* will work just as well.) That's not the only reserved range, either! Each network class has a specific IP address range reserved for *private* networks—traffic from these networks doesn't get routed to the Internet at large. Class A's private range goes from 10.0.0.1 to 10.255.255.255. Class B has two private address ranges: 172.16.0.1 up to 172.16.255.255 for manually configured addresses and 169.254.0.1 to 169.254.255.254 (link-local addresses) to accommodate the Automatic Private IP Addressing (APIPA) function discussed later. Class C's private addresses range from 192.168.0.0 to 192.168.255.255.

Table 13.1	Class A, B, and C Addresses		
Network Class	**Address Range**	**No. of Network Addresses Available**	**No. of Host Nodes (Computers) Supported**
A	1–126	~~129~~ 126	16,777,214
B	128–191	16,384	65,534
C	192–223	2,097,152	254

Subnet Mask The subnet mask is a value that distinguishes which part of the IP address is the network address and which part of the address is the host address. The subnet mask blocks out (or masks) the network portions (octets) of an IP address. Certain subnet masks are applied by default. The default subnet mask for Class A addresses is 255.0.0.0; for Class B, it's 255.255.0.0; and for Class C, 255.255.255.0. For example, in the Class B IP address 131.190.4.121 with a subnet mask of 255.255.0.0, the first two octets (131.190) make up the network address and the last two (4.121) make up the host address.

A New Kind of Port

The term "port" has several meanings in the computer world. Commonly, port defines the connector socket on an Ethernet NIC, where you insert an RJ-45 jack. That's how I've used the term for the most part in this book. It's now time to see another use of the word port.

In TCP/IP, ports are 16-bit numbers between 0 and 65,535, assigned to a particular TCP/IP session. All TCP/IP packets (except for some really low-level maintenance packets) contain port numbers that the two communicating computers use to determine not only the kind of session—and thus what software protocol—to use to handle the data in the packet, but also how to get the packet or response back to the sending computer.

Each packet has two ports assigned, a destination port and an ephemeral port. The destination port is a fixed, predetermined number that defines the function or session type. Common TCP/IP session types use destination port numbers in the range 0–1023. The ephemeral port is an arbitrary number generated by the sending computer; the receiving computer uses the ephemeral port as a destination address so that the sending computer knows which application to use for the returning packet. Ephemeral ports usually fall in the 1024–5000 range, but this varies slightly among the different operating systems.

Ports enable one computer to serve many different services, such as a Web server and e-mail server, at the same time.

TCP/IP Services

TCP/IP is a different type of protocol. Although it supports File and Printer Sharing, it adds a number of special sharing functions unique only to it, lumped together under the umbrella term TCP/IP services. The most famous TCP/IP service is called Hypertext Transfer Protocol (HTTP), the language of the World Wide Web. If you want to surf the Web, you must have TCP/IP. But TCP/IP supplies many other services beyond just HTTP. By using a service called Telnet, for example, you can access a remote system as though you were actually in front of that machine.

Another example is a handy utility called PING. PING enables one machine to check whether it can communicate with another machine. Figure 13.11 shows an example of PING running on a Windows Vista system. Isn't it interesting that many TCP/IP services run from a command prompt? Good thing you know how to access one! I'll show you other services in a moment.

The goal of TCP/IP is to link any two hosts (remember, a host is just a computer in TCP/IP lingo), whether the two computers are on the same LAN or on some other network within the WAN. The LANs within the WAN are linked together with a variety of connections, ranging from basic dial-ups to

Pinging the loopback is the best way to test whether a NIC is working properly. To test a NIC's loopback, the other end of the cable must be in a working switch or you must use a loopback device such as a loopback adapter/plug.

Tech Tip

Link-local Addresses
If APIPA is enabled and the DHCP-configured client can't reach a DHCP server, the client will automatically be configured with an APIPA link-local IP address in the range between 169.254.0.1 to 169.254.255.254 and get a Class B subnet mask of 255.255.0.0 until the DHCP server can be reached.

The CompTIA A+ Practical Application exam does not require you to break down IP addresses and subnet masks into their binary equivalents or to deal with non-standard subnet masks such as 255.255.240.0, but you should know what IP addresses and subnet masks are and how to configure your PC to connect to a TCP/IP network.

```
Administrator: C:\Windows\system32\cmd.exe

C:\>ping www.totalsem.com

Pinging www.totalsem.com [209.29.33.25] with 32 bytes of data:
Reply from 209.29.33.25: bytes=32 time=60ms TTL=53
Reply from 209.29.33.25: bytes=32 time=60ms TTL=53
Reply from 209.29.33.25: bytes=32 time=60ms TTL=53
Reply from 209.29.33.25: bytes=32 time=66ms TTL=53

Ping statistics for 209.29.33.25:
    Packets: Sent = 4, Received = 4, Lost = 0 (0% loss),
Approximate round trip times in milli-seconds:
    Minimum = 60ms, Maximum = 66ms, Average = 61ms

C:\>
```

• **Figure 13.11** PING in action

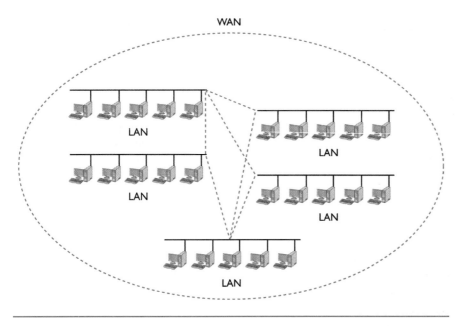

• **Figure 13.12** WAN concept

• **Figure 13.13** Typical router

dedicated high-speed (and expensive) data lines (Figure 13.12). To move traffic between networks, you use routers (Figure 13.13). Each host sends traffic to the router only when that data is destined for a remote network, cutting down on traffic across the more expensive WAN links. The host makes these decisions based on the destination IP address of each packet.

TCP/IP Settings

TCP/IP has a number of unique settings that you must set up correctly to ensure proper network functioning. Unfortunately, these settings can be quite confusing, and there are quite a few of them. Not all settings are used for every type of TCP/IP network, and it's not always obvious where you go to set them.

Windows makes this fairly easy by letting you configure both dial-up and network connections by using the Network Connections dialog box (Figure 13.14). To get there, right-click on My Network Places (Windows 2000/XP) or Network (Windows Vista/7) and select Properties. In Vista/7, you have to click the *Manage network connections* button, but in 2000 and XP, you simply select the connection you wish to configure and then set its TCP/IP properties.

The CompTIA A+ Practical Application exam assumes that someone else, such as a tech support person or some network

• **Figure 13.14** Network Connections dialog box showing dial-up and LAN connections

guru, will tell you the correct TCP/IP settings for the network. Your only job is to understand roughly what they do and to know where to enter them so the system works. Following are some of the most common TCP/IP settings.

Default Gateway A computer that wants to send data to another machine outside its LAN is not expected to know exactly how to reach every other computer on the Internet. Instead, all IP hosts know the address of at least one router to which they pass all of the data packets they need to send outside the LAN. This router is called the **default gateway**, which is just another way of saying "the local router" (Figure 13.15).

Domain Name Service (DNS) Knowing that users could not remember lots of IP addresses, early Internet pioneers came up with a way to correlate those numbers with more human-friendly computer designations. Special computers, called **domain name service (DNS) servers, keep databases of IP addresses and their corresponding names.** For example, a machine called TOTALSEMINAR1 will be listed in a DNS directory with a corresponding IP address, such as 209.34.45.163. So instead of accessing the \\209.34.45.163\FREDC share to copy a file, you can ask to see \\TOTALSEMINAR1\FREDC. Your system will then query the DNS server to get TOTALSEMINAR1's IP address and use that to find the right machine. Unless you want to type in IP addresses all of the time, a TCP/IP network will need at least one DNS server (Figure 13.16).

The Internet has regulated domain names. If you want a domain name that others can access on the Internet, you must register your domain name and pay a small yearly fee. In most cases, your ISP can handle this for you.

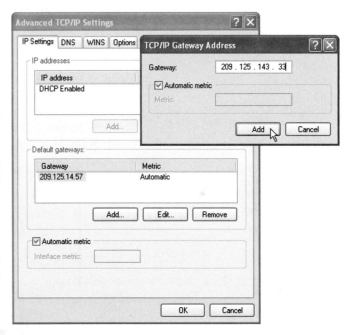

• **Figure 13.15** Setting a default gateway

• **Figure 13.16**   Adding two DNS servers in Windows Vista

Originally, DNS names all ended with one of the following seven domain name qualifiers, called *top level domains* (*TLDs*):

.com General business	**.org** Nonprofit organizations
.edu Educational organizations	**.gov** Government organizations
.mil Military organizations	**.net** Internet organizations
.int International	

As more and more countries joined the Internet, an entire new level of domains was added to the original seven to indicate a DNS name in a particular country, such as .uk for the United Kingdom. It's common to see DNS names such as www.bbc.co.uk or www.louvre.fr. The *Internet Corporation for Assigned Names and Numbers* (*ICANN*) announced the creation of several more new domains, including .name, .biz, .info, and others. Given the explosive growth of the Internet, these are unlikely to be the last ones! For the latest developments, check ICANN's Web site at www.icann.org.

WINS   Before Microsoft came fully on board with Internet standards such as TCP/IP, the company implemented its own type of name server: *Windows Internet Name Service (WINS)*. WINS enables NetBIOS network names such as SERVER1 to be correlated to IP addresses, just as DNS does, except these names are *Windows* network names such as SERVER1, not fully qualified domain Internet names (FQDNs) such as server1.example.com. NetBIOS names must be unique and contain 15 or fewer characters, but other than that there isn't much to it. Assuming that a WINS server exists on your network, all you have to do to set up WINS on your PC is type in the IP address for the WINS server (Figure 13.17). Windows 2000–7 based networks don't use WINS; they use an improved "dynamic" DNS (DDNS) that supports both Internet names and Windows names. On older networks that still need to support the occasional legacy Windows NT 4.0 server, you may need to configure WINS, but on most TCP/IP networks you can leave the WINS setting blank.

DHCP   The last feature that most TCP/IP networks support is **dynamic host configuration protocol (DHCP)**. To understand DHCP, you must first remember that every machine must be assigned an IP address, a subnet mask, a default gateway, and at least one DNS server (and maybe a WINS server). These settings can be added manually by using the TCP/IP Properties window. When you set the IP address manually, the IP address will not change and is called a **static IP address** (Figure 13.18).

DHCP enables you to create a pool of IP addresses that are given temporarily to machines. DHCP is especially handy for networks of a lot of laptops that join and leave the network on a regular basis. Why give a

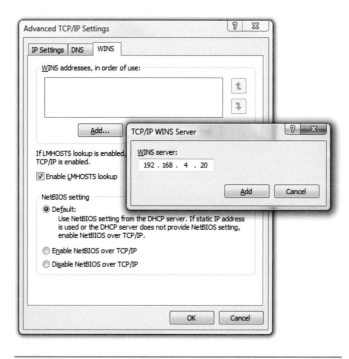

• **Figure 13.17**   Setting up WINS to use DHCP

Figure 13.18 • Setting a static IP address

Figure 13.19 • Automatically obtain an IP address

machine that is on the network for only a few hours a day a static IP address? For that reason, DHCP is quite popular. If you add a NIC to a Windows system, the default TCP/IP settings are set to use DHCP. When you accept those automatic settings, you're really telling the machine to use DHCP (Figure 13.19).

TCP/IP Tools

All versions of Windows come with handy tools to test TCP/IP. Those you're most likely to use in the field are PING, IPCONFIG, NSLOOKUP, and TRACERT. All of these programs are command prompt utilities. Open a command prompt to run them; if you just place these commands in the Run command, you'll see the command prompt window open for a moment and then quickly close!

PING You've already seen PING, a really great way to see if you can talk to another system. Here's how it works. Get to a command prompt and type **ping** followed by an IP address or by a DNS name, such as **ping www.chivalry.com**. Press the ENTER key on your keyboard and away it goes! Figure 13.20 shows the common syntax for PING.

Choosing to obtain an IP address automatically will disable DHCP.

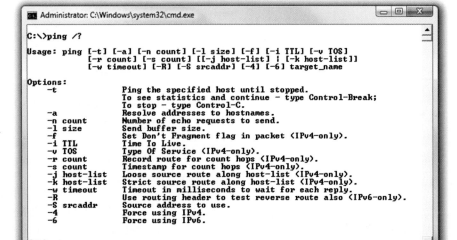

Figure 13.20 • PING syntax

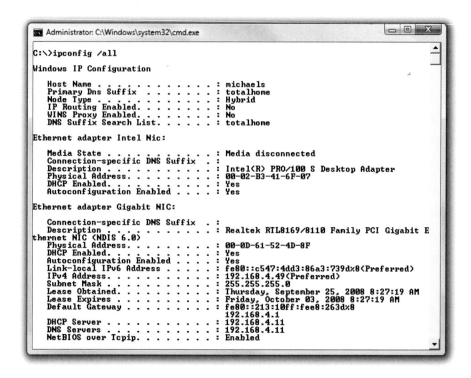

```
Administrator: C:\Windows\system32\cmd.exe

C:\>ipconfig /all

Windows IP Configuration

    Host Name . . . . . . . . . . . . : michaels
    Primary Dns Suffix  . . . . . . . : totalhome
    Node Type . . . . . . . . . . . . : Hybrid
    IP Routing Enabled. . . . . . . . : No
    WINS Proxy Enabled. . . . . . . . : No
    DNS Suffix Search List. . . . . . : totalhome

Ethernet adapter Intel Nic:

    Media State . . . . . . . . . . . : Media disconnected
    Connection-specific DNS Suffix  . :
    Description . . . . . . . . . . . : Intel(R) PRO/100 S Desktop Adapter
    Physical Address. . . . . . . . . : 00-02-B3-41-6F-07
    DHCP Enabled. . . . . . . . . . . : Yes
    Autoconfiguration Enabled . . . . : Yes

Ethernet adapter Gigabit NIC:

    Connection-specific DNS Suffix  . :
    Description . . . . . . . . . . . : Realtek RTL8169/8110 Family PCI Gigabit E
thernet NIC (NDIS 6.0)
    Physical Address. . . . . . . . . : 00-0D-61-52-4D-8F
    DHCP Enabled. . . . . . . . . . . : Yes
    Autoconfiguration Enabled . . . . : Yes
    Link-local IPv6 Address . . . . . : fe80::c547:4dd3:86a3:739d%8(Preferred)
    IPv4 Address. . . . . . . . . . . : 192.168.4.49(Preferred)
    Subnet Mask . . . . . . . . . . . : 255.255.255.0
    Lease Obtained. . . . . . . . . . : Thursday, September 25, 2008 8:27:19 AM
    Lease Expires . . . . . . . . . . : Friday, October 03, 2008 8:27:19 AM
    Default Gateway . . . . . . . . . : fe80::213:10ff:fee8:263d%8
                                        192.168.4.1
    DHCP Server . . . . . . . . . . . : 192.168.4.11
    DNS Servers . . . . . . . . . . . : 192.168.4.11
    NetBIOS over Tcpip. . . . . . . . : Enabled
```

• **Figure 13.21**   IPCONFIG /ALL on Windows Vista

PING has a few options beyond the basics that CompTIA wants you to know about. The first option is –*t*. By using the –*t* switch, PING continuously sends PING packets until you stop it with the break command (CTRL-C). The second option is the –*l* switch, which enables you to specify how big a PING packet to send. This helps in diagnosing specific problems with the routers between your computer and the computer you PING.

IPCONFIG   Windows offers the command-line tool **IPCONFIG** for a quick glance at your network settings. Click Start | Run and type **CMD** to get a command prompt. From the prompt, type **IPCONFIG /ALL** to see all of your TCP/IP settings (Figure 13.21).

When you have a static IP address, IPCONFIG does little beyond reporting your current IP settings, including your IP address, subnet mask, default gateway, DNS servers, and WINS servers. When using DHCP, however, IPCONFIG is also the primary tool for releasing and renewing your IP address. Just type **ipconfig /renew** to get a new IP address or **ipconfig /release** to give up the IP address you currently have.

NSLOOKUP   **NSLOOKUP** is a powerful command-line program that enables you to determine exactly what information the DNS server is giving you about a specific host name. Every version of Windows makes NSLOOKUP available when you install TCP/IP. To run the program, type **NSLOOKUP** from the command line and press the ENTER key (Figure 13.22). Note that this gives you a little information but the prompt has changed? That's because you're running the application. Type **exit** and press the ENTER key to return to the command prompt.

TRACERT   The TRACERT utility shows the route that a packet takes to get to its destination. From a command line, type **TRACERT** followed by a

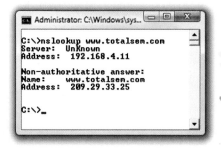

```
Administrator: C:\Windows\sys...

C:\>nslookup www.totalsem.com
Server:  UnKnown
Address:  192.168.4.11

Non-authoritative answer:
Name:    www.totalsem.com
Address:  209.29.33.25

C:\>_
```

• **Figure 13.22**   NSLOOKUP in action

You can do some cool stuff with NSLOOKUP, and consequently some techs absolutely love the tool. It's way outside the scope of CompTIA A+ certification, but if you want to play with it, type **HELP** at the NSLOOKUP prompt and press ENTER to see a list of common commands and syntax.

space and an IP address. The output describes the route from your machine to the destination machine, including all devices the packet passes through and how long each hop takes (Figure 13.23). TRACERT can come in handy when you have to troubleshoot bottlenecks. When users complain of difficulty reaching a particular destination by using TCP/IP, you can run this utility to determine whether the problem exists on a machine or connection over which you have control or if it is a problem on another machine or router. Similarly, if a destination is completely unreachable, TRACERT can again determine whether the problem is on a machine or router over which you have control.

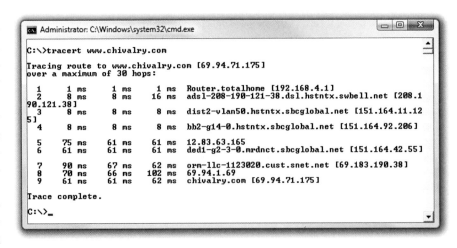

● **Figure 13.23** TRACERT in action

Configuring TCP/IP

By default, TCP/IP is configured to receive an IP address automatically from a DHCP server on the network (and automatically assign a corresponding subnet mask). As far as the CompTIA A+ Practical Application exam is concerned, Network+ techs and administrators give you the IP address, subnet mask, and default gateway information and you plug them into the PC. That's about it, so here's how to do it manually:

Try This!

Running TRACERT

Ever wonder why your e-mail takes *years* to get to some people but arrives instantly for others? Or why some Web sites are slower to load than others? Part of the blame could lie with how many hops away your connection is to the target server. You can use TRACERT to run a quick check of how many hops it takes to get to somewhere on a network, so Try This!

1. Run TRACERT on some known source, such as www.microsoft.com or www.totalsem.com.

2. How many hops did it take? Did your TRACERT time out or make it all of the way to the server? Try a TRACERT to a local address. If you're in a university town, run a TRACERT on the campus Web site, such as www.rice.edu for folks in Houston, or www.ucla.edu for those of you in Los Angeles. Did you get fewer hops with a local site?

1. In Windows XP, open the Control Panel and double-click the Network Connections applet. Double-click the Local Area Connection icon. In Windows 2000, click Start | Settings | Network and Dial-up Connections, and double-click the Local Area Connection icon. In Windows Vista/7, right-click on Network and then click *Manage network connections*. After that, double-click the Local Area Network icon.

2. Click the Properties button, highlight Internet Protocol (TCP/IP), and click the Properties button. In Windows Vista/7, you should highlight Internet Protocol Version 4 (TCP/IPv4) because Vista and 7 both have IPv4 and IPv6 installed by default.

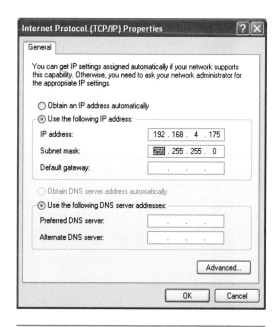

Figure 13.24 Setting up IP

3. In the dialog box, click the radio button next to *Use the following IP address*.

4. Enter the IP address in the appropriate fields.

5. Press the TAB key to skip down to the Subnet mask field. Note that the subnet mask is entered automatically, although you can type over this if you want to enter a different subnet mask (see Figure 13.24).

6. Optionally, enter the IP address for a default gateway (a router or another computer system that will forward transmissions beyond your network).

7. Optionally, enter the IP addresses of a primary and a secondary DNS server.

8. Click the OK button to close the dialog box.

9. Click the Close button to exit the Local Area Connection Status dialog box.

10. Windows will alert you that you must restart the system for the changes to take effect.

Automatic Private IP Addressing

Windows supports a feature called Automatic Private IP Addressing (APIPA) that automatically assigns an IP address to the system when the client cannot obtain an IP address automatically. The Internet Assigned Numbers Authority, the nonprofit corporation responsible for assigning IP addresses and managing root servers, has set aside the range of addresses from 169.254.0.1 to 169.254.255.254 for this purpose.

If the computer system cannot contact a DHCP server, the computer randomly chooses an address in the form of 169.254.*x.y* (where *x.y* is the computer's identifier) and a 16-bit subnet mask (255.255.0.0) and broadcasts it on the network segment (subnet). If no other computer responds to the address, the system assigns this address to itself. When using APIPA, the system can communicate only with other computers on the same subnet that also use the 169.254.*x.y* range with a 16-bit mask. APIPA is enabled by default if your system is configured to obtain an IP address automatically.

A computer system on a network with an active DHCP server that has an IP address in this range usually indicates a problem connecting to the DHCP server.

Sharing and Security

Windows systems can share all kinds of resources: files, folders, entire drives, printers, faxes, Internet connections, and much more. Conveniently for you, the CompTIA A+ Practical Application exam limits its interests to folders, printers, and Internet connections. You'll see how to share folders and printers now; Internet connection sharing is discussed in Chapter 15, "Mastering the Internet."

Sharing Drives and Folders

All versions of Windows share drives and folders in basically the same manner. Simply right-click any drive or folder and choose Properties. Select the Sharing tab (Figure 13.25). Select *Share this folder*, add something in the

Comment or User Limit fields if you wish (they're not required), and click Permissions (Figure 13.26).

Hey! Doesn't NTFS have all those wild permissions such as Read, Execute, Take Ownership, and all that? Yes, it does, but NTFS permissions and network permissions are totally separate beasties. Microsoft wanted Windows to support many different file systems (NTFS, FAT16, FAT32), old and new. Network permissions are Microsoft's way of enabling you to administer file sharing on any type of partition supported by Windows, no matter how ancient. Sure, your options will be pretty limited if you are working with an older file system, but you *can* do it.

The beauty of Windows is that it provides another tool—NTFS permissions—that can do much more. NTFS is where the power lies, but power always comes with a price: you have to configure two separate sets of permissions. If you are sharing a folder on an NTFS drive, as you normally are these days, you must set *both* the network permissions and the NTFS permissions to let others access your shared resources. Some good news: this is actually no big deal! Just set the network permissions to give everyone full control, and then use the NTFS permissions to exercise more precise control over *who* accesses the shared resources and *how* they access them. Open the Security tab to set the NTFS permissions.

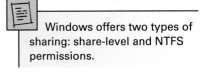

● **Figure 13.25** Windows XP Sharing tab on NTFS volume

Accessing Shared Drives/Directories

Once you have set up a drive or directory to be shared, the final step is to access that shared drive or directory from another machine. Windows 2000 and XP use My Network Places and Windows Vista and Windows 7 use Network, although you'll need to do a little clicking to get to the shared resources (Figure 13.27).

You can also map network resources to a local resource name. For example, the FREDC share can be mapped to be a local hard drive such as E: or F:. From within any Explorer window (such as My Documents or Documents), choose Tools | Map Network Drive to open the Map Network Drive dialog box (Figure 13.28). In Windows Vista/7, you'll need to press the ALT key once to see the menu bar. Click the Browse button to check out the neighborhood and find a shared drive (Figure 13.29).

In Windows 2000, you can also use the handy Add Network Place icon in My Network Places to add network locations you frequently access without using up drive letters. Windows XP removed the icon but added the menu option in its context bar on the left; Windows Vista and Windows 7 have removed it altogether. Here's how it looks on a Windows 2000 system (Figure 13.30).

Mapping shared network drives is a common practice, as it makes a remote network share look like just another drive on the local system. The only downside to drive mapping stems from the fact that users tend to forget they are on a network. A classic example is the user who always accesses a particular folder or file on the network and then suddenly gets a "file not found" error when the workstation is disconnected from the network. Instead of recognizing this as a network error, the user often imagines the problem is a missing or corrupted file.

> Windows offers two types of sharing: share-level and NTFS permissions.

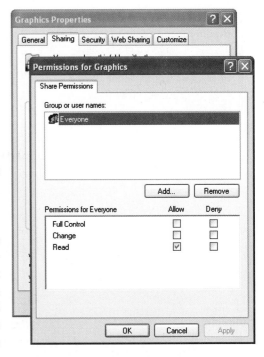

● **Figure 13.26** Network permissions

• **Figure 13.27**   Shared resources in Network

All shared resources should show up in My Network Places (or Network in Vista/7). If a shared resource fails to show up, make sure you check the basics first: Is File and Printer Sharing activated? Is the device shared? Don't let silly errors fool you!

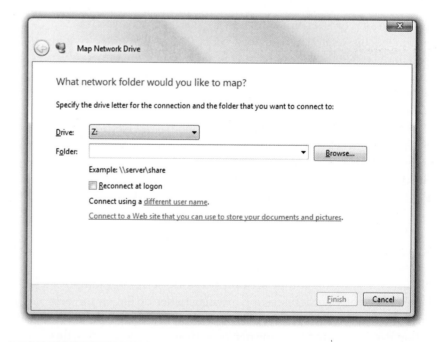

• **Figure 13.28**   Map Network Drive dialog box in Vista

UNC

All computers that share must have a network name, and all of the resources they share must also have network names. Any resource on a network can be described by combining the names of the resource being shared and the system sharing. If a machine called SERVER1 is sharing its C: drive as FREDC, for example, the complete name would look like this:

`\\SERVER1\FREDC`

This is called the **universal naming convention (UNC)**. The UNC is distinguished by its use of double backslashes in front of the sharing system's name and a single backslash in front of the shared resource's name. A UNC name can also point directly to a specific file or folder:

~~`\\SERVER1\FREDC\INSTALL-FILES\SETUP.EXE`~~

In this example, INSTALL-FILES is a subdirectory in the shared folder FREDC (which may or may not be called FREDC on the server), and SETUP.EXE is a specific file.

NET Command

Windows enables you to view a network quickly from the command line through the **NET command**. This works great when you plug into a network for the first time and, naturally, don't know the names of the other computers on that network. To see the many options that NET offers, type **net** at a command prompt and press ENTER. The VIEW and USE options offer excellent network tools.

You can think of NET VIEW as the command-line version of My Network Places. When run, NET VIEW returns a list of Windows computers on the network. Once you know the names of the computers, you type **NET VIEW** followed by the computer name. NET

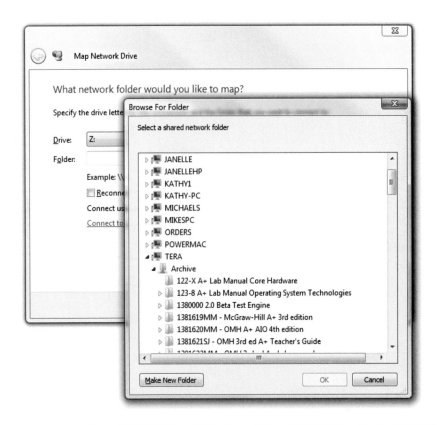

• **Figure 13.29**   Browsing for shared folders

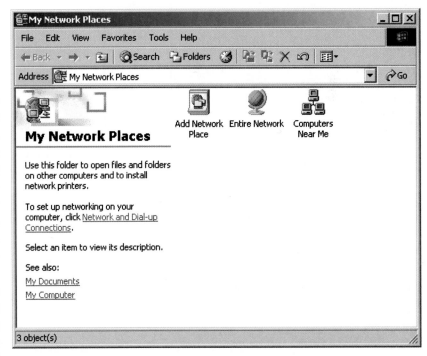

• **Figure 13.30**   Add Network Place icon in Windows 2000

VIEW will show any shares on that machine and whether they are mapped drives.

```
C:\>NET VIEW SERVER1
Shared resources at SERVER1
Share name   Type   Used as   Comment
----------------------------------------------------------------
FREDC        Disk
Research     Disk   W:
The command completed successfully.
```

NET USE is a command-line method for mapping network shares. For example, if you wanted to map the Research share shown in the previous example to the X drive, you simply type:

```
C:\>NET USE X: \\SERVER1\Research
```

This will map drive X to the Research share on the SERVER1 computer.

Sharing Printers

Sharing printers in Windows is just as easy as sharing drives and directories. Assuming that the system has printer sharing services loaded, just go to the Printers folder in the Control Panel or Start menu and right-click the printer you wish to share. Select Sharing; then click *Shared as* (Windows 2000) or *Share the printer* (Windows XP/Vista/7) and give it a name (see Figure 13.31).

To access a shared printer in any version of Windows, simply click the Add Printer icon in the Printers folder. When asked if the printer is Local or Network, select Network; browse the network for the printer you wish to access, and Windows takes care of the rest! In almost all cases, Windows will copy the printer driver from the sharing machine. In the rare case where it doesn't, it will prompt you for drivers.

One of the most pleasant aspects of configuring a system for networking under all versions of Microsoft Windows is the amazing amount of the process that is automated. For example, if Windows detects a NIC in a system, it automatically installs the NIC driver, a network protocol (TCP/IP), and Client for Microsoft Networks (the NetBIOS part of the Microsoft networking software). So if you want to share a resource, everything you need is automatically installed. Note that although File and Printer Sharing is also automatically installed, you still must activate it by clicking the appropriate checkbox in the Local Area Connection Properties dialog box.

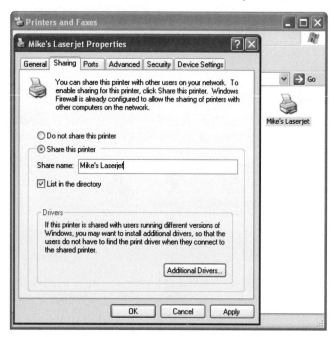

Remember that you can use the /? modifier with any command to learn its syntax. Use NET /? if you forget how the NET command works!

• **Figure 13.31**   Giving a name to a shared printer on Windows XP

Chapter 13 Review

■ Chapter Summary

After reading this chapter and completing the exercises, you should understand the following about networking.

Explain network operating systems

■ An NOS communicates with the PC hardware to make connections between machines. At least one machine on a network must play the server role, sharing data and services, while client machines access these shared resources. To make Windows networking happen, you have to install a network protocol, set up server software to share resources, and set up client software to access shared resources.

■ The three types of network organization are client/server, peer-to-peer, and domain-based. All Windows PCs can function as network clients and servers.

■ A client/server network dedicates one machine to act as a server. The server has a dedicated NOS optimized for sharing files, with powerful caching software that enables high-speed file access, extremely high levels of protection, and an organization that permits extensive control of the data.

■ A peer-to-peer network enables any or all of the machines on the network to act as a server. Every computer can perform both server and client functions. A peer-to-peer network comprising only client machines requires you to place a local account on every system, which the system administrator must add and delete individually.

■ In a domain-based network environment, the security database for all systems is centralized on one or more servers called domain controllers. This database holds a single list of all users and passwords. When you log on to any computer in the network, the logon request goes to an available domain controller for verification.

■ Every Windows system contains a very special account called administrator that has complete and absolute power over the entire system. When you install Windows, you must create a password for the administrator account. Anyone who knows the administrator password has the ability to read any file and run any program.

■ Network protocol software takes the incoming data received by the network card, keeps it organized, sends it to the application that needs it, and then takes outgoing data from the application and hands it to the NIC to be sent out over the network. All networks use some protocol; most networks today use TCP/IP.

■ IBM developed NetBEUI, the default protocol for Windows for Workgroups, LANtastic, and Windows 95. NetBEUI was small and relatively high speed, but it couldn't be used for routing.

■ To access data or resources across a network, a Windows PC needs to have client software installed for every kind of server that you want to access. When you install a network card and drivers, Windows installs at least one set of client software, called Client for Microsoft Networks, which enables your system to connect to a Microsoft network.

■ You can turn any Windows PC into a server simply by enabling File and Print Sharing to share files, folders, and printers. Windows installations come with this feature, but it is not activated by default. Activating takes only a click in a checkbox.

Install and configure wired networks

■ When you install a NIC, by default, Windows installs the TCP/IP protocol (configured for Dynamic DHCP), the Client for Microsoft Networks, and File and Printer Sharing for Microsoft Networks upon setup.

■ To establish network connectivity, you need a network client installed and configured properly. The Client for Microsoft Networks is installed as part of the OS installation.

■ Systems in a TCP/IP network use IP addresses rather than names. IP addresses are four sets of eight binary numbers (octets) separated by periods (dotted-octet notation). The first part of the address identifies the network; the second part identifies the local computer (host) address. The subnet mask is a value that distinguishes which part of the IP address is the network address and which part is the host address. The subnet mask blocks out (masks) the network portions (octets) of an IP address.

■ A traditional TCP/IP network divides IP addresses into classes, which correspond with the potential size of the network: Class A, Class B, and Class C.

Class A networks use the first octet to identify the network address, and the remaining three octets to identify the host. Class B networks use two and two. Class C networks use three and one.

- TCP/IP not only supports File and Print Sharing, but it also adds a number of special sharing functions unique only to it, called TCP/IP services, such as HTTP, the language of the World Wide Web. Another example is Telnet, which enables you to access a remote system as though you were actually in front of that machine.

- TCP/IP uses a 16-bit number called a port number to control the connection between two systems. Each packet has two ports assigned, a destination port and an ephemeral port. The destination port is a fixed, predetermined number that defines the type of server connected, such as port 80 for a Web server.

- The goal of TCP/IP is to link together multiple LANs to make a WAN. You use routers to move traffic between networks. Each host sends traffic to the router only when that data is destined for a remote network, cutting down on traffic across the more expensive WAN links.

- On a Windows system, you can configure both dial-up and network connections by using the Network Connections dialog box. Simply select the connection you wish to configure, and then set its TCP/IP properties.

- A computer that wants to send data to a machine outside its LAN is not expected to know all of the IP addresses of all of the computers on the Internet. Instead, all IP machines know the name of one computer, called the default gateway, to which they pass the data they need to send outside the LAN. The default gateway is the local router.

- DNS servers keep databases of IP addresses and their corresponding names. Virtually all TCP/IP networks require you to set up DNS server names.

- If you want an Internet domain name that others can access on the Internet, you must register your domain name and pay a small yearly fee. Originally, DNS names all ended with one of the following top level domains: .com, .org, .edu, .gov, .mil, .net, and .int.

- DHCP automatically assigns IP address settings (including IP, subnet mask, default gateway, DNS servers, and WINS server, if necessary). If you add a NIC to a Windows system, the TCP/IP settings are set to use DHCP. A manually assigned IP address is known as a static IP address.

- All versions of Windows come with handy tools to test TCP/IP. The four you're most likely to use in the field are PING, IPCONFIG, NSLOOKUP, and TRACERT. You can use PING to test connections between hosts. You can use IPCONFIG both to display your current IP address settings and to renew and release your DHCP-assigned settings. NSLOOKUP is a powerful command-line program that enables you to determine the name of a DNS server, among many other things. The TRACERT utility shows the route that a packet takes to get to its destination.

- By default, TCP/IP is configured to receive an IP address automatically from a DHCP server, but you can assign a static IP address. Use the Network Connections applet in Windows XP/Vista/7; Network and Dial-up Connections from the Start menu in Windows 2000.

- Windows supports Automatic Private IP Addressing (APIPA). APIPA automatically assigns an IP address to the system when the client cannot obtain an IP address. If your PC gets an address with 169.254.x.y, you know the PC is not connecting to your DHCP server. Check your connection!

- All versions of Windows share drives and folders in basically the same manner. Simply right-click any drive or folder, choose Properties, and then select the Sharing tab. Click the *Share this folder* radio button and type a share name.

- When sharing a folder on an NTFS drive, you must set the network permissions to give everyone full control, and then use the NTFS permissions (on the Security tab) to exercise more precise control over who accesses the shared resources and how they access them.

- Network resources can be mapped to a local resource name. This can be done from Windows Explorer by clicking the Tools Menu and choosing Map Network Drive.

- All computers that share must have a share name, and all of the resources they share must also have names. Any resource on a network can be described by combining the names of the resource being shared and the system sharing. The complete UNC name of the FREDC share on SERVER1, for example, would be \\SERVER1\FREDC.

- Windows provides the NET utility to help explore and diagnose a Windows network. One of the more popular options is NET VIEW, which lists other Windows systems on the network. Another popular option is the NET USE command to map a remote share as a network drive.

- To share a printer in Windows, open the Printers folder in the Control Panel and right-click the printer you want to share. Select Properties and go to the Sharing tab; then click *Shared as* and give the printer a name. To access a shared printer in any version of Windows, simply click the Add Printer icon in the Printers folder.

■ Key Terms

administrator account *(395)* 3
Automatic Private IP Addressing (APIPA) *(402)* 5
client/server network *(393)*
default gateway *(405)*
destination port *(403)*
directory service *(395)*
domain name service (DNS) *(405)*
domain-based network *(395)*
dynamic host configuration protocol (DHCP) *(406)*
ephemeral port *(403)*
Hypertext Transfer Protocol (HTTP) *(403)*
IP address *(401)*
IPCONFIG *(408)*
NET command *(413)*

NetBIOS Extended User Interface (NetBEUI) *(398)*
network operating system (NOS) *(393)* 1
NSLOOKUP *(408)*
peer-to-peer network *(394)*
PING *(403)* 2
port *(403)*
resource *(393)*
router *(398)*
static IP address *(406)*
subnet mask *(403)*
TCP/IP *(398)* 4
TCP/IP service *(403)* 7
TRACERT *(408)* 6
universal naming convention (UNC) *(413)*

■ Key Term Quiz

Use the Key Terms list to complete the sentences that follow. Not all terms will be used.

1. A(n) _____ enables a PC to act as a server and share data and services over a network.

2. The command-line utility called _____ enables one machine to check whether it can communicate with another machine.

3. A person logged into the _____ on a Windows system can read any file and run any program on the system.

4. The most popular networking protocol is _____.

5. Windows supports a feature called _____ that automatically assigns an IP address to the system when the client cannot obtain an IP address automatically.

6. You can use the _____ command to follow the path a data packet takes.

7. HTTP and TELNET are both examples of special sharing functions called _____.

■ Multiple-Choice Quiz

1. Everything worked fine on your 1000BaseT network yesterday, but today no one can connect to the server. The server seems to be in good running order. Which of the following is the most likely problem?

    A. Someone changed all of the passwords for server access.

    B. A switch is malfunctioning.

    C. Someone's T connector has come loose on the bus.

    D. The server's cable is wired as TIA/EIA 568A and all of the others are wired as TIA/EIA 568B.

2. Simon's system can't contact a DHCP server to obtain an IP address automatically, but he can still communicate with other systems on his subnet. What feature of Windows makes this possible?

   A. Subnet masking

   B. WINS

   C. APIPA

   D. Client for Microsoft Networks

3. Which of the following is the correct NET syntax for discovering which network shares on a particular server are mapped on your computer?

   A. NET VIEW \\fileserver

   B. NET \\fileserver

   C. NET MAP \\fileserver

   D. NET SHARE \\fileserver

4. What command-line utility would you run to show a list of network computers?

   A. NET SEND

   B. SHOW NET_SERVERS

   C. NET USE

   D. NET VIEW

5. How do you share drives and folders in Windows?

   A. You must be running a copy of Windows Server to share files.

   B. Use the NET SHARE [file path] command.

   C. Right click on the drive or folder, select Properties, and then click *Share this folder* in the Sharing tab.

   D. Use the IPCONFIG /SHAREALL command.

6. What is the proper UNC location for a subfolder called "Vacation" located in a folder named "Photos" on a computer called "Mike?"

   A. \\Mike\Photos\Vacation

   B. \\Vacation\Photos\Mike

   C. \\Mike\Vacation\Photos

   D. \\Photos\Mike\Vacation

7. What is the host address of the Class C IP address 192.168.1.42?

   A. 192.168

   B. 168.1.42

   C. 1.42

   D. 42

8. What is another common name for a local router?

   A. Hub

   B. Switch

   C. Default gateway

   D. Repeater

9. What is the purpose of APIPA?

   A. It enables your computer to operate on a local area network.

   B. It enables your computer to connect to the Internet.

   C. It gives your computer a link-local IP address if it cannot obtain one otherwise.

   D. It enables your computer to send broadcast traffic.

10. What command-line utility enables one machine to check for connectivity with another machine?

    A. PING

    B. NETSTAT

    C. DIR

    D. CHKDSK

11. What new utility did Vista add that enables you to easily check connectivity, manage file and printer sharing, and toggle network discovery on and off?

    A. Connection Properties

    B. Network Sharing Center

    C. Network Command Center

    D. Network Properties

■ Essay Quiz

1. You get a late-night telephone call from a senior network tech with a crisis on his hands. "I need help getting 20 PCs networked within 24 hours, and your boss told me you might be able to assist me. I'll buy all of the pizza you can eat, and when the project's over, the beer is on me. Do you know the basics of a network? What must you do to get a PC ready to network?" Write a

short essay responding to his question. (Hint: Discuss four things in response to his last question.)

2. Your boss has a serious problem: the network tech is gone for the day and he can't access the file server. Tag; you're it. Write a brief essay

describing what yo
about your netwo
troubleshooting;
use if your netw

Lab Projects

• Lab Project 13.1

This chapter described how Windows automatically generates an IP address if there is no DHCP server. Experiment with this idea. If you have a network of Windows PCs that you can play with, make sure there is no DHCP server on the network. Use

IPCONFIG and see what your IP address is, and try sharing it and pinging other systems. Try to share resources and to access shared resources on other machines in the lab.

• Lab Project 13.2

The Internet is a big, sprawling place with big routers that move packets from place to place around the world. Using the TRACERT command,

see how many hops it takes to get to various Web sites in other countries.

Mastering Wireless

> "Having wires strewn across your couch and across the floor is a big deal to a lot of people."
>
> —J Allard

In this chapter, you will learn how to

- **Install and configure wireless networks**
- **Troubleshoot wireless networks**

Wireless networks have been popular for many years now, but unlike wired networks, so much of how wireless works continues to elude people. Part of the problem might be that a simple wireless network is so inexpensive and easy to configure that most users and techs never really get into the *hows* of wireless. The chance to get away from all the cables and mess and just *connect* has a phenomenal appeal. Well, let's change all that and dive deeply into installing and troubleshooting wireless networks.

■ Installing and Configuring Wireless Networking

The mechanics of setting up a wireless network don't differ much from a wired network. Physically installing a wireless network adapter is the same as installing a wired NIC, whether it's an internal PCI card, a PC Card, or an external USB device. Simply install the device and let plug and play handle detection and resource allocation. Install the device's supplied driver when prompted, and you're practically finished. Unless you're using Windows XP and later, you also need to install the wireless network configuration utility supplied with your wireless network adapter so you can set your communication mode, SSID, and so on.

Wireless devices want to talk to each other, so communicating with an available wireless network is usually a no-brainer. The trick is in configuring the wireless network so that only specific wireless nodes are able to use it and securing the data that's being sent through the air.

> The CompTIA A+ Practical Application exam assumes you know the names and connectors (or lack thereof) in wireless networking.

Wi-Fi

Wi-Fi networks support ad hoc and infrastructure operation modes. Which mode you choose depends on the number of wireless nodes you need to support, the type of data sharing they'll perform, and your management requirements.

Ad Hoc Mode

Ad hoc wireless networks don't need a **wireless access point (WAP)** or wireless router. The only requirements in an **ad hoc mode** wireless network are that each wireless node be configured with the same network name (SSID) and that no two nodes use the same IP address. Figure 14.1 shows a wireless network configuration utility with ad hoc mode selected.

The only other configuration steps to take are to make sure that no two nodes are using the same IP address (this step is usually unnecessary if all PCs are using DHCP) and ensuring that the File and Printer Sharing service is running on all nodes.

Infrastructure Mode

Typically, **infrastructure mode** wireless networks employ one or more WAPs connected to a wired network segment, a corporate intranet or the Internet, or both. As with ad hoc mode wireless networks, infrastructure mode networks require that the same SSID be configured on all nodes and WAPs. Figure 14.2 shows a NETGEAR Wi-Fi configuration screen set to infrastructure mode and using WPA security.

● **Figure 14.1**   Selecting ad hoc mode in wireless configuration utility

● Figure 14.2   Selecting infrastructure mode in wireless configuration utility

● Figure 14.3   Security login for Linksys WAP

WAPs have an integrated Web server and are configured through a **browser-based setup utility**. Typically, you fire up your Web browser on one of your network client workstations and enter the WAP's default IP address, such as 192.168.1.1, to bring up the configuration page. You will need to supply an administrative password, included with your WAP's documentation, to log in (see Figure 14.3). Setup screens vary from vendor to vendor and from model to model. Figure 14.4 shows the initial setup screen for a popular Linksys WAP/router.

Configure the SSID option where indicated. Channel selection is usually automatic, but you can reconfigure this option if you have particular needs in your organization (for example, if you have multiple wireless networks operating in the same area). Remember that it's always more secure to configure a unique SSID than it is to accept the well-known default one. You should also make sure that the option to allow broadcasting of the SSID is disabled. This ensures that only wireless nodes specifically configured with the correct SSID can join the wireless network.

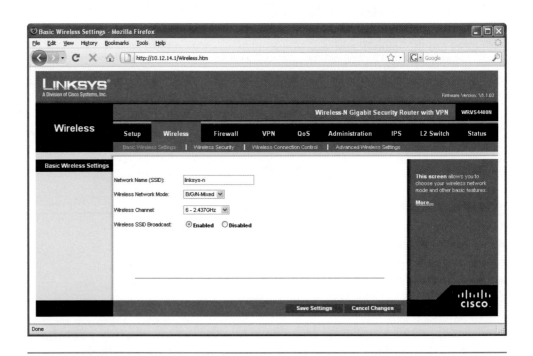

● Figure 14.4   Linksys WAP setup screen

● **Figure 14.5**   MAC filtering configuration screen for a Linksys WAP

To increase security even more, use **MAC address filtering**. Figure 14.5 shows the MAC filtering configuration screen on a Linksys WAP. ~~Simply enter the MAC address of a wireless node that you wish to allow (or deny) access to your wireless network.~~ Set up encryption by turning encryption on at the WAP and then generating a unique security key. Then configure all connected wireless nodes on the network with the same key information. Figure 14.6 shows the WEP key configuration dialog for a Linksys WAP.

When setting up **Wired Equivalent Privacy (WEP)** encryption, you have the option of automatically generating a set of encryption keys or doing it manually; save yourself a headache and use the automatic method. Select an encryption level—the usual choices are either 64-bit or 128-bit—and then enter a unique passphrase and click the Generate button (or whatever the equivalent button is called on your WAP). Then select a default key and save the settings. The encryption level, key, and passphrase must match on the wireless client node or communication will fail. Many WAPs have the capability to export the WEP encryption key data onto a media storage device for easy importing onto a client workstation, or you can manually configure encryption by using the vendor-supplied configuration utility, as shown in Figure 14.7.

WPA and WPA2 encryption is configured in much the same way as WEP. There are two ways to set up WPA/WPA2: Pre-shared Key (PSK)

> The WEP protocol provides security, but it's easily cracked. Use WPA2 or, if you have older equipment, settle for WPA until you can upgrade.

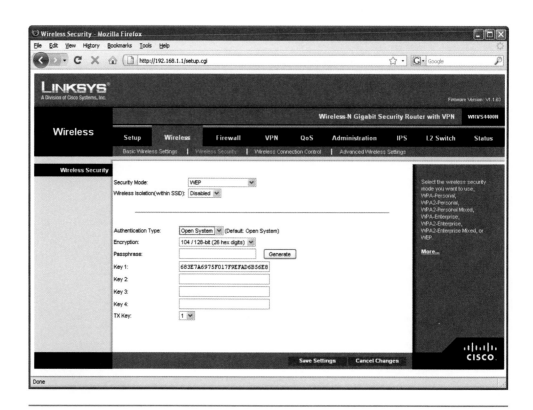

• **Figure 14.6** WEP encryption key configuration screen on Linksys WAP

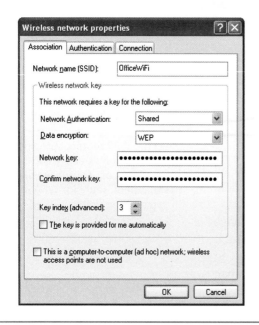

• **Figure 14.7** WEP encryption screen on client wireless network adapter configuration utility

Always try WPA2-PSK first. If you then have wireless computers that can't connect to your WAP, fall back to WPA-PSK.

or Enterprise. WPA/WPA2-PSK is the most common for small and home networks. Enterprise is much more complex, requires extra equipment (a RADIUS server), and is only used in the most serious and secure wireless networks.

If you have the option, choose WPA2 encryption for the WAP as well as the NICs in your network. You configure WPA2 the same way you would WPA. Note that the settings such as WPA2 for the Enterprise assume you'll enable authentication by using a device called a RADIUS server (Figure 14.8). This way, businesses can allow only people with the proper credentials to connect to their Wi-Fi networks. For home use, select the PSK version of WPA/WPA2. Use the best encryption you can. If you have WPA2, use it. If not, use WPA. WEP is always a last choice.

With most home networks, you can simply leave the channel and frequency of the WAP at the factory defaults, but in an environment with overlapping Wi-Fi signals, you'll want to adjust one or both features. To adjust the channel, find the option in the WAP configuration screens and simply change it. Figure 14.9 shows the channel option in a Linksys WAP.

With dual-band 802.11n WAPs, you can choose which band to put 802.11n traffic on, either 2.4 GHz or 5 GHz. In an area with overlapping signals, most of the traffic will be on the 2.4-GHz frequency, because most devices are either 802.11b or 802.11g. In addition to other wireless devices (such as cordless phones), microwaves also use 2.4-GHz

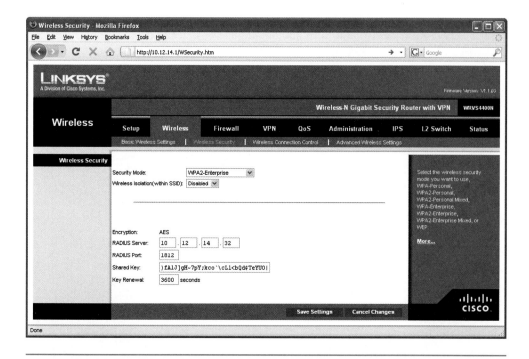

● **Figure 14.8**   Encryption screen with RADIUS option

frequency and can cause a great deal of interference. You can avoid any kind of conflict with your 802.11n devices by using the 5-GHz frequency instead. Figure 14.10 shows the configuration screen for a dual-band 802.11n WAP.

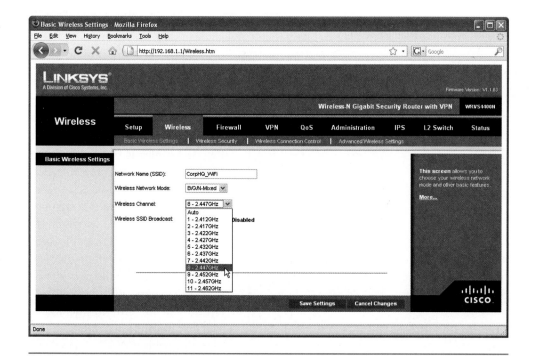

● **Figure 14.9**   Changing the channel

● **Figure 14.10**   Selecting frequency

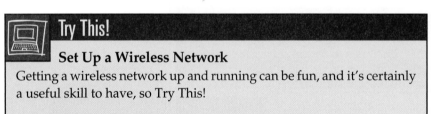

Try This!

Set Up a Wireless Network

Getting a wireless network up and running can be fun, and it's certainly a useful skill to have, so Try This!

1. Install wireless NICs in two or more PCs and then get them chatting in ad hoc mode. Don't forget to change the SSID!

2. Once you've got them talking in ad hoc mode, add a WAP and get them chatting in infrastructure mode.

3. If you don't have a lab but you have access to an Internet café (or coffee shop offering wireless), go there and ask someone to show you how they connect. Don't be shy. People love showing off technology!

Placing the Access Point(s)

The optimal location for an access point depends on the area you want to cover, whether you care if the signal bleeds out beyond the borders, and what interference exists from other wireless sources. You start by doing a site survey. A site survey can be as trivial as firing up a wireless-capable laptop and looking for existing SSIDs. Or it can be a complex job where you hire people with specialized equipment to come in and make lots of careful plans, defining the best place to put WAPs and which wireless channels to use. To make sure the wireless signal goes where you want it to go and not where you don't, you need to use the right antenna. Let's see what types of antennae are available.

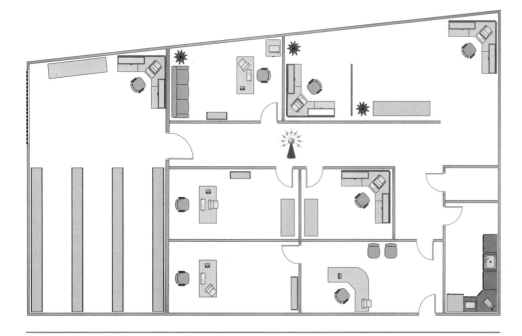

• **Figure 14.11**   Room layout with WAP in the center

Omnidirectional and Centered   For a typical network, you want blanket coverage and would place a WAP with an omnidirectional antenna in the center of the area (Figure 14.11). With an omnidirectional antenna, the radio wave flows outward from the WAP. This has the advantage of ease of use—anything within the signal radius can potentially access the network. Most wireless networks use this combination, especially in the consumer space. The standard straight-wire antennae that provide the most omnidirectional function are called dipole antennae.

Gaining Gain   An antenna strengthens and focuses the radio frequency (RF) output from a WAP. The ratio of increase—what's called **gain**—is measured in decibels (dB). The gain from a typical WAP is 2 dB, enough to cover a reasonable area but not a very large room. Increasing that signal requires a bigger antenna. Many WAPs have removable antennae that you can replace. To increase the signal in an omnidirectional and centered setup, simply replace the factory antennae with one or more bigger antennae (Figure 14.12). Get a big enough antenna and you can crank it all the way up to 11!

Bluetooth Configuration

As with other wireless networking solutions, **Bluetooth** devices are completely plug and play. Just connect the adapter and follow the prompts to install the appropriate drivers and configuration utilities (these are supplied by

• **Figure 14.12**   Replacement antenna on a WAP

Cross Check

It's Still a NIC!

Just because you've gone wireless, don't think for a minute that any of the rules you learned in Chapter 13, "Mastering Local Area Networking," have changed. A wireless NIC works the same as a wired NIC. Keep in mind the rules for accomplishing things with wired NICs and see if you can answer these questions:

1. How do you access the TCP/IP settings for the wireless NIC?
2. What IP address is your wireless NIC set to use right now?
3. Can you enable and disable the wireless NIC?

your hardware vendor). Once they're installed, you have little to do: Bluetooth devices seek each other out and establish the master/slave relationship without any intervention on your part.

Connecting to a Bluetooth **personal area network (PAN)** is handled by specialized utility software provided by your portable device or Bluetooth device vendor. Figure 14.13 shows a screen of an older PDA running the Bluetooth Manager software to connect to a Bluetooth access point. Like their Wi-Fi counterparts, Bluetooth access points use a browser-based configuration utility. Figure 14.14 shows the main setup screen for a Belkin Bluetooth access point. Use this setup screen to check on the status of connected Bluetooth devices; configure encryption, MAC filtering, and other security settings; and use other utilities provided by the access point's vendor.

Cellular Configuration

There is no single standard for configuring a cellular network card, because the cards and software vary based on which company you have service through. Fortunately those same cell phone companies have made the process of installing their cards very simple. All that is required in most cases is to install the software and plug in the card.

Once you've installed all of the correct drivers, simply plug in the card and start up the application. From here, just follow the instructions that came with the software; in this case, double-click on the VZAccess network

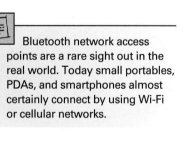

• **Figure 14.13** iPAQ Bluetooth Manager software connected to Bluetooth access point

Bluetooth network access points are a rare sight out in the real world. Today small portables, PDAs, and smartphones almost certainly connect by using Wi-Fi or cellular networks.

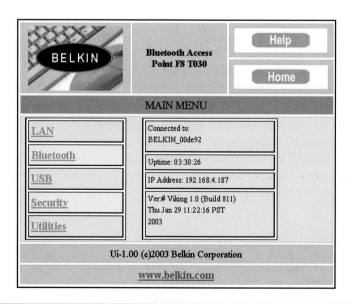

• **Figure 14.14** Belkin Bluetooth access point

● **Figure 14.15**   VZAccess Manager

listed in the window (Figure 14.15). This initiates the connection to (in this case) Verizon's network. You can also go to the Options menu and select Statistics and see the specifics of your connection, as shown in Figure 14.16.

The key thing to remember about cellular Internet access is that it is almost completely configured and controlled by the cellular company. A tech has very little to do except to make sure the cellular card is plugged in, is recognized by the computer, and its drivers are properly installed.

■ Troubleshooting Wi-Fi

Wireless networks are a real boon when they work right, but they can also be one of the most vexing things to troubleshoot when they don't. Let's turn to some practical advice on how to detect and correct wireless hardware, software, and configuration problems.

As with any troubleshooting scenario, your first step in troubleshooting a wireless network is to break down

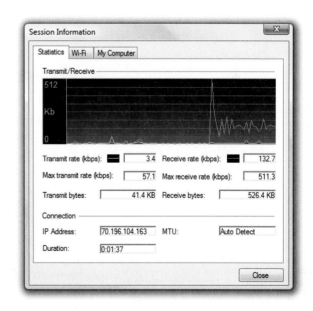

● **Figure 14.16**   Session statistics for VZAccess Manager

your tasks into logical steps. Your first step should be to figure out the scope of your wireless networking problem. Ask yourself *who*, *what*, and *when*:

- Who is affected by the problem?
- What is the nature of their network problem?
- When did the problem start?

The answers to these questions dictate at least the initial direction of your troubleshooting.

So, who's affected? If all machines on your network—wired and wireless—have lost connectivity, you have bigger problems than that the wireless machines cannot access the network. Troubleshoot this situation the way you'd troubleshoot any network failure. Once you determine which wireless nodes are affected, it's easier to pinpoint whether the problem lies in one or more wireless clients or in one or more access points.

After you narrow down the number of affected machines, your next task is to figure out specifically what type of error the users are experiencing. If they can access some, but not all, network services, it's unlikely that the problem is limited to their wireless equipment. For example, if they can browse the Internet but can't access any shared resources on a server, they're probably experiencing a permissions-related issue rather than a wireless one.

Finally, determine when the problem started. What has changed that might explain your loss of connectivity? Did you or somebody else change the wireless network configuration? For example, if the network worked fine two minutes ago, and then you changed the WEP key on the access point, and now nobody can see the network, you have your solution—or at least your culprit! Did your office experience a power outage, power sag, or power surge? Any of these also might cause a WAP to fail.

Once you figure out the who, what, and when, you can start troubleshooting in earnest. Typically, your problem is going to center on your hardware, software, connectivity, or configuration.

Hardware Troubleshooting

Wireless networking hardware components are subject to the same kind of abuse and faulty installation as any other hardware component. Troubleshooting a suspected hardware problem should bring out the technician in you.

Open Windows Device Manager and look for an error or conflict with the wireless adapter. If you see a big yellow exclamation point or a red X next to the device, you have either a driver error or a resource conflict. Reinstall the device driver or manually reset the IRQ resources as needed.

If you don't see the device listed at all, perhaps it is not seated properly in its PCI slot or not plugged all the way into its PC Card or USB slot. These problems are easy to fix. One thing to consider if you're using an older laptop and PC Card combination is that the wireless adapter may be a CardBus type of PC Card device. CardBus cards will not snap into a non-CardBus slot, even though both new and old cards are the same size. If your laptop is older than about five years, it may not support CardBus, meaning you need to get a different PC Card device. Or, if you've been looking for a reason to get a new laptop, now you have one!

As with all things computing, don't forget to do the standard PC troubleshooting thing and reboot the computer before you do any configuration or hardware changes!

Software Troubleshooting

Because you've already checked to confirm that your hardware is using the correct drivers, what kind of software-related problems are left to check? Two things come immediately to mind: the wireless adapter configuration utility and the WAP's firmware version.

As I mentioned earlier, some wireless devices won't work correctly unless you install the vendor-provided drivers and configuration utility before plugging in the device. This is particularly true of wireless USB devices. If you didn't do this, go into Device Manager and uninstall the device; then start again from scratch.

Some WAP manufacturers (I won't name names here, but they're popular) are notorious for shipping devices without the latest firmware installed. This problem often manifests as a device that enables clients to connect, but only at such slow speeds that the devices experience frequent timeout errors. The fix for this is to update the access point's firmware. Go to the manufacturer's Web site and follow the support links until you find the latest version. You'll need your device's exact model and serial number—this is important, because installing the wrong firmware version on your device is a guaranteed way of rendering it unusable!

Again, follow the manufacturer's instructions for updating the firmware to the letter. Typically, you need to download a small executable updating program along with a data file containing the firmware software. The process takes only minutes, and you'll be amazed at the results.

Connectivity Troubleshooting

Properly configured wireless clients should automatically and quickly connect to the desired SSID. If this isn't taking place, it's time for some troubleshooting. Most wireless connectivity problems come down to either an incorrect configuration (such as an incorrect password) or low signal strength. Without a strong signal, even a properly configured wireless client isn't going to work. Wireless clients use a multi-bar graph (usually five bars) to give an idea of signal strength: zero bars indicates no signal and five bars indicates maximum signal.

Whether configuration or signal strength, the process to diagnose and repair uses the same methods you use for a wired network. First, check the wireless NIC's link light to see whether it's passing data packets to and from the network. Second, check the wireless NIC's configuration utility. Typically the utility has an icon in your system tray that shows the strength of your wireless signal. Figure 14.17 shows Windows XP Professional's built-in wireless configuration utility—called Wireless Zero Configuration (or just Zeroconf)—displaying the link state and signal strength.

The link state defines the wireless NIC's connection status to a wireless network: connected or disconnected. If your link state indicates that your computer is currently disconnected, you may have a problem with your WAP. If your signal is too weak to receive a signal, you may be out of range of your access point, or there may be a device causing interference.

You can fix these problems in a number of ways. Because Wi-Fi signals bounce off of objects, you can try small adjustments to your antennae to see if the signal improves. You can swap out the standard antenna for one or

• **Figure 14.17**   Windows XP Professional's wireless configuration utility

If you're lucky enough to have a laptop with an internally installed NIC (instead of a PC Card), your device may not have a link light.

more higher-gain antennae. You can relocate the PC or access point, or locate and move the device causing interference.

Other wireless devices that operate in the same frequency range as your wireless nodes can cause interference as well. Look for wireless telephones, intercoms, and so on as possible culprits. One fix for interference caused by other wireless devices is to change the channel your network uses. Another is to change the channel the offending device uses, if possible. If you can't change channels, try moving the interfering device to another area or replacing it with a different device.

Configuration Troubleshooting

With all due respect to the fine network techs in the field, the most common type of wireless networking problem is misconfigured hardware or software. That's right—the dreaded *user error*! Given the complexities of wireless networking, this isn't so surprising. All it takes is one slip of the typing finger to throw off your configuration completely. The things you're most likely to get wrong are the SSID and security configuration.

Verify SSID configuration on your access point first, and then check on the affected wireless nodes. With most wireless devices you can use any characters in the SSID, including blank spaces. Be careful not to add blank characters where they don't belong, such as trailing blank spaces behind any other characters typed into the name field.

If you're using MAC address filtering, make sure the MAC address of the client that's attempting to access the wireless network is on the list of accepted users. This is particularly important if you swap out NICs on a PC, or if you introduce a new PC to your wireless network.

Check the security configuration to make sure that all wireless nodes and access points match. Mistyping an encryption key prevents the affected node from talking to the wireless network, even if your signal strength is 100 percent! Remember that many access points have the capability to export encryption keys onto a floppy disk or other removable media. It's then a simple matter to import the encryption key onto the PC by using the wireless NIC's configuration utility. Remember that the encryption level must match on access points and wireless nodes. If your WAP is configured for 128-bit encryption, all nodes must also use 128-bit encryption.

Chapter 14 Review

Chapter Summary

After reading this chapter and completing the exercises, you should understand the following about wireless networking.

Install and configure wireless networks

- The mechanics of setting up a wireless network don't differ much from a wired network. Physically installing a wireless network adapter is the same as installing a wired NIC, whether it's an internal PCI card, a PC Card, or an external USB device. Simply install the device and let plug and play handle detection and resource allocation. Unless you're using Windows XP or greater, you also need to install the wireless network configuration utility supplied with your wireless network adapter so you can set your communication mode, SSID, and so on.

- Wi-Fi networks support ad hoc and infrastructure operation modes. Which mode you choose depends on the number of wireless nodes you need to support, the type of data sharing they'll perform, and your management requirements.

- Ad hoc wireless networks don't need a WAP. The only requirements in an ad hoc mode wireless network are that each wireless node be configured with the same network name (SSID) and that no two nodes use the same IP address. You may also have to select a common channel for all ad hoc nodes.

- Typically, infrastructure mode wireless networks employ one or more WAPs connected to a wired network segment, a corporate intranet or the Internet, or both. As with ad hoc mode wireless networks, infrastructure mode networks require that the same SSID be configured on all nodes and WAPs.

- WAPs have an integrated Web server and are configured through a browser-based setup utility. Typically, you enter the WAP's default IP address to bring up the configuration page and supply an administrative password, included with your WAP's documentation, to log in.

- Set up WEP encryption—if that's your only option— by turning encryption on at the WAP and then generating a unique security key. Then configure all connected wireless nodes on the network with the same key information. WPA and WPA2 encryption are configured in much the same way. You may be required to input a valid user name and password to configure encryption by using WPA/WPA2.

- As with other wireless networking solutions, Bluetooth devices are completely plug and play. Just connect the adapter and follow the prompts to install the appropriate drivers and configuration utilities. Connecting to a Bluetooth PAN is handled by specialized utility software provided by your portable device or Bluetooth device vendor.

Troubleshoot wireless networks

- As with any troubleshooting scenario, your first step should be to figure out the scope of your wireless networking problem. Ask yourself *who*, *what*, and *when*. This helps you focus your initial troubleshooting on the most likely aspects of the network.

- Hardware troubleshooting for Wi-Fi devices should touch on the usual hardware process. Go to Device Manager and check for obvious conflicts. Check the drivers to make sure you have them installed and up to date. Make certain you have proper connectivity between the device and the PC.

- Software troubleshooting involves checking configuration settings, such as the SSID, WEP, MAC address filtering, and encryption levels. Be sure to check configuration settings on both the WAP and the wireless NIC.

Key Terms

ad hoc mode *(421)*
Bluetooth *(427)*
browser-based setup utility *(422)*
dipole antenna *(427)*
gain *(427)*
infrastructure mode *(421)*

MAC address filtering *(423)*
personal area network (PAN) *(428)*
Wi-Fi *(421)*
Wired Equivalent Privacy (WEP) *(423)*
wireless access point (WAP) *(421)*

Key Term Quiz

Use the Key Terms list to complete the sentences that follow.

1. Computers are in _____ when they connect directly together without using a WAP.

2. If you need to share an Internet connection or connect to a wired network through your wireless network, you would use _____.

3. _____ enables you to block certain computers from gaining access to your wireless network.

4. Most consumer routers come with a(n) _____ that makes configuration a snap.

5. The most common signal broadcasting method for wireless is using a(n) _____.

6. The amount that an antenna strengthens and focuses the radio frequency (RF) output from a WAP is called _____.

Multiple-Choice Quiz

1. Personal area networks are created by what wireless technology?
   A. Bluetooth
   B. IrDA
   C. Wi-Fi
   D. Cellular wireless

2. Which of these Wi-Fi security protocols is the least secure and easily hacked?
   A. WEP
   B. WAP
   C. WINS
   D. WPA2

3. What is a cheap and easy way to extend the range of a WAP?
   A. Upgrade the antenna.
   B. Buy a WAP that advertises a longer range.
   C. You can't easily boost range.
   D. Upgrade the wireless NICs.

4. Which of the following 802.11 standards can make use of both the 2.4- and 5-GHz bands?
   A. 802.11a
   B. 802.11b
   C. 802.11g
   D. 802.11n

5. Leo has several laptops with wireless NICs that he wants to network wirelessly but doesn't have a WAP. How can he turn these laptops into a small wireless network without a WAP?

   A. He can set each laptop to ad hoc mode.
   B. He can set each laptop to infrastructure mode.
   C. He can set each laptop to PAN mode.
   D. He cannot create a wireless network without a WAP.

6. What is the first thing you should check if you're having connectivity issues with your wireless network?
   A. The SSID.
   B. Your NIC's link lights.
   C. Your computer's IP address.
   D. What mode your wireless NIC is set to.

7. Where can you check for hardware problems when troubleshooting a wireless network?
   A. Look in Device Manager.
   B. Check the Performance monitor.
   C. Look at the Wireless Configuration window.
   D. Check the Network Sharing Center.

8. Angie just changed the WPA key on her wireless router, and now her laptop can't connect to her wireless network. What is most likely the problem?
   A. Something in her house is causing interference.
   B. She forgot to reset her router after changing the WPA key.
   C. Her laptop isn't configured for the new WPA key yet.
   D. She set an invalid WPA key.

9. What is the primary benefit of using an ad hoc wireless network?

   A. You don't need a wireless NIC in your computer.

   (B) You don't need a WAP.

   C. You can use 802.11n with an 802.11g NIC.

   D. Ad hoc networks speed up Internet traffic.

10. How do many modern WAPs make it easy for you to change your network settings?

   (A) They have a W

   B. A technician them at no a

   C. They don't

   D. You can c the comm

Essay Quiz

1. Write a few paragraphs describing the proper procedure for troubleshooting wireless networks. Your answer should contain information on hardware, software, connectivity, and configuration troubleshooting.

Lab Project

• Lab Project 14.1

If you have access to a WAP, a wireless NIC expansion card, and a lab computer that you are able to work on, try installing the NIC in the lab computer, setting up a wireless network using the WAP, and connecting the lab computer to the network you set up. For an extra challenge, try using different encryption methods or try disabling SSID broadcast and then connecting.

Mastering the Internet

"The Internet is not something that you just dump something on. It's not a big truck. It's a series of tubes."

—Ted Stevens

In this chapter, you will learn how to

- **Connect to the Internet**
- **Use Internet software tools**

RJ 45 -

RJ 11 -

Imagine coming home from a long day at work building and fixing PCs, sitting down in front of your shiny new computer, double-clicking the single icon that sits dead center on your monitor...and suddenly you're enveloped in an otherworldly scene where 200-foot trees slope smoothly into snow-white beaches and rich blue ocean. Overhead, pterodactyls soar through the air while you talk to a small chap with pointy ears and a long robe about heading up the mountain in search of a giant monster. TV show from the SciFi channel? Spielberg's latest film offering? How about an interactive game played by millions of people all over the planet on a daily basis by connecting to the Internet? If you guessed the last one, you're right.

This chapter covers the skills you need as a PC tech to help people connect to the Internet. It starts with a brief section on how the Internet works, along with the concepts of connectivity, and then it goes into the specifics on hardware, protocols, and software that you use to make the Internet work for you (or for your client). Let's get started!

Connecting to the Internet

PCs commonly connect to an ISP by using one of seven technologies that fit into four categories: dial-up, both analog and ISDN; dedicated, such as DSL, cable, and LAN; wireless; and satellite. Analog dial-up is the slowest of the bunch and requires a telephone line and a special networking device called a modem. ISDN uses digital dial-up and has much greater speed. All the others use a regular Ethernet NIC like you played with in Chapter 13, "Mastering Local Area Networking." Satellite is the odd one out here; it may use either a modem or a NIC, depending on the particular configuration you have, although most folks will use a NIC. Let's take a look at all these various connection options.

Dial-up

A dial-up connection to the Internet requires two pieces to work: hardware to dial the ISP, such as a modem or ISDN terminal adapter, and software to govern the connection, such as Microsoft's **Dial-Up Networking (DUN)**. Let's look at the hardware first, and then we'll explore software configuration.

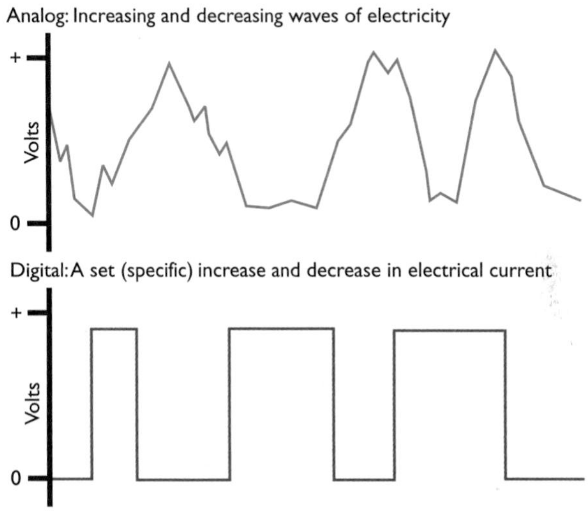

Modems

At some point in the early days of computing, some bright guy or gal noticed a colleague talking on a telephone, glanced down at a PC, and then put two and two together: why not use telephone lines for data communication? The basic problem with this idea is that traditional telephone lines use analog signals, while computers use digital signals (Figure 15.1). Creating a dial-up network required equipment that could turn digital data into an analog signal to send it over the telephone line and then turn it back into digital data when it reached the other end of the connection. A device called a modem solved this dilemma.

A modem enables computers to talk to each other via standard commercial telephone lines by converting analog signals to digital signals, and vice versa. The term *modem* is short for modulator/demodulator, a description of transforming the signals. Telephone wires transfer data via analog signals that continuously change voltages on a wire. Computers hate analog signals. Instead, they need digital signals, voltages that are either on or off, meaning the wire has voltage present or it does not. Computers, being binary by nature, use only two states of voltage: zero volts and positive volts. Modems take analog signals from telephone lines and turn them into digital signals that the PC can understand (Figure 15.2). Modems also

Analog: Increasing and decreasing waves of electricity

Digital: A set (specific) increase and decrease in electrical current

• **Figure 15.1** Analog signals used by a telephone line versus digital signals used by the computer

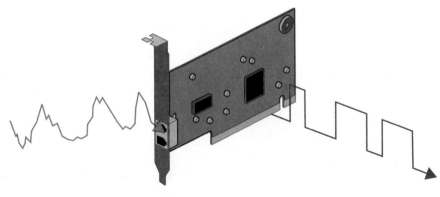

• **Figure 15.2** Modem converting analog signal to digital signal

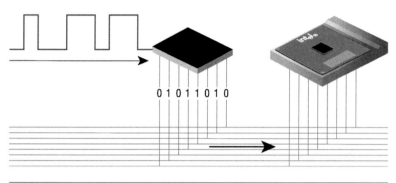

• **Figure 15.3** CPUs can't read serial data.

• **Figure 15.4** The UART chip converts serial data to parallel data that the CPU can read.

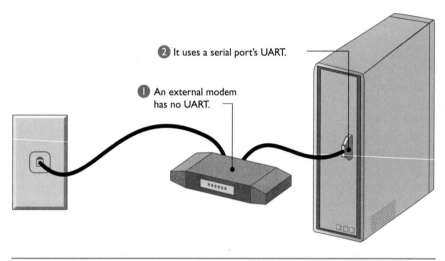

01011010

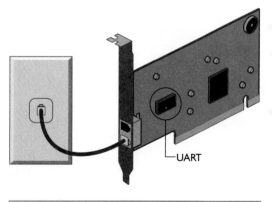

2 It uses a serial port's UART.

1 An external modem has no UART.

• **Figure 15.5** An external modem uses the PC's serial port.

UART

• **Figure 15.6** An internal modem has UART built in.

take digital signals from the PC and convert them into analog signals for the outgoing telephone line.

A modem does what is called *serial communication*: it transmits data as a series of individual ones and zeroes. The CPU can't process data this way. It needs parallel communication, transmitting and receiving data in discrete 8-bit chunks (Figure 15.3). The individual serial bits of data are converted into 8-bit parallel data that the PC can understand through the universal asynchronous receiver/transmitter (UART) chip (Figure 15.4).

There are many types of UARTs, each with different functions. All serial communication devices are really little more than UARTs. *External* modems can convert analog signals to digital ones and vice versa, but they must rely on the serial ports to which they're connected for the job of converting between serial and parallel data (Figure 15.5). Internal modems can handle both jobs because they have their own UART built in (Figure 15.6).

Phone lines have a speed based on a unit called a *baud*, which is one cycle per second. The fastest rate that a phone line can achieve is 2,400 baud. Modems can pack multiple bits of data into each baud; a 33.6 kilobits per second (Kbps) modem, for example, packs 14 bits into every baud: 2,400 × 14 = 33.6 Kbps. Thus, it is technically incorrect to say, "I have a 56 K baud modem." The correct statement is, "I have a 56 Kbps modem." But don't bother; people have used the term "baud" instead of **bits per second (bps)** so often for so long that the terms have become functionally synonymous.

Modern Modem Standards: V.90 vs. V.92 The fastest data transfer speed a modem can handle is based on its implementation of one of the international standards for modem technology: the **V** standards. Set by the International Telecommunication Union (ITU), the current top standards are V.90 and V.92. Both standards offer download speeds of just a hair under 56 Kbps, but they differ in upload speeds: up to 33.6 Kbps for V.90 and up to 48 Kbps for V.92 modems. To get anywhere near the top speeds of a V.90 or V.92 modem requires a comparable modem installed on the other line and connecting telephone lines in excellent condition.

In practice, you'll rarely get faster throughput than about 48 Kbps for downloads and 28 Kbps for uploads.

Flow Control (Handshaking)   Flow control, also known as handshaking, is the process by which two serial devices verify a conversation. Imagine people talking on a CB radio. When one finishes speaking, he says "over." That way the person listening can be sure that the sender is finished speaking before she starts. Each side of the conversation is verified. During a file transfer, two distinct conversations take place that require flow control: local (between modem and COM port) and end-to-end (between modems).

The modems themselves handle end-to-end flow control. PCs can do local flow control between the modem and COM port in two ways: hardware and software. Hardware flow control employs extra wires in the serial connection between the modem and the COM port to let one device tell the other that it is ready to send or receive data. These extra wires are called *ready to send* (*RTS*) and *clear to send* (*CTS*), so hardware handshaking is often called RTS/CTS. Software flow control uses a special character called XON to signal that data flow is beginning, and another special character called XOFF to signal that data transmission is finished; therefore, software handshaking is often called XON/XOFF. Software handshaking is slower and not as dependable as hardware handshaking, so you rarely see it.

Bells and Whistles   Although the core modem technology has changed little in the past few years, modem manufacturers have continued to innovate on many peripheral fronts—pardon the pun and the bad grammar. You can walk into a computer store nowadays, for example, and buy a V.92 modem that comes bundled with an excellent fax machine and a digital answering machine. You can even buy modems that you can call remotely that will wake up your PC (Figure 15.7). What will they think up next?

Modem Connections   Internal modems connect to the PC very differently than external modems. Almost all internal modems connect to a PCI or PCI Express expansion bus slot inside the PC, although cost-conscious manufacturers may use smaller modems that fit in special expansion slots designed to support multiple communications features such as modems, NICs, and sound cards (Figure 15.8). Older AMD motherboards used Audio/Modem Riser (AMR) or Advanced Communication Riser (ACR) slots, while Intel motherboards used Communication and Networking Riser (CNR) slots.

External modems connect to the PC through an available serial port (the old way) or USB port (Figure 15.9). Many older PCs came with 9-pin serial ports, whereas most external modems designed to connect to a serial port come with a 25-pin connector. That means you will probably need a 9-to-25-pin converter, available at any computer store, to connect your external modem. Serial ports are now quite rare as virtually all computers today have two or more USB ports.

● **Figure 15.7**   Some of the many features touted by the manufacturer of the SupraMax modem

 You can test a modem by plugging in a physical device called a *loopback plug* and then running diagnostics.

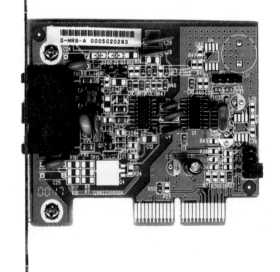

● **Figure 15.8**   A CNR modem

AMR, ACR, and CNR slots have gone away, though you'll still find them on older systems. Current systems use built-in components or PCIe ×1 slots for modems, sound, and NICs.

• **Figure 15.9** A USB modem

Cross Check

Installing a PCI Modem

Installing a PCI modem card involves pretty much the same process as installing any other PCI card. Refer to Chapter 3, "Mastering Motherboards," and cross check your knowledge of the process.

1. What do you need to guard against when installing a PCI card?

2. Any issues involving drivers, plug and play, or other hardware topics?

Don't fret about USB versus serial for your modem connection, as the very low speeds of data communication over a modem make the physical type of the connection unimportant. Even the slow, aging serial interface more than adequately handles 56 Kbps data transfers. If you have the option, choose a USB modem, especially one with a volume control knob. USB offers simple plug and play and easy portability between machines, plus such modems require no external electrical source, getting all the power they need from the USB connection.

Dial-up Networking

The software side of dial-up networks requires configuration within Windows to include information provided by your ISP. The ISP provides a dial-up telephone number or numbers, as well as your user name and initial password. In addition, the ISP will tell you about any special configuration options you need to specify in the software setup. The full configuration of dial-up networking is beyond the scope of this book, but you should at least know where to go to follow instructions from your ISP. Let's take a look at the Network and Internet Connections applet in Windows XP.

Network Connections   To start configuring a dial-up connection in Windows XP, open the Control Panel. Select Network and Internet Connections from the Pick a category menu and then choose *Set up or change your Internet connection* from the Pick a task menu The Internet Properties dialog box opens with the Connections tab displayed (Figure 15.10). All your work will proceed from here.

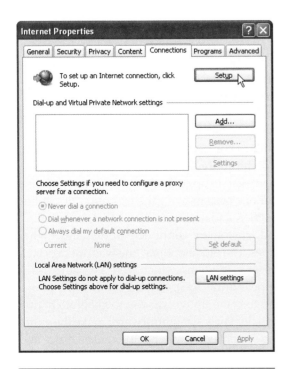

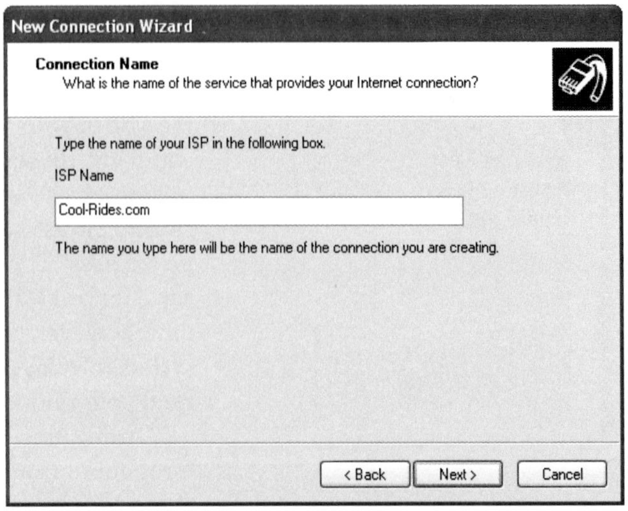

Figure 15.11 The New Connection Wizard

Figure 15.10 The Connections tab in the Internet Properties dialog box

Click the Setup button to run the New Connection Wizard (Figure 15.11), and then work through the screens. At this point, you're going to need information provided by your ISP to configure your connection properly. When you finish the configuration, you'll see a new Connect To option on the Start menu if your system is set up that way. If not, open up Network Connections, and your new dial-up connection will be available. Figure 15.12 shows the option to connect to a fictitious ISP, Cool-Rides.com.

PPP Dial-up links to the Internet have their own special hardware protocol called **Point-to-Point Protocol (PPP)**. PPP is a streaming protocol developed especially for dial-up Internet access. To Windows, a modem is nothing more than a special type of network adapter. Modems have their own configuration entry in the Network Connections applet.

Most dial-up "I can't connect to the Internet"–type problems are user errors. Your first area of investigation is the modem itself. Use the modem's properties to make sure the volume is turned up. Have the user listen to the connection. Does she hear a dial tone? If she doesn't, make sure the modem's line is plugged into a good phone jack. Does she hear the modem dial and then hear someone saying, "Hello? Hello?" If so, she probably dialed the wrong number! Wrong password error messages are fairly straightforward—remember that the password may be correct but the user name may be wrong. If she still fails to connect, it's time to call the network folks to see what is not properly configured in the Dial-up Networking settings.

Figure 15.12 Connection options in Network Connections

ISDN

A standard telephone connection comprises many pieces. First, the phone line runs from your phone out to a network interface box (the little box on the side of your house) and into a central switch belonging to the telephone company. (In some cases, intermediary steps are present.) Standard metropolitan areas have a large number of central offices, each with a central switch. Houston, Texas, for example, has nearly 100 offices in the general metro area. These central switches connect to each other through high-capacity *trunk lines*. Before 1970, the entire phone system was analog; over time, however, phone companies began to upgrade their trunk lines to digital systems. Today, the entire telephone system, with the exception of the line from your phone to the central office, and sometimes even that, is digital.

During this upgrade period, customers continued to demand higher throughput from their phone lines. The old telephone line was not expected to produce more than 28.8 Kbps (56 K modems, which were a *big* surprise to the phone companies, didn't appear until 1995). Needless to say, the phone companies were very motivated to come up with a way to generate higher capacities. Their answer was actually fairly straightforward: make the entire phone system digital. By adding special equipment at the central office and the user's location, phone companies can now achieve a throughput of up to 64 K per line (see the paragraphs following) over the same copper wires already used by telephone lines. This process of sending telephone transmission across fully digital lines end-to-end is called integrated services digital network (ISDN) service.

ISDN service consists of two types of channels: Bearer, or B, channels and Delta, or D, channels. B channels carry data and voice information at 64 Kbps. D channels carry setup and configuration information and carry data at 16 Kbps. Most providers of ISDN allow the user to choose either one or two B channels. The more common setup is two B/one D, usually called a *basic rate interface* (BRI) setup. A BRI setup uses only one physical line, but each B channel sends 64 K, doubling the throughput total to 128 K. ISDN also connects much faster than modems, eliminating that long, annoying, mating call you get with phone modems. The monthly cost per B channel is slightly more than a regular phone line, and usually a fairly steep initial fee is levied for the installation and equipment. The big limitation is that you usually need to be within about 18,000 feet of a central office to use ISDN.

The physical connections for ISDN bear some similarity to analog modems. An ISDN wall socket usually looks something like a standard RJ-45 network jack. The most common interface for your computer is a device called a *terminal adapter* (TA). TAs look much like regular modems, and like modems, they come in external and internal variants. You can even get TAs that are also hubs, enabling your system to support a direct LAN connection.

> Another type of ISDN, called a primary rate interface (PRI), is composed of twenty-three 64-Kbps B channels and one 64-Kbps D channel, giving it a total throughput of 1.5 megabits per second. PRI ISDN lines are also known as T1 lines.

> The two most common forms of DSL you'll find are *asynchronous* (*ADSL*) and *synchronous* (*SDSL*). ADSL lines differ between slow upload speed (such as 384 Kbps, 768 Kbps, and 1 Mbps) and faster download speed (usually 3–7 Mbps). SDSL has the same upload and download speeds, but telecom companies charge a lot more for the privilege. DSL encompasses many such variations, so you'll often see it referred to as *x*DSL.

DSL

Digital subscriber line (DSL) connections to ISPs use a standard telephone line but special equipment on each end to create always-on Internet connections at blindingly fast speeds, especially when compared with analog dial-up connections. Service levels vary around the United States, but the typical upload speed is ~768 Kbps, while download speed comes in at a very sweet ~3+ Mbps!

DSL requires little setup from a user standpoint. A tech comes to the house to install the DSL receiver, often called a DSL modem (Figure 15.13), and possibly hook up a wireless router. The receiver connects to the telephone line and the PC (Figure 15.14). The tech (or the user, if knowledgeable) then configures the DSL modem and router (if there is one) with the settings provided by the ISP, and that's about it! Within moments, you're surfing at blazing speeds. You don't need a second telephone line. You don't need to wear a special propeller hat or anything. The only kicker is that your house has to be within a fairly short distance from a main phone service switching center, something like 18,000 feet.

• **Figure 15.13**   A DSL receiver

Cable

Cable offers a different approach to high-speed Internet access, using regular cable TV cables to serve up lightning-fast speeds. It offers faster service than most DSL connections, with a 1–10 Mbps upload and 6–50+ Mbps download. Cable Internet connections are theoretically available anywhere you can get cable TV.

Cable Internet connections start with an RG-6 or RG-59 cable coming into your house. The cable connects to a cable modem that then connects to a NIC in your PC via UTP Ethernet cable. Figure 15.15 shows a typical cable setup. One nice advantage of cable over DSL is that if you have a TV tuner card in your PC, you can use the same cable connection (with a splitter) to watch TV on your PC. Both DSL and cable modem Internet connections can be used by two or more computers if they are part of a LAN, including those in a home.

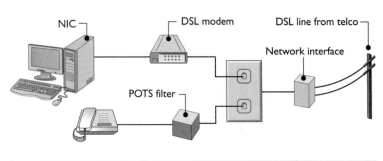

• **Figure 15.14**   DSL connections

LAN

Most businesses connect their internal local area network (LAN) to an ISP via some hardware solution that Network+ techs deal with. Figure 15.16

> The term *modem* has been warped and changed beyond recognition in modern networking. Both DSL and cable fully digital Internet connections use the term *modem* to describe the box that takes the incoming signal from the Internet and translates it into something the PC can understand.

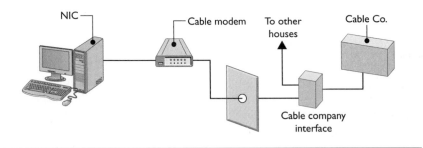

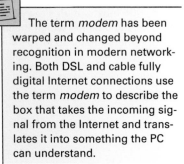

• **Figure 15.15**   Cable connections

shows a typical small-business wiring closet with routers that connect the LAN to the ISP. You learned all about wiring up a LAN in Chapter 13, "Mastering Local Area Networking," so there's no need to go through any basics here. To complete a LAN connection to the Internet, you need to add a second NIC or a modem to one of the PCs and then configure that PC as the default connection. We'll revisit this idea in a moment with Internet Connection Sharing.

Wireless

Every once in a while a technology comes along that, once the kinks are smoothed out, works flawlessly, creating a magical computing experience. Unfortunately, the various wireless networking technologies out there today don't fulfill that dream yet. When they work, it's like magic. You walk into a coffee shop, sit down, and flip open your laptop computer. After firing up your Internet browser, suddenly you're quaffing lattes and surfing Web sites—with no wires at all.

Suffice it to say that connecting to the Internet via wireless means that you must connect to a cellular network or to a LAN that's wired to an ISP. The local Internet café purchases high-speed Internet service from the cable or telecom company, for example, and then connects a wireless access point (WAP) to its network. When you walk in with your portable PC with wireless NIC and open a Web browser, the wireless NIC communicates with the *fully wired* DHCP server via the WAP and you're surfing on the Internet. It appears magically wireless, but the LAN to ISP connection still uses wires.

Cellular networking is even more seamless. Anywhere you can connect with your cell phone, you can connect with your cellular network–aware portable or laptop computer.

• **Figure 15.16**   A wiring closet

One form of wireless communication does not require local wires. For *wireless broadband*, the ISP must put up a tower, and then any building within the line of sight (perhaps up to 10 miles) can get a high-speed connection.

Satellite

Satellite connections to the Internet get the data beamed to a satellite dish on your house or office; a receiver handles the flow of data, eventually sending it through an Ethernet cable to the NIC in your PC. I can already sense people's eyebrows rising. "Yeah, that's the download connection. But what about the upload connection?" Very astute, me hearties! The early days of satellite required you to connect via a modem. You would upload at the slow 26- to 48-Kbps modem speed but then get super-fast downloads from the dish. It worked, so why complain? You really can move to that shack on the side of the Himalayas to write the great Tibetan novel and still have DSL- or cable-speed Internet connectivity. Sweet!

Satellite might be the most intriguing of all the technologies used to connect to the Internet today. As with satellite television, though, you need to have the satellite dish point at the satellites (toward the south if you live in the United States). The only significant issue to satellite is that the distance the signal must travel creates a small delay called the *satellite latency*. This latency is usually unnoticeable unless the signal degrades in foul weather such as rain and snow.

Windows Internet Connection Sharing

Internet Connection Sharing (ICS) enables one system to share its Internet connection with other systems on the network, providing a quick and easy method for multiple systems to use one Internet connection. Modern Windows versions (Windows 2000 through Windows 7) also provide this handy tool. Figure 15.17 shows a typical setup for ICS. Note the terminology used here. The PC that connects to the Internet and then shares that connection via ICS with other machines on a LAN is called the *ICS host* computer. PCs that connect via LAN to the ICS host computer are simply called *client* computers.

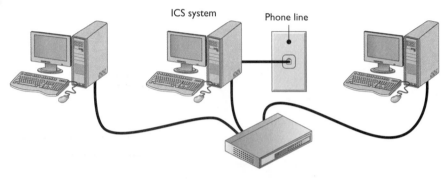

• **Figure 15.17**   Typical ICS setup

To connect multiple computers to a single ICS host computer requires several things in place. First, the ICS host computer has to have a NIC dedicated to the internal connections. If you connect via dial-up, for example, the ICS host computer uses a modem to connect to the Internet. It also has a NIC that plugs into a switch. Other PCs on the LAN likewise connect to the switch. If you connect via some faster service, such as DSL that uses a NIC cabled to the DSL receiver, you'll need a second NIC in the ICS host machine to connect to the LAN and the client computers.

Setting up ICS in Windows is very simple. If you are using Windows 2000 or XP, open the properties dialog for My Network Places. If you are using Windows Vista or 7, open the Network and Sharing Center and click on *Manage network connections* (Vista) or *Change adapter settings* (7) in the left-hand task list. Now access the properties of the connection you wish to share.

Click the Sharing tab (Windows 2000, Vista, and 7) or the Advanced tab (Windows XP), and select *Enable Internet connection sharing for this connection* (Windows 2000) or *Allow other network users to connect through this computer's Internet connection* (Windows XP–7, Figure 15.18). Clients don't need any special configuration but should simply be set to DHCP for their IP address and other configurations.

• **Figure 15.18**   Enabling Internet Connection Sharing in Windows Vista

Hardware Connection Sharing

Although Windows Internet Connection Sharing works, it has a major drawback—you must leave the computer running all the time so the other computers on the network can access the Internet. This is where the small home router fits perfectly. Several manufacturers offer robust, easy-to-configure routers that enable multiple computers to connect to a single Internet connection. These boxes require very little configuration and provide firewall protection between the primary computer and the Internet, which you'll learn more about in Chapter 16, "Mastering Computer Security." All it

takes to install one of these routers is simply to plug your computer into any of the LAN ports on the back, and then to plug the cable from your Internet connection into the port labeled Internet or WAN.

A great example of a home router is the Linksys WRT54G (Figure 15.19). This little DSL/cable router, for example, has four 10/100 Ethernet ports for the LAN computers, and a WiFi radio for any wireless computers you may have. The Linksys, like all home routers, uses a technology called Network Address Translation, or NAT for short. NAT performs a little network subterfuge: it presents an entire LAN of computers to the Internet as a single machine. It effectively hides all of your computers and makes them appear invisible to other computers on the Internet. All anyone on the Internet sees is your *public* IP address. This is the address your ISP gives you, while all the computers in your LAN use private addresses that are invisible to the world. NAT therefore acts as a firewall, protecting your internal network from probing or malicious users from the outside.

● **Figure 15.19**   Common home router with Wi-Fi

Basic Router Configuration

These small routers require very little in the way of configuration if all you need is basic Internet connection sharing. In some cases, though, you may have to deal with a more complex network that requires changing the router's settings. The vast majority of these routers have built-in configuration Web pages that you access by typing the router's IP address into a browser. The address varies by manufacturer, so check the router's documentation. If you typed in the correct address, you should then receive a prompt for a user name and password, as in Figure 15.20. As with the IP address, the default user name and password change depending on the model/manufacturer. Once you enter the correct credentials, you will be greeted by the router's configuration page (Figure 15.21). From these pages, you can change any of the router's settings. Now look at a few of the basic settings that CompTIA wants you to be familiar with.

● **Figure 15.20**   Router asking for user name and password

Changing User Name and Password   One of the first changes you should make to your router after you have it working is to change the user name and password to something other than the default. This is especially important if you have open wireless turned on, which you'll recall from Chapter 14, "Mastering Wireless." If you leave the default user name and password, anyone who has access to your LAN can easily gain access to the router and change its settings. Fortunately, router manufacturers make it easy to change a router's login credentials. On this Linksys of mine, for example, I just click on the Administration tab and fill in the appropriate boxes as shown in Figure 15.22.

Disabling DHCP   If you are configuring a router for a small office, the router's built-in DHCP server might conflict with a domain controller on

● **Figure 15.21** Configuration home page

your network. These conflicts, although not dangerous, can cause a lot of frustration and shouting as everyone's network connections stop working. To avoid this blow to inter-office relations, you should disable the DHCP server in the router before you plug it into the network. To do this, use a separate computer such as a laptop, or unplug your computer from the wall and plug it into the new router to log on.

● **Figure 15.22** Changing the user name and password

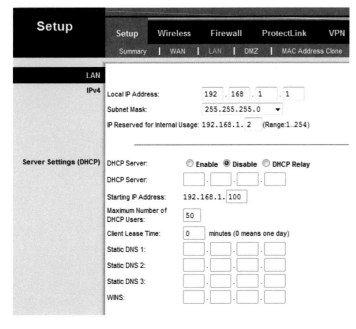

• Figure 15.23 Configuring DHCP server

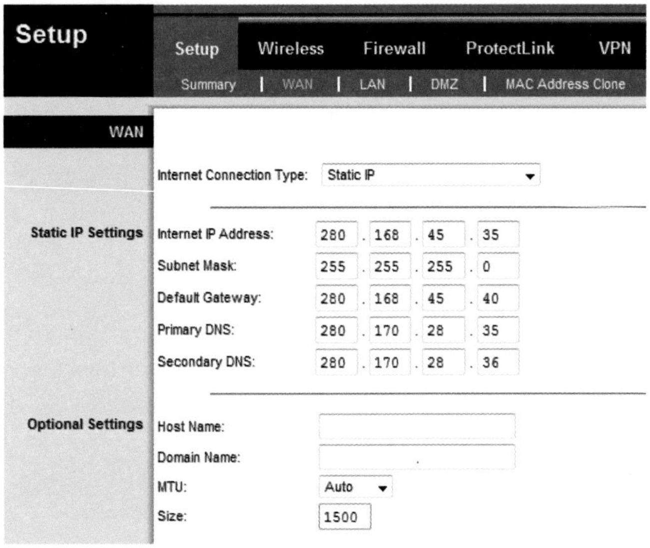

• Figure 15.24 Entering a static IP address

Once on the configuration screen, you will see a configuration page similar to the one in Figure 15.23. A word of warning: Once the DHCP server is disabled, the router will no longer hand out IP addresses, so you must make sure that the router's IP address is in the correct subnet of your office's LAN. If it isn't, you need to change it before you disable DHCP. On my router, all that is needed is to enter the new address and subnet at the top of the screen shown in Figure 15.23. If you are unsure what address you need, ask your network administrator or CompTIA Network+ tech. Once you have the router's IP address taken care of, all you need to do is click the Disable radio button and save the settings. Now you can safely plug your router into the LAN without risking the ire of Internet-less coworkers.

Setting Static IP Addresses   With that all taken care of, let's look at setting up the router to use a static IP address for the Internet or WAN connection. In most cases, when you plug in the router's Internet connection, it receives an IP address using DHCP just like any other computer. Of course, this means that your Internet IP address will change from time to time, which can be a bit of a downside. This does not affect most people, but for some home users and businesses, it can present a problem. To solve this problem, most ISPs enable you to order a static IP. Once your ISP has allocated you a static IP address, you must manually enter it into your router. You do this the same way as all the previous changes you've just looked at. My router has a WAN configuration tab where I can enter all the settings that my ISP has provided me (Figure 15.24). Remember, you must change your connection type from Automatic/ DHCP to Static IP to enter the new addresses.

Updating Firmware

Routers are just like any other computer in that they run software—and software has bugs, vulnerabilities, and other issues that sometimes require updating. The router manufacturers call these "firmware updates" and make them available on their Web sites for easy download. To update a modern router, you simply have to download the latest firmware from the manufacturer's Web site to your computer. Then you enter the router's configuration Web page and find the firmware update screen. On my router, it looks like Figure 15.25. From here, just follow the directions and click Update. A quick word of caution: unlike a Windows update, a firmware update gone bad can *brick* your router. In other words, it can destroy the hardware and make it as useful as a brick sitting on your desk. This rarely happens, but you should keep it in mind when doing a firmware update.

● **Figure 15.25**   Firmware update page

Internet Software Tools

Once you've established a connection between the PC and the ISP, you can do nothing on the Internet without applications designed to use one or more TCP/IP services, such as Web browsing and e-mail. TCP/IP has the following commonly used services:

- World Wide Web (HTTP and HTTPS)
- E-mail (POP and SMTP)
- Newsgroups
- FTP
- TELNET
- VoIP

Each of these services (sometimes referred to by the overused term *TCP/IP protocols*) operates by using defined ports, requires a special application, and has special settings. You'll look at all six of these services and learn how to configure them. As a quick reference, Table 15.1 has some common port numbers CompTIA would like you to know.

Table 15.1	TCP/IP Service Port Numbers
TCP/IP Service	**Port Number**
HTTP	80
HTTPS	443
FTP	20, 21
POP	110
SMTP	25
TELNET	23

NETSTAT

Try using the command prompt utility NETSTAT to see the connections your applications are making. NETSTAT shows the local and remote IP address as well the port numbers used for all applications running on your system. To make things easier to read, NETSTAT defaults to using computer and service names instead of numbers. For extra geek points, try running NETSTAT-n to see the IP addresses and port numbers.

NETSTAT is a powerful tool for determining who you're connected to at any moment. For example, if you see an FTP connection but you're not knowingly running an FTP client or server, you might have an unauthorized access or even a malware problem.

The World Wide Web

The Web provides a graphical face for the Internet. *Web servers* (servers running specialized software) provide Web sites that you access by using the HTTP protocol on port 80 and thus get more or less useful information. Using Web-browser software, such as Internet Explorer or Mozilla Firefox, you can click a link on a Web page and be instantly transported—not just to some Web server in your home town—to anywhere in the world. Figure 15.26 shows Firefox at the home page of my company's Web site, www.totalsem.com. Where is the server located? Does it matter? It could be in a closet in my office or on a huge clustered server in Canada. The great part about the Web is that you can get from here to there and access the information you need with a click or two of the mouse.

Although the Web is the most popular part of the Internet, setting up a Web browser takes almost no effort. As long as the Internet connection is working, Web browsers work automatically. This is not to say you can't make plenty of custom settings, but the default browser settings work almost every time. If you type in a Web address, such as the best search engine on the planet— www.google.com—and it doesn't work, check the line and your network settings and you'll figure out where the problem is.

● **Figure 15.26**   Mozilla Firefox showing a Web page

Configuring the Browser

Web browsers are highly configurable. On most Web browsers, you can set the default font size, choose whether to display graphics, and adjust several other settings. Although all Web browsers support these settings, where you go to make these changes varies dramatically. If you are using the popular Internet Explorer that comes with Windows, you will find configuration tools in the Internet Options Control Panel applet or under the Tools menu.

Proxy Server Many corporations use a proxy server to filter employee Internet access, and when you're on their corporate network you have to set your proxy settings within the Web browser (and any other Internet software you want to use). A proxy server is software that enables multiple connections to the Internet to go through one protected PC, much as ICS works on a home network. Unlike ICS, which operates transparently to the client PCs by manipulating IP packets, proxy servers communicate directly with the browser application. Applications that want to access Internet resources send requests to the proxy server instead of trying to access the Internet directly, both protecting the client PCs and enabling the network administrator to monitor and restrict Internet access. Each application must therefore be configured to use the proxy server. To configure proxy settings in Internet Explorer, choose Tools | Internet Options. Select the Connections tab. Then click the LAN Settings button to open the Local Area Network (LAN) Settings dialog box (Figure 15.27).

Note that you have three options here, with automatic detection of the proxy server being the default. You can specify an IP address and port for a proxy server by clicking the third checkbox and simply typing it in as shown in Figure 15.27.

In some cases, companies have different proxy servers for different programs, such as FTP. You can enter those proxy addresses by clicking the Advanced button and entering the individual addresses. You can also add addresses that should not go through the proxy servers, such as intranet sites. These sites can be added in the Exceptions box down at the bottom of the dialog (Figure 15.28). Your network administrator will give you information on proxy servers if you need it to configure a machine. Otherwise, you can safely

Tech Tip

PING

*The command-line tool PING may be your best friend for diagnosing TCP/IP errors. PING always works; you don't need to log on to a server or even log on to a system. Simply type PING followed by a DNS name or an IP address. To run PING, get to a command prompt (Start | Run | type **cmd** | click OK in Windows 2000/XP, or simply Start and type **cmd** in the dialog in Windows Vista/7) and type **ping** followed by a DNS name or IP address, like this:*

`c:\>ping www.totalsem`
`.com`

Then press the ENTER key. If the Web server is up, you'll get a reply to that effect.

*You can even ping yourself: just type **ping 127.0.0.1** (127.0.0.1 is known as the loopback address). This can give you a quick check to make sure your NIC is functional. If you ping an address and get the famous "Request timed out" message, the device you are trying to ping is not available. Be aware, however, that "Request timed out" messages are fairly common when you use PING on the Internet because many servers turn off the PING reply as a security measure.*

• **Figure 15.27** The LAN Settings dialog box

leave the browser configured to search automatically for a proxy server. If proxy servers are not used on your network, the automatic configuration will fail and your browser will try to connect to the Internet directly, so there is no harm in just leaving *Automatically detect settings* checked.

Security and Scripts   While we're on the subject of configuration, make sure you know how to adjust the security settings in your Web browser. Many Web sites come with programs that download to your system and run automatically. These programs are written in specialized languages and file formats such as Java and Active Server Pages (ASP). They make modern Web sites powerful and dynamic, but they can also act as a portal to evil programs. To help with security, all better Web browsers let you determine whether you want these potentially risky programs to run. What you decide depends on personal factors. If your Web browser refuses to run a Java program (you'll know because you'll get a warning message, as in Figure 15.29), check your security settings because your browser may simply be following orders! To get to the security configuration screen in Internet Explorer, choose Tools | Internet Options and open the Security tab (Figure 15.30).

Internet Explorer gives you the option of selecting preset security levels by clicking the Custom level button on the Security tab and then using the pull-down menu (Figure 15.31). Changing from Medium to High security, for example, makes changes across the board, disabling everything from ActiveX to Java. You can also manually select which features to enable or disable in the scrolling menu, also visible in Figure 15.31.

Security doesn't stop with programs. Another big security concern relates to Internet commerce. People don't like to enter credit card information, home phone numbers, or other personal information for fear this information might be intercepted by hackers. Fortunately, there are methods for encrypting this information, the most common being **Hypertext Transfer Protocol Secure (HTTPS)**. Although HTTPS looks a lot like HTTP from the point of view of a Web

● **Figure 15.28**   Specifying the proxy server address

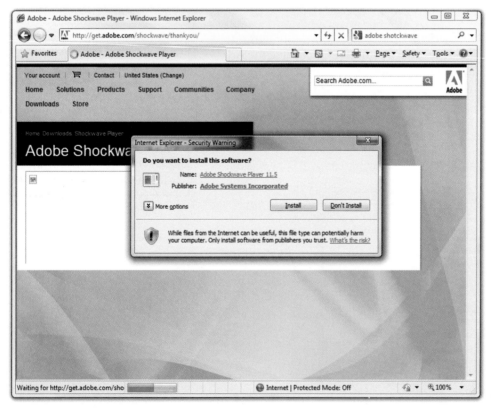

● **Figure 15.29**   Warning message about running ActiveX

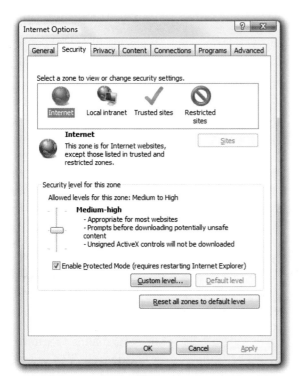

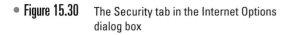

• **Figure 15.30**   The Security tab in the Internet Options dialog box

• **Figure 15.31**   Changing security settings

browser, HTTPS uses port 443. It's easy to tell if a Web site is using HTTPS because the Web address starts with *HTTPS*, as shown in Figure 15.32, instead of just *HTTP*. The Web browser also displays a lock symbol in the lower-right corner to remind you that you're using an encrypted connection.

There's one security risk that no computer can completely defend against: you. In particular, be very careful when downloading programs from the Internet. The Internet makes it easy to download programs that you can then install and run on your system. There's nothing intrinsically wrong with this unless the program you download has a virus, is corrupted, contains a Trojan horse, or is incompatible with your operating system. The watchword here is *common sense*. Only download programs from reliable sources. Take time to read the online documentation so you're sure you're downloading a version of the program that works on your operating system. Finally, always run a good antivirus program, preferably one that checks incoming programs for viruses before you install them! Failure to do this can lead to lockups, file corruption, and boot problems that you simply should not have to deal with.

E-mail

You can use an e-mail program to access e-mail. The three most popular are Microsoft's Outlook Express, Windows Mail, and Mozilla's Thunderbird. E-mail clients need a little more setup. First, you must provide your e-mail address and password. All e-mail addresses come in the now-famous

Depending on the Web site and your Web browser, you might also see a lock in the address bar or even different colors appearing on the address bar when accessing an HTTPS site. While these extras may vary from site to site and browser to browser, you can always count on seeing the lock in the bottom-right corner and the HTTPS in the address.

See Chapter 16, "Mastering Computer Security," for the scoop on Trojans and other viruses.

● **Figure 15.32** A secure Web page

accountname@Internet domain format. Figure 15.33 shows e-mail information entered into the Windows Mail account setup wizard.

Next you must add the names of the **Post Office Protocol version 3 (POP3)** or **Internet Message Access Protocol version 4 (IMAP4)** server and the **Simple Mail Transfer Protocol (SMTP)** server. The POP3 or IMAP server is the computer that handles incoming (to you) e-mail. POP3 is by far the most widely used standard, although the latest version of IMAP, *IMAP4*, supports some features POP3 doesn't. For example, IMAP4 enables you to search through messages on the mail server to find specific keywords and select the messages you want to download onto your machine. Even with the advantages of IMAP4 over POP3, the vast majority of incoming mail servers use POP3.

Tech Tip

Web-based Mail

Many people use Web-based e-mail, such as Yahoo! Mail or Gmail from Google, to handle all of their e-mail needs. Web-based mail offers the convenience of having access to your e-mail from any Internet-connected computer. The benefit to using a standalone program is that most offer a lot more control over what you can do with your e-mail, such as flagging messages for later review. Web-based mail services, especially Gmail, are catching up, though, and might surpass traditional e-mail programs in features and popularity.

Make sure you know your port numbers for these e-mail protocols! POP3 uses port 110, IMAP uses port 143, and SMTP uses port 25.

● **Figure 15.33** Adding an e-mail account to Windows Mail

The SMTP server handles your outgoing e-mail. These two systems may often have the same name, or close to the same name, as shown in Figure 15.34. Your ISP should provide you with all these settings. If not, you should be comfortable knowing what to ask for. If one of these names is incorrect, you will either not get your e-mail or not be able to send e-mail. If an e-mail setup that has been working well for a while suddenly gives you errors, it is likely that either the POP3 or SMTP server is down or that the DNS server has quit working.

When I'm given the name of a POP3 or SMTP server, I use PING to determine the IP address for the device, as shown in Figure 15.35. I make a point to write this down. If I ever have a problem getting mail, I'll go into my SMTP or POP3 settings and type in the IP address (Figure 15.36). If my mail starts to work, I know the DNS server is not working.

Newsgroups

Newsgroups are one of the oldest services available on the Internet. To access a newsgroup, you must use a newsreader program. A number of third-party newsreaders exist, such as the popular Forté Free Agent, but Microsoft Outlook Express is the most common of all newsreaders (not surprising since it comes free with most versions of Windows). To access a newsgroup, you must know the name of a news server. *News servers* run the Network News Transfer Protocol (NNTP). You can also use public news servers, but these are extremely slow. Your ISP will tell you the name of the news server and provide you with a user name and password if you need one (Figure 15.37).

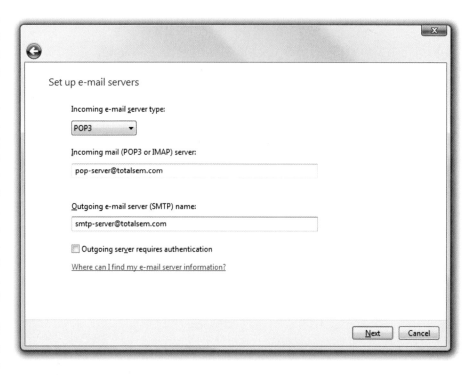

● **Figure 15.34**   Adding POP3 and SMTP information in Windows Mail

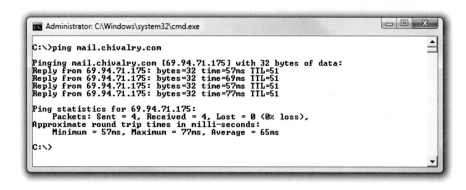

● **Figure 15.35**   Using PING to determine the IP address

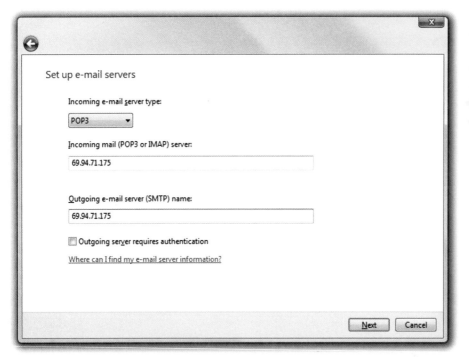

File Transfer Protocol (FTP)

File Transfer Protocol (FTP)

File transfer protocol (FTP), using ports 20 and 21, is a great way to share files between systems. FTP server software exists for most operating systems, so you can use FTP to transfer data between any two systems regardless of the operating system. To access an FTP site, you must use an FTP client such as FileZilla, although most Web browsers provide at least download support for FTP. Just type in the name of the FTP site. Figure 15.38 shows Firefox accessing ftp.kernel.org.

Although you can use a Web browser, all FTP sites require you to log on. Your Web browser will assume that you want to log on as "anonymous."

• **Figure 15.36**   Entering IP addresses into POP3 and SMTP settings

If you want to log on as a specific user, you have to add your user name to the URL. (Instead of typing **ftp://ftp.example.com**, you would type **ftp://mikem@ftp.example.com**.) An anonymous logon works fine for most public FTP sites. Many techs prefer to use third-party programs such as FileZilla (Figure 15.39) for FTP access because these third-party applications can store user name and password settings. This enables you to access the FTP site more easily later. Keep in mind that FTP was developed during a more trusting time, and that whatever user name and password you send over the network is sent in clear text. Don't use the same password for an FTP site that you use for your domain logon at the office!

Telnet and SSH

Telnet is a terminal emulation program for TCP/IP networks that uses port 23 and enables you to connect to a server or fancy router and run commands on that machine as if you were sitting in front of it. This way, you can remotely administer a server and communicate with other servers on your network. As you can imagine, this is rather risky. If *you* can remotely control a computer, what's to stop others from doing the same? Of course, Telnet does not allow just *anyone* to log on and wreak havoc with your network. You must enter a special user name and password to run Telnet. Unfortunately, Telnet shares FTP's bad

• **Figure 15.37**   Configuring Outlook Express for a news server

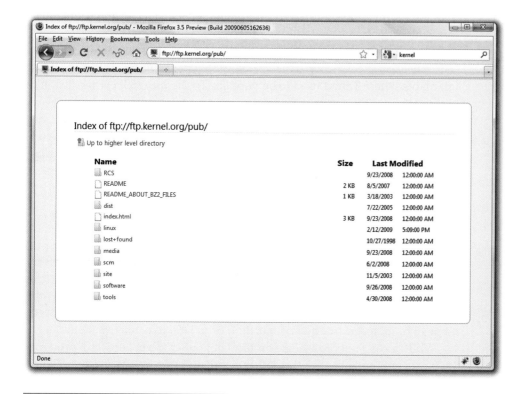

● **Figure 15.38**   Accessing an FTP site in Firefox

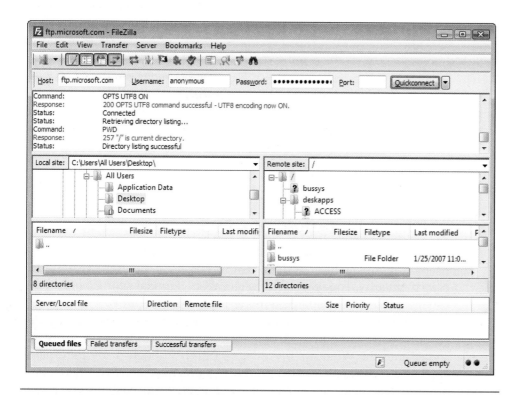

● **Figure 15.39**   The FileZilla program

habit of sending passwords and user names as clear text, so you should generally use it only within your own LAN.

If you need a remote terminal that works securely across the Internet, you need **Secure Shell (SSH)**. In fact, today SSH has replaced Telnet in almost all places where Telnet used to be popular. To the user, SSH works just like Telnet. Behind the scenes, SSH uses port 22, and the entire connection is encrypted, preventing any eavesdroppers from reading your data. SSH has one other trick up its sleeve: it can move files or any type of TCP/IP network traffic through its secure connection. In networking parlance, this is called **tunneling**, and it is the core of a technology called VPN which enables users to access local area networks remotely over the Internet.

Voice over IP

You can use **Voice over IP (VoIP)** to make voice calls over your computer network. Why have two sets of wires, one for voice and one for data, going to every desk? Why not just use the extra capacity on the data network for your phone calls? That's exactly what VoIP does for you. VoIP works with every type of high-speed Internet connection, from DSL to cable to satellite.

VoIP doesn't refer to a single protocol but rather to a collection of protocols that make phone calls over the data network possible. Venders such as Skype and Vonage offer popular VoIP solutions, and many corporations use VoIP for their internal phone networks. A key to remember when installing and troubleshooting VoIP is that low network latency is more important than high network speed. Latency is the amount of time a packet takes to get to its destination and is measured in milliseconds. The higher the latency, the more problems, such as noticeable delays during your VoIP call.

Try This!

Checking Latency with PING

Latency is the bane of any VoIP call because of all the problems it causes if it is too high. A quick way to check your current latency is to use the ever-handy PING, so Try This!

1. Run PING on some known source, such as www.microsoft.com or www.totalsem.com.

2. When the PING finishes, take note of the average round-trip time at the bottom of the screen. This is your current latency to that site.

Terminal Emulation

In Microsoft networking, we primarily share folders and printers. At times it would be convenient to be transported in front of another computer—to feel as if your hands were actually on its keyboard. This is called **terminal emulation**. Terminal emulation is old stuff; Telnet is one of the oldest TCP/IP applications, but the introduction of graphical user interfaces cost it much of its popularity. Today when techs talk about terminal emulation, they are usually referring to graphical terminal emulation programs.

Like so many other Windows applications, graphical terminal emulation originally came from third-party companies and was eventually absorbed into the Windows operating system. Although many third-party emulators are available, one of the most popular is the University of Cambridge's VNC. VNC is free and totally cross-platform, enabling you to run and control a Windows system remotely from your Macintosh system, for example. Figure 15.40 shows VNC in action.

Windows 2000 Server (not Professional) was the first version of Windows to include a built-in terminal emulator called Windows Terminal Services. Terminal Services has a number of limitations: the server software runs only on Windows Server and the client software runs only on Windows—although the client works on *every* version of Windows and is free. Figure 15.41 shows Windows Terminal Services running on a Windows 2000 computer.

Windows XP and Vista offer an alternative to VNC: Remote Desktop. **Remote Desktop** provides control over a remote server with the fully graphical interface. Your desktop *becomes* the server desktop (Figure 15.42). It's quite incredible—although it's only for Windows XP and later.

Wouldn't it be cool if, when called about a technical support issue, you could simply see what the client sees? (I'm not talking voyeur cam here.) When the client says that something doesn't work, it would be great if you could transfer yourself from your desk to your client's desk to see precisely what the client sees. This would dramatically cut down on the miscommunication that can make a tech's life so tedious. Windows Remote Assistance does just that. Based on the Shared Desktop feature that used to come with the popular MSN Messenger program, Remote Assistance enables you to give anyone control of your desktop. If a user has a problem,

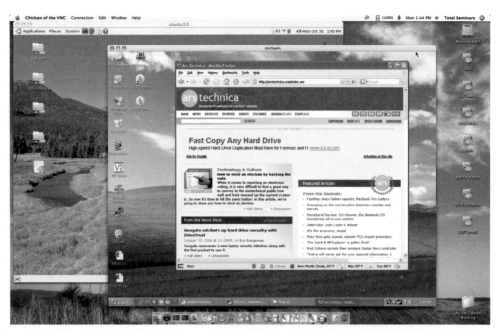

● **Figure 15.40**   VNC in action

● **Figure 15.41**   Old Terminal Services

that user can request support directly from you. Upon receiving the support request e-mail, you can then log on to the user's system and, with permission, take the driver's seat. Figure 15.43 shows Remote Assistance in action.

With Remote Assistance, you can do anything you would do from the actual computer. You can troubleshoot some hardware configuration or driver problem. You can install drivers, roll back drivers, download new ones, and so forth. You're in command of the remote machine as long as the client allows you to be. The client sees everything you do, by the way, and can stop you cold if you get out of line or do something that makes the client nervous! Remote Assistance can help you teach someone how to use a particular application. You can log on to a user's PC and fire up Outlook, for example, and then walk through the steps to configure it while the user watches. The user can then take over the machine and walk through the steps while you watch, chatting with one another the whole time. Sweet!

The new graphical terminal emulators provide everything you need to access one system from another. They are common, especially now that Microsoft provides free terminal emulators. Whatever type of emulator you use, remember that you will always need both a server and a client program. The server goes on the system you want to access and the client goes on the system you use to access the server. On many solutions, the server and client software are integrated into a single product.

• **Figure 15.42** Windows Vista Remote Desktop Connection dialog box

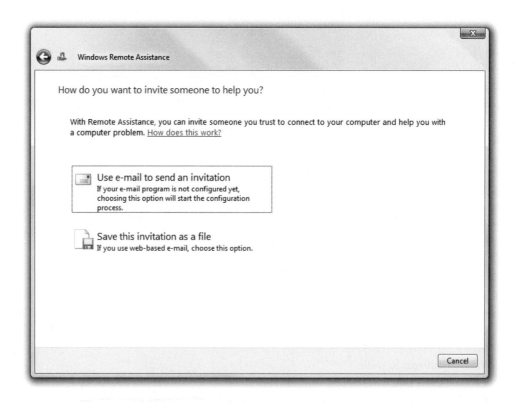

• **Figure 15.43** Remote Assistance in action

■ Chapter Summary

After reading this chapter and completing the exercises, you should understand the following about the Internet.

Connect to the Internet

■ Seven technologies are commonly used to connect a PC to an ISP. These technologies fit into four categories: (1) dial-up (analog and ISDN), (2) dedicated (DSL, cable, and LAN), (3) wireless, and (4) satellite. Analog dial-up, the slowest connection, uses a telephone line and a modem. ISDN is a much faster digital dial-up method. With the exception of satellite, which may use either a modem or a NIC, all the technologies use an Ethernet NIC.

■ A dial-up connection needs hardware, such as a modem or ISDN terminal adapter, and software, such as Microsoft's DUN.

■ A modem converts digital signals from the PC into analog signals that travel on telephone lines, and vice versa. An example of serial communication, the modem transmits data as a series of ones and zeros. On the other hand, the computer processes data by using parallel communication or data in discrete 8-bit chunks. A UART chip converts serial to parallel and parallel to serial. An external modem uses the UART chip in the computer's serial port, while an internal modem has its own built-in UART.

■ Phone lines measure speed in bauds, or cycles per second. However, the fastest baud rate a phone line can achieve is 2400 baud. Today's modems pack multiple bits of data into each baud. Although not technically correct, people use the term *baud* instead of *bps* so often that the terms have become synonymous.

■ The International Telecommunication Union (ITU) sets V standards to define the fastest data transfer speed a modem can handle. Currently V.90 and V.92 are the highest standards, downloading data at just a little under 56 Kbps. Upload speeds differ, with 33.6 Kbps being the fastest for V.90 and 48 Kbps proving the fastest for V.92 modems.

■ Modems may be internal or external. The less-expensive internal modems usually connect to a PCI or PCI Express expansion bus slot. Some motherboards include special expansion slots used

for multiple communications features such as modems, NICs, and sound cards. AMD calls such slots ACRs, while Intel has named them CNR slots. Many motherboards come with integrated modems. External modems attach to the PC's serial port or USB port. Most motherboards today include two or more USB ports. It is a good idea to choose a USB modem because you won't need an external electrical source and it will likely include a volume control knob.

■ Windows includes configuration options to set up dial-up networks. Windows XP uses the Network and Internet Connections applet, Windows 2000 calls this feature Network and Dial-up Connections, and Vista uses the *Set up a connection or network* wizard. To configure dial-up networking, you'll need information from your ISP. Dial-up links to the Internet use PPP streaming hardware protocol.

■ If you can't connect to the Internet, look at the modem's properties to make sure the volume is turned up. Listen, too, for a befuddled voice on the other end that would indicate your modem is dialing the wrong number. Other things to check: be sure the line is plugged into a good phone jack, and make sure the number and password are correct. If you still can't connect to the Internet, call the network technicians to check that the dial-up networking settings are correct.

■ An ISDN consists of two types of channels: Bearer, or B, channels that carry data and voice at 64 Kbps and Delta, or D, channels that transmit setup and configuration information at 16 Kbps. Users can use one or two B channels, but the most common setup is the BRI, consisting of two B channels and one D to provide a throughput total of 128 Kbps. Except for the steep cost of installation and equipment, ISDN lines are only slightly more expensive than regular phone lines, but this service is limited to an area within about 18,000 feet of a central office. ISDN uses a terminal adapter that looks like a regular modem and may be either external or internal.

■ DSL modems connect to an ISP by using a standard telephone line and special connections on each end. Although service levels vary, typical upload speed is ~768 Kbps with a download speed of ~2+ Mbps. A tech usually comes to the house to install a DSL receiver (often called a DSL modem) as well as a NIC in the PC. DSL is usually limited to about 18,000 feet from a main phone service switching center.

- Cable TV companies offer high-speed Internet access, with an upload speed of about 1+ Mbps and download transmission rates of 5+ Mbps. With a TV tuner card, cable enables you to watch TV on your PC.

- Wireless Internet service requires connecting to a LAN that's wired to an ISP. The other wireless option is a satellite connection. Although early satellite technology required uploads through a slow modem (26–48 Kbps) and fast downloads through the dish, newer technology uses the modem only for the initial setup, sending both downloads and uploads through the dish.

- ICS enables multiple systems to use one Internet connection. Included in all current Windows versions, ICS uses an ICS host computer connected to the Internet that then shares the connection via a LAN with client computers. The ICS host computer must have a NIC or modem to connect to the Internet and a NIC that plugs into a hub. The other PCs then connect to the hub.

- Small home routers allow multiple users to easily share a broadband connection without leaving a Windows computer running all the time. They provide NAT that allows you to share a single IP address while acting as an effective firewall. Configuration of small home routers is done through special Web pages built into the routers.

Use Internet software tools

- Applications provide TCP/IP services, including Web, e-mail, newsgroups, FTP, Telnet, and VoIP. Using Web browser software such as Internet Explorer or Mozilla Firefox, you can access Web sites and pages from Web servers throughout the world. If you are unsuccessful in connecting to a site, use the command-line tool PING to determine whether the server is up. Simply type **ping** followed by either the DNS name or the IP address. If the device you are trying to ping is not available, you'll see a "Request timed out" message. You can use the loopback address (127.0.0.1) to ping yourself.

- A proxy server is software that enables multiple connections to the Internet to go through one protected PC. Configure proxy settings through the Local Area Network Settings dialog box. Although

automatic detection of the proxy server is the default setting, you can also specify an IP address for a proxy server.

- You should also know how to adjust security settings in your Web browser. In IE, choose Tools | Internet Options and open the Security tab. You can set different security levels or manually select the features you want to enable or disable.

- Security also includes encrypting information such as credit card numbers, home phone numbers, or other personal information. The most common method of encrypting this information is HTTPS. You'll identify Web sites using HTTPS by the *HTTPS:* that appears at the beginning of the Web address and the little lock icon located on the right side of the address bar or in the lower-right corner of the Web browser.

- You need an e-mail program such as Mozilla Thunderbird to receive e-mail. To set up an e-mail client, provide your e-mail address and password. E-mail addresses use the *accountname@Internet domain* format. You must also add the names of the POP3 or IMAP server for incoming mail and the SMTP server for outgoing mail.

- You'll need a newsreader such as Outlook Express to access a newsgroup. News servers run Network News Transfer Protocol (NNTP). Check with your ISP to get the name of the news server, along with a user name and password if you need them.

- FTP enables you to send and receive files. You may use an FTP client such as FileZilla, although later versions of IE and other Web browsers provide support for FTP. You'll have to log on to an FTP site, but most public FTP sites allow anonymous logon.

- Telnet is a terminal emulation program for TCP/IP networks. It lets you connect to a server and run commands as if you were sitting in front of the server. Telnet requires a special user name and password. The user name and password will be sent over the network in clear text.

- Voice over IP (VoIP) enables you to make voice calls over your computer network and refers to a collection of protocols. Venders such as Skype and Vonage offer VoIP solutions.

- Today, terminal emulation usually means graphical terminal emulation programs from third-party companies or in the Windows operating system. Terminal emulation programs require separate server and client programs. Windows 2000 Server was the first Windows version to include a built-in terminal emulator called Windows Terminal Services. The modern client is called Remote Desktop and is built into every version of Windows since XP.

- Remote Assistance, available with Windows XP and later, enables you to give anyone control of your

desktop. Useful for giving a tech control of a computer to troubleshoot a hardware configuration or driver problem, you can also use Remote Assistance to install drivers or teach someone how to use a particular application.

Key Terms

baud *(438)*
bits per second (bps) *(438)*
Dial-Up Networking (DUN) *(437)*
digital subscriber line (DSL) *(442)*
file transfer protocol (FTP) *(456)* 3
handshaking *(439)*
Hypertext Transfer Protocol Secure (HTTPS) *(452)* 1
integrated services digital network (ISDN) *(442)*
Internet Connection Sharing (ICS) *(445)*
Internet Message Access Protocol version 4 (IMAP4), port 143 *(454)*
latency *(458)*
modem *(437)*
Network Address Translation (NAT) *(446)*
Network News Transfer Protocol (NNTP) *(455)*

Point-to-Point Protocol (PPP) *(441)*
Post Office Protocol version 3 (POP3), port 110 *(454)*
proxy server *(451)* 2
Remote Assistance *(459)*
Remote Desktop *(459)* 5
Secure Shell (SSH), port 22 *(458)*
Simple Mail Transfer Protocol (SMTP), port 25 *(454)*
Telnet *(456)*
terminal emulation *(458)*
tunneling *(458)*
universal asynchronous receiver/transmitter (UART) *(438)*
V standards *(438)* 4
Voice over IP (VoIP) *(458)* 6

Key Term Quiz

Use the Key Terms list to complete the sentences that follow. Not all terms will be used.

1. The most common method used to encrypt information, such as credit card numbers, on the Internet is _____.

2. A(n) _____ is software that enables multiple connections to go to the Internet through one protected PC.

3. By using an anonymous logon, _____ allows you to send and receive files from a public site.

4. Set by the International Telecommunication Union (ITU), _____ define the fastest data transfer speed a modem can handle.

5. _____ enables tech support to control a user's computer from a distance, saving both time and effort.

6. The protocol that enables you to use your Internet connection like a phone is called _____.

Multiple-Choice Quiz

1. If your modem cannot connect to the Internet, which of the following can you eliminate as a cause of the problem?

   A. The phone line is dead.

   B. All lines on the Internet are busy.

   C. You dialed the wrong number.

   D. The modem is bad.

2. Which term describes hardware or software that protects your computer or network from probing or malicious users?

   A. Router

   B. Firewall

   C. Protocol

   D. Spyware

3. Liz can receive her e-mail, but she cannot send e-mail. Which of the following is most likely causing her problem?

   A. POP3

   B. SMTP

   C. IMAP

   D. UART

4. Which technology enables you to make voice calls over your computer network?

   A. Internet Voice Protocol

   B. Voice over IP

   C. Digital Telephony Subscriber Service

   D. Universal Asynchronous Receiver Transmitter

5. A user on Windows XP has asked you to teach her how to use a feature of Microsoft Word. What tool should you use?

   A. Remote Assistance

   B. Remote Desktop

   C. Telnet

   D. Secure Shell (SSH)

6. John walked up to a computer that couldn't connect to the Internet and immediately opened a command-line window and typed **ping 127.0.0.1**. Why?

   A. He wanted to test the connection to the default gateway.

   B. He wanted to test the connection to the nearest Tier 2 router.

   C. He wanted to test the NIC on the local machine.

   D. He wanted to test the NIC on the default gateway.

7. Where would you go first if you needed to configure a small Linksys router to use a static IP address?

   A. The router configuration applet in the Control Panel.

   B. The router's configuration Web page.

   C. Plug in a Yost cable and start PuTTY.

   D. There is no way to give the router a static IP.

8. What matters more when setting up a VoIP connection: latency or bandwidth?

   A. Latency.

   B. Bandwidth.

   C. They are equally important.

   D. They are the same thing.

9. What protocol enables sensitive data, such as addresses and credit card numbers, to be transmitted securely over the Internet?

   A. TCP

   B. PPP

   C. ISDN

   D. HTTPS

10. What technology enables one system to share its Internet connection with other systems on a network?

   A. Internet connection sharing (ICS)

   B. Network sharing (NS)

   C. Internet sharing (IS)

   D. Network connection sharing (NCS)

■ Essay Quiz

1. With the rash of worms and viruses that attack computers connected to the Internet, how can you protect your computer?

2. Andrew's wife, Talena, collects pottery. Andrew found a shop on the Internet that has a piece she's been wanting. He'd love to get it for her birthday next week, but the only way it can arrive by then is if he pays for it with his credit card. He's a bit apprehensive about giving his credit card number over the Internet. He wants you to tell him whether you think the site is safe or not. How can you evaluate the site to determine whether it uses encryption for credit card numbers?

3. With a child in high school and another at a local college, it's always a struggle in Tom's house about who gets to use the computer to do Internet research. It's not feasible for Tom to have two DSL con second compute solve his proble

Lab Projects

• Lab Project 15.1

Remote Desktop is a great feature of Windows. However, making it work when the computer you want to connect to is behind a router or firewall can be difficult. You need to consider and configure many things, such as the computer's public IP address and port forwarding or network address translation on the router. Using the Internet, find a tutorial or a step-by-step "how-to" article that guides you through configuring a remote computer and router to make a Remote Desktop connection possible.

• Lab Project 15.2

Remote Desktop provides the same functionality as some third-party software and services, such as the open source VNC software, Symantec's commercial pcAnywhere software, and the online service GoToMyPC.com. Each has its own benefits, such as no cost, ease of configuration, and cross-platform use. Research two other solutions that offer remote control functionality similar to Remote Desktop and compare and contrast the three. What are the similarities? What are the unique benefits of each? Which one would you be more likely to use yourself? Why?

• Lab Project 15.3

Have you heard of WebDAV? Web Distributed Authoring and Versioning is a set of extensions added to Hypertext Transfer Protocol to support collaborative authoring on the Web. While HTTP is a reading protocol, WebDAV is a writing protocol created by a working group of the Internet Engineering Task Force (IETF). WebDAV offers a faster, more secure method of file transfer than FTP, and some predict that it may make FTP obsolete. It's already incorporated into most current operating systems and applications. Some authors say that WebDAV will change the way we use the Web. Use the Internet to learn more about WebDAV and its features. Apple calls it "a whole new reason to love the Net." After learning about WebDAV, see if you agree.

Mastering Computer Security

Distrust and caution are the parents of security."
—BENJAMIN FRANKLIN

In this chapter, you will learn how to

- ■ **Explain the threats to your computers and data**
- ■ **Describe key security concepts and technologies**
- ■ **Explain how to protect computers from network threats**

Your PC is under siege. Through your PC, a malicious person can gain valuable information about you and your habits. He can steal your files. He can run programs that log your keystrokes and thus gain account names and passwords, credit card information, and more. He can run software that takes over much of your computer processing time and use it to send spam or steal from others. The threat is real and right now. Worse, he's doing one or more of these things to your clients as I write these words. You need to secure your computer and your users from these attacks.

But what does computer security mean? Is it an antivirus program? Is it big, complex passwords? Sure, it's both of these things, but what about the fact that your laptop can be stolen easily?

To secure computers, you need both a sound strategy and proper tactics. From a strategic sense, you need to understand the threat from unauthorized access to local machines as well as the big threats posed when computers go onto networks. Part of the big picture means to know what policies, software, and hardware to put in place to stop those threats. From a tactical in-the-trenches sense, you need to master the details, to know how to implement and maintain the proper tools. Not only do you need to install antivirus programs in your users' computers, for example, but you also need to update those programs regularly to keep up with the constant barrage of new viruses.

■ Analyzing Threats

Threats to your data and PC come from two directions: accidents and malicious people. All sorts of things can go wrong with your computer, from users getting access to folders they shouldn't see to a virus striking and deleting folders. Files can be deleted, renamed, or simply lost. Hard drives can die, and optical discs get scratched and rendered unreadable. Accidents happen and even well-meaning people can make mistakes.

Unfortunately, a lot of people out there intend to do you harm. Add that intent together with a talent for computers, and you have a deadly combination. Let's look at the following issues:

- Unauthorized access
- Social engineering
- Data destruction, accidental or deliberate
- Administrative access
- Catastrophic hardware failures
- Physical theft
- Viruses/spyware

Unauthorized Access

Unauthorized access occurs when a person accesses resources without permission. Resources in this case mean data, applications, and hardware. A user can alter or delete data; access sensitive information, such as financial data, personnel files, or e-mail messages; or use a computer for purposes the owner did not intend.

Not all unauthorized access is malicious—often this problem arises when users who are randomly poking around in a computer discover that they can access resources in a fashion the primary user did not intend. Unauthorized access becomes malicious when outsiders knowingly and intentionally take advantage of weaknesses in your security to gain information, use resources, or destroy data!

One of the ways to gain unauthorized access is through intrusion. You might imagine someone kicking in a door and hacking into a computer, but more often than not it's someone sitting at a home computer, trying various passwords over the Internet. Not quite as glamorous, but still. . .

Dumpster diving is the generic term for anytime a hacker goes through your refuse, looking for information. This is also a form of intrusion. The amount of sensitive information that makes it into any organization's trash bin boggles the mind! Years ago, I worked with an IT security guru who gave me and a few other IT people a tour of our office's trash. In one 20-minute tour of the personal wastebaskets of one office area, we had enough information to access the network easily, as well as to embarrass seriously more than a few people. When it comes to getting information, the trash is the place to look!

Social Engineering

Although you're more likely to lose data through accident, the acts of malicious users get the vast majority of headlines. Most of these attacks come under the heading of social engineering—the process of using or manipulating people inside the networking environment to gain access to that network from the outside—which covers the many ways humans can use other humans to gain unauthorized information. This unauthorized information may be a network logon, a credit card number, company customer data—almost anything you might imagine that one person or organization may not want a person outside of that organization to access.

Social engineering attacks aren't hacking—at least in the classic sense of the word—although the goals are the same. Social engineering means people attacking an organization through the people in the organization or physically accessing the organization to get the information they need. Following are a few of the more classic types of social engineering attacks.

It's common for social engineering attacks to be used together, so if you discover one of them being used against your organization, it's a good idea to look for others.

Infiltration

Hackers can physically enter your building under the guise of someone who might have a legitimate reason for being there, such as cleaning personnel, repair technicians, or messengers. They then snoop around desks, looking for whatever they can find. They might talk with people inside the organization, gathering names, office numbers, and department names—little things in and of themselves but powerful tools when combined later with other social engineering attacks.

Dressing the part of a legitimate user—with fake badge and everything—enables malicious people to gain access to locations and thus potentially your data. Following someone through the door, for example, as if you belong, is called tailgating. Tailgating is a common form of infiltration.

Telephone Scams

Telephone scams are probably the most common social engineering attacks. In this case, the attacker makes a phone call to someone in the organization to gain information. The attacker attempts to come across as someone inside the organization and uses this to get the desired information. Probably the most famous of these scams is the "I forgot my user name and password" scam. In this gambit, the attacker first learns the account name of a legitimate person in the organization, usually using the infiltration method. The attacker then calls someone in the organization, usually the help desk, in an attempt to gather information, in this case a password.

Hacker: "Hi, this is John Anderson in accounting. I forgot my password. Can you reset it, please?"

Help Desk: "Sure, what's your user name?"

Hacker: "j_w_Anderson"

Help Desk: "OK, I reset it to e34rd3."

Certainly telephone scams aren't limited to attempts to get network access. There are documented telephone scams against organizations aimed at getting cash, blackmail material, or other valuables.

Phishing

Phishing is the act of trying to get people to give their user names, passwords, or other security information by pretending to be someone else electronically. A classic example is when a bad guy sends you an e-mail that's supposed to be from your local credit card company asking you to send them your user name and password. Phishing is by far the most common form of social engineering done today.

Data Destruction

Often an extension of unauthorized access, data destruction means more than just intentionally or accidentally erasing or corrupting data. It's easy to imagine some evil hacker accessing your network and deleting all your important files, but authorized users may also access certain data and then use that data beyond what they are authorized to do. A good example is the person who legitimately accesses a Microsoft Access product database to modify the product descriptions, only to discover that she can change the prices of the products too.

This type of threat is particularly dangerous when users are not clearly informed about the extent to which they are authorized to make changes. A fellow tech once told me about a user who managed to mangle an important database when someone gave them incorrect access. When confronted, the user said: "If I wasn't allowed to change it, the system wouldn't let me do it!" Many users believe that systems are configured in a paternalistic way that wouldn't allow them to do anything inappropriate. As a result, users often assume they're authorized to make any changes they believe are necessary when working on a piece of data they know they're authorized to access.

Administrative Access

Every operating system enables you to create user accounts and grant those accounts a certain level of access to files and folders in that computer. As an administrator, supervisor, or root user, you have full control over just about every aspect of the computer. Windows XP, in particular, makes it entirely too easy to give users administrative access to the computer, especially Windows XP Home, which allows only two kinds of users: administrators and limited users. Because you can't do much as a limited user, most home and small office systems simply use multiple administrator accounts. If you need to control access, you really need to use non-Home versions of Windows.

System Crash/Hardware Failure

As with any technology, computers can and will fail—usually when you can least afford for it to happen. Hard drives crash, the power fails—it's all part of the joy of working in the computing business. You need to create redundancy in areas prone to failure (such as installing backup power in case of electrical failure) and perform those all-important data backups. Chapter 7, "Securing Windows Resources," goes into detail about using backups and other issues involved in creating a stable and reliable system.

Physical Theft

A fellow network geek once challenged me to try to bring down his newly installed network. He had just installed a powerful and expensive firewall router and was convinced that I couldn't get to a test server he added to his network just for me to try to access. After a few attempts to hack in over the Internet, I saw that I wasn't going to get anywhere that way. So I jumped in my car and drove to his office, having first outfitted myself in a techy-looking jumpsuit and an ancient ID badge I just happened to have in my sock drawer. I smiled sweetly at the receptionist and walked right by my friend's office (I noticed he was smugly monitoring incoming IP traffic by using some neato packet-sniffing program) to his new server. I quickly pulled the wires out of the back of his precious server, picked it up, and walked out the door. The receptionist was too busy trying to figure out why her e-mail wasn't working to notice me as I whisked by her carrying the 65-pound server box. I stopped in the hall and called him from my cell phone.

> **Me (cheerily):** "Dude, I got all your data!"
>
> **Him (not cheerily):** "You rebooted my server! How did you do it?"
>
> **Me (smiling):** "I didn't reboot it—go over and look at it!"
>
> **Him (really mad now):** "YOU <EXPLETIVE> THIEF! YOU STOLE MY SERVER!"
>
> **Me (cordially):** "Why, yes. Yes, I did. Give me two days to hack your password in the comfort of my home, and I'll see everything! Bye!"

I immediately walked back in and handed him the test server. It was fun. The moral here is simple: never forget that the best network software security measures can be rendered useless if you fail to protect your systems physically!

Virus/Spyware

Networks are without a doubt the fastest and most efficient vehicles for transferring computer viruses among systems. News reports focus attention on the many virus attacks from the Internet, but a huge number of viruses still come from users who bring in programs on floppy disks, writable optical discs, and USB drives. The "Network Security" section of this chapter describes what you need to do to prevent virus infection of your networked systems.

■ Security Concepts and Technologies

Once you've assessed the threats to your computers and networks, you need to take steps to protect those valuable resources. Depending on the complexity of your organization, this can be a small job encompassing some basic security concepts and procedures, or it can be exceedingly complex. The security needs for a three-person desktop publishing firm, for example, would differ wildly from those of a defense contractor supplying top-secret toys to the Pentagon.

From a CompTIA A+ certified technician's perspective, you need to understand the big picture (that's the strategic side), knowing the concepts and available technologies for security. At the implementation level (that's the tactical side), you're expected to know where to find such things as security policies in Windows. A CompTIA Network+ or CompTIA Security+ tech will give you the specific options to implement. (The exception to this level of knowledge comes in dealing with malicious software such as viruses, but we'll tackle that subject in the last part of the chapter.) So let's look at three concept and technology areas: access control, data classification and compliance, and reporting.

Cross Check

Securing Windows Resources

Part of establishing local control over resources involves setting up the computer properly in the first place, a topic covered in depth in Chapter 7, "Securing Windows Resources." Check your memory of proper setup techniques from that chapter and see if you can answer these questions: How do you establish control over a computer's resources? What file system must you use?

Access Control

Access is the key. If you can control access to the data, programs, and other computing resources, you've secured your systems. Access control is composed of four interlinked areas that a good security-minded tech should think about: physical security, authentication, users and groups, and security policies. Much of this you know from previous chapters, but this section should help tie it all together as a security topic.

Secure Physical Area and Lock Down Your System

The first order of security is to block access to the physical hardware from people who shouldn't have access. This isn't rocket science. Lock the door. Don't leave a PC unattended when logged in. In fact, don't ever leave a system logged in, even as a limited user. God help you if you walk away from a server still logged in as an administrator. You're tempting fate.

For that matter, when you see a user's computer logged in and unattended, do the user and your company a huge favor and lock the computer. Just walk up and press the WINDOWS LOGO KEY-L on the keyboard to lock the system. It works in all versions of Windows.

Authentication

Security starts with properly implemented authentication, which means in essence how the computer determines who can or should access it, and once accessed, what that user can do. A computer can authenticate users through software or hardware, or a combination of both.

Software Authentication: Proper Passwords It's still rather shocking to me to power up a friend's computer and go straight to his or her desktop, or with my married-with-kids friends, to click one of the parents' user account icons and not be prompted for a password. This is just wrong! I'm always tempted to assign passwords right then and there—and not tell them the passwords, of course—so they'll see the error of their ways when they try to log on next. I don't do it, but always try to explain gently the importance of good passwords.

Cross Check

Proper Passwords

So, what goes into making a good password? Turning once again to Chapter 7, "Securing Windows Resources," see if you can answer these questions: What sorts of characters should make up a password? Should you ask for a user's password when working on that user's PC? Why or why not? If you're in a secure environment and know you'll have to reboot several times, is it okay to ask for a password then? What should you do?

You know about passwords from Chapter 7, "Securing Windows Resources," so I won't belabor the point here. Suffice it to say that you need to make certain that all of your users have proper passwords. Don't let them write passwords down or tape them to the underside of their mouse pads either!

It's not just access to Windows that you need to think about. There's always the temptation for people to hack the system and do mean things, such as changing CMOS settings, opening up the case, and even stealing hard drives. Any of these actions render the computer inoperable to the casual user until a tech can undo the damage or replace components. All modern CMOS setup utilities come with a number of tools to protect your computer, such as drive lock, intrusion detection, and of course system access passwords such as the one shown in Figure 16.1. Refer to Chapter 3, "Mastering Motherboards," to refresh yourself on what you can do at a BIOS level to protect your computer.

• **Figure 16.1** CMOS access password request

Hardware Authentication Smart cards and biometric devices enable modern systems to authenticate users with more authority than mere passwords. Smart cards are credit-card-sized cards with circuitry that can identify the bearer of the card. Smart cards are relatively common for such tasks as authenticating users for mass transit systems, for example, but are fairly uncommon in computers. Figure 16.2 shows a smart card and keyboard combination.

People can guess or discover passwords, but forging someone's fingerprints is a lot harder. The keyboard in Figure 16.3 authenticates users on a local machine by using fingerprints. Other devices that will do the trick are key fobs, retinal scanners, and PC cards for laptop computers. Devices that require some sort of physical, flesh-and-blood authentication are called **biometric devices**.

Clever manufacturers have developed key fobs and smart cards that use radio frequency identification (RFID) to transmit authentication information so users don't have to insert something into a computer or card reader. The Privaris plusID combines, for example, a biometric fingerprint fob with an RFID tag that makes security as easy as opening a garage door remotely! Figure 16.4 shows a plusID device.

• **Figure 16.2** Keyboard-mounted smart card reader being used for a commercial application (*photo courtesy of Cherry Corp.*)

● **Figure 16.3**   Microsoft keyboard with fingerprint accessibility

NTFS, not FAT32!

The file system on a hard drive matters a lot when it comes to security. On a Windows machine with multiple users, you simply must use NTFS or you have no security at all. Not just primary drives but also any secondary drives in computers in your care should be formatted as NTFS, with the exception of removable drives such as the one you use to back up your system.

When you run into a multiple-drive system that has a second or third drive formatted as FAT32, you can use the CONVERT command-line utility to go from FAT to NTFS. The syntax is pretty straightforward. To convert a D: drive from FAT or FAT32 to NTFS, for example, you'd type the following:

```
CONVERT D: /FS:NTFS
```

You can substitute a mount name in place of the drive letter in case you have a mounted volume. The command has a few extra switches as well, so at the command prompt, type a **/?** after the CONVERT command to see all of your options.

Users and Groups

Windows uses user accounts and groups as the bedrock of access control. A user account is assigned to a group, such as Users, Power Users, or Administrators, and by association gets certain permissions on the computer. Using NTFS enables the highest level of control over data resources.

Assigning users to groups is a great first step in controlling a local machine, but this feature really shines once you go to a networked environment. Let's go there now.

User Account Control Through Groups

Access to user accounts should be restricted to the assigned individuals, and those who configure the permissions to those accounts must remember the Principle of Least Privilege discussed in Chapter 7, "Securing Windows Resources": *Accounts should have permission to access only the resources they need*

● **Figure 16.4**   plusID (*photo courtesy of Privaris, Inc.*)

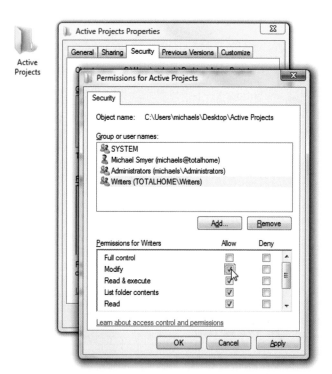

● **Figure 16.5**   Giving a group permissions for a folder in Windows Vista

and no more. Tight control of user accounts is critical to preventing unauthorized access. Disabling unused accounts is an important part of this strategy, but good user account control goes far deeper than that. One of your best tools for user account control is groups. Instead of giving permissions/rights to individual user accounts, give them to groups; this makes keeping track of the permissions assigned to individual user accounts much easier. Figure 16.5 shows me giving permissions to a group for a folder in Windows Vista. Once a group is created and its permissions set, you can then add user accounts to that group as needed. Any user account that becomes a member of a group automatically gets the permissions assigned to that group. Figure 16.6 shows me adding a user to a newly created group in the same Windows Vista system.

Groups are a great way to achieve increased complexity without increasing the administrative burden on network administrators, because all network operating systems combine permissions. When a user is a member of more than one group, which permissions does that user have with respect to any particular resource? In all network operating systems, the permissions of the groups are *combined*, and the result is what you call the **effective permissions** the user has to access the resource. As an example, if Rita is a member of the Sales group, which has List Folder Contents permission to a folder, and she is also a member of the Managers group, which has Read and Execute permissions to the same folder, Rita will have both List Folder Contents *and* Read and Execute permissions to that folder.

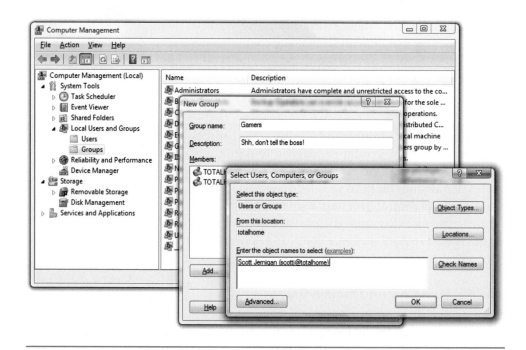

● **Figure 16.6**   Adding a user to a newly created group in Windows Vista

Watch out for *default* user accounts and groups—they can become secret backdoors to your network! All network operating systems have a default Everyone group that can be used to sneak into shared resources easily. This Everyone group, as its name implies, literally includes anyone who connects to that resource. Windows gives full control to the Everyone group by default, for example, so make sure you know to lock this down!

All of the default groups—Everyone, Guest, Users—define broad groups of users. Never use them unless you intend to permit all of those folks to access a resource. If you use one of the default groups, remember to configure them with the proper permissions to prevent users from doing things you don't want them to do with a shared resource!

All of these groups and organizational units only do one thing for you: they let you keep track of your user accounts, so you know they are only available for those who need them and they can only access the resources you want them to use.

Security Policies

Although permissions control how users access shared resources, there are other functions you should control that are outside the scope of resources. For example, do you want users to be able to access a command prompt on their Windows system? Do you want users to be able to install software? Would you like to control what systems a user can log onto or at what time of day a user can log on? All network operating systems provide you with some capability to control these and literally hundreds of other security parameters, under what Windows calls *policies*. I like to think of policies as permissions for activities as opposed to true permissions, which control access to resources.

A policy is usually applied to a user account, a computer, or a group. Let's use the example of a network composed of Windows XP Professional systems with a Windows 2003 Server system. Every Windows XP system has its own local policies program, which enables policies to be placed on that system only. Figure 16.7 shows the tool you use to set local policies on an individual system, called Local Security Settings, being used to deny the user account Danar the capability to log on locally.

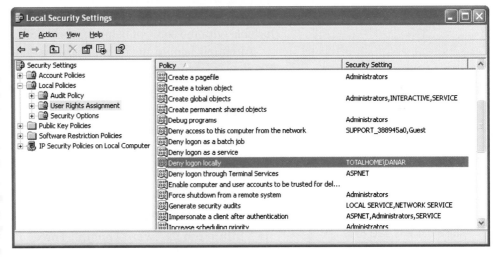

• **Figure 16.7**   Local Security Settings

Local policies work great for individual systems, but they can be a pain to configure if you want to apply the same settings to more than one PC on your network. If you want to apply policy settings *en masse*, you need to step up to Windows Active Directory domain-based Group Policy. By using Group Policy, you can exercise deity-like—Microsoft prefers to use the term *granular*—control over your network clients.

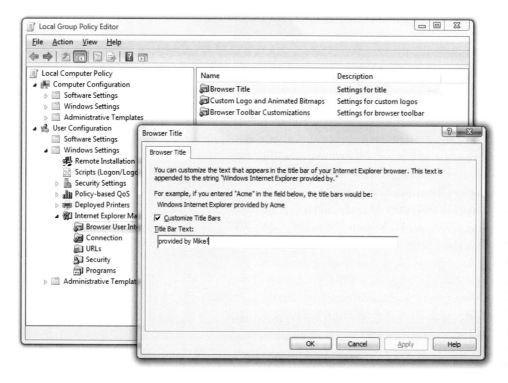

● **Figure 16.8** Using Group Policy to make IE title say "provided by Mike!"

Want to set default wallpaper for every PC in your domain? Group Policy can do that. Want to make certain tools inaccessible to everyone except authorized users? Group Policy can do that, too. Want to control access to the Internet, redirect home folders, run scripts, deploy software, or just remind folks that unauthorized access to the network will get them nowhere fast? Group Policy is the answer. Figure 16.8 shows Group Policy; I'm about to change the default title on every instance of Internet Explorer on every computer in my domain!

That's just one simple example of the settings you can configure by using Group Policy. You can apply literally hundreds of tweaks through Group Policy, from the great to the small, but don't worry too much about familiarizing yourself with each and every one. Group Policy settings are a big topic on most of the Microsoft certification tracks, but for the purposes of the CompTIA A+ Practical Application exam, you simply have to be comfortable with the concept behind Group Policy.

Although I could never list every possible policy you can enable on a Windows system, here's a list of some commonly used ones:

- **Prevent Registry Edits**   If you try to edit the Registry, you get a failure message.

- **Prevent Access to the Command Prompt**   Keeps users from getting to the command prompt by turning off the Run command and the MS-DOS Prompt shortcut.

- **Log on Locally**   Defines who may log on to the system locally.

- **Shut Down System**   Defines who may shut down the system.

- **Minimum Password Length**   Forces a minimum password length.

- **Account Lockout Threshold**   Sets the maximum number of logon attempts a person can make before being locked out of the account.

- **Disable Windows Installer**   Prevents users from installing software.

- **Printer Browsing**   Enables users to browse for printers on the network, as opposed to using only assigned printers.

Although the CompTIA A+ Practical Application exam doesn't expect you to know how to implement policies on any type of network, you are expected to understand that policies exist, especially on Windows networks, and that they can do amazing things to control what users can do on their systems. If you ever try to get to a command prompt on a Windows system only to discover the Run command is dimmed, blame it on a policy, not the computer!

Data Classification and Compliance

Larger organizations, such as government entities, benefit greatly from organizing their data according to its sensitivity—what's called data classification—and making certain that computer hardware and software stay as uniform as possible. In addition, many government and internal regulations apply fairly rigorously to the organizations.

Data classification systems vary by the organization, but a common scheme classifies documents as public, internal use only, highly confidential, top secret, and so on. Using a classification scheme enables employees such as techs to know very quickly what to do with documents, the drives containing documents, and more. Your strategy for recycling a computer system left from a migrated user, for example, will differ a lot if the data on the drive was classified as internal use only or top secret.

Compliance means, in a nutshell, that members of an organization or company must abide by or comply with all of the rules that apply to the organization or company. Statutes with funny names such as Sarbanes-Oxley impose certain behaviors or prohibitions on what people can and cannot do in the workplace.

From a technician's point of view, the most common compliance issue revolves around software, such as what sort of software users can be allowed to install on their computers or, conversely, why you have to tell a user that he can't install the latest application that may help him do the job more effectively because that software isn't on the approved list. This can lead to some uncomfortable confrontations, but it's part of a tech's job.

The concepts behind compliance in IT are not, as some might imagine at first blush, to stop people from being able to work effectively. Rather they're designed to stop users with not quite enough technical skill or knowledge from installing malicious programs or applications that will destabilize their systems. This keeps technical support calls down and enables techs to focus on more serious problems.

Reporting

As a final weapon in your security arsenal, you need to report any security issues so a network administrator or technician can take steps to make them go away. You can set up two tools within Windows so that the OS reports problems to you: Event Viewer and Auditing. You can then do your work and report those problems. Let's take a look.

Event Viewer

Event Viewer is Window's default tattletale program, spilling the beans about many things that happen on the system. You can find Event Viewer in Administrative Tools in the Control Panel. By default, Event Viewer has three sections: Application, Security, and System. If you've downloaded Internet Explorer 7, you'll see a fourth option for the browser, Internet

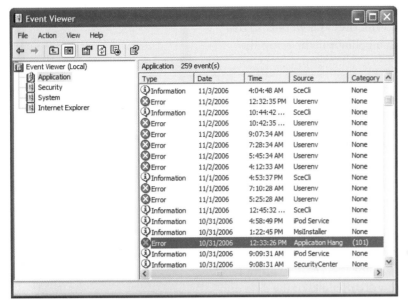

● **Figure 16.9**   Event Viewer

Explorer (Figure 16.9). As you'll recall from Chapter 8, "Maintaining and Troubleshooting Windows," the most common use for Event Viewer is to view application or system errors for troubleshooting (Figure 16.10).

One very cool feature of Event Viewer is that you can click the link to take you to the online Help and Support Center at Microsoft.com, and the software reports your error (Figure 16.11), checks the online database, and comes back with a more or less useful explanation (Figure 16.12).

Auditing

The Security section of Event Viewer doesn't show you anything by default. To unlock the full potential of Event Viewer, you need to set up auditing. ~~Auditing in the security sense means to tell Windows to create an entry in the Security Log~~ when certain events happen, for example, a user logs on—~~called event auditing~~—or tries to access a certain file or folder—called **object access auditing**. Figure 16.13 shows Event Viewer tracking logon and logoff events.

The CompTIA A+ Practical Application exam doesn't test you on creating a brilliant auditing policy for your office—that's what network administrators do. You simply need to know what auditing does and how to turn it on or off so you can provide support for the network administrators in the field. To turn on auditing at a local level, go to Local Security Settings in Administrative Tools. Select Local Policies and then click Audit Policies. Double-click one of the policy options and select one or both of the checkboxes. Figure 16.14 shows the Audit object access dialog box.

Incidence Reporting

Once you've gathered data about a particular system or you've dealt with a computer or network problem, you need to complete the mission by telling your supervisor. This is called **incidence reporting**. Many companies have pre-made forms that you simply fill out and submit. Other places are less formal. Regardless, you need to do this!

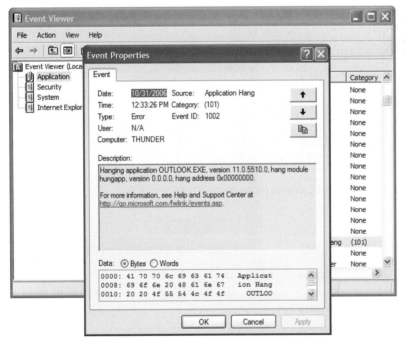

● **Figure 16.10**   Typical application error message

Event Viewer stores log files in %SystemRoot%\System32\ Config.

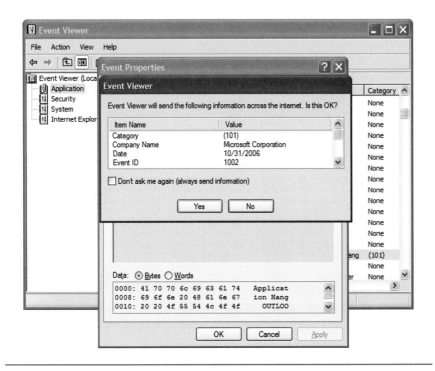

● **Figure 16.11**   Details about to be sent

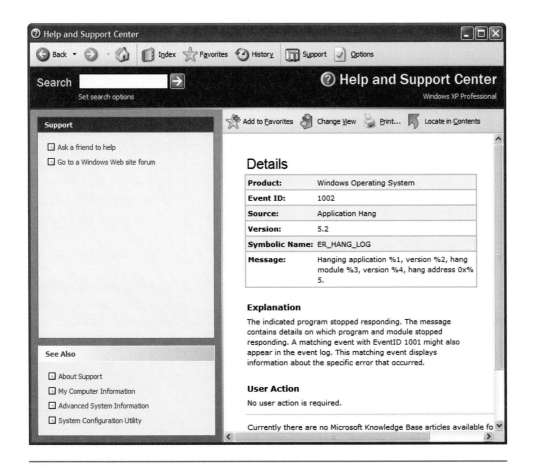

● **Figure 16.12**   Help and Support Center being helpful

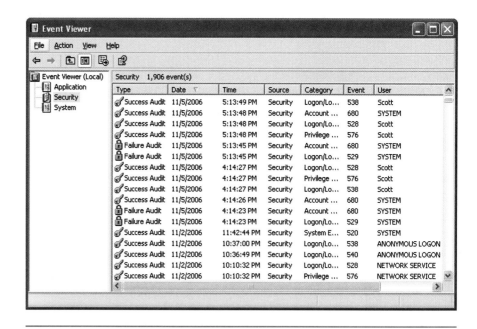

● **Figure 16.13**   Event Viewer displaying security alerts

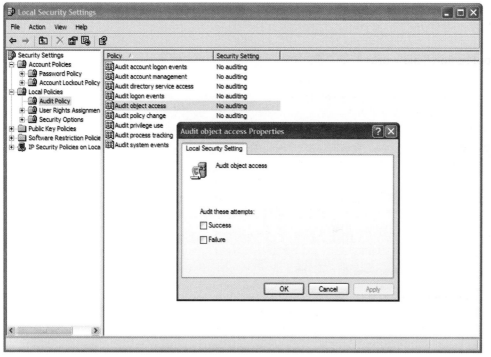

● **Figure 16.14**   Audit object access, with the Local Security Settings dialog box open in the background

Incidence reporting does a couple of things for you. First, it provides a record of work you've accomplished. Second, it provides a piece of information that, when combined with other information you might or might not know, reveals a pattern or bigger problem to someone higher up the chain. A seemingly innocuous security audit report, for example, might match other such events in numerous places in the building at the same time and thus show that conscious, coordinated action rather than a glitch was at work.

■ Network Security

Networks are under threat from the outside as well, so this section looks at issues involving Internet-borne attacks, firewalls, and wireless networking. This content is the security bread and butter for a CompTIA A+ technician, so you need to understand the concepts and procedures and be able to implement them properly.

Virus Prevention and Recovery

The only way to protect your PC permanently from getting a virus is to disconnect from the Internet and never permit any potentially infected software to touch your precious computer. Because neither scenario is likely these days, you need to use a specialized antivirus program to help stave off the inevitable virus assaults. When you discover infected systems, you need to know how to stop the spread of the virus to other computers and how to fix infected computers.

Antivirus Programs

An **antivirus program** protects your PC in two ways. It can be both sword and shield, working in an active seek-and-destroy mode and in a passive sentry mode. When ordered to seek and destroy, the program scans the computer's boot sector and files for viruses and, if it finds any, presents you with the available options for removing or disabling them. An antivirus program can also operate as a **virus shield** that passively monitors your computer's activity, checking for viruses only when certain events occur, such as a program executing or a file being downloaded.

Antivirus programs use different techniques to combat different types of viruses. They detect boot sector viruses simply by comparing the drive's boot sector to a standard boot sector. This works because most boot sectors are basically the same. Some antivirus programs make a backup copy of the boot sector. If they detect a virus, the programs use that backup copy to replace the infected boot sector. Executable viruses are a little more difficult to find because they can be on any file in the drive. To detect executable viruses, the antivirus program uses a library of signatures. A **signature** is the code pattern of a known virus. The antivirus program compares an executable file to its library of signatures. There have been instances where a perfectly clean program coincidentally held a virus signature. Usually the antivirus program's creator provides a patch to prevent further alarms. Now that you understand the types of viruses and how antivirus programs try to protect against them, let's review a few terms that are often used when describing certain traits of viruses.

Polymorphics/Polymorphs A polymorph virus attempts to change its signature to prevent detection by antivirus programs, usually by continually scrambling a bit of useless code. Fortunately, the scrambling code itself can be identified and used as the signature—once the antivirus makers become aware of the virus. One technique used to combat unknown polymorphs is to have the antivirus program create a checksum on every file in the drive. A *checksum* in this context is a number generated by the software based on the contents of the file rather than the name, date, or size of that file. The algorithms for creating these checksums vary among different antivirus programs (they are also usually kept secret to help prevent virus makers from coming up with ways to beat them). Every time a program is run, the antivirus program calculates a new checksum and compares it with the earlier calculation. If the checksums are different, it is a sure sign of a virus.

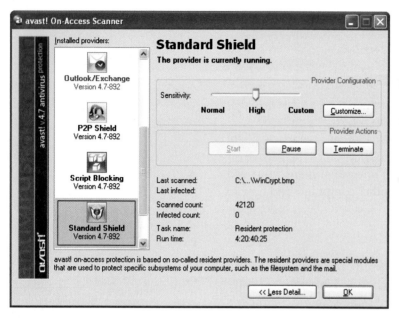

• Figure 16.15 A virus shield in action

Stealth The term "stealth" is more of a concept than an actual virus function. Most **stealth virus** programs are boot sector viruses that use various methods to hide from antivirus software. The AntiEXE stealth virus hooks on to a little-known but often-used software interrupt, for example, running only when that interrupt runs. Others make copies of innocent-looking files.

Virus Prevention Tips

The secret to preventing damage from a malicious software attack is to keep from getting a virus in the first place. As discussed earlier, all good antivirus programs include a virus shield that scans e-mail, downloads, running programs, and so on automatically (see Figure 16.15).

Use your antivirus shield. It is also a good idea to scan PCs daily for possible virus attacks. All antivirus programs include terminate-and-stay resident programs (TSRs) that run every time the PC is booted. Last but not least, know the source of any software before you load it. Although the chance of commercial, shrink-wrapped software having a virus is virtually nil (there have been a couple of well-publicized exceptions), that illegal copy of Unreal Tournament you borrowed from a local hacker should definitely be inspected with care.

Keep your antivirus program updated. New viruses appear daily, and your program needs to know about them. The list of virus signatures your antivirus program can recognize is called the **definition file,** and you must keep that definition file up to date so your antivirus software has the latest signatures. Fortunately, most antivirus programs update themselves automatically. Further, you should periodically update the core antivirus software programming—called the *engine*—to employ the latest refinements the developers have included.

Virus Recovery Tips

When the inevitable happens and either your computer or one of your user's computers gets infected by a computer virus, you need to follow certain steps to stop the problem from spreading and get the computer back up safely into service. Try this five-step process.

1. Recognize
2. Quarantine
3. Search and destroy
4. Remediate
5. Educate

Recognize and Quarantine The first step is to recognize that a potential virus outbreak has occurred. If you're monitoring network traffic and one computer starts spewing e-mail, that's a good sign. Or users might complain that a computer that was running snappily the day before seems very sluggish.

Many networks employ software such as the open source PacketFence that automatically monitors network traffic and can cut a machine off the network if that machine starts sending suspicious packets. You can also quarantine a computer manually by disconnecting the network cable. Once you're sure the machine isn't capable of infecting others, you're ready to find the virus and get rid of it.

Be sure to turn off System Restore before cleaning up a virus. Otherwise, Windows might keep a copy of the virus in the system backup files!

Search and Destroy Once you've isolated the infected computer (or computers), you need to get to a safe boot environment and run your antivirus software. You can try Windows Safe mode first, because it doesn't require anything but a reboot. If that doesn't work, or you suspect a boot sector virus, you need to turn to an external bootable source, such as a bootable CD or flash memory drive.

Get into the habit of keeping around an antivirus CD-R—a bootable CD-R disc with a copy of an antivirus program. If you suspect a virus, use the disc, even if your antivirus program claims to have eliminated the virus. Turn off the PC and reboot it from the antivirus disc. (You might have to change CMOS settings to boot to an optical disc.) This will put you in a clean boot environment that you know is free from any boot-sector viruses. If you only support fairly recent computers, most have an option to boot to a USB flash drive, so you can put a boot environment on a thumb drive for even faster start-up speeds.

You have several options for creating the bootable CD-R or flash drive. First, some antivirus software comes in a bootable version, such as the avast! Virus Cleaner tool (Figure 16.16).

Second, you can download a copy of Linux that offers a LiveCD option such as Ubuntu. With a LiveCD, you boot to the CD and install a complete working copy of the operating system into RAM, never touching or accessing the hard drive, to give you full Internet-ready access to many online antivirus sites. (You'll obviously need Internet access for those tools.) Kaspersky Labs provides a nice option at www.kaspersky.com.

• **Figure 16.16**   avast! Virus Cleaner tool

Finally, you can download and burn a copy of the Ultimate Boot CD. It comes stocked with several antivirus programs, so you wouldn't need any other tool. Find it at www.ultimatebootcd.com. The only downside is that the antivirus engines will be out of date, as will their virus encyclopedias.

Once you get to a boot environment, run your antivirus program's most comprehensive virus scan. Then check all removable media that were exposed to the system, as well as any other machine that might have received data from it or that is networked to the cleaned machine. A virus or other malicious program can often lie dormant for months before anyone knows of its presence.

E-mail is still a common source of viruses, and opening infected e-mails is a common way to get infected. Viewing an e-mail in a preview window opens the e-mail message and exposes your computer to some viruses. Download files only from sites you know to be safe, and of course the less reputable corners of the Internet are the most likely places to pick up computer infections.

Remediate   Virus infections can do a lot of damage to a system, especially to sensitive files needed to load Windows, so you might need to remediate formerly infected systems after cleaning off the drive or drives. Remediation simply means that you fix things the virus harmed. This can mean replacing corrupted Windows Registry files or even startup files.

If you can't start Windows after the virus scan is finished, you need to follow the steps outlined in Chapter 7, "Securing Windows Resources," to boot to the Recovery Console in Windows 2000/XP, or boot into a repair environment in Windows Vista.

Once in the Recovery Console, you'll have access to tools to repair the boot sector (or *boot blocks*, as CompTIA calls them) through the FIXMBR and FIXBOOT commands. You can run BOOTCFG to rebuild a corrupted BOOT.INI file. EXPAND will enable you to grab any replacement files from the Windows CAB files.

With the Windows Vista repair environment, you have access to more repair tools, such as Startup Repair, System Restore, Windows Complete PC Restore, and the command prompt (Figure 16.17). Run the appropriate option for the situation and you should have the machine properly remediated in a jiffy.

Educate   The best way to keep from having to deal with harmful software (generally referred to as malware or grayware) is education. It's your job as the IT person to talk to users, especially the ones whose systems you've just spent the last hour cleaning of nasties, about how to avoid these programs. Show them samples of dangerous e-mails they should not open, Web sites to avoid, and the types of programs they should not install and use on the network. Any user who understands the risks of questionable actions on their computers will usually do the right thing and stay away from malware.

Finally, have your users run antivirus and antispyware programs regularly. Schedule them while interfacing with the user so you know it will happen.

Firewalls

Firewalls are an essential tool in the fight against malicious programs on the Internet. A *firewall* is a device or software that protects an internal network from unauthorized access to and from the Internet at large. Hardware firewalls use a number of methods to protect networks, such as hiding IP addresses and blocking TCP/IP ports. Most SOHO networks use a hardware firewall, such as the Linksys router in Figure 16.18. These devices do a great job.

Every version of Windows since Windows XP Service Pack 2 comes with an excellent software firewall, called the Windows Firewall (Figure 16.19). It can also handle the heavy lifting of port blocking, security logging, and more.

You can access the Windows Firewall by opening the Windows Firewall applet in the Control Panel. If you're running the Control Panel in Category view, click the Security Center icon (Figure 16.20) and then click the Windows Firewall option in the Windows Security Center dialog box. Figure 16.21 illustrates the Exceptions tab on the Windows Firewall, showing the applications allowed to use the TCP/IP ports on my computer.

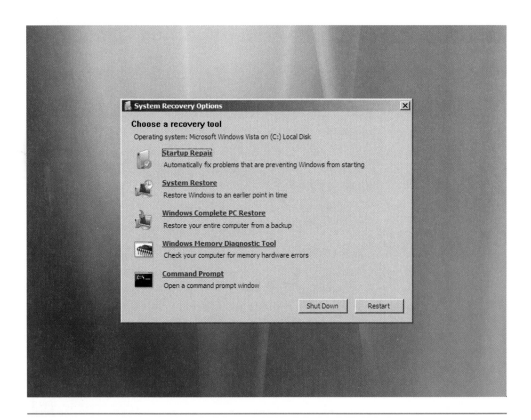

Figure 16.17 System Recovery options in Windows Vista

Figure 16.18 Linksys router as a firewall

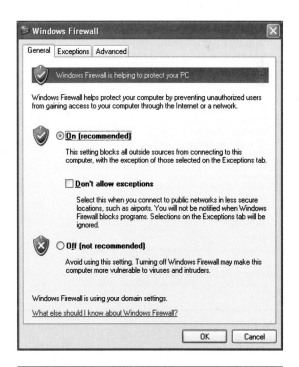

Figure 16.19 Windows Firewall

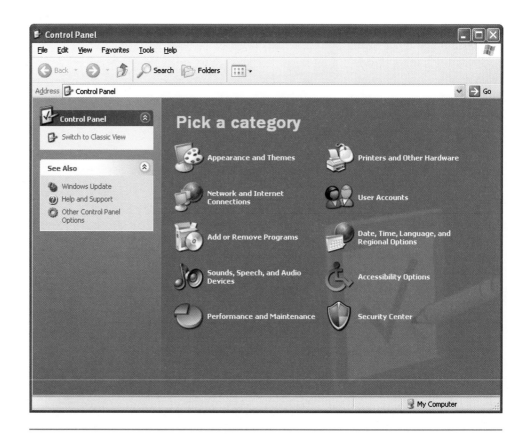

● Figure 16.20   Control Panel, Category view

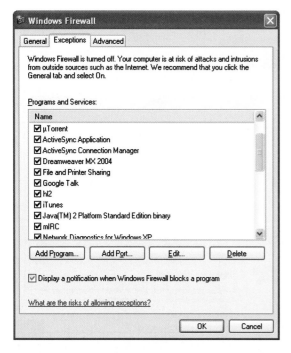

● Figure 16.21   Essential programs (doesn't everyone need to run Half-Life 2?)

Authentication and Encryption

You know from previous chapters that the first step in securing data is authentication, through a user name and password. But when you throw in networking, you're suddenly not just a single user sitting in front of a computer and typing. You're accessing a remote resource and sending logon information over the Internet. What's to stop someone from intercepting your user name and password?

Firewalls do a great job of controlling traffic coming into or out of a network from the Internet, but they do nothing to stop interceptor hackers who monitor traffic on the public Internet looking for vulnerabilities. Worse, once a packet is on the Internet itself, anyone with the right equipment can intercept and inspect it. Inspected packets are a cornucopia of passwords, account names, and other tidbits that hackers can use to intrude into your network. Because we can't stop hackers from inspecting these packets, we must turn to encryption to make them unreadable.

Network encryption occurs at many levels and is in no way limited to Internet-based activities. Not only are there many levels of network encryption, but each encryption level also provides multiple standards and options, making encryption one of the most complicated of all networking issues. You need to understand where encryption comes into play, what options are available, and what you can use to protect your network.

Network Authentication

Have you ever considered the process that takes place each time a person types in a user name and password to access a network, rather than just a local machine? What happens when this *network* authentication is requested? If you're thinking that when a user types in a user name and password, that information is sent to a server of some sort to be authenticated, you're right—but do you know how the user name and password get to the serving system? That's where encryption becomes important in authentication.

In a local network, authentication and encryption are usually handled by the NOS. In today's increasingly interconnected and diverse networking environment, there is a motivation to enable different network operating systems to authenticate any client system from any other NOS. Modern network operating systems such as Windows and OS X use standard authentication encryptions such as MIT's **Kerberos**, enabling multiple brands of servers to authenticate multiple brands of clients. These LAN authentication methods are usually transparent and work quite nicely, even in mixed networks.

Unfortunately, this uniformity falls away as you begin to add remote access authentications. There are so many different remote access tools, based on UNIX/Linux, Novell NetWare, and Windows serving programs, that most remote access systems have to support a variety of authentication methods.

PAP   ~~Password Authentication Protocol (PAP) is the oldest and most~~ basic ~~form of authentication. It's also the least safe, because it sends all passwords in clear text.~~ No NOS uses PAP for a client system's logon, but almost all network operating systems that provide remote access service support PAP for backward compatibility with a host of older programs (such as Telnet) that only use PAP.

CHAP   **Challenge Handshake Authentication Protocol (CHAP)** is the most common remote access protocol, by which the serving system challenges the remote client by asking the remote client some secret—usually a password. If the remote client responds appropriately, the host allows the connection.

MS-CHAP   **MS-CHAP** is Microsoft's variation of the CHAP protocol, using a slightly more advanced encryption protocol. The version of MS-CHAP that comes with Vista is version 2 (MS-CHAP v2).

Configuring Dial-up Encryption

It's the server, not the client, that controls the choice of dial-up encryption. Whoever configures the dial-up server determines how you have to configure the dial-up client. Microsoft clients handle a broad selection of authentication encryption methods, including no authentication at all. On the rare occasion when you have to change your client's default encryption settings for a dial-up connection, you'll need to journey deep into the bowels of its properties. Figure 16.22 shows the Windows Vista dialog box, called Advanced Security Settings, where you configure encryption. The person who controls the server's configuration will tell you which encryption method to select here.

• **Figure 16.22**   Setting dial-up encryption in the Windows Vista Advanced Security Settings dialog box

Data Encryption

Encryption methods don't stop at the authentication level. There are a number of ways to encrypt network *data* as well. The choice of encryption method is dictated to a large degree by the method used by the communicating systems to connect. Many networks consist of multiple networks linked together by some sort of private connection, usually some kind of telephone line such as ISDN or T1. Microsoft's encryption method of choice for this type of network is called **IPSec** (derived from *IP security*). IPSec provides transparent encryption between the server and the client. IPSec also works in VPNs, but other encryption methods are more commonly used in those situations.

Application Encryption

When it comes to encryption, even TCP/IP applications can get into the swing of things. The most famous of all application encryptions is Netscape's **Secure Sockets Layer (SSL)** security protocol, which is used to create secure Web sites. Microsoft incorporates SSL into its more far-reaching HTTPS (HTTP secure, or HTTP over SSL) protocol. These protocols make it possible to create the secure Web sites people use to make purchases over the Internet. You can identify HTTPS Web sites by the *HTTPS://* included in the URL (see Figure 16.23).

• **Figure 16.23** A secure Web site

To make a secure connection, your Web browser and the Web server must encrypt their data. That means there must be a way for both the Web server and your browser to encrypt and decrypt each other's data. To do this, the server sends a public key to your Web browser so the browser knows how to decrypt the incoming data. These public keys are sent in the form of a **digital certificate**. This certificate is signed by a trusted authority that guarantees that the public key you are about to get is actually from the Web server and not from some evil person trying to pretend to be the Web server. A number of companies issue digital certificates to Web sites, probably the most famous being VeriSign, Inc.

Your Web browser has a built-in list of trusted authorities. If a certificate comes in from a Web site that uses one of these highly respected companies, you won't see anything happen in your browser; you'll just go to the secure Web page, where a small lock will appear in the lower-right corner of your browser. Figure 16.24 shows the list of trusted authorities built in to the Firefox Web browser.

However, if you receive a certificate from someone *not* listed in your browser, the browser will warn you and ask you if you wish to accept the certificate, as shown in Figure 16.25.

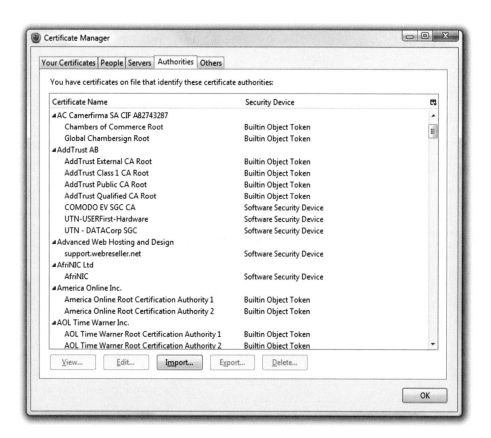

• **Figure 16.24**   Trusted authorities

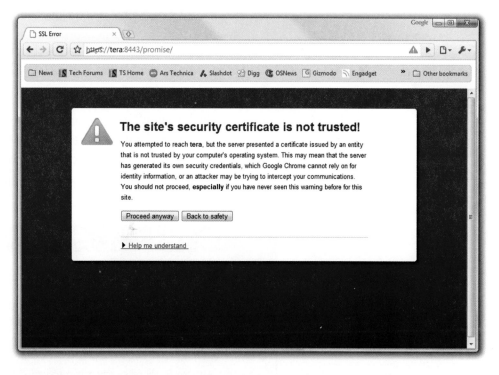

• **Figure 16.25**   Incoming certificate

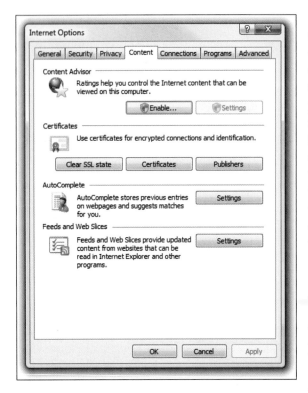

Figure 16.26 The Internet Options Content tab

What you do here is up to you. Do you wish to trust this certificate? In most cases, you simply say yes, and this certificate is added to your SSL cache of certificates. However, an accepted certificate may become invalid, usually because of something boring; for instance, it may go out of date or the public key may change. This never happens with the "big name" certificates built in to your browser—you'll see this more often when a certificate is used, for example, in-house on a company intranet and the administrator forgets to update the certificates. If a certificate goes bad, your browser issues a warning the next time you visit that site. To clear invalid certificates, you need to clear the SSL cache. The process varies in every browser, but in Internet Explorer, go to the Content tab under Internet Options and click the *Clear SSL state* button (Figure 16.26).

Wireless Issues

Wireless networks add a whole level of additional security headaches for techs to face, as you know from Chapter 14, "Mastering Wireless." Some of the points to remember or to go back and look up are as follows:

■ Set up wireless encryption, at least WEP but preferably WPA or the more secure WPA2 and configure clients to use them.

■ Disable DHCP and require your wireless clients to use a static IP address.

■ If you need to use DHCP, only allot enough DHCP addresses to meet the needs of your network to avoid unused wireless connections.

■ Change the WAP's SSID from default and disable SSID broadcast.

■ Filter by MAC address to allow only known clients on the network.

■ Change the default user name and password. Every hacker has memorized the default user names and passwords.

■ Update the firmware as needed.

■ If available, make sure the WAP's firewall settings are turned on.

 Cross Check

Securing Wireless Networks

Wireless networks are all the rage right now, from your local Starbucks to the neighbors around you. Securing wireless networks has, therefore, become an area that CompTIA A+ certified technicians must master. You read a lot about wireless networks in Chapter 14, "Mastering Wireless," so turn there now and see if you can answer these questions: What is the minimum level of encryption to secure a wireless network? What types of wireless will you find for connecting at your local coffee shop?

Chapter 16 Review

■ Chapter Summary

After reading this chapter and completing the exercises, you should understand the following about computer security.

Explain the threats to your computers and data

■ Threats to your data come from two sources: accidents and malicious people.

■ Unauthorized access occurs when a user accesses resources in an unauthorized way. Not all unauthorized access is malicious and some is even accidental. Authorized access can lead to data destruction by users who do not intend to be malicious. When users have access to a file or database, they typically believe the system won't let them make any changes they are not authorized to make.

■ Most computer attacks are accomplished through social engineering rather than hacking. Telephone scams are one of the most common social engineering tactics. Dumpster diving involves physically going through an organization's trash looking for documents that might reveal user names, passwords, or other sensitive information. Be sure to secure your computer equipment in a locked room to prevent physical theft.

■ Windows XP Home has only two types of user accounts: administrative and limited. If you need to control access, you are better off using a non-Home version of Windows.

■ Computers, hard drives, and power all fail. As a tech, you need to plan for redundancy in these areas. You also need to protect your computers against viruses distributed through the network and removable media. You should implement good access policies and implement methods for tracking computer usage.

Describe key security concepts and technologies

■ Controlling access to programs, data, and other computing resources is the key to securing your system. Access control includes four interlinked areas requiring your attention: physical security, authentication, users and groups, and security policies.

■ Store computers with sensitive data in a locked room and never walk away from your computer while logged in. Log out or lock the computer by pressing the WINDOWS LOGO KEY-L.

■ For software authentication, every user account should have a password to protect against unauthorized access. Additionally, CMOS setup should have a password for any computer in a public place.

■ For hardware authentication, try smart cards or biometric devices. Smart cards are the size of credit cards and contain circuitry that can identify the card holder. Biometric devices identify users by physical characteristics such as fingerprints or retinal scans. Some smart cards use radio frequency identification to transmit authentication information so users don't have to insert something into a computer or card reader.

■ Accounts should be given permissions to access only what they need and no more. Unused accounts should be disabled.

■ When a user account is a member of several groups, and permissions have been granted to groups, the user account will have a set of combined permissions that may conflict. The resulting permissions that ultimately control access are referred to as the effective permissions.

■ Make sure to lock down the default Everyone group of which all users are automatically members. Windows 2000 gives full control to the Everyone group by default. Never use the default Everyone or Users groups or the default Guest account unless you intend to permit all those accounts access to resources.

■ Policies control permissions for activities, such as installing software, access to a command prompt, or time of day a user can log on. A policy is usually applied to a user account, computer, or group. Use the Local Security Settings tool to manage policies for an individual computer.

■ Group Policy enables you to control such things as deploying software or setting each computer in a domain to use the same wallpaper. Commonly used policies include Prevent Registry Edits,

Prevent Access to the Command Prompt, Log On Locally, and Minimum Password Length.

- Data classification systems vary by the organization, but a common scheme classifies documents as public, internal use only, highly confidential, top secret, and so on. Using a classification scheme enables employees such as techs to know very quickly what to do with documents, drives containing documents, and more.

- Compliance means that members of an organization or company must abide by or comply with all of the rules that apply to the organization or company. From a technician's point of view, the most common compliance issue revolves around software, such as what sort of software users can be allowed to install on their computers. Compliance keeps technical support calls down and enables techs to focus on more serious problems.

- Use Event Viewer to track activity on your system. Event Viewer offers three sections: Application, Security, and System. By default, the Security section doesn't show you everything, so it is good practice to enable event auditing and object auditing. Event auditing creates an entry in the Security Log when certain events happen, such as a user logging on, while object auditing creates entries in response to object access, such as someone trying to access a certain file or folder.

- Incidence reporting means telling your supervisor about the data you've gathered regarding a computer or network problem. This provides a record of what you've done and accomplished. It also provides information that, when combined with other information you may or may not know, may reveal a pattern or bigger problem to someone higher up the chain.

Explain how to protect computers from network threats

- To help protect a computer from malware, make sure to run up-to-date antivirus software, use a firewall, and apply all security patches for your software and operating system. Run Windows Update automatically, or at least weekly if you choose to configure it for manual updates.

- Antivirus software works in active mode to scan your file system for viruses and in passive mode by monitoring your computer's activity and checking for viruses in response to an action, such as

running a program or downloading a file. The software detects boot-sector viruses by comparing the drive's boot sector to a standard boot sector. To detect executable viruses, a library of virus signatures is used.

- Polymorph viruses attempt to change their signature to prevent detection by antivirus software. Fortunately, the scrambled code itself can be used as a signature. A checksum, based on file contents, can be created for every file on the drive. If the checksum changes, it is a sign of a virus infection. Most stealth viruses are boot sector viruses that hide from antivirus software.

- The best way to prevent damage from a virus is to keep from getting a virus in the first place. Use your passive antivirus shield, scan the PC daily, know where software has come from before you load it, and keep your antivirus definitions updated. Don't view e-mail messages in a preview pane, and only download files from sites you know to be safe.

- When the inevitable happens and either your computer or one of your user's computers is infected by a computer virus, you need to follow a process to stop the problem from spreading and get the computer back up safely into service.

- First, recognize the symptoms of a computer virus attack, such as a suddenly very sluggish computer. Follow up by quarantining the infected computer to make certain the virus doesn't spread. Third, boot the computer in Safe mode or an alternative safe boot environment and run your antivirus software. To finish up, remediate the formerly infected machine by fixing boot sector problems and so on, and educate your users so infection doesn't happen again.

- Hardware firewalls protect networks by hiding IP addresses and blocking TCP/IP ports. Windows XP and later come with a built-in software firewall that is accessible from the Control Panel Security Center applet.

- Encryption makes network packets unreadable by hackers who intercept network traffic. You are especially vulnerable when using the Internet over a public network. Modern operating systems use Kerberos to encrypt authentication credentials over a local network.

- PAP sends passwords in clear text, so it is not very safe. CHAP is the most common remote access protocol, by which the serving system challenges the remote system by asking some secret, such as a password. MS-CHAP is Microsoft's version of CHAP and uses a more advanced encryption protocol.

- Network data can be encrypted similar to authentication credentials. Microsoft's encryption method of choice is called IPSec. Netscape's Secure Sockets Layer (SSL) creates secure Web sites. Microsoft's HTTPS protocol incorporates SSL into

HTTP. Web sites whose URLs begin with HTTPS:// (rather than HTTP://) are used to encrypt credit card purchases.

- To secure a wireless network, use wireless encryption and disable DHCP. Require wireless clients to use a static IP address or allot only enough DHCP addresses to meet the needs of your network. Definitely change the default administrator user name and password on the WAP!

■ Key Terms

access control *(471)*
antivirus program *(481)*
authentication *(471)*
biometric device *(472)*
Challenge Handshake Authentication Protocol (CHAP) *(487)* 6
compliance *(477)*
data classification *(477)* 1
definition file *(482)* 2
digital certificate *(489)*
dumpster diving *(468)*
effective permissions *(474)*
encryption *(486)*
event auditing *(478)*
Event Viewer *(477)*
firewall *(484)*
Group Policy *(475)*
incidence reporting *(478)*

IPSec *(488)*
Kerberos *(487)*
Local Security Settings *(475)*
MS-CHAP *(487)*
object access auditing *(478)* 3
Password Authentication Protocol (PAP) *(487)*
phishing *(469)*
polymorph virus *(481)*
remediation *(484)*
Secure Sockets Layer (SSL) *(488)* 7
signature *(481)*
smart card *(472)*
social engineering *(468)* 5
stealth virus *(482)*
tailgating *(468)*
telephone scam *(468)*
unauthorized access *(467)* 4
virus shield *(481)*

■ Key Term Quiz

Use the Key Terms list to complete the sentences that follow. Not all terms will be used.

1. Mary's company routinely labels data according to its sensitivity or potential danger to the company if someone outside accesses the data. This is an example of _____.

2. Antivirus software uses updatable _____ to identify a virus by its _____.

3. Enable _____ to create Event Viewer entries when a specific file is accessed.

4. Although not all _____ is malicious, it can lead to data destruction.

5. Most attacks on computer data are accomplished through _____.

6. _____ is the most common remote authentication protocol.

7. Before making a credit card purchase on the Internet, be sure the Web site uses the _____ security protocol, which you can verify by checking for the HTTPS protocol in the address bar.

Multiple-Choice Quiz

1. What is the process of using or manipulating people to gain access to network resources?

   A. Cracking

   B. Hacking

   C. Network engineering

   D. Social engineering

2. Which of the following might offer good hardware authentication?

   A. Strong password

   B. Encrypted password

   C. NTFS

   D. Smart card

3. Which of the following tools would enable you to stop a user from logging on to a local machine but still enable him to log on to the domain?

   A. AD Policy

   B. Group Policy

   C. Local Security Settings

   D. User Settings

4. Which type of encryption offers the most security?

   A. MS-CHAP

   B. PAP

   C. POP3

   D. SMTP

5. Which of the following should Mary set up on her Wi-Fi router to make it the most secure?

   A. NTFS

   B. WEP

   C. WPA

   D. WPA2

6. A user account is a member of several groups, and the groups have conflicting rights and permissions to several network resources. The culminating permissions that ultimately affect the user's access are referred to as what?

   A. Effective permissions

   B. Culminating rights

   C. Last rights

   D. Persistent permissions

7. What does Windows use to encrypt the user authentication process over a LAN?

   A. PAP

   B. MS-CHAP

   C. HTTPS

   D. Kerberos

8. Which threats are categorized as social engineering? (Select two.)

   A. Telephone scams

   B. Dumpster diving

   C. Trojans

   D. Spyware

9. Which security threat is most often committed by well-meaning but uninformed employees messing with things they shouldn't?

   A. Theft

   B. Data destruction

   C. Phishing

   D. Dumpster diving

10. What tool can you use to get a log of any unauthorized access or other security errors on a Windows system?

    A. Event Viewer

    B. Task Manager

    C. Safe Mode

    D. Security Center

11. What does a Web server transmit to a client in order to show that it is making a secure Internet connection?

    A. A firewall

    B. A polymorph

    C. A PAP

    D. A digital certificate

■ Essay Quiz

1. A coworker complains that he is receiving a high amount of spam on his home computer through a personal e-mail account. What advice can you give him to alleviate his junk mail?

2. The boss's assis... a new coffee m... nervous about... credit card. ... online purc...

Lab Project

• Lab Project 16.1

You have learned a little bit about the Local Security Policy in Windows. Fire up your Web browser and do a search for Local Security Policy. Make a list of at least five changes you might consider making to your personal computer by using the Local Security Policy tool. Be sure to include what the policy is, what it does, and where in the tool it can be configured.

Mapping to the CompTIA A+ Practical Application Objectives

CompTIA A+ Practical Application Objectives Map

Topic	Chapter(s)
Domain 1.0 Hardware	
1.1 Given a scenario, install, configure, and maintain personal computer components	
Storage devices	5, 9, 11
HDD	5
SATA	5, 11
PATA	5, 11
Solid state	5
FDD	9
Optical drives	9
CD / DVD / RW / Blu-Ray	9
Removable	9
External	9
Motherboards	2, 3, 4, 5, 7, 8, 9
Jumper settings	3
CMOS battery	3
Advanced BIOS settings	3
Bus speeds	3
Chipsets	3
Firmware updates	3
Socket types	3
Expansion slots	2, 3, 10
Memory slots	2, 3
Front panel connectors	3
I/O ports	3, 9, 10, 11, 12, 13
Sound, video, USB 1.1, USB 2.0, serial, IEEE 1394 / Firewire, parallel, NIC, modem, PS/2	3, 9, 10, 11, 12, 13
Power supplies	4
Wattages and capacity	4
Connector types and quantity	4
Output voltage	4

Topic	Chapter(s)
Processors	2, 3
Socket types	2
Speed	2
Number of cores	2
Power consumption	2
Cache	2
Front side bus	3
32bit vs. 64bit	2, 3
Memory	2
Adapter cards	3, 5, 10
Graphics cards	10
Sound cards	10
Storage controllers	5, 9
RAID cards (RAID array – levels 0,1,5)	5
eSATA cards	9
I/O cards	9
Firewire	9
USB	9
Parallel	9
Serial	9
Wired and wireless network cards	13, 14
Capture cards (TV, video)	10
Media reader	9
Cooling systems	2, 4
Heat sinks	2
Thermal compound	2
CPU fans	2
Case fans	2, 4
1.2 Given a scenario, detect problems, troubleshoot and repair/replace personal computer components	
Storage devices	5, 9, 11, 13
HDD	5
SATA	5, 11
PATA	5, 11
Solid state	5
FDD	9
Optical drives	9
CD / DVD / RW / Blu-Ray	9
Removable	9
External	9
Motherboards	2, 3, 4, 5, 8, 9, 10
Jumper settings	2, 3
CMOS battery	3

Topic	Chapter(s)
Advanced BIOS settings	3
Bus speeds	3
Chipsets	3
Firmware updates	3
Socket types	2, 3
Expansion slots	2, 3, 10
Memory slots	2, 3
Front panel connectors	3
I/O ports	3, 9, 11, 13
Sound, video, USB 1.1, USB 2.0, serial, IEEE 1394 / Firewire, parallel, NIC, modem, PS/2	3, 9, 10, 11, 13
Power supplies	4
Wattages and capacity	4
Connector types and quantity	4
Output voltage	4
Processors	2, 3, 5, 8, 9
Socket types	2, 3
Speed	2
Number of cores	2
Power consumption	2
Cache	2
Front side bus	3
32bit vs. 64bit	2
Memory	2, 3
Adapter cards	3, 10
Graphics cards – memory	10
Sound cards	10
Storage controllers	5
RAID cards	5
eSATA cards	5, 9
I/O cards	9
Firewire	9
USB	9
Parallel	9
Serial	9
Wired and wireless network cards	13, 14
Capture cards (TV, video)	10
Media reader	13
Cooling systems	2, 3, 4, 10
Heat sinks	2, 5
Thermal compound	2, 5

Topic	Chapter(s)
CPU fans	2, 3, 4, 5
Case fans	2, 3, 4, 5, 10
1.3 Given a scenario, install, configure, detect problems, troubleshoot and repair/replace laptop components	
Components of the LCD including inverter, screen and video card	11
Hard drive and memory	11
Disassemble processes for proper reassembly	11
Document and label cable and screw locations	11
Organize parts	11
Refer to manufacturer documentation	11
Use appropriate hand tools	11
Recognize internal laptop expansion slot types	11
Upgrade wireless cards and video card	11
Replace keyboard, processor, plastics, pointer devices, heat sinks, fans, system board, CMOS battery, speakers	11
1.4 Given a scenario, select and use the following tools	
Multimeter	4, 12
Power supply tester	4
Specialty hardware / tools	4, 12
Cable testers	13
Loopback plugs	13
Anti-static pad and wrist strap	3
Extension magnet	12
1.5 Given a scenario, detect and resolve common printer issues	
Symptoms	12
Paper jams	12
Blank paper	12
Error codes	12
Out of memory error	12
Lines and smearing	12
Garbage printout	12
Ghosted image	12
No connectivity	12
Issue resolution	12
Replace fuser	12
Replace drum	12
Clear paper jam	12
Power cycling	12
Install maintenance kit (reset page count)	12
Set IP on printer	13
Clean printer	12

Topic	Chapter(s)
Domain 2.0 Operating Systems – unless otherwise noted, operating systems referred to within include Microsoft Windows 2000, Windows XP Professional, XP Home, XP MediaCenter, Windows Vista Home, Home Premium, Business and Ultimate.	
2.1 Select the appropriate commands and options to troubleshoot and resolve problems	
MSCONFIG	8
DIR	6
CHKDSK (/f /r)	5, 6, 8
EDIT	6
1COPY (/a /v /y)	6, 8
XCOPY	6
FORMAT	6, 8
IPCONFIG (/all /release /renew)	13
PING (–t –l)	13
MD / CD / RD	6, 8
NET	13
TRACERT	13
NSLOOKUP	13
[command name] /?	5, 6, 13, 16
SFC	6
2.2 Differentiate between Windows Operating System directory structures (Windows 2000, XP, and Vista)	
User file locations	8
System file locations	8
Fonts	8
Temporary files	8
Program files	8
Offline files and folders	8
2.3 Given a scenario, select and use system utilities / tools and evaluate the results	
Disk management tools	5, 6, 8
DEFRAG	5
NTBACKUP	8
CheckDisk	5, 6, 8
Disk Manager	5
Active, primary, extended, and logical partitions	5
Mount points	5
Mounting a drive	5
FAT32 and NTFS	5
Drive status	5
Foreign drive	5
Healthy	5
Formatting	5

Topic	Chapter(s)
Active, unallocated	5
Failed	5
Dynamic	5
Offline	5
Online	5
System monitor	8
Administrative tools	8
Event Viewer	8
Computer Management	8
Services	8
Performance Monitor	8
Device Manager	8
Enable	8
Disable	8
Warnings	8
Indicators	8
Task Manager	2, 10
Process list	10
Resource usage	2, 10
Process priority	10
Termination	10
System Information	10
System Restore	8
Remote Desktop Protocol (Remote Desktop / Remote Assistance)	15
Task Schedule	8
Regional settings and language settings	5
2.4 Evaluate and resolve common issues	
Operational problems	4, 8, 12
Windows-specific printing problems	12
Print spool stalled	12
Incorrect / incompatible driver/form printing	12
Auto-restart errors	8
Blue Screen error	2, 8
System lock-up	2, 4, 8
Device drivers failure (input / output devices)	8
Application install, start, or load failure	8
Service fails to start	8
Error messages and conditions	8
Boot	8
Invalid boot disk	8

Topic	Chapter(s)
Inaccessible boot drive	8
Missing NTLDR	8
Startup	8
Device / service failed to start	8
Device / program in Registry not found	8
Event Viewer (errors in the event log)	8
System performance and optimization	8, 10
Aero settings	8
Indexing settings	8
UAC	8, 16
Side bar settings	8
Startup file maintenance	8
Background processes	8, 10
Domain 3.0 Networking	
3.1 Troubleshoot client-side connectivity issues using appropriate tools	
TCP/IP settings	13, 15
Gateway	13
Subnet mask	13
DNS	13
DHCP (dynamic vs. static)	13, 15
NAT (private and public)	15
Characteristics of TCP/IP	13, 15
Loopback addresses	13
Automatic IP addressing	13, 15
Mail protocol settings	15
SMTP	15
IMAP	15
POP	15
FTP settings	15
Ports	15
IP addresses	15
Exceptions	15
Programs	15
Proxy settings	15
Ports	15
IP addresses	15
Exceptions	15
Programs	15

Topic	Chapter(s)
Tools (use and interpret results)	13, 15
Ping	13, 15
Tracert	13
Nslookup	13
Netstat	15
Net use	13
Net /?	13
Ipconfig	13
telnet	15
SSH	15
Secure connection protocols	15
SSH	15
HTTPS	15
Firewall settings	16
Open and closed ports	16
Program filters	16
3.2 Install and configure a small office home office (SOHO) network	
Connection types	14, 15
Dial-up	15
Broadband	15
DSL	15
Cable	15
Satellite	15
ISDN	15
Wireless	14
All 802.11	14
WEP	14
WPA	14
SSID	14
MAC filtering	14
DHCP settings	14
Routers / access points	13, 14
Disable DHCP	13
Use static IP	13
Change SSID from default	14
Disable SSID broadcast	14

Topic	Chapter(s)
MAC filtering	14
Change default username and password	14
Update firmware	14
Firewall	16
LAN (10/100/1000BaseT, speeds)	13
Bluetooth (1.0 vs. 2.0)	14
Cellular	14
Basic VoIP (consumer applications)	15
Basics of hardware and software firewall configuration	15, 16
Port assignment / setting up rules (exceptions)	15
Port forwarding / port triggering	15
Physical installation	13
Wireless router placement	15
Cable length	13
Domain 4.0 Security	
4.1 Given a scenario, prevent, troubleshoot, and remove viruses and malware	
Use antivirus software	16
Identify malware symptoms	16
Quarantine infected systems	16
Research malware types, symptoms, and solutions (virus encyclopedias)	16
Remediate infected systems	16
Update antivirus software	16
Signature and engine updates	16
Automatic vs. manual	16
Schedule scans	16
Repair boot blocks	16
Scan and removal techniques	16
Safe mode	16
Boot environment	16
Educate end user	16
4.2 Implement security and troubleshoot common issues	
Operating systems	14, 15, 16
Local users and groups: Administrator, Power Users, Guest, Users	16
Vista User Access Control (UAC)	8
NTFS vs. Share permissions	6, 16
Allow vs. deny	16
Difference between moving and copying folders and files	6
File attributes	6

appendix **B**

About the CD

ike Meyers has put together a bunch of resources to help you prepare for the CompTIA A+ Practical Application exam. You will also find them invaluable even after taking the exam in your career as a PC Tech. The CD-ROM included with this book comes complete with a sample version of the Total Tester practice exam software, with one full practice exam plus all the Chapter Review questions from the book, a searchable electronic copy of the book, a document from CompTIA with a list of acronyms you should know for the CompTIA A+ Practical Application exam, a complete list of the objectives for the Practical Application exam, a copy of several freeware and shareware programs that Mike talks about in the book, and a sample of LearnKey's online training featuring Mike Meyers. The practice test and video software are easy to install on any Windows 98/NT/2000/XP/Vista/7 computer and must be installed to access the Total Tester practice exam and LearnKey video sample. The eBook and CompTIA A+ acronyms and objectives lists are Adobe Acrobat files. If you don't have Adobe Acrobat Reader, it is available for installation on the CD-ROM.

■ System Requirements

The software on the CD-ROM requires Windows 98 or higher, Internet Explorer 5.0 or above, and 50 MB of hard disk space for full installation. To access the online training from LearnKey, you must have Windows Media Player 9 or higher, which will be automatically installed when you launch the online training.

■ Installing and Running Total Tester

If your computer's CD-ROM drive is configured to Autorun, the CD-ROM will automatically start when you insert the disk. If the Autorun feature does not launch the CD's splash screen, browse to the CD-ROM and double-click the Launch.exe icon.

From the splash screen, you may install Total Tester by clicking *Install A+ Practice Exams*. This will begin the installation process, create a program group named Total Seminars, and put an icon on your desktop. To run Total Tester, go to Start | Programs | Total Seminars or just double-click the icon on your desktop.

To uninstall the Total Tester software, go to Start | Settings | Control Panel | Add/Remove Programs and select the A+ Total Tester program. Select Remove, and Windows will completely uninstall the software.

About Total Tester

The best way to prepare for the CompTIA A+ Practical Application exam is to read the book and then test your knowledge and review. We have included a sample of Total Seminars' practice exam software to help you test your knowledge as you study. Total Tester provides a simulation of the actual exam. There is a suite called A+ 702 Split that contains a sample 702 exam you can take in either practice or final mode. Practice mode provides an assistance window with hints, references to the book, explanations of the answers, and the ability to check your answers as you take the test. Both practice and final modes provide an overall grade and a grade broken down by certification objective. There is also a four-exam suite called A+ 702 Review. Each exam covers chapter review questions from four chapters. To launch a test, select Suites from the menu at the top, and then select an exam. Additional practice exams are available for both of the CompTIA A+ exams. Visit our Web site at www.totalsem.com or call 800-446-6004 for more information.

Accessing the eBook, CompTIA A+ Acronyms, and CompTIA A+ Exam Objectives

You will find these documents useful in your preparation for the exam. To access these PDF documents, first be sure you have a copy of Adobe Acrobat Reader installed. If you don't have Acrobat Reader installed on your system, you can install it from the CD-ROM by clicking *Install Adobe Acrobat Reader*. Once you have installed Acrobat Reader, simply select the document you want to view from the CD-ROM's splash screen to open and view the document.

Shareware and Freeware

Mike has put together copies of some of his favorite freeware and shareware programs that are mentioned in this book. The CD-ROM includes a list with short descriptions of the programs. To use these programs, select the Shareware and Freeware option on the CD-ROM splash screen to see a list of programs. Select a program and follow the installation instructions to load the utility on your system.

LearnKey Online Training

If you like Mike's writing style, you will love listening to him in his LearnKey video training. The CD-ROM includes sample videos of Mike covering several different topics. Check out Mike's video training. If you like it, you can purchase the full 21 hours of interactive video training by contacting Mike's company, Total Seminars, at www.totalsem.com or 800-446-6004. The *Install LearnKey demo* button will launch a wizard to install the software on your computer. Follow the instructions on the wizard to complete the installation. To run the LearnKey demo, use Start | Programs | LearnKey or just double-click the icon on your desktop. Enter a user name and password to begin your video training.

■ Technical Support

For questions regarding the Total Tester software, visit www.totalsem.com, e-mail support@totalsem.com, or visit http://mhp.softwareassist.com/. For customers outside the United States, e-mail international_cs@mcgraw-hill.com.

LearnKey Technical Support

For technical problems with the software (installation, operation, or uninstalling the software) and for questions regarding LearnKey Video Training, e-mail techsupport@learnkey.com.

10BaseT Ethernet LAN designed to run on UTP cabling. 10BaseT runs at 10 megabits per second. The maximum length for the cabling between the NIC and the hub (or switch, repeater, etc.) is 100 meters. It uses baseband signaling. No industry standard spelling exists, so sometimes written 10BASE-T or 10Base-T.

100BaseT Generic term for an Ethernet cabling system designed to run at 100 megabits per second on UTP cabling. It uses baseband signaling. No industry standard spelling exists, so sometimes written 100BASE-T or 100Base-T.

1000BaseT Gigabit Ethernet on UTP.

2.1 Speaker setup consisting of two stereo speakers combined with a subwoofer.

3.5-inch floppy drive All modern floppy disk drives are of this size; the format was introduced in 1986 and is one of the longest surviving pieces of computer hardware.

34-pin ribbon cable Type of cable used by floppy disk drives.

3-D graphics Video technology that attempts to create images with the same depth and texture as objects seen in the real world.

40-pin ribbon cable PATA cable used to attach EIDE devices (such as hard drives) or ATAPI devices (such as optical drives) to a system. (*See* PATA.)

5.1 speaker system Four satellite speakers plus a center speaker and a subwoofer.

8.3 naming system File-naming convention that specified a maximum of eight characters for a filename, followed by a 3-character file extension. Has been replaced by LFN (long filename) support.

80-wire ribbon cable PATA cable used to attach fast EIDE devices (such as ATA/100 hard drives) or ATAPI devices (such as optical drives) to a system. (*See* PATA.)

802.11a Wireless networking standard that operates in the 5-GHz band with a theoretical maximum throughput of 54 Mbps.

802.11b Wireless networking standard that operates in the 2.4-GHz band with a theoretical maximum throughput of 11 Mbps.

802.11g Wireless networking standard that operates in the 2.4-GHz band with a theoretical maximum throughput of 54 Mbps and is backward compatible with 802.11b.

802.11n Wireless networking standard that can operate in both the 2.4-GHz and 5-GHz bands and uses MIMO to achieve a theoretical maximum throughput of 100+ Mbps.

A/V sync Process of synchronizing audio and video.

AC (alternating current) Type of electricity in which the flow of electrons alternates direction, back and forth, in a circuit.

AC'97 Sound card standard for lower-end audio devices; created when most folks listened to stereo sound at best.

access control Security concept using physical security, authentication, users and groups, and security policies.

ACPI (Advanced Configuration and Power Interface) Power management specification that far surpasses its predecessor, APM, by providing support for hot-swappable devices and better control of power modes.

activation Process of confirming that an installed copy of a Microsoft product (most commonly Windows or a Microsoft Office application) is legitimate. Usually done at the end of software installation.

active matrix Type of liquid crystal display that replaced the passive matrix technology used in most portable computer displays. Also called *TFT* (*thin film transistor*).

active partition On a hard drive, primary partition that contains an operating system.

active PFC (power factor correction) Circuitry built into PC power supplies to reduce harmonics.

...de   Decentralized wireless network mode, ...se known as peer-to-peer mode, where each ...less node is in meshed contact with every other ...ode.

Add or Remove Programs   Applet allowing users to manually add or remove a program from the system.

address bus   Wires leading from the CPU to the memory controller chip (usually the Northbridge) that enable the CPU to address RAM. Also used by the CPU for I/O addressing. An internal electronic channel from the microprocessor to random access memory, along which the addresses of memory storage locations are transmitted. Like a post office box, each memory location has a distinct number or address; the address bus provides the means by which the microprocessor can access every location in memory.

address space   Total amount of memory addresses that an address bus can contain.

administrative shares   Administrator tool to give local admins access to hard drives and system root folders.

Administrative Tools   Group of Control Panel applets, including Computer Management, Event Viewer, and Reliability and Performance Monitor.

Administrator account   User account, created when the OS is first installed, that is allowed complete, unfettered access to the system without restriction.

Administrators group   List of members with complete administrator privileges.

ADSL (asymmetric digital subscriber line)   Fully digital, dedicated connection to the telephone system that provides average download speeds of 7 Mbps and upload speeds of 512 Kbps.

Advanced Startup Options menu   Menu that can be reached during the boot process that offers advanced OS startup options, such as boot in Safe mode or boot into Last Known Good Configuration.

adware   Type of malicious program that downloads ads to a user's computer, generating undesirable network traffic.

Aero   The Windows Vista desktop environment. Aero adds some interesting aesthetic effects such as window transparency and Flip 3D.

AGP (Accelerated Graphics Port)   32/64-bit expansion slot designed by Intel specifically for video that runs at 66 MHz and yields a throughput of at least 254 Mbps. Later versions (2×, 4×, 8×) give substantially higher throughput.

algorithm   Set of rules for solving a problem in a given number of steps.

ALU (arithmetic logic unit)   CPU logic circuits that perform basic arithmetic (add, subtract, multiply, and divide).

AMD (Advanced Micro Devices)   CPU and chipset manufacturer that competes with Intel. Produces the popular Phenom, Athlon, Sempron, Turion, and Duron microprocessors; also produces video card processors under its ATI brand.

AMI (American Megatrends, Inc)   Major producer of BIOS software for motherboards, as well as many other computer-related components and software.

amperes (amps or A)   Unit of measure for amperage, or electrical current.

amplitude   Loudness of a sound card.

AMR (Audio/Modem Riser)   Proprietary slot used on some motherboards to provide a sound inference–free connection for modems, sound cards, and NICs.

analog   Device that uses a physical quantity, such as length or voltage, to represent the value of a number. By contrast, digital storage relies on a coding system of numeric units.

anti-aliasing   In computer imaging, blending effect that smoothes sharp contrasts between two regions—e.g., jagged lines or different colors. Reduces jagged edges of text or objects. In voice signal processing, process of removing or smoothing out spurious frequencies from waveforms produced by converting digital signals back to analog.

anti-static bag   Bag made of anti-static plastic into which electronics are placed for temporary or long-term storage. Used to protect components from electrostatic discharge.

anti-static mat   Special surface on which to lay electronics. These mats come with a grounding connection designed to equalize electrical potential between a workbench and one or more electronic devices. Used to prevent electrostatic discharge.

anti-static wrist strap   Special device worn around the wrist with a grounding connection designed to equalize electrical potential between a technician and an electronic device. Used to prevent electrostatic discharge.

antivirus program Software designed to combat viruses by either seeking out and destroying them or passively guarding against them.

API (application programming interface) Software definition that describes operating system calls for application software; conventions defining how a service is invoked.

APIPA (Automatic Private IP Addressing) Feature of Windows that automatically assigns an IP address to the system when the client cannot obtain an IP address automatically.

APM (advanced power management) BIOS routines that enable the CPU to turn selected peripherals on and off.

applet Generic term for a program in the Windows Control Panel.

archive To copy programs and data onto a relatively inexpensive storage medium (disk, tape, etc.) for long-term retention.

archive attribute Attribute of a file that shows whether the file has been backed up since the last change. Each time a file is opened, changed, or saved, the archive bit is turned on. Some types of backups turn off this archive bit to indicate that a good backup of the file exists on tape.

ARP (Address Resolution Protocol) Protocol in the TCP/IP suite used with the command-line utility of the same name to determine the MAC address that corresponds to a particular IP address.

ASCII (American Standard Code for Information Interchange) Industry-standard 8-bit characters used to define text characters, consisting of 96 upper- and lowercase letters, plus 32 nonprinting control characters, each of which is numbered. These numbers were designed to achieve uniformity among computer devices for printing and the exchange of simple text documents.

aspect ratio Ratio of width to height of an object. Standard television has a 4:3 aspect ratio.

ASR (Automated System Recovery) Windows XP tool designed to recover a badly corrupted Windows system; similar to ERD.

assertive communication Means of communication that is not pushy or bossy but is also not soft. Useful in dealing with upset customers as it both defuses their anger and gives them confidence that you know what you're doing.

AT (Advanced Technology) Model name of the second-generation, 80286-based IBM computer. Many aspects of the AT, such as the BIOS, CMOS, and expansion bus, have become de facto standards in the PC industry. The physical organization of the components on the motherboard is called the AT form factor.

ATA (AT Attachment) Type of hard drive and controller designed to replace the earlier ST506 and ESDI drives without requiring replacement of the AT BIOS—hence, AT attachment. These drives are more popularly known as IDE drives. (*See* IDE.) The **ATA/33** standard has drive transfer speeds up to 33 MBps; the **ATA/66** up to 66 MBps; the **ATA/100** up to 100 MBps; and the **ATA/133** up to 133 MBps. (*See* Ultra DMA.)

ATA/ATAPI-6 Also known as ATA-6 or "Big Drive." Replaced the INT13 extensions and allowed for hard drives as large as 144 petabytes (144 million GBs).

ATAPI (ATA packet interface) Series of standards that enable mass storage devices other than hard drives to use the IDE/ATA controllers. Popular with optical drives. (*See* EIDE.)

ATAPI-compliant Devices that utilize the ATAPI standard. (*See* ATAPI.)

Athlon Name used for a popular series of CPUs manufactured by AMD.

ATTRIB.EXE Command used to view the specific properties of a file; can also be used to modify or remove file properties, such as read-only, system, or archive.

attributes Values in a file that determine the hidden, read-only, system, and archive status of the file.

ATX (AT eXtended) Popular motherboard form factor that generally replaced the AT form factor.

authentication Any method a computer uses to determine who can access it.

authorization Any method a computer uses to determine what an authenticated user can do.

autodetection Process through which new disks are automatically recognized by the BIOS.

Automatic Updates Feature allowing updates to Windows to be retrieved automatically over the Internet.

AutoPlay Windows 2000/XP/Vista/7 setting, along with autorun.inf, enabling Windows to automatically detect media files and begin using them. (*See* AUTORUN.INF.)

AUTORUN.INF File included on some media that automatically launches a program or installation routine when the media is inserted/attached to a system.

autosensing Better quality sound cards use autosensing to detect a device plugged into a port and to adapt the features of that port.

auto-switching power supply Type of power supply able to detect the voltage of a particular outlet and adjust accordingly.

Award Software Major producer of BIOS software for motherboards.

backlight One of three main components used in LCDs to illuminate an image.

backside bus Set of wires that connect the CPU to Level 2 cache. First appearing in the Pentium Pro, all modern CPUs have a backside bus. Some buses run at the full speed of the CPU, whereas others run at a fraction. Earlier Pentium IIs, for example, had backside buses running at half the speed of the processor. (*See also* frontside bus and external data bus.)

Backup or Restore Wizard Utility contained within Windows that allows users to create system backups and set system restore points.

ball mouse Input device that enables users to manipulate a cursor on the screen by using a ball and sensors that detect the movement and direction of the ball.

bandwidth Piece of the spectrum occupied by some form of signal, such as television, voice, fax data. Signals require a certain size and location of bandwidth to be transmitted. The higher the bandwidth, the faster the signal transmission, allowing for a more complex signal such as audio or video. Because bandwidth is a limited space, when one user is occupying it, others must wait their turn. Bandwidth is also the capacity of a network to transmit a given amount of data during a given period.

bank Total number of SIMMs or DIMMs that can be accessed simultaneously by the chipset. The "width" of the external data bus divided by the "width" of the SIMM or DIMM sticks. DIMM slots must be populated to activate dual- or triple-channel memory.

bar code reader Tool to read Universal Product Code (UPC) bar codes.

basic disks Hard drive partitioned in the "classic" way with a master boot record (MBR) and partition table. (*See also* dynamic disks.)

baud One analog cycle on a telephone line. In the early days of telephone data transmission, the baud rate was often analogous to bits per second. Due to advanced modulation of baud cycles as well as data compression, this is no longer true.

BD-RE (Blu-ray Disc-REwritable) Blu-ray Disc equivalent of the rewritable DVD, allows writing and rewriting several times on the same BD. (*See* Blu-ray Disc.)

BD-ROM Blu-ray Disc equivalent of a DVD-ROM or CD-ROM. (*See* Blu-ray Disc.)

beaming Term used to describe transferring data from one PDA to another by means of IrDA.

beep codes Series of audible tones produced by a motherboard during the POST. These tones identify whether the POST has completed successfully or whether some piece of system hardware is not working properly. Consult the manual for your particular motherboard for a specific list of beep codes.

binary numbers Number system with a base of 2, unlike the number systems most of us use that have bases of 10 (decimal numbers), 12 (measurement in feet and inches), and 60 (time). Binary numbers are preferred for computers for precision and economy. An electronic circuit that can detect the difference between two states (on–off, 0–1) is easier and more inexpensive to build than one that could detect the differences among ten states (0–9).

biometric device Hardware device used to support authentication; works by scanning and remembering unique aspects of a user's various body parts (e.g., retina, iris, face, or fingerprint) by using some form of sensing device such as a retinal scanner.

BIOS (basic input/output system) Classically, software routines burned onto the system ROM of a PC. More commonly seen as any software that directly controls a particular piece of hardware. A set of programs encoded in read-only memory (ROM) on computers.

These programs handle startup operations and low-level control of hardware such as disk drives, the keyboard, and monitor.

bit   Single binary digit. Also, any device that can be in an on or off state.

BitLocker Drive Encryption   Drive encryption software offered in Windows Vista/7 Ultimate and Enterprise editions. BitLocker requires a special chip to validate hardware status and to ensure that the computer hasn't been hacked.

bit depth   Number of colors a video card is capable of producing. Common bit depths are 16-bit and 32-bit, representing 65,536 colors and 16.7 million colors, respectively.

Bluetooth   Wireless technology designed to create small wireless networks preconfigured to do specific jobs, but not meant to replace full-function networks or Wi-Fi.

Blu-ray Disc (BD)   Optical disc format that stores 25 or 50 GB of data, designed to be the replacement media for DVD. Competed with HD DVD.

boot   To initiate an automatic routine that clears the memory, loads the operating system, and prepares the computer for use. Term is derived from "pull yourself up by your bootstraps." PCs must do that because RAM doesn't retain program instructions when power is turned off. A cold boot occurs when the PC is physically switched on. A warm boot loads a fresh OS without turning off the computer, lessening the strain on the electronic circuitry. To do a warm boot, press the CTRL-ALT-DELETE keys twice in rapid succession (the three-fingered salute).

boot sector   First sector on a PC hard drive or floppy disk, track 0. The boot-up software in ROM tells the computer to load whatever program is found there. If a system disk is read, the program in the boot record directs the computer to the root directory to load the operating system.

BOOT.INI   Text file used during the boot process that provides a list of all OSs currently installed and available for NTLDR. Also tells where each OS is located on the system. Used in Windows XP and earlier Microsoft operating systems.

bootable disk   Disk that contains a functional operating system; can also be a floppy disk, USB thumb drive, or optical disc.

bootstrap loader   Segment of code in a system's BIOS that scans for an operating system, looks specifically for a valid boot sector, and, when one is found, hands control over to the boot sector; then the bootstrap loader removes itself from memory.

bps (bits per second)   Measurement of how fast data is moved from one place to another. A 56K modem can move ~56,000 bits per second.

broadband   Commonly understood as a reference to high-speed, always-on communication links that can move large files much more quickly than a regular phone line.

browser   Program specifically designed to retrieve, interpret, and display Web pages.

BSoD (Blue Screen of Death)   Infamous error screen that appears when Windows encounters an unrecoverable error.

BTX (Balanced Technology eXtended)   Motherboard form factor designed as an improvement over ATX.

buffered/registered DRAM   Usually seen in motherboards supporting more than four sticks of RAM, it is required to address interference issues caused by the additional sticks.

buffer underrun   Inability of a source device to provide a CD-burner with a constant stream of data while burning a CD-R or CD-RW.

bug   Programming error that causes a program or a computer system to perform erratically, produce incorrect results, or crash. The term was coined when a real bug was found in one of the circuits of one of the first ENIAC computers.

burn   Process of writing data to a writable optical disc, such as a DVD-R.

burn-in failure   Critical failure usually associated with manufacturing defects.

bus   Series of wires connecting two or more separate electronic devices, enabling those devices to communicate.

bus mastering   Circuitry allowing devices to avoid conflicts on the external data bus.

bus topology   Network configuration wherein all computers connect to the network via a central bus cable.

byte Unit of eight bits; fundamental data unit of personal computers. Storing the equivalent of one character, the byte is also the basic unit of measurement for computer storage.

CAB files Short for cabinet files. These files are compressed and most commonly used during OS installation to store many smaller files, such as device drivers.

cache (disk) Special area of RAM that stores the data most frequently accessed from the hard drive. Cache memory can optimize the use of your systems.

cache (L1, L2, L3, etc.) Special section of fast memory, usually built into the CPU, used by the onboard logic to store information most frequently accessed by the CPU.

calibration Process of matching the print output of a printer to the visual output of a monitor.

card reader Device with which you can read data from one of several types of flash memory.

card services Uppermost level of PCMCIA services. Card services level recognizes the function of a particular PC Card and provides the specialized drivers necessary to make the card work. (*See also* socket services.)

CardBus 32-bit PC cards that can support up to eight devices on each card. Electrically incompatible with earlier PC cards (3.3 V versus 5 V).

CAT 5 Category 5 wire; a TIA/EIA standard for UTP wiring that can operate up to 100 megabits per second.

CAT 5e Category 5e wire; TIA/EIA standard for UTP wiring that can operate up to 1 gigabit per second.

CAT 6 Category 6 wire; TIA/EIA standard for UTP wiring that can operate up to 10 gigabits per second.

catastrophic failure Occurs when a component or whole system will not boot; usually related to a manufacturing defect of a component. Could also be caused by overheating and physical damage to computer components.

CCFL (cold cathode fluorescent lamp) Light technology used in LCDs and flatbed scanners. CCFLs use relatively little power for the amount of light they provide.

CD (CHDIR) Shorthand for "Change Directory." Allows you to change the focus of the command prompt from one directory to another.

CD (compact disc) Originally designed as the replacement for vinyl records, CDs have become the primary method of long-term storage of music and data.

CD quality CD-quality audio has a sample rate of 44.4 KHz and a bit rate of 128 bits.

CDDA (CD-Digital Audio) Special format used for early CD-ROMs and all audio CDs; divides data into variable length tracks. A good format to use for audio tracks but terrible for data because of lack of error checking.

CD-R (compact disc recordable) CD technology that accepts a single "burn" but cannot be erased after the one burn.

CD-ROM (compact disc/read only memory) Read-only compact storage disk for audio or video data. Recordable devices, such as CD-Rs, are updated versions of the older CD-ROM players. CD-ROMs are read by using CD-ROM drives.

CD-RW (compact disc rewritable) CD technology that accepts multiple reads/writes like a hard drive.

Celeron Lower-cost brand of Intel CPUs.

Cellular WAN Technology that allows laptops and other mobile devices to access the Internet over a cell phone network.

cellular wireless networks Networks that enable cell phones, PDAs, and other mobile devices to connect to the Internet.

Centrino Marketing name for an Intel laptop solution including the mobile processor, support chips and wireless networking.

Centronics connector Connector used with older printers.

certification License that demonstrates competency in some specialized skill.

Certified Cisco Network Associate (CCNA) One of the certifications demonstrating a knowledge of Cisco networking products.

CHAP (Challenge Handshake Authentication Protocol) Common remote access protocol; serving system challenges the remote client, usually by means of asking for a password.

chassis intrusion detection Feature offered in some chassis that trips a switch when the chassis is opened.

chipset Electronic chips, specially designed to work together, that handle all of the low-level functions of a PC. In the original PC, the chipset consisted of close to 30 different chips; today, chipsets usually consist of one, two, or three separate chips embedded into a motherboard.

CHKDSK (Checkdisk) Hard drive error detection and, to a certain extent, correction utility in Windows. Originally a DOS command (CHKDSK.EXE); also the executable for the graphical Error-checking tool.

clean installation Operating system installed on a fresh drive, following a reformat of that drive. Often the only way to correct a problem with a system when many of the crucial operating system files have become corrupted.

client Computer program that uses the services of another computer program. Software that extracts information from a server; your auto-dial phone is a client, and the phone company is its server. Also, a machine that accesses shared resources on a server.

client/server Relationship in which client software obtains services from a server on behalf of a person.

client/server network Network that has dedicated server machines and client machines.

clock cycle Single charge to the clock wire of a CPU.

clock-multiplying CPU CPU that takes the incoming clock signal and multiples it inside the CPU to let the internal circuitry of the CPU run faster.

clock speed Speed at which a CPU executes instructions, measured in MHz or GHz. In modern CPUs, the internal speed is a multiple of the external speed. (*See also* clock-multiplying CPU.)

clock (CLK) wire Charge on the CLK wire to tell the CPU that another piece of information is waiting to be processed.

cluster Basic unit of storage on a floppy or hard disk. Multiple sectors are contained in a cluster. When Windows stores a file on a disk, it writes those files into dozens or even hundreds of contiguous clusters. If there aren't enough contiguous open clusters available, the operating system finds the next open cluster and writes there, continuing this process until the entire file is saved. The FAT or MFT tracks how the files are distributed among the clusters on the disk.

CMOS (complementary metal-oxide semiconductor) Originally, the type of nonvolatile RAM that held information about the most basic parts of your PC, such as hard drives, floppies, and amount of DRAM. Today, actual CMOS chips have been replaced by Flash-type nonvolatile RAM. The information is the same, however, and is still called CMOS—even though it is now almost always stored on Flash RAM.

CMOS setup program Program enabling you to access and update CMOS data.

CNR (Communications and Network Riser) Proprietary slot used on some motherboards to provide a sound inference–free connection for modems, sound cards, and NICs.

coaxial cable Cabling in which an internal conductor is surrounded by another, outer conductor, thus sharing the same axis.

code Set of symbols representing characters (e.g., ASCII code) or instructions in a computer program (a programmer writes source code, which must be translated into executable or machine code for the computer to use).

codec (compressor/decompressor) Software that compresses or decompresses media streams.

color depth Term to define a scanner's ability to produce color, hue, and shade.

COM port(s) Serial communications ports available on your computer. When used as a program extension, .COM indicates an executable program file limited to 64 KB.

command A request, typed from a terminal or embedded in a file, to perform an operation or to execute a particular program.

command prompt Text prompt for entering commands.

command-line interface User interface for an OS devoid of all graphical trappings.

CompactFlash (CF) One of the older but still popular flash media formats. Its interface uses a simplified PC Card bus, so it also supports I/O devices.

compatibility modes Feature of Windows 2000 and beyond to allow software written for previous versions of Windows to operate in newer operating systems.

compliance Concept that members of an organization must abide by the rules of that organization. For a technician, this often revolves around what software can or cannot be installed on an organization's computer.

component failure Occurs when a system device fails due to manufacturing or some other type of defect.

compression Process of squeezing data to eliminate redundancies, allowing files to use less space when stored or transmitted.

CompTIA A+ 220-701 (Essentials) One half of the CompTIA A+ exam, concentrating on understanding terminology and technology, how to do fundamental tasks, and basic Windows operating system support.

CompTIA A+ 220-702 (Practical Application) The other half of the CompTIA A+ exam, covering advanced troubleshooting and configuration.

CompTIA A+ certification Industry-wide, vendor-neutral computer certification program that demonstrates competency as a computer technician.

CompTIA Network+ certification Industry-wide, vendor-neutral certification for network technicians, covering network hardware, installation, and trouble-shooting.

Computer (Vista) Default interface in Windows Vista and 7 for Windows Explorer; displays drives and network locations. (*See* My Computer.)

Computer Administrator One of three types of user accounts, the Administrator account has access to all resources on the computer.

Computer Management Applet in Windows' Administrative Tools that contains several useful snap-ins, such as Device Manager and Disk Management.

computing process Four parts of a computer's operation: input, processing, output, and storage.

Computing Technology Industry Association (CompTIA) Nonprofit IT trade association that administers the CompTIA A+ and CompTIA Network+ exams.

conditioning charger Battery charger that contains intelligent circuitry that prevents portable computer batteries from being overcharged and damaged.

connectors Small receptacles used to attach cables to a system. Common types of connectors include USB, PS/2, and DB-25.

consumables Materials used up by printers, including paper, ink, ribbons, and toner cartridges.

container file File containing two or more separate, compressed tracks, typically an audio and a moving picture track. Also known as a wrapper.

context menu Small menu brought up by right-clicking on objects in Windows.

Control Panel Collection of Windows applets, or small programs, that can be used to configure various pieces of hardware and software in a system.

controller card Card adapter that connects devices, such as a disk drive, to the main computer bus/motherboard.

convergence Measure of how sharply a single pixel appears on a CRT; a monitor with poor convergence produces images that are not sharply defined.

copy backup Type of backup similar to Normal or Full, in that all selected files on a system are backed up. This type of backup does not change the archive bit of the files being backed up.

COPY command Command in the command-line interface for making a copy of a file and pasting it in another location.

Core Name used for the family of Intel CPUs that succeeded the Pentium 4.

counter Used to track data about a particular object when using the Performance console.

CPU (central processing unit) "Brain" of the computer. Microprocessor that handles primary calculations for the computer. CPUs are known by names such as Core i5 and Phenom.

CRC (cyclic redundancy check) Very accurate mathematical method used to check for errors in long streams of transmitted data. Before data is sent, the main computer uses the data to calculate a CRC value from the data's contents. If the receiver calculates a CRC value different from the received data, the data was corrupted during transmission and is re-sent. Ethernet packets have a CRC code.

C-RIMM or CRIMM (continuity RIMM) Passive device added to populate unused banks in a system that uses Rambus RIMMs.

crossover cable Special UTP cable used to connect hubs or to connect network cards without a hub. Crossover cables reverse the sending and receiving wire pairs from one end to the other.

CRT (cathode ray tube) Tube of a monitor in which rays of electrons are beamed onto a phosphorescent screen to produce images. Also a shorthand way to describe a monitor that uses CRT rather than LCD technology.

CSMA/CA (carrier sense multiple access with collision avoidance) Networking scheme used by wireless devices to transmit data while avoiding data collisions, which wireless nodes have difficulty detecting.

CSMA/CD (carrier sense multiple access with collision detection) Networking scheme used by Ethernet devices to transmit data and resend data after detecting data collisions.

cylinder Single track on all the platters in a hard drive. Imagine a hard drive as a series of metal cans, nested one inside another; a single can would represent a cylinder.

daily backup Backup of all files that have been changed on that day without changing the archive bits of those files. Also called *daily copy backup*.

daisy-chaining Method of connecting several devices along a bus and managing the signals for each device.

data classification System of organizing data according to its sensitivity. Common classifications include public, highly confidential, and top secret.

data structure Scheme that directs how an OS stores and retrieves data on and off a drive. Used interchangeably with the term file system. (*See also* file system.)

DB connectors D-shaped connectors used for a variety of connections in the PC and networking world. Can be male (with prongs) or female (with holes) and have a varying number of pins or sockets. Also called *D-sub*, *D-subminiature*, or *D-shell connectors*.

DB-15 A two- or three-row DB connector (female) used for 10Base5 networks, MIDI/joysticks, and analog video.

DB-25 connector DB connector (female), commonly referred to as a parallel port connector.

DC (direct current) Type of electricity in which the flow of electrons is in a complete circle in one direction.

DDR SDRAM (double data rate SDRAM) Type of DRAM that makes two processes for every clock cycle. (*See also* DRAM.)

DDR2 SDRAM Type of SDRAM that sends four bits of data in every clock cycle. (*See also* DDR SDRAM.)

DDR3 SDRAM Type of SDRAM that transfers data at twice the rate of DDR2 SDRAM.

debug To detect, trace, and eliminate errors in computer programs.

decibels Unit of measurement typically associated with sound. The higher the number of decibels, the louder the sound.

dedicated server Machine that is not used for any client functions, only server functions.

default gateway In a TCP/IP network, the nearest router to a particular host. This router's IP address is part of the necessary TCP/IP configuration for communicating with multiple networks using IP.

definition file List of virus signatures that an antivirus program can recognize.

defragmentation (DEFRAG) Procedure in which all the files on a hard disk are rewritten on disk so that all parts of each file reside in contiguous clusters. The result is an improvement in disk speed during retrieval operations.

degauss Procedure used to break up the electromagnetic fields that can build up on the cathode ray tube of a monitor; involves running a current through a wire loop. Most monitors feature a manual degaussing tool.

DEL (Erase) command Command in the command-line interface used to delete/erase files.

desktop User's primary interface to the Windows operating system.

desktop extender Portable computer that offers some of the features of a full-fledged desktop computer but with a much smaller footprint and lower weight.

desktop replacement Portable computer that offers the same performance as a full-fledged desktop computer; these systems are normally very heavy to carry and often cost much more than the desktop systems they replace.

device driver Program used by the operating system to control communications between the computer and peripherals.

Device Manager Utility that enables techs to examine and configure all the hardware and drivers in a Windows PC.

DHCP (Dynamic Host Configuration Protocol) Protocol that enables a DHCP server to set TCP/IP settings automatically for a DHCP client.

differential backup Similar to an incremental backup. Backs up the files that have been changed since the last backup. This type of backup does not change the state of the archive bit.

digital camera Camera that simulates film technology electronically.

digital certificate Form in which a public key is sent from a Web server to a Web browser so that the browser can decrypt the data sent by the server.

digital zoom Software tool to enhance the optical zoom capabilities of a digital camera.

digitally signed driver All drivers designed specifically for Windows are digitally signed, meaning they are tested to work stably with these operating systems.

DIMM (dual inline memory module) 32- or 64-bit type of DRAM packaging, similar to SIMMs, with the distinction that each side of each tab inserted into the system performs a separate function. DIMMs come in a variety of sizes, with 184- and 240-pin being the most common on desktop computers.

dipole antennae Standard straight-wire antennae that provide the most omnidirectional function.

DIR command Command used in the command-line interface to display the entire contents of the current working directory.

directory Another name for a folder.

directory service Centralized index that each PC accesses to locate resources in the domain.

DirectX Set of APIs enabling programs to control multimedia, such as sound, video, and graphics. Used in Windows Vista to draw the Aero desktop.

Disk Cleanup Utility built into Windows that can help users clean up their disks by removing temporary Internet files, deleting unused program files, and more.

disk cloning Taking a PC and making duplicates of the hard drive, including all data, software, and configuration files and transferring it to another PC. (*See* image installation.)

disk duplexing Type of disk mirroring using two separate controllers rather than one; faster than traditional mirroring.

Disk Management Snap-in available with the Microsoft Management Console that enables techs to configure the various disks installed in a system; available in the Computer Management Administrative Tool.

disk mirroring Process by which data is written simultaneously to two or more disk drives. Read and write speed is decreased but redundancy in case of catastrophe is increased.

disk quota Application allowing network administrators to limit hard drive space usage.

disk striping Process by which data is spread among multiple (at least two) drives. Increases speed for both reads and writes of data. Considered RAID level 0 because it does not provide fault tolerance.

disk striping with parity Method for providing fault tolerance by writing data across multiple drives and then including an additional drive, called a parity drive, that stores information to rebuild the data contained on the other drives. Requires at least three physical disks: two for the data and a third for the parity drive. This provides data redundancy at RAID levels 3–5 with different options.

disk thrashing Hard drive that is constantly being accessed due to lack of available system memory. When system memory runs low, a Windows system will utilize hard disk space as "virtual" memory, thus causing an unusual amount of hard drive access.

display adapter Handles all the communication between the CPU and the monitor. Also known as a video card.

Display applet Tool in Windows 2000 and Windows XP used to adjust display settings, including resolution, refresh rate, driver information, and color depth.

DMA (direct memory access) modes Technique that some PC hardware devices use to transfer data to and from the memory without using the CPU.

DMA controller Resides between the RAM and the devices and handles DMA requests.

DNS (domain name system) TCP/IP name resolution system that translates a host name into an IP address.

DNS domain Specific branch of the DNS name space. First-level DNS domains include .COM, .GOV, and .EDU.

docking station Device that provides a portable computer extra features such as a DVD drive or PC Card, in addition to legacy and modern ports. Similar to a port replicator.

document Steps a technician uses to solve a problem: To record the relevant information. For a technician, this would be recording each troubleshooting job: what the problem was, how it was fixed, and other helpful information.

Documents folder Windows Vista/7 folder for storing user-created files. Replaces the My Documents folder previously used in Windows 2000/XP. (*See* My Documents.)

Dolby Digital Technology for sound reductions and channeling methods used for digital audio.

domain Groupings of users, computers, or networks. In Microsoft networking, a domain is a group of computers and users that share a common account database, called a SAM, and a common security policy. On the Internet, a domain is a group of computers that share a common element in their hierarchical name. Other types of domains exist—e.g., broadcast domain, etc.

domain-based network Network that eliminates the need for logging in to multiple servers by using domain controllers to hold the security database for all systems.

DOS (Disk Operating System) First popular operating system available for PCs. A text-based, single-tasking operating system that was not completely replaced until the introduction of Windows 95.

dot pitch Value relating to CRTs, showing the diagonal distance between phosphors measured in millimeters.

dot-matrix printer Printer that creates each character from an array of dots. Pins striking a ribbon against the paper, one pin for each dot position, form the dots. May be a serial printer (printing one character at a time) or a line printer.

double-sided RAM RAM stick with RAM chips soldered to both sides of the stick. May only be used with motherboards designed to accept double-sided RAM. Very common.

DPI (dots per inch) Measure of printer resolution that counts the dots the device can produce per linear (horizontal) inch.

DPMS (Display Power-Management Signaling) Specification that can reduce CRT power consumption by 75 percent by reducing/eliminating video signals during idle periods.

DRAM (dynamic random access memory or dynamic RAM) Memory used to store data in most personal computers. DRAM stores each bit in a "cell" composed of a transistor and a capacitor. Because the capacitor in a DRAM cell can only hold a charge for a few milliseconds, DRAM must be continually refreshed, or rewritten, to retain its data.

DriveLock CMOS program enabling you to control the ATA security mode feature set. Also known as *drive lock*.

driver signing Digital signature for drivers used by Windows to protect against potentially bad drivers.

DS3D (DirectSound3D) Introduced with DirectX 3.0, DS3D is a command set used to create positional audio, or sounds that appear to come from in front, in back, or to the side of a user. (*See also* DirectX.)

DSL (digital subscriber line) High-speed Internet connection technology that uses a regular telephone line for connectivity. DSL comes in several varieties, including asynchronous (ADSL) and synchronous (SDSL), and many speeds. Typical home-user DSL connections are ADSL with a download speed of 7 Mbps and an upload speed of 512 Kbps.

D-subminiature *See* DB connectors.

DTS (Digital Theatre Systems) Technology for sound reductions and channeling methods, similar to Dolby Digital.

dual boot Refers to a computer with two operating systems installed, enabling users to choose which operating system to load on boot. Can also refer to kicking a device a second time just in case the first time didn't work.

DualView   Microsoft feature enbling Windows to use two or more monitors simultaneously.

dual-channel architecture   Using two sticks of RAM (either RDRAM or DDR) to increase throughput.

dual-channel memory   Form of DDR, DDR2, and DDR3 memory access used by many motherboards that requires two identical sticks of DDR, DDR2, or DDR3 RAM.

dual-core   Dual-core CPUs have two execution units on the same physical chip but share caches and RAM.

dual-scan passive matrix   Manufacturing technique for increasing display updates by refreshing two lines at a time.

dumpster diving   To go through someone's trash in search of information.

DUN (Dial-Up Networking)   Software used by Windows to govern the connection between the modem and the ISP.

duplexing   Similar to mirroring in that data is written to and read from two physical drives, for fault tolerance. Separate controllers are used for each drive, both for additional fault tolerance and additional speed. Considered RAID level 1. Also called *disk duplexing* or *drive duplexing*.

Duron   Lower-cost version of AMD's Athlon series of CPUs.

DVD (digital versatile disc)   Optical disc format that provides for 4–17 GB of video or data storage.

DVD-ROM   DVD equivalent of the standard CD-ROM.

DVD-RW   Rewritable DVD media.

DVD-Video   DVD format used exclusively to store digital video; capable of storing over 2 hours of high-quality video on a single DVD.

DVI (Digital Visual Interface)   Special video connector designed for digital-to-digital connections; most commonly seen on PC video cards and LCD monitors. Some versions also support analog signals with a special adapter.

Dxdiag (DirectX Diagnostics)   Diagnostic tool for getting information about and testing a computer's DirectX version.

dye-sublimation printers   Printer that uses a roll of heat-sensitive plastic film embedded with dyes, which are vaporized and then solidified onto specially coated paper to create a high-quality image.

dynamic disks   Special feature of Windows that enables users to span a single volume across two or more drives. Dynamic disks do not have partitions; they have volumes. Dynamic disks can be striped, mirrored, and striped or mirrored with parity.

EAX (Environment Audio eXtensions)   3-D sound technology developed by Creative Labs but now supported by most sound cards.

ECC (error correction code)   Special software, embedded on hard drives, that constantly scans the drives for bad sectors.

ECC RAM/DRAM (error correction code DRAM)   RAM that uses special chips to detect and fix memory errors. Commonly used in high-end servers where data integrity is crucial.

effective permissions   User's combined permissions granted by multiple groups.

EFI (Extensible Firmware Interface)   Firmware created by Intel and HP that replaced traditional 16-bit BIOS and added several new enhancements.

EFS (encrypting file system)   Encryption tool found in NTFS 5.

EIA/TIA   *See* TIA/EIA.

EIDE (enhanced IDE)   Marketing concept of hard drive–maker Western Digital, encompassing four improvements for IDE drives, including drives larger than 528 MB, four devices, increase in drive throughput, and non–hard drive devices. (*See* ATAPI, PIO mode.)

electrostatic discharge (ESD)   Movement of electrons from one body to another. A real menace to PCs, as it can cause permanent damage to semiconductors.

eliciting answers   Communication strategy designed to help techs understand a user's problems better. Works by listening to a user's description of a problem and then asking cogent questions.

e-mail (electronic mail)   Messages, usually text, sent from one person to another via computer. Can also be sent automatically to a group of addresses (mailing list).

electromagnetic interference (EMI)   Electrical interference from one device to another, resulting in poor performance of the device being interfered with. Examples: Static on your TV while running a blow dryer, or placing two monitors too close together and getting a "shaky" screen.

emergency repair disk (ERD)   Saves critical boot files and partition information and is the main tool for fixing boot problems in Windows 2000.

encryption   Making data unreadable by those who do not possess a key or password.

erase lamp   Component inside laser printers that uses light to make the coating of the photosensitive drum conductive.

Error-checking   Windows XP/Vista/7 name for the Checkdisk and ScanDisk tools.

eSATA   Serial ATA-based connector for external hard drives and optical drives.

escalate   Process used when person assigned to repair a problem is not able to get the job done, such as sending the problem to someone else.

Ethernet   Name coined by Xerox for the first standard of network cabling and protocols. Based on a bus topology.

Ethic of Reciprocity   Golden Rule: Do unto others as you would have them do unto you.

EULA (end-user license agreement)   Agreement that accompanies a piece of software, to which user must agree before using the software. Outlines the terms of use for the software and also lists any actions on the part of the user that violate the agreement.

event auditing   Feature of Event Viewer's Security section that creates an entry in the Security Log when certain events happen, such as a user logging on.

Event Viewer   Utility made available as an MMC snap-in that enables users to monitor various system events, including network bandwidth usage and CPU utilization.

EXPAND   Command-line utility program included with Windows used to access files within CAB files.

expansion bus   Set of wires going to the CPU, governed by the expansion bus crystal, directly connected to expansion slots of varying types (PCI, AGP, PCIe, etc.). Depending on the type of slots, the expansion bus runs

at a percentage of the main system speed (8.33–133 MHz).

expansion bus crystal   Controls the speed of the expansion bus.

expansion slots   Connectors on a motherboard that enable users to add optional components to a system. (*See also* AGP and PCI.)

ExpressCard   Serial PC Card designed to replace CardBus PC Cards. ExpressCards connect to either a Hi-Speed USB (480 Mbps) or PCI Express (2.5 Gbps) bus.

extended partition   Type of non-bootable hard disk partition. May only have one extended partition per disk. Purpose is to divide a large disk into smaller partitions, each with a separate drive letter.

extension   Three or four letters that follow a filename and identify the type of file. Common file extensions are .ZIP, .EXE, and .DOC.

external data bus (EDB)   Primary data highway of all computers. Everything in your computer is tied either directly or indirectly to the external data bus. (*See also* frontside bus and backside bus.)

fast user switching   Account option that is useful when multiple users share a system; allows users to switch without logging off.

FAT (file allocation table)   Hidden table that records how files on a hard disk are stored in distinct clusters; the only way DOS knows where to access files. Address of first cluster of a file is stored in the directory file. FAT entry for the first cluster is the address of the second cluster used to store that file. In the entry for the second cluster for that file is the address for the third cluster, and so on until the final cluster, which gets a special end-of-file code. There are two FATs, mirror images of each other, in case one is destroyed or damaged.

FAT32   File allocation table that uses 32 bits for addressing clusters. Commonly used with Windows 98 and Windows Me systems. Some Windows 2000 Professional and Windows XP systems also use FAT32, although most modern Windows systems use the more robust NTFS.

FDISK   Disk-partitioning utility included with Windows.

fiber optics   High-speed channel for transmitting data, made of high-purity glass sealed within an opaque tube. Much faster than conventional copper wire such as coaxial cable.

file Collection of any form of data that is stored beyond the time of execution of a single job. A file may contain program instructions or data, which may be numerical, textual, or graphical information.

file allocation unit Another term for cluster. (*See also* cluster.)

file association Windows term for the proper program to open a particular file; for example, file association for opening .MP3 programs might be Winamp.

file format How information is encoded in a file. Two primary types are binary (pictures) and ASCII (text), but within those are many formats, such as BMP and GIF for pictures. Commonly represented by a suffix at the end of the filename; for example, .txt for a text file or .exe for an executable.

file server Computer designated to store software, courseware, administrative tools, and other data on a local- or wide-area network. It "serves" this information to other computers via the network when users enter their personal access codes.

file system Scheme that directs how an OS stores and retrieves data on and off a drive; FAT32 and NTFS are both file systems. Used interchangeably with the term "data structure." (*See also* data structure.)

filename Name assigned to a file when the file is first written on a disk. Every file on a disk within the same folder must have a unique name. Filenames can contain any character (including spaces), except the following: \ / : * ? " < > |

firewall Device that restricts traffic between a local network and the Internet.

FireWire (IEEE 1394) Interconnection standard to send wide-band signals over a serialized, physically thin connector system. Serial bus developed by Apple and Texas Instruments; enables connection of 63 devices at speeds up to 800 megabits per second.

firmware Embedded programs or code stored on a ROM chip. Generally OS-independent, thus allowing devices to operate in a wide variety of circumstances without direct OS support. The system BIOS is firmware.

Flash ROM ROM technology that can be electrically reprogrammed while still in the PC. Overwhelmingly the most common storage medium of BIOS in PCs today, as it can be upgraded without a need to open the computer on most systems.

flatbed scanner Most popular form of consumer scanner; runs a bright light along the length of the tray to capture an image.

FlexATX Motherboard form factor. Motherboards built in accordance with the FlexATX form factor are very small, much smaller than microATX motherboards.

Flip 3D In the Aero desktop environment, a three-dimensional replacement for ALT-TAB. Accessed by pressing the WINDOWS KEY-TAB key combination.

floppy disk Removable storage media that can hold between 720 KB and 1.44 MB of data.

floppy drive System hardware that uses removable 3.5-inch disks as storage media.

flux reversal Point at which a read/write head detects a change in magnetic polarity.

FM synthesis Producing sound by electronic emulation of various instruments to more-or-less produce music and other sound effects.

folders list Toggle button in Windows Explorer for Windows 2000 and XP that displays the file structure on the left side of the window. In Windows Vista and 7, the folders list is active by default.

form factor Standard for the physical organization of motherboard components and motherboard size. Most common form factors are ATX and BTX.

FORMAT command Command in the command-line interface used to format a storage device.

formatting Magnetically mapping a disk to provide a structure for storing data; can be done to any type of disk, including a floppy disk, hard disk, or other type of removable disk.

FPU (floating point unit) Formal term for math coprocessor (also called a *numeric processor*) circuitry inside a CPU. A math coprocessor calculates by using a floating point math (which allows for decimals). Before the Intel 80486, FPUs were separate chips from the CPU.

fragmentation Occurs when files and directories get jumbled on a fixed disk and are no longer contiguous. Can significantly slow down hard drive access times and can be repaired by using the DEFRAG utility included with each version of Windows. (*See also* defragmentation (DEFRAG).)

freeware   Software that is distributed for free, with no license fee.

frequency   Measure of a sound's tone, either high or low.

frontside bus   Wires that connect the CPU to the main system RAM. Generally running at speeds of 66–133 MHz. Distinct from the expansion bus and the backside bus, though it shares wires with the former.

front-view projector   Shoots the image out the front and counts on you to put a screen in front at the proper distance.

FRU (field replaceable unit)   Any part of a PC that is considered to be replaceable "in the field," i.e., a customer location. There is no official list of FRUs—it is usually a matter of policy by the repair center.

FTP (File Transfer Protocol)   Protocol used when you transfer a file from one computer to another across the Internet. FTP uses port numbers 20 and 21.

fuel cells   Power source that uses chemical reactions to produce electricity. Lightweight, compact, and stable devices expected to replace batteries as the primary power source for portable PCs.

full-duplex   Any device that can send and receive data simultaneously.

Full-Speed USB   USB standard that runs at 12 Mbps.

fuser assembly   Mechanism in laser printers that uses two rollers to fuse toner to paper during the print process.

gain   Ratio of increase of radio frequency output provided by an antenna, measured in decibels (dB).

GDI (graphical device interface)   Component of Windows that utilizes the CPU rather than the printer to process a print job as a bitmapped image of each page.

general protection fault (GPF)   Error code usually seen when separate active programs conflict on resources or data.

geometry   Numbers representing three values: heads, cylinders, and sectors per track; define where a hard drives stores data.

giga   Prefix for the quantity 1,073,741,824 or for 1 billion. One gigabyte would be 1,073,741,824 bytes, except with hard drive labeling, where it means 1 billion bytes. One gigahertz is 1 billion hertz.

GPU (graphics processing unit)   Specialized processor that helps CPU by taking over all of the 3-D rendering duties.

grayscale depth   Number that defines how many shades of gray the scanner can save per dot.

grayware   Program that intrudes into a user's computer experience without damaging any systems or data.

group   Collection of user accounts that share the same access capabilities.

Group Policy   Means of easily controlling the settings of multiple network clients with policies such as setting minimum password length or preventing Registry edits.

Guest/Guest groups   Very limited built-in account type for Windows.

GUI (graphical user interface)   Interface that enables user to interact with computer graphically, by using a mouse or other pointing device to manipulate icons that represent programs or documents, instead of using only text as in early interfaces. Pronounced "gooey."

HAL (hardware abstraction layer)   Part of the Windows OS that separates system-specific device drivers from the rest of the NT system.

handshaking   Procedure performed by modems, terminals, and computers to verify that communication has been correctly established.

hang   When a computer freezes and does not respond to keyboard commands, it is said to "hang" or to have "hung."

hang time   Number of seconds a too-often-hung computer is airborne after you have thrown it out a second-story window.

hardware   Physical computer equipment such as electrical, electronic, magnetic, and mechanical devices. Anything in the computer world that you can hold in your hand. A floppy drive is hardware; Microsoft Word is not.

hardware protocol   Defines many aspects of a network, from the packet type to the cabling and connectors used.

HBA (host bus adapter)   Connects SATA devices to the expansion bus. Also known as the SATA controller.

HD (Hi-Definition)   Multimedia transmission standard that defines high-resolution images and 5.1, 6.1, and 7.1 sound.

HDA (High-Definition Audio)   Intel-designed standard to support features such as true surround sound with many discrete speakers.

HDD (hard disk drive)   Data-recording system using solid disks of magnetic material turning at high speeds to store and retrieve programs and data in a computer.

HDMI (Hi-Definition Multimedia Interface)   Single multimedia connection that includes both high-definition video and audio. One of the best connections for outputting to television. Also contains copy protection features.

heads   Short for read/write heads; used by hard drives to store data.

heat dope   See thermal compound.

hex (hexadecimal)   Base-16 numbering system using 10 digits (0 through 9) and six letters (A through F). In the computer world, shorthand way to write binary numbers by substituting one hex digit for a four-digit binary number (e.g., hex 9 = binary 1001).

hibernation   Power management setting in which all data from RAM is written to the hard drive before going to sleep. Upon waking up, all information is retrieved from the hard drive and returned to RAM.

hidden attribute   File attribute that, when used, does not allow DIR command to show a file.

hierarchical directory tree   Method by which Windows organizes files into a series of folders, called *directories*, under the root directory. (*See also* root directory.)

high gloss   Laptop screen finish that offers sharper contrast, richer colors, and wider viewing angles than a matte finish, but is also much more reflective.

high-level formatting   Format that sets up a file system on a drive.

high-voltage anode   Component in a CRT monitor that has very high voltages of electricity flowing through it.

Hi-Speed USB   USB standard that runs at 480 Mbps.

honesty   Telling the truth—a very important thing for a tech to do.

host   On a TCP/IP network, single device that has an IP address—any device (usually a computer) that can be the source or destination of a data packet. In the mainframe world, computer that is made available for use by multiple people simultaneously.

hot-swappable   Any hardware that may be attached to or removed from a PC without interrupting the PC's normal processing.

HotSync (synchronization)   Program used by PalmOS-based PDAs to synchronize files between a PDA and a desktop computer.

HRR (horizontal refresh rate)   Amount of time it takes for a CRT to draw one horizontal line of pixels on a display.

HTML (Hypertext Markup Language)   ASCII-based, script-like language for creating hypertext documents such as those on the World Wide Web.

HTTP (Hypertext Transfer Protocol)   Extremely fast protocol used for network file transfers in the WWW environment.

HTTPS (Hypertext Transfer Protocol Secure)   Secure form of HTTP used commonly for Internet business transactions or any time when a secure connection is required. (*See also* HTTP.)

hub   Electronic device that sits at the center of a star topology network, providing a common point for the connection of network devices. Hubs repeat all information out to all ports and have been replaced by switches, although the term is still commonly used.

hyperthreading   CPU feature that enables a single pipeline to run more than one thread at once.

I/O (input/output)   General term for reading and writing data to a computer. "Input" includes data from a keyboard, pointing device (such as a mouse), or loaded from a disk. "Output" includes writing information to a disk, viewing it on a CRT, or printing it to a printer.

I/O addressing   Using the address bus to talk to system devices.

I/O Advanced Programmable Interrupt Controller (IOAPIC)   Typically located in the Southbridge, the IOAPIC acts as the traffic cop for interrupt requests to the CPU.

I/O base address   First value in an I/O address range.

ICH (I/O controller hub)   Official name for Southbridge chip found in Intel's chipsets.

icon   Small image or graphic, most commonly found on a system's desktop, that launches a program when selected.

ICS (Internet Connection Sharing)   Allowing a single network connection to be shared among several machines. ICS was first introduced with Windows 98.

IDE (Integrated Drive Electronics)   PC specification for small- to medium-sized hard drives in which the controlling electronics for the drive are part of the drive itself, speeding up transfer rates and leaving only a simple adapter (or "paddle"). IDE only supported two drives per system of no more than 504 megabytes each, and has been completely supplanted by Enhanced IDE. EIDE supports four drives of over 8 gigabytes each and more than doubles the transfer rate. The more common name for PATA drives. Also known as *intelligent drive electronics*. (*See* PATA.)

Identify the problem.   To question the user and find out what has been changed recently or is no longer working properly. (One of the steps a technician uses to solve a problem.)

IEC-320   Connects the cable supplying AC power from a wall outlet into the power supply.

IEEE (Institute of Electronic and Electrical Engineers)   Leading standards-setting group in the United States.

IEEE 1284   IEEE standard governing parallel communication.

IEEE 1394   IEEE standard governing FireWire communication. (*See also* FireWire.)

IEEE 1394a   FireWire standard that runs at 400 Mbps.

IEEE 1394b   FireWire standard that runs at 800 Mbps

IEEE 802.11   Wireless Ethernet standard more commonly known as Wi-Fi.

image file   Bit-by-bit image of data to be burned on CD or DVD—from one file to an entire disc—stored as a single file on a hard drive. Particularly handy when copying from CD to CD or DVD to DVD.

image installation   Operating system installation that uses a complete image of a hard drive as an installation media. Helpful when installing an operating system on a large number of identical PCs.

impact printer   Uses pins and inked ribbons to print text or images on a piece of paper.

impedance   Amount of resistance to an electrical signal on a wire. Relative measure of the amount of data a cable can handle.

incident report   Record of the details of an accident, including what happened and where it happened.

incremental backup   Backs up all files that have their archive bits turned on, meaning that they have been changed since the last backup. Turns the archive bits off after the files have been backed up.

Information Technology (IT)   Field of computers, their operation, and their maintenance.

infrastructure mode   Wireless networking mode that uses one or more WAPs to connect the wireless network nodes to a wired network segment.

inheritance   NTFS feature that passes on the same permissions in any sub-folders/files resident in the original folder.

ink cartridge   Small container of ink for inkjet printers.

inkjet printer   Uses liquid ink, sprayed through a series of tiny jets, to print text or images on a piece of paper.

installation disc   Typically a CD-ROM or DVD that holds all the necessary device drivers.

instruction set   All of the machine-language commands that a particular CPU is designed to understand.

integrity   Always doing the right thing.

interface   Means by which a user interacts with a piece of software.

Interrupt 13 (INT13) extensions   Improved type of BIOS that accepts EIDE drives up to 137 GB.

interrupt/interruption   Suspension of a process, such as the execution of a computer program, caused by an event external to the computer and performed in such a way that the process can be resumed. Events of this kind include sensors monitoring laboratory equipment or a user pressing an interrupt key.

inverter   Device used to convert DC current into AC. Commonly used with CCFLs in laptops and flatbed scanners.

IP (Internet Protocol)   Internet standard protocol that provides a common layer over dissimilar networks; used to move packets among host computers and through gateways if necessary. Part of the TCP/IP protocol suite.

IP address   Numeric address of a computer connected to the Internet. An IPv4 address is made up of 4 octets of 8-bit binary numbers translated into their shorthand numeric values. An IPv6 address is 128 bits long. The IP address can be broken down into a network ID and a host ID. Also called *Internet address*.

IPCONFIG   Command-line utility for Windows servers and workstations that displays the current TCP/IP configuration of the machine. Similar to WINIPCFG and IFCONFIG.

IPSec (Internet Protocol Security)   Microsoft's encryption method of choice for networks consisting of multiple networks linked by a private connection, providing transparent encryption between the server and the client.

IrDA (Infrared Data Association)   Protocol that enables communication through infrared devices, with speeds of up to 4 Mbps.

IRQ (interrupt request)   Signal from a hardware device, such as a modem or a mouse, indicating that it needs the CPU's attention. In PCs, IRQs are sent along specific IRQ channels associated with a particular device. IRQ conflicts were a common problem in the past when adding expansion boards, but the plug-and-play specification has removed this headache in most cases.

ISA (Industry Standard Architecture)   Industry Standard Architecture design was found in the original IBM PC for the slots that allowed additional hardware to be connected to the computer's motherboard. An 8-bit, 8.33-MHz expansion bus was designed by IBM for its AT computer and released to the public domain. An improved 16-bit bus was also released to the public domain. Replaced by PCI in the mid-1990s.

ISDN (integrated services digital network)   Standard from the CCITT (Comité Consultatif Internationale de Télégraphie et Téléphonie) that defines a digital method for communications to replace the current analog telephone system. ISDN is superior to POTS telephone lines because it supports up to 128 Kbps transfer rate for sending information from computer to computer. It also allows data and voice to share a common phone line. DSL reduced demand for ISDN substantially.

ISO 9660   CD format to support PC file systems on CD media. Supplanted by the Joliet format.

ISO file   Complete copy (or image) of a storage media device, typically used for optical discs.

ISP (Internet service provider)   Company that provides access to the Internet, usually for money.

jack (physical connection)   Part of a connector into which a plug is inserted. Also referred to as ports.

Joliet   Extension of the ISO 9660 format. Most popular CD format to support PC file systems on CD media.

joystick   Peripheral often used while playing computer games; originally intended as a multipurpose input device.

joule   Unit of energy describing (in this book) how much energy a surge suppressor can handle before it fails.

jumper   Pair of small pins that can be shorted with a shunt to configure many aspects of PCs. Usually used in configurations that are rarely changed, such as master/slave settings on IDE drives.

Kerberos   Authentication encryption developed by MIT to enable multiple brands of servers to authenticate multiple brands of clients.

kernel   Core portion of program that resides in memory and performs the most essential operating system tasks.

keyboard   Input device. Three common types of keyboards: those that use a mini-DIN (PS/2) connection, those that use a USB connection, and those that use wireless technology.

Knowledge Base   Large collection of documents and FAQs that is maintained by Microsoft. Found on Microsoft's Web site, the Knowledge Base is an excellent place to search for assistance on most operating system problems.

KVM (keyboard, video, mouse switch)   Hardware device that enables multiple computers to be viewed and controlled by a single mouse, keyboard, and screen.

LAN (local area network)   Group of PCs connected via cabling, radio, or infrared that use this connectivity to share resources such as printers and mass storage.

laptop   Traditional clamshell portable computing device with built-in LCD monitor, keyboard, and trackpad.

laser Single-wavelength, in-phase light source that is sometimes strapped to the head of sharks by bad guys. Note to henchmen: Lasers should never be used with sea bass, no matter how ill-tempered they might be.

laser printer Electro-photographic printer in which a laser is used as the light source.

Last Known Good Configuration Option on the Advanced Startup Options menu that allows your system to revert to a previous configuration to troubleshoot and repair any major system problems.

latency Amount of delay before a device may respond to a request; most commonly used in reference to RAM.

LBA (logical block addressing) Translation (algorithm) of IDE drives promoted by Western Digital as a standardized method for breaking the 504-MB limit in IDE drives. Subsequently adopted universally by the PC industry and now standard on all EIDE drives.

LCD (liquid crystal display) Type of display commonly used on portable PCs. Also have mostly replaced CRTs as the display of choice for most desktop computer users, due in large part to rapidly falling prices and increasing quality. LCDs use liquid crystals and electricity to produce images on the screen.

LED (light-emitting diode) Solid-state device that vibrates at luminous frequencies when current is applied.

Level 1 (L1) cache First RAM cache accessed by the CPU, which stores only the absolute most-accessed programming and data used by currently running threads. Always the smallest and fastest cache on the CPU.

Level 2 (L2) cache Second RAM cache accessed by the CPU. Much larger and often slower than the L1 cache, and accessed only if the requested program/data is not in the L1 cache.

Level 3 (L3) cache Third RAM cache accessed by the CPU. Much larger and slower than the L1 and L2 caches, and accessed only if the requested program/data is not in the L2 cache. Seen only on high-end CPUs.

Li-Ion (lithium-ion) Battery commonly used in portable PCs. Li-Ion batteries don't suffer from the memory effects of Ni-Cd batteries and provide much more power for a greater length of time.

limited account/user User account in Windows XP that has limited access to a system. Accounts of this type cannot alter system files, cannot install new programs, and cannot edit settings by using the Control Panel.

Linux Open-source UNIX-clone operating system.

Local Security Settings Windows tool used to set local security policies on an individual system.

local user account List of users allowed access to a system.

Local Users and Groups Tool enabling creation and changing of group memberships and accounts for users.

log files Files created in Windows to track the progress of certain processes.

logical drives Sections of a hard drive that are formatted and assigned a drive letter, each of which is presented to the user as if it were a separate drive.

login screen First screen of the Windows interface, used to log in to the computer system.

loopback plug Device used during loopback tests to check the female connector on a NIC.

Low-Speed USB USB standard that runs at 1.5 Mbps.

LPT port Commonly referred to as a printer port; usually associated with a local parallel port.

LPX First slimline form factor; replaced by NLX form factor.

lumens Unit of measure for amount of brightness on a projector or other light source.

Mac (Also **Macintosh**.) Apple Computers' flagship operating system, currently up to OS Xv10.6 "Snow Leopard" and running on Intel-based hardware.

MAC (Media Access Control) address Unique 48-bit address assigned to each network card. IEEE assigns blocks of possible addresses to various NIC manufacturers to help ensure that the address is always unique. The Data Link layer of the OSI model uses MAC addresses for locating machines.

MAC address filtering Method of limiting wireless network access based on the physical, hard-wired address of the units' wireless NIC.

machine language   Binary instruction code that is understood by the CPU.

maintenance kits   Commonly replaced printer components provided by many manufacturers.

mass storage   Hard drives, CD-ROMs, removable media drives, etc.

matte   Laptop screen finish that offers a good balance between richness of colors and reflections, but washes out in bright light.

MBR (master boot record)   Tiny bit of code that takes control of the boot process from the system BIOS.

MCC (memory controller chip)   Chip that handles memory requests from the CPU. Although once a special chip, it has been integrated into the chipset on all PCs today.

MCH (memory controller hub)   Intel-coined name for what is now commonly called the Northbridge.

MD (MKDIR) command   Command in the command-line interface used to create directories.

mega-   Prefix that usually stands for the binary quantity 1,048,576 (2^{20}). One megabyte is 1,048,576 bytes. One megahertz, however, is a million hertz. Sometimes shortened to *Meg*, as in "a 286 has an address space of 16 Megs."

megapixel   Term used typically in reference to digital cameras and their ability to capture data.

memory   Device or medium for temporary storage of programs and data during program execution. Synonymous with storage, although it most frequently refers to the internal storage of a computer that can be directly addressed by operating instructions. A computer's temporary storage capacity is measured in kilobytes (KB), megabytes (MB), or gigabytes (GB) of RAM (random-access memory). Long-term data storage on disks is also measured in kilobytes, megabytes, gigabytes, and terabytes.

memory addressing   Taking memory address from system RAM and using it to address nonsystem RAM or ROM so the CPU can access it.

Memory Stick   Sony's flash memory card format; rarely seen outside of Sony devices.

mesh topology   Network topology where each computer has a dedicated line to every other computer, most often used in wireless networks.

MFT (master file table)   Enhanced file allocation table used by NTFS. (*See also* FAT.)

microATX   Variation of the ATX form factor, which uses the ATX power supply. MicroATX motherboards are generally smaller than their ATX counterparts but retain all the same functionality.

microBTX   Variation of the BTX form factor. MicroBTX motherboards are generally smaller than their BTX counterparts but retain all the same functionality.

microprocessor   "Brain" of a computer. Primary computer chip that determines relative speed and capabilities of the computer. Also called *CPU*.

Microsoft Windows Logo Program   Testing program for hardware manufacturers, designed to ensure compatibility with the Windows OS.

MIDI (musical instrument digital interface)   Interface between a computer and a device for simulating musical instruments. Rather than sending large sound samples, a computer can simply send "instructions" to the instrument describing pitch, tone, and duration of a sound. MIDI files are therefore very efficient. Because a MIDI file is made up of a set of instructions rather than a copy of the sound, modifying each component of the file is easy. Additionally, it is possible to program many channels, or "voices" of music to be played simultaneously, creating symphonic sound.

migration   Moving users from one operating system or hard drive to another.

MIMO (multiple in/multiple out)   Feature of 802.11n devices that enables the simultaneous connection of up to four antennae, allowing for increased throughput.

mini-audio connector   Very popular, 1/8-inch diameter connector used to transmit two audio signals; perfect for stereo sound.

mini connector   One type of power connector from a PC power supply unit. Supplies 5 and 12 volts to peripherals. Also known as a floppy connector,

mini PCI   Specialized form of PCI designed for use in laptops.

mini power connector   Connector used to provide power to floppy disk drives.

mini-DIN   Small connection most commonly used for keyboards and mice. Many modern systems implement USB in place of mini-DIN connections. Also called *PS/2*.

mirrored volume   Volume that is mirrored on another volume. (*See also* mirroring.)

mirroring   Reading and writing data at the same time to two drives for fault tolerance purposes. Considered RAID level 1. Also called *drive mirroring*.

MMC (Microsoft Management Console)   Means of managing a system, introduced by Microsoft with Windows 2000. The MMC allows an Administrator to customize management tools by picking and choosing from a list of snap-ins. Available snap-ins include Device Manager, Users and Groups, and Computer Management.

MMX (multimedia extensions)   Specific CPU instructions that enable a CPU to handle many multimedia functions, such as digital signal processing. Introduced with the Pentium CPU, these instructions are used on all ×86 CPUs.

mode   Any single combination of resolution and color depth set for a system.

modem (modulator/demodulator)   Device that converts a digital bit stream into an analog signal (modulation) and converts incoming analog signals back into digital signals (demodulation). Analog communications channel is typically a telephone line, and analog signals are typically sounds.

module   Small circuit board that DRAM chips are attached to. Also known as a "stick."

Molex connector   Computer power connector used by CD-ROM drives, hard drives, and case fans. Keyed to prevent it from being inserted into a power port improperly.

monaural   Describes recording tracks from one source (microphone) as opposed to stereo, which uses two sources.

monitor   Screen that displays data from a PC. Can use either a cathode ray tube (CRT) or a liquid crystal display (LCD) to display images.

motherboard   Flat piece of circuit board that resides inside your computer case and has a number of connectors on it. You can use these connectors to attach a variety of devices to your system, including hard drives, CD-ROM drives, floppy disk drives, and sound cards.

motherboard book   Valuable resource when installing a new motherboard. Normally lists all the specifications about a motherboard, including the type of memory and type of CPU that should be used with the motherboard.

mount point   Drive that functions like a folder mounted into another drive.

mouse   Input device that enables users to manipulate a cursor on the screen to select items.

MOVE command   Command in the command-line interface used to move a file from one location to another.

MP3   Short for MPEG, Layer 3. MP3 is a type of compression used specifically for turning high-quality digital audio files into much smaller, yet similar sounding, files.

MPA (Microsoft Product Activation)   Introduced by Microsoft with the release of Windows XP, Microsoft Product Activation prevents unauthorized use of Microsoft's software by requiring users to activate the software.

MPEG-2 (Moving Picture Experts Group)   Standard of video and audio compression offering resolutions up to 1280 × 720 at 60 frames per second.

MPEG-4 (Moving Picture Experts Group)   Standard of video and audio compression offering improved compression over MPEG-2.

MS-CHAP   Microsoft's variation of the CHAP protocol, which uses a slightly more advanced encryption protocol. Windows Vista uses MS-CHAP v2 (version 2), and does not support MS-CHAP v1 (version 1).

MSCONFIG (System Configuration utility)   Executable file that runs the Windows System Configuration utility, which enables users to configure a system's boot files and critical system files. Often used for the name of the utility, as in "just run MSCONFIG."

MSDS (material safety data sheet)   Standardized form that provides detailed information about potential environmental hazards and proper disposal methods associated with various PC components.

MSINFO32   Provides information about hardware resources, components, and the software environment. Also known as System Information.

multiboot   OS installation in which multiple operating systems are installed on a single machine. Can also refer to kicking a device several times in frustration.

multimedia extensions Originally an Intel CPU enhancement designed for graphics-intensive applications (such as games). It was never embraced but eventually led to improvements in how CPUs handle graphics.

multimeter Device used to measure voltage, amperage, and resistance.

multisession drive Recordable CD drive capable of burning multiple sessions onto a single recordable disc. A multisession drive also can close a CD-R so that no further tracks can be written to it.

multitasking Process of running multiple programs or tasks on the same computer at the same time.

Music CD-R CD using a special format for home recorders. Music CD-R makers pay a small royalty to avoid illegal music duplication.

My Computer Applet that allows users to access a complete list of all fixed and removable drives contained within a system.

My Documents Introduced with Windows 98 and used in Windows 2000 and Windows XP, the My Documents folder provides a convenient place for users to store their documents, log files, and any other type of files.

My Network Places Folder in Windows XP that enables users to view other computers on their network or workgroup.

native resolution Resolution on an LCD monitor that matches the physical pixels on the screen. CRTs do not have fixed pixels and therefore do not have a native resolution.

NET Command in Windows that allows users to view a network without knowing the names of the other computers on that network.

NetBIOS (Network Basic Input/Output System) Protocol that operates at the Session layer (Layer 5) of the OSI seven-layer model. This protocol creates and manages connections based on the names of the computers involved.

network Collection of two or more computers interconnected by telephone lines, coaxial cables, satellite links, radio, and/or some other communication technique. Group of computers that are connected and that communicate with one another for a common purpose.

Also, the name of Vista's version of the My Network Places folder.

network ID Number that identifies the network on which a device or machine exists. This number exists in both IP and IPX protocol suites.

network printer Printer that connects directly to a network.

NIC (network interface card) Expansion card that enables a PC to physically link to a network.

Ni-Cd (nickel-cadmium) Battery that was used in the first portable PCs. Heavy and inefficient, these batteries also suffered from a memory effect that could drastically shorten the overall life of the battery. (*See also* Ni-MH, Li-Ion.)

Ni-MH (nickel-metal hydride) Battery used in portable PCs. Ni-MH batteries had fewer issues with the memory effect than Ni-Cd batteries. Ni-MH batteries have been replaced by lithium-ion batteries. (*See also* Ni-Cd, Li-Ion.)

nit Value used to measure the brightness of an LCD displays. A typical LCD display has a brightness of between 100 and 400 nits.

NLQ (near-letter quality) Designation for dot-matrix printers that use 24-pin printheads.

NLX Second form factor for slimline systems. Replaced the earlier LPX form factor. (NLX apparently stands for nothing; it's just a cool grouping of letters.)

NMI (non-maskable interrupt) Interrupt code sent to the processor that cannot be ignored. Typically manifested as a BSOD.

NNTP (Network News Transfer Protocol) Protocol run by news servers that enable newsgroups.

non-system disk or disk error Error that occurs during the boot process. Common causes for this error are leaving a non-bootable floppy disk, CD, or other media in the drive while the computer is booting.

nonvolatile Memory that retains data even if power is removed.

normal backup Full backup of every selected file on a system. Turns off the archive bit after the backup.

Northbridge Chip that connects a CPU to memory, the PCI bus, Level 2 cache, and AGP activities. Communicates with the CPU through the frontside bus. Newer CPUs feature an integrated Northbridge.

NOS (network operating system) Standalone operating system or part of an operating system that provides basic file and supervisory services over a network. Although each computer attached to the network has its own OS, the NOS describes which actions are allowed by each user and coordinates distribution of networked files to the user who requests them.

notification area Contains icons representing background processes, the system clock and volume control. Located by default at the right edge of the Windows taskbar. Most users call this area the system tray.

NSLOOKUP Command-line program in Windows used to determine exactly what information the DNS server is providing about a specific host name.

NTDETECT.COM One of the critical Windows NT/2000/XP startup files.

NTFS (NT file system) Robust and secure file system introduced by Microsoft with Windows NT. NTFS provides an amazing array of configuration options for user access and security. Users can be granted access to data on a file-by-file basis. NTFS enables object-level security, long filename support, compression, and encryption.

NTFS permissions Restrictions that determine the amount of access given to a particular user on a system using NTFS.

NTLDR Windows NT/2000/XP boot file. Launched by the MBR or MFT, NTLDR looks at the BOOT.INI configuration file for any installed operating systems.

NVIDIA One of the foremost manufacturers of graphics cards and chipsets.

object System component that is given a set of characteristics and can be managed by the operating system as a single entity.

object access auditing Feature of Event Viewer's Security section that creates an entry in the Security Log when certain objects are accessed, such as a file or folder.

ohm(s) Electronic measurement of a cable's impedance.

OpenGL One of two popular APIs used today for video cards. Originally written for UNIX systems but now ported to Windows and Apple systems. (*See also* DirectX.)

optical disc/media Types of data discs (such as DVDs, CDs, Blu-ray Discs, etc.) that are read by a laser.

optical drive Drive used to read/write to optical discs, such as CDs or DVDs.

optical mouse Pointing device that uses light rather than electronic sensors to determine movement and direction the mouse is being moved.

optical resolution Resolution a scanner can achieve mechanically. Most scanners use software to enhance this ability.

optical zoom Mechanical ability of most cameras to "zoom" in as opposed to the digital ability.

option ROM Alternative way of telling the system how to talk to a piece of hardware. Option ROM stores BIOS for the card onboard a chip on the card itself.

OS (operating system) Series of programs and code that create an interface so users can interact with a system's hardware, for example, DOS, Windows, and Linux.

OS X Current operating system on Apple Macintosh computers. Based on a UNIX core, early versions of OS X ran on Motorola-based hardware; current versions run on Intel-based hardware. Pronounced "ten" rather than "ex."

OSI seven-layer model Architecture model based on the OSI protocol suite that defines and standardizes the flow of data between computers. The seven layers are:
Layer 1 The Physical layer Defines hardware connections and turns binary into physical pulses (electrical or light). Repeaters and hubs operate at the Physical layer.
Layer 2 The Data Link layer Identifies devices on the Physical layer. MAC addresses are part of the Data Link layer. Bridges operate at the Data Link layer.
Layer 3 The Network layer Moves packets between computers on different networks. Routers operate at the Network layer. IP and IPX operate at the Network layer.
Layer 4 The Transport layer Breaks data down into manageable chunks. TCP, UDP, SPX, and NetBEUI operate at the Transport layer.
Layer 5 The Session layer Manages connections between machines. NetBIOS and Sockets operate at the Session layer.
Layer 6 The Presentation layer Can also manage data encryption; hides the differences between various types of computer systems.
Layer 7 The Application layer Provides tools for programs to use to access the network (and the lower layers). HTTP, FTP, SMTP, and POP3 are all examples of protocols that operate at the Application layer.

overclocking   To run a CPU or video processor faster than its rated speed.

P1 power connector   Provides power to ATX motherboards.

P4 12V connector   Provides additional 12-volt power to motherboards that support Pentium 4 and later processors.

P8 and P9 connectors   Provides power to AT-style motherboards.

packet   Basic component of communication over a network. Group of bits of fixed maximum size and well-defined format that is switched and transmitted as a single entity through a network. Contains source and destination address, data, and control information.

page fault   Minor memory-addressing error.

page file   Portion of the hard drive set aside by Windows to act like RAM. Also known as virtual memory or swap file.

PAN (personal area network)   Small wireless network created with Bluetooth technology and intended to link PCs and other peripheral devices.

parallel port   Connection for the synchronous, high-speed flow of data along parallel lines to a device, usually a printer.

parallel processing   When a multicore CPU processes more than one thread.

parental controls   Tool to allow monitoring and limiting of user activities; designed for parents to control the content their children can access.

parity   Method of error detection where a small group of bits being transferred is compared to a single parity bit set to make the total bits odd or even. Receiving device reads the parity bit and determines if the data is valid, based on if the parity bit is odd or even.

parity RAM   Earliest form of error-detecting RAM; stored an extra bit (called the *parity bit*) to verify the data.

partition   Section of the storage area of a hard disk. Created during initial preparation of the hard disk, before the disk is formatted.

partition table   Table located in the boot sector of a hard drive that lists every partition on the disk that contains a valid operating system.

partitioning   Electronically subdividing a physical hard drive into groups called *partitions* (or *volumes*).

passive matrix   Technology for producing colors in LCD monitors by varying voltages across wire matrices to produce red, green, or blue dots.

password   Key used to verify a user's identity on a secure computer or network.

Password Authentication Protocol (PAP)   Oldest and most basic form of authentication. Also the least safe, because it sends all passwords in clear text.

password reset disk   Special type of floppy disk with which users can recover a lost password without losing access to any encrypted, or password-protected, data.

PATA (parallel ATA)   Implementation that integrates the controller on the disk drive itself. (*See also* ATA, IDE, SATA.)

patch   Small piece of software released by a software manufacturer to correct a flaw or problem with a particular piece of software.

path   Route the operating system must follow to find an executable program stored in a subdirectory.

PC bus   Original 8-bit expansion bus developed by IBM for PCs; ran at a top speed of 4.77 MHz. Also known as the XT bus.

PC Card   Credit-card–sized adapter cards that add functionality in many notebook computers, PDAs, and other computer devices. Come in 16-bit and CardBus parallel format and ExpressCard serial format. (*See also* PCMCIA.)

PC tech   Someone with computer skills who works on computers.

PCI (Peripheral Component Interconnect)   Design architecture for the expansion bus on the computer motherboard, which enables system components to be added to the computer. Local bus standard, meaning that devices added to a computer through this port will use the processor at the motherboard's full speed (up to 33 MHz) rather than at the slower 8 MHz speed of the regular bus. Moves data 32 or 64 bits at a time rather than the 8 or 16 bits the older ISA buses supported.

PCIe (PCI Express)   Serialized successor to PCI and AGP, which uses the concept of individual data paths called *lanes*. May use any number of lanes, although single lanes (×1) and 16 lanes (×16) are the most common on motherboards.

PCI-X (PCI Extended)   Enhanced version of PCI, 64 bits wide. Typically seen in servers and high-end systems.

PCL   Printer control language created by Hewlett-Packard and used on a broad cross-section of printers.

PCM (Pulse Code Modulation)   Sound format developed in the 1960s to carry telephone calls over the first digital lines.

PCMCIA (Personal Computer Memory Card International Association)   Consortium of computer manufacturers who devised the PC Card standard for credit-card–sized adapter cards that add functionality in many notebook computers, PDAs, and other computer devices. (*See also* PC Card.)

PDA (personal digital assistant)   Handheld computer that blurs the line between calculators and computers. Early PDAs were calculators that enabled users to program in such information as addresses and appointments. Modern PDAs, such as the Palm and PocketPC, are fully programmable computers. Most PDAs use a pen/stylus for input rather than a keyboard. A few of the larger PDAs have a tiny keyboard in addition to the stylus.

Pearson VUE   One of the two companies that administers the CompTIA A+ exams, along with Prometric.

peer-to-peer networks   Network in which each machine can act as both a client and a server.

Pentium   Name given to the fifth and later generations of Intel microprocessors; has a 32-bit address bus, 64-bit external data bus, and dual pipelining. Also used for subsequent generations of Intel processors—the Pentium Pro, Pentium II, Pentium III, and Pentium 4. Pentium name was retired after the introduction of the Intel Core CPUs.

pen-based computing   Input method used by many PDAs that combines handwriting recognition with modified mouse functions, usually in the form of a pen-like stylus.

Performance console   Windows tool used to log resource usage over time.

Performance Logs and Alerts   Snap-in enabling the creation of a written record of most everything that happens on the system.

Performance Options   Tool allowing users to configure CPU, RAM, and virtual memory settings.

peripheral   Any device that connects to the system unit.

permission propagation   Term to describe what happens to permissions on an object when you move or copy it.

persistence   Phosphors used in CRT screens continuing to glow after being struck by electrons, long enough for the human eye to register the glowing effect. Glowing too long makes the images smeary, and too little makes them flicker.

Personalization applet   Windows Vista/7 applet with which users can change display settings such as resolution, refresh rate, color depth, and desktop features.

PGA (pin grid array)   Arrangement of a large number of pins extending from the bottom of the CPU package. There are many variations on PGA.

Phillips-head screwdriver   Most important part of a PC tech's toolkit.

Phoenix Technologies   Major producer of BIOS software for motherboards.

phosphor   Electro-fluorescent material that coats the inside face of a cathode ray tube (CRT). After being hit with an electron, it glows for a fraction of a second.

photosensitive drum   Aluminum cylinder coated with particles of photosensitive compounds. Used in a laser printer and usually contained within the toner cartridge.

picoBTX   Variation of the BTX form factor. picoBTX motherboards are generally smaller than their BTX or microBTX counterparts but retain the same functionality.

pin 1   Designator used to ensure proper alignment of floppy disk drive and hard drive connectors.

ping (packet Internet groper)   Slang term for a small network message (ICMP ECHO) sent by a computer to check for the presence and aliveness of another. Used to verify the presence of another system. Also the command used at a prompt to ping a computer.

PIO mode   Series of speed standards created by the Small Form Factor Committee for the use of PIO by hard drives. Modes range from PIO mode 0 to PIO mode 4.

pipeline Processing methodology where multiple calculations take place simultaneously by being broken into a series of steps. Often used in CPUs and video processors.

pixel (picture element) In computer graphics, smallest element of a display space that can be independently assigned color or intensity.

plug Hardware connection with some sort of projection that connects to a port.

plug and play (PnP) Combination of smart PCs, smart devices, and smart operating systems that automatically configure all necessary system resources and ports when you install a new peripheral device.

polygons Multi-sided shapes used in 3-D rendering of objects. In computers, video cards draw large numbers of triangles and connect them to form polygons.

polymorph virus Virus that attempts to change its signature to prevent detection by antivirus programs, usually by continually scrambling a bit of useless code.

polyphony Number of instruments a sound card can play at once.

POP3 (Post Office Protocol) Refers to the way e-mail software such as Eudora gets mail from a mail server. When you obtain a SLIP, PPP, or shell account, you almost always get a POP account with it. It is this POP account that you tell your e-mail software to use to get your mail. Also called *point of presence*.

pop-up Irritating browser window that appears automatically when you visit a Web site.

port (networking) In networking, the number used to identify the requested service (such as SMTP or FTP) when connecting to a TCP/IP host. Examples: 80 (HTTP), 20 (FTP), 69 (TFTP), 25 (SMTP), and 110 (POP3).

port (physical connection) Part of a connector into which a plug is inserted. Physical ports are also referred to as jacks.

port replicator Device that plugs into a USB port or other specialized port and offers common PC ports, such as serial, parallel, USB, network, and PS/2. By plugging your notebook computer into the port replicator, you can instantly connect the computer to nonportable components such as a printer, scanner, monitor, or full-sized keyboard. Port replicators are

typically used at home or in the office with the nonportable equipment already connected.

positional audio Range of commands for a sound card to place a sound anywhere in 3-D space.

POST (power-on self test) Basic diagnostic routine completed by a system at the beginning of the boot process to make sure a display adapter and the system's memory are installed; it then searches for an operating system. If it finds one, it hands over control of the machine to the OS.

PostScript Language defined by Adobe Systems, Inc. for describing how to create an image on a page. The description is independent of the resolution of the device that will actually create the image. It includes a technology for defining the shape of a font and creating a raster image at many different resolutions and sizes.

potential Amount of static electricity stored by an object.

power conditioning Ensuring and adjusting incoming AC wall power to as close to standard as possible. Most UPS devices provide power conditioning.

power good wire Used to wake up the CPU after the power supply has tested for proper voltage.

power supply fan Small fan located in a system power supply that draws warm air from inside the power supply and exhausts it to the outside.

power supply unit Provides the electrical power for a PC. Converts standard AC power into various voltages of DC electricity in a PC.

Power User(s) Group Second most powerful account and group type in Windows after Administrator/Administrators.

ppm (pages per minute) Speed of a printer.

PPP (Point-to-Point Protocol) Enables a computer to connect to the Internet through a dial-in connection and enjoy most of the benefits of a direct connection.

primary corona Wire located near the photosensitive drum in a laser printer, that is charged with extremely high voltage to form an electric field, enabling voltage to pass to the photosensitive drum, thus charging the photosensitive particles on the surface of the drum.

primary partition Partition on a Windows hard drive designated to store the operating system.

print resolution   Quality of a print image.

print spooler   Area of memory that queues up print jobs that the printer will handle sequentially.

printer   Output device that can print text or illustrations on paper. Microsoft uses the term to refer to the software that controls the physical print device.

printhead   Case that holds the printwires in a dot-matrix printer.

printed circuit boards   Copper etched onto a non-conductive material and then coated with some sort of epoxy for strength.

printwires   Grid of tiny pins in a dot-matrix printer that strike an inked printer ribbon to produce images on paper.

PRML (Partial Response Maximum Likelihood)   Advanced method of RLL that uses powerful, intelligent circuitry to analyze each flux reversal on a hard drive and to make a best guess as to what type of flux reversal it just read. This allows a dramatic increase in the amount of data a hard drive can store.

product key   Code used during installation to verify legitimacy of the software.

program/programming   Series of binary electronic commands sent to a CPU to get work done.

Programs and Features   Windows Vista/7 replacement for the Add or Remove Programs applet.

projector   Device for projecting video images from PCs or other video sources, usually for audience presentations. Available in front and rear view displays.

Prometric   One of the two companies that administers the CompTIA A+ exams, along with Pearson VUE.

prompt   A character or message provided by an operating system or program to indicate that it is ready to accept input.

proprietary   Technology unique to a particular vendor.

protocol   Agreement that governs the procedures used to exchange information between cooperating entities. Usually includes how much information is to be sent, how often it is sent, how to recover from transmission errors, and who is to receive the information.

proxy server   Device that fetches Internet resources for a client without exposing that client directly to the Internet. Usually accept requests for HTTP, FTP, POP3, and SMTP resources. Often caches, or stores, a copy of the requested resource for later use. Common security feature in the corporate world.

public folder   Folder that all users can access and share with all other users on the system or network.

queue   Area where objects wait their turn to be processed. Example: the printer queue, where print jobs wait until it is their turn to be printed.

Quick Launch toolbar   Enables you to launch commonly used programs with a single click.

QVGA   Video display mode of 320 × 240.

RAID (redundant array of inexpensive devices)   Six-level (0–5) way of creating a fault-tolerant storage system:
Level 0   Uses byte-level striping and provides no fault tolerance.
Level 1   Uses mirroring or duplexing.
Level 2   Uses bit-level striping.
Level 3   Stores error-correcting information (such as parity) on a separate disk, and uses data striping on the remaining drives.
Level 4   Level 3 with block-level striping.
Level 5   Uses block-level and parity data striping.

RAID-5 volume   Striped set with parity. (*See also* RAID.)

rails   Separate DC paths within an ATX power supply.

RAM (random access memory)   Memory that can be accessed at random; that is, which you can write to or read from without touching the preceding address. This term is often used to mean a computer's main memory.

RAMDAC (random access memory digital-to-analog converter)   Circuitry used on video cards that support analog monitors to convert the digital video data to analog.

raster image   Pattern of dots representing what the final product should look like.

raster line   Horizontal pattern of lines that form an image on the monitor screen.

RD (RMDIR)   Command in the command-line interface used to remove directories.

RDRAM (Rambus DRAM) Patented RAM technology that uses accelerated clocks to provide very high-speed memory.

read-only attribute File attribute that does not allow a file to be altered or modified. Helpful when protecting system files that should not be edited.

rear-view projector Projector that shoots an image onto a screen from the rear. Rear-view projectors are usually self-enclosed and very popular for TVs, but are virtually unheard of in the PC world.

Recovery Console Command-line interface boot mode for Windows that is used to repair a Windows 2000 or Windows XP system suffering from massive OS corruption or other problems.

Recycle Bin When files are deleted from a modern Windows system, they are moved to the Recycle Bin. To permanently remove files from a system, they must be emptied from the Recycle Bin.

REGEDIT.EXE Program used to edit the Windows Registry.

register Storage area inside the CPU used by the onboard logic to perform calculations. CPUs have many registers to perform different functions.

registration Usually optional process that identifies the legal owner/user of the product to the supplier.

Registry Complex binary file used to store configuration data about a particular system. To edit the Registry, users can use the applets found in the Control Panel or REGEDIT.EXE or REGEDT32.EXE.

Reliability and Performance Monitor Windows Vista's extended Performance applet.

remediation Repairing damage caused by a virus.

remnant Potentially recoverable data on a hard drive that remains despite formatting or deleting.

Remote Assistance Feature of Windows that enables users to give anyone control of his or her desktop over the Internet.

Remote Desktop Connection Windows tool used to enable a local system to graphically access the desktop of a remote system.

REN (RENAME) command Command in the command-line interface used to rename files and folders.

resistance Difficulty in making electricity flow through a material, measured in ohms.

resistor Any material or device that impedes the flow of electrons. Electronic resistors measure their resistance (impedance) in ohms. *See* ohm(s).

resolution Measurement for CRTs and printers expressed in horizontal and vertical dots or pixels. Higher resolutions provide sharper details and thus display better-looking images.

resources Data and services of a PC.

respect What all techs should feel for their customers.

response rate Time it takes for all of the sub-pixels on the panel to go from pure black to pure white and back again.

restore point System snapshot created by the System Restore utility that is used to restore a malfunctioning system. (*See also* System Restore.)

RET (resolution enhancement technology) Technology that uses small dots to smooth out jagged edges that are typical of printers without RET, producing a higher-quality print job.

RFI (radio frequency interference) Another form of electrical interference caused by radio-wave emitting devices, such as cell phones, wireless network cards, and microwave ovens.

RG-58 Coaxial cabling used for 10Base2 networks.

RIMM Individual stick of Rambus RAM. The letters don't actually stand for anything; they just rhyme with SIMM and DIMM.

RIP (raster image processor) Component in a printer that translates the raster image into commands for the printer.

riser card Special adapter card, usually inserted into a special slot on a motherboard, that changes the orientation of expansion cards relative to the motherboard. Riser cards are used extensively in slimline computers to keep total depth and height of the system to a minimum. Sometimes called a daughterboard.

RJ (registered jack) connector UTP cable connector, used for both telephone and network connections. RJ-11 is a connector for four-wire UTP; usually found in telephone connections. RJ-45 is a connector for eight-wire UTP; usually found in network connections.

RJ-11 *See* RJ (registered jack) connector.

RJ-45 *See* RJ (registered jack) connector.

ROM (read-only memory) Generic term for nonvolatile memory that can be read from but not written to. This means that code and data stored in ROM cannot be corrupted by accidental erasure. Additionally, ROM retains its data when power is removed, which makes it the perfect medium for storing BIOS data or information such as scientific constants.

root directory Directory that contains all other directories.

root keys Five main categories in the Windows Registry:

    HKEY_CLASSES_ROOT
    HKEY_CURRENT_USER
    HKEY_USERS
    HKEY_LOCAL_MACHINE
    HKEY_CURRENT_CONFIG

router Device connecting separate networks; forwards a packet from one network to another based on the network address for the protocol being used. For example, an IP router looks only at the IP network number. Routers operate at Layer 3 (Network) of the OSI seven-layer model.

RS-232C Standard port recommended by the Electronics Industry Association for serial devices.

Run dialog box Command box in which users can enter the name of a particular program to run; an alternative to locating the icon in Windows.

S.M.A.R.T. (Self-Monitoring, Analysis, and Reporting Technology) Monitoring system built into hard drives.

S/PDIF (Sony/Philips Digital Interface Format) Digital audio connector found on many sound cards. Users can connect their computers directly to a 5.1 speaker system or receiver. S/PDIF comes in both a coaxial and an optical version.

Safe Mode Important diagnostic boot mode for Windows that only runs very basic drivers and turns off virtual memory.

sampling Capturing sound waves in electronic format.

SATA (serial ATA) Serialized version of the ATA standard that offers many advantages over PATA (parallel ATA) technology, including thinner cabling, keyed connectors, and lower power requirements.

SATA bridge Adapter that allows PATA devices to be connected to a SATA controller.

SATA power connector 15-pin, L-shaped connector used by SATA devices that support the hot-swappable feature.

satellites Two or more standard stereo speakers to be combined with a subwoofer for a speaker system (i.e., 2.1, 5.1, etc.).

scan code Unique code corresponding to each key on the keyboard sent from the keyboard controller to the CPU.

SCSI (small computer system interface) Powerful and flexible peripheral interface popularized on the Macintosh and used to connect hard drives, CD-ROM drives, tape drives, scanners, and other devices to PCs of all kinds. Normal SCSI enables up to seven devices to be connected through a single bus connection, whereas Wide SCSI can handle 15 devices attached to a single controller.

SCSI chain Series of SCSI devices working together through a host adapter.

SCSI ID Unique identifier used by SCSI devices. No two SCSI devices may have the same SCSI ID.

SD (Secure Digital) Very popular format for flash media cards; also supports I/O devices.

SDRAM (synchronous DRAM) DRAM that is synchronous, or tied to the system clock and thus runs much faster than traditional FPM and EDO RAM. This type of RAM is used in all modern systems.

SEC (single-edge cartridge) CPU package where the CPU was contained in a cartridge that snapped into a special slot on the motherboard called Slot 1.

sector Segment of one of the concentric tracks encoded on the disk during a low-level format. A sector holds 512 bytes of data.

sector translation Translation of logical geometry into physical geometry by the onboard circuitry of a hard drive.

sectors per track (sectors/track) Combined with the number of cylinders and heads, defines the disk geometry.

serial port   Common connector on a PC. Connects input devices (such as a mouse) or communications devices (such as a modem).

server   Computer that shares its resources, such as printers and files, with other computers on a network. Example: Network File System Server that shares its disk space with a workstation that does not have a disk drive of its own.

service pack   Collection of software patches released at one time by a software manufacturer.

SetupAPI.log   Log file that tracks the installation of all hardware on a system.

Setuplog.txt   Log file that tracks the complete installation process, logging the success or failure of file copying, Registry updates, and reboots.

SFC (system file checker)   Scans, detects, and restores Windows system files, folders, and paths.

shadow mask   CRT screen that allows only the proper electron gun to light the proper phosphors.

shared documents   Windows pre-made folder accessible by all users on the computer.

shared memory   Means of reducing the amount of memory needed on a video card by borrowing from the regular system RAM, which reduces costs but also decreases performance.

share-level security   Security system in which each resource has a password assigned to it; access to the resource is based on knowing the password.

shareware   Program protected by copyright; holder allows (encourages!) you to make and distribute copies under the condition that those who adopt the software after preview pay a fee to the holder of the copyright. Derivative works are not allowed, although you may make an archival copy.

shunt   Tiny connector of metal enclosed in plastic that creates an electrical connection between two posts of a jumper.

SID (security identifier)   Unique identifier for every PC that most techs change when cloning.

sidebanding   Second data bus for AGP video cards; enables the video card to send more commands to the Northbridge while receiving other commands at the same time.

signal-to-noise ratio   Measure that describes the relative quality of an input port.

signature   Code pattern of a known virus; used by antivirus software to detect viruses.

SIMM (single in-line memory module)   DRAM packaging distinguished by having a number of small tabs that install into a special connector. Each side of each tab is the same signal. SIMMs come in two common sizes: 30-pin and 72-pin.

simple file sharing   Allows users to share locally or across the network but gives no control over what others do with shared files.

simple volume   Volume created when setting up dynamic disks. Acts like a primary partition on a dynamic disk.

single-sided RAM   Has chips on only one side as opposed to double-sided RAM.

slimline   Motherboard form factor used to create PCs that were very thin. NLX and LPX were two examples of this form factor.

slot covers   Metal plates that cover up unused expansion slots on the back of a PC. Useful in maintaining proper airflow through a computer case.

smart battery   Portable PC battery that tells the computer when it needs to be charged, conditioned, or replaced.

smart card   Hardware authentication involving a credit-card-sized card with circuitry that can be used to identify the bearer of that card.

SmartMedia   Format for flash media cards; no longer used with new devices.

SMM (System Management Mode)   Special CPU mode that enables the CPU to reduce power consumption by selectively shutting down peripherals.

SMTP (Simple Mail Transport Protocol)   Main protocol used to send electronic mail on the Internet.

snap-ins   Small utilities that can be used with the Microsoft Management Console.

social engineering   Using or manipulating people inside the networking environment to gain access to that network from the outside.

socket services Device drivers that support the PC Card socket, enabling the system to detect when a PC Card has been inserted or removed, and providing the necessary I/O to the device.

SODIMM (small outline DIMM) Memory used in portable PCs because of its small size.

soft power Characteristic of ATX motherboards, which can use software to turn the PC on and off. The physical manifestation of soft power is the power switch. Instead of the thick power cord used in AT systems, an ATX power switch is little more than a pair of small wires leading to the motherboard.

software Single group of programs designed to do a particular job; always stored on mass storage devices.

solid ink printers Printer that uses solid sticks of non-toxic "ink."

sound card Expansion card that can produce audible tones when connected to a set of speakers.

Southbridge Part of a motherboard chipset; handles all the inputs and outputs to the many devices in the PC.

spam Unsolicited e-mails from both legitimate businesses and scammers that accounts for a huge percentage of traffic on the Internet.

spanned volume Volume that uses space on multiple dynamic disks.

SPD (serial presence detect) Information stored on a RAM chip that describes the speed, capacity, and other aspects of the RAM chip.

speaker Device that outputs sound by using magnetically driven diaphragm.

sprite Bitmapped graphic such as a BMP file used by early 3-D games to create the 3-D world.

spyware Software that runs in the background of a user's PC, sending information about browsing habits back to the company that installed it onto the system.

SRAM (static RAM) RAM that uses a flip-flop circuit rather than the typical transistor/capacitor of DRAM to hold a bit of information. SRAM does not need to be refreshed and is faster than regular DRAM. Used primarily for cache.

SSH (Secure Shell) Terminal emulation program similar to Telnet, except that the entire connection is encrypted.

SSD (solid state drive) Data storage device that uses solid state memory to store data.

SSID (service set identifier) Parameter used to define a wireless network; otherwise known as the network name.

SSL (Secure Sockets Layer) Security protocol used by a browser to connect to secure Web sites.

standard account/user User account in Windows Vista that has limited access to a system. Accounts of this type cannot alter system files, cannot install new programs, and cannot edit some settings by using the Control Panel without supplying an administrator password. Replaces the Limited accounts in Windows XP.

standouts Small connectors that screw into a computer case. A motherboard is then placed on top of the standouts, and small screws are used to secure it to the standouts.

star topology Network topology where the computers on the network connect to a central wiring point, usually called a *hub*.

Start button Button on the Windows taskbar that enables access to the Start menu.

Start menu Menu that can be accessed by clicking the Start button on the Windows taskbar. Enables you to see all programs loaded on the system and to start them.

static charge eliminator Device used to remove a static charge.

static IP address Manually set IP address that will not change.

stealth virus Virus that uses various methods to hide from antivirus software.

stepper motor One of two methods used to move actuator arms in a hard drive. (*See also* voice coil motor.)

stereo Describes recording tracks from two sources (microphones) as opposed to monaural, which uses one source.

stick Generic name for a single physical SIMM, RIMM, or DIMM.

STP (shielded twisted pair) Cabling for networks, composed of pairs of wires twisted around each other at specific intervals. Twists serve to reduce interference (also called *crosstalk*)—the more twists, the less interference. Cable has metallic shielding to protect the wires from external interference.

streaming media   Broadcast of data that is played on your computer and immediately discarded.

stream loading   Process a program uses to constantly download updated information.

stripe set   Two or more drives in a group that are used for a striped volume.

strong password   Password containing at least eight characters, including letters, numbers, and punctuation symbols.

stylus   Pen-like input device used for pen-based computing.

subnet mask   Value used in TCP/IP settings to divide the IP address of a host into its component parts: network ID and host ID.

sub-pixel   Tiny liquid crystal molecules arranged in rows and columns between polarizing filters used in LCDs.

subwoofer   Powerful speaker capable of producing extremely low-frequency sounds.

super I/O chip   Chip specially designed to control low-speed, legacy devices such as the keyboard, mouse, and serial and parallel ports.

surge suppressor   Inexpensive device that protects your computer from voltage spikes.

SVGA (super video graphics array)   Video display mode of 800 × 600.

swap file   See page file.

switch   Device that filters and forwards traffic based on some criteria. A bridge and a router are both examples of switches.

SXGA   Video display mode of 1280 × 1024.

SXGA+   Video display mode of 1400 × 1050.

syntax   The proper way to write a command-line command so that it functions and does what it's supposed to do.

Sysprep   Windows tool that makes cloning of systems easier by making it possible to undo portions of the installation.

System BIOS   Primary set of BIOS stored on an EPROM or Flash chip on the motherboard. Defines the BIOS for all the assumed hardware on the mother-

board, such as keyboard controller, floppy drive, basic video, and RAM.

system bus speed   Speed at which the CPU and the rest of the PC operates; set by the system crystal.

system crystal   Crystal that provides the speed signals for the CPU and the rest of the system.

system disk   Any device with a functional operating system.

system fan   Any fan controlled by the motherboard but not directly attached to the CPU.

System Management Mode (SMM)   Provided CPUs the ability to turn off high-power devices (monitors, hard drives, etc.). Originally for laptops; later versions are incorporated in all AMD and Intel CPUs.

System Monitor   Utility that can evaluate and monitor system resources, such as CPU usage and memory usage.

system resources   In classic terms, the I/O addresses, IRQs, DMA channels, and memory addresses. Also refers to other computer essentials such as hard drive space, system RAM, and processor speed.

System Restore   Utility in Windows that enables you to return your PC to a recent working configuration when something goes wrong. System Restore returns your computer's system settings to the way they were the last time you remember your system working correctly—all without affecting your personal files or e-mail.

System ROM   ROM chip that stores the system BIOS.

System Tools   Menu containing tools such as System Information and Disk Defragmenter, accessed by selecting Start | Programs or All Programs | Accessories | System Tools.

system tray   Contains icons representing background processes and the system clock. Located by default at the right edge of the Windows taskbar. Accurately called the *notification area*.

system unit   Main component of the PC, in which the CPU, RAM, CD-ROM, and hard drive reside. All other devices—the keyboard, mouse, and monitor—connect to the system unit.

Tablet PC   Small portable computer distinguished by the use of a touch screen with stylus and handwriting recognition as the primary modes of input. Also the name of the Windows XP-based operating system designed to run on such systems.

tailgating Form of infiltration and social engineering that involves following someone else through a door as if you belong.

take ownership Special permission allowing users to seize control of a file or folder and potentially preventing others from accessing the file/folder.

Task Manager Shows all running programs, including hidden ones, accessed by pressing CTRL-SHIFT-ESC. Able to shut down an unresponsive application that refuses to close normally.

taskbar Contains the Start button, the system tray, the Quick Launch bar, and buttons for running applications. Located by default at the bottom of the desktop.

TCP/IP (Transmission Control Protocol/Internet Protocol) Communication protocols developed by the U.S. Department of Defense to enable dissimilar computers to share information over a network.

tech toolkit Tools a PC tech should never be without, including a Phillips-head screwdriver, a pair of tweezers, a flat-head screwdriver, a hemostat, a Torx wrench, a parts retriever, and a nut driver or two.

telephone scams Social engineering attack in which the attacker makes a phone call to someone in an organization to gain information.

TELNET Terminal emulation program for TCP/IP networks that allows one machine to control another as if the user were sitting in front of it.

tera- Prefix that usually stands for the binary number 1,099,511,627,776 (2^{40}). When used for mass storage, it's often shorthand for a trillion bytes.

terminal Dumb device connected to a mainframe or computer network that acts as a point for entry or retrieval of information.

terminal emulation Software that enables a PC to communicate with another computer or network as if the PC were a specific type of hardware terminal.

termination Using terminating resistors to prevent packet reflection on a network cable.

terminator Resistor that is plugged into the end of a bus cable to absorb the excess electrical signal, preventing it from bouncing back when it reaches the end of the wire. Terminators are used with coaxial cable and on the ends of SCSI chains. RG-58 coaxial cable requires resistors with a 50-ohm impedance.

Test the theory Attempt to resolve the issue by either confirming the theory and learning what needs to be done to fix the problem, or by not confirming the theory and forming a new one or escalating. (One of the steps a technician uses to solve a problem.)

texture Small picture that is tiled over and over again on walls, floors, and other surfaces to create the 3-D world.

TFT (thin film transistor) Type of LCD screen. (*See also* active matrix.)

theory of probable cause One possible reason why something is not working; a guess.

thermal compound Paste-like material with very high heat-transfer properties. Applied between the CPU and the cooling device, it ensures the best possible dispersal of heat from the CPU. Also called *heat dope*.

thermal printer Printers that use heated printheads to create high-quality images on special or plain paper.

thermal unit Combination heat sink and fan designed for BTX motherboards; blows hot air out the back of the case instead of just into the case.

thread Smallest logical division of a single program.

throttling Power reduction/thermal control capability allowing CPUs to slow down during low activity or high heat build-up situations. Intel's version is known as SpeedStep, AMD's as PowerNow!

throw Size of the image a projector displays at a certain distance from the screen.

TIA/EIA Telecommunications Industry Alliance/Electronic Industries Alliance. Trade organization that provides standards for network cabling and other electronics.

tiers Levels of Internet providers, ranging from the Tier 1 backbones to Tier 3 regional networks.

timbre Qualities that differentiate the same note played on different instruments.

toner A fine powder made up of plastic particles bonded to iron particles, used by laser printers to create text and images.

toner cartridge   Object used to store the toner in a laser printer. (*See also* laser printer, toner.)

touchpad   Flat, touch-sensitive pad that serves as a pointing device for most laptops.

touch screen   Monitor with a type of sensing device across its face that detects the location and duration of contact, usually by a finger or stylus.

TRACERT   Command-line utility used to follow the path a packet takes between two hosts. Also called TRACEROUTE.

traces   Small electrical connections embedded in a circuit board.

track   Area on a hard drive platter where data is stored. A group of tracks with the same diameter is called a *cylinder*.

trackball   Pointing device distinguished by a ball that is rolled with the fingers.

TrackPoint   IBM's pencil-eraser-sized joystick used in place of a mouse on laptops.

transfer corona   Thin wire, usually protected by other thin wires, that applies a positive charge to the paper during the laser printing process, drawing the negatively charged toner particles off of the drum and onto the paper.

transparency (Windows Vista Aero)   Effect in the Aero desktop environment that makes the edges of windows transparent.

triad   Group of three phosphors—red, green, blue—in a CRT.

Trojan   Program that does something other than what the user who runs the program thinks it will do.

troubleshooting theory   Steps a technician uses to solve a problem: identify the problem, establish a theory of probable cause, test the theory, establish a plan of action, verify functionality, and document findings.

TV tuner   Typically an add-on device that allows users to watch television on a computer.

TWAIN (Technology Without an Interesting Name)   Programming interface that enables a graphics application, such as a desktop publishing program, to activate a scanner, frame grabber, or other image-capturing device.

UAC (User Account Control)   Windows Vista feature that enables Standard accounts to do common tasks and provides a permissions dialog when Standard and Administrator accounts do certain things that could potentially harm the computer (such as attempt to install a program).

UART (universal asynchronous receiver/transmitter)   Device that turns serial data into parallel data. The cornerstone of serial ports and modems.

UDF (universal data format)   Replaced the ISO-9660 formats, allowing any operating system and optical drive to read UDF formatted disks.

UEFI (Unified Extensible Firmware Interface)   Consortium of companies that established the UEFI standard that replaced the original EFI standard.

Ultra DMA   Hard drive technology that enables drives to use direct memory addressing. Ultra DMA mode 3 drives—called *ATA/33*—have data transfer speeds up to 33 MBps. Mode 4 and 5 drives—called *ATA/66* and *ATA/100*, respectively—transfer data at up to 66 MBps for mode 4 and 100 MBps for mode 5. Both modes 4 and 5 require an 80-wire cable and a compatible controller to achieve these data transfer rates.

unauthorized access   Anytime a person accesses resources in an unauthorized way. This access may or may not be malicious.

Unicode   16-bit code that covers every character of the most common languages, plus several thousand symbols.

unsigned driver   Driver that has not gone through the Windows Hardware Quality Labs or Microsoft Windows Logo Program to ensure compatibility.

UPC (Universal Product Code)   Bar code used to track inventory.

Upgrade Advisor   The first process that runs on the XP installation CD. It examines your hardware and installed software (in the case of an upgrade) and provides a list of devices and software that are known to have issues with XP. It can also be run separately from the Windows XP installation, from the Windows XP CD. The Upgrade Advisor is also available for Windows Vista and Windows 7.

upgrade installation   Installation of Windows on top of an earlier installed version, thus inheriting all previous hardware and software settings.

UPS (uninterruptible power supply)   Device that supplies continuous clean power to a computer system the whole time the computer is on. Protects against power outages and sags.

URL (uniform resource locator)   An address that defines the location of a resource on the Internet. URLs are used most often in conjunction with HTML and the World Wide Web.

USB (universal serial bus)   General-purpose serial interconnect for keyboards, printers, joysticks, and many other devices. Enables hot-swapping devices.

USB host controller   Integrated circuit that is usually built into the chipset and controls every USB device that connects to it.

USB hub   Device that extends a single USB connection to two or more USB ports, almost always directly from one of the USB ports connected to the root hub.

USB root hub   Part of the host controller that makes the physical connection to the USB ports.

USB thumb drive   Flash memory device that uses the standard USB connection.

User account   Container that identifies a user to an application, operating system, or network, including name, password, user name, groups to which the user belongs, and other information based on the user and the OS or NOS being used. Usually defines the rights and roles a user plays on a system.

User Accounts applet   Windows XP (and later versions) applet that replaced the Users and Passwords applet of Windows 2000.

user interface   Visual representation of the computer on the monitor that makes sense to the people using the computer, through which the user can interact with the computer.

user profiles   Settings that correspond to a specific user account and may follow users regardless of the computers where they log on. These settings enable the user to have customized environment and security settings.

User's Files   Windows Vista's redux of the My Documents folder structure. It is divided into several folders such as Documents, Pictures, Music, and Video.

Users and Passwords applet   Windows 2000 application that allowed management of user accounts and passwords.

Users group   List of local users not allowed, among other things, to edit the Registry or access critical system files. They can create groups, but can only manage the groups they create.

USMT (User State Migration Tool)   Advanced application for file and settings transfer of multiple users.

UTP (unshielded twisted pair)   Popular type of cabling for telephone and networks, composed of pairs of wires twisted around each other at specific intervals. The twists serve to reduce interference (also called *crosstalk*). The more twists, the less interference. Unlike its cousin, STP, UTP cable has no metallic shielding to protect the wires from external interference. 1000BaseT uses UTP, as do many other networking technologies. UTP is available in a variety of grades, called categories, as follows:
Category 1 UTP   Regular analog phone lines—not used for data communications.
Category 2 UTP   Supports speeds up to 4 megabits per second.
Category 3 UTP   Supports speeds up to 16 megabits per second.
Category 4 UTP   Supports speeds up to 20 megabits per second.
Category 5 UTP   Supports speeds up to 100 megabits per second.
Category 5e UTP   Supports speeds up to 1000 megabits per second.
Category 6 UTP   Supports speeds up to 10 gigabits per second.

V standards   Standards established by CCITT for modem manufacturers to follow (voluntarily) to ensure compatible speeds, compression, and error correction.

verify   Making sure that a problem has been resolved and will not return. (One of the steps a technician uses to solve a problem.)

vertices   Used in the second generation of 3-D rendering, vertices have a defined X, Y, and Z position in a 3-D world.

VESA (Video Electronics Standards Association) Consortium of computer manufacturers that standardized improvements to common IBM PC components. VESA is responsible for the Super VGA video standard and the VLB bus architecture.

VGA (video graphics array) Standard for the video graphics adapter that was built into IBM's PS/2 computer. It supports 16 colors in a 640 × 480 pixel video display and quickly replaced the older CGA (Color Graphics Adapter) and EGA (Extended Graphics Adapter) standards.

video capture Computer jargon for the recording of video information, such as TV shows or movies.

video card Expansion card that works with the CPU to produce the images displayed on your computer's display.

video display *See* monitor.

virus Program that can make a copy of itself without your necessarily being aware of it. Some viruses can destroy or damage files. The best protection is to back up files regularly.

virus definition or data file Files that enable the virus protection software to recognize the viruses on your system and clean them. These files should be updated often. They are also called *signature files*, depending on the virus protection software in use.

virus shield Passive monitoring of a computer's activity, checking for viruses only when certain events occur.

VIS (viewable image size) Measurement of the viewable image that is displayed by a CRT rather than a measurement of the CRT itself.

voice coil motor One of two methods used to move actuator arms in a hard drive. (*See also* stepper motor.)

VoIP (Voice over Internet Protocol) Collection of protocols that make voice calls over a data network possible.

volatile Memory that must have constant electricity to retain data. Alternatively, any programmer six hours before deadline after a non-stop, 48-hour coding session, running on nothing but caffeine and sugar.

volts (V) Measurement of the pressure of the electrons passing through a wire, or voltage.

volume Physical unit of a storage medium, such as tape reel or disk pack, that is capable of having data recorded on it and subsequently read. Also refers to a contiguous collection of cylinders or blocks on a disk that are treated as a separate unit.

volume boot sector First sector of the first cylinder of each partition; stores information important to its partition, such as the location of the operating system boot files.

voucher Means of getting a discount on the CompTIA A+ exams.

VPN (virtual private network) Encrypted connection over the Internet between a computer or remote network and a private network.

VRM (voltage regulator module) Small card supplied with some CPUs to ensure that the CPU gets correct voltage. This type of card, which must be used with a motherboard specially designed to accept it, is not commonly seen today.

VRR (vertical refresh rate) The amount of time it takes for a CRT to draw a complete screen. This value is measured in hertz, or cycles per second. Most modern CRTs have a VRR of 60 Hz or better.

wait state Occurs when the CPU has to wait for RAM to provide code. Also known as pipeline stalls.

WAP (Wireless Access Point) Device that centrally connects wireless network nodes.

wattage (watts or W) Measurement of the amps and volts needed for a particular device to function.

wave table synthesis Technique that supplanted FM synthesis, wherein recordings of actual instruments or other sounds are embedded in the sound card as WAV files. When a particular note from a particular instrument or voice is requested, the sound processor grabs the appropriate prerecorded WAV file from its memory and adjusts it to match the specific sound and timing requested.

Web browser Program designed to retrieve, interpret, and display Web pages.

webcam PC camera most commonly used for Internet video.

Welcome screen Login screen for Windows XP. Enables users to select their particular user account by clicking on their user picture.

WEP (Wired Equivalent Privacy) Wireless security protocol that uses a standard 40-bit encryption to scramble data packets. Does not provide complete end-to-end encryption and is vulnerable to attack.

Wi-Fi Common name for the IEEE 802.11 wireless Ethernet standard.

wildcard Character used during a search to represent search criteria. For instance, searching for *.doc will return a list of all files with a .doc extension, regardless of the filename. The * is the wildcard in that search.

Windows 2000 Windows version that succeeded Windows NT; it came in both Professional and Server versions.

Windows 9x Term used collectively for Windows 95, Windows 98, and Windows Me.

Windows Explorer Windows utility that enables you to manipulate files and folders stored on the drives in your computer.

Windows Logo'd Product List List of products that have passed the Microsoft Windows Logo Program and are compatible with Windows operating system. Formerly called the *Hardware Compatibility List* (or *HCL*).

Windows NT Precursor to Windows 2000, XP, and Vista, which introduced many important features (such as HAL and NTFS) used in all later versions of Windows.

Windows sidebar User interface feature in Windows Vista that enables users to place various gadgets, such as clocks, calendars, and other utilities, on the right side of their desktop.

Windows Update Microsoft application used to keep Windows operating systems up to date with the latest patches or enhancements. (*See* Automatic Updates.)

Windows Vista Version of Windows; comes in many different editions for home and office use, but does not have a Server edition.

Windows XP Version of Windows that replaced both the entire Windows 9x line and Windows 2000; does not have a Server version.

worm Very special form of virus. Unlike other viruses, a worm does not infect other files on the computer. Instead, it replicates by making copies of itself on other systems on a network by taking advantage of security weaknesses in networking protocols.

WPA (Wi-Fi Protected Access) Wireless security protocol that uses encryption key integrity-checking and EAP and is designed to improve on WEP's weaknesses.

WPA 2 (Wi-Fi Protected Access 2) Wireless security protocol, also known as IEEE 802.11i. Uses the Advanced Encryption standard and replaces WPA.

WQUXGA Video display mode of 2560 × 1600.

wrapper *See* container file.

WSXGA Video display mode of 1440 × 900.

WSXGA+ Video display mode of 1680 × 1050.

WUXGA Video display mode of 1920 × 1200.

WVGA Video display mode of 800 × 480.

WWW (World Wide Web) System of Internet servers that support documents formatted in HTML and related protocols. Can be accessed by using Gopher, FTP, HTTP, Telnet, and other tools.

www.comptia.org CompTIA's Web site.

WXGA Video display mode of 1280 × 800.

x64 Describes 64-bit operating systems and software.

x86 Describes 32-bit operating systems and software.

XCOPY command Command in the command-line interface used to copy multiple directories at once, which the COPY command could not do.

xD (Extreme Digital) picture card Very small flash media card format.

Xeon Line of Intel CPUs designed for servers.

XGA (extended graphics array) Video display mode of 1024 × 768.

XPS (XML Paper Specification) print path Improved printing subsystem included in Windows Vista. Has enhanced color management and better print layout fidelity.

XT bus *See* PC bus.

ZIF (zero insertion force) socket Socket for CPUs that enables insertion of a chip without the need to apply pressure. Intel promoted this socket with its overdrive upgrades. The chip drops effortlessly into the socket's holes, and a small lever locks it in.

Internet Options applet, 141
Internetwork Packet Exchange/
   Sequenced Packet Exchange
   (IPX/SPX), 398
interrupt requests (IRQs), 340
intrusion, 467, 468
invalid media type error
   messages, 142
inverters, 333–334
I/O. *See* input/output
IP addresses:
   Automatic Private IP
      Addressing, 402, 410
   and configuring TCP/IP,
      401–402
   of e-mail servers, 455
   of routers, 448
   static, 406, 407, 448
   and subnet masks, 403
iPAQ Bluetooth Manager, 428
IPCONFIG command, 408
iPhone, 349
IPSec, 488
IPv4 addresses, 402
IPv6 addresses, 402
IPX/SPX (Internetwork Packet
   Exchange/Sequenced Packet
   Exchange), 398
IRQs (interrupt requests), 340
ISDN (integrated services digital
   network) service, 437, 442
ISO files, 296, 304
ISPs, 437
   configuration information
      from, 440
   connecting LANs to,
      443–444
   e-mail settings from, 455
   news server information
      from, 455
   static IP addresses
      from, 448
IT (Information Technology),
   1, 477
ITU (International
   Telecommunication
   Union), 438
iTunes, 336

J

Java applets, 141
joystick ports, 57
jumpers:
   and cabling, 93–94
   and CPU installation, 22
   on/off, 80
   soft power, 84

K

Kaspersky Labs, 483
Kerberos, 487
keyboard protectors, 362
keyboards:
   hardware authentication
      for, 472
   laptop, 350, 354
   USB, 285, 286
keypads, 365
"known good" devices, 289

L

Lagerweij, Bart, 484
LAN (local area network),
   392–417
   configuring network client
      for, 401
   configuring TCP/IP for,
      401–410
   connecting to Internet with,
      443, 444
   encryption in, 487
   installing NIC for,
      400–401
   and Internet Connection
      Sharing, 445
   IP addresses for, 402
   and NAT, 446
   and NetBEUI, 398
   and network operating
      systems, 393–400
   sharing with, 410–414
   and TCP/IP services, 403
landscape mode (monitors), 318
language preferences, 123, 124
laptop locks, 364
laptops. *See* portable computers

laser printing, 372–376
   printer maintenance,
      383–384
   problems with, 384–387
   process of, 372–374
   raster images in, 375
   and resolution, 375–376
   troubleshooting with,
      383–387
Last Known Good Configuration
   boot option, 262, 265
latency:
   satellite, 444
   and VoIP, 458
LCD monitors:
   cleaning, 334
   native resolution of, 316
   on portable computers, 361
   replaceable controls
      for, 330
   rotating, 318
   troubleshooting, 333–334
LearnKey video training,
   507, 508
LEDs (light-emitting diodes), 42,
   64, 364
LFN (long filenames), 163
LFX12V power supply, 87
license agreements, 119, 125
light ghosting, 385
light-emitting diodes. *See* LEDs
limited user accounts, 203, 204
link state (Wi-Fi), 431
Linksys routers, 422–425,
   446–449, 484, 485
Linux systems, 106, 107, 147,
   159, 483
liquid-cooling systems, 24
List Folder Contents
   permissions, 216
lithium ion batteries, 355–357
lithography, 19
live CDs, 147–148, 483
local area network. *See* LAN
local flow control, 439
Local Security Settings, 475
local shares, 223
local user accounts, 199, 206, 213

RTS (ready to send) wire, 439
Run dialog box, 162

■ S

Safe Mode, 263–264, 329, 483
Safe Mode with Command
    Prompt, 163, 264
Safe Mode with Networking, 264
Safely Remove Hardware
    tool, 354
SATA (serial ATA) drives:
        and autodetection, 97, 98
        installing, 95, 291
        for portable computers, 353
        power connectors for, 77
satellite Internet connection, 444
satellite latency, 444
saving:
        batch files, 181
        CMOS settings, 49
scams, 468–469
ScanDisk, 139
Scheduled Tasks, 247
scheduling (exams), 8
screen(s):
        appearance of, 313–315
        boot-order, 98
        classic Logon, 205, 206
        Integrated Peripherals,
            46, 47
        on portable computers,
            364–365
        Welcome, 202, 203, 205, 206
screen cleaners, 361
screws, 62, 63
scripts, 452–454
SCSI drives, 96
SDRAM, 95, 352
SDSL (synchronous DSL), 442
search and destroy (viruses),
    483–484
secondary controllers, 97
sectors:
        boot, 43, 101, 102
        corrupted data on, 144
        information on status
            of, 109
Secure Boot Setting, 200, 201

Secure Shell (SSH), 458
Secure Sockets Layer (SSL)
    security protocol, 488
security, 7, 198–228, 466–493
        access control, 471–477
        administrative access, 469
        authentication, 199–214,
            471–473, 486–490
        authorization, 199,
            214–218, 469
        data classification and
            compliance, 477
        data destruction, 469
        in infrastructure mode of
            wireless networks,
            421–424
        with NAT, 446
        network, 432, 480–490
        NTFS, 114, 115
        on peer-to-peer
            networks, 394
        physical theft, 470
        policies, 475–477
        for portable computers,
            363–364
        reporting, 477–479
        sharing, 218–225
        social engineering, 468–469
        system crash/hardware
            failure, 470
        unauthorized access,
            467–468
        viruses and spyware, 470,
            481–485
        for Wi-Fi networks, 432
        on World Wide Web,
            452–454
Security Center, 247
Security domain, 504–505
see-through power supply units,
    85, 86
Select Users, Computers, or
    Groups dialog box, 213, 214
sensitive information, 468
serial ATA drives. See SATA
    (serial ATA) drives
serial communication, 438
serial connections, 439
serial ports, 281–283

serial presence detect (SPD), 30
server machines, 133
server software, 399–400
servers:
        in client/server
            networks, 393
        e-mail, 454–456
        news, 455
        proxy, 451–452
        Web, 450, 489
services, 252, 254–255,
    267, 268
Services applet, 252, 254–255
SET command, 183
Set Password dialog box, 202
Settings tab, 315–318
SFC. See System File Checker
SFX12V power supply, 87
Shared Documents, 219, 220
shared folders, 222–223
Shared Folders tool, 222, 223
shared memory, 352–353
Shared Music folder, 220
Shared Pictures folder, 220
shareware, 507
sharing, 218–225. See also file
    sharing
        administrative shares, 223
        drives, 410–413
        folders, 219, 222–223,
            410–411
        hardware connection,
            445–449
        Internet Connection
            Sharing, 445, 451
        with local area networking,
            410–414
        locating shared folders,
            222–223
        multiple printers, 381
        Network and Sharing
            Center, 399
        Network Sharing
            Center, 445
        printers, 399, 400, 414
        protecting data with
            encryption, 223–225
        targeted, 221
        in Windows 7, 411